SOCIOLOGY

# SOCIOLOGY

## *A SYNOPSIS OF PRINCIPLES*

BY

JOHN F. CUBER

*Professor of Sociology*
*The Ohio State University*

*New York*

APPLETON-CENTURY-CROFTS, INC.

488

PRINTED IN THE UNITED STATES OF AMERICA

TO

MY PARENTS

—for their faith

TO

MY PARENTS

for their faith

# PREFACE

This volume is a product of thirteen years of struggle with the problems of elementary sociology instruction in liberal arts colleges and state universities. Like most of his colleagues the author is not satisfied with the results. He offers this volume as one tentative approach to the textbook aspect of the total problem. The underlying sociological theory and the pedagogical philosophy are explained in the introductory section for the instructor, in which problems of sociology instruction are discussed at some length.

Like most authors, this one is indebted to a great number of sociologists and other students of society and human behavior whose work has been heavily drawn upon. Specific acknowledgements are inadequate because the long and wide stream of sociological thoughtways is so overwhelming.

Numerous persons have made notable contributions to this project, chiefly, but not exclusively, my colleagues and graduate students in the Department of Sociology at the Ohio State University. Dr. Read Bain criticized the complete manuscript and made numerous helpful suggestions most of which have been subsequently incorporated. Other major indebtedness is due the following persons for reading and criticizing portions of the earlier manuscript: Dr. Paul Hatt for the chapters on social psychology, race, demography, and human ecology; Dr. C. C. North for the chapters on social stratification, social problems, and social organization and disorganization, and Dr. John Bennett, anthropologist, for the chapters in the section on culture and society. Acknowledgements of a less specific, but not necessarily less important, nature are due Dr. R. C.

Angell, the late Dr. R. D. McKenzie, Dr. Herbert Blumer and Dr. Walter Terpenning who over the long period of incubation of these ideas have made important contributions. Among my recent associates, the following have been of definite assistance in various ways: Miss Irene Osborne, Dr. James T. Laing, Dr. Kurt Wolff, Mr. Melvin Seeman, Mr. Paul B. Horton, Dr. Robert Harper, Mr. Herman Lantz, and Mr. Chester M. Stephenson.

Dr. Perry P. Denune, Chairman of the Department of Sociology at the Ohio State University, contributed greatly to the early maturation of the project by arranging numerous administrative matters in such a way as to expedite the writing in its later phases.

Most of all, the inestimable services of my wife have made the completion of this task possible. Her accomplishment of the vast and onerous stenographic labors almost single handed has been exceeded only by her complete devotion to the enterprise and her unfailing faith in its ultimate success.

The faith of all these people in the eventual utility of the project can only be vindicated by the value it may have to the student—the ultimate consumer of the sociological product—upon whom the final appraisal must rest.

J. F. C.

*Columbus, Ohio*

## CONTENTS

# INTRODUCTION FOR THE TEACHER: THE PROBLEM OF TEACHING INTRODUCTORY SOCIOLOGY

Some early American sociologists thought that the study of sociology should be limited to graduate students. While modern sociologists have not followed the advice of their forebears, we appear not always to have been mindful of the mental immaturity of the students with whom we work in the elementary course. We may have erred seriously by presenting sociology with a scope and a depth better fitted to more advanced instruction. We need to be more realistic about the kind of people who take the beginning course in the principles of sociology. Failure to meet students where they are seems not only to be wasteful of much of our writing and instructional effort, but may also have a serious negative public relations angle. The uncomplimentary popular estimate that sociologists are "too theoretical" and "in the ivory tower" may result as much from the way in which we present our "stuff" as in the inherent nature of it.

In most colleges and universities the students who enroll for courses in introductory sociological principles are freshmen and sophomores. They do not read theoretical materials well at the outset, although they gradually learn to do better under guidance. They have almost no abilities, as a rule, in reading tables, graphs, and maps. Carefully prepared footnote references are not read by the overwhelming mass of these beginners, and are rarely regarded by them as a necessary part of the textbook. Unless the teacher and textbook writer are mindful of such facts as these much sociology will continue to get lost "between the producer and the consumer" of sociological instruction.

### *Scope of the Beginning Principles Course*

The planner of an introductory course confronts a serious initial problem of scope. Should one include major units on culture and on social psychology? Some of the younger sociologists especially, feel that they would prefer that their students secure instruction in these areas from courses in anthropology and social psychology, and then begin their study of sociology with the treatment of groups, social organization, and institutions, which they regard as the essence of sociology proper. In most colleges and universities, however, one cannot assume that students have had adequate training in cultural anthropology or social psychology, even if they should have had courses in these subjects since such courses, too, vary greatly in content and point of view. Thus, there seems no alternative but to follow the sociological traditions and include two major introductory units which introduce the student to the basic cultural anthropological and the social psychological understandings which he should have. Moreover, this approach has the added pedagogical advantage of enabling students to gain these basic understandings from a sociological "slant."

### *The Teaching Function of an Elementary Text*

Considerations of pedagogy seem to necessitate forms of statement, modes of organization, and emphases not wholly justifiable if a textbook were being written as a systematic sociology for the advanced student. Pedagogical considerations have materially modified the makeup of this book. For example, repetitions are frequent; the student is reminded from time to time that earlier he has touched the idea now under discussion, or that further discussion is to follow. The style is "conversational." Sometimes even the same illustrations are used to clarify different principles. These teaching practices have proved effective in lectures and discussions and ought also to prove so in a textbook.

Part I is designed as the students' orientation to the study of sociology. Some instructors prefer to begin the course with the consideration of such methodological matters as objectivity and the scientific nature of sociological study. Others prefer to launch directly into subject matter and end the course with such an emphasis, using it as a review device. In such an event Part I may be left for the end of the course, and the student be started out with Part II which really begins the treatment of materials per se.

*Documentation and Bibliographies*

Failure to make frequent footnote references to sources grows out of no unwillingness to acknowledge the vast indebtedness to sociologists and other scholars whose work has been heavily drawn upon. Every writer in every field of science is primarily parasitic; his "own contributions" are usually both few and minor. To that generalization this writer is certainly no exception. The relative absence of footnotes in this book stems instead from the fact that it is primarily a textbook for the beginning student who, experience has shown, finds frequent citations not only useless but somewhat distracting. Since a beginning textbook rarely contains much of basic theoretical innovation, it seemed best to assume that instructors are familiar with the content of the field of sociology, both in the realm of empiric materials and of theory. Should this assumption be incorrect, the bibliographies found at the end of each chapter will serve to direct both the instructor and the more able student to some of the better known and more useful sources of sociology.

These bibliographies are certainly not exhaustive. The number has been kept to a minimum, there being not over 200 separate items cited. Selection is, of course, somewhat arbitrary, but an effort was made to select readings which vary in degree of difficulty, are representative of points of view not found in the text, contain many of the "classics" of sociology, and are usually available in college libraries. Bibliographic comment is also included. It is designed to assist both student and instructor by pointing out the general content of the reference, its degree of difficulty, its relation to the text and to other bibliographic items.

*Presentation of Statistical Data*

Many of the necessary data and manipulations of data in sociology involve quantitative designation. This has not been overlooked. It does not follow, however, that magnitudinal data need be presented only in the form of statistical tables or graphs. Verbal presentation may also be both precise and graphic, and may, in fact, even surpass more formal modes of presentation in functional integration of statistical data with pertinent theory. As with documentation, it has been found that very few beginning students can be motivated to study tables and graphs, and then integrate the resulting conceptions with theory. Better, it seems, to present quantitative data in verbal form at the appropriate place in the development of the basic frame of reference of the subject matter. To be sure, one might choose to teach students how to use graphical, tabular, and cartographic devices, and some teachers may choose to do so. Thus, a number of graphs are to be found in various parts of this book which deal with magnitudinal phenomena.

### *"Principles" and "Problems"*

Sociologists have sometimes tended to dichotomize the study of the principles of sociology (theory) and the study of social problems. While there is much to justify such a separation, there are many considerations also which favor a more integrated treatment of the two. After all, if principles of sociology are sound, these principles should be valid when used for the purpose of understanding the problem aspects as well as the more "normal" aspects of social life, and should be pertinent to studying social dynamics as well as the static aspect of society. While this book is organized around principles primarily, it contains much discussion of social change, social problems, and social control of problems. These are not treated in separate sections of the book, but recur throughout the topics treated, and in almost every chapter. This seems not to detract from the study of principles, in fact adds much, and makes the book quite usable in a combined principles-problems course, although probably not for the specialized problems course.

# *Part I*

# ORIENTATION TO SOCIOLOGY

# Chapter I

## MODERN SOCIOLOGY AS A FIELD OF KNOWLEDGE

"Man, know thyself" is old advice. Yet in many ways man knows less about himself than he does about dogs or the fleas which inhabit them. Man started to study himself scientifically many centuries after he had built up fairly impressive sciences of many other things varying from the planets to the insects. There are, of course, numerous reasons why man was so tardy in studying himself *scientifically*. First, there have always been persons who have opposed the application of scientific modes of study to man, either because to study himself seemed unbecoming or because it seemed impossible. Eventually, however, after concentrating scientifically for centuries on virtually every phenomenon in the universe *except* himself, man is coming at last to try to understand himself by the use of an analytical method of study called "science." The result is a group of knowledges called "the social sciences," one of them being sociology.

To most of the students using this book the study of sociology will constitute a new learning experience. In this fact lies both an opportunity and a difficulty. The opportunity arises from the novelty and the freshness of new experience; the difficulty results from the possibility that the novelty will be too great, so new and so confusing that the novice may get lost in it. For this reason the first two chapters of this book will be devoted to orienting the student to the study of sociology, and acquainting him with its point of view.

At the onset it seems necessary to point out that *sociology consists of tested knowledge built up gradually and painstakingly over the years,* often by the lifelong efforts of numerous men and women. Originators of new knowledge, in whatever field they work, represent as a rule a rare combination of inventive genius and hard work. Each is dependent upon the work of those who have gone before and each, if he is truly inventive, adds the results of his work to the accumulated product of knowledge. Sometimes it turns out that what appears to be "true" at one time in the development of a field of knowledge, eventually comes to be recognized as not true or only partially true and has to be discarded. In its place is then substituted the better knowledge. Every field of knowledge goes through this constant sorting process; each truth must always stand the test of careful scrutiny if it is to be continued as truth. That is the way in which each generation of mankind can best be guaranteed that its knowledge is up to date.

*The specialized body of knowledge which we call sociology is vast.* It numbers hundreds of worthy books and thousands of other writings. Some of these books are quite old, but despite their age still contain the essential truths which later sociologists' researches have found to be fundamentally correct. On other books the printer's ink is hardly dry, but their significance is already evident. In view of the vastness of the sociological library which we now have, it is impossible to present within the pages of any one book all that we know about this field. Much less can an *introductory* book cover the field completely. In this book we shall, so to speak, cover only the ABC's of sociology. Thus the student should not expect that a mastery of this book will make him a sociologist, any more than the mastery of a college textbook in physics will make him a physicist. That objective would constitute a career.

Another way of describing the content and purpose of this book would be to call it a resumé or synopsis of the whole field of sociology; it aims to introduce and discuss briefly the major findings of sociology. It does not contain *all* of the findings and most assuredly does not give *all of the evidence* underlying even the findings which are discussed. It will be reasonably complete, however, and the more interested student will secure from it a sufficiently well-rounded preparation in the subject, permitting him later to go on to more specialized courses in sociology and encounter no serious difficulty with his basic understanding, his technical vocabulary, or his point of view.

### *Definition of Sociology*

Some introductory textbooks contain brief, one-sentence definitions of sociology. Other writers prefer not to attempt a formal definition, because they believe that such synoptical definitions are not only too brief to be meaningful to the beginner, but also may lead to serious misunderstandings. These writers simply offer "the whole book" as the student's best working notion of the scope of sociology. While there may be merit in this approach, there seems greater merit in at least attempting an approximate, terse definition, even though both writer and student realize that it has serious limitations. At least it is a beginning.

Sociology may be defined as *a body of scientific knowledge about human relationships.* The word *relationships* is a key word. Sociology is not concerned, for example, primarily with man as a biological being, nor with his history, nor with his accomplishments. Sociology is concerned with man's behavior in relation to other men, with human interaction. When we pointed out that sociology is not concerned "primarily" with man's biology, his history, or his accomplishments, it was not intended to imply that sociology is not at all concerned with these phenomena. Sociology is concerned with these phenomena, but *only as they are a part of, affect, or result from human interrelationships.* Digestion, the Constitution, and the atomic bomb, then, are of interest to sociology but not in themselves; we are only concerned with the ways in which these phenomena affect human association or are affected by human interaction.

## THE POINT OF VIEW OF MODERN SOCIOLOGY

Probably the most fundamental idea with which the beginning student of sociology must familiarize himself is what we call the "point of view." Many beginning students encounter unnecessary difficulty in this field because they launch too soon into the study of the materials without first knowing why the materials are to be studied.

### *Confusion among Laymen Regarding the Nature of Sociology*

A long time ago the word *layman* came into our vocabulary to designate the person not professionally trained in some field. Now the word is widely used in referring to people who may be fairly "well informed" about "things in general" but who lack the precise training and the carefully disciplined mind of the professional person in his field of competence. To the superficial observer the fairly well-informed layman often appears to know as much about certain fields as the professional physician or lawyer or clergyman. But almost invariably a more careful observation discloses that there are no short-cuts to real understanding of any field of knowledge, that there is no substitute for the precise and painstaking mastery of a field by the methods required. Professional standards are the result of many years of experience in training persons for the field in question. So it is with sociology, too. In fact it may even be possible that sociology is misrepresented and misunderstood more than many fields by lay efforts to "tell us all about it."

There are several reasons why this layman's confusion concerning the nature of sociology should exist. First, as fields of knowledge go, sociology is youthful. One is not to assume, of course, that sociology was "just born yesterday." It has been taught in American colleges and universities for three-quarters of a century under the name of *sociology* and some of its teachings have been incorporated in college curricula for a much longer period under other labels. As fields of knowledge go, however, three-fourths of a century is hardly a venerable age. There are people high in academic, professional, and social position who have either never been exposed during their formal education to sociology *as it is regarded by its highest ranking scholars today*, or have been exposed to learnings bearing the *name* of sociology but constituting less than a "reasonable facsimile thereof." The nature of sociology has changed so much during the last thirty years that a person studying with reputable sociologists of thirty years ago, and remembering what he learned, might find himself seriously out of touch with sociology as it is conceived today. To some extent, of course, all fields of knowledge have changed, but the more youthful ones have changed more radically, probably because they were so youthful.

Many people, moreover, become confused because of the loose usage of the terms *sociology* and *sociologists* which one hears and reads on every hand. Social workers who administer relief and counsel to destitute people are often called "sociologists," ultra-wealthy persons who contribute vast sums to philanthropic organizations are often designated as "sociologists." Such loose usage of the word is as much "off the beam" as one would be if he attached the word *physician* to a kindly neighbor who sits up all night with a sick friend. His service may be valuable, he is bound to know *something* about his friend's illness, and certainly he has been "close to" the malady. But none of these things, however virtuous or interesting, makes him a doctor. One does not get to be a physician by any procedure except that of being schooled in the knowledge and techniques of the medical profession, being schooled slowly and meticulously over a considerable period of time.

Small wonder, then, with the word *sociology* so indiscriminately employed by seemingly well-informed people, that the beginning student should often have a vague or even wholly incorrect notion of what sociology "is all about." We turn, in the next paragraph to the basic question of what sociology is—and also what it disclaims being.

### *Sociology Is Knowledge, Not Therapy*

Broadly speaking, there are two distinct kinds of competence which man has built up. One is *knowledge about things* and the other is *knowledge of how to do things*. Much needless confusion arises from the failure to distinguish these two. Before discussing sociology itself it may be well to illustrate this distinction by reference to another area. Suppose we use biology and medicine. Certainly these two fields of knowledge are related in that both of them are concerned with the human body. But a biologist is not a physician and a physician is not a biologist. Each one knows a great deal about things about which the other is, in all probability, quite ignorant. Even more fundamental, however, is the *difference in purpose*. The biologist is a seeker after knowledge about living things. His chief interest is in knowing, in discovering what, and to some extent why, his knowledges are true. The physician, on the other hand, is professionally interested only in the knowledges which will assist him in making sick people well or keeping people well. His knowledge must be "practical," that is, it must be immediately useful in treating people. We call him a "therapist"; the biologist is not a therapist, he is a discoverer of knowledge—virtually any knowledge pertaining to living things, not only the immediately practical and not only about humans.

Similarly sociology is a field of knowledge and the sociologist's chief, if not sole, duty is to build up the most accurate body of knowledge about human relationships that is possible. The *use* of this knowledge, like the use of the biologist's knowledge, remains for others to carry out. Thus, social workers, juvenile court judges, teachers, psychiatrists, parents, and many other people may put sociological information into practical use either in a professional way or in their own "personal" lives, very much in the same way that the physician puts into practical use the knowledges discovered by biologists, chemists, and other discoverers. Persons who use sociological knowledge, however, do not thereby become sociologists, any more than the physician becomes a chemist or a biologist merely by using some chemical or biological knowledge. In summary, one should not expect to find in sociology a set of knowledges ready to be used in the alleviation of human problems or in the treatment of social ills. These belong largely in the province of a related field of therapy called "social work" or "social administration" for which, as a rule, training in sociology is considered a basic prerequisite. Sociology, then, is a body of knowledge about the behavior of human beings, it has "practical value" often, but is usually put into practical operation by others than sociologists.

*Sociological Knowledge Is Based on Evidence*

Persons unfamiliar with the large amount of painstaking research which underlies sociological truth have often made a fundamental error, an error to which so many have become addicted that it seems necessary to state the sociologists' position very clearly. A sociological statement is not true because some sociologist *says* it is, or for that matter because five hundred sociologists say it is. It is only true if and when sufficient numbers of observations and/or experiments have been made and critically examined to formulate a factual (or "empiric") basis for the statement. Thus, sociology is a field of knowledge *based on evidence*. This evidence consists of *observations of phenomena*, on *repeated* observations of the same and related phenomena, which observations then constitute the basis, or authority, for the statement.

When we use the term *observation* we do not mean merely "looking at" something. Observation is a technical process involving much training in ways and means of *accurate* observation. The astronomer uses a telescope, the biologist a microscope, the physician a stethoscope; what all three have in common in the use of these precision tools is the purpose, namely, to improve the accuracy of observations. Each field of knowledge develops its own technical tools to improve the reliability and accuracy of its observation of the materials within its scope of study. The telescope is, of course, of no greater use to the physician than the stethoscope would be to the astronomer, and neither would be of much use to an economist. But the economist has developed certain other observational procedures, not necessarily instruments, which help him to improve the accuracy and precision of his observations. And so with the sociologist. He, too, has devised various technical procedures which enable him to observe his data more accurately than the person who merely "looks at" the people and things about him. In summary, sociological truths are carefully tested by repeated observations, by the use of technical methods of observation, before they can qualify as true.

### *Sociology Is the Study of What "Is"*

The prime concern of sociology, as we have already seen, is to discover what is true about human beings and their relations to one another. Sociologists are not advocates, are not reformers, are not preachers, and have no "axe to grind" other than this interest in building up the most nearly perfect body of knowledge about human beings that they can. Of course, every sociologist is a citizen too, and *as a citizen* he usually has preferences for one political party over another, for one religion over another, or for one philosophy over another. But this part of him is his citizen-self, not his sociologist-self. Other specialists, of course, have the same compartments in their thinking. An architect may be a Democrat, a Catholic, and a conservative. He is these three things not, however, because he is an architect, but because he is a person. A second architect may be a Republican, a Protestant, and a radical. But in their professional capacities, studying, applying, and discovering the best possible principles for the design and constructing of edifices, their citizen rôles, even their differences, are of no significance. And so it is with the sociologists; the personal predilections of sociologist *A* or of sociologist *B* are not a part of the subject matter of sociology.

In strict fairness it ought to be pointed out that there is a group of sociologists, mostly older men and women, who believe that it is within the professional province of the sociologist to make recommendations as to what "*ought* to be," what changes are desirable in human affairs.

C. C. Bowman says: [1]

It is maintained that the scientific interest in society cannot be marked off sharply from an interest in societal welfare, since the two are interrelated. Stimulated by training along religious and humanitarian lines, a number of persons have entered the field of sociology in order to participate in the "solution" of social problems. As their study progressed, at least some have come to realize that humanitarian sentiment per se is not enough. Consequently they have turned to science in order to implement their ideals with a substantial fund of knowledge.

On the other hand, and more relevant to our present purpose, a student of society may start out to be strictly scientific and develop a social-welfare interest as his knowledge grows. In any scientific pursuit, particularly in its applied aspects, it is an easy and natural step from objective knowledge to interest in improvement. This is especially true in the United States where knowledge for its own sake is an ideal that runs counter to our pragmatic tendencies. Thus, the improvement of health becomes a professional goal of the medical scientist that develops directly out of his interest in the human organism. In the normal course of professional development the welfare interest emerges as a concomitant of scientific endeavor and provides an ethical orientation for the social scientist. The ethical evolves, *pari passu,* with the objective orientation. Moreover, there are external forces working to the same end: people see problems in which they and their friends are personally involved and they seek expert assistance. An economist does not need to justify a welfare interest, for the economic ills of mankind have led to public interest in ameliorative measures. It is the same with a physician. His heart need not bleed for suffering humanity. If he opens an office after obtaining proper training, the sick will seek him out.

This normal connection between scientific and welfare interests may be blocked by various factors. In this country conflicts between strictly scientific and welfare sociologists are apparent from time to time. A polarity of relationship tends to exist wherein the scientists are too detached and the welfare group too impatient. Such misunderstanding represents an early stage in the evolution of a new field of knowledge that is trying to free itself from moralistic pre-conceptions and the unsubstantiated opinions of common sense. It probably has no permanency. Certain sociologists become excited whenever the term *welfare* is mentioned, for in their minds it connotes the limited approach of traditional social work or "up-lift" activities based upon great passion but little understanding. In the present discussion the term is free from these connotations. The whole purpose is to oppose the view that interest in social betterment is imposed upon the scientific quest arbitrarily, if at all. It is maintained that, although the welfare interest is to be classified as ethical, it

[1] C. C. Bowman, "Must the Social Sciences Foster Moral Skepticism?" *American Sociological Review,* X, p. 714.

emerges readily from the professional interest and activities of the social scientist and from the needs of the public.

Most sociologists, however, appear to regard their primary if not sole purpose as that of *studying the existing scheme of things* with the view to learning what is true. This book is written largely from that point of view. This is in line with the leading sociological scholarship of our time, and it seems more fundamental to learn, first, what is true, before attempting to pass judgment on it or to advocate something else.

### *Sociology Is Amoral*

The word *amoral* is not to be confused with *immoral. Immoral* implies that there is an accepted moral code which has been violated, that one has "gone against the moral." *Amoral* means simply that the matter in question is *outside the scope or realm of morals* or is perhaps *not concerned with morals*. Now what does this distinction have to do with the study of sociology? Simply this: The findings of sociologists very frequently contain truths which are the precise opposite of some of the beliefs or teachings or popular prejudices or precious sentiments which people hold. The sociologist, like most scientists, takes the position that truth is truth regardless of who or how many persons may happen to have prejudices to the contrary. Truth should never be subordinated to ignorance, however time honored or precious the ignorance may appear to be. Thus, for example, for many centuries we have been taught that it is "natural for all women, because they have a mother instinct, to love little children." This has long been a very precious and meaningful sentiment to many people. In recent years, however, psychologists, anthropologists, and sociologists have made repeated observations and have conducted numerous experiments which tend to show, first, that the so-called "mother instinct" does not exist, and second, that many women, as a matter of *fact,* do not love, or even like, small children. (We shall not at this point study the evidence pertaining to research on instinct, but shall do so later. We are using this point here simply as an illustration.) Perhaps it is unfortunate that so lofty an idea as inherent mother love should have to be questioned, but truth is truth. It is the scientists' position that we get the farthest in the long run by teaching and knowing truth, not nonsense. After all, if astronomers had hesitated to stand against the sacred idea that Jupiter's horses dragged the sun across the sky each day, we might still be in the doldrums of scientific ignorance regarding the sun! There is no doubt that numerous persons have been made seriously unhappy each time that science has made a great stride in knowledge, but it hardly seems wise, even if we could, to stop the clock of progress so that each generation may live its full "three score and ten" in undisturbed ignorance.

*The Problem of Bias*

The student should understand that it is the goal of the sociologist to be free from prejudice and bias in his study of human beings and social situations, but that all sociologists do not find it possible to attain this ideal all of the time. Many factors work against the attainment of complete freedom from prejudice. Many prejudice patterns are so subtle as to escape discovery in one's thinking, even though he is ever on the alert to detect bias. From time to time in this book, attention will be called to instances in which sociologists and other scientists of human behavior and society have made errors due to the unconscious operation of some bias. Such instances are, however, not common, and need not detract from the basic principle, namely, that freedom from bias is vigorously sought, in fact is a fundamental professional ideal or ethic of the scientific student of human beings and society.

*Sociology in Relation to Other Social Sciences*

Sociology is not the only modern field which studies man. Biology, anthropology, psychology, social psychology, economics, political science, and others study some aspect or other of the behavior of human beings. These various fields study different aspects of man's behavior for the most part, although in some cases several may study the same aspect. During very recent years there has arisen an attempt to integrate sociology, psychology, and anthropology into one science of human behavior. While we cannot at present be certain that this movement to integrate the three fields will stand the test of time, there are many reasons to applaud the movement as a step in the right direction. It is not to be assumed, however, that progress in human knowledge could not continue if the various fields of knowledge remained separate. Up to the present time great strides in knowledge have been made even though these closely related fields have remained somewhat distinct. Border line studies like social psychology, with one foot in sociology and the other in psychology, have served as integrating points. Also numerous individual scholars have done their research on problems in which two or more social sciences converge and have made some important discoveries thereby.

One should not overlook the fact, however, that many individual students who have occasion to borrow ideas and points of view from fields which they know less well than they do their own, often do their borrowing and integrating very erroneously. Sociologists frequently note the naïveté displayed by non-sociologists who, on the basis of very little knowledge, become confident that they know precisely what "sociologists" have found to be true on this or that problem. It is not improbable that sociologists commit the same error when they attempt to transplant parts of some other "ology" into their own. The point is not that all those students do not wish to be accurate in transplanting discoveries from one field to another, but rather that they are so often insufficiently versed in the fields other than their own to be able to discriminate carefully on the finer points. And it is so often the "finer points" which represent the difference between truth and error.

The writer has been impressed many times with the fact that the "findings" of some persons who are amateurs in the field of sociology and who are therefore not highly regarded by sociologists, are frequently cited to him as evidence of what "sociologists have discovered!" One must, therefore, utilize great diligence to assure himself that he has really gotten the *accurate* content of some field, and not a mangled version of it instead. Scientific accuracy is not easily achieved, but it must be constantly striven for. It is probably the chief reason why many thoughtful scholars of today advocate the abandonment of the present-day subject matter divisions in the social sciences. But they have not yet demonstrated that there is any real solution to the problem of specialization which does not in itself also have problems at least equally serious.

As the matter now stands, we have several fields of knowledge all studying man's behavior, each presenting an impressive accumulation of tested knowledge, and staffed by a sizable group of professionally competent people. The truly educated person has no choice but to acquaint himself as fully and as precisely as he can with the main knowledges of *all* of these fields, and then put them together as best he can. To do anything less is to leave gaps of ignorance in his understanding of himself and of other people.

### *Professional Differences Within the Field of Sociology*

When one has studied any field of knowledge carefully, he will find that it has within it some rather marked differences of point of view and some downright conflicts concerning the validity of this or that discovery. Not all physicians agree, for example, on what is reliably known concerning vitamins. Not all psychologists agree on the correctness or value of psychoanalysis, and certainly not all political scientists and historians agree on the utility of the United Nations. Several factors are involved in these intra-professional differences of opinion. Not all persons are equally familiar with the facts involved, or are equally unprejudiced or, for that matter, equally capable of interpreting them. Sometimes two or more points of view may both be correct or at least both tenable for the time being.

But it is easy to exaggerate the extent and seriousness of these professional disagreements. If one could make a complete catalogue of the many items of information within the fields of say, medicine, or psychology, or history, and then have each physician, psychologist, or historian check those on which he agreed with others in his field, one would find an overwhelming agreement on an overwhelming proportion of items. A 2 per cent disagreement may cause a riot of controversy; the 98 per cent agreement goes unnoticed!

Most modern fields of knowledge welcome, however, the somewhat varied viewpoints among their scholars. It is from differences that progress arises. If all sociologists agreed precisely on everything, one could only conclude that all possible knowledge was already known. Knowledge, quite to the contrary, is dynamic and ever changing. Today's truth may be tomorrow's error. The "knowledge" taught in a dozen departments of a modern college of thirty years ago would have to be repudiated today. In each instance some one discovered that his predecessors, and perhaps also he himself, were wrong about something.

Throughout this book there will occur frank admissions that on this or that problem, two or more points of view are currently tenable in the light of existing knowledge. In the vast majority of instances, however, that will not be necessary because substantial agreement has already been reached. This does not mean, however, that at some future time new discoveries may not revolutionize sociology as biology and physics have been revolutionized by the discoveries of evolution and relativity during recent decades.

*Summary*

In this section we have discussed the "point of view" of modern sociology. It has been noted, first, that among people not too well acquainted with sociology, or acquainted with an obsolete model of it, there is confusion concerning what it is. Among professional sociologists, however, there now exists a rather clear consensus concerning the field. These agreements are: (1) that modern sociology is a field of knowledge, not a reform movement, and not a therapy; (2) that the subject matter of sociology should consist only of the knowledges which are based on careful and repeated observations and by the use of well-trained persons employing tested methods of observation; (3) that sociology should be concerned with the study of what *is*, not with speculation about what ought to be; (4) that modern sociology is largely amoral, that is, is concerned with the discovery of what is true, regardless of what older moral sentiments such knowledge may call into question; (5) that sociology is only one of a group of social sciences which study human behavior, each of which has its own subject matter, point of view, and personnel, none having a corner on the whole truth; and (6) sociology, like all fields of knowledge, contains differences in professional viewpoint, but we cherish these differences because out of them usually comes progress in human knowledge.

## IS SOCIOLOGY A SCIENCE?

For decades an argument, almost an academic feud, has held sway over the issue whether sociology and other social sciences are really "sciences." The intensity of the argument has been reduced somewhat during recent years as a result of the growing realization of one cardinal fact, namely, that *science is one, but fields of science are many*. Basically all fields, whether astronomy or speech correction or dietetics seek to discover as best they can, the most accurate knowledge about the matters they study. Obviously, since they study different things, the details of their methods of investigation are somewhat different. A telescope is a scientific instrument useful to the astronomer, but useless to the dietitian. An oven thermometer may be useful to the dietitian but of no particular use to the astronomer. Neither instrument is of any particular use to the psychologist, but the lie detector or a recording apparatus is useful to him. While all of the fields have in common the desire to know and the necessity for repeated observations, the precise *way* they observe, *what apparatus is used* in observing, and many other details *will be found to vary* greatly.

### *What Are the Requirements of Science?*

Science (not any particular science) as we know it, is a method of knowing, a method which is based on certain assumptions that are now "taken for granted." We assume, first, that items in the universe, whether we are talking about the planets, the composition of blood, or the operation of the human mind, show uniformities and regularities which man can discover if he searches ably enough. The so-called "unpredictability of things" is not really inherent unpredictability at all, but rather current human ignorance concerning "how the things work." Much that was unpredictable yesterday is readily predictable today, and many things unpredictable to the layman are readily predictable to the expert. Accurate prediction is possible only for the person who knows how the matter in question "works."

A further assumption of science is that we learn the uniformities in the universe through *observation,* rechecking our observations many, many times in order that we might learn more precisely and certainly what the uniformities are. It is the *method of verification* through which we validate our findings. As we have pointed out before, the precise ways in which we observe and verify vary for each field of knowledge, but fundamentally there is no substitute for the verification process.

After verified observation has demonstrated that something is true, it becomes necessary to *codify* the finding in some definite way. The well-known chemical formula $H_2O$ is such a statement. What it really means is that after repeated observations water has been found to consist of two "parts" hydrogen and one "part" oxygen. The finding could just as well be stated in a sentence as in a formula, but usage seems to have favored the formula $H_2O$ rather than a sentence. Other findings of sciences cannot be stated so tersely. For example, the theory of evolution as discovered by biologists cannot be stated as a formula and can, in fact, hardly be stated accurately in a sentence. It is too involved for either, but is no less certain and certainly no less important than some other finding which can be stated more tersely.

Scientific findings when stated in words are usually classified into *laws, theories,* and *hypotheses.* If the evidence indicates that the finding is clearly established, and can be stated definitely without too many "ifs, ands and provideds," then it is called a "law." Examples are the "Law of Falling Bodies" in physics, "Boyle's Law" in chemistry, the "Law of Diminishing Returns" in economics. Discoveries which are probably true, but for which the evidence is not quite so conclusive, are usually called "theories." It is necessary to emphasize, however, that a theory is not a guess, it is not "a notion spun out of thin air" but is a truth for which there exists considerable but not final and conclusive evidence. Finally, there are "hypotheses." A hypothesis is an idea about which we are not yet sufficiently certain to permit us to call it a law or a theory, but there is, nevertheless, some evidence to support it. An idea usually does not remain a hypothesis very long. It is usually soon tested and if found true becomes a theory or a law, if found to be false is discarded.

Most fields of knowledge have some laws, some theories, and some hypotheses, although they do not always call their findings by these labels. Very often the term *principles* is used to cover all three. The point, however, to our discussion is simply that the findings of each field of knowledge vary in degree of definiteness depending on how much research underlies them, that the findings can be expressed in various ways, but that fundamentally they constitute a statement of what has been found to be true.

The final step in science is to organize the laws, theories, and hypotheses into *systems* or *patterns of knowledge.* Some principles are large, overall truths which are fundamental to the rest of the science such as evolution in biology or relativity in physics. Other truths are very specific, almost minute in nature, such as the law that water will solidify at 0° centigrade and vaporize at 100° centigrade at sea level and under other specified conditions. Obviously the broad principles, the subordinate principles, and the minute principles have to be arranged and woven together into the overall pattern of knowledge which makes up what we call the "field."

We can summarize our discussion of science in this way: Science is a method of discovery of the uniformities in the universe through the process of observation and re-observation, the results of which eventually come to be stated in principles and arranged and organized into fields of knowledge. The ultimate purpose of this knowledge is to enable us to predict for the future on the basis of the observations of the past.

*Does Sociology Qualify as a Science?*

There are two ways in which this question can be answered in the light of existing evidence. The first consists of going over the above-mentioned criteria of science and determining whether the principles of sociology have been built up in the way indicated. Such an examination would indicate that sociology is a science, because its findings are based upon repeated observation, are formalized into statements called principles, and woven into a pattern of knowledges such as this book contains. The other way of answering the question is a way which is employed by many persons who preoccupy themselves with consideration of "definiteness" and "precise predictability" as the ultimate measure of science. It is obvious, of course, that there are few mathematically precise and infallibly predictable truths in sociology (although there are some) as well as in many other fields. The conclusion drawn by this logic then, is that sociology is not a science in the sense that some other sciences are, for example, physics. Such analysis frequently misses two points: (*a*) that certain aspects of human behavior *can* be accurately and precisely predicted, although admittedly not entirely so, and (*b*) that even where sociologists are not able to predict accurately, their researches are directed along lines designed to further their knowledge and improve the accuracy of their predictions. No one contends that a field so new as all of the behavior sciences could possess a body of predictive knowledge equal to other fields five or twenty times as old. Although the question should not be glibly and incautiously answered, the preponderant evidence would seem to indicate that sociology does qualify as scientific, even though not with as long and as imposing a record for accurate predictions as certain other fields may properly claim.

*"Exactness"*

The student should guard against exaggeration of the importance of the difference between the so-called "exact" natural sciences and the "inexact" social sciences. *There are many phenomena in the realm of natural science*—astronomy, physics, chemistry, and biology—*which are unknown, cannot be predicted, and about which the sciences are really very inexact.* It has been pointed out that (1) the meteorologist cannot accurately predict the weather five days in the future—even approximately; (2) the most capable doctor of medicine must "wait until tomorrow" in order to "decide whether Junior's rash is measles or something else"; (3) "the zoologist cannot tell us which rabbit [if any] will eat the tops off our newly arisen peas"; (4) "the botanist cannot predict which seeds [or even how many] out of a package will germinate"; (5) "the bacteriologist would hesitate to say which of a dozen children exposed to mumps will contract the illness"; (6) "the geologist would not like to have us press him for a statement where the next earthquake will occur"; (7) the physicist would be utterly unable to "predict which railroad rail [if any] will crack during the next heavy frost"; [2] and (8) no one knows anything reliable about the nature or treatment of the common cold despite the tremendous and long-standing practical need for such information. The list could be extended indefinitely. It is not intended by presenting these facts to cast any aspersions on these fields of science, but simply to "get the record straight" about the alleged categorical differences of "exactness" between the natural and the social sciences.

Many of the exactnesses of the natural sciences, moreover, pertain to phenomena which are of very *limited practical significance, uncontrollable* even though accurately predictable (the orbits of the planets), and are *virtually useless under "natural" or uncontrolled conditions.* On the other hand, numerous matters in the realm of the social sciences are known exactly, but the exactness is of such limited importance that it is hardly worth mentioning. It is possible, for example, to measure the average expectancy of life to fifty

[2] Chester Alexander, "Is Sociology An Exact Science?" *American Sociological Review*, XI, p. 5.

places to the right of the decimal point, but is it of any significance that the average length of life is "63.009001742 years" instead of "approximately 63"? Is it of any significance that we have measured some phase of anti-Negro prejudice and have found that 37.92713 per cent of the people of the United States possess that prejudice? What would we then know which is not already known, even though now quite inexactly? There is a fundamental difference in *significance* between the phenomena of the physical and the social sciences which may be of far more importance than the mere matter of exactness. We shall discuss this problem further in connection with prediction in the following chapter.

*Research Instruments*

Some sciences build up their knowledge in laboratories where the researchers wear white coats, use delicate balances, and prepare precise charts. Other sciences send their students to far away places, or into the stratosphere or down into the bowels of the earth, but these are the details of the observation, not the essence of science. One must observe the data where the data exist and by whatever procedures the data require. But one must be careful lest he unconsciously assume that it is the white coat or the far-away place or the microscope which makes the science. The reverse is nearer the truth. Science, the method of knowing which requires careful observation and verification, is the fundamental and necessary thing. Microscopes and stethoscopes are only the tools of the specific sciences, tools necessitated by the nature of the things which the specific sciences choose to study. An anthropologist with schedules and a pencil and a knowledge of the language of the Zulus is doing scientific observation, using the approved methods of his field, quite as much as is the astronomer who gazes into his telescope and charts the orbits of the planets.

*Values and the Scientist*

People cherish certain ideas which are called "values." These ideas contain or express the prevailing estimates which people have of the relative worth of things. Some values can be expressed in money terms, but most values concern non-economic matters. In America we characteristically value highly success, beauty, a high standard of living, and education. It might not be so in another part of the world. Speed, for example, is highly valued in America, but is much less highly valued in parts of China. Democracy is highly valued by some people in the United States, but not by others.

Once a person accepts a value, he becomes somewhat biased or prejudiced thereby. This does not mean that all people who accept the value of democracy are necessarily *equally* biased or prejudiced, but merely that they are all likely to be *somewhat* blinded to the possible values of a non-democratic social system. Similarly one may prefer rural life to city life, the Republican party to the Democratic party. Thus, one can not escape having some values, and once he has them they operate as prejudices or biases in his thinking.

In terms of values, then, we have said in the preceding part of this chapter that science of all kinds seeks truth, irrespective of what or whose values may be jeopardized by the results. By seeking to avoid bias and be amoral, science might seem to have nothing to do with values whatsoever. While this *is true for the method* of science, it is *not true for the goal* of science. The scientist seeks accurate knowledge, regardless of whose "ox may be gored" thereby, but *why* does he seek that knowledge? Why, *ultimately*, does he wish to discover accurate scientific knowledge?

### *Science Is a Value*

The scientist seeks scientific truth because he accepts, on faith and faith alone, that out of the quest for accurate knowledge will eventually come some good for human kind. He cannot be sure that that will be the result, because harm as well as good has resulted from scientific knowledge up to the present. Currently, one of thinking men's greatest fears is the atomic bomb which scientific man has created and which may destroy him. Even though less dramatically than in the case of the atomic bomb, many other scientific inventions have *so far* been of doubtful good. Yet science goes on apace, spurred by the hope and the faith that eventually, when there is *enough* knowledge, man may be the better for it. Thus, science as a goal, is basically a value.

In summary, then, the *method of science disavows values and seeks to eliminate them, but the eventual goal of science is itself a value, the faith in the ultimate good of knowing the truth.*

## SUMMARY

In this chapter the student has been introduced to the field of sociology and its relation to other fields of knowledge. We have pointed out that the youth of sociology has made for certain misunderstandings regarding its nature, and we have sought to correct those popular misunderstandings in the mind of the beginner by pointing out how, and to some extent why, they are incorrect. The complete story cannot be told in one chapter, or for that matter in one book, but at least the broad outlines of the point of view of modern sociology as a field of knowledge have been charted.

The content of sociology as a field of knowledge constitutes the rest of this book, or more properly, the whole sociological library of which this book is an elementary synopsis.

Before we turn to the subject matter of sociology proper, however, it seems necessary to devote one more chapter to orientation. Chapter II contains numerous study suggestions which experience in teaching beginning college students for over a dozen years has indicated are needed. Many errors and study difficulties can perhaps be avoided or reduced by doing one more orientation reading before launching into sociology itself.

## SUGGESTED READINGS

Since Chapters I and II constitute a single unit which is divided into separate chapters only for purposes of convenience, the readings for both chapters are combined and will be found on page 43 at the conclusion of Chapter II.

## STUDY QUESTIONS

1. Why has man been so slow in studying himself scientifically?
2. Why is it difficult to give a one-sentence definition of sociology?
3. Why is sociology often misrepresented and misunderstood?
4. In what ways is the term *sociologist* often improperly applied?
5. Why is sociology not "therapy"? Illustrate.
6. What is the "field of knowledge" of sociology?
7. Why is it necessary for each field of knowledge to develop its own technical tools?
8. Why are modern professional sociologists not advocates of any particular "ought to be"?
9. How may an interest in welfare grow out of a professional interest in sociology?
10. Why are most sociologists primarily interested in studying the existing scheme of things?

11. Why is it difficult to be entirely free from prejudice? Illustrate.
12. Why is it difficult to "integrate" the various present-day subject matter divisions in the social sciences?
13. How do different points of view arise in any one field of knowledge? Why is this often overemphasized?
14. How do differences among scholars promote progress in a science?
15. What is the basis for accurate prediction in any field of knowledge?
16. What is the ultimate purpose of science?
17. Is sociology a science? Why and why not?

# Chapter II

## SOME FUNDAMENTAL ATTITUDES AND UNDERSTANDINGS

Probably every field of study presents its own peculiar problems to the novice. Sociology is certainly no exception. Beginning students in sociology frequently have difficulty mastering the materials because they do not understand, first, what kind of attitudes or "mind sets" will be called for. This chapter is an attempt to acquaint the student with some of the more prominent attitudes which are taken for granted, in fact required, if one is to master the materials and understanding of sociology. They may be regarded as the mental tools of the trade. Eventually the student would probably "catch on" to these and learn how to use them, even if no specific directions were given in this introduction, but it should prove helpful to point out some of them in advance, and explain why they are so essential.

### OBJECTIVITY

The basic attitude or point of view which is essential for successful work in any science is objectivity. Objectivity means *the ability and the willingness to study the facts of a given field without prejudice.* It is essential to see things as they "really" are, even if this seeing is uncomfortable or not to one's liking or not to one's best interest. For example, a student who is proud of his scholastic record may find it difficult to acknowledge that his success is the result not solely of his hard work or of his perseverance, but also of the superior mind which it was his good fortune to inherit and develop. It would be much more satisfying to his ego if he could assume that all people are born equal in mental endowment and that therefore any superiority in achievement which might appear later would simply constitute evidence of his personal virtue. But if he is truly objective, he will have to accept the facts when they are presented to him, instead of resisting them or denying them or trying to explain them away. To carry our illustration further. This student probably would think, being as honest as he could, that taking account of his superior mental ability would constitute a reflection on his work habits. The point, however, is that his superior mental ability is a factor in his success. A second irrefutable fact is that basic capacity for learning *is* a biological trait, and the person has little control over it. Refusal to recognize facts like these is evidence of a lack of objectivity in a person's thinking processes. Since much of the subject matter of sociology consists of understandings as close if not closer to the existing prejudices of people as this one, the student must be especially conscious both of the need for being objective and of the hindrances to objectivity which are constantly being encountered.

*Lack of Training in Objectivity*

We have not been trained to be objective. As a matter of fact, most persons are actually trained not to be objective. Every one is more or less indoctrinated with prejudices about many things. It is always easy to recognize that the other person's views constitute prejudices, but it requires a considerable measure of objectivity to be able to recognize equally clearly that one is prejudiced himself. A man once complained to the writer that a friend of his who belonged to the opposite political party was "very prejudiced on political matters." He said that he had argued almost all night with the prejudiced man and could not change his political views. This complainant seemed quite innocent of the fact that *both* he and his political opponent were prejudiced, and that it was quite as significant that his own mind was not changed during the discussion as it was that the other man's was not. What he really said could be paraphrased this way: "I have intelligent ideas; he who agrees with me also does, but he who disagrees is either unintelligent, stupid, or prejudiced." This is more or less true of everyone although, of course, all persons are not equally prejudiced or necessarily prejudiced in the same direction or about the same things.

Not only is everyone indoctrinated with prejudices, but also often with the idea that not to be prejudiced constitutes "disloyalty" to some person or to some principle. A student recently reported, for example, that in the study of history she had learned certain facts about the private lives of some of our nation's heroes which were not wholly complimentary to their characters. She protested the teaching of such information on the ground that it was "disloyal" not to be able to continue to believe that these men were above reproach. One is forced to conclude, then, that she would prefer to remain ignorant and keep her "loyalties" rather than know the truth and lose them. This is by no means an exceptional case. Illustrations of the same point could be found in the thinking of almost anyone. It is a quite natural outcome of our teaching children to be loyal to groups and to ideals. Every group with which we are affiliated indoctrinates us with prejudicial views of many things. This is true of our church, our political party, our race, our social class, even our age-groups.

With this prejudice-producing background, which none of us can escape, it becomes exceedingly difficult suddenly to become objective and open minded about the things which yesterday we were admonished to regard as unquestionably true, eternally right, or inviolable. But that is precisely what one must stand ready to do if he is to be liberally educated in any field of knowledge. He must free his mind of all impediments to objective thinking. That does not mean that it is necessary to become a "doubting Thomas" about any and every thing all at once. Such would be mental anarchy and would lead to hopeless confusion. All that is required is the willingness and the ability to stand ready to accept evidence when it *is* evidence, even though that evidence may jeopardize the security of existing prejudice. Perhaps one further step is the recurrent searching of one's own thinking processes for the purpose of determining as far as possible what one's own prejudices actually are, and frequently asking oneself what evidence he has for the notions he accepts as "true."

### *"Factual Information" Is Often Wrong*

It will be noted before very many pages of this book are mastered that many of the "facts which every one knows are true" are really false. For example, practically everyone has heard, and probably has also repeated, the time-honored phrase, "He's a chip off the old block." Few think to question just what this means, and how accurate it is in the light of existing scientific knowledge about heredity. Let us do just that. First, we note, that "he" had two parents, not just one. Potentially, then, he is a chip off *two* "blocks." But the known facts about heredity do not permit us to stop even here. No one's heredity is acquired simply from his parents. Instead he inherits traits from his ancestors for many generations back, and usually *possesses traits which neither of his parents possess.* Analyzing still further, practically none of a person's behavior traits, other than some obviously physical ones, comes to him simply through inheritance. Many of them have to be *learned;* and *if they were learned by the parent they cannot be biologically transmitted by him to his child.* What then does the cliché that "He's a chip off the old block" really amount to? It is misleading, if not downright erroneous.

To illustrate the point a bit more vividly, try to answer the following short test of five factual questions. All are questions about which you must have thought and for which you could easily have found the correct answers if you were interested or if you had doubted that you had the right answer already. How many can you answer? The correct answer will be found in a footnote at the bottom of this page, but first try to answer each question as best you can before looking up the correct answers.

1. What is the population of the world?
2. What proportion of the population of the United States is Negro?
3. What percentage of the population of the world lives in the United States?
4. What percentage of divorces in the United States are secured by going to states with more lenient laws?
5. Does Virginia or West Virginia have the higher rate of illiteracy?
6. Is there any difference between the chemical composition of Negro and white blood?[1]

This test was recently given to over three hundred freshmen and sophomores in a midwestern university. Not one of them had as many as three answers even approximately correct. A majority of

[1] 1. Slightly over two billion.
2. One out of ten.
3. Between six and seven per cent.
4. Three per cent.
5. Virginia, by almost 60 per cent.
6. No.

them had no answers correct. The significant point, however, is not that they were incorrect but that *in a majority of cases they said they were sure they were right!* There is a great difference between realizing that one does not know the answer and assuming that something is true when it really is false.

*Interpretation of Facts Is Vital*

Even when one has the given *fact* correctly, he may err so badly in his interpretation of what it *means,* that his having the fact may be a liability rather than an asset. For example, it is generally known that due to recent medical advances, public health progress, and other factors, the average length of life in the United States has increased. It is not uncommon to hear persons say that, therefore, "people live to be older than they formerly did." Such an interpretation is wholly incorrect. One's chance of living to seventy or eighty is not much, if any, better now than it was previously. The average length of life has increased because a large proportion of the infants who would formerly have died during the first year of life are now saved. This raises the *average* length of life. Let us take a simple illustration based upon five people. Suppose that:

*A* dies at 1 year of age
*B* dies at 27 years of age
*C* dies at 38 years of age
*D* dies at 49 years of age
*E* dies at 71 years of age.

The average age of these five people would be computed by adding their five ages and dividing the sum by five. This average age is 37.2 years. Now, let us suppose that *A* lives to be 20 years of age instead of only 1, and all others to live exactly the same age as they did in our first illustration. By computing the average length of life in the same way as we previously did, we find that the *average increased by almost three years,* and yet no one lived to be older than 71 in either case. Now let us take a third condition. This time we shall have *E* live to be only 65 instead of 71. Computing the average age now we note that it is 39.8 years, almost one and one-half years longer than the average age we found in the first illustration, and yet no one lived even as long as the eldest did in the first illustration. What has occurred in the population of the United States through the increase of average age is simply that *more people live for a while*, not that a person at 20 years of age has a much better chance of living to "ripe old age" than he formerly did. The adage that "a little knowledge is a dangerous thing" is apropos much amateur interpretation of social facts like this one.

### *Lack of Objectivity Results Also from Attempts to Justify Social Position*

One frequently finds it necessary, or at least comfortable, to justify the things he does or the privileges he possesses. It is also useful to alibi his failures and mistakes. For example, during the great depression when millions of Americans were unable to secure means of employment, many of the more fortunate people were finding it easier to say that "anyone who really wants a job can get one" or "the more capable people get jobs when jobs are scarce," than to acknowledge the fact of the matter, namely, that for many people employment was simply not available irrespective of ability, character, or need. The same principle extends to our group affiliations—we learn popular clichés to justify the actions or ideas of our groups. Thus, numerous whites are quick to "explain" the superior advantages of whites in terms of the "lower capability of Negroes," omitting the remainder of the truth, namely, that Negroes are less well trained than whites, on the average, because whites, being in control, will not permit Negroes to utilize their skills along many lines by denying them job and educational opportunities. It is easier to say that the Negro "does not have the necessary experience to do a white man's work" than to say that one has denied him the opportunity to acquire the experience.

Sometimes unobjective information regarding one's community appears. For example, in one Ohio city located adjacent to a large city, the "Boosters' Club" boasts of the low death rate as compared to that of the larger adjacent city. The facts are correct as stated, but the reason is less complimentary. The city with the low death rate has no hospital, and its ill go to the adjacent city's hospitals for treatment and, when they die, the deaths are recorded in the city which has the hospitals within its borders! But yet, somehow, it is comforting to many to be able to live in the city with the low death rate, even if it is only a statistical trick! The trick, however, is at the expense of those who really believe that they live in "a more healthful city."

*Summary*

Perhaps enough has been said to indicate that coming to the right conclusions regarding truths in social science is not made easy by the mere fact that one has been exposed to some of its raw materials in the course of growing up. As a matter of fact, it is largely because one has been exposed to many of the prejudicial interpretations that it is difficult for him to be objective, and then come to correct conclusions. One can see the "superstitions" in the other person's religion better than those in his own. He can see the "logical errors" in someone else's philosophy better than he can the equally logical errors in his own. He is taught to do this, and is indoctrinated with numerous socially acceptable ways of thinking which make prejudice easy and objectivity difficult. Yet despite the difficulties, some measure of objectivity is attainable for almost everyone, and if they will work at it diligently, a great deal of objectivity about social phenomena is attainable by most. One of the by-products of studying this book will be a sharpened sense of objectivity about the matters with which it deals. The chief point to our discussion of objectivity was to show its importance, in fact indispensability, to successful scientific work in sociology, and to point out some of the handicaps to attaining objectivity "overnight." Progress in mastering objectivity is usually slow.

### THE PURPOSES FOR STUDYING INTRODUCTORY SOCIOLOGY

It has been pointed out previously that one cannot hope to learn the whole body of knowledge called sociology from the study of any one book or from any one course. Obviously, then, the writer should indicate just what parts or aspects of the whole field of sociology he is striving to present. Four objectives are sought:

1. To acquaint the student with the basic *point of view of sociology*. This has already been outlined in broad terms in the preceding chapter, but will need to be made more specific from time to time as we proceed.

2. To teach the student the *basic and more important information* which sociologists have discovered.

3. To give the student something of an idea of the *research procedures which sociologists use* in the discovery and testing of

their research, that is, how sociological evidence is gathered and interpreted.

4. To acquaint the student with the *basic technical vocabulary* of sociology. Each field of knowledge develops a specialized vocabulary, with a precise and often technical meaning attached to words. In order that a person be competent, even in an elementary way, to do work in a field, he must familiarize himself with some of the specialized terminology.

These, then, are the results which should be expected from your first adventure in the principles of sociology.

### *Technical and "Common-sense" Knowledge*

One of the notions which one hears so often and which he unconsciously eventually tends to accept because it is repeated so often, is the high respect for what is called "common sense." No one quite knows how to define it, but is forced to conclude that the trait must indeed be very *uncommon,* else its results would be more in evidence than they seem to be. Somehow, the notion persists that if a person is "close to" some phenomenon that he, therefore, secures some deeper insight into its nature and workings, that he acquires "practical" or "common-sense" knowledge about it which is as good as, if not better than, the knowledge which the more formally and technically trained "expert" has. While it may be possible that sometimes such experience yields important knowledge, it is certain that such revelations are very rare indeed. One is reminded of the well-known instance in which a mature woman dismissed the proffered services of a young, unmarried specialist in child care with the comment, "My dear, you can't tell *me* anything I don't already know about the care of babies, for I have already buried six of them." Much so-called "practical experience" may really constitute nothing more useful than prolonged practice in doing something the wrong way for a long time, or the habit of repeating the same mistake so often that it eventually seems "natural." Man has long since learned that observation, if it is to be used for the purpose of discovering what is true or for testing some assumption, is a highly difficult technical process. If it were not, then perhaps lovers would know more about the planets than astronomers do, because they have spent more time in the presence of this phenomenon of nature! One will do well not to commit the error of assuming that fighting off mosquitoes for a fortnight or a lifetime will make him any more competent as an entomologist! The time has long passed when a person could learn basic truths by informal speculation based on untrained observation; more reliable is the person who knows *by scientific processes* "whereof he speaks." There may be those who resent their reliance upon the experts, but the wise person with the problem will consult him who *knows* rather than rely upon his too-common "sense."

## THE USE OF CASES IN SOCIOLOGICAL WORK

### *The Case and Its Limitations*

One of the most difficult things for beginning students to understand about their work in sociology is how to use their own experiences. That raises the whole question of the individual "case." A case is a single unit of something which is observed as a whole. John Doe who lives on Center Street; Harvard University; World War I; the Office of Price Administration; your home town; the 1945 World Series, are all cases, as the term is employed in research and study. Before we can come to any general and reliable conclusion about "people" we must certainly study many more than just John Doe. Before we can come to any very reliable conclusions regarding the nature of universities, we must study many more universities than Harvard. Before we can come to any very accurate knowledge concerning government agencies, we must study more agencies than simply the O.P.A. This point seems obvious enough and usually no one takes exception to it when it is stated in the abstract. Yet there is a strong and pervasive tendency, which almost every layman manifests, to make or change generalizations on the basis of one or only a few cases. On every hand one sees this misuse of experience with one or a few cases. The following quotations reveal the persistent error.

"I understand children; I reared three."

"Polish people are stupid; I once had a Polish cook who didn't know how to defrost a refrigerator."

"Farm boys are hard workers; all three of the boys who got A's last semester grew up on farms."

"Jews are dishonest; a Jewish lawyer tried to bribe me."

"Women are unstable; my wife can never make up her mind about anything."

"Dogs are more intelligent than horses; my dog understands more words than my horse does."

"Coal dealers always cheat you on weight; that happened to me three different times."

In each of the above sentences the second clause is probably true, at least we shall so assume. The error in each sentence lies in the first clause. The implication is clear that the first clause is regarded as true *because* the second clause is true, that is, the second clause is given as evidence or proof that the first is true. The criticism is obvious enough. One Polish cook proves nothing about Polish cooks in general, one Jewish lawyer proves nothing about Jewish lawyers in general, and three experiences with coal dealers proves nothing about the other five thousand dealers. When one understands the cases thoroughly, which he rarely ever does, he still has no way of determining whether his one case is an example of the rule or constitutes an exception. Perhaps if one studied a great many Polish cooks, he might find that they were more capable, instead of less capable, than the others. Or if one made a study of all the coal dealers he might find that they gave more honest weight than other merchants who sell merchandise by weight. Even, however, after one has observed a considerable number of cases, he cannot be certain that he does not still have the exception rather than the rule. How many cases, then, are "enough" cases to justify a conclusion? This question can be answered, but not here nor anywhere in this book. There are technical statistical formulas which can be employed to test the adequacy of samples but they are beyond the province of this book. All that we are attempting to establish at this point, however, is the caution against drawing conclusions from one or a few cases of anything. That is a persistent error among amateurs in sociology.

There is, perhaps, one sort of conclusion which can be drawn from a given case. Suppose that it is alleged that all universities require English courses during the freshman year, but you know of one university which does not require English during the freshman year. The knowledge of this one case is useful in that it destroys the validity of the generalization that *all* universities require English during the freshman year. Thus, carefully employed, single cases may be useful to test generalizations which allege universal truths. When, of course, the generalization is stated as "usually" or "in 90 per cent of the instances," the "one case I know" ceases to have any utility.

*The Valid Use of Cases*

But cases, even single cases, are useful in sociological study and also in formal sociological research, provided one employs the individual case correctly. What, then, is the valid use of a case? Cases are valuable—almost invaluable—for the purpose of *illustration*. They make theoretical points more vivid and graphic. They add interest—even drama—to the study process. First, however, one must have had the principle tested and know by that procedure that it is correct, and then he may seek some one concrete example of it for use as an illustrative case. For example, suppose we are studying "white collar criminals." It may be helpful to read an autobiography of Joe Blow, who is a white collar criminal. Or suppose we are studying an abstract phenomenon such as "ambivalence," and have defined it as "the state of having simultaneous or intermittent opposite attitudes toward some person or thing." It might be helpful, then, to use the case of Mary Smith who both loved and hated her husband at the same time. She ordered him out of the house and before he could leave begged his pardon. She offered him a kiss, but when he accepted her offer, it rekindled her hatred and she again became angry. One must be careful, however, not to assume from the case cited that "ambivalence is what Mary did," because ambivalence exists in many different forms. Mary is only one instance. Other cases of ambivalent behavior may show striking contrasts from Mary's.

*Each Case Is, as a Whole, Unique*

"No two cases are alike." Each case is made up of a great many "attributes," that is, of specific traits or aspects. Some single attributes of many different cases may be the same, but the rest of the attributes may be different, making each case still unique. Two men are each twenty-seven years old today. They have this one attribute, age, in common, but in a hundred other ways they are different. John Doe is a radical and a member of a labor union. Joe Blow is also a radical but he is a union hater. With respect to the attribute of radicalness John and Joe are similar, but we note that regarding unions the two are opposite. Because two cases have one attribute in common, one must not assume that they necessarily have any other in common.

*One Case May Illustrate Many Different Things at the Same Time*

Here lies another difficulty with the use of cases. A given case may be used by one person because it illustrates one thing, but another person observing it "sees" some attribute entirely different. An English professor assigned a novel to a student because it contained a certain type of plot, but the student became so engrossed in the sensational descriptions of some love scenes that he did not even notice the plot! Or a given case may be used at different times to illustrate different things. A man tips his hat to a woman. This one act illustrates "deference," an "attitude," the "double standard" of conduct, "folkway," and "overt behavior." The man himself illustrates a Republican, a bibliophile, a "marginal man," a student, and a husband. Thus a case of one momentary act of one man may quite properly be used to illustrate at least five different phenomena, and the man at least five different attributes. When one is using a case he should be careful to indicate exactly what he intends to illustrate, and when a case is presented for illustration one should be equally certain that he understands of what it is supposed to be illustrative. Otherwise, confusion or error is probable.

## THE PROBLEM OF CAUSE AND EFFECT

The words *cause* and *effect* are of such common usage that it may elicit surprise to have them introduced here. It is not our intention to get into involved analyses of them as, sooner or later, every truly educated person should. The purpose to be achieved here is, simply, to point out a serious misuse of the "cause and effect" logic which arises so frequently in the thinking of beginners in sociological study.

A child once confided to his mother that he wished he had a "bushy tail like a squirrel." Upon inquiry as to why he wanted the bushy tail, he replied that then he "could crack nuts with my teeth." This almost incredible episode is almost tailor-made for the point under discussion. The child, unconsciously, assumed that the two most apparent attributes of the squirrel, bushy-tail-ness and nut-cracking-ness, were related causally merely because they were coincident attributes at the opposing ends of the squirrel. A more mature mind would immediately point out that the nut-cracking propensities of the squirrel are in no way affected by the bushiness of the tail. The two merely "happen" to exist together.

Many mature adults "think" about sociological matters in such a way as to commit the same error as this child did. A recent newspaper editorial pointed out that during the administration of a certain governor there had occurred an increase in the volume of business transacted in the state. The editorial called for the re-election of the governor on the ground that he "has been good for prosperity." While it is possible that certain decisions which a state governor makes *might* have some effect on the business activity of the state, it certainly does not follow that because a man's term of office coincided with a prosperity period, he caused the prosperity. The two just happened to coexist; the prosperity was related much more probably to the business boom of the war. It is almost an axiom in American politics that a man who is president when a business depression occurs finds it almost impossible to become re-elected at the next election. Few seem to be either willing or able to ask, first, what if anything he did could have caused or aggravated the depression; it is sufficient, apparently, that his being president at the time of the misfortune made him somehow responsible for it.

Much of the folklore of almost any people contains the same error in cause and effect thinking. Someone had a "bad night" and in the morning learns that a close friend died the night before. Not infrequently the two facts become causally related in his mind. He did not sleep well *because* Joe was dying. Instead of searching for possible—or even obvious—reasons why one could have had difficulty sleeping, such as ill-health, worry, improper eating the evening before, and so on, the tendency is to seek the "cause" in the most spectacular thing which occurred simultaneously, whether it has any demonstrable connection or not. As this is being written many persons are claiming that this or that occurrence—especially if it is undesirable—has been "caused" by the war. All that they really *know* about the matter in question, as a rule, is that it occurred *during* the war. This fact is insufficient proof of causation, although it might suggest a feasible hypothesis of causality. The correctness of the hypothesis, however, must first be established by careful research procedures before we have any scientific or moral right to assume that it is true. It may be "just a coincidence."

## LOGIC IS NOT THE SAME AS TRUTH

Many conclusions may seem "logical" but not be true. For example, one might "reason" that since a college education costs a great deal of money and since Americans are usually eager to get their money's worth, that, therefore, the student in college always works as hard as he possibly can, never misses a class, and resents an unexpected day of vacation because these would short-change him! Obviously, despite the logic, the truth is otherwise. Again, it is logical to assume that if people *know* the harmful effects of eating certain foods and/or drinks and want to live healthfully and long, that they would abstain from the harmful acts in order to insure their health or longevity. But, again, as we all know, for many persons the facts of the matter are quite otherwise.

Many students, unfortunately, approach the study of sociology too much disposed to reach "logical" conclusions instead of correct ones. Logical answers to questions are easier to reach than empirically correct ones are. One can sit in his armchair and "reason out" how men will act when in battle, but if he actually observes real men in real battle, he will probably find that they do not, *as a matter of fact*, act as he had reasoned that they would. Many generalizations pertaining to human behavior which the untrained brush aside as "unreasonable and therefore untrue" have been found by trained observers to be correct. This book contains many such principles, which, although often logically improbable as seen by the untrained mind of the gentleman in the armchair, have actually been found to be true by the trained student who has taken the trouble to study the facts.

## THE IMPORTANCE OF QUALIFICATION IN GENERALIZATIONS

In studying sociology the student should be careful to note the qualifying words such as *sometimes, rarely, usually, on the average, as far as we know, presumably*, and so on. There is an important difference between the statements that "all men are born equal" and that "all men are born equal *in legal rights*." The first is unqualified (and, incidentally, incorrect); the second is more nearly correct, although the word *all,* not further qualified as to place and time, would certainly raise grave doubts, because in numerous times and places great inequalities in legal rights have existed and still exist. In the United States at the present time, to be more exact, all people are born equal in legal rights *except* Negroes in some states, women, children born out of wedlock, orphans, and Japanese-Americans. And, also, since abstract legal rights are often of no particular significance to the person unable to afford competent legal counsel, we might need to add income or wealth or prestige as an additional inequality. Our original statement would be much more nearly in accord with the facts, and hence more nearly correct or true, if we restated it this way: "In America at about 1947 all legitimate, white, males have the same theoretical, but not actual legal equality."

Too much qualification can, of course, impede one unduly. Important as precision in scientific work is, it can be overdone, and render the resultant generalization ridiculous. It is recorded that a scientist and a layman were riding through the country and passed a flock of sheep that had recently been shorn. The layman remarked that, "Those sheep have just been shorn." The scientist is reported to have replied, after careful scrutiny of the sheep, "Well, it appears from where I am, that those which I can see have been shorn, on the side which I am observing, if my eyesight is correct." It is hardly necessary to qualify generalizations as guardedly as that.

It is doubtful that the beginning student will overdo the qualifications of his statements and thoughts. Experience shows that he is much more likely to err on the side of omitting much-needed qualification than he is to include it. This is especially important in reading sociological material or understanding correctly the instructor's statements. Laymen are usually not trained to see or to hear the finer distinctions, and it is the fine distinctions, often, which mark the difference between correctness and error. The writer once publicly read a paper which contained the following statement: "There are probably instances in which parental sex education of children is so inadequately or incorrectly done that the school is left with no choice but to take over this important task." The newspaper on the following morning, under the headline "Sociologist Advocates Sex Education in Public Schools," carried a story, containing some accurate fragmentary quotation, but which made no mention whatsoever of the qualifications in the recommendation that "probably" there were "cases" in which sex education had to be done by the schools which were "left with no choice but" to do it. This illustrates how a person (the reporter) who heard the entire paper and probably intended to report it correctly, committed a serious error by not noting the important qualifications in the general statement.

In studying this book the student will do well to watch carefully for qualifying words and phrases of the following sorts:

1. Regarding the *degree of generality*—words like all, always, sometimes, rarely, usually.
2. Regarding the *time referred to*—all time, since the beginning, during our generation, before the Civil War.
3. Regarding the *place referred to*—the world, this continent, Ohio, the South Pacific peoples, North of the Mason-Dixon line, in cities, in large cities.
4. Regarding the *group referred to*—everyone, males, persons 30-34, white collar workers, students in state universities.
5. Regarding the *conclusiveness of the evidence*—"on the basis of this one experiment," "in all cases studied," "on the basis of research conducted in the United States."
6. Regarding the *extent of professional agreement* on point under discussion—a majority of scholars, a few scholars, almost without exception, "a growing agreement," "an increasing skepticism."

The difference between understanding correctly, passably, or being entirely wrong may, and often does, lie in the qualifying phrase. Frequently the difference between the scientifically correct generalization and the popular one is in the qualification of the scientific one. "Like begets like," says the laymen to genetics. "Yes and No," says the geneticist, as he goes on to qualify the statement in the light of the whole truth, as the truth is known to scholars in that field.

### PREDICTION AND FORECASTING

Suppose that we were to assemble a group of capable—in fact distinguished—physicists, chemists, and automotive engineers and set before them this problem: Please predict the number of statute miles which this automobile will run on a gallon of "regular" gasoline. Our assembled scientists would no doubt refuse the task, not because they were poor scientists but because they were good ones.

They would explain, no doubt, that such a prediction could not be made, because they knew nothing about the many "variables" entering into the experiment such as, at what speed would the car be driven, what is the nature of the terrain over which it is to be driven, what is the mechanical condition of the car, how is it adjusted, what would the temperature be, the wind velocity and direction, *ad infinitum.* And yet the value of knowing such a "fact" as how far a given car can be driven on a gallon of gasoline might be great. The importance of the problem notwithstanding, the correct answer cannot be given in the *real* situation, but only "under controlled conditions." The scientist's predictions are valid only, he explains, under *known* conditions; if the conditions are unknown, the outcomes of a test cannot be foretold, or if the conditions change any forecast may be expected, therefore, to be inaccurate.

The social scientist recurrently faces the counterpart of the hypothetical automobile problem which we tried to have the physicists and chemists solve for us. At every hand someone wants to know the future in the realm of social and economic and political matters. Like the owner of our auto they have very urgent need for the information. For example, when will the post-war depression occur, and how severe will it be as compared with the last depression? Like our formerly assembled scientists, the sociologists and the economists will refuse to forecast—and for the identical reasons, namely, that the pertinent conditions are at the time this is being written not known, such as the policies of the government, the nature of the peace settlement, the rate and type of demobilization and many other facts.

It is not intended, in pointing out the basic similarity of the prediction problem in the two fields of science, to imply that the physical scientists are no better equipped to predict accurately than the social scientists are. One must admit that they are. But it is necessary also to note the *basic similarity of the prediction problem*—in fact the identity of it. Its essence lies in the *importance of the interrelation of the factors and variables.* Give either scientist the necessary information concerning the pertinent variables and then the prediction becomes relatively easy.

Forecasting, however, is different. It *foretells the future without regard to conditions or by guessing at the variables.* Many times such attempts are inescapable. Tomorrow's weather, your graduation date, the next war are foretold, correctly or otherwise, by many. What one does in forecasting is to estimate, or guess, at the variables, at the "other conditions" which he knows may change the result if they are other than operative as he anticipates them to be. The point to note is that we cannot avoid forecasting from time to time, because we must make plans for the future, and we must therefore come to some idea regarding what the conditions will be when the future arrives. We expect, also, that our forecasts will be wrong, or partly wrong, much of the time.

It is an error to assume, however, that the knowledge we possess has no predictive value. We know, for example, that in the United States during time of prosperity, high wages, and high employment, divorce rates rise. We cannot forecast the number of divorces for 1949 because at present we do not know what the wage and employment rates will be. But we can predict from our previous experience that in high probability the divorce rate will go up as prosperity does. Likewise we know that wars or threats of wars increase marriage and birth rates markedly, and so also with many other similar mass-phenomena.

Moreover, everyone makes a large number of day-to-day predictions and forecasts about his own behavior and that of his associates. Overwhelmingly his predictions and forecasts are correct, but not always so. He makes his correct ones on the basis of his knowledge of how the same or similar persons have behaved under the same or similar conditions in the past. It is safe to forecast, on the basis of our existing knowledge, many if not most of the questions, misunderstandings, and problems which will arise in a beginning class in sociology, particularly if one has taught such classes for very long. And so you usually predict your father's reaction when you ask for money, your own behavior if an important "date" fails to materialize, or your feelings at failing a course in college. If you have actually had each of these experiences a number of times you will probably predict more accurately, but even if the experience is a first one, your anticipations will not be wholly wrong. The point is not that our foretelling is infallible, it is, rather, that it is frequently correct and, as knowledge grows and becomes more precise, our foretelling does also.

In conclusion, then, we have pointed out the difference between forecasting and prediction, showing how prediction is the more precise, technical process of foretelling, necessarily useful only when one has knowledge of all of the pertinent "other factors" which may affect the occurrence being anticipated. *A* will cause *B*, provided *C*, *D*, and *E* are so and so, but if any one of them changes then *A* may not cause *B*. To illustrate: If you work reasonably diligently you will pass the course in mathematics, provided you do not become ill, provided you have the necessary mental ability, and provided you do not drop out of school. Should any of these occur or prove true, then you probably shall not pass the course. For you to assert now that you shall, in fact, pass the course would be a forecast: it might prove right or wrong.

Most sciences strive to predict and most can predict some things. Some predict more accurately and can predict more items than others can. Sociology can predict some occurrences, but by no means all. Its predictive value is being improved.

## SUMMARY

In this chapter an effort has been made to anticipate the students' difficulties in studying sociology. These difficulties may be reduced to some extent by observing the cautions and points of view discussed, but they probably cannot be wholly eliminated thereby. Instead, both student and teacher will need to strive from day to day to implement these study aids. Objectivity, for example, almost always comes slowly and then only through considerable effort. The proper use of cases is likewise a perennial problem, as is also the unguarded abuse of cause and effect and logical thinking. Once achieved, however, these mental tools will prove invaluable assets to more successful, and more zestful, living as well as constituting an aid to the mastery of the subject matter of sociology and related behavior science fields.

## SUGGESTED READINGS

Each item in the bibliography is followed by the letter **A** or **B**. **A** indicates that the reading is somewhat advanced and best suited, therefore, to the instructor or to the advanced or unusual student. **B** indicates that the reading is probably within the comprehension of the ordinary student. This procedure will be followed in each bibliography throughout the book.

BERNARD, L. L., editor, *The Fields and Methods of Sociology* (New York, Ray Long and Richard R. Smith, Inc., 1934). **A**

This symposium volume was prepared by the American Sociological Society for the purpose of setting forth the major fields of sociology and the chief research methods by which sociological data are gathered and interpreted. The book is valuable as an historical work.

Cooley, C. H., Angell, R. C., and Carr, L. J., *Introductory Sociology* (New York, Charles Scribner's Sons, 1933), Chapter XXIX. **B**

Chapter XXIX, entitled "Social Science and Values," treats a number of the same topics as are included in Chapters I and II in this book. In addition it presents a short resumé of the relations between social science and social philosophy (values) and of the history of sociology both in Europe and in America.

Gillin, J. L. and Gillin, J. P., *An Introduction to Sociology* (New York, The Macmillan Co., 1942), Chapter I. **B**

This chapter contains a useful definition of sociology for the beginner. There is also a well-balanced discussion of scientific method and scientific attitude with reference to sociology.

House, F. N., *The Development of Sociology* (New York, McGraw-Hill Book Co., 1936). **A**

A somewhat exhaustive and detailed treatment of the history and emergence of sociology in the intellectual currents of Europe and America.

Jensen, H. E., "Cultural Values as Data for Social Science," *Social Science*, Vol. VIII (1933), pp. 349-53. **AB**

A clear formulation of the basic idea that sociology is concerned with values *as data*. A very useful antidote to the student who "overlearns" the methodological point that sociology is amoral and thus fails to see that values are of the essence as materials for study.

Lumley, F. E., *Principles of Sociology* (New York, McGraw-Hill Book Co., 1935), pp. 3-19. **B**

An excellent elementary statement of the point of view needed for the successful study of sociology.

Lundberg, G. A., *Social Research*, revised edition (New York, Longmans, Green, and Co., 1942). **AB**

Chapter I, entitled "Theory and Planning of Social Research," is a clear statement of the way in which an objective, empiric social scientist proceeds in setting up a research problem.

Lundberg, G. A., *Foundations of Sociology* (New York, The Macmillan Co., 1939), Chapters I and II, especially. **A**

An advanced treatment of the "Postulates" of natural science and their application to sociological data. Quantification is stressed throughout. A somewhat controversial book, but a classic presentation of its point of view.

Lynd, R. S., *Knowledge for What?* (Princeton, New Jersey, Princeton University Press, 1939). **AB**

This is a widely known and important book. Lynd's thesis is that scientific objectivity among sociologists and other social scientists results in the loss of much of the scientist's contribution. He seems to advocate that sociologists espouse values and make their efforts "practical" in the sense that they orient their research and writing to public affairs and participate actively in championing the application of their findings to the direct improvement of social life.

## STUDY QUESTIONS

1. Why is objectivity essential to the study of sociology?
2. Why is it difficult to be objective in regard to human affairs?
3. Of what significance is current inaccurate factual information?
4. How do erroneous conclusions arise from the misinterpretation of facts?
5. How is lack of objectivity often a result of an attempt to justify position?
6. What is necessary besides "common sense" and "practical experience" to be an expert in any field? Why?
7. Why can't valid generalizations be based upon one or a few "cases?"
8. How may a single case be employed to test a "universal" truth?
9. Why is care necessary in the use of cases for illustrations?
10. Why are many logical conclusions often not correct?
11. Why is it necessary to qualify many generalizations?
12. What six general types of qualification are used in this text? Illustrate each.
13. Why are controlled conditions necessary for scientific prediction?
14. How do "forecasts" and "predictions" differ?
15. Why do we forecast in one situation and predict in another? Illustrate.

# *Part II*

# BACKGROUND UNDERSTANDINGS FROM CULTURAL ANTHROPOLOGY

# Chapter III

## CULTURE AND SOCIETY

### A NOTE ON LANGUAGE: TERMS AND CONCEPTS

One of the fundamental problems which one faces when he begins work in a new field is the necessity of learning the concepts which are employed and the words or terms which stand for the concepts. Until one learns what the biologist means by "vertebrates" or the economist by "marginal utility" or the political scientist by "sovereignty," he cannot penetrate very deeply into any of these fields. The student's problem here is more than just learning words; it is learning the *ideas* for which the words merely stand.

Fortunately, in all three of the cases just mentioned the terms have no popular meaning. If one hears the term *vertebrate, marginal utility,* or *sovereignty,* it is probable that the user of it has at least an approximate idea of what it means in the technical usage of the field of knowledge from which it comes. Unfortunately not all technical language consists of words which have no popular usage. Words like *sympathy, emotion, race,* or *accommodation,* while technically employed in one or more of the social sciences, also have other meanings in the everyday language of laymen. Thus, one must not assume that he knows what the psychologist means by "intelligence" merely because he already has a notion that intelligence has something to do with "smart people." He must first learn exactly what the psychologist means *by* intelligence before he can ever understand what the psychologist can tell him *about* intelligence. That it is unfortunate and confusing to have several usages of the same word in existence at the same time is admitted. But one has no recourse; he must use the language as it is. He must learn the correct usages of words and terms in the several contexts to which they customarily apply, if he is to be literate.

There is nothing inherent or essential about the particular word which happens to be used to represent a given idea. The word *cow* could just as well stand for the animal we now call *horse, so long as we all knew what it represented.* In the course of time, the various ideas which man has invented, as well as the various objects which he has experienced, have gotten more or less customary names to represent them. In other words, a *consensus* has arisen concerning what we shall call this thing or that idea.

All this discussion of language may be illustrated by considering "justice" as a *concept* and as a word. The word is only the label which is used when one wishes to refer to the idea of justice. Any other word could "do," but why use any other word when most people know already that the concept and the word *justice* "go together." But, do persons really *all* know what justice means? Does justice mean the same to a lawyer as it does to a layman? Does it mean the same to an employer during a strike as it does to an employee? Probably not. But, nevertheless, there is a rather general agreement or consensus on what it means, even though different persons' ideas of justice may be somewhat different. Each person's conception of justice, however, needs to be close to that of others' so that when they communicate there may be a meeting of minds.

In summary, it has been shown that while ideas are represented by words, the word (or term) and the idea (or concept) are distinct. Usually it is more difficult to learn the concept or idea, than it is merely to learn the label or terms. It has also been shown that a given term may have somewhat different meanings to different people, but despite these differences there may still be a general agreement or consensus. Finally, two or more quite distinct meanings or concepts may coexist for a given word, and be basically and uncompromisingly different, such as the professional and the popular use of the word *culture* to which we now turn.

## CULTURE

### *Introduction*

The basic discovery of social science, not just of sociology, is the phenomenon termed *culture.* While some of the social sciences can perhaps "get by" without a formal and precise consideration of the nature of culture, certain social sciences, particularly social anthropology, social psychology, and sociology probably cannot. Culture is fundamental to the understanding of the human being and of groups. Most of the other social science ideas grow out of it or are dependent on it.

For the present it is sufficient to define a culture as the way of life of any society. This way of life includes innumerable details of behavior. . . . They all represent the normal, anticipated (expected) response (acts) of any of the society's members to a particular situation. Thus, in spite of the infinite number of minor variations which can be found in the responses of various individuals, or even in those of the same individual at different times, it will be found that most of the people in a society will respond to a given situation in much the same way. In our society, for example, nearly everybody eats three times a day and takes one of these meals approximately at noon. Moreover, individuals who do not follow this routine are regarded as queer. Such a consensus (uniformity) of behavior and opinion constitutes a culture pattern; the culture as a whole is a more or less organized aggregate of such patterns.[1]

### *Popular Meanings of the Word* Culture

One frequently hears reference to some person as "cultured" or some act as "cultural." The implication is often clear in such usage that some other person is not cultured or some other act is not cultural. In other words, culture is popularly conceived in an evaluative way. Certain things are good or highly desirable or supposedly possessed of virtue, and are, therefore, called "cultural" to set them aside from the less good, the less valuable, and the less highly regarded things. *Social scientists do not use the term that way. All people have culture; although different persons and different groups have different cultures.*

### *The Technical Meaning of Culture*

How then, precisely, is culture defined in social science? What is the concept for which the word *culture* stands? Although there are several ways in which the idea can be worded, this way of stating it seems to be essentially accurate and yet reasonably simple: *Culture is the continually changing patterns of learned behavior and the products of learned behavior (including attitudes, values,*

[1] Ralph Linton, *The Cultural Background of Personality* (New York, D. Appleton-Century Co., 1945), p. 19.

*knowledges and material objects) which are shared by and transmitted among the members of society.* Like most definitions this one needs to be explained phrase by phrase and illustrated. That task will cover the next six pages.

1. "*. . . learned behavior. . . .*" This technical meaning of the word *behavior* should not be confused with the popular one implied in such sentences as "Now, son, behave," because technically the son is behaving whether he is doing the approved thing or the disapproved thing. Putting a tack on the teacher's chair, playing truant from school, or telling a lie are all "behavior," even though one could hardly regard any of them as praiseworthy. Not all behavior is learned, but most of it is. Combing one's hair, standing in line, telling jokes, criticising the President, going to the movie, and kissing one's aunt all constitute behaviors which had to be learned. So, also, is feeling angry or hurt because someone laughed at you, solving a problem in mathematics, or worrying about your health. Each of these had to be learned. One readily recognizes that he had to learn how to solve the mathematics problem, but he is apt to overlook the fact that he also had to learn to worry, to love his mother, or to use the latest slang word. Sometimes the words *conscious* learning and *unconscious* learning are used to distinguish the learnings which one does deliberately from the learnings which "just seemed to happen" in the course of living.

2. "*. . . pattern of learned behavior. . . .*" Our definition of culture indicated that the learned behavior of people is *patterned.* One's behavior is not just a list of items. There is a *relationship among these items.* Why are you reading this book at this moment? Whatever your reason, you will find that it is related to some other item of your total behavior. Perhaps you are curious to know what culture is. Perhaps you are just fulfilling a requirement in a course. If you think a bit you will observe that you either like or dislike this book, and perhaps, if you think long enough and accurately enough, you may be able to discover why you like it or dislike it. Thus the act of reading, the reason for reading, your attitudes and feelings toward the reading, as well as many, many other behaviors are interrelated. And so, of course, with everyone else. It would be difficult indeed, for almost any normal person to find a wholly isolated or unrelated unit of learned behavior. Even should this be done in one or, even several instances, it would only serve to rein-

force the general point since one had to search so hard to find an exception to the rule.

Another way in which behavior is patterned or fitted together is in the relationship between the behaviors of people when they are in contact. In order that one person may give, another must receive. Many of the learned behaviors making up each person's life have complementary behaviors in the life of someone else. If one will reflect for a moment upon the many behaviors involved in the following reciprocal and complementary relationships, this phase of patterning will be more clear: husband-wife behavior, parent-child interaction, teacher-pupil relationship, employer-employee interdependence, and so on. Each person's behaviors often depend upon some particular behaviors of someone else. The point is not that the behaviors fit perfectly, or that they fit every time, or that one is necessarily conscious of the fitting. It is rather that, as a rule, behaviors are somewhat integrated or organized with related behaviors of other persons.

The learned behaviors of whole peoples also constitute a sort of pattern—a pattern of living. Putting together all of the innumerable separate acts of the men, women, adults and children, rich and poor, urban and rural, of present day America one finds that there is a total or overall configuration which has been called the "American way of life." There is, of course, also an "urban way of life," a "rural way of life," a man's "way of life," a woman's "way of life," a child's "way of life," a politician's "way of life," a factory worker's "way of life," and so on, *ad infinitum.*

We have now shown that much human behavior is learned and is patterned for both the person and the group.

3. "*. . . and the results of behavior. . . .*" As one lives among other people he acquires a great many behaviors from them, likes and dislikes, notions of right and wrong, explanations of what is supposedly true and what is not true. He probably seldom wonders how the right and the wrong, the true and the untrue came so to be regarded. If as a child he were to ask why these things came to be, he in all probability would receive an answer which would boil down to something like this: "Things are right and wrong because they are right and wrong. Decent people do things this way; if you wish to be a decent person you will too." This explanation more than likely would carry with it considerable "punch"—ex-

pressed or implied threats of dire consequences which would follow should one observe other conceptions of right and wrong than those prescribed.

Thus far our point is obvious enough. But what is frequently missed is the fact that the ideas which come to one are ready-made *by man,* had to be fashioned by someone, somewhere, somehow. It is not necessary at this point to consider the specific questions of where and how some one notion or practice came into being; for example, why women powder their faces and cut their hair now, whereas well-dressed men in George Washington's day cut their hair quite similarly and then powdered it. The point is that the upper-class man of Washington's era who wished to be well groomed, powdered his hair, because this unit of behavior was correct. It was "correct" simply because it resulted from the experience of the men who had preceded Washington. One learns behavior from others, and they in turn from others, until we get back eventually to the point of origin of the particular behavior in question. The act originally came into use as a result of someone's initiating behavior.

Another sense in which cultural learnings are the "results" of behavior may be seen in this way. As the person behaves, performs the acts making up his life, there occur changes *in him.* He acquires the ability to swim, to feel hatred toward someone, to think objectively, or to sympathize with someone. These attributes of his being are real, and can be demonstrated by him quite readily. They have grown out of his previous behaviors.

In both ways, then, human behavior is the result of behavior. The experiences of other people are impressed on one as he grows up, and also many of his traits and abilities have grown out of his own past behaviors. Of what, now, do these results consist? The next paragraphs will amplify somewhat more fully what is included among the "results" of behavior.

*a.* "*. . . including attitudes, values, knowledges. . . .*" There is a widespread error in the thinking of many people who tend to regard the ideas, attitudes, and notions which they have as "their own," that is, that they are unique to one because they result from his "own experience." It is easy to overestimate the uniqueness of one's own attitudes and ideas. When there is agreement with other people it is largely unnoticed, but when there is a disagreement or difference one is usually conscious of it. Let us take a simple instance. Select some friend of approximately your own age and sex and think of all the ways in which you are alike, of the things which you both do, the ideas on which you both agree, and the likes and dislikes which you both have. The list of these close similarities in behavior would be impressive. Yet how could it be otherwise? You have both grown up, very roughly speaking, in the same or similar cultures. Therefore, obviously you both speak the English language, and you both want to have more money. Your differences, however, may also be cultural. Suppose you are a Protestant and the other person a Catholic. You came in contact with one cultural religious stream of ideas, prejudices, and practices called "Protestant"; the other person came in contact with a somewhat different pattern of ideas, prejudices, and practices called "Catholic." (We shall not define attitudes and values at this point, but shall do so later.)

And so it is also with knowledge. How does one really *know,* for example, that the major ideas and truths which he accepts as correct are correct in fact? How can he determine that they are correct? He thinks about them, no doubt, but with what does he think? He thinks with his other knowledges, with the prevailing prejudices, and the things which he "takes for granted" because others do too. How does one know that one hundred fifty million divided by three is fifty million? He certainly has not carefully counted out one hundred fifty million items of something into three equal piles and then found that there are fifty million in each pile! Rather he learned a thinking method called "arithmetic," one of the mental processes of which is division. And so with other kinds of logic and other thought systems.

*b. "... and objects...."* Frequently as people behave, their behavior results in creating objects. Man's behavior has created an impressive array of material objects all the way from the crude flint choppers of the stone age to the sky-scrapers, flying fortresses, and electron microscopes of today. Men were behaving when they made these things. To make these objects required numerous and various skills which human beings have gradually built up through the ages. Man has invented the "know how," he has preserved his knowledge, and he has organized and integrated it with other knowledge he had. And, behaving again, he has invented something else and so on and on.

Occasionally one encounters the view that man does not really "make" baseball bats, steel, or a battleship. All these things, it is sometimes argued, first existed in a "state of nature"; man merely modified their form, changed them from a state in which they were to the state in which he now uses them. The chair was first a tree which man surely did not make. The glue which holds the pieces together probably came from the hoofs of a horse which man certainly did not make. But the chair is more than trees and horse hoofs, and the flying fortress is more than iron ore, sap from a rubber tree, and so forth. Undeniably man *uses* nature, but the significant question is, *how* does he use nature? Nature contained wood, but not chairs. Nature contained dogs, but not Great Danes. Nature contained sand, but not the lens of a telescope. It seems a very unreal and indefensible point of view to deny that man has created these things which were fashioned not by nature, but by the ingeniousness of man's mind.

4. "*. . . shared by . . . the members of society. . . .*" The patterns of learned behavior and the results of behavior are possessed not by one or a few persons, but usually by a large proportion. Thus, many millions of persons share such behavior patterns as Christianity, the use of automobiles, or the English language.

As has been pointed out previously, the numerous persons whose mode of life contains some one pattern of behavior need not be otherwise identical. Persons may share some part of a culture unequally as, for example, Americans do the Christian religion. To some persons Christianity is the all-important, predominating idea in life. To others it is less preoccupying, and to still others it is of marginal significance only. Not only do the various people share unequally in Christianity, but they share different aspects of it—Catholic and Protestant, liberal or conservative, as clergymen or as laymen. But Christianity is nevertheless shared, even though unequally and somewhat variously. The point to our discussion is not that culture or any part of it is shared identically, but that it is shared by the members of society to a sufficient extent that, given a person's cultures, one can have a reasonably accurate idea of what that person does, how he looks, what he believes, and numerous other facts about him, even though not everything about him.

5. "*. . . transmitted by. . . .*" These cultural ways which we have been discussing are learned *by* persons *from* persons. Many of them

are handed down by one's elders, by parents, teachers, and others of a somewhat older generation. Other cultural behaviors are "handed up" to elders. Most children have taught their parents more about the child culture than either the parents or the child are likely to recognize. Home economists, for example, have frequently pointed out that one of the ways of improving home-making standards for adults is to teach better standards to their children. Many a parent likewise comes gradually to be educated in the precisely correct and latest adolescent slang. Finally, some of the transmission of culture is among contemporaries, neither down from the elders nor up from the juniors. Styles of dress, recreational fads, political views, and the use of recent labor saving devices all tend to illustrate the point.

It is necessary to point out that the phrase "transmitted by" may not indicate too clearly, exactly what is involved in the handing along of patterns of learned behavior. Transmission is really a shorthand word for the process of *teaching and learning,* which must go on whenever a behavior is passed along. One does not acquire a behavior pattern spontaneously. He learns it. That means that someone teaches him and he learns what is being taught. The parent who learns a slang phrase from his child probably does not recognize that he is learning something, any more than the child realizes that he has momentarily served as teacher. We see here again an example of the basic principle involved in cultural learning, namely, that much of the learning process both for the teacher and the learner is quite unconscious, unintentional, or accidental, but it is learning and teaching nevertheless.

6. "*. . . continually changing. . . .*" There is one fundamental attribute of culture: the *fact of unending change*. Few if any persons who live to maturity leave the identical culture which existed at the time of their birth. Phrases like "stagnant cultures" and "unchanging cultures" are misleading. All that squares with the facts is that some societies at some times change slowly, and hence in comparison to other societies seem not to be changing at all. But they are changing, even though not radically or obviously so.

People frequently (but not always) have a deep-seated distrust and fear of change. It is usually easier not to change—to drift along in the accustomed ruts, doing as one always did. That requires less thinking, and there is less chance for making a mistake. But the behavior patterns of culture really constitute the techniques through which the people of the society meet and solve the many problems which periodically confront them. From moment to moment as one lives, he encounters problems and obstacles. When he is confronted with a problem he turns to the solutions for situations like that, which he has learned in the course of participating in culture. Man does not meet each recurring situation in *exactly* the same way each time, however. He makes modifications, large and small. He tries new ways, or he accidentally stumbles on to new ways of handling the situation. These new ways are transmitted to others, and already the culture is changed. The person who sets for himself the task of preserving the culture of the society permanently as it is at any one time, has cut out for himself a hopeless and impossible task. At best all he can do, and even that is not as easy as it appears, is sometimes to slow down the unending and uncontrollable process of change. Repeatedly man sets up social systems—government, requirements for the A.B. degree, and rules for the game of football—because above all else man seems to want security and predictability in his affairs. But he wants the impossible—the impossible in terms of the nature of his being. He often wants security, but he manifests ceaseless change. The saving grace in the situation is that man has the kind of a mind which enables him to solve problems in new ways as they arise. The point is not that his new solutions are perfect or permanent, but simply that they are new, and thus give him another chance at controlling his destiny. The only certainty is uncertainty, the only security is the security which comes from having the kind of mind which gives him at least a "fighting chance" to create something new to give his life, for the time being at least, the semblance of being secure.

### *Summary*

We have tried in this section to clarify the meaning of the fundamental concept, *culture*. To recapitulate: culture is a continually changing pattern of learned behavior and the products of learned behavior (including attitudes, values, knowledge, and material objects) which are shared by and transmitted among the members of society. Attention has been called to the facts:

1. That the behaviors of people are largely learned;
2. That they are organized into patterns;

3. That these patterns result from the teaching (conscious or unconscious) of other people;
4. That they exist both in the form of material objects and intangible thought-habits like attitudes and knowledges;
5. That they tend to be somewhat uniformly shared by the members of society, learned from and taught to each other largely unconsciously;
6. These ways of doing and ways of thinking make up the pattern of human lives;
7. These ways are constantly changing.

We shall go on, now, to a further consideration and a somewhat more detailed analysis of culture.

### *Culture: the General and the Specific*

It is common knowledge that different groups around the world have different "ways of life," that is, different cultures. It is equally true that different groups in a modern American city have markedly different cultures. The Cadillac-driving social class is different from the jalopy-driving American classes in many more ways than just the automobile. Almost every person has had the experience at some time of being in "an uncomfortable spot," when he found himself abruptly in the midst of a group of people whose ways were sufficiently different that he felt confused, embarrassed, or conspicuous. The different cultures around the world or around your home town are not different in all respects, although they are different in enough respects to be obvious. We shall treat this matter of cultural variability at length in another chapter. The fact of difference in human cultures is mentioned here because it is necessary to establish a basic distinction in the use of the concept. Some sociological generalizations refer to *a* culture, like the culture of the Zulus, the Roman culture during the Empire, or the culture of the Mormons in Utah during the 1880's. Many of the findings of sociologists pertain only to a *given culture.* Other findings pertain to *culture in general,* that is, are true of all cultures, or at least of all cultures studied thus far. Thus, we refer to "language" which is found in all cultures, but a specific language, English, Sanscrit, or Latin, when referring to the means of communication found in some given group at some given time. It is important always to bear in mind that *both kinds of generalization are valid and useful in their places,* but to assume that because something is true in one culture it is therefore true in all cultures, is a frequent and serious source of confusion. It will be recalled that in an earlier chapter a discussion of the value and limitation in the use of cases was presented. To some extent one may think of *a* culture as a case, having all of the utility and all of the limitations pertaining to the use of cases which were there discussed.

It is well perhaps not to make too much of the language distinction between *a* culture and cultures *in general,* because it is not a radical departure from standard usage in the English language. The word *man* may refer to *a* man or may refer to *all* mankind. The word *state* may refer to a specific state or it may be used generically as *the* state referring to all states in existence. It may be useful to add that *a* culture is somewhat tangible; it can be seen, studied, described, experimented upon, and even, using the word loosely, "felt." Culture, in the general sense is, of course, an abstraction. It cannot be seen or experienced by any of the ordinary senses, although one may conceive of it in the same way that he can conceive the idea "dog" as distinct from any specific dog, of any specific size, specific color, or specific appearance.

In order to be able to "understand people," it has been found necessary for social scientists to study both specific cultures and culture in the abstract. Certain conclusions regarding cultures in general may be reached by studying the specific details of the many individual cultures. Other conclusions consist of generalizations based upon specific informations about some one culture and are applicable only to that culture. Neither type of study is necessarily to be considered as any more useful or any more important than the other. Both are needed, are in fact, indispensable to an adequate understanding of human beings.

### *Do Animals Have Culture?*

Man is only one of several "higher vertebrate species"; one of which, the ape, is similar enough to man in several respects to suggest that it might be "near enough" to man to possess a culture. Animals possess learned behavior, and animals *may* learn some behaviors from others of their species. But there are important differences between animal and human learning. First, man learns many *more* things than any animals appear capable of learning. Second, and much more important, human learning differs in its nature. Humans can learn in one basic and significant way in which animals seem not to be able to, namely *through the medium of abstract language.* Animals can learn imitatively, by trial and error, and by rote training, but seem unable to learn symbolically or purposively. There is no evidence that a mother cat, for example, "reasons" that if she brings a half-live mouse to her kittens, that that will enable the kittens to learn how to handle a live mouse. Nor do we know how much of animal behavior is instinctive and how much is learned. There are probably elements of both in animal behavior. Moreover, animals appear to lack the ability to think abstractly, that is, to abstract the *attributes* of a thing from the *total* thing. For example, a dog may be taught the word *ball* and to associate the word with the object. He may be taught to "bring" the "ball." Some animals can be taught to distinguish red balls from green balls. But animals cannot be taught, even by humans expert in animal training, to *abstract the attribute* "red" from the total red-ball so that it can thereafter identify redness as a trait wherever found, in a ball, a coat, or a sunset. Also, the ape can be taught numerous acts denoting kindness such as bowing or giving food to a newcomer. But he *cannot be taught the idea "kindness,"* so that he can act *in original ways to show kindness* the way that humans do.

It is doubtful, then, that one may attribute culture to animals, because learned behavior among animals lacks certain characteristics which are essential to culture as humans have it.

1. Animals *cannot purposively* teach other animals—at least the evidence is lacking which would permit us to say that they do. Even though some cultural transmission is unconscious, much of it also is taught deliberately.

2. Animals *cannot learn abstractions.* Much human behavior is taught by language symbols or precepts which animals apparently cannot comprehend.

3. Animals *cannot accumulate* their learnings. Each generation starts more or less "from scratch." Each human generation starts where the last one left off. Whether the song of the "Bob White" is learned or instinctive, it is the same song for all quail and is not consciously or deliberately modified from generation to generation.

4. Animals *cannot solve as complex problems* as humans, although animals appear to be able to solve some problems with originality. The basis of their learning, like ours, is trial and error, however.

All this would seem to indicate a rather fundamental and important difference between animal and human mentality. In short, the abilities which are indispensable to the creation and transmission of culture, animals appear not to have or not to have in sufficient degree to be capable of the kind of cultural life which characterizes humans.

## SOCIETY

Culture, however, is not the people. Although no analogy is useful without being at the same time inaccurate, we shall risk one which has served for some time to help clarify the distinction between society and culture. In some ways culture may be considered to be like a play, and the people of the society where the culture prevails may be considered as actors enacting the play. The play is, of course, visible only through the enactments of the actors. The actors get their lines from the play; although they are given some freedom of choice in interpreting the play, not very much "leeway" is usually permitted. The only tangible existence which the play has is in the portrayal of the players; the only knowledge one has of the players is the play which they enact.

Society, thus, may be thought of as the organized group of people who enact a culture. There are, of course, many weaknesses to this analogy. The people of the society do not "play" their culture. It is the only existence which, for the most part, they know; the very essence of their lives is that one culture. Moreover, the members of the society do not merely "enact" the culture; they create culture as they go along, carrying on, like the bride, with "something old and something new." But the illustration is useful in showing both the close relationship of culture and society, and yet also the basic distinction.

### *Definition of Society*

A society may be defined as a *group of people who have lived together long enough to become organized and to consider themselves and be considered as a unit* more or less distinct from other human units. The key phrase in the definition is a *group of people.* A culture, on the other hand, is a *group of behavior patterns.* The behavior patterns of the culture determine both the behavior and the organization of the persons of the society, but the behaving *people constitute the society.*

*Society and Societies*

The same basic distinction which was pointed out with respect to *a* culture and culture needs to be pointed out again regarding *a* society and society. One is the specific; the other the general. Study of both is needed and cautions must be observed in speaking and writing so that the reader or the listener may know whether the generalization applies to the society of the Tschambuli in 1900 or to all human societies that have ever been studied.

## SUMMARY

In this chapter we have defined and explained the fundamental concepts of sociology—culture and society. This has been only a beginning, of course, because the whole book is about culture and society. Culture is the constantly changing patterns of learned behavior and the products of learned behavior (including attitudes, values, knowledges and material objects) which are shared by and transmitted among the members of society. Society is the group of people who have lived together long enough to become organized and to consider themselves and be considered as a unit.

The distinction between the general and the specific use of these terms has been stressed, because it has been found that much error results from the failure of students to keep that distinction clear. We have also discussed the fundamental paradox inherent in the nature of both culture and society—the illusion of stability and the fact of constant change.

## SUGGESTED READINGS

Blumenthal, Albert, *Culture Consists of Ideas* (Marietta, Ohio, Marietta College Press, 1937). **A**

A somewhat hypercritical evaluation of definitions of culture and a formulation of a "best" one. This short work is useful, however, for (1) emphasis on the fact that culture consists basically of ideas, and (2) evidence of the difficulty of synoptical definitions.

Gillin, J. L., and Gillin, J. P., *An Introduction to Sociology* (New York, The Macmillan Co., 1942), Chapter VI. **B**

A somewhat different, but by no means inconsistent, treatment of culture on the elementary textbook level. Terse and interesting.

House, F. N., *Development of Sociology* (New York, McGraw-Hill Book Co., 1936), Chapter XXII. **A**

An historical treatment of the concept of culture from its beginnings in the social thought of European and American theorists.

Linton, Ralph, *The Cultural Background of Personality* (New York, D. Appleton-Century Co., 1945), Chapter II. **A B**

A clear and direct statement of the nature of culture. Similar to the formulation presented in this book.

Lowie, R. H., "American Indian Cultures," *American Mercury*, Vol. XX, (July 1930). **B**

A readable and illuminating account of the cultures of several American Indian peoples. Useful in correcting many of the current myths about "the" American Indians.

## STUDY QUESTIONS

1. Why is it necessary to learn technical terms and concepts when one begins the study of a new field of knowledge? Does the seasoned scholar need to learn new language and concepts? Why?
2. What is the relationship between terms and concepts? Illustrate.
3. What difficulties arise when one term represents two or more concepts? Illustrate.
4. Why will most people in a society respond to a given situation in much the same way?
5. What differences do you observe between the technical meaning and the popular meanings of the word *culture*?
6. How do we acquire our behavior patterns? How are they "patterned?"
7. If we are acquainted with a person's culture, why can we predict to a certain extent that person's behavior? Illustrate.
8. How is cultural learning a mutual interaction between contemporary people rather than a "handing-down" process?
9. What are the differences between animal and human learning? How do these differences relate to culture?
10. Distinguish between culture and *a* culture. Why is the distinction essential?
11. What is the relationship between society and culture? Illustrate.
12. Why must the so-called "basic" groupings of people be stated in general terms? Give examples.
13. Why are there no static societies or unchanging cultures?

# *Chapter IV*

## VARIABILITY AND UNIFORMITY AMONG CULTURES AND SOCIETIES

One of the interesting by-products of American participation in the global World War II, is the contact which millions of American young men in the armed services have had with peoples of greatly different cultures from our own. Especially in North Africa, the Pacific, and the Near East, servicemen have rubbed elbows with folk whose ways of life have been so alien as to tax the credulity of many of the folk "back home" who read the soldiers' and sailors' letters describing their experiences. Probably the letters provide the "home folk," however, with more amazement and amusement than understanding. Knowledge about these peoples is, of course, "old stuff" to professional anthropologists and sociologists who have been writing libraries of books and articles describing and interpreting the cultures of the various societies around the world. Not infrequently the writer and his colleagues have been amused by some veteran's offer to "let us in" on his "discoveries" or experiences. It usually turns out that what the soldier thought was an unusual interpretation or a newly-discovered fact has actually been a commonplace fact or interpretation well known to behavior scientists long before the war. But G. I. Joe's personal experience, though of limited use in the discovery and interpretation of anthropological data, has not been valueless; it has provided him with a few vivid first-hand observations which are useful as background, not only for him but also for those persons whom he has told about it. Usually these experiences should be used with care, however.

Two cautions to the person who has observed other cultures at first hand should be understood at the outset. First, much of the content of the culture observed tends to escape the observation of the untrained observer. Suppose that an Arab soldier was suddenly stationed in the United States and remained here for six months or two years. How much of American culture would he *really* see? How much of the culture would we permit him to see? With the limited knowledge of English which he could master in that time, how much of American culture could he grasp, even if we associated with him freely and used no caution whatsoever in interacting with him? Obviously, he could leave America after a reasonably long stay with only very superficial observation of American material culture, and with very confused and often mistaken ideas of our modes of thought. The American in Melanesia or Tokio comes back with equally distorted and incomplete ideas about these places and people for the same reasons that the hypothetical Arab would return to Arabia with distorted ideas about America. But he does not often realize this.

A second caution centers around the *interpretation* of other cultures, assuming for the moment that the actual observation has been 100 per cent accurate. "What of it," if one has observed that the New Georgians decorate their graves with elaborate artifacts made from coral, and "what of it" if the graves contain human skulls? Whose skulls are they, members of the dead men's families, his enemies, or of whom? Why are they there? What purpose do they fulfill in the scheme of things of the New Georgian natives? And, what is most important of all, after these questions have been answered correctly, what does this knowledge contribute to understanding mankind as a whole, not just the New Georgian natives or the Veddah, but Americans, Canadians, Republicans, and New Yorkers? These are, of course, technical questions which in order to be answered correctly require many other pertinent knowledges which have been built up through research, criticism, and more research down through the many years during which the sciences of human behavior have been built up. "A little knowledge is a dangerous thing," runs the adage, and it certainly applies to the ever-present tendency to assume that one "knows all about" the people in another society merely because he lived there as an unwilling and grudgingly-received foreigner for six days, six months, or six years.

## SCIENTIFIC INTEREST IN COMPARING CULTURES

Everyone, it seems, is interested in the "quaint, queer folk" of other societies. Souvenir hunting among strange peoples is a common hobby. Travelers' tales are always amusing. But *scientific* study of cultural variability has advanced considerably beyond the curio-hunting and naïve sensationalism of the layman. Modern behavior scientists' interest in cultural variability centers around certain *theoretical problems* pertaining to the different cultures in which man lives and has lived.

1. *How wide is the variation among cultures?* Is it literally true that "the ideas of some society make anything right, and of the next society make the same thing wrong?" Or are there some limits beyond which the variability does not go?

2. *Why do these variabilities exist?* Since man as a species is biologically constituted the same, why does he not behave everywhere the same, as the members of other species do?

3. *Are there uniformities common to all cultures?*

This chapter contains a treatment of these three basic problems.

## VARIABILITY AMONG CULTURES

It would be impossible to summarize even a very small fraction of the available material on cultural variability which ethnologists have discovered. There are hundreds of cultures in the world, and thousands of patterns in each culture. It must suffice to give a few examples, so that the student may get some understanding of the general situation. We shall therefore treat very briefly the extent of cultural variability in certain characteristic parts of culture.

### 1. *Variability in Sex-Marriage-Family Behavior*

Everywhere the human race is divided into two sexes, and everywhere human beings reproduce by the same biological process. There is, however, seemingly no end to culturally formed variations in how, when, and where the basic biological processes are to be carried out.

*a. The makeup of the family* illustrates variability convincingly. Some societies, like ours, are *monogamous,* that is, each adult person is permitted to have only one legal mate at a time. He is permitted remarriage only after the death of the previous mate or after a court decision (divorce) sets the marriage aside. Some societies have stricter monogamy than we do, because they prohibit divorce, and in some cases do not permit remarriage, even after the death of the mate. In many parts of the world *polygyny* is and has been permitted or required. Under the polygynous system, a man has multiple wives. If the man has great prestige, wealth, or power, the number of wives may run into the hundreds, as in the well-known case of King Solomon. Usually, of course, the number of wives is much lower, and often even in a polygynous society a man may not take advantage of the privilege of having multiple wives. Then, also there is *polyandry*, the practice of one woman having multiple husbands. Polyandry is and has been much less common than polygyny. Finally, *group marriage* exists. Under this system a group of men are married to a group of women, not necessarily of equal number, each person having sexual access and economic and legal rights to all or a number of the others. Group marriage is not widespread, but does exist in a few societies. It is important to note that there are innumerable details which make up a polygynous or polyandrous society, just as there are innumerable details which have to be observed in a society like ours in order to carry out our specific kind of monogamous system. For example, the colonial American mating system was monogamous, many native American Indian cultures were monogamous, and we are monogamous, but the details of each of these three systems varied greatly. Likewise in some polyandrous societies it is required that the multiple husbands be brothers, while in other societies it makes no difference. Thus, we see that in the mating arrangement every possible combination of the sexes has somewhere come to be accepted—one man to one woman; one man to several women; one woman to several men; and several men to several women.

*b. Mate choice.* In some societies a woman is not eligible for marriage until after she has borne one or more children. It is said that the logic of this practice is that child bearing is such an important function, that no respectable man would want to risk marrying a woman who might prove to be infertile. Obviously, under such conditions pre-marital sex behavior is not only permitted, but necessary. In other societies the unmarried men and women must not only remain chaste, but are prevented from speaking to each other from the time of puberty until marriage. Frequently girls are not eligible for marriage until all older sisters are already married. Sometimes wives are purchased either in exchange for money, for property, or for the young man's labor. Sometimes the marrying persons choose each other, and sometimes their marriage is arranged by parents or some other persons. In some cases marriages are arranged between older men and infant girls, the marriage to be physically consummated when the girl attains maturity. Sometimes mates are "selected" by "falling in love."

A very prevalent aspect of mate selection arises from cultural patterns relative to the group from which the mate must be chosen, regardless of who does the choosing. Under *endogamy* the mate must be chosen from within some designated group to which the chooser also belongs. Thus in some cultures one must marry within his social class, his village, or his circle of blood relatives. The latter may operate so as to permit or even require first-cousin, brother-sister, or father-daughter marriage, although such cultures are not common. The opposite of endogamy is *exogamy,* the obligation to choose the mate from outside the group to which one belongs. Again, as in endogamy, "the group" may refer to blood relationship, class, or territorial group, although most generally it refers to blood relationship. It is to be noted, of course, that a culture may require *both* endogamy and exogamy. Thus, for example, our culture requires exogamous marriage so far as close blood relationship is concerned, but endogamy regarding race and to some extent in regard to social class and religion also.

*c. Family rule.* Under the *patriarchal* family form—the most prevalent—authority is vested in the male head of the family. Sometimes that authority is so absolute as to include the right of life or death over the women and children. Usually, there are some limitations imposed by law or by informal custom. Less common than the patriarchate is the *matriarchal* family—authority vested in the woman head of the family with the male being subordinate. Contemporary American families are said to be "democratic," that is, not clearly patriarchal or matriarchal. But legally and by custom, male dominance is still quite in evidence, although it is increasingly being abridged.

*d. Other variability in the sex-marriage-family sphere.* Conspicuous in the encyclopedia of curios are such practices as sexual hospitality (lending of wives to overnight guests) or Sutteeism (burning the wife on the funeral pyre of her deceased husband) and many others. Little would be added to an already adequately described generalization of wide variability. So vast are the variations among cultures, that most persons find it impossible to "think up" a practice which does not already exist or has not already existed. Man has shown himself to be truly inventive in his social inventions centering around sex, marriage, and the family.

2. *Variability in Religion*

Man has, likewise, endowed almost everything at some time or other with supernatural power or existence: animals of various kinds, plants, planets, mountains, rivers, people (insane people, old people, children), storms, ancestors, dreams, dead people. In fact it is very difficult to conceive of anything which is not or has not somewhere been regarded by man as "sacred." Moreover, in the name of religion, man performs the most varied and antithetical acts: meditation and dancing, feasting and fasting, silence and shouting, sex abstinence and sacred prostitution, acts of kindness and acts of cruelty, child care and infanticide (killing babies), love and hate. In fact, there seems again to be no end to man's ingenuity at inventing and building religions. No end, either, to the range of "explanations" as to *why* he does what he does, thinks what he thinks, or has "authority" to act in the way he does.

3. *Variability in Governmental Systems*

Every college student has studied, at least cursorily, enough history to permit him to illustrate governmental variability without much aid. Somewhere, men have lived and loved—even fought and died—for governmental systems as varied as democracy and dictatorship. Dictatorial or *absolutistic governments are of various sorts*—hereditary monarchies, elected persons given or taking permanent and complete authority, small cliques with power and indefinite tenure, autocratic powers by exclusive groups of the wealthy, and so on. *Democracy is likewise of very different varieties*—the British is not like the American, neither is it like the Swiss, and the democracy of primitive peoples is not like any of them. Nor is the American democracy of the 1940's like the American democracy of the 1860's, when neither Negroes nor women voted.

4. *Variability in Economic Pursuits and Ideas*

Americans, living as they do in a highly competitive and wealth-conscious society, tend to "take for granted" that it is inherent in the "nature" of good human beings to "keep up with the Joneses," work hard, and be thrifty. Such a view is, of course, quite incorrect. There are numerous cultures in which pecuniary matters have no prominence, in fact are subordinated to other matters. Likewise, there are societies in which there is no concept of saving or notions of the virtue of hard work as we know them. Instead one lives in these societies on the assumption that he works each day for the purpose of meeting that day's needs—tomorrow is another day. Regular work is not a sign of commendable character, but rather of stupidity, because a clever person should see that there are other values in life, and that there are ways of avoiding regularity of work. "Savings" in some cultures are non-existent.

Another widespread American notion which does not square with the facts, is that people always work harder and more efficiently when there is "incentive of profit" or at least of "personal reward for work." Such a notion is understandable as a rationalization to support the prejudices of our economic system, but as a scientific statement is, simply, incorrect. People are activated to exert effort by many different motives, only one of which is pecuniary self-interest. Much of the world's work, even in this culture, is done for reasons quite aside from financial gain.

The careful study of many cultures gives one perspective on many of his own cultural ideas. From such study he learns that our notions of what is valuable and important are by no means shared generally by people of other societies, that not all peoples *want* what we call "high standards" of living, that wealth does not necessarily bring power and prestige to its possessors, that people are motivated by many other considerations than money or wealth, that people work very effectively in coöperation as well as in competition, that people take pride and interest in and will sacrifice for communally-owned property, and that what is customarily regarded as private property in one society may be owned collectively in the next or at another time in the same society. All economic systems seem "natural" and work fairly well, although not perhaps equally well, to provide man with the satisfactions of his basic needs.

*Are Each Society's Ways The Best For It?*

Frequently one encounters a point of view to the effect that each society's ways constitute "the best adjustment" which that people can make "to the existing situation." In one sense such a view is correct, provided that one recognizes that the idea "best" is itself a cultural definition and subject, therefore, to variation from culture to culture. Thus the "best adjustment" which a people "can" make depends on the ideas, knowledges, and values of the rest of their culture.

> A tribe which tries to stop a typhoid epidemic by organizing large-scale witch hunts operates logically in terms of the culturally established fact that witches are responsible for disease. When we try to achieve the same end by innoculation and boiling drinking water we also are acting logically on the basis of our culturally established knowledge that disease is caused by bacteria. Most members of our society have never seen a germ, but they have been taught that germs exist and accept their existence without further proof. Our own not very remote ancestors would have found the witch hunt more logical than the innoculations.[1]

Frequently it is noted that the practices of some peoples involve consequences which jeopardize the health of members of the society. On the surface it would appear that it would be better if the practice were to be discontinued. The difficulty, however, is that the practice cannot be discontinued without doing violence to the basic values of the society. For example, it is well known that there are many ways of "making love," one of which is known as kissing. It is well known in our society that the act of osculation spreads disease germs of many kinds, and, therefore, is clearly a menace to sound health. Knowledge of this fact, however, seems not to have resulted in the discontinuance of osculatory behavior. The conclusion is inescapable that even though kissing entails risk of infection with disease, the other values implicit in the behavior are regarded as important enough to justify the risk of infection. Is it, then, logical to say that kissing is the best adjustment to the existing conditions in American life?

Many other practices involve the same principle as has just been illustrated. It seems better to say merely that practices are customary or habitual, than that they can be interpreted as the

[1] Ralph Linton, *Cultural Background of Personality* (New York, D. Appleton-Century Co., 1945), p. 102.

best adjustments. As will be discussed later, the origins of many practices are lost in antiquity. All that one knows is simply the observed fact that the practice exists, that it is not too poor an adjustment, because the group still exists, and that the practice usually seems more or less logical in the culture in which it is found.

*Summary: Variability among Cultures*

The culturally approved and entrenched practices of the various societies are replete with variety, contrast, and antithesis. One is forced to the conclusion that man is so constituted biologically as to permit of highly varied modes of living, so varied that opposite practices can each meet his "needs" as an organism. It is also to be noted that each of these variant practices claims the loyalty of its practitioners, and thus may be regarded as satisfactory to them. Many persons are quick to observe when commenting on alien customs that "these people really don't know about other systems, because they are habituated to their own and do not get a chance to see others." What such superficial observation misses is that this identical logic could with equal justification be directed toward the practices of the observer's society! The view is sound enough, but not until one includes also his own ways, does he "get the point." Man is so constituted biologically that he can secure the satisfaction of his basic needs by any one of many different modes of life, and after he has become thoroughly habituated to one mode he tends to regard that mode as intrinsically better than any other.

## UNIFORMITIES AMONG CULTURES

Variability, of course, is not the whole truth. While there are no universal cultural practices, in the strict sense of the word *universal*, there are numerous very widespread or near-universal practices and ideas. Thus, in order to complete our treatment of cultures, we must consider also those practices and ideas which stand out because they are so much more common. To illustrate this point, it was noted earlier that in some societies father-daughter marriages have been known to exist. While it is well to recognize this fact, one should not lose sight of the overwhelming fact that *as a rule* the societies prohibit such marriages. The *incest taboo* (the prohibition of marriage to and/or sexual relations with persons of close blood relationship) is nearly universal, although there is considerable variation as to how close "close" is. Thus, for example, in some American states first-cousin marriage is prohibited, because it is regarded as incestuous, while in other states it is permitted. Another near-universal, although apparently not nearly as universal as the incest taboo, is monogamy. Even though there are and have been numerous societies which have permitted or required polygyny, polyandry, and group marriage, closer observation reveals that among the rank and file of the people one spouse rather than multiple spouses has been the rule.

It would be impossible to catalogue here the many specific practices which show a high frequency among cultures. Such a list would be imposing. We shall, however, confine ourselves to a consideration of the more general similarities among the cultures of the world.

*The Main Uniformities among Cultures*

Although, as we have seen, there is wide variability in the specific practices centering around sex, marriage, and the family, it is well also to note that every society has had *some kind* of a sex-marriage-family pattern. It is significant, then, first, that in no society is the individual free to do as he pleases, but instead must observe numerous taboos and other behavior requirements. Furthermore, this fact shows that every society which has survived has had some kind of formalized arrangements pertaining to the care of children by adults. (It is worth noting at this point, however, that there *may* have been societies in which adults did not protect children and, very possibly because they did not protect children, they failed to survive.)

On the basis of existing data it is possible to catalogue at least the following group of behavior patterns found in every known human society.

1. Language—not necessarily written language.
2. A sex-marriage-family system—widely variable as to details of content, but always present.
3. Age and sex differentiation, that is, a somewhat different and often strikingly different set of behaviors required of males and females and of persons of different ages.
4. Government functions—a generally recognized set of ideas and prac-

tices designed to handle disputes between persons, between groups, and to make for coöperation to preserve the society from aggression.
5. Religion—a set of ideas and practices relating to the societies' conceptions of the sacred.
6. Knowledges—a system of propositions regarded as true or correct, sometimes built up as a mythology, and sometimes by more or less scientific derivation.
7. Economic system—a set of beliefs and practices pertaining to making a living, property rights, and the relative importance of economic matters in the whole scheme of life.
8. Recreational or play activities—participation in certain activities for amusement.
9. Art—some kind of attempt to portray situations and create objects in non-utilitarian form.

It is to be noted carefully that the above list of *universal patterns* in culture is to be kept entirely distinct from the variabilities in the *content of culture.* For example, Nazi Germany, United States of America, the natives of the New Hebrides and the Roman Empire all had government, but in the rights of citizens, in the authority of rulers, in the standards of justice, a long list of differences between these four societies could be made. Similarly the family is universal, but one should always bear in mind that there are many specific content differences from society to society and from time to time.

## REASONS FOR CULTURAL VARIABILITY

From days of antiquity thinking men have speculated concerning the causes or reasons for the wide variety of cultural practices. Before social science developed it was fashionable to regard alien peoples as "bedeviled people" upon whom the wrath of God had been visited for some assumed sin. Their ways were frequently regarded as "perverted ways." They were "uncivilized," "savage," "barbarian," and certainly "backward." The naïveté implied in this mode of thinking is obvious, perhaps, to the person reading this book, but to many less-schooled (or differently schooled) contemporaries, it still seems quite plausible.

Somewhat later in the development of interest in societies a number of explanations of variability were advanced. These ideas still enjoy considerable respectability among some laymen. They will be discussed here and their fallacies pointed out, because the student will almost inevitably encounter them at some time or another. Because they seem fairly "plausible" the untrained person may assume them to be correct.

*Geographical Environment Is Not a Sufficient Explanation*

It is an obvious fact that geographical conditions vary throughout the world. It is not surprising, therefore, that not-very-critical people tried to explain variations in culture simply on the basis of variations in geography. It seemed an obvious explanation.

Before discussing the relation between geography and culture it is necessary to draw a fundamental distinction between geographical factors which *prevent* certain cultural practices and those which are assumed to *require* certain cultural practices. It is easy to demonstrate that the conditions of the natural environment may sometimes prevent a people's culture from containing certain elements. Thus, for example, the Eskimo cannot have banana culture as one of their food producing arts, and the Central Americans cannot construct their dwellings out of snow—at least not at sea level.

But one must be careful not to carry this explanation too far. In many societies people will be observed to be doing things which the conditions of their immediate environment would seem to prohibit. A Kentucky Colonel sipping his ice-cold lemonade on the Fourth of July is a case in point. Lemons do not grow naturally within hundreds of miles of the Colonel's veranda, and the ice would have to be made artificially at that time of year or preserved artificially from the preceding winter. Thus, even though the environment would seem to preclude the ice-cold lemonade on the Fourth of July, the Colonel still goes on with his sipping. Throughout the world, man has for centuries been turning deserts into oases, forests into cornfields, swamps into truck gardens, through the application of his scientific knowledge. Less and less is man dependent upon the immediate benefits of his natural environment. Tersely, but accurately, man modifies his geographical environment radically. Or, if one prefers to state the matter otherwise, man may use his geographical environment in such a way as radically to change its effects on him.

The chief difficulty, however, with regarding the geographical environment as an explanation for cultural variability lies in another direction. The geographical environment always presents man with *alternatives.* As an example, let us consider the presence of snakes in some environment. If snakes are abundant in a given area, what does that fact determine so far as man's behavior is concerned? In one place or another man has been observed to make the following use of snakes: (1) man may eat the snakes; (2) man may make pets out of snakes as we do out of dogs, and therefore because of sentiment refuse to eat them; (3) man may worship the snakes; (4) man may largely ignore the snakes, as he often does. What then, about a culture is determined because of this condition in the natural geographical environment? There are numerous cases in which vast natural resources, as they appear to us, remain largely or entirely ignored by the peoples of the area where the resources abound. To these people they are not resources at all. It is difficult, if not impossible, to find an inhabitable area in the world in which the environment does not present to man alternative usages of the elements which it contains. The geographical environment can never tell man what to do with it; that is always up to man.

Finally, it is to be noted that there are innumerable and important practices which have no connection whatsoever with the natural environment. Questions of etiquette and morals are cases in point. History records a series of evolutions and revolutions in the cultures of Europe during the last few hundred years during which period the seasons, temperature, rainfall, climate, topography, and native plants and animals of that part of the world have not changed. Obviously "something else" must constitute the explanation.

One should not assume from the foregoing paragraphs that the geographical environment has absolutely nothing to do with the specific content of culture. The geographical environment, as we have pointed out, presents certain limitations and prohibitions to man as a cultural builder. Although sometimes, to be sure, man circumvents these limitations by the application of his knowledge, some of them do persist. Even when man modifies the existing geography of his area, he still must work within the limitations imposed by the natural order. But all of this is indeed a long way from explaining the vast variability among cultures which we have already observed.

*Race Is Not an Explanation*

"Race" is sometimes offered as an explanation of cultural variability. It is suggested that some races are "slower," or "less intelligent," or "temperamentally different," or possess "special skills," or have "different needs and interests." The evidence is entirely to the contrary. Three factual tests of this explanation can be made and each demonstrates its falsity.

1. *The contemporary test.* Each of the three major races—White, Negro, Mongoloid—at the present time are found in a number of cultures showing wide variation. There are Negroes in Harlem and in the professions in America, and there are several primitive Negro groups in Africa. Likewise with whites. Within the United States there are the "hillbilly whites" and "the poor white trash" of some areas in the South. They are quite as "white" as are the members of the President's Cabinet. And so, also, there are wide cultural variations among the Mongoloids. *If* any one race were inherently different, then we should find the people of that race with a culture having distinct features. But, *in fact,* we do not find such.

2. *The historical test.* Furthermore since "race traits" are inherited, race differences, if they are valid as any explanation of culture differences, would have to be consistent over long periods of time. If one race is different from others in 1940, it should also be in 1840 or in 1140 B.C. The evidence, again, shows that at one period of history some culture possessed by some one race is in the ascendency, and at another period the culture of a different race is. Compare, for example, the white and the yellow races at about 4000 B.C. The yellow race in China had the world's most highly developed culture at that time. The white race at that time, and for a long time thereafter, was exceedingly primitive. We observe also that cultures rise and fall in their prestige and power positions in the world. Sometimes the cultures of one race are in the seemingly "higher" position, but other cultures of the same race at the same time are "lower." At a later time still another culture becomes the "leader." If the theory of racial determination of culture were true, such oscillation would not be possible.

3. *The clinical-psychological test.* Finally, it is now possible to test representative samples of persons of various races in psycho-

logical laboratories to determine their relative intelligence, temperament, and special aptitudes. Such tests show conclusively that the commonly alleged differences among the races do not exist. The several races are essentially the same in the mental endowments needed to make cultures. (Chapter XVI will treat the evidence in some detail.) Thus we see that the racial explanation of cultural variability is entirely incorrect and must, *because of the evidence*, be discarded.

### *Why, Then, Do Cultures Vary?*

At the present stage of our knowledge this question is not satisfactorily answerable, although certain data permit some tentative generalizations. Reviewing, we already have seen that:

1. Man's biological "needs" for food, sex activity, and protection *can* be "satisfied" in any one of a number of quite different ways.
2. The geographical environments differ.
3. Man invents new ways of doing and of thinking from time to time, that is, he is a problem-solving animal.

Here are the *raw materials of culture making*—biological needs, the natural environment, and man's ingenuity. Thus, due to his constant inventiveness and reflective thinking, man strives always to have his interests and needs fulfilled. He has, here and there, somewhat different materials to work on, as provided by the natural environment. In one instance he comes out with behavior *A*—let us say, pre-marital chastity—as a "good policy." But in another instance he comes out with behavior *B*—which is pre-marital promiscuity—which for him in this situation also "works." Thus, we have two different—in fact opposite—cultural practices. Both fulfill needs; they *must* fulfill needs or they could not exist.

Similarly with food. One man perhaps finds a fish accidently thrown out of the water. He is hungry and eats it. His hunger is satisfied, and there are no "bad after effects." Fish eating is "in the culture" as soon as others take on his invention. Meanwhile in culture *B* no one "happens" on to a fish, but does experiment with snake eggs. They meet the hunger needs, and snake egg eating comes into culture *B*.

This trial and error process of culture building has sometimes been called "historical accident," and so it appears to be. Obviously, a large element of chance enters into the "choice" of practice *A* over practice *B*. Some students of behavior science have objected to the phrase "historical accident," because it is vague, and is really only a cover for our ignorance relative to *why* culture *A* invented fish-eating and culture *B* invented egg-eating when both had, theoretically, access to both fish and eggs. Eventually, we have reason to hope for a more precise explanation than the historical accident theory, but for the time being it is not possible to offer much more accurate explanation than the "historical accident" statement of the case.

To take a more current case. Why does some movie star or some popular singer or some hair styling "catch" the popular fancy and sweep the nation overnight? Actually, we do not know, but it is altogether possible, if not probable, that the necessary facts *could* be determined if there were the necessary time and financial support to study the process. The history of science is replete with examples of scientific problems which are regarded as mere "chance outcomes" at one time, but which, after study, have been found to be causally determined and later predictable. It may be that, eventually, when more study has gone into analysis of the "historical accident" in culture building, we shall have a better answer to the question. But for the time being one must be content with some such statement as the following regarding culture variability: Within the limitations imposed by the geographical environment, man's problem-solving activities result in the selection of some behaviors which meet his biological and psychic needs. This behavior may then become prevalent among the group, and thus culturally established. Both the invention of the behavior and its acceptance depend on many interacting factors, most of which are themselves cultural. At the present stage of our knowledge of the factors involved, the outcome can rarely be predicted successfully. Negatively, we may say that neither race nor geography constitute an acceptable explanation of most cultural variability because of the empiric (factual) tests which have been made and reported in the preceding paragraphs.

## SUMMARY

This chapter has been devoted to an examination of the variations and uniformities among the cultures of the world. While there is great, in fact almost infinite, variation in the specific *content* of the various cultures, the overall *patterns* of culture possess notable uniformities. A number of these have been listed and briefly discussed.

Although it is difficult to establish the fact empirically, it appears probable that the uniformities stem from the inherent biological-psychological uniformities and/or needs of man as a species. Variations are somewhat more difficult to account for. The theological and other mystical theories which in the past purported to explain cultural variability, have now been superseded by two popular explanations which are completely untenable in the light of present knowledge, but still hold many adherents. Neither the fact of race difference nor the fact of difference in the geographical environment can be accepted as explanations for cultural variability. Both arise from false historical inference, and from inadequate factual evidence regarding man's cultural experience. Whereas it can be shown that the racial and the geographical explanations are both erroneous, it is not possible to substitute a wholly acceptable hypothesis in their place. Many social scientists use the "historical accident" explanation, but it is not entirely accurate because it implies that man is a more passive agent in culture formation than he in fact is.

## SUGGESTED READINGS

BLUMENTHAL, Albert, *Small Town Stuff* (Chicago, University of Chicago Press, 1932). **A B**

A well-known and intimate study of a small town, showing many of the characteristics of the local culture.

FOLSOM, J. K., *The Family and Democratic Society* (New York, John Wiley and Sons, 1943), Chapters I, II. **A B**

This is a combination textbook and treatise on the family. Chapter I contains an interesting comparison of the American and the Trobriand Island family cultures. The comparison is made in parallel columns under a series of headings so that the reader can observe both the similarities and the differences under each subject such as family rule, kinship arrangements, and so forth. Chapter II deals with similarities and differences among all family systems. The treatment of "limits to cultural variation" seems especially good.

KIRK, William, "Culture Patterns Among the Ainus of Japan," *Sociology and Social Research,* XXIV, pp. 303-17. **B**

A description and interpretation of the culture of the Ainus of Japan. These people are of interest to the social scientist because they are a "white" people resident for centuries in a small area of Japan.

Mead, Margaret, *Growing Up in New Guinea* (New York, William Morrow and Co., 1930). **B**

A very interesting study of the Manus people with emphasis upon the culturization of the Manus child. Very readable.

Mead, Margaret, *Sex and Temperament in Three Primitive Societies* (New York, William Morrow and Co., 1935). **A**

A comparison of the sex, marriage, and family roles of persons in each of three widely different primitive societies. Gives an excellent perspective on the cultural formation and expression of such "temperament" patterns as aggression, submission, and pleasure seeking.

Sherman, Mandel and Henry, T. R., *Hollow Folk* (New York, The Thomas Y. Crowell Co., 1933). **B**

A small and very readable volume describing and interpreting the life and culture of people in several "hollows" in the southern Appalachians. This book takes one as much "out of his world" as does a volume on some primitive South Seas people.

Tumin, Melvin, "Culture, Genuine and Spurious: A Re-evaluation," *American Sociological Review*, X, 199-207. **A**

A somewhat technical treatment of the hypothesis of "folk" and "urban" or "sacred" and "secular" culture types. It is probably preferable first to examine Redfield, R., *The Folk Culture of Yucatan* (Chicago, University of Chicago Press, 1941), where the formulation of the "folk-urban" theory is expressly set forth.

Whyte, W. F., "A Slum Sex Code," *American Journal of Sociology*, XLIX, pp. 24-32. **AB**

Discusses an American sub-culture. Readable and frank presentation of a somewhat elaborate analysis of the values and overt behavior of a specialized urban community in an American city. A preview of the same author's *Street Corner Society* (Chicago, University of Chicago Press).

## STUDY QUESTIONS

1. Why do the observations of an untrained observer in an alien culture have limited value? Illustrate.
2. What are the similarities and differences among the three types of family rule?
3. Why is there no one "superior" governmental or religion or economic system? Illustrate.
4. What determines "the best adjustment" people make "to the existing situation?" Illustrate.
5. What general behavior patterns are found in every human society?
6. Why are these patterns *general* rather than specific?
7. How does the geographic environment limit, but not determine, cultural practices? Illustrate.
8. How does the biological nature of man limit, but not determine culture? Illustrate.
9. How does the culture of a group limit, but not determine cultural additions? Illustrate.

10. Why is race not a sound explanation for cultural variability? Explain with illustrations.
11. Why must a cultural practice fulfill a need in order to exist? What determines the "need?"
12. How do the three raw materials of culture-making permit cultural variability? Illustrate.
13. Criticise: "Cultural variability is inevitable for human kind."

# Chapter V

## ETHNOCENTRISM AND ITS IMPLICATIONS

Attention has already been drawn to the fact that the people of each society usually find it difficult, if not impossible, to think or act in ways other than those to which they have become habituated. Thus everyone tends to be "culture bound," although not all persons are bound in exactly the same way or to the same extent. The purpose of this chapter is to consider how the culture of a people limits its ability to participate in or to evaluate other culture *realistically*.

### ETHNOCENTRISM A SOCIAL REALITY

*Ethnocentrism Defined*

Ethnocentrism may be defined as *the tendency of persons to judge other cultures by the standards of judgment prevailing in their own.* When, for example, one has been reared in a culture, such as ours, in which women are accorded social privileges comparable to those enjoyed by men, and in which great pride is taken in having "freed" women, it is difficult to observe another culture in which women are accorded a different rôle without coming to the conclusion that the second culture is not a "good" culture. A person from the second culture would probably come to the same negative conclusion about ours. A simpler but perhaps more terse illustration was suggested once by a school boy in whose community a foreign language speaking family lived. Like most of his neighbors the boy was inclined to speak disparagingly of "these queer funny-talking people." When it was pointed out to him that, after all, language was only a medium for communicating ideas and that any language is about as good as any other after one has learned it, he listened politely as if he understood the explanation. He then dismissed the subject with the confident conclusion that "the trouble with foreign languages is that you can't say anything in them that makes any sense."

It is virtually inevitable that a person will use the judgments and thoughtways of his own culture in thinking about other cultures. It is practically unavoidable, therefore, that persons tend to conclude that their cultural ways are the "best ways" of thinking and of doing. As a result, most persons come to regard other cultures with contempt and distrust. If one lives in a society in which people wear clothing, it is only natural to regard the people in the society which do not as "crude people" lacking somehow the "refinements" of "good taste." In our culture many people apparently feel that it is altogether proper for us to send missionaries all over the world to acquaint the people there with the religious as well as many other aspects of our culture. In fact many persons feel quite virtuous about such an undertaking, but would themselves oppose the efforts of other nations to instill their culture here. Again it is not uncommon to hear somewhat sophisticated Americans amused if not disgusted by some of the unhygienic food habits of other peoples, it not somehow occurring to them that many of our own food habits are as dangerous, if not more dangerous, to sound health.

### *Conformity Does Not Necessarily Denote Ethnocentrism*

The fact that a person adheres to the modes of thought and action prevailing in his society does not in itself prove that he is ethnocentric. The underlying *reason* for his conformity is the important criterion. One may conform to the laws and customs of his society merely because it is more expedient to do so. A white may refuse to marry a Negro not because he necessarily regards Negroes as inferior, but simply because he realizes that a Negro-white marriage creates numerous and severe problems for the married pair and for their children. On the basis of *rational or realistic choice* he abstains from the Negro-white marriage.

"Loyalty," likewise, may or may not reflect ethnocentrism, depending upon its source. One may be loyal to some particular religion, school, or nation because after a careful objective examination of pertinent facts, he comes to the conclusion that that religion, school, or nation is the best for him. It should not be assumed, however, that such "rational loyalty" as we have just described is either common or easily attainable. It requires a high and uncommon degree of objectivity and a considerable amount of effort to attain even a measure of perspective on one's own culture. In a complete sense probably the goal is impossible to attain, but in a relative degree it can be approximated. It should at least be clear that not all loyalty is equally "blind." The member of the local "booster" club is not necessarily ignorant of the advantages of living in another town, but since he makes his living here, he can quite rationally concentrate upon the virtues of the local community for the sake of the benefits he might derive therefrom.

*Ethnocentrism Is Largely Inescapable*

One should not dismiss lightly the patterns of thinking called ethnocentric. There is often the tendency among people unfamiliar with the ramifications of ethnocentrism in their own thinking to conclude that "broad-minded persons" like themselves, who strive to "free their minds of prejudice," are able to rise above such "narrow-minded attitudes" as these. The breadth or narrowness of one's "mind" is not, however, the point. Rather it is the knowledge and thinking *content of the mind* which determines the degree of ethnocentrism of a given person. The point is not so much *that a person is unwilling to think in terms of another cultural context, but that he is unable to.*

One says to a man, for example, "put yourself in this woman's place." But can he? Can he know how this woman, as a woman, views many things? He may consider what she says about it, but there is so much at the same time which she cannot verbalize—in fact the really basic values, the values ingrained in a person's existence by decades of living are the hardest to verbalize. And even if these values and sentiments were accurately put into words, can the man interpret the words the way the woman means them? But this has been a relatively simple example.

Suppose we had said to a white man "now put yourself in a Negro's position." Can he? Or, again, suppose you put yourself in the position of a cannibal. Can you imagine yourself in a cultural context of habits, sentiments, religion, joking, and so on, which might conceivably fit a cannibalistic pattern? In a very superficial way perhaps one could, but it would be indeed superficial. In the first place one of the most deep-seated ideas of our culture is a "respect for human life." So great is that respect that the practice of putting people to death is a very repulsive thought—except perhaps under the necessity of war or police action. Then, when eating the body of the victim is considered, innumerable other sentiments arise which one would be obliged, somehow, to neutralize before he could really understand the cannibalistic pattern. Cannibalism is, of course, of no great significance numerically or otherwise. We have used it as an illustration only. One would encounter the same difficulties in trying to understand any cultural pattern the values and practices of which are foreign to those of his own culture. Many have heard discussions between Catholics and Protestants regarding their religious thinking. So often each has occasion to say to the other, "But it isn't like that." Each recognizes that the other, however "openminded" he may care to be, is not really able to participate even vicariously in the other's culture, because as he participates he does so as an outsider, using unconsciously the judgments, prejudices, and assumptions of his own cultural patterns, because he cannot escape them.

### *Ethnocentrism Is Taught*

Everywhere there is evidence of this fact. Often one is taught "loyalty" to his community, his school, his social class, his country, or his religion, he is being taught to be ethnocentric about it. One is admonished in a half-hearted, conventional way to be "tolerant," but at the same time in innumerable ways is being taught that tolerance toward certain other cultures constitutes "disloyalty" to his own. Not only is one taught the sufficiency of his own religion, his own country, his own social class, but is taught it in such a way that the others seem stupid, or inferior, or even dangerous. Frequently these teachings are couched in the most unctious language and thinking. For example, "The Zulus are not necessarily bad; they are simply ignorant." After they have been educated—educated, that is, to accept *our prejudices* on matters—they can be as "good" as we are. One, therefore, would presumably have no prejudice against the Zulus—after they stop being Zulus, and think and act as we do.

*Unconscious learning and teaching of ethnocentrism.* Not only is ethnocentrism taught formally, but much of it comes to the person through informal learnings. Note, for example, the ethnocentrism implied in the innumerable jokes which are supposed to demonstrate the penury of the Scotch, the business acumen of the Jew, and the ignorance of the "hillbilly." Seldom are these jokes told in a context which could be considered deliberately defamatory to these people or to their way of life. Instead they are told as jokes, *as if* for amusement only. They have the effect, however, of fixing certain ideas in the minds of people hearing and telling the stories. For example, the Scotch stories convey at least three notions: (1) that the Scotch are "tight" in money matters; (2) that being a Scotsman is per se evidence that a person is penurious; and (3) that it is not good to be penurious—one ought to be "like us." Not one of the above three has been proved factually. The first two could be empirically proved either to be true or to be false, if some one took the trouble. The third is virtually indeterminable. There is no way in which one can determine, without prejudice due to the basic assumptions with which he approaches the problem, whether it is better to be penurious or somewhat more free with money. It is a matter of values. It all depends on what one has as his goal or objective, whether it is better to be thrifty or not. It is much like the age-old value issue, whether it is better to have loved and lost or never to have loved at all!

Movies, radio, and stage in modern society also reinforce our ethnocentrism, and at least for the young help to create it. Stage characterizations of Negroes, primitive peoples, and foreign peoples, are portrayed in such a way as to lead to the uncontestable conclusion that their ways are the wrong ways and our ways the right ways—and for the most obviously convincing reasons! Again, as in the case of jokes, the intention to be ethnocentric is probably seldom deliberately planned, but the effect is the same as if it had been planned: intensification of the "this is right" ideology and, "therefore we do it," but the other way is "unwise, wrong, indecent," although "they" do it.

*Deliberate teaching of ethnocentrism.* In other instances ethnocentrism is deliberately taught through our strongest conformity-producing social institutions and agencies. Often such teaching is called "indoctrination." Many institutions in society have indoctrination as either their primary or incidental function. In the case of organizations for Americanization or for teaching religious doctrine, indoctrination is obvious enough. But in many other ways it occurs often in spite of our intentions. For example, it has become fashionable for American schools to disavow all indoctrination. Such a point of view may or may not be commendable, depending in part upon how ethnocentric one may be, but it is hardly attainable. If the schools did not indoctrinate with the thoughtways and the folkways what, then, would they teach? Indoctrination is virtually inescapable in the course of teaching the child about his country, its literature, its history, its achievements, even its language per se which is replete with ethnocentric words and ideas. Although much has been achieved in recent years in the direction of less extremely and narrowly ethnocentric teaching of history in the public schools, it is easy to overemphasize the change. In studying about the Civil War a child in the North and a child in the South does not, somehow, get the same version. Nor does the English child read the same account of the American revolution as the American child does. The tendency invariably is to interpret the facts so that they fit into the basic prejudice patterns of the society.

It is not to be assumed throughout this discussion that ethnocentrism is necessarily undesirable—or that it is desirable. It is our purpose to describe, not to evaluate. One is entitled as a citizen of a democracy quite as much to the view that it is right to be ethnocentric as he is to the view that ethnocentrism is a distorted view of the truth. Rather it is our purpose to find out as much as possible about the phenomenon of ethnocentrism, how and why it operates, and what its advantages and disadvantages to a society are.

### *An Experiment in Ethnocentric Thinking among Adults*

Perhaps what we have been saying about ethnocentrism could be illustrated by the results of an experiment performed with the assistance of approximately one hundred adults. These persons were all native Americans and members of a parent-teacher's association who volunteered for the experiment. A speaker spoke to them for about fifteen minutes concerning a custom known as sexual hospitality, which is and has been practiced in several societies. In this pattern the male overnight guest is expected to spend the night with the host's wife, or one of his wives. The custom is observed, of course, quite openly, and is defined by those who practice it as an ordinary form of etiquette which is supposed to prevail between host and guest. All these things were explained to these hundred adults by the speaker. Immediately afterward the persons who heard the address were asked to write a few sentences explaining their reactions to the practice and to the people who practiced it. In examining the written statements two facts stand out. (1) Over 90 per cent of these statements contained obvious ethnocentric comments and (2) the persons differed greatly in the manner in which ethnocentrism showed up. Roughly one could classify the 90 per cent who were ethnocentric into three groups. First, there was a group of almost 15 per cent who denied that the practice existed. They wrote in one way or another that they did not believe that "such a thing could go on openly anywhere." It seems significant that so many persons took this position even after the speaker, who was a respected professional man, said that he had read reputable accounts of it. A second group, nearly 40 per cent, wrote simply that the practice was categorically wrong, that "people shouldn't act like that because it is contrary to human nature." (It seems important to note that this group apparently identified human nature with *our kind* of human nature. *For us* sexual hospitality is, no doubt, contrary to human nature, but for the people being described it obviously was "not contrary to" their human nature, but actually a part of human nature.) A third group, about 20 per cent, felt also that sexual hospitality as a practice was undesirable, and attributed its existence to the fact that these people were "unintelligent people" or "just need enlightenment" or have been "misled" by someone. The phrases in these quotations contain vivid evidence of ethnocentrism. Because the society described had a culture different from ours, the people there were thought to be "unintelligent." It apparently did not occur to many, that their intelligence might simply have been used to work out an etiquette of sexual hospitality instead of an etiquette which excluded the sexual aspect from hospitality. The suggestion that these people need enlightenment, really means not enlightenment per se, but *our kind* of it, that is, they ought to replace their prejudices with our prejudices. The notion of their having been "misled" is a common form of modern American ethnocentrism. Some sinister person or group somehow hoodwinked these innocent people! The fact that the practice may be many centuries old, or that it might have counterparts among the very peoples from whom the Americans themselves have descended, seems not to have occurred to anyone. The final group, about 15 per cent, stated that the practice while "possibly alright" is really "impractical" and "fraught with dangerous implications and consequences" such as the danger of male jealousy, the possibility of permanent infatuations between the guest and the wife, spread of venereal infection, and so forth. Here we note ethnocentrism in another form. While not exactly puritanical, the people in the group were trying to be tolerant, open-minded, unprejudiced and altogether objective, but had still made the mistake of assuming that the sort of "complications," like jealousy and infatuations, which very probably would result if the practice occurred in this culture, would necessarily also occur there. In America a man usually would not oppose his spouse dancing with someone else because of the danger of jealousy of infatuation, because while these consequences are admittedly possible, the way we interpret dancing makes such outcomes improbable. In spite of the speaker having pointed out that the primitive group in question regard sex hospitality as casually as we do dancing, these American adults still were unable to think about sex hospitality in terms of standards other than those which might apply if the practice occurred in our society in violation of our standards.

This is, of course, only one experiment with only a hundred people, but it constitutes an excellent illustration of the virtual impossibility of most persons rising very far above the limitations of their own culture—even when they try to think consciously of some other way of doing and try to be what is conventionally called "tolerant." It also illustrates the many devious and subtle ways in which ethnocentrism operates, varying all the way from flat denials that another practice is possible, to various sorts of "reasonings" which are designed to show, "objectively," of course, that the practice is impracticable or undesirable.

Similar results have been obtained with other experiments using thoughtways and folkways from religion, government, the economic system, property, and the treatment of children. The results are invariably similar. A negligible minority is fairly free of ethnocentrism. The vast majority show evidence of it in various ways. We are forced, then, to the conclusion that one of the fundamental truths about humans in relation to culture is the fact of ethnocentrism. Not only does the society teach people to be ethnocentric, but it accomplishes the teaching with enough effectiveness, so that ethnocentrism is virtually inescapable.

*Ignorance of a Culture's Sources Aids Ethnocentrism*

The people of each society tend to regard their culture as their "own," as if all of the existing objects and ideas were invented by persons in that culture stream. Even among the somewhat better informed persons, there is a tendency to minimize the culture's debt to other cultures. As a matter of historical *fact*, each culture contains a minimum of traits and patterns unique to it or actually invented by it. Instead it is the rule for cultures to draw very heavily upon other cultures for their culture objects and ideas. If the whole truth were known to them, it would be difficult for intelligent people to be as ethnocentric as they tend to be. Somehow the unique contributions or inventions in a culture are played up, and the items borrowed or "stolen" from other cultures tend to be played down. As an illustration let us consider the following realistic account of the cultural content of a "one hundred per cent" American citizen. It is written as satire, but the point it makes is irrefutable. The author is a distinguished anthropologist and well acquainted with the facts which it contains.[1]

> There can be no question about the average American's Americanism or his desire to preserve this precious heritage at all costs. Nevertheless, some insidious foreign ideas have already wormed their way into his civilization without his realizing what was going on. Thus dawn finds the unsuspecting patriot garbed in pajamas, a garment of East Indian origin; and lying in a bed built on a pattern which originated in either Persia or Asia Minor. He is muffled to the ears in un-American materials: cotton, first domesticated in India; linen, domesticated in the Near East; wool from an animal native to Asia Minor; or silk whose uses were first discovered by the Chinese. All these substances have been transformed into cloth by methods invented in Southwestern Asia. If the weather is cold enough he may even be sleeping under an eiderdown quilt invented in Scandinavia.
>
> On awakening he glances at the clock, a medieval European invention, uses one potent Latin word in abbreviated form, rises in haste, and goes to the bathroom. Here, if he stops to think about it, he must feel himself in the presence of a great American institution; he will have heard stories of both the quality and frequency of foreign plumbing and will know that in no other country does the average man perform his ablutions in the midst of such splendor. But the insidious foreign influence pursues him even here. Glass was invented by the ancient Egyptians, the use of glazed tiles for floors

[1] Ralph Linton, "One Hundred Per Cent American," *The American Mercury*, XL, pp. 427-29.

and walls in the Near East, porcelain in China, and the art of enameling on metal by Mediterranean artisans of the Bronze Age. Even his bathtub and toilet are but slightly modified copies of Roman originals. The only purely American contribution to the ensemble is the steam radiator.

In this bathroom the American washes with soap invented by the ancient Gauls. Next he cleans his teeth, a subversive European practice which did not invade America until the latter part of the eighteenth century. He then shaves, a masochistic rite first developed by the heathen priests of ancient Egypt and Sumer. The process is made less of a penance by the fact that his razor is of steel, an iron-carbon alloy discovered in either India or Turkestan. Lastly, he dries himself on a Turkish towel.

Returning to the bedroom, the unconscious victim of un-American practices removes his clothes from a chair, invented in the Near East, and proceeds to dress. He puts on close-fitting tailored garments whose form derives from the skin clothing of the ancient nomads of the Asiatic steppes and fastens them with buttons whose prototypes appeared in Europe at the close of the Stone Age. This costume is appropriate enough for outdoor exercise in a cold climate, but is quite unsuited to American summers, steam-heated houses, and Pullmans. Nevertheless, foreign ideas and habits hold the unfortunate man in thrall even when common sense tells him that the authentically American costume of gee string and moccasins would be far more comfortable. He puts on his feet stiff coverings made from hide prepared by a process invented in ancient Egypt and cut to a pattern which can be traced back to ancient Greece, and makes sure they are properly polished, also a Greek idea. Lastly, he ties about his neck a strip of bright-colored cloth which is a vestigial survival of the shoulder shawls worn by seventeenth-century Croats. He gives himself a final appraisal in the mirror, an old Mediterranean invention, and goes downstairs to breakfast.

Here a whole new series of foreign things confronts him. His food and drink are placed before him in pottery vessels, the popular name of which—china—is sufficient evidence of their origin. His fork is a medieval Italian invention and his spoon a copy of a Roman original. He will usually begin the meal with coffee, an Abyssinian plant first discovered by the Arabs. The American is quite likely to need it to dispel the morning-after effects of over-indulgence in fermented drinks, invented in the Near East; or distilled ones, invented by the alchemists of medieval Europe. Whereas the Arabs took their coffee straight, he will probably sweeten it with sugar, discovered in India; and dilute it with cream, both the domestication of cattle and the technique of milking having originated in Asia Minor.

If our patriot is old-fashioned enough to adhere to the so-called American breakfast, his coffee will be accompanied by an orange, domesticated in the Mediterranean region, a cantaloupe domesticated in Persia, or grapes, domesticated in Asia Minor. He will follow this with a bowl of cereal made from grain domesticated in the Near East and prepared by methods also invented there. From this he will go on to waffles, a Scandinavian invention, with plenty of butter, originally a Near-Eastern cosmetic. As a side dish he may have the egg of a bird domesticated in Southeastern Asia or strips of the flesh of an animal domesticated in the same region, which have been salted and smoked by a process invented in Northern Europe.

Breakfast over, he places upon his head a molded piece of felt, invented by the nomads of Eastern Asia, and, if it looks like rain, puts on outer shoes of rubber, discovered by the ancient Mexicans, and takes an umbrella, invented in India. He then sprints for his train—the train, not the sprinting, being an English invention. At the station he pauses for a moment to buy a newspaper, paying for it with coins invented in ancient Lydia. Once on board he settles back to inhale the fumes of a cigarette invented in Mexico, or a cigar invented in Brazil. Meanwhile, he reads the news of the day, imprinted in characters invented by the ancient Semites by a process invented in Germany upon a material invented in China. As he scans the latest editorial pointing out the dire results to our institutions of accepting foreign ideas, he will not fail to thank a Hebrew God in an Indo-European language that he is a one hundred per cent (decimal system invented by the Greeks) American (from Americus Vespucci, Italian geographer).

The last paragraph of the above quotation is very significant. It points out how the very *basic components* of the "American" way of life—language, religion, the number system, and so on—are really not American at all, except by importation and subsequent usage. It is true that each culture adds, subtracts, modifies these importations, but its basic debt to the other civilizations should not be overlooked although it usually is.

## ADVANTAGES OF ETHNOCENTRISM TO CULTURAL STABILITY

The word *advantage* in the above caption requires comment. "Advantage" is meaningless unless it is specified "for whom" or "for what" it is advantageous. In this section we shall consider the effect of ethnocentrism on the preservation of a society. Whether such preservation be desirable or not is quite another matter, but outside the scope of this discussion.

### *Ethnocentric Thinking Reduces or Even Prevents Criticism of the Status Quo*

Insofar, however, as ethnocentric thinking occurs, it has the effect of strengthening the *status quo*. If, for example, one's religion is the "only true religion revealed to man by God," then there is not only no good reason to consider another religion, but every reason to shun and ridicule the others. If capitalism is the only really good and workable economic system, then one need have no concern about its being replaced by another, because no other system will be found to be good enough. On the other hand, other religions and other economic systems do "creep in" in places where ethnocentrism is insufficiently strong to prevent a consideration of the possible merits of other systems. One is not to assume, of course, that the only factor resisting or facilitating change is ethnocentrism; obviously there are many others, but ethnocentrism is certainly one of them. Ethnocentric thinking must in some way be weakened or reduced or destroyed, before the existing scheme of things can be successfully criticised and a competing system substituted, if found or thought to be better.

### *Loyalty to One's Society*

Groups are often "strong" in proportion to the "loyalty" which their members give them. Insofar, therefore, as a society is able to maintain the ethnocentrism of its members, that is, can keep the members believing that the purposes and functions of that society are right, good, and desirable, that group is more secure. There is less danger of its going out of existence due to its members' apathy. A nation at war is a case in point. To the extent that the people of a nation agree that their cause is a just one, they will coöperate in fighting the war, even at great personal danger or loss of property. Their nation may, of course, actually lose the war, but the point is that their chances of winning are greatly enhanced by loyalty and that their loyalty is greater if their ethnocentrism is more deeply entrenched. On both sides in World War II, millions of men have died, each believing that he was fighting for the perpetuation of a culture which was "right." Both sides believed that they were obliged to fight the opposing society, and were involved in a righteous attempt to "protect" themselves. Naziism would have offered much less successful and certainly shorter resistance, if the Germans who adhered to that culture had been less ethnocentric about it.

### *Ethnocentrism Increases Uniformity Within the Society*

To the extent that one does not question the logic of the prevailing thoughtways, he is in harmony with them. And to the extent that a society can indoctrinate sufficient numbers of persons in the same way, its conflicts within itself tend to be reduced. There are thoughtful people today who believe that the chief problem of America as a nation, is the diversity which one finds in the values of different classes, races, creeds, and religions. The multiplicity of value systems, it is argued, makes for no real meeting of minds even when persons actually meet to talk things over, because there is no common basis of agreement which all can take as a point of departure for discussion. Whether this be a correct diagnosis of the problems of American culture or not, we shall discuss at a later point in this book. The proponents of this point of view, however, are probably correct when they point out that to the extent that we have common prejudices, that is, are ethnocentric with respect to the same social system, the resulting uniformity makes for a smoother functioning of the society.

### *Ethnocentrism May Be Ego-Satisfying*

It is comforting to one's apparent need for feeling superior, if he can accept the idea that his people are the chosen people singled out by God or by history for some special mission in the universe, even though that mission might entail hardship and deprivation. It is of considerable assurance to some, likewise, to "belong" to a nation which carries the "white man's burden" to the "unenlightened peoples of the world." It makes one feel important, or at least not neglected, in the larger scheme of things.

Numerous controlling groups in this and other nations have made excellent use of this principle as a means of keeping the rank and file of folk from becoming restless and ill-contented when things have not gone well for them. During the great depression the unfortunate people were admonished to keep faith in the American economic culture despite current deprivations. One should go with fewer than three meals per day in 1932, and perhaps his grandchildren would have air-conditioned row boats, because America is like that! There is no limit to her progress. There is no way of determining precisely how many people have been effectively held in control by this sort of ideology. The blind loyalty inspired by the Nazi régime in Germany certainly indicates that much can be accomplished by such deliberate attempts. Thus the American who is very sure that automobiles, sky-scrapers, air-conditioning, and television are wonderful achievements of this culture seems not often to pause to consider that these things may not be intrinsically valuable or may also contain harmful aspects which could conceivably counterbalance the alleged benefits.

### *Ethnocentrism and Vicarious Cultural Participation*

The extent to which a person may receive satisfaction through identifying himself with the alleged achievements of the culture, even though he cannot personally benefit from the alleged benefits, should not be overlooked. Thus a semi-literate New York taxicab driver who once sensed the writer's unfamiliarity with the city, proceeded to enumerate the many "cultural advantages" of that great metropolitan center. It was obvious that he was very proud of them, proud of the art galleries, the universities, the music conservatories, and the penthouse "dream homes," none of which he had been able to participate in himself or appeared likely to. It was enough somehow for him to know that these things were supposed to be great, that they were in New York City, he was in New York City, and somehow he was the better because those things were there. Moreover, one frequently hears urban dwellers extol the virtues of the increasing size of their city *as if* the increasing size were somehow inherently good, and an obvious evidence of progress. If such persons are asked specifically of what use it is *to them personally* if the city in which they live increases by 10 per cent in a decade, they are embarrassed to know what the advantages are. They are embarrassed because they had not thought of it that way; after all "bigger things are better than smaller things, aren't they?" Like many of the artisans of medieval Europe who spent years of their lives and much of their fortune on building great cathedrals which they never lived to see completed, found satisfaction in their work, so numerous Americans unable to afford television, air-conditioning, or aeroplane rides receive satisfaction from belonging to a society in which some people enjoy these things.

### *Summary*

Ethnocentrism, measuring the worth of things in terms of the standards of value of the existing culture is, of course, circular thinking. The person gets indoctrinated with a set of values, Catholic or Protestant, Republican or Democrat, Christian or non-Christian, capitalist or communist, and thereafter judges other cultural streams in terms of the already indoctrinated ideas. It is not surprising, then, that he usually concludes that his ways are the best ways, and that the anemic bird in the hand is worth more than a fatter bird in a theoretical bush! In this section we have seen how ethnocentrism helps to keep a culture from changing, by reducing or eliminating some of the criticism and discouraging really objective thinking about the culture. The more thoroughly ethnocentric person is likely to be more loyal when the society needs loyalty from him. Ethnocentric thinking, because it works against the introduction of new ideas and ways, makes for uniformity and temporary stability of the culture. Meanwhile the ethnocentric person receives certain measures of contentment and satisfaction from his confident acceptance of the all-sufficiency of his scheme of things, either because he is actually convinced that his culture benefits him, or because he identifies himself with it in ways which he cannot or does not wish to measure selfishly. The net result of the operation of these and other influences is to make for a more closely-knit and integrated society. In the sense that such conditions make for a permanent and strong group organization, ethnocentrism may be said to be an advantage to the perpetuation of the group and of its culture. But there are also disadvantages of ethnocentrism to the group, and we now turn to a consideration of some of them.

### DISADVANTAGES OF ETHNOCENTRISM

Ethnocentrism also has its negative aspects from the point of view of group preservation. No society lives in a vacuum; instead it lives among other societies, and the conditions of its existence are determined in no small part by what goes on in the other societies. A more ethnocentric society, while it has advantages through the blind loyalty of its members and through its refusal to accept disorganizing changes in its culture, faces certain disadvantages, especially in relation to other societies. For example, Nazi Germany and Japan certainly constituted two of the most ethnocentric large modern nations. In neither case did their ethnocentrism save them. At best we might say that their ethnocentrism put off the day of their final doom. In other respects it can be shown that their ethnocentrism may have been largely responsible for getting them into the conflicts as a result of which they were annihilated. Although it is not altogether clear in the case of these two nations that their ethnocentrism alone was the determining factor in this chapter of their history, certainly it was a contributing factor.

*Ethnocentrism Hinders Intercultural Relations*

Frequently societies, like persons, get along better with others, whether in competition or not, when they understand each other, respect each other, and in general can work together. Frequently societies may find it to their greater advantage to work together in order to attain mutually advantageous objectives. The too-ethnocentric society or group often finds that its ethnocentrism stands in the way and prevents or reduces the understanding necessary to work in harmony. Loyalty or patriotism may be so intense that essential coöperation between societies becomes difficult.

Russian and American future relations are an important case in point. Twenty-five years ago when Russia overthrew capitalism by revolution, capitalistic peoples like ourselves became uneasy lest the communistic experiment in Russia should work. Many influential persons in America, however, not only hoped the communistic experiment would fail, but were confident that it would. During the 1920's it was a fashionable indoor sport for many somewhat informed and sophisticated Americans to debate the number of years it would take for the communistic experiment to fail, as if the fact of failure was a foregone conclusion. The experiment did not fail. Anti-Russian feelings ran high again just prior to World War II when Russia seemed to be casting her lot with the Nazis in Germany. This further intensified the suspicion and hatred of the Russian "scheme." When Russia finally entered the war on the side of the Allies, many were actually only half-hearted about her assistance. They regarded her as a somewhat impotent nation, large to be sure, but not a very decisive force, because her economic system was so backward as compared with ours. When Russia began giving a rather convincing account of herself in both an economic and military way, the ethnocentrism of millions of Americans concerning this "impossible Russian experiment" received a rather severe jolt. Here this "impotent, backward, ignorant, people," without the spur of private property and profit, had become a powerful nation. Instead of ridiculing Russia, many came to fear her, and despite governmental efforts to stop it, a persistent rumor circulated widely both in the army and among civilians that the large American armed force was being built up not really to fight Germany and Japan at all, but to fight Russia. International tension is great between Russia and the Anglo-American "bloc" in the United Nations.

Relations between that nation and ours will probably continue to be strained as a result of the fears, ill-feelings, and misunderstanding which have been built up on both sides for over twenty-five years. It is not to be assumed that coöperation between Russia and United States will be impossible in the future, but rather that it will be made more difficult than it needs to be by the strong ethnocentric beliefs common in America and in Russia.

*Ethnocentrism Hinders Assimilation*

From time to time groups break up into sub-groups and small groups are absorbed into large ones. The process of absorption of persons or groups of one culture into a larger group of a different culture is called *assimilation.* One of the chief characteristics of the United States of the nineteenth and early twentieth centuries was the assimilation of millions of Europeans of various cultures into the American society. Under such conditions, and in the long run, assimilation is virtually inevitable, but the length of the run may be appreciably shortened if the members of each group are not too ethnocentric in their appraisals of the other group's culture. Two conditions made the Americanization of the European immigrant difficult. First, and probably chiefly, the native American usually had no real appreciation of the culture which the immigrant brought with him. The immigrant was treated by most "Americanization" organizations as if he had no culture at all before coming here. Insofar as there was superficial recognition of the culture with which he came, the incoming culture was regarded as an unpleasant and unfortunate perversion of these people which had to be destroyed at the earliest possible moment. Partly as a result of the prevailing native attitude, but also as a result of ethnocentrism of the Europeans themselves, the immigrants frequently resisted assimilation by America as long as they could. They organized clubs, lodges, and even political groups; they sponsored foreign language newspapers, and sent their children to foreign language schools. They tried to impose the foreign ways and ideas upon their children who thus were torn between the American ways and the ways they were taught at home. The result was a great deal of conflict between parents and children of the second generation and a disproportionate amount of delinquency and crime in the second generation. This latter fact was seized upon by the one-hundred-per centers as evidence that immigration was a mistake, that these foreigners were really inferior people anyway, and should be kept in inferior social position. Thus the ethnocentrism of both sides aggravated a difficult situation, caused a great deal of unhappiness in both groups, and prolonged the solution of the problem for many years unnecessarily.

It is thought by many persons, also, that coöperative action between religious groups in America could be facilitated greatly if there were less ethnocentrism in this phase of modern culture. The situation frequently arises that all sides really wish to accomplish the same objective upon which their leaders agree, but the folk in the rank and file of both groups find it so completely impossible to acknowledge that any good thing could possibly come out of the other camp with its altogether mistaken ideas, that the official agreements are not translated into action as was originally planned. Eventually probably, some degree of assimilation will take place, but ethnocentrism will prolong the process and strew many hurdles along the way.

## WHY STUDY ETHNOCENTRISM?

Students frequently assume that the sociologists' purpose in studying ethnocentrism is to destroy it. Only in a very limited and very professional sense is this true. In order to be objective about the behavior of persons in other cultures, it is necessary to free oneself of the ethnocentrism from his own. But so far as one's personal beliefs as citizen, church member, alumnus, husband, and American are concerned, his ethnocentric views pertaining to these things will no doubt continue. As a sociologist, for example, one must recognize that sexual hospitality among the persons who practice it with the approval of their mores, is a normal and natural practice. To practice sexual hospitality in America, however, is defined as criminal and immoral. In professional capacity the sociologist and the student of sociology need to be able to objectify ethnocentrism so that they know what it is, are able to recognize its causes and effects. In their personal lives both the sociologist and the student of sociology are still both probably quite ethnocentric.

Most of the organizations to which they belong can be depended upon to reinforce and to perpetuate much of the conventional ethnocentrism. Perhaps coming to understand the things with which this chapter has dealt, however, might tend to reduce at least a few of the too-blatant ethnocentrisms.

## SUMMARY

In this chapter attention has been drawn to the phenomenon called *ethnocentrism.* It has been shown that ethnocentrism is virtually universal among humans, and that it varies in degree and form among different cultures and among the different persons in a given society as well. The essence of ethnocentrism is evaluation—judging the worth of other ways of doing and ways of thinking in terms of the values with which one has become indoctrinated by his own cultural experience. It results in prejudicial language and overt behaviors taking such organizational forms as the missionary movement, wars, and educational and religious indoctrination. Ethnocentrism has both advantages and disadvantages to the society as a result of its tendency to insulate the thoughts and ways of the people from the thoughts and ways of other peoples. The ability to recognize and analyze ethnocentrism is a basic professional prerequisite of the sociologist and also of the successful student of sociology.

## SUGGESTED READINGS

ARNOLD, Thurman, *The Folklore of Capitalism* (New Haven, Conn., Yale University Press, 1937), esp. Chapter VII. **A B**

A very realistic book on government and economics in the United States. Chapter VII, "Traps Which Lie in Definitions and Polar Words," is an excellent treatment of the uncritical, ethnocentric acceptance of word symbols.

GILLIN, J. L., and GILLIN, J. P., *An Introduction to Sociology* (New York, The Macmillan Co., 1942), pp. 195-98. **B**

This short reading covers the same general scope of ideas as that covered by the chapter just completed. The Gillins, however, illustrate their material with data from primitive society.

JOHNSON, Charles, *Growing Up in The Blackbelt,* American Council on Education, Washington, D. C., 1941. **B**

A very readable and non-technical treatment of how the person "grows up" in the culture of the South. See especially Chapters I ("Personality Profiles"), X, ("Color and Status"), XI ("Relations with Whites") and IX ("Intra-Race Attitudes").

LIVINGSTON, Sigmund, *Must Men Hate?* (Cleveland, Crane Press, 1944). **AB**

A book designed to expose the Jewish myth as it is entrenched in American culture by a factual examination of the "truths" which have wide currency. While the book may not be wholly unbiased, it is certainly a useful antidote to the institutionalized nonsense regarding Jews which one hears *ad nauseum.*

Symposium, "Controlling Group Prejudice," *Annals of the American Academy of Political and Social Science,* Vol. 224, March, 1946. **AB**

A timely discussion by a number of distinguished authors of various theoretical and practical aspects of the problem of controlling prejudice among groups.

WEST, James, *Plainville, U. S. A.* (New York, Columbia University Press, 1945). **AB**

An intimate study of a "small town in the central part of the United States." Excellent description. Chapter III is on the class system and contains interesting material on ethnocentrism.

WISSLER, Clark, "The Contribution of the Indian," in Brown, F. J. and Roucek, J., *Our Racial and National Minorities* (New York, Prentice-Hall, Inc., 1937). **AB**

A highly interesting statement of the many and varied culture elements which the Indians have contributed to present-day American culture. A useful companion article to the "One Hundred Per Cent American" quoted in this chapter.

## STUDY QUESTIONS

1. Why do people tend to judge other cultures by the standards of their own?
2. Why do Americans send missionaries to China?
3. Why is a person unable to think in terms of another cultural context? Illustrate.
4. How does society "teach" people to be ethnocentric? Illustrate with examples of unconscious fostering of ethnocentrism.
5. What is the relation between prejudice and enlightenment? Is either any more "cultural" than the other?
6. Why is the term *pure American culture* a myth?
7. Why is ethnocentrism a relative term? In what ways is it relative?
8. How does ethnocentrism tend to produce cultural stability?
9. What is the relation between ethnocentrism and "nationalism?"
10. Are local "boosters' clubs" ethnocentric? Or only "rationally loyal?"
11. How has ethnocentrism created majority-minority problems in the United States?
12. Why does the sociologist need to be able to "objectify" ethnocentrism? Illustrate.
13. How is ethnocentrism "a system of evaluation?" Illustrate.

# *Chapter VI*

# THE CONTENT AND ORGANIZATION OF CULTURE

---

The purpose of this chapter is to examine the makeup and the organization of culture. It has already been pointed out that the various parts of culture are "patterned," but nothing has been presented to indicate what the various parts are, or how and why the parts are organized in the manner in which they are.

A more basic purpose must be achieved first, however. One should become as familiar as possible with the technical language used by sociologists and anthropologists for the designation of the parts of culture and the organization of culture.

## CULTURE AND CULTURE OBJECTS

### *The Distinction*

In the preceding chapter brief mention was made of the fact that culture contains both material objects, like shoes and trains, and intangible behaviors, like a belief in democracy or the ability to tell a lie. The point was made that while a sky-scraper, as a material object, and woman suffrage, as a non-material practice, are radically different in form, both consist of man-made inventions, and are the results of man's attempt to solve problems. Both, then, are products of man's mind.

### *Similarities in the Evolution of Culture and Culture Objects*

And yet it seems, particularly to the beginner, that an automobile is unlike a symphony in a way so fundamental that the two should not be linked. The difficulty probably arises from a failure to see the material object in its correct historical and functional perspective. First, looking at the material object historically, one notes that it has a long evolution, an evolution characterized by a long series of changes, modifications, and combinations of what went before. Thus, the automobile when it was invented consisted of the combination of two objects which were already common in the culture, one of them was the four-wheel vehicle, and the other was the internal combustion engine. The "horseless carriage," as the automobile was first called, was exactly that. It was a carriage which was propelled by a power-producing engine instead of by a horse. Furthermore the carriage itself shows an evolution. Before the carriage or wagon there was a two-wheel cart, and before there could be a two-wheel cart man had to discover the wheel itself. Now let us look at the evolution process from the other end, from the time the wheel was invented. At that point some man or group of men conceived the idea that materials or people could be moved with less energy if placed upon a revolving circular object than if carried or dragged along. Whether the wheel was discovered "accidentally" or "thought out" before the experiment was tried, is a question which cannot be answered. The point, however, is that when man built the first crude wheel he had a *purpose* for building it. The purpose consisted of the notion that the wheel would be useful to him.

The non-material items of culture have the same kind of history. Let us use the Revolutionary War period and the Constitution of the United States as an example. The people who lived in the America of Colonial times had known a modified autocratic type of government with a monarch at the head. He was limited in the power which he held over other people, but yet was by no means a mere figurehead. Until the time when the British government passed certain specific laws such as the Stamp Act, there was no very widespread vocal opposition to the existing government. But after a series of governmental regulations disturbed the purposes of the colonists sufficiently, there were a few episodes like the Boston Tea Party, then the war to resist the British government's attempts to enforce their laws, and eventually the War of Independence. The American Revolution did not start out as a revolution for American Independence, but more as *a war of protest.*

Later the *idea* that the thirteen colonies ought to be entirely free of European control became common. That idea, of course, was not invented on this side of the Atlantic, but rather on the other. It had a precedent not only in the revolutionary political philosophies widely circulated in France, but also in the ideas pertaining to self government since the Magna Carta in Britain itself. "Taxation without representation" became a problem not because life was so unbearable that way, but merely because some of the people in America invented the idea that no group ought to be taxed unless it could be represented in the making of the laws fixing the taxes. There were then as there are now, millions of people all over the world who are being taxed without representation. To them it is no "problem" unless their culture contains the idea that it is not right to be taxed without representation and unless it is called to their attention that they are being so taxed.

When the war for Independence was won, the colonies faced a new problem. Was it possible and was it wise to continue as thirteen separate nations, or should they somehow combine? And if they should combine, how should they combine? There was the experiment with the Articles of the Confederation, but finally the Constitutional Convention was called in an attempt to "provide a more perfect union." As one reads Madison's *Journals,* the most authentic "play-by-play description" we have of the deliberations of the Convention, one sees the process of social invention going on. They had a new problem. They tried to solve it in terms of the existing culture they had. It is not surprising that one group wanted a king or at least a hereditary presidency, because that was the kind of executive officer with which they had had experience. But eventually they drafted the Constitution, which was new in the sense that it contained a combination of political ideas never before assembled in one document. But the specific ideas in the Constitution had practically all been widely discussed in books on political philosophy written in Europe, which the libraries of many of the "founding fathers" contained.

Like the "horseless carriage" the American Constitution was new only in the sense that it contained a combination of already existing things. Basic to both was the fact that certain persons wanted certain problems solved. They "put their minds to work" using the experiences which they already had, and the knowledges with which they were already familiar, and invented something new. Thus we see that the development of material and non-material culture follows the same general lines.

### REGULARITIES OR PATTERNS WITHIN CULTURE

So-called "pressure" to conform to the ways of other people is evident to almost everyone, particularly to the young who in onerous ways experience one or another kind of "control" recurrently. Pressure to conform is no less strong for more mature people, but they, because of their maturity, usually are so thoroughly habituated to the patterns that the pressure is largely unnoticed except under unusual circumstances. Society contains numerous devices to facilitate and assure conformity. Basically there exists a reward and punishment system—one is rewarded for doing the appropriate things and punished for doing the inappropriate things. Why is man so docile?

The individual is virtually powerless to resist indoctrination as he participates in his culture. He has few real choices as to the fundamentals in the pattern. He speaks the language which prevails, engages as a rule in the activities which he is supposed to, and acquires the knowledges, the prejudices, and the fears that are current. He seems bribed into conformity, coerced into being and doing what is expected.

It has been suggested by some writers, mostly not sociologists, that this molding of the person by his culture results in making a person a mere automaton, that by virtue of the fact of cultural conformity man is "everywhere in chains." But is the figure of speech apt? Is one, because he speaks English and is a Christian, therefore enslaved? Or is he, by virtue of his participation in these cultural traditions, really more free to experience and enjoy many things which would otherwise be denied him? Persons who are irked by some behavior patterns which are required of them often react categorically against "culture," not realizing that they resent conformity only because they are also participating in *another* stream of culture which is different.

Conformity to the patterns of one's culture is, however, not complete; the person still has choices, even if only the choices among the several alternatives contained in the culture.

### *All Behavior Not Equally Patterned*

The persons of a society do not behave identically, even though similarities are often marked. People in culture attach different degrees of importance to the various patterns of behavior. The situation may be graphically portrayed in the following way. Suppose one thinks of the following continuum, graduated into degrees like a thermometer or a speedometer, as representing the various degrees of uniformity in behavior among the persons in a society.

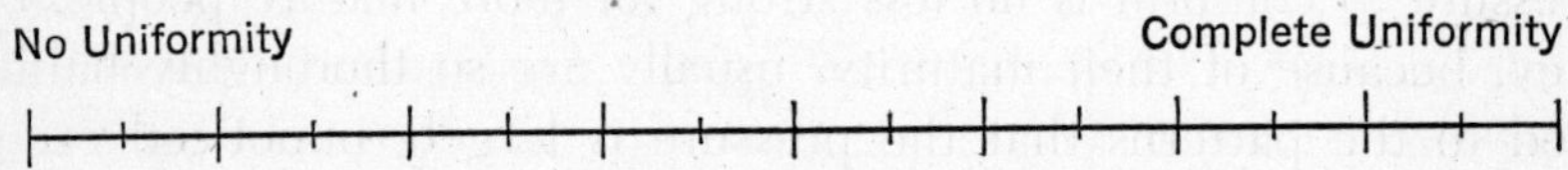


One could then distribute the various behaviors of people along this continuum. Thus, the following items for contemporary urban Americans may be approximately located.

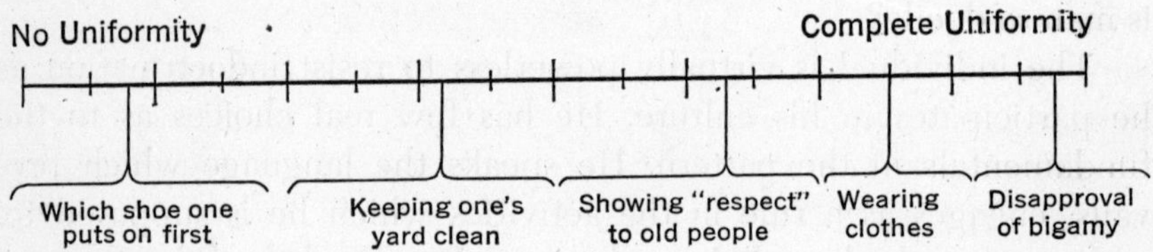


The location of the various items along the continuum is, of course, very approximate. One cannot prove, for example, that showing "respect for one's elders" is 50 per cent more uniformly observed than is "wearing clothes." The basis for locating "respect for elders" on the continuum is *in relation to other items,* that is, "respect for elders" is less uniform than "wearing clothes," but presumably more frequently found than is "keeping one's yard clean." Thus, each of the many acts making up the mode of life can be placed *somewhere* along this continuum. The point to our discussion is not that it is possible or necessary to place every act in its precisely correct position, but that each act *could* be placed as soon as sufficient research were done. Many acts can be approximately placed without formal research, as in the above examples.

### *"Folkways," "Mores," and "Undefined Acts"*

Sociologists have attached the words *mores, folkways,* and *undefined acts* to certain ranges along this continuum. *Mores* are usually defined as the must-behaviors, the basic and important patterns of ideas and acts of a people. Monogamy, wearing clothes, and loyalty to the government, especially in time of war, are illustrations of the mores. There may be some variations granted under a few "exceptional circumstances" which might arise, but on the whole these behaviors are said to be required if one is to live in present-day American society without suffering disprivilege. Some of the mores are written down in the law and carry stipulated penalties to be imposed upon violators. Many of the mores are not so formally set forth, but observance of them is no less compulsive. Informal methods of enforcement consist of such patterns as ridicule, gossip, and ostracism by one's associates. Many persons' behavior is said to be "held in line" not by fear of legal action but by fear of social ostracism, which can be more seriously and permanently harmful than formal legal action. For example, the loss of "reputation" of a physician is a far more serious penalty to him professionally, than the fine which might be imposed for some malpractice. In one way or another, then, the society rigidly enforces some of its most important patterns of behavior—its mores.

*Folkways* are construed as somewhat less compulsive than the mores of the same society. Many of the folkways are not even really enforced, but rather are the expected or taken-for-granted things which most persons within the society perform similarly, even though under no rigid requirement so to do. It will be observed, for example, that in most urban, middle-class, residential communities, Monday is recognized as "wash-day." The housewife is not under any legal or other pressure to wash the family's clothes on Monday. Instead, she lives among other housewives who generally observe that practice. It seems only natural to do likewise. Besides other activities in the week are so organized that to observe this day for this purpose fits better than some other arrangement. Other folkways may be somewhat more compulsive. For example, the appropriate clothing for students to wear to class, while somewhat varied from campus to campus and region to region, is more or less agreed upon. Should a woman appear in a long gown or a man in overalls, neither would probably be disprivileged in any official way for so doing, but both would constitute "bad taste," and the wearers would probably be regarded as somewhat eccentric or "queer." Perhaps some mild pressure would be imposed, like ridicule or laughing at them. But few would consider this to be a serious breach of the moral code, or consider taking formal action to punish the students involved. The point is best illustrated perhaps by the fact that cases like the above are very few. Persons rarely *want* to wear other than the appropriate clothes, do not consider very seriously wearing anything other than the regularly accepted clothing for the occasion. Such is the nature of the folkways.

Finally, some acts are regarded as outside the province of social dictation, and it is of no real concern to anyone else what one does. No one cares which arm goes into the coat sleeve first or whether one prefers his coffee with or without sugar. Such acts are regarded as in the realm of one's own preference; any way is socially acceptable.

In terms of the already familiar continuum, folkways, mores, and undefined acts may be represented thus:

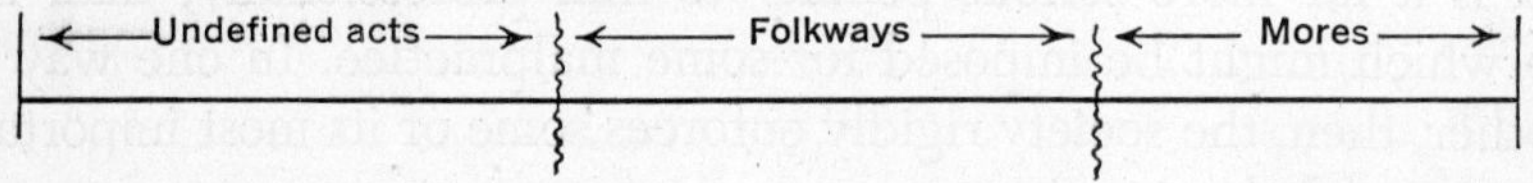


Again, the range covered by each of these three terms is only approximate. It might be difficult to determine, for example, whether taking frequent baths constitutes a folkway or a mos (singular of mores). Is daily bathing required for social acceptability or is it "just the expected, natural thing to do?" The answer would vary from social class to social class; it would then be a "borderline case," somewhere between folkway and mos for the general community. But, it is still regarded as convenient to have the terms *mores, folkways,* and *undefined acts* for quick and approximate designation even though the distinctions are not always clear-cut.

### *Position Along the Continuum Varies with Time*

There is nothing final or permanent about the position of any specific act along the continuum we have just discussed. Behavior considered essential at one time may gradually lose its compulsion until eventually it becomes largely undefined. The history of woman's dress contains numerous illustrations. What would have been considered as "immoral, indecent exposure" in beach costume in 1900 is undefined and largely unnoticed conventional dress today. The reverse may also be true. Undefined acts and folkways may with the passing of time become regarded as increasingly important and hence "in the mores" of the group. At one time a person with a disease such as measles or whooping cough could come and go as he wished, whereas now he is required by both law and public opinion to remain isolated so that he will not infect others. The history of morals contains numerous examples of radical shifts in the societal definition of various acts.

### *Emphasis on Cultural Compulsion Is Misleading*

Although it has been traditional for some sociologists and anthropologists to stress the compulsion feature underlying societal behavior patterns, this point of view leads to basic misunderstanding. At its worst, the view sets the person and the culture apart *as if* the culture were an active thing ordering people around and forcing them to do what they do not wish to do. Actually, of course, the culture is inseparable from the people of a society; the people are participants in the culture. To say that culture "forces" people to abide by social standards would be like saying that the game of football forces quarterbacks to call signals or centers to lean over the ball. The point is not that the game of football forces these men to behave in these ways, but rather that these men are participants in the culture of football, and the pattern simply consists of these behaviors.

### *Groups and Individuals, Not Cultures, Force Persons to Behave in Stipulated Ways*

There is no denying the fact that persons are often required to act in ways which they do not prefer. The existence of laws tabooing some acts and requiring others illustrates the fact of social compulsion. But it is well always to note that the acts tabooed may reflect culturally patterned behavior quite as much as the acts approved. The member of a boys' gang which steals automobile tires is manifesting the boys' gang culture in which he is participating. The fact that this behavior is illegal, according to the standards of behavior set up by the people who made the laws, reflects merely a difference in judgments between the two groups. The controlling group of citizens, lawmakers, and law-enforcing officials are the ones trying to force the boys' gang to do what it does not wish to do, namely, refrain from the behavior pattern of automobile pilfering. *We may, then, speak of "social" compulsion but not of "cultural" compulsion.*

*Compulsion Is Not Entirely Arbitrary: Values*

Compulsion is not entirely a hit-or-miss thing which societies "just happen upon" or devise merely for the sake of making living onerous. Instead, compulsion may arise from the *ideas of importance* which the culture contains with respect to certain behaviors. These are called the cultural *values*. Compulsion is logical *if* it is important that an act be performed, or that it be performed in some precise way. If, for example, the Puritans of New England considered that man's chief responsibility was to God and that church-going was the minimum, inescapable evidence of devotion to God, then it was logical for them to pass strict laws requiring men and women to attend church services regularly. Moreover, if it is considered a serious moral wrong to murder a fellow-man, then severe penalties for murder are in order, assuming, of course, that such penalties deter murderers. And so on. In a later chapter attention will be drawn to the interesting and significant problem of what determines such ideas as logic and right, but here we are only concerned with making the point that the prevailing notions of the importance of certain behavior is the basis for requiring adherence to the societal standards of conduct.

*Mores Formulated in Terms of Taboo or of Required Action*

Sometimes it is easier to describe a mos in terms of the requirement that the individual abstain from some act—*taboo*. The Ten Commandments constitute an excellent case in point. The "Thou shalt nots" of the Mosaic code are, moreover, the same kinds of prohibitions which are recorded in the laws of the United States. In other instances it is conventional to express the mores positively, that is, in terms of what one is under *obligation* to do. Thus, according to both law and custom, a man must support his wife and children, and adults are responsible for the maintenance of aged and indigent parents. Likewise, during time of war a person is under more or less obligation to serve his nation in some capacity suited to his talents, age, and marital status, and he is supposed to show more concern for his country's welfare and less for his own than under more normal circumstances.

*Law and Informal Mores May Not Be Consistent*

There are numerous examples of discrepancies between what the law prescribes pertaining to human conduct, and what the more informal mores of the people condone. Thus, despite clear and overwhelming evidence of murder, few juries will convict a man if the murder can be shown to have been in "self defense" or if the victim had been involved in adulterous behavior with the murderer's wife, even though the law states nothing whatsoever about the legality of such exceptions. "You cannot legislate morality" is an adage containing much that is sociologically sound. When the mores conflict with law, in the long run the mores seem usually to "win out." Prohibition during the 1920's illustrates the difficulty of setting up laws which a substantial minority of the population do not consider to be in the true realm of moral taboos. Under such conditions "lawlessness becomes normal."

The sovereignty of the mores over law occurs also in societies which are not democratic. It would be difficult, for example, to conceive of more severe or more certain punishment of nonconformers to law than that meted out by the Nazis in the occupied countries during the Second World War. Yet throughout the period of Nazi occupation in almost every country involved, fairly large and effective underground organizations flourished for the express purpose of circumventing the operation of the conqueror's law. In the United States prior to the Civil War, despite Supreme Court decisions and laws to the contrary, prominent and highly respected people in the North supported another type of widespread underground movement called the "Underground Railway" which made it possible for escaped Negro slaves to secure safe passage into the North. Every conceivable device was used and many of the devices employed were in themselves clearly illegal, but because the moral conscience of the people justified the objective of freeing Negroes, the illegality of their behavior seemed to be regarded as of little consequence. Many of the early extreme reforms of the Russian revolution had to be modified or abandoned because the mores of the peasants of the vast country run so completely counter to the laws passed by the new government, that it was found necessary to make changes in the law providing for greater consistency with the prevailing mores.

*The Phrase "The Mores" is Frequently An Oversimplification*

Particularly under the conditions of modern urban civilization, the mores may be changing so rapidly or there may be so many different sets of mores in existence, that it is difficult for a person who is completely objective to determine what the mores of his community are. For example, do the mores of America condone or condemn contraception (birth control by medical means)? Studies have shown that the majority of married pairs, in numerous samples that have been investigated, either have practiced contraception or at least are not opposed to its practice. Yet several large and prominent church bodies with millions of members have endorsed resolutions specifically condemning the practice, and the laws of at least one American state make it illegal even for members of the medical profession to give advice on contraception. What, then, are "the mores" regarding contraception? Perhaps one can become more realistic with respect to behavior patterns if attention is drawn to the basic distinction between real and ideal patterns.

## "REAL" AND "IDEAL" CULTURE PATTERNS

When one closely observes the people participating in a culture, he will find that they actually show two kinds of uniformities. The first of these may be called *ideal* patterns. These are the models of exemplary conduct which are held up as standards of perfection. They represent what one "should do" or "ought to do" if he were to behave ideally. Thus, in our culture a person does not lie and he does not act as "tattle tale" or "stool pigeon." Ideal patterns are usually formulated in such a way that they are more or less unreal. If a person carried them out exactly, he would not only be regarded as naïve and queer, but probably would get into numerous practical difficulties in "reward" for his very virtuous conduct. Suppose one were at a party at which inferior food was served and where the guests were dull, and altogether he had had a bad evening. At the end of the evening when paying the hostess the customary compliment, should one lie and be "diplomatic," or should he tell the truth and offend her? Whichever he chooses to do, he thereby violates one or another of the social codes. It is probable that in most cases diplomacy takes precedence over the truth. Yet one does believe in telling the truth, even though he lies to his hostess. And he will no doubt punish his child for the serious offense of telling a lie!

There is a second set of behavior patterns. These are called *real.* They are "real" in the sense that they are what the people actually do, irrespective of what they are ideally supposed to do, or what they themselves believe they should do. In the previously mentioned dilemma regarding one's "honors" to the hostess, the real pattern is probably one of lying to the hostess if necessary in order to compliment her. In similar vein one notes that most people agree with the ideal that it is wrong to steal, but many compute their income tax in such a way as to pay the government less than they know they ought to, without regarding such behavior as theft.

In a strictly logical sense real and ideal patterns constitute inconsistencies. But if one is realistic in his observation of human beings, the conclusion cannot be escaped that ideal patterns and real patterns pertaining to the same acts are not so much inconsistent as only different. That is not to say, however, that the ideal patterns are of no significance. Quite to the contrary. So long as ideal patterns exist they tend to serve as checks upon real patterns, even though at some times the checks seem not to be very effective. There always seem to be some morally sensitive people in a society, who take ideal standards somewhat seriously. Such persons perform the function of periodically reminding the members of the society of the inconsistencies between the real and ideal behavior patterns, and frequently have originated significant changes making for a greater agreement between real and ideal patterns.

### *The "Strain Toward Consistency"*

This phrase was coined by Sumner nearly forty years ago. The phrase may or may not be a useful one. It calls attention to the fact that inconsistencies in culture constitute potential problems and that *in the long run some* of the inconsistent patterns *tend* to be eliminated. Thus, before 1850 the United States was more or less dedicated to the "all men are born equal" idea and yet contained at the same time an appreciable number of men (Negroes) to whom freedom was denied. Of course, there were those who attempted to explain away the inconsistency by stating that "Negroes" were not "men" and that, therefore, there was no inconsistency in denying them freedom. The illogic of this reasoning, however, was shown in the long run, and was well phrased by Lincoln in his "no nation can exist half slave and half free" statement. On the other hand, there are inconsistencies which tend to persist even over long periods. At least one of the nations loud in its advocacy of the Atlantic Charter, which contained among other things the assertion that one people has no right to subject another people, continues to subject several millions of them! Very probably this inconsistency will continue to cause the British Commonwealth of Nations increasing difficulty as time goes on, in very much the same way that Negro slavery gave the American republic considerable difficulty until it was finally abolished.

There is some evidence to indicate that societies like ours and the British, which are highly literate and somewhat democratic, may find it more difficult to tolerate such inconsistencies as we have been discussing, than less literate and less democratic societies would. When a high level of public information is achieved, and when people are free to speak their minds, there is greater opportunity for some one to discover the inconsistency, point it out, and eventually win enough supporters to force a change.

This discussion would be seriously incomplete if the point were not emphatically made that the strain for consistency is *only a tendency, not a certainty,* and that even when it occurs it operates *in the long run*—and the "run" can be *very* long. Moreover, there may be inconsistencies which are never made consistent, and new inconsistencies may arise more rapidly than old ones are removed.

## THE ORGANIZATION OF CULTURE

It has become customary to use specific language to characterize the various parts of culture. It is necessary for the student, therefore, to acquaint himself with this nomenclature.

The smallest unit of culture is called a *culture trait.* A group of related traits is called a *culture complex.* In contemporary America, for example, the automobile complex consists of a great many culture objects and behavior patterns having to do with the automobile and its usage; automobiles, filling stations, roadside parks, traffic laws, and automobile clubs are merely a few of the ramifications of the automobile complex.

The difference between a culture trait and a culture complex is not always as simple a distinction as the above paragraph seems to imply. What appears to one observer to be a culture trait might appear to another observer, who is able to analyze it further, to be a culture complex. Both usages are correct; it is a matter of the observer's ability to distinguish the different degrees or minutia. Thus, an automobile would be called a "trait" if one were describing American culture to an Arab, yet to an automobile engineer an automobile is a culture "complex" consisting of such traits as the wheel, the internal combustion engine, four-wheel brakes, and the incredible number of technical features which taken together constitute an automobile. At the outset the student may have some difficulty in determining when to use the word *trait* and when to use *complex*. Generally speaking, if one is aware that the segment of culture being described is readily divisible into parts, then the word complex would probably be employed.

Complexes, like traits, are related to each other. The term, *the culture pattern*, is sometimes used to designate the overall organization of the culture, but sometimes is used in a more limited way also. Thus one finds both in sociological and anthropological writing, such phrases as "the culture pattern of the Eskimo" when it is quite clear from the context that the writer means the entire culture of the Eskimo. More commonly, major segments of the culture are referred to as patterns, for example, "the family pattern of the Trobrianders" or "the religious pattern of the Todas."

### *Trait-Complex-Pattern Unity*

It should be emphasized that the various traits of a culture derive their meaning and significance from the way in which they fit into the large complex to which they are related. Objects *or units of behavior have no meaning outside of their contexts.* This can readily be illustrated by observing a material culture object from another culture. Frequently the observer does not even know for what the object is used or how valuable it is in relation to other objects, unless and until he knows something else about the rest of the culture. A breastplate from the New Georgia Island natives is as meaningless to an American as a "number 2 iron" would be to a New Georgian.

At many points in this book attention will be devoted to the problems which center around the interrelation of the parts of culture. One of the greatest problems of living for the individual, and one of the greatest problems of controlling societies, is that of changing one aspect of behavior without upsetting a great many others which are related to it. The problems of war and the problems of reconversion to peace have both been greatly increased because of the lack of knowledge concerning how the parts of modern culture really fit together, or a refusal to follow the course of action which our knowledge would seem to indicate. This important principle shall be treated in considerable detail in several of its ramifications from time to time in subsequent chapters.

## SUMMARY

The first purpose of this chapter has been to introduce the technical nomenclature customarily used in describing and analyzing cultures: culture and culture objects; patterns or uniformities in culture; folkways and mores; real and ideal culture patterns; and traits and complexes. Although sociological and anthropological writers are not entirely consistent in the use of these terms, each concept has a somewhat standardized core of meaning which has been defined and illustrated.

Cultures are organized and/or integrated. This does not mean that every single item of each culture is neatly and precisely integrated with everything else. It means rather that it is normal for the parts to be somewhat integrated and organized, and that culture traits receive their significance and meaning out of their relation to the rest of the culture.

## SUGGESTED READINGS

BAIN, Read, "Our Schizoid Culture," *Sociology and Social Research*, XIX, pp. 266-76. **A B**

A clever description of the "irrational, contradictory" behavior characterizing our culture. Very tersely written in terms of a series of antitheses. An idea which should become familiar to everyone. The more serious student will profit by Bain's "Cultural Integration and Social Conflict," *American Journal of Sociology,* XLIV, pp. 499-509. The treatment here is more profound and more implications are considered. (**A**)

BENEDICT, Ruth, *Patterns of Culture* (Boston, Houghton Mifflin Co., 1934). **A**

An important basic volume in the anthropological tradition. Treats both similarities and differences in culture on a somewhat sophisticated level.

BENNETT, John, SMITH, Harvey, and PASSIN, Herbert, "Food and Culture in Southern Illinois—A Preliminary Report," *American Sociological Review*, VII, pp. 645-61. **A**

A realistic study of food habits in relation to the whole culture of the various groups and classes in a southern Illinois river valley community. Contains considerable theoretical treatment of culture per se.

CAPLOW, Theodore, "Transiency as a Culture Pattern," *American Sociological Review*, V, pp. 731-40. **A B**

A summary of factual data from several sources dealing with the nature and extent of transiency in the United States and an attempt to interpret transiency as a "way of life."

DAY, G. M., "Folkways vs. Stateways," *Sociology and Social Research*, XXIII, pp. 334-44. **B**

Discussion of the conflict brought about in Russia after the Revolution when the government introduced behavior patterns and values which seemed desirable on a rational basis but ran counter to the folkways long observed by the people. In general, the author feels that the folkways "won" over the superimposed "stateways."

TUMIN, Melvin, "Culture, Genuine and Spurious." (See p. 80 for bibliographic note.)

## STUDY QUESTIONS

1. Why should one learn the technical terms used by sociologists in their study of culture?
2. How are both material objects and "intangible" behavior part of culture?
3. How are culture objects and non-material behavior related? Illustrate.
4. How does the reward-punishment system produce conformity to a culture?
5. Why is it impossible for the individual to be wholly "indoctrinated" by this culture?
6. Why do not all people show the same degree of conformity to all expected types of behavior?
7. How is conformity to culture "a relative matter?"
8. Why are some forms of behavior mores, others folkways, while others are just "undefined acts?"
9. How do behavior patterns vary from society to society, and in the same society at different times? Illustrate.
10. How may mores be "sins of omission" as well as "sins of commission?"
11. Criticise: "For every mos there is a law, and for every law there is a mos."
12. What is the relation of the "real" to the "ideal" culture patterns? Illustrate.
13. How is the presence of "inconsistent" culture patterns a source of problems for a society? How does one know that they are "inconsistent" patterns? Illustrate.
14. What is the relation of the culture trait and culture complex to the culture pattern? Illustrate.
15. Give some examples of folkways becoming mores, and vice versa.

# Chapter VII

## SOCIETY AND THE PERSON

It has probably already occurred to most readers of the foregoing chapters that the culture and the society in which a person lives profoundly influence him. But how profound and how complete is this influence? It is obvious enough that one's society requires certain overt behaviors like shaking hands, paying taxes, and wearing tuxedos. But does societal influence extend on into the "deeper aspects" of the person, to determine how he "feels" about his overt acts, how he thinks, how he reaches conclusions, or how he values the artifacts of his and other cultures? Do people in a given culture think as much alike as they dress alike or play alike? The complete answer to some of these questions must be delayed until after we have studied the materials in Part II, "The Development of Personality," but even at this early point, certain basic and important factors can be discussed.

### CULTURAL PARTICIPATION AND A PERSON'S "NEEDS"

*Food Needs*

At first thought most persons will probably be inclined to question the idea that society fashions a person's "needs." Are not one's needs determined by something more basic than the particular society in which he chances to be reared? Is not the recurring need for food, for example, an organically generated need which one has because he is a human being, irrespective of any society? Suppose you have gone without food for twelve hours. What are your food needs? You say you are so hungry that you "could eat anything edible." But is this true? Suppose, further, that you were then served a stew which you were told contained substantial amounts of skunk meat, human flesh, and dog milk, all prepared in a thoroughly sanitary manner and seasoned in the conventional way. It is almost certain that few, if any, persons would—not to say "could"—eat this stew. Now there is nothing biologically harmful about any of the ingredients of our hypothetical stew; in fact it could be so balanced as to constitute a better meal dietetically than most people ordinarily eat. Nevertheless it would not be acceptable to most Americans if they knew what the ingredients were. Persons in some other culture might have no difficulty eating and enjoying a meal of this sort. Organically or biologically they may have the same food "needs" as an American would, but that similarity is, in the practical situation, without any significance. The fact remains that one person would be unable to eat what another person, from another culture, would regard, perhaps, as a delicacy. Realistically, when any person refers to his "food needs" he means, his needs for some specific kind or kinds of food, often requiring some particular (and often "unnatural") mode of preparation. Among many peoples the mode of serving food is as important even as is the food itself. The same is true of time for eating.

*Needs for Harmful Commodities*

It should be noted, also, that social living often conditions persons to need foods (or other things) which are actually harmful to the human body. Frequently these "needs" are among the most pressing needs which people feel. For example, the consumption of coffee, tobacco, and alcohol cannot in any sense of the word be considered as needs of the human organism. Yet during the recent war many Americans felt more seriously deprived because of shortages of coffee, cigarettes, and liquor than from almost any other scarce article. Anyone familiar with the rudiments of the science of dietetics could cite innumerable examples in which the people in our culture prefer or even highly prize certain kinds of food or modes of preparing food which are either not nutritious or positively harmful to the human organism. So deeply ingrained are these habits, moreover, that despite our scientific knowledge and our desire to be healthy, it has become virtually impossible to get people to change their food habits, even though they know that they are endangering their health and shortening their lives through continuing their present practices.

*Other Needs*

Other kinds of needs, when analyzed, will be seen to be even more arbitrary than the food needs that we have just discussed. Take, for example, the urban dweller's so-called need for an automobile. He will usually justify his need in terms of transportation to work, transportation to the points of recreation, and transportation of food stuffs and other supplies. As compared with his grandfather who may have lived in the same city, the contemporary citizen works fewer hours and has better public transportation to serve him. In an abstract sense grandfather needed the automobile much more than we do, but since he did not have access to it he was quite content with a mode of life without an automobile. The mere fact that the contemporary man knows that he works shorter hours, does lighter work, and has speedier and more convenient public transportation to serve him, does not in any way really alter the fact that he needs the automobile or that he would feel seriously deprived if he were denied the use of it.

*Necessities and Luxuries*

This raises the whole question of "luxuries *versus* necessities." If one is realistic he immediately encounters difficulty in distinguishing luxuries and necessities. A man is quick to note that a woman's fifth pair of shoes is surely a luxury; she can certainly get along with four. He is less likely, however, to be equally aware of the more luxurious aspect of the items in his own wardrobe. Does he "really need" the fourth suit, or the golf shoes? Similarly, persons who do not smoke are usually quite sure that tobacco is a luxury, and people who are not interested in football are equally certain that football tickets constitute luxury. The detached observer, however, comes sooner or later to the conclusion that in modern cultures such as ours, so many of the objects and activities become necessary, but not necessary because they are physiologically required. They are needed because they are defined in the culture as being important and necessary to satisfactory psychological living. It is easy to demonstrate this fact by comparing the needs of people in two or more quite different cultures. By so doing one recognizes that a person needs the things he needs because he is a participant in culture *A* instead of culture *B*. One needs an education, a new suit, an eight-room house, a larger automobile, or a new refrigerator because participation in his culture has taught him a mode of life in which he needs these things in order to live correctly or successfully or with a feeling of satisfaction.

*Psychological Needs*

Thus far needs have been considered largely in terms of needs for material objects or for overt behaviors. The same principle which we have already discussed applies also to feelings, ideas, and other forms of covert experience. Students of religion have, for example, pointed out that many persons seem to need "a belief in a personal God" in order to feel secure in the world. Psychiatrists have frequently pointed out that mentally disturbed people have sometimes been helped by a rediscovery of faith in such a Divine being. The evidence presented in these individual cases is possibly correct *for the case mentioned*. But frequently an erroneous conclusion is drawn from these facts, namely, that there is something about human beings per se which requires belief in a personal Deity. What is overlooked often is the fact that many people require a belief in a personal Deity in order to feel well adjusted because they have grown up in a culture in which the need for a personal Deity has been taught to them either by formal instruction or through the suggestion of living among people who are so oriented. In much the same way the Japanese "need" their emperor whom some regard as sacred, the people of India "need" their sacred cows, and the British "need" their King.

Many errors in thinking about government in relation to the person spring from a failure to understand the nature of culturally derived needs. It is common for Americans, who have experienced a democratic form of government, to assume that *all* peoples have a need for exercising a voice in their government. Perhaps the chief error which the Allies made at the conclusion of World War I was in the supposition that once they provided the German people with a democratic form of government that these people would have the desire and the knowledge necessary to continue it. Numerous peoples have neither the desire nor the required techniques for accomplishing such objectives. Instead their need consists of a desire *to be* governed, or of the necessity for believing that their despot is a good despot. Humans find security in many diverse forms of social organization, once they are habituated to that particular mode of organization.

### CULTURE PARTICIPATION GIVES MEANINGS

"What does it *mean?*" is a recurrent question. And it is among the hardest of questions to answer completely. All that one can ever say, with accuracy and assurance, is what it means *to him,* that is, what it means in the light of the cultural *perspective* through which he observes it. What does "democracy" mean—to a Japanese or to an American? And to which American? What does "God" mean —to a Christian or to an Atheist? And to which Christian? What, even, does life itself mean? What is life for? Are there obligations with respect to it? If so, what obligations? Does one have the right to dispense with his life if he wishes to? Obviously the answer to any and all of these questions depends upon the culture from the context of which the answer comes, and, also, the answer will vary radically if not antithetically from culture to culture and from time to time in the same culture.

But our chief concern here is not with meanings of such magnitude and profundity as the above mentioned ones. Everyday acts and thoughts, however trivial, involve assumptions of meaning. You observe that someone tells a "lie." What does that mean? Is the person, therefore, not trustworthy? Will you cultivate his friendship, tend to shun him, or remain unchanged in your relationship to him? Perhaps the falsehood was a "white lie." What makes one lie "whiter" than another? Perhaps the lie was a cleverly concealed partial-truth, that is, technically not a lie at all, such as is so often encountered in some business transactions. Does that make it mean anything different to you? Is a lie on the income tax return the same as a lie in a court trial?

Suppose, moreover, that you suddenly feel a pain in your left side. What does it mean? With the knowledge which we have regarding physiology, it is not likely that you will attribute the pain to supernatural forces. You are not likely to go over your list of "sins" of yesterday and today to seek the reason for your discomfort. You might, however, take inventory of your recent behavior to discover possible injuries, dietary excesses, and so forth, which might provide some clues to the source of your pain. But to you the pain would not mean punishment by an angry Deity. If you were worried about the pain and needed help, you would call or visit a physician, not a witch-chaser. In other words, to you (1) the pain would *mean* mere physical malfunction and have no relation to moral conduct; (2) having the pain—if it persisted—would *mean* to you that "something ought to be done about it"; (3) seeking a cure would *mean* finding a professional functionary called a doctor who is supposed to know what to do for you. In another culture all three of the meanings might be different—the pain would have different meaning, your reaction to it would be different, your behavior would be different.

### *"But It's Natural...."*

A common belief among humans is that their particular *modus operandi* or their particular "way of looking at it" is more "natural" than some other. This implies that there is some one basically correct way of doing or thinking which is inherent to man as man, irrespective of any particular culture or of any particular time. All of the evidence points to the fallacy of this point of view. Virtually anything seems natural to one whose culture habituates him to it. It is "natural" for a cannibal to eat human flesh—but not for an American. It is "natural" for an Eskimo to get hungry for whale blubber—but not for you. It is "natural" for men in several different cultures to lend their wives to overnight guests as a demonstration of genuine hospitality—but not in the United States. What then, does "natural" mean? It may refer to the acts and thoughts to which one becomes so thoroughly habituated that it is difficult if not impossible, to conceive of any other proper or fitting way of acting or thinking. When the conditioning is complete enough, the person acquires the *illusion of inherency* of the act, that is, the notion that the act results not from mere habit, but from "the nature of things." Here lies the error, but it is a persistent error. One should recognize that often what seems natural to him has become so by the long process of habit formation and habit exercise.

It is not intended to deny that there are some behaviors which are natural in the universal and organic sense, such as sleeping, eating, resting, or belching. But sleeping in beds, a given number of hours, or at given times of the day, being afraid to sleep in the dark or ashamed of sleeping during the day, are neither universal nor organically natural. They are the variable behaviors of some particular culture. Whether or not one uses the *word* "natural" is of little consequence; the important point lies in the recognition of the *fact* that one should be ever cautious lest he confuse habituation with organic necessity.

Perhaps the best test to apply in a specific case where "naturalness" is at issue is the *test of universality*. Do all peoples regardless of the culture in which they live, do or think or feel in the manner in question? If the answer is found—*found, not assumed*—to be "yes," then it seems scientifically justifiable to consider the behavior inherent and not culturally habituated. If, on the other hand, one people behaves in one way and another in another way, then if we call either's mode of behaviors "natural" we must recognize that we mean natural *by habituation*—not inherently. Invariably, of course, each culture's ways seem "natural" (that is, *as if* inherent) to the persons habituated to them.

### *"But It's Logical. . . ."*

Here again, as with the notion of naturalness, one may easily be ethnocentric without knowing it. The error again lies in the assumption that there is only one correct logical conclusion which can be drawn from given conditions. On the contrary there are several, perhaps innumerable, conclusions which can be reached logically from given conditions. Logicalness always depends upon the amount and kind of other knowledge which one possesses at the time he draws his conclusions. It also depends on what might be called "basic assumptions." For example, if one starts with the idea that the universe was the work of some purposive Being, then it seems logical to ascribe its normal workings and its irregularities to that Being's wishes or intents. The storm struck here instead of there because the storm director wanted for some reason or other to have it so. On the other hand, if one begins with the assumption that the universe is not the creation of a purposive Being, then the above storm's explanation is not only not logical but ridiculous. Again, if one assumes that the earth is flat, then it follows logically that he should not go out near the edge so that he will not fall off, an explanation common in Columbus' time.

The point to note is that *logic is itself a cultural creation or invention.* Logic is a mode of thinking about certain items in the universe in an orderly fashion. The logic invented, or modified, by one culture is, therefore, not necessarily, or likely, to be exactly like that of the second culture. Science is one logic. Religion is another logic. Mathematics is a logic with a formal language of its own. Each is quite logical—but each is different. It is also noteworthy that logic is used often as a mode of buttressing or "proving" some way of thinking after one has by non-logical methods come to accept it. In this way logic may come to be used as a kind of formalized "sales talk" for some point of view. One cannot fail to have noted that opposite ideas or programs are both more or less logically supported by their proponents and more or less logically attacked by their opponents. Logic supports the Catholic faith and the Protestant faith and the non-Christian faiths, logic supports the Republican party platform and the Democratic party platform. But *which* logic?

In summary, we see that logicalness, like naturalness, is a mode of thinking which one derives from the cultural stream in which he functions. It is common to find persons resorting to the "it's natural" or "it's logical" mode of thought as a means of justifying their particular prejudice-system. These words are often used because in our culture "logic" and "nature" have become "virtue words." We are, on the whole, favorably disposed toward education and science. If something can be made to appear "natural," that is, inherent in the assumed scheme of things and not alterable by man, it takes on a certain authority and finality. Likewise, if some act or idea can be made to appear reasonable or logical, its authority and respectability are accordingly enhanced. Both of the ideas, logical and natural, are useful, but the problem arises out of their misuse, or at least their vulgarization, by persons who understand their implications incompletely, or have an insufficient knowledge of the facts and other data in the fields to which the terms are properly applied.

### *"But It's Abnormal. . . ."*

What makes an act or an idea normal? Would it be regarded as normal if one of your classmates were to claim that he had had another life on earth before this one, that he had been a cat, or a goldfish in Mr. Vanderbilt's aquarium the first time? Surely, the student's mental faculties would be questioned. "A normal person would not believe that." A normal person *in this culture* and *at this time* would *usually* not accept such an interpretation of himself. But, again, there are cultures in which such an explanation would seem altogether plausible, if not obvious, to the people. There the "abnormal" person would be one who did not accept the reincarnation idea. Thus, we see "normality" is essentially of the same cultural origin as the logical or the natural. It is a word to label the act or idea or person which is out of the ordinary, too-different to be acceptable. Obviously, what is regarded as normal or abnormal varies from culture to culture and from time to time in the same culture. It is certainly not abnormal for a woman to smoke, wear cosmetics, and dress in slacks at the present time, but not long ago any one of these behaviors would have rendered her not only abnormal but criminally so.

*"But It's Immoral. . . ."*

Morality, again, is a cultural definition as we have already seen in the chapter on cultural variability. History is replete with examples of acts and their opposite, ideas and their antitheses, which are both regarded as moral and both as immoral by each of two contemporary or successive cultures. It would be immoral to hold a Negro in slavery today in the United States, but one hundred years ago it was not so. Some people regard birth control as immoral but others regard it as immoral to refrain from limitation of offspring.

### SOCIETY AND FEARS

While the psychological process of fear is found in all humans, fears, that is, the specific things feared and the ways in which fear is expressed, are societal and therefore, highly variable. It has sometimes been carelessly or ignorantly asserted that "men fear the things they do not understand." We understand pneumonia, war, and lightning, but we may fear any or all of them. In fact, many fears result from knowledge; if the person were ignorant of the fact, he would not have the fear. It is also noteworthy that we do not fear all of the things we do not understand—such as love or the supernatural. More accurate, it seems, is the point of view that men as a rule fear the things which they learn to fear by participation in their culture. Items in one's universe tend all to be defined in some way or other by culture. Part of the definition process consists of the formulation of emotional responses, like fear, to the object, person, or behavior which has been defined. *If* germs bring illness or death, and *if* illness and death are undesirable, then one fears germs. But if war brings death, but death from war is a glorious thing, as with some of the Nazis, then war is not to be feared even though one may die in it.

Experiments with babies show that there are very, very few innate (that is, inborn) fears. Therefore most of the fears must be explained by learning. It does not follow, of course, that because most fears are learned, that therefore they are societally relevant fears, because a person might acquire some fear due to an unusual and unique experience which he has had. Most fears are, however, culturally learned. Moreover, once they are learned it is usually very difficult to eliminate them from the person. Fears tend to persist, even though one has learned rationally that they are not correctly grounded or originally grew up from false knowledge.

Make a list of the five things you fear most. By "fears" we do not necessarily mean that they need to worry you unduly or that you are necessarily preoccupied with thoughts about them. We mean simply that they are things or occurrences or persons or conditions with which you are unable to cope, and from which you would prefer escaping because you believe that they would harm you in some way. The author has collected lists of "five fears" from several hundreds of students over a period of years. These lists showed usually the effects of the times; during the war men feared the draft or the war or being 4F, and during the depression they feared unemployment or their father's cut in income, and so forth. But taking an overall view, six fears recurred consistently: (1) loss of fiancé, (2) failure in college, (3) unemployment after graduation, (4) poverty—really inadequate income, not actual poverty, (5) certain diseases—mostly cancer, syphilis, and polio, and (6) loss of popularity. The similarity among these people was striking; they feared the same small group of things. They feared the things which they had been taught to fear. A smaller number of adults were interrogated also and they showed similarity among themselves. But the adults had somewhat different fears than college students did. The chief adult fears were unemployment, illness, and tragedy which might befall their children. A large proportion of the women around forty feared cancer, but the men feared "heart trouble." Almost none feared witches and similar supernatural phenomena which would appear prominently in list of fears compiled from a study of persons in some other cultures.

### CULTURE AND CONSCIENCE

Although the idea of conscience is of somewhat uncertain meaning, it calls attention to an important aspect of human behavior. The essential conception involved in conscience is that human beings have standards or criteria in the light of which they evaluate their behavior. It amounts to a sort of self-discipline. Almost any person has had the experience of refraining from some act which he acknowledges he would find pleasurable. He restrains himself because the act is not regarded as right, or not becoming to a gentleman, or to an officer, or to a mature man. Another common evidence of the existence of conscience is the so-called "pain" of "injured conscience." It refers, of course, to the psychological discomfort which persons feel when they have performed some act which is contrary to the standards involved in their conscience. It is not necessary at this point to consider the recurrent argument of whether everyone has conscience, whether conscience, when violated, always "hurts." It is sufficient to note that the vast majority of persons will readily acknowledge that they have observed conscience, as here defined, in themselves or in other person's reactions.

While introspection readily reveals the existence of conscience, it gives little clue to the origin of it. Conscience is so deeply rooted in human nature that it carries, like other aspects of behavior, the illusion of inherency, the "feeling" that it must somehow be innate because it is so potent. Scientific evidence, on the other hand, clearly establishes the learned basis for conscience. Conscience consists, largely, of the personalized application of what we have already termed culturally patterned behavior. If one is habituated to a culture in which pre-marital chastity is the pattern, the unchaste person is likely to have a conscience which tends to deter him from unchaste acts, and which will pain him afterward if he should perform such acts. In another culture the content of conscience may be, as we have already seen many times, precisely the reverse. Thus, many Catholics have consciences which prevent or deter them from seeking a divorce in case their marriages are unhappy, but most Protestants do not have this item of conscience in the same way or to the same degree. Both, however, would probably have consciences which would taboo murder, rape, or wife-beating. These things both have been learned in essentially the same way, but on the matter of divorce, differences were learned.

Conscience, of course, may change as a result of new learnings or new experiences, and possibly also as a result of maturity. Acts which might be tabooed by the conscience of a child would not necessarily be so tabooed by an adult and vice versa. Conscience, however, does not change readily because it is acquired in a context of experience which results in its being more indelibly fixed in a person's mind than less valued behavior is.

Society sometimes makes fine distinctions among behaviors or rationalizes opposite standards in such a way as to create problems for some persons. War is a case in point. Christians are usually taught the sanctity of human life and a more or less qualified notion of the "brotherhood of men." Taking human life becomes an important taboo. Then a war arises and military duty requires the taking of human life. Most men make the adjustment in time, but some never make it and many find it difficult, especially in hand to hand combat or when women and children might lose lives as a result of the man's action. Less extreme instances occur in everyday civilian life. Persons sometimes find some of the practices of certain occupations or of certain social groups so offensive to their consciences that mental conflict or a change in group affiliation results.

## CULTURE AND INTELLIGENCE

The researches of psychologists have clearly established certain principles regarding intelligence, although some issues regarding the measurement of it still remain. The findings regarding the nature of intelligence are as follows: (1) a person's intelligence is based on biological factors; (2) persons differ from one another radically in the degree of intelligence which they have; (3) persons cannot learn, regardless of the amount and kind of effort they expend, beyond the limits of their native intelligence; and (4) ill-health, isolation, certain kinds of temperament and other factors as well, may seriously limit the proportion of one's intelligence which he may actually be able to put to *use*. It probably cannot be stressed too fully that intelligence of itself means little so far as the actual behavior, knowledge, and skill of a person are concerned. A person may have extremely high intelligence and be unable to read and write until such time as he *learns* to read and write. *Having high intelligence only increases the ease with which the person learns. He cannot learn anything with which he does not come in contact, regardless of how intelligent he may be.* This is a basic point.

This last principle is of great importance in relation to culture. The content of a person's behavior, that is, the specific things he can do, come largely from his culture. An average Zulu has the necessary intelligence and physical makeup to typewrite, but since the Zulu culture does not contain typewriters or typewriting, he will not learn to type. This fact is obvious enough in the case of physical skills, but is apt to be overlooked in other and perhaps more important respects, notably in modes of thinking or techniques for reaching conclusions. "Superstitions" constitute a case in point. It is easy to find examples from other cultures than one's own which demonstrate faulty thinking. We "know" that the dancing, chanting and other antics of the native "medicine man" do not actually cure the tropical fever from which the patient suffers. That does not prove, however, that the people who believe that the medicine man cures tropical fever are unintelligent. They may be of very high intelligence. What these people lack is knowledge, not intelligence. An Einstein or a "quiz kid" born in such a society would also believe in the medicine man's powers. How could he do otherwise? The mind can only think with the materials with which it comes in contact.

The fact of invention constitutes no contradiction of the principle contained in the preceding paragraph. The inventor, it should always be noted, invents, first, relatively few new things or ideas and, second, invents only such things as are more or less "in line with" the rest of the culture, because he must use the materials and ideas at hand in the course of formulating the innovation. The inventor is the recipient of the accumulated knowledges of all the myriads of generations of inventors which have preceded him.

The best contemporary inventor, if left to himself from birth, would not even learn to talk and would, in all probability, perish.

The manipulation of intelligence through cultural participation can, perhaps, be illustrated by reference to a few obvious questions. Are Catholics more intelligent or less intelligent than Protestants? Obviously, their differences are not matters of inborn intelligence at all but are, instead, differences in the *learned content of mind,* that is, of knowledges, beliefs, logics, and so forth. The same for Republicans and Democrats. Both groups contain persons of extremely high intelligence, but there are still two or more distinct "sides" to many political issues because there are two or more distinct knowledge and attitude configurations (that is, cultures). Likewise the Nazis, the Japanese, the Russians, and the Eskimos are of essentially the same intelligence *as a group,* but their cultures are radically different. Therefore, the persons in each of these groups have their intelligence trained differently. Thus the social scientist does not find the clue to cultural differences in the factor of different intelligence, but instead finds that intelligence may be expressed in any one of an infinite variety of behaviors depending on the culture to which it is exposed.

## SUMMARY

Although we shall pursue the question of the relation between the person and culture somewhat more fully and precisely in a later series of chapters (Part III), certain relationships have already been noted in this chapter. The culture in which a person participates profoundly influences him. From those experiences he acquires his needs and interests, his fears and hopes. He derives from it meanings of things, the definitions of what is logical and natural and right. He learns these notions so clearly and so indelibly that often he requires no external force to keep him in conformity to the societal requirements. His "conscience" is sufficient as a guide, at least for certain of the more important behaviors. So thoroughly does cultural participation influence one, that the illusion is fostered that the behavior is inherent, not actually learned as it really is. Through participation in culture innate and undefined intelligence is translated into concrete behavior skills and abilities. It is a mistake to regard any one society as any more or any less intelligent than another, because high or low or mediocre intelligence may be shaped to fit any culture. One may have a moral right to believe literally anything about anything or entertain any preferences for or against any custom or idea, but as a realist one must recognize the incontestable fact of social domination of the content of mind regardless of what degree of native intelligence is possessed.

## SUGGESTED READINGS

COOLEY, C. H., ANGELL, R. C., and CARR, L. J., *Introductory Sociology* (New York, Charles Scribner's Sons, 1933), Chapter V, "Individual and Society," and VIII, "Culture and Personality." **B**

An excellent treatment of the individual in relation to culture and society. The latter chapter is especially useful in its emphasis upon the way in which culture "defines" experience for the person. This is a significant factor.

CUBER, John, "Sociological Aspects and Implications of Science," in Roucek, J., and others, *Sociological Foundations of Education* (New York, The Thomas Y. Crowell Co., 1942). **B**

This is an attempt to appraise the impact of scientific thinking upon the person living in the modern era.

LINTON, Ralph, *The Study of Man* (New York, D. Appleton-Century Co., 1936). Chapter on "Interests." **A B**

Shows the way in which the person participating in culture acquires characteristic interest patterns.

MEAD, Margaret, *Sex and Temperament in Three Primitive Societies* (New York, William Morrow and Co., 1935). (See bibliographic note p. 80.) **A**

MINEHAN, Thomas, *Boy and Girl Tramps of America* (New York, Farrar and Rinehart, Inc., 1934). **B**

A study of over 1000 boy and girl migrants made during the great depression of the 1930's. The author lived among these people and writes intimately about their culture. Interesting and significant for the way it shows how cultural patterning of behavior takes place among these people.

SHAW, Clifford, *The Natural History of a Delinquent Career* (Chicago, University of Chicago Press, 1931). **B**

A book-length life history of a delinquent boy. Contains much material on the behavior patterns of the boys' gang culture of the great city and also of the law enforcement agencies and personnel.

SHERMAN and HENRY, *Hollow Folk.* (See bibliographic note p. 80.) **B**

## STUDY QUESTIONS

1. Why does the American eat ham with his eggs instead of dog meat?
2. How do we acquire the "need" for coffee, soap, and "spike" heels?

3. What determines the difference betwen a luxury and a necessity?
4. Why do some people require a belief in a personal God in order to feel well "adjusted?" What determines the "meaning" of this personal God?
5. On what does a logical conclusion depend? Illustrate.
6. Why may different persons arrive at more than one logical conclusion from the same set of given facts or conditions?
7. What determines whether a particular mode of conduct is normal or abnormal? Moral or immoral?
8. Why do people in the same society have similar fears?
9. How could one become involved in difficulties if he "let his conscience be his guide?" Illustrate.
10. Why do we not always obey the commandmant, "Thou shall not kill?"
11. What besides our inherited capacity to learn determines the amount and kinds of knowledge and skills that we acquire?
12. Can you think of any exceptions to the Golden Rule as a guide for conduct? Explain.
13. How does one determine whether he or someone else is a success or a failure? What criteria are used? Where do the criteria come from?

# *Chapter VIII*

# DEVELOPMENT OF CULTURE

## A TIME PERSPECTIVE ON MODERN CULTURE

### *Culture Origins*

It might be expected that this chapter would contain information about the origins of culture. Unfortunately there is no scientific knowledge as to *precisely* when, where, or how man first began to create culture. The quest for knowledge about culture origins, however, has preoccupied many scholars' time and energies for centuries. Not all of these scholars were scientists; many were theologians or philosophers and some of them have created "explanations," "theories," or sheer guesses. None can, however, stand the test of empiric examination, because the *prehistoric* past is veiled in such utter obscurity. The problem persists largely because of the almost inconceivable antiquity of man's original activities in culture creation.

Science is not, however, entirely devoid of reliable information on some aspects of the genesis of human culture. While many facts about man's remote past have been lost, all of the evidence from the earliest cultures has not. Certain items of early material culture which did not decompose, such as stone tools, pottery, some paintings on the interior of caves, and other artifacts are present even today and can be observed and handled. The early non-material culture, on the other hand, cannot be reconstructed, because prior to the appearance of writing and art, no tangible evidence of how the people lived, what they thought about, why they happened on one invention instead of another, can be determined. We can, however, derive certain *inferences* concerning the folkways of some prehistoric peoples. If, for example, a people's skeletel remains are found in proximity with one another accompanied by apparently valuable items like jewelry and are usually found in a characteristic position, it would seem reasonable to assume that these people buried their dead instead of simply abandoning the corpses. Again, if the people left paintings showing campfire scenes and men riding astride horses, one might infer that horse riding and campfire fraternization were among their folkways. Caution must be observed, however, not to assume too much from such inferential "evidence." From the above illustrations regarding primitive drawings of men riding horses, one still does not know whether to conclude that these people rode horses for pleasure or economic reasons or both, whether horseback riding gave a man higher or lower status than did some other form of locomotion, whether the horses were used solely for riding or only incidentally for riding, their chief function possibly being to provide meat or milk. For that matter we do not even know whether the horses were kept for utilitarian reasons or were regarded as sacred beasts like the sacred cattle of India. Thus, great caution must be observed in drawing inferences concerning a people's *habits* from the mere fact that a given artifact (material culture object) was possessed by or known to them. The even more significant question, namely, what did it *mean* to them, is almost impossible to determine from material remains alone. Prior to the preservation of writings, and to some extent even after that, this vital information has not been available.

### *Culture History*

Anthropologists have, nevertheless, secured some sufficiently reliable information regarding human cultural beginnings and early development to permit one to piece together an approximate—but *very* approximate—chronology of some of man's early cultural evolution.

The earliest traces of culture are regarded by archaeological authorities to have appeared about a million years B.C. Translating such a time span into units which are more familiar, a million years is five hundred times as long as the period which has elapsed since the birth of Christ, or more than six thousand times as long as the period since the American Constitution was written.

The artifacts from these early cultures are, of course, quite crude. They consist of chipped stone tools probably used by the people of that time for chopping or hewing. There is little evidence that for the next half million years, almost half the way up to the present time, much change in man's production of artifacts occurred. It seems probable, however, that non-material culture could and did change during this tremendous era, but we have no artifacts or other definitive evidence to prove it, except by inference.

By around 100,000 B.C. stone tools were supplemented by tools made of bone and some tools showed technical work which was becoming increasingly precise. Noteworthy, perhaps, is the fact that tools which were made apparently around 100,000 B.C. were decorated with carvings and other evidences of non-utilitarian workmanship and interest.

From about 75,000 to 14,000 B.C. culture seems to have developed more rapidly. Specifically, for example, there is evidence that by around 14,000 B.C. men began to bury their dead, live in cave communities, use wood for tools in addition to bone and stone, and to draw and paint recognizable images. By 10,000 B.C. human culture contained numerous material and non-material elements familiar to us such as agriculture, domestic animals, and pottery.

Several cautions should be observed by the student in thinking about the above data. (1) The dates are *very* approximate. It is not difficult to find two or more archaeologists of comparable ability and training whose judgment differs by several thousand years concerning the age of some item. While the sequence is roughly as we have indicated, the transition dates, that is, the dates chosen to mark the end of one period and the beginning of the next, are very arbitrarily chosen and can be justified only by convenience. (2) Many of the data are inferential, that is, our "facts" are often deductions from other facts and may be faulty, particularly when artifacts are used as the basis for determining the behavior of the people, as mentioned in preceding paragraphs. When one speculates concerning what this or that practice "meant" to this or that people, and "why" they behaved as they did, he is treading on very thin academic ice. (3) Development was *very* slow. A period like the span of years between the discovery of America and the present would be a mere moment in the history of civilization. The rapid change which characterizes modern life is something exceedingly new in human experience. Throughout most of man's existence the amount of culture change from generation to generation was almost imperceptible. (4) European civilization (and modern America also, since it is an offshoot of the European) was one of the last major cultures to develop. The Near Eastern, the Oriental and the Mediterranean cultures were well advanced while the Europeans were still primitive. The Chinese, for example, were living in palaces and the Egyptians had bronze plumbing at the time our European ancestors were wearing bearskins, eating raw meat and living in crude huts.

## SOME PRINCIPLES REGARDING CULTURAL CHANGE

### *Selective Addition and Loss of Traits*

One of the persistent errors in much thinking about culture change is the notion that man's culture "just accumulated" as if it were like the proverbial snowball rolling downhill, gaining size with each revolution, picking up virtually everything with which it came in contact, gathering momentum as it rolled, and guided by no purpose except the laws of the physical universe. Although culture does tend to accumulate new traits and patterns from time to time, it also loses such elements. Culture loses traits in several ways. Sometimes a people discards a culture trait because it has found something "better" to take the place of the outmoded trait. We are not concerned here with the important question of whether the new trait is "really better" than the old one or *why* it is better, but simply with the fact that under existing conditions the people whose prerogative it is to make the choice, either consciously or unconsciously choose to employ folkway *A* instead of folkway *B*, or artifact *A* instead of artifact *B*. The result is that down through time there are numerous instances of culture losing certain elements.

The additions to culture are not random, but are what is usually called "selective." As a rule there are numerous alternatives or choices. In the area of religion, for example, a people have an almost infinite range of phenomena which they may worship. For one culture it seems "fitting and logical" that people worship the moon, to another group it seems equally fitting and logical that they venerate ancestors, and to a third it seems fitting and logical to worship nothing at all. Adding or discarding a culture trait stems not so much from the mere availability of the trait as from the relationship between that trait and the rest of the culture into which it may or may not ultimately be absorbed.

### *"Resistances" to Culture Change*

Much popular comment has centered around the "resistances" of peoples to new ideas and artifacts. In characteristic ethnocentric fashion it has become conventional to decry the "ignorance and superstition" of, for example, the mountaineer who refuses to bathe. The mountaineer's critic, however, may himself also manifest ignorance and superstition by eating his steak so rare that he is vulnerable to infestation with tapeworm or rendering himself increasingly susceptible to various degenerative diseases while he cavorts his scientific self from night club to night club as he "does" New York City. With all his "ignorance and superstition" the mountaineer may yet outlive the sophisticate! The point is that the folkways of each will continue to be observed only if and as they fit into the large overall pattern of the culture in which he is functioning. The mountaineer deserves no particular credit, either morally or intellectually, if he goes to bed when the birds do, because he has no electricity, no interesting world of amusement awaiting him. Moreover, when one considers the way he has to bathe, if he does, and the conditions within which he must live his life, it is small wonder that he finds little "necessity" for keeping his skin clean. Frequently what is called "superstition and ignorance" by the observer from the other culture is simply another system of values which the observer does not understand or does not approve.

This is not to deny the unmistakable fact that unfounded beliefs and assumptions ("superstitions") do exist and tend to prevent the acceptance of new and perhaps objectively better culture traits. In the above illustration, for example, the objective point of view need not justify the mountaineer's uncleanliness; incontrovertibly he would be better off if he were cleaner. The point, however, is that one of the chief factors underlying a person's or a group's ability and willingness to accept a new *modus operandi* or to refuse to discard an old one, is the nature of the rest of the prevailing culture. The whole way of life must at least seem to "make sense" to the person who lives it; any part of it which does not fit, impedes smooth and comfortable functioning. If one has grown up with the idea that Negroes "are not really men," then it would be very difficult, if not impossible, to vote for a Negro or for that matter even to permit the Negro to vote. The overall culture sets up the criteria on the basis of which the specific new idea or practice is evaluated.

Culture is then a unity; its various parts, while they need not fit perfectly together, need in some measure to be consistent, or at least need to seem to be consistent with one another. On the basis of this "strain for consistency," the selective adding and discarding of culture traits takes place down through time.

### *Great Men and Cultural Change*

One of the persistent errors in thinking about culture development is the overemphasis upon the influence of a few great men as inventors or innovators in culture. This is a gross oversimplification and leads to a recurring and serious error when one attributes some invention solely to "the work of this great man." It is well to consider the *other factors* which account for both the inventor himself and the incorporation of the invention into the culture.

1. *Few, if any, inventors ever created anything wholly new.* The inventor of the automobile, for example, only combined the four-wheel carriage and the internal combustion engine both of which had been in existence for some time. The inventor of the carriage simply combined two of the two-wheel carts which were in existence before the four-wheel carriage. In other words each inventor draws on the accumulated cultural storehouse of objects and ideas which are given to him by the persons and groups which came before him.

The same principle is operative in non-material invention, that is, innovations in the folkways and thoughtways, the mores and laws of a society. The writers of the American Constitution, for example, did not start from scratch. Practically all of the ideas embodied in the American Constitution are to be found in the writings of the political philosophers in Europe for many years prior to the American Revolution. These ideas were known to many among the intelligentsia of America. The American Constitution was new, to be sure, but new only at that time in the sense that it consisted of a selection and integration of these radical political ideas from Europe and of the governmental experiments and experiences of America itself. In short, the Constitutional Convention of 1787 picked and chose *from among the available ideas* about government, integrated their choices, and the result was the American Constitution.

Similarly, the New Deal, often erroneously accredited to President Roosevelt, presents such an illustration. Most of the ideas and philosophies underlying the Rooseveltian program of reform in America were common in the reform literature of America and Europe at least since the 1920's. Social security, greater rights for labor, a more systematic attack on problems of social welfare, farm relief, reciprocity in trade relations among nations, were all in the intellectual "air" long before Roosevelt became President. His "invention" consisted of putting into practice, modifying and choosing from among the prevailing ideas the precise kinds of social reforms which America would have. In the realm of new ideas as well as in gadgets, the "miracle" of invention only seems to be a miracle to the persons not familiar with the cultural context from which the invention came.

The atomic bomb looked like a miracle to the man on the street, but the principles of atomic energy were common classroom discussions in courses in physics in American universities for years. The atomic bomb inventors did create something new, but in the making of it were privileged to draw upon the accumulated knowledge and experimentation of generations of scientists and engineers without which knowledge no atomic bomb could possibly have been achieved in our time.

2. The inventor's *invention must be accepted by the society* before it can become a vital part of any people's existence. It is customary to refer to "men ahead of their times." This expression embodies an important principle pertaining to invention, namely, that the final determination of whether an invention will have acceptance lies not so much in the nature of the invention as in the conditions affecting its acceptance or rejection. Several years before streamlined automobiles came into general public acceptance, one company placed on the market a streamlined automobile closely resembling the contemporary motor car. The public did not "take" to it presumably because they were not ready for it. Ten years later even more radically designed streamlined cars are in vogue. Clothing styles and hair dress are other obvious cases in point. The "greatness," as well as the mere appropriateness of an invention, usually stems from the extent of its subsequent adoption and is frequently

determined not so much by the intrinsic qualities of the invention itself as from how the invention is accepted and used.

3. Since inventions must draw upon preceding knowledges and techniques and must depend upon popularity for their eventual appraisal, they *can often be anticipated before they actually occur.* Moreover, there have been numerous instances in which the same invention has been invented several different times by different persons working independently.

The purpose in pointing out these facts regarding invention is obviously not to detract from the prestige of the inventor who is usually a person of somewhat superior ability, but rather to correct the false belief that a few great men have largely chartered the course of human development. It would be more accurate to say that these innovators in material and non-material culture were as much the product of their cultures as they were the creators of it, even in the areas of culture to which their inventions pertained.

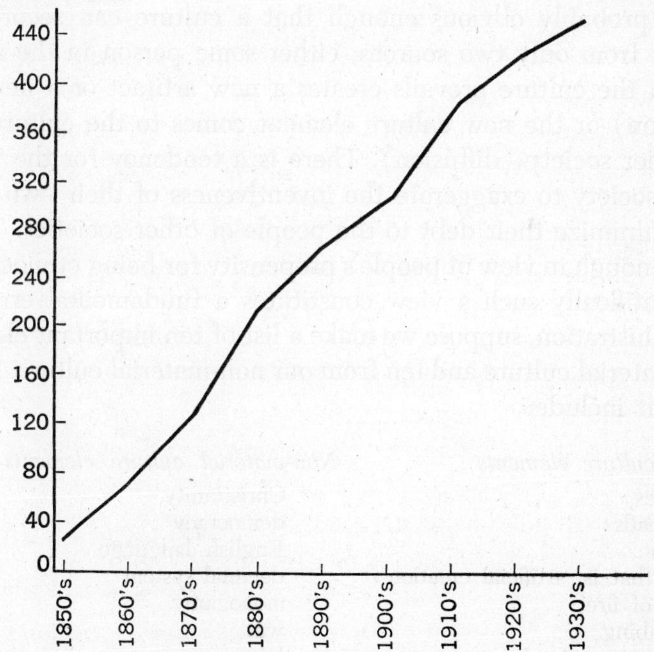


CULTURAL ACCUMULATION AS MEASURED BY INVENTIONS PATENTED IN THE UNITED STATES PATENT OFFICE, 1850-1940

Data from United States Department of Commerce, Bureau of the Census, *Statistical Abstract of the United States,* 1941, Government Printing Office, p. 1912.

### *The Ease of Invention*

One frequently hears that "so many things have been invented that it must be very difficult to make an invention now." The reverse is the truth. The more elements a culture has the more a prospective inventor has with which to work. Since, as we have seen, all invention is really a combination of preëxisting elements, then the greater number of elements in a culture (the *culture base*) the greater is the number of new possible combinations which can be created. A recent study of applications for patents in the United States Patent Office has shown that over a period of years the number of new patents per year has been expanding at an ever increasing rate. There is no reason to expect any change in the immediate future.

## INVENTION AND DIFFUSION

It is probably obvious enough that a culture can secure new elements from only two sources; either some person in the society in which the culture prevails creates a new artifact or a new idea (invention) or the new culture element comes to the culture from some other society (diffusion). There is a tendency for the people of each society to exaggerate the inventiveness of their own group and to minimize their debt to the people of other societies. This is natural enough in view of people's propensity for being ethnocentric; but scientifically such a view constitutes a fundamental error. By way of illustration, suppose we make a list of ten important elements of our material culture and ten from our non-material culture. Such a list might include:

| *Material culture elements* | *Non-material culture elements* |
|---|---|
| houses | Christianity |
| railroads | democracy |
| radio | English language |
| fire, that is, artificial creation of fire | decimal system |
| plumbing | monogamy |
| domestic animals | war |
| tilling the soil—agriculture | law |
| atomic bomb | education |
| printing | music |
| factory system | marriage |

Now let us go over the lists to determine how many of these material cultural objects and practices originated in the United States of America. The only one would be the atomic bomb and that was with the assistance of the scientists from other nations, although from nations whose cultures are similar to ours. In the non-material list, none is exclusively and originally "American." While another person might make a different list, certainly it cannot be doubted that each of the items on our list is fundamental. There has been so much diffusion among cultures that practically no culture is without a great deal of indebtedness to the other cultures of the world. If a Russian or a Japanese were to make a similar list he, too, would be forced to the same conclusion that we were—the overwhelming force of diffusion as a culture builder.

This importance of diffusion will become more clear, perhaps, if the student will review pp. 90-92, in which it was shown through dozens of illustrations that the great majority of both material and non-material culture contents prevalent in the United States came from other culture areas, some of them from simpler cultures upon which America often tends to look condescendingly.

*Basic Similarity of Invention and Diffusion As Culture Modifiers*

The separation of invention and diffusion and the discussion of them as if in opposition to one other, may easily lead to the erroneous notion that "invention and diffusion are opposites." Actually they have much in common as factors in culture building. Both have in common the crucial factor of necessity for *acceptance* of the innovation, regardless of the source from which it comes. The final test determining whether or not something new will actually be incorporated into a culture depends upon how well the innovation "fits" with the rest of the culture, particularly with the value system which prevails. If, for example, "efficiency" through the saving of labor and time is a prevailing value, then a labor-saving device, whether invented or diffused, will probably receive a favorable reception, but if the society does not regard labor saving as a desirable objective, the trait, whether invented or diffused, will probably be rejected. The ultimate test is the fitness of the new trait for the prevailing scheme of things. Thus, rural groups have often refused to accept "cityfied" ways—the new patterns did not "fit" rural values. They seemed, and were, "foreign."

*Some Subordinate Principles of Cultural Innovation*

1. Innovations in material culture seem not to be as strongly resisted as innovations in non-material culture. New ideas in government or morals take longer to accept and are more bitterly opposed than innovations in automobile design or kitchen equipment. Apparently people can appraise the value of a material object more readily than they can an idea, particularly if the previous competing idea has had a high value and is deeply ingrained in the prejudice structure.

2. Innovation seems to occur more readily during times of crisis, such as war or depression. Presumably, when attention is focused on a serious problem, like winning a war, less attention is given to the social controls which ordinarily tend to impede change. Although we cannot be certain which is cause and which is effect, it appears probable that crisis periods conduce to, or at least permit, many changes to occur; however, in the very nature of the case one cannot prove that the change would not have taken place if the crisis had not occurred.

The World War II period contains numerous examples of marked changes in the culture which were being effectively resisted for many years before the war, but which during the war became incorporated in our ways of behavior. The forthright discussion and treatment of the venereal disease problem as a health rather than a moral problem, has long been advocated by authorities in that field. It was not until the war period in many communities that the problem was attacked in the manner in which the authorities had long said it should be attacked. Also it took a serious manpower shortage to permit many American employers to allow women to work at jobs previously exclusively held by men. Illustrations could be produced *ad infinitum,* but seem not to be necessary.

*Is Culture Static or Dynamic?*

It is probably already clear that constant change in culture is normal and is in fact inherent in the nature of culture itself. It is unfortunate that some earlier writers on culture have somewhat overemphasized the static aspect of culture through the undue emphasis upon the importance of the social controls which society imposes on persons. This emphasis upon stability leads often to the erroneous notion that constancy in human affairs is normal and change abnormal. Human life does, however, present something of a paradox. Through the folkways and mores and other social controls, society indoctrinates people and enforces conformity to standards which are not of their making. Yet even while these standards are being imposed, they are already in the process of change. Thus at any given time, in any given society, there is to be observed something of a struggle or conflict between sets of forces, some making for permanence and stability, and others for change. *But they are all cultural products; one is quite as normal and inevitable as is the other.*

*The "Ultimate" Effects of Innovation*

One of the most difficult problems regarding culture change is the attempt to anticipate or foresee the rate and direction of change in a society. When new artifacts or ideas are introduced one cannot foresee what all of their ramifications will be. The complications and implications resulting from some one culture trait may forge an endless chain of cause and effect which can entirely revolutionize a society. The Industrial Revolution in England is a case in point. From the strictly economic point of view, the Industrial Revolution meant merely the shift from the manufacturing of goods in homes or in small groups to manufacturing in large groups. The factory system was made necessary in order to utilize power more efficiently, and later in order to secure lower production costs through the advantages of division of labor. What was originally simply a change in the means of production, however, ushered in a whole new era in all human living. It brought cities of a size never dreamed of before the Industrial Revolution. It brought a standard of living so different that the lowest workman may today enjoy comforts and luxuries unattainable by kings before the Industrial Revolution. The factory system also brought problems. The congestion of cities brought health, traffic, and recreational problems. Crime became more difficult to deal with effectively. Slums developed. Capital and labor, formerly closely allied, have become sharply estranged, and as this is being written the nation is almost paralyzed by strikes in key industries affecting millions of workmen and creating serious problems for countless millions more. A solution will ultimately be reached, of course, but that solution will become but another link in the endless chain of solution, problem, and solution. A change in one segment of culture seems almost never to confine its influence to the segment of culture for which it was intended. Discoveries in science bring changes in religion; changes in styles of dress, make and break whole industries. The web of interrelationship in culture is so intricate that nothing is isolated or isolatable from anything else.

A study just published attempts to anticipate the probable effects of the discovery of atomic energy upon the social life of this and other nations. Most important perhaps is the strong probability that atomic energy will necessitate the "breaking up of large cities." At first glance when one thinks of slums, traffic congestion and health hazards, the breaking up of large cities looks like a welcome solution to many old and persistent problems. But large cities also have great advantages which might be lost with decentralization. The author of the study likens the coming revolution brought about by the discovery of atomic energy to the Industrial Revolution.[1]

> Wind on sails and windmills had led to some social changes, but not to the extent that steam did. The range of the influence of the metal machine using steam has been so great that hardly a single branch of the social sciences dealing with modern times is not concerned to some extent with the industrial revolution. Steam made possible the cities with their urban civilization; though steam was not used on the farms directly, yet indirectly it shifted farming from the subsistence type to commercial farming and thus radically altered agriculture. With the factories and railroads run by steam, there came a new economic organization. The social classes were altered and new ones created. A new division and distribution of wealth followed. The ranking of nations in military power was shifted, and the nature of warfare changed. The nations with blast furnaces became the great powers. Before steam, the factories of production were in the household. Steam destroyed the household economy, eliminated the women's work, and gave them jobs in factories, stores, and offices. Both the family as an organization and the position of women in society were radically changed by steam. Steam brought to cities many new problems of health, crime, education, divorce, recreation, morals, religion, justice. The foregoing are only a few of the important social changes precipitated by the use of this first great source of mechanical power. Now there comes from the atom a new source of energy, enormous in quantity. Does atomic energy foreshadow social consequences comparable to those that followed the discovery of steam power and the invention of machines to use it?
>
> The answer to these questions depends, first, upon when the uses of atomic energy will become widespread industrially. This we do not know. We

[1] W. F. Ogburn, "Sociology and The Atom," *American Journal of Sociology*, LI (1946), pp. 273-274.

already have cheap sources of power in coal, oil, and electricity. If these are cheaper than atomic power, they will be used. In countries where there is no coal, it is imported. The energy from the atom, if used industrially, must, of course, be used in machines, almost surely such as are used now. These machines are made of metals which must be processed as now. Indeed, power is only a small part of the total costs of production. Hence it may be argued that atomic energy is, at best, merely the substitution of one type of power for another and that all we can expect is the continuation of present trends.

The same argument could have been used in the early 1700's regarding the steam engine. Steam would be only a substitute for human or animal energy and would be used only if it was cheaper. People were already living together in communities. Steam would only make them grow, and hence it would mean only a continuance of trends. Yet, within two centuries, steam had profoundly altered civilization and had left unchanged hardly a single social institution.

It is only necessary to state that the evolution of the release of atomic fission bears watching and that there are factors which make it possible that the social effects will be many, radical, and profound. This conception of probability is strengthened by the precedent of steam and by the enormous energy that becomes available.

Without allowing too much speculation, it is possible that very cheap power might work out to increase greatly the standard of living. Production in factories might be done with fewer and fewer human laborers. The hours of labor might become very much shorter. If atomic energy could be used for transportation purposes, community life and the structure of nations might be tremendously changed. If used in airplanes by jet propulsion, it would make practicable travel at supersonic speeds; and if these sources of energy for aircraft were cheap, the size and interconnections of the great variety of social organization and communities would lead to very many interesting possibilities in diffusion and in collective effort. The social changes due to the peacetime uses of atomic energy might become vastly greater than the social changes that may follow the bomb alone.

However, these possible changes are not all likely to come as suddenly as did the bomb in Hiroshima; for, the parts of civilization being so highly integrated, when one part changes its effects are slowed up because of the interconnections of the other parts. The accumulated cultural lag is great, and the resulting inertia slows change and, of course, produces maladjustments and social problems.

Whether these analyses and views are exactly right or wrong, it is clear that the mode of life to come may be profoundly influenced as a result of atomic researches which were motivated chiefly if not solely by the desire to build a more effective weapon of war more quickly than our enemies could. This is just another of the several far-reaching social revolutions which could not be foreseen because they stemmed from a chain of causes and effects, the ultimate end of which could not be anticipated even by the most brilliant minds of the time.

## SUMMARY

In this chapter we have taken a broad sweep of human development from the dawn of civilization about which we know little to the dawn of the atomic age about which we know less. The reasons for our ignorance are, however, not the same in the two cases. We do not know all we would like to know about cultural origins because of the obscurity of antiquity. We are bewildered about the atomic age because we know just enough about the forces of change to be both awe-stricken and somewhat panic-stricken when we attempt to fathom the implications.

No attempt has been made to chronicle the events of human history. That is for the historian to do. Instead attention has been focused in this chapter upon a number of principles involved in the process of social change. These knowledges have been derived inductively from many researches in many different cultures. These principles seem to be:

1. Man's cultural development covers vast periods of time.
2. Throughout most of that time social change has mostly been slow, but the rate of change has been rapidly accelerated in recent years.
3. Many of the basic characteristics of modern society like democracy, science, and high standards of living are so new to man's experience that he has difficulty often in knowing what to do with them.
4. Change in culture is inevitable; no culture fails to show evidence of change.
5. The factors making for stability and the factors making for change are equally aspects of culture.
6. The rates at which cultures change are very variable. Some societies change very rapidly; others very slowly. Some societies change rapidly for a time, then slowly; others, vice versa.
7. Culture changes by the addition of traits, the loss of traits, or the changed emphasis on existing traits.
8. New cultural elements can arise within the culture (invention) or come from some other culture (diffusion).
9. Invention inevitably involves the use of existing cultural elements in some new combinations. Therefore, the larger the cul-

tural base, other things being equal, the greater the wealth of elements from which the new inventions can be fashioned. This applies both to culture objects and to ideas.

10. With the possible exception of a few primitive societies, all societies have secured more of their content from diffusion than from their own invention.

11. Most of the inventions represent minor modifications or changes in the details of the culture; the basic patterns of the society are less frequently or radically modified.

12. The eventual effects of inventions are so far-reaching that it is almost impossible to envisage in advance what aspects of a total culture will be changed by some given innovation.

13. The determining factor in the integration of a new artifact or thoughtway into a culture is how the new item fits into the prevailing scheme. No trait is intrinsically of high or low value; it always comes to be evaluated in terms of the standards prevailing in the culture, the standards themselves, of course, having been innovations originally.

These, then, are some of the fundamental knowledges about man's cultural development and the processes involved in it. Later chapters (especially in Part IV) will take up in some detail the nature of the society which modern culture change is producing and will analyze some of the problems resulting therefrom.

## SUGGESTED READINGS

BARNES, H. E., *Society in Transition* (New York, Prentice-Hall, Inc., 1939), Chapters I, II, and III. **B**

A well-written historical treatment of the emergence of Western culture beginning with the Industrial Revolution. Emphasizes the significance of capitalism, urbanization, secularization, and science. Written as a textbook.

CRESSEY, P. F., "Chinese Traits in European Civilization: A Study in Diffusion," *American Sociological Review*, X, pp. 595-605. **B**

An historical study of the diffusion of traits from Chinese to European culture. Material traits such as gunpowder came first as isolated units of cultural transmission. These have always been materially altered in function however. "The basic ethos of the West has not been modified by the adoption of these Chinese innovations."

GILFILLAN, S. C., *Sociology of Invention* (Chicago, Follett Publishing Co., 1935). **A B**

A significant study of the social context of invention. Reveals how "society" is both cause and effect of invention.

Lowie, R. H., *Are We Civilized?* (New York, Harcourt, Brace and Co., 1929). **B**

An excellent semi-popular discussion of the existing knowledge regarding the origin and development of such varied cultural aspects as domesticated plants and animals and institutions such as the family and government.

Lowie, R. H., "The Transition of Civilizations in Primitive Society," *American Journal of Sociology*, XLVII, pp. 527-43. **A B**

Primitive societies are not necessarily any more static than modern ones are. We have made too many studies of change in primitive society in terms of change *toward our kind* of society, and thus have gotten an exaggerated idea of their so-called "resistance" to change.

Ogburn, W. F., "The Great Man *vs.* Social Forces," *Social Forces*, V, pp. 225-31. **B**

An attempt to appraise the relative importance of impersonal social change and the purposive influence of the "great man."

Ogburn, W. F., *Social Change* (New York, B. W. Huebsch, Inc., 1922). **A**

A classic study of the process of social change. Written by the author of the famous "culture lag" theory which, although it is somewhat in disrepute in several of its applications, still contains some measure of basic truth about the differential diffusion of material and non-material culture patterns. Should be read in connection with Mueller, J., "Present Status of the Culture Lag Theory," *American Sociological Review*, III, pp. 320-332, and especially J. W. Woodard, "Critical Notes on the Culture Lag Concept," *Social Forces*, XII, pp. 388-398.

## STUDY QUESTIONS

1. Why are we unable to state definitely how, when, and where man first began to create culture?
2. Why do we have definite information about some of man's earliest material culture, but only "inferential information" about his non-material culture?
3. Why must we be cautious in the use of "inferential" conclusions from data about culture before the use of writing? Does the use of writing remove the possibility for error? Why?
4. Why is culture not an accumulation of all the culture traits that ever existed?
5. What determines whether culture traits are accepted, rejected, or modified?
6. On what do both material and non-material inventions depend?
7. How do inventions illustrate the proverb that "there is nothing new under the sun?" How do they disprove the adage?
8. Why is it often necessary for an invention to be introduced more than once?
9. What has made possible the increasing rate of inventions?
10. Why is it incorrect to say that a society creates its culture traits?
11. How are invention and diffusion similar? Related?
12. Why do we accept innovations in material culture more readily than we do in non-material culture?

13. How is necessity often the "mother of acceptance" instead of the "mother of invention?" Illustrate.
14. How may the introduction of a new culture trait result in unforeseen changes in a society? Illustrate.
15. How is invention the mother of necessity? Illustrate.

# *Part III*

# BACKGROUND UNDERSTANDINGS FROM SOCIAL PSYCHOLOGY

# *Chapter IX*

## SOCIALIZATION AND MATURATION

Not so many years ago you came into the world a polymorphous-perverse little ape with a billion years of biological evolution precipitated, so to speak, in your dimpled organism. You came naked, without shame, without language, food habits, or manual dexterity; ideas, or religious faith; without respect for law and order and with no discernible admiration for Mr. Herbert Hoover. You came with no higher desires than to have your capacious belly filled with milk and your somatic and visceral itches scratched by loving hands.[1]

Now you are sophisticated and supercilious [students], weary young intellectuals in a decadent era, murmuring over this, that, and the other in your daily routine, "What a beastly bore!" You are clothed in the choicest fabrics and adorned with the totemic symbols of your respective fraternities. You speak and write the English language—fairly well; and you know better than to eat pie with a knife, at least in public. Some of you can probably play eighteen holes of golf in less than a hundred strokes; some of you can lie beautifully to that effect. Some of you think you know what da Vinci tried to convey by the smile of Mona Lisa. Your desires have multiplied; so have your doubts and fears. You still have somatic and visceral itches, but your scratching technique has, I trust, become much more complicated and effective. Think of yourself as a bawling and puking brat with your nose and bladder in perennial flux, and then look at yourself now. *Mirabile visu!* Isn't Nature wonderful? How did you get this way? That's the first question we shall try to answer.

It is common knowledge that in the course of his development to adulthood a human being is influenced by his inherited physical makeup, usually called his "heredity," and his learnings from experience, often loosely called his "environment." Like other prescientific explanations of phenomena, "heredity plus environment equals person" is scientifically not very valuable. The conception

[1] Excerpts from "The Noble Animal," in R. G. Smith, *Fugitive Papers* (New York, Columbia University Press, 1930).

is vague and implies several fundamental untruths as we shall shortly demonstrate.

Perhaps every one has encountered the recurrent argument, "heredity *versus* environment." Some persons are inclined to credit heredity with "greater influence" (whatever that means) and others give greater credit to environment. To argue which of the two is the more important to the development of the human being would seem to be about as futile as an argument whether the male's sperm or the female's ovum is the "more important" in effecting a conception Either without the other is essentially useless. And yet the popular argument goes on, as endless as it is senseless. Fortunately the scientist has discovered some techniques of analysis which make it possible for him, through the use of experimentation and other research devices, to study the process of human development with greater precision and more valid eventual understandings.

### THE THREE FACTORS AFFECTING HUMAN DEVELOPMENT

The human being is molded by three separable sets of influences which we may designate at the outset as:

1. his inborn characteristics ("Original Nature");
2. the culture, or cultures, in which he lives; and
3. the unique personal experiences he has.

Our first task is to analyze somewhat more carefully the nature and content of these three sets of forces.

#### *Original Nature*

The term *original nature* is essentially synonymous with heredity. It consists of all those traits and characteristics which a person possesses because he is a specimen of the species *Homo sapiens.* On the surface it would seem easy enough to determine what one owes, so to speak, to the fact of biological transmission, yet this scientific problem has been one of the most baffling. Our first step shall consist of separating "heredity" into its parts.

Much needless confusion concerning man's original nature has resulted from the failure to distinguish three quite distinct parts of one's inherited nature. All three are, of course, transmitted to the person through the germ plasm.

1. In a very general sense practically all of the individuals of the species are *approximately* the same. Humans usually have two eyes, the heart is on the left side, they have the necessary mechanism to enable them to walk erect, they can learn, they require sleep, and so forth.

2. But no two human beings are exactly alike, and sometimes the *extent of individual differences is very great*. Both the genius and the moron are human beings (and might be brothers). Sometimes these marked differences, especially the extremes, result from accidental biological products called "sports," but other inherited individual differences are the result of more normal heredity and are due to somewhat modified general characteristics which are handed down from individual to individual in the *specific ancestral* line. It is well established, for example, that similar intelligence tends usually to run in families. This applies to both high intelligence and low intelligence.

3. Aside from the occasional sport (and the mutation) every human being also has a number of *unpredictable hereditary uniquenesses,* which are still only partially understood by geneticists (specialists in the study of heredity). These are usually termed *continuous variation.*

Thus, we see that human inheritance presents something of a paradox. Because he is a human being, Joe inherits a collection of traits roughly characteristic of all human beings, but Joe also inherits an almost innumerable array of uniquenesses, some due to the specific parentage he has had and others, as far as we now can determine, to sheer "chance," a term we use to cover occurrences the causal factors of which we do not understand or cannot measure.

### *Culture*

The culture in which a person is reared might seem on first thought to constitute a set of influences which could easily be studied. Such is, however, not the case. As we have already seen, the culture of a society is not uniform for everyone. Persons of different ages, sexes, social classes, and regions, may be exposed to radically different patterns of cultural behavior. In fact it is altogether normal for such cultural specialization to occur. It will, therefore, be necessary in subsequent parts of this and later chapters to break down the totality of culture into more detailed units in order to assay more precisely its many relations to the individual's behavior.

*Unique Experience*

Finally, each individual in the course of living has some experiences which are more or less unique to him. Sometimes a person's unique experiences are such that he develops ideas and overt behavior patterns diametrically opposite to those manifested by the majority of persons in his society. The "woman hater," the hermit, the homosexual, the religious fanatic are only a few of many cases in point. It should be noted, however, that all of the above illustrations could also be "normal" behaviors for persons whose cultures contained such norms. But by no means can all persons in such categories be accounted for by their special group-culture connections. Many of our individual likes and dislikes, hopes and fears, are the result of the unusual specific experiences each individual has had.

In the past many writers on sociology and anthropology have ignored or have insufficiently emphasized the unique experience factor in the development of the person. This concept is indispensable if one is to have a more adequate understanding of the forces which shape the human being. At the same time, however, one must be careful not to overemphasize the unique experience factor. Humans are rarely as unique as they think they are. Most of the "original ideas" to which persons lay claim are ideas which thousands of other people have had previously in almost precisely the same way. What is often called "my own idea" usually turns out to be a carbon copy of half a million others! Yet there is a bona fide element of unique experience which will be treated at length in this and later chapters.

## THE INTERACTION OF ORIGINAL NATURE, CULTURE, AND UNIQUE EXPERIENCE

*The Three Factors Interact*

One must be careful not to think of any of these three factors as being operative independently of the other two. A person's behavior is not the result of original nature *plus* culture *plus* unique experience. Instead it results from the *interplay* of them. Each imposes limitations on the others, and each also facilitates the others. A person, for example, might live in an "excellent environment," as the prevailing values of the culture rate it, and yet not have sufficient intelligence to be able to take advantage of the opportunities which the environment has presented to him. Suppose, again, that there is an individual with an exceedingly high intelligence born into a group which does not have access to schools and in which there is hostility toward formal education. Such a child might conceivably not even learn to read. When he is an adult he would be illiterate, but he would not be illiterate because of any deficiency in his inherited intelligence; he would be illiterate because his inherited capacities for great learning could not be realized in the environment in which he was reared. Thus, we see that either factor may limit or even prevent the realization of the possibilities of either or both of the other two.

It is possible to state the above proposition in the form of three direct principles.

1. The original nature of a person may prevent his utilizing his culture. A society may contain universities, but if a person has insufficient intelligence to learn beyond the elementary school level, the opportunities presented by the university have no practical existence to this person. Similarly, a color-blind person cannot participate in the enjoyment of fine color shadings even though the culture contains them.

2. The culture in which a person is participating may limit or prevent the realization of the potentialities of a person's original nature. For many centuries women were not permitted to participate in the same kinds of higher education that men were. Throughout these years women of superior intelligence were being born and died without any of them being permitted to utilize their intelligence on the higher intellectual planes. The same is found today with respect to some Negroes. In some parts of the United States Negroes are given poorer educational opportunities than whites receive in the same communities. Suppose that there are two children, one white and one Negro, who have identical native intelligence and thus the identical potential capacity for learning. It is obvious that the white child, having greater opportunity to participate in an environment in which his intelligence could be trained, will be able to attain greater educational achievements, not

because he is by heredity any brighter but only because he has greater opportunities to utilize the hereditary qualities he natively possesses.

Perhaps the extreme illustration of this principle is found in the *feral.* Ferals are human beings who become isolated from all human contacts at a very early age and are reared by animals. Wolves, bears, and apes have been known to "adopt" very young human infants and rear them as they would their own young. Such persons at the age of ten years, although they were normal human beings capable potentially of the same achievements as most readers of this book were at the age of ten, would actually be unable to read, write or speak, frequently have been observed to be unable to walk except on all fours, and would refuse to eat most "civilized" foods. Such ferals, of course, would wear no clothes, and if forced into clothes would tear them off as any wild animal would. Here, then, we have practically a laboratory experiment, without deliberately planning it that way, which gives us a graphic account of what human beings would be like "naturally" that is, if not influenced by any human culture.

3. Unique experience may limit or prevent even the mutual potentialities of both the culture and the original nature.

Billy has unusual high intelligence and comes from a family of distinguished men and women. His family is wealthy and therefore able to provide him with the finest educational opportunities that money can buy, plus all the comforts and luxuries which Billy might want. But Billy has developed a hatred of schools, books and teachers. He is now nineteen. He has spent six years in high school but was still unable to graduate because he refused to do any work, would skip school whenever he could. And for the last two years has refused even to take an examination.

Here we have an instance of a boy "favored" with an unusual mind and physical health. He also has access to an advanced intellectual level of culture. Both his original nature and his environment contained unusually good opportunities for Billy's personal development. But the potentialities have not been realized, and probably never will, because of certain unique experiences which Billy has had. It is not necessary to go into all of the details here, but the facts in Billy's case history show a series of very unfortunate experiences at the hands of a tactless governess who tried in many ingenious ways to force Billy to study at a time when Billy was too young to study the kinds of things she tried to teach him. As a result Billy developed an intense hatred of books, learning, and, of course, of the governess. Later, when he went to school he carried all of his animosities toward learning with him and readily transferred his antagonism for the governess to an antagonism toward the teacher. No teacher has been able successfully to break down that antagonism. Billy's case is obviously an exceptional one. Most children of superior ability who have opportunities for a superior education do not turn out like Billy. The point is that Billy had also had an unusual set of traumatic experiences with the governess which, fortunately, were unique to him and not typical.

Perhaps enough has already been written to explain what we mean by saying that original nature and culture alone cannot create behavior; they only contain *capacities or potentialities* for the development of behavior, and may or may not actually be translated into acts and thoughts, depending upon the exact kind of personal experiences which the person has had.

### POTENTIAL AND REALIZED HEREDITY AND CULTURE

It may be useful for the student to distinguish two distinct meanings of heredity and culture which we may term *potential* and *realized.* Only those items in the environment which can be and are actually experienced by a person can affect him. Frequently what appears on the surface to be a "good" environment may, for the specific person in it, not be good at all. Billy's environment seemed to be a good one, that is, it had the potentialities from which a rich childhood experience could come. But *for Billy* it was decidedly not good, at least so far as his education was concerned. Billy's governess was a potentially valuable person who might have given Billy a splendid educational start. In fact she had tutored several other children very successfully. But Billy did not actually experience what the governess potentially presented to him. He experienced instead almost the antithesis of what one might expect, namely, a hatred for books, learning, and teachers. Another illustration. It is often said that "City dwellers are privileged to live a broad experience since they have daily access to libraries, art galleries, museums, and symphonies." But what proportion of the people of Chicago or New York City avail themselves regularly, if ever, of libraries, art galleries, museums and symphonic music? Potentially the environment contains these items, but they are not really experienced in the behavior of most people.

The same principle is illustrated on the college or university campus. Potentially each student can secure a rich intellectual and aesthetic development if he devotes all of his time and energy to these opportunities, but as everyone acquainted with the realities of college life in America knows, most students do not actually experience the potentialities of their college. It might be added that their native intellectual acumen is, almost certainly, not the reason for this lack of participation. Rather it is in part at least, due to the system of values which many students have acquired and which make other things, such as "coke" parties, football rallies, and bull sessions more important than a visit to the art gallery or an evening at a symphony concert. It goes perhaps without saying that if the student's parents and the college faculty could control the situation they would prefer, as a rule, that a different system of values obtain, but of course, neither are in a position to control the out-of-school and away-from-home experiences of youth from which the values arise.

*Recapitulation*

Thus far in this chapter we have made some preliminary inquiries into the factors which shape the human being, but it may be useful to pause and take account of what has already been presented. The human being develops through the *interplay* of three sets of influences which impinge upon him—his inherited organism and all of its functions, the culture which he contacts, and the unique personal experiences he undergoes. It cannot be stressed too emphatically that both the culture and the original nature are significant for human behavior as *reservoirs of potentials* and *not as behavior* per se. If a man inherits a strong physique, good muscular coördination and a superior mind he has the potentials for any or several kinds of athletic activity. But that does not mean that he will necessarily become any kind of athlete. He still must learn any game he plays. If he is not given a chance to learn any game or if he is not interested in learning, he may never participate in any athletic contest. He may prefer one game to another, stress the one he likes and never go on to another in which he might excel far more conspicuously than he does in the one he plays. *The factor of unique experience translates the potentials into behavior.* When the above-mentioned athlete first tried to play a game he began the process of transforming his potentialities into the actual behavior skills of the game. It could happen that he did not like the game as a result of his early experience with it, and he could easily form a dislike for it or for his coach or his fellow-players or for all of them. Thus, his unique experience forms not only his overt skills but his attitudes as well. Potentially he is capable of likes and dislikes, and potentially any game could result in likes or dislikes.

## OF WHAT DOES ORIGINAL NATURE CONSIST?

At the outset it should be stressed that the term *original nature* or *heredity* is an abstraction. No one can see it or otherwise experience it through his senses. One can see certain *evidences* in humans' behavior, but that which is called "heredity" can be experienced only as an *idea.* It cannot be perceived; it can only be conceived. The idea original nature is a sort of summary of a number of related facts and interpretations of facts which the scientist has discovered in the course of his experiments and observations. Thus, we observe that at birth the infant cries, he has eyes, even though he sees very little, he can move his arms and legs, but with apparently no purpose or with little dexterity. Later he gets larger and his dexterity improves. Still later his sexual organs change and he becomes capable of reproduction. Finally, if he lives that long, he usually becomes gray, gets wrinkled, has less physical vigor. Eventually he dies. We say these acts and characteristics are "due to heredity." But that neither tells us what heredity *is* nor gives us any assurance that our observations are correct. All that one can say with any measure of scientific objectivity, is that heredity is a general term used to cover those items of human behavior and makeup which we *think* one gets from the fact that he is a specimen of his species and a descendant of his particular ancestral line. All learned behavior and all acquired changes in him are something other than hereditary. When we say that heredity is what we "think" it is, we do not mean to imply that we are guessing; we mean simply that one cannot observe heredity directly and is forced to utilize inferences from observations of overt behavior. Errors are therefore common.

### *How Can the Influence of Heredity or Original Nature Be Objectively Determined?*

We say that sexual maturity is due to heredity. But why? At about the same age at which he is sexually mature a boy often is able to drive an auto. Why do we say that he acquires the former from heredity but learns the latter from his culture? Probably the reasoning is clear enough in this case, because it is obvious that he has had to learn to drive the auto. But how about the ability to walk? Is walking a result of heredity or of learning? How can that question be scientifically answered? One way, certainly, would be to isolate some children from all opportunities to learn walking or to imitate walking and then observe whether or not they walked voluntarily. The difficulty, of course, is that such an experiment could not be carried out because of our moral scruples. Hence we are forced to infer the answer to our original question from observations of normal children and of those occasional cases of ferals or isolated children. Consequently there is "room for argument" concerning a number of questions when the essential issue is whether some unit of behavior, like walking, is hereditary or learned.

The overall trend of research on human behavior in the last quarter-century has been a consistent reduction of the items of behavior regarded as attributable to heredity and an increasing number explainable on the basis of learning. This generalization applies to experiments on animal behavior as well as to experiments on humans. More unsophisticated early scholars attributed too much to inheritance because they did not know enough about psychology to be able to understand some of the more subtle aspects of the learning process, such as learning by imitation but more especially by suggestion. People learn a great deal through unconscious learning processes of which they are not aware and which other observers, except those trained in psychological science, are usually equally unaware. This is not to be taken as a sweeping denial that any human behavior can be native to the organism, but simply as a statement summarizing the general trend of research on human behavior in the last quarter-century.

There are certain types of behavior and potentialities for behavior which at the present stage of our knowledge seem to be the result primarily of one's original nature. Briefly these include:

1. *The body structure* consisting of muscles, bones, and internal organs, and the organic processes such as circulation, respiration, and digestion.

2. *Intelligence,* that is, the capacity to learn new reactions and modify old ones as a result of experience.

3. *Reflexes.* Reflexes are simple units of behavior which show up under stimulation such as, the blink reflex, swallowing reflex, "knee-jerk" reflex, reaction reflex, (withdrawal from pain), and so forth. Whenever the appropriate sense mechanisms are stimulated the organism reacts. It should always be borne in mind, however, that *reflexes can be conditioned.* An organism can be taught to behave in some way other than the way originally determined by the reflexes.

4. *Endocrine glandular influences on behavior.* These seem to have considerable importance. The ductless or endocrine glands, such as the thyroid, the pituitary and the adrenal, secrete "hormones" into the blood stream and thus seem to affect behavior rather markedly. Much more clinical research needs to be done before we can be at all certain concerning the effect of the endocrines, and especially before we can control the endocrines artificially with any high degree of certainty as to results. Enough research has already been done, however, to establish the fact of considerable individual variation in endocrine functioning from person to person. Some persons, for example, are more excitable than others under comparable conditions. This fact of differential sensitivity can easily be a factor influencing how much and what kind of experience a person can actually realize in a given environment. There is one caution which the beginner must observe in thinking about endocrine glandular influences on behavior. There is a tendency to attribute too much, often, to this factor. Excessive secretion of some hormones, for example, makes for irritability in some persons, but this fact in itself does not really explain why a particular person is irritable. The person still had to learn the kind of behavior which we call 'irritable" and the hormones do not explain why he is irritable about item *A* and not about item *B.* Furthermore, there are numerous factors making for irritability in persons besides their endocrine secretion.

5. *Drives.* The term *drive* has come into usage as a convenient word to designate the organically stimulated motivations which ap-

parently prompt people to activity. When there is no longer food in the stomach, for example, a person begins to "feel hungry" and will be stimulated to some kind of activity as a means of securing food. This motivation to act is called the *drive*.

*Drives, however, should not be confused with overt behavior.* This is a common and serious error. The hunger drive may explain why one is hungry and why he seeks food, but is not the explanation for his desire to get a chocolate malted milk or a broiled steak. The specific desires and their related behavior had to be learned by the person. All that the inherited drive provides is the internal stimulation to do *something* about the food need, not any particular thing. One learns to go to the ice box or to turn on the oven, or to walk over to the restaurant, but the food drive could be satisfied in an infinite number of other ways.

Two decades ago it was common to find long lists of drives in psychology and sociology textbooks, but present scholarship is unable to justify more than three or four. These we may roughly designate as:

*a.* the drive to secure food (and drink);
*b.* the drive for sex expression;
*c.* the activity drive, a somewhat vague motivation, most conspicuously evidenced in children, to exercise body muscles;
*d.* the drive to maintain a constant body temperature.

Other motivations formerly thought to be drives such as "curiosity," "maternity," "self preservation," "hoarding," and many others are not now so regarded, because research has shown that (1) *they are not universal to mankind* and (2) that *the cultures in which they are found are the cultures in which these values are taught.*

These, then, are the basic inherited components of the human organism which are considered to be significant either directly as behavior or as the potentialities for behavior.

## ORIGINAL NATURE IS PLURIPOTENTIAL (OR MULTIPOTENTIAL)

Perhaps the chief error which is often made when persons seek to discover relationships between original nature and actual behavior, is the assumption that a given original nature can result in only one kind or type of behavior. In other words, if a man is a capable lawyer he is assumed to have inherited an intelligence for law. The fact of the matter is, on the other hand, that the man has a high intelligence which might just as well have been used in medicine, business, politics, agriculture, or crime as in the legal profession. This particular man's culture and unique experience resulted in his becoming a capable lawyer. A different culture and unique experience could just as well have resulted in an equally capable personality along some other line which required comparable intelligence.

It will be recalled from early chapters dealing with culture variability that very wide differences in human behavior norms can be seen among different peoples of the world. Yet all of these peoples have essentially the same original nature, with the occasional exception of such irrelevant things as skin color, size, and head shape. Thus, apparently man's original nature is sufficiently versatile as to permit him to acquire such divergent behavior norms as monogamy and polygamy, Christianity and Shintoism, democracy and dictatorship, capitalism and communism. While each of the above systems is not exactly the opposite of the other, differences are certainly tremendous.

Within a given culture one can also find rather marked behavior differences between persons of similar if not identical heredity. Instances are known in which identical twins, the closest to identical heredity that is possible, show marked differences and contradictions in their behavior. The evidence from the behavior of ferals is also pertinent to this principle of multiple potentiality in human original nature.

The wide range of possible conditioning of drives also illustrates the multiplicity of divergent behavior of which human original nature is capable. Everyone has the sex drive, but some people remain celibate while others marry, some are monogamous and others polygamous, some are preoccupied with sex and to others sex is of minor interest. One can discover no actual behavior which the existence of the sex drive requires. It can apparently be "satisfied" by such divergent behaviors as prostitution and the writing of romantic poetry!

It is often an interesting speculation what one would have become if he had not become what he did. Obviously there is no definitive empiric proof that he could have become anything else, but the preponderant *inference* from what we have learned is that he certainly could have become a different person if his culture or his unique experience had been different. An excellent exercise which may be helpful in appreciating the multipotentiality of one's original nature is to assume that at birth one changed place with a newborn Japanese or Zulu or Mexican peon infant. In what ways, under such circumstances, would one be different: language, morals, values, interests, dress and personal appearance, skills, education, religion? Certainly if one had not contacted American culture, he could not have the characteristic traits of behavior of American society.

## SOCIALIZATION AND MATURATION

*Socialization* is a generic term to cover all of the processes and results of learning from other people, either directly in face-to-face interaction or indirectly through reading. It is through socialization that one learns the folkways and mores, the real and the ideal culture patterns of his society, shaped, of course, by the vicissitudes of one's unique experience. *Maturation* refers to those changes in the characteristics and behavior of the person due to biological changes resulting from increasing age, irrespective of one's experience. Children attain puberty and adults usually get gray hair in all cultures. Obviously all of the changes which take place in a human being from birth to death take place because of maturation and/or because of socialization. A persistent and not yet completely solved problem arises, as we have already seen, when one attempts to discover whether socialization or maturation is the sole or more important factor in some *specific* change. When a child goes through the stage known as puberty, for example, there are certain physical changes which occur and which are undeniably due to maturation. This would occur in any culture. But puberty and adolescence are also characterized by numerous psychological changes and characteristics. Are these psychological changes due to the fact of maturation or to the accompanying changes in the culture of the child which may result from the adult's differing conceptions and treatment of the child after he has attained puberty? The answer to this problem is not completely known, but there is growing emphasis among authorities upon the significance of the changed rôle of the person as a major causative factor in the psychological disturbances attending adolescence. The point is that many of the differences in the behaviors of the persons in different age-groups are not so much the result of the difference of their ages per se as of the fact that the social codes require or expect or suggest different behaviors for persons in the different age-groups.

*Socialization Defines Organic Factors*

It has already been shown in preceding chapters that society requires certain behaviors and exerts strong pressures toward certain others. The culture of every people, for example, contains certain requirements and prohibitions concerning the human body and its functioning. All modern cultures define certain parts of the human body as taboo for public exhibition. Quite consistently the genital organs are cases in point. So strong is this taboo that violations of it are regarded with disgust and such acts are said to be obscene. Precisely how much exposure is to be permitted and how close to the genitals the exposure may properly come, is simply a matter of style, the standards for which vary greatly from time to time even within the same society. Urination and defecation are also defined, and more or less elaborate rules for their "correct" execution exist.

Almost nothing involved in the organic makeup of the human being has escaped cultural definition and, of course, for practically every approved practice in some culture, a radically different practice in another culture can be found. Thus, the prevailing attitudes derived from the culture determine for a person how and what he ought to think about every part of his anatomy and every function of his organs. This fact of cultural definition is so thoroughly ingrained in a person's experience that most persons believe, for example, that "it is natural for all humans to be modest" about exposure of certain organs and "ashamed of" certain acts. So long as the principle is stated thus generally it is not entirely incorrect. The idea frequently overlooked, however, is that cultural variability is so great and that cultural definitions are so varied, that modesty norms from one group become meaningless in another. In one culture a woman would be ashamed if her face were seen in public but need have no concern about the exposure of her buttocks. Modesty taboos in some cultures require women to conceal their breasts while in others they may be exposed with perfect propriety.

If one wishes to understand human behavior he must recognize that feelings like shame, troubled consciences, or disgust constitute no evidence whatsoever that any given organic act is any more natural or unnatural than another. Man's capacity for variously defining vice and virtue, propriety and impropriety, fastidiousness and boorishness is almost endless. Likewise his propensity for building elaborate cultural mechanism to enforce conformity to some particular standards seems almost boundless. The potentiality of the human organism for antithetical behaviors is almost beyond comprehension. But it must also be clearly understood that in no society is a person really permitted to make up his own mind concerning matters of propriety and impropriety, right and wrong. Instead he comes into a world which is already equipped with all of the "right" answers to the question of how he shall behave, right down to the most intimate and personal act. In fact no one really knows or can know how he would really feel if his body and body processes were defined through another set of mores.

## SUMMARY

This chapter began with a preliminary discussion of the factors of original nature, culture, and unique experience as forces molding the human being. It was stressed that both original nature and culture contained potentialities for behavior but not behavior per se. They are always in interaction with each other and operate in such a way that (1) the original nature of a person may prevent the utilization of the available culture, (2) the culture of a person may be such as to prevent the realization of the potentialities of his original nature and (3) a person's unique experience may be such as even to limit or prevent the potentialities present in both the original nature and the culture. Whatever behavior is made possible by a person's original nature and by his culture, it still has to be learned by him through his unique experience. The outcome of the unique experience may create traits and personalities markedly different from what one might expect to find if he knew only the culture in which the person was socialized.

It was then pointed out that the original nature of a person consists of his body structure, intelligence, reflexes, endocrine glandular influences, and drives. It has been stressed that these parts of man's original nature are pluripotential or multipotential. Evidence for this principle comes from many sources, chiefly from the facts of cultural variability, ferals, and identical twins reared separately. Out of all of the many potentialities for behavior which a given person possesses, socialization eventually molds a single human being with one aggregate of potentialities tangibly realized, and the other potentialities never become expressed in any behavior at all.

One persistent problem is that of drawing the line between socialization and maturation. Sometimes it is of practical importance to determine whether a given behavior is due to socialization or due to maturation. Although existing techniques for the delineation of maturation and socialization are by no means perfected, they are gradually becoming better.

It must be borne in mind, particularly by the beginning student of behavior science, that the culture in which a person is reared defines virtually every physiological process and physical organ of the body with some of the most deeply ingrained emotional imprints of which man is capable. After these prejudice patterns are entrenched some persons try to think introspectively about their behavior and notice that it is easier to behave in one way than in another, and that certain alternative ways of behaving, though physically quite possible, are so revolting and disgusting as to be really unthinkable. The tendency is then to jump to the conclusion that the accustomed way of acting or thinking is a necessary part of the original nature of man. Acts or thoughts contrary to the approved ways are presumed to be contrary to original nature. The error lies in omitting consideration of the large amount, and of the intensity of, socialization which accompanies the maturation of the physical organism. It is this socialization which defines which one or ones of all of the physically possible behaviors are to be regarded as approved and habituated and which ones are to be disapproved and discarded. After years of repeated practice of some one mode of behavior, it is easy to overlook the fact that any one of several other alternative practices could in the first place have just as well been established in one's habit structure.

In succeeding chapters the unique experience factor will be somewhat more completely analyzed and several of the more specialized aspects of socialization will be treated.

## SUGGESTED READINGS

BERNARD, L. L., *Instinct; A Study in Social Psychology* (New York, Henry Holt and Co., 1924). **A B**

A classic examination of the instinct hypothesis in the light of the evidence. The student may be interested in considering the implications of the fact that as early as 1924 the instinct idea was in disrepute in the scientific world and yet the idea has wide popular currency today.

COOLEY, C. H., *Human Nature and the Social Order* (New York, Charles Scribner's Sons, 1922). **A**

This is a classic on human behavior in relation to group participation. While some of its ideas are in disrepute today, the major contributions are unassailable. Especially important seem to be Cooley's treatment of "sympathy," "self," and the nature of society.

COOLEY, C. H., ANGELL, R. C., and CARR, L. J., *Introductory Sociology* (New York, Charles Scribner's Sons, 1933), Chapter III, "The Psycho-Social Basis of Association—Communication and Sympathetic Insight." **B**

This chapter is based largely upon the work and ideas of Cooley. It stresses the fact of communication as the source of social learning and the rôle of "insight" in learning.

DAVIS, Kingsley, "A Case of Extreme Social Isolation in a Child," *American Journal of Sociology,* 45, 554-565. **A B**

An excellent study of the effects of isolation. While it is not as graphic, perhaps, as studies of ferals, it is more authentic in that the case came from "our own" culture and society and was studied by contemporary scientists.

KIRKPATRICK, Clifford, "Original Human Nature," in Bossard, J., editor, *Man and His World* (New York, Harper and Bros., 1932). **A**

A clear statement of what the human being owes to the fact of human transmission. Some of the formulations do not square exactly with those contained in this book or in other readings, such as for example the discussion of instinct, but differences are largely terminological and need not confuse unduly.

LAPIERE, Richard, and FARNSWORTH, Paul, *Social Psychology* (New York, McGraw-Hill Book Co., 1936), Part II, "The Processes of Socialization." **A**

A splendid interpretation of the socialization process; the emphasis upon the "symbolic" nature of socio-cultural behavior and meaning is basic. Contains, also, a splendid bibliography for further reading.

OUTLAND, George, "Culture, Intelligence, and the Learning Process," in Roucek and others, *Sociological Foundations of Education* (New York, The Thomas Y. Crowell Co., 1942). **B**

A good discussion of "the nature and meaning of intelligence" as used by the modern psychologists and other behavior scientists (pp. 172-176). Writes cautiously regarding the relation of culture to the learning process, but caution is needed.

## STUDY QUESTIONS

1. Why is "heredity *versus* environment" a futile argument? Illustrate.
2. Why is the concept *heredity* an "abstraction?" Illustrate.
3. Why does each person inherit a unique original nature? What are the sources of the uniqueness?
4. Why is it difficult to evaluate the influence of culture upon human development?
5. Why do identical twins reared in the same home develop into different personalities?
6. Evaluate: "A person's behavior is the result of original nature plus culture plus unique experience?"
7. How is original nature only a *potential* influence upon the development of behavior? Illustrate.
8. Why do we emphasize the *experienced* part of the environment? Illustrate.
9. Would Babe Ruth have been an outstanding baseball star in Switzerland? Why?
10. What types of behavior and potentialities for behavior appear to be the result of original nature? How may these be modified by learning?
11. How have we (the scientists) changed our conception of "drives?"
12. Why is one person a Christian lawyer, another a Mormon physician, and another a bigamous counterfeiter?
13. Why is it difficult to determine the "relative influences" of socialization and maturation upon the behavior of the individual?
14. How do the mores of a society determine the naturalness or unnaturalness of normal organic acts? Illustrate.

# *Chapter X*

# SOCIAL EXPERIENCE AND THE PERSONALITY

## VARIABLE SOCIETAL NORMS AND UNIQUE EXPERIENCE

It has already been shown that persons who grow up in the same society do not necessarily behave in the same manner. Most Americans, for example, speak and write the English language sufficiently alike so that ordinary communication is possible among them. But not everyone has learned the English language in the same way or from the same sources, nor are the results exactly the same. Some people are very conscious of their language; they take pride in speaking and writing it with precision and nicety. Others give little thought to language as an art, and are quite content with numerous imperfections, often not even being aware that they are speaking and writing as poorly as they are. Similarly with other areas of culturally patterned learning. The conditions under which human beings interact seem to involve a considerable range of variation, a sort of "tolerance range" permitted or even provided by the culture.

### *Meaning of the Concept "Unique"*

The word *unique* has, like many words, a number of somewhat varied connotations. One of these meanings implies complete singularity, something "new and different" for which there is no counterpart. We do not use the term in that way here. By "unique experience" we merely mean that the experience in question is the experience of that one person, and we do not intend to imply that no other person has had a similar experience. The word is used as an antonym of "common" or "universal." Like many language usages, the word is employed relatively. There are all degrees of uniqueness varying from insignificant and barely distinguishable variation to diametrical opposites. Uniqueness, moreover, is relative to some standard or norm. Thus, automobile theft is a unique form of behavior as compared to the norms of the whole American society, but is a common behavior form among a group of auto thieves. Many behavior differences among persons are comparable to this illustration. Thus if we are going to study human behavior realistically, we must provide understanding and explanations which will treat both the similarities and the dissimilarities of behavior among persons. The word *unique* may seem too "strong" a word to use when one is intending to convey the sort of meaning which we have just outlined, but this usage seems to be quite reasonable and, after all, so long as its meaning is made clear, it can serve as a useful language tool.

It should not be overlooked that uniqueness of experience can as easily be underestimated as overestimated. There is a common misapprehension to the effect that, for example, if one man loses a son he therefore "knows how another man feels" or "what he experiences" when he also loses a son. But does he? Can the two experiences be that parallel in view of what we know about individual differences in behavior? True, the man who has lost a son might understand how the second man "feels" or what he "experiences" somewhat better than some third person who has not had a comparable experience. But there is still ample opportunity for differences between the two men who have lost their sons. The objective student of behavior must be as cautious not to exaggerate as not to minimize the uniqueness of behavior.

Sometimes a person's uniqueness is only a somewhat singular *combination* of separate behaviors and experiences which are themselves quite typical, but which are "unique" in the particular pattern which they form as they converge *in that one person*. Some uniquenesses in persons are merely the somewhat infrequent combinations of quite normal reactions to typical experiences or quite ordinary reactions to unusual circumstances. Perhaps this point will be made more clear if we turn to specific examples. By discussing specific aspects of behavior and various sources of influence on behavior we may bring the factor of social experience into sharper focus.

*The Family*

Some persons speak or write glibly, for example, about what "family life means to the child." But *what kind* of family life? Studies of the actual kinds of relationships existing between husbands, wives, and children show not only a great variety of overt behaviors and attitudes, but reveal also a number of virtual opposites in the realm of family experience. This is true even for families living under what appear to be the same or similar circumstances. Some parents give their children a great deal of freedom even while the children are very young, while other parents dominate almost every act of the child on into adulthood. Some children live in homes where the parents are devoted to one another, where they are considerate of one another's wishes, and where relative harmony exists most of the time, while other children grow up in tension-fraught domestic circles in which for days upon end they can observe nothing but conflict, quarreling, outbursts of ill-temper, and evidences of distrust. With the widespread practice of divorce in the United States numerous children grow up actually having had several different persons in the rôle of parent, while others have only two parents and sometimes only one. Some parents instruct their children in the ways of good social usage with patience and tact, others by coercion, intimidation, and bribery. Some parents teach their children to be tolerant of different races, nationalities, social classes, and persons of varying religious and political viewpoints, while other parents indoctrinate their children, either deliberately or unconsciously, with bitter prejudices, hatreds, and intolerance of many persons and groups with whom they must later live. Some children see in their family circles evidences of high and noble ethical principles of human interaction, of justice, magnanimity and service, while other children receive object lessons in injustice, dishonesty and vicious selfishness. What, then, does "*American* family life mean to *the* child?" Obviously it means different things to different children—and the differences are sometimes radical. Of course, there are some basic similarities such as the fact that the American family almost everywhere is monogamous, that most mothers give daily attention to the rearing of their children, that most families grow up in single family dwelling units. But these are only the superficials. The really fundamental factors in the formation of character and personality spring from the more detailed and intimate interpersonal relationships, and are profoundly affected by the specific conditions under which the child comes of age.

*The Play Group*

The child's play group, likewise, provides him with a galaxy of unique experiences which leave their mark upon personality as indelibly as do the experiences in his family group. Children, for example, can be unbelievably cruel to one another. The child who is outcast from the play group because he is a stranger in the community or because he lacks the necessary physical prowess to participate in the traditional games or who is conspicuously dull in his school work or who speaks a foreign tongue, frequently becomes the object of painful ridicule and ostracism from the group in which he would like to participate. Case studies of maladjusted adults have shown graphically how the rejection of the child in his play group or school group may lead to serious and permanent animosities and insecurity feelings which may seriously impede or completely prevent normal adult participation in work, recreational, or other groups.

Participations in the play group have also a positive function in the development of virtuous personal traits. Many persons first secure experience in leadership, responsibility, and the necessity for adjusting to other people while they are children and functioning in play groups. But all children do not have the same experiences in the play groups—even though superficially they may *seem* to.

## EXPERIENCES ARE DEFINED SUBJECTIVELY

It is important to note, however, that it is not simply the experience itself which a person has had that leaves the lasting influence upon him, but it is the way in which the experience is *interpreted* or *defined* by the person himself. It is not uncommon to find cases in which a child or an adult feels rejected by his associates and very sensitive about his social position, when the objective fact of the matter is that he is quite well accepted and is afforded an average or superior prestige. Here is a fundamental principle of social experience. It matters little what the objective fact or circumstance may be; it is the definition or interpretation of the fact or circumstance which determines its real effect upon the person. A few illustrations may help to fix this principle in mind.

Suppose a woman believes that her husband is unfaithful, that whenever he is out of her sight he is pursuing or being pursued by some other woman. Suppose, further, that the facts of the matter are entirely to the contrary, that is, that the husband is and has been completely faithful to his wife. Which is the more significant fact *in determining the behavior of the woman toward her husband and toward other people,* her personal conviction that her husband has been unfaithful or the objective truth that he has not? Obviously since she does not know or will not believe the objective fact, it can only be her subjective interpretation which can form the basis for her judgment and overt behavior. Another illustration. A young man feels that he is "unpopular with girls." The facts are, however, that girls say they like him and are attentive and courteous to him. He says, however, that they are "just putting on an act" because they "feel sorry for" him and that their apparent interest in him is feigned and not sincere. Meanwhile he is embarrassed by what he regards as the absence of personal prestige among women, a loss which he feels very bitterly. This mistaken idea not only causes him much personal unhappiness, but forms the basis for certain objectionable traits in his behavior by which some of his associates are becoming increasingly irked. So far as this man's judgment and resulting behaviors are concerned, it is of absolutely no significance that his interpretations do not square with the objective facts. So far as he is concerned it *is* a fact that he is socially outcast by women; to him there is no other and can be no other "fact." In most other respects the young man is essentially a normal personality—he is a good athlete, successful in his profession, was a good student in school, and is very popular with men.

Thus we see that, so far as the significance to human behavior may be concerned, there are two distinct kinds of "reality"; *objective* reality, which can be verified by the observation of almost any number of persons capable of viewing the situation, and *subjective* reality which consists of what *seems* real to the persons involved. It should be borne in mind that objective reality and subjective reality are not necessarily different for all people all of the time.

The point is that they *may* be different, as shown in the above illustrations, and that when they are different it can be only the subjective definition which can have significance to the person's behavior. This important fact has led one pioneer student of sociology to write the classic statement that: "The imaginations which people have of one another are the solid facts of human life." In our language, the subjective definitions which a person has of himself, of his fellow-men, and of the situations in which he finds himself are the significant influences on his life. What the facts "really are" may coincide with what the person believes they are, or they may not. That is of little consequence to the person, however, who can act and react only on the basis of what he has experienced, not on the basis of something else. If a person is color-blind and cannot distinguish between red and green then there is no difference between red and green *for him.* The fact that some one else can see the difference is entirely irrelevant to his experience. Likewise, if a man has an insecurity complex and believes that no one likes him, it is of no consequence to him that *some other* person knows that people really do like him. To him the fact of being socially disliked is real.

In this and later chapters it will be explained in somewhat greater detail why persons develop characteristic patterns of subjective definitions of situations which differ from the objective facts as seen by the majority of others. Obviously such discrepancy represents a kind of deficiency in social judgment, an ineptness in "sizing up" the world of people for what they really are. But to give it a name, or for that matter to explain how it arises, does not in any way solve the problem. The problem persists and is at the root of many of the misunderstandings between persons and groups whose conflicts constitute so important a part of the web of social life.

### WHY ARE EXPERIENCES UNIQUE?

We turn now to a somewhat more systematic treatment of some of the reasons for discrepancies between the subjective and objective realities.

A factor in the environment has no consequence to a human being until it is experienced. The process of experiencing one's environment is limited by numerous factors. As you read these words, for example, of how much of your environment are you actually conscious? If you are giving your attention to your reading, and particularly if you are interested in it, there are sounds, smells, and sights in the room of which you are largely unaware and will remain unaware until you cease reading or give less attention to your reading. The same would be true for any activity in which you are engaged. Out of all of the potentials present in any environment, only a part are actually being experienced at a given time by the person "in" that environment.

What conditions may be responsible for the person's failure to participate in all of the potentialities of his environment?

1. *Physical limitations.* A tone-deaf person is unable to distinguish the differences in tonal quality which a normal person can. A person of low intelligence cannot assimilate verbal stimuli as fast as a person of higher intelligence. An ill person may be less alert and, therefore, see and hear less than when he is well.

Such factors as these are known to have important practical significances in the ability of children (and adults) to learn. In the classroom situation, where the level of activity must be set on the basis of an average ability, a child may "get behind" because of such factors as these. Then after he has gotten behind, he may lose status in his group or with the teacher and may also encounter difficulty at home because of inferior school work. There are numerous instances, for example, in which a child was thought to have been dull when he was merely hard of hearing, or had poor eyesight, or was undernourished. If these conditions were not corrected, however, they could become the genesis of objectionable personality traits which would become a part of his adult personality. Case studies have shown instances in which a man's choice of occupation could be traced to his being chronically ill as a child, thus forcing him to secure his satisfactions from the world of books instead of the more normal world of childhood.

2. *Previous education* may limit a person's ability to participate in his environment. It has been estimated, for example, that when the late President Roosevelt delivered his fireside chats to the nation, his voice was frequently heard by as many as forty million people representing many varied age-groups, regions, degrees of education, religions, and political viewpoints. Could all of these people possibly hear the same thing? Obviously not. Many of the

President's utterances would be largely unintelligible to an unschooled mind, because in order to understand them as he meant them, one would have to have at least some technical knowledge about government, economics, and social conditions. Moreover, frequently the President stated a position on a topic on which some listeners had previously reached a contrary opinion, while others had reached the same opinion which the President had. It would be only natural for the person with whose view the President was disagreeing to have a different "reaction" from that of the person's whose view the President was endorsing.

Another illustration. Suppose a person who has lived his entire life in New York City were to take a walk through the country in company with a farmer who had also been trained as a biologist. Would they see the same things? Obviously not. The city dweller could probably identify a number of the flora and fauna by their popular names. He could probably identify "butterflies," but the scientist could distinguish several dozens of distinct kinds of butterflies. The layman, moreover, would have only the vaguest conceptions of the relationships between the various biological phenomena present. The experience of the two would thus be quite different, not because of any difference in basic intelligence or capacity for observation, but simply due to the differences in their previous training. It is often one's education which gives him the ability to experience the finer distinctions and to understand their meanings. Thus learnings influence learnings *ad infinitum*.

3. *A person may be "blocked" emotionally* in such a way as to limit his experiencing his environment. From time to time people have very vivid experiences which often leave their mark in the form of intense emotional feelings. These strong feelings are called into operation whenever the person is reminded of the unfortunate episode. Sex education, for example, is often made difficult for some persons because they have previously acquired emotionalized definitions of the wrongness or sinfulness of discussing such a subject. There is a case on record of a college girl who became hysterical during a lecture on the physiology of coitus and rushed from the lecture hall screaming "*My* mother never did anything like that! *My* mother never did anything like that!" Obviously, such a person would not have the same experience in listening to the professor's lecture as another student would whose background of experience

had brought her to the lecture with a different emotional orientation to the subject of sex.

Almost everyone has observed instances, either in his own behavior or in the behavior of others, which demonstrate that persons under emotional stress such as anger or grief or love or hilarity give evidence that they do not hear what is being said to them, even though other persons present and not under the emotional stress, do. Most of the illustrations of this point which have been presented have been of an extreme sort. But it should be borne in mind that in many other far less dramatic ways, the day-to-day experiences of people are colored by the emotional part of the total experience. Thus, previous emotional experience constitutes a modifying influence accounting in part for the uniqueness of the individual's participation in his immediate environment.

4. Another factor affecting the uniqueness of experience is the *unequal participation* of different persons who are theoretically "of the same culture." Almost everyone participates in only a part of what might be regarded as "his culture." The family in which one is reared opens up for him certain channels of the culture and closes certain others. If the family is a professional family, the children will probably have more contact with the children of other professional families than with children of working class or farm occupations. If the family is Protestant the child will probably not have an opportunity to participate in the religion of the Catholic church. The child's school and play groups will be largely limited to the children who happen to live in the surrounding neighborhood. The same is true on an adult level. Our education, our occupation, our race, our income level, our sex and many other similar factors limit the extent to which we can participate in groups not appropriate to our categories. Consequently it is normal for each person to have somewhat limited understandings of the way of life, and consequently of the problems and points of view, typical of people with other group affiliations.

One of the unfortunate things, many think, about modern specialized urban living is the fact that the different groups in the community who are dependent on each other often find it almost impossible to reach a common meeting ground of ideas and actions because they live in such utterly different social worlds, even though living only a stone's throw from one another geographically. Neither employers nor laborers, as a rule, *really* understand the problems and difficulties of the other, because neither is participating, as a rule, in the society of the other. The same is true of the different races, different nationality groups, and to some extent different age-groups.

5. Some persons, moreover, *do not have normal opportunity to participate thoroughly in that part of the society to which they supposedly do have access.*

The writer recalls a girl with whom he went to high school who actually did not participate in the high school as it was; she only went to classes. Her parents rarely permitted her to attend parties, extra-curricular clubs, or athletic games. On those rare instances when she was permitted to go, she was chaperoned by her father who remained closely at her side throughout the event. On the surface one might think that she had had a high school experience but actually she did not. Her high school experience omitted many things which her classmates' education did not. Although she was a very able girl, she developed into "an odd person," say most of her acquaintances.

In similar manner other factors may work to limit a person's participation in the culture to which he seems to have ready access, such as insufficient money, low family prestige, illness, or lack of popularity.

When one considers all of the possible limitations on participation, it is not difficult to understand why persons whose situations appear to the outsider to be "identical" are really not so. It helps to explain, for example, why children in the same family, perhaps twins, even though they are of similar or identical heredity and have the "same environment," turn out to be such utterly different people. The point is that the selected and realized part of the total environment may be very different for each and even that will, in all probability, be defined and interpreted in different ways due to the unique ingredients of the total experience for each individual.

## PERSONALITY

### *Definition*

The term *personality* is employed by different behavior scientists in different ways. The precise reasons behind the different conceptions and statements involve somewhat advanced considerations, and are, therefore, outside the province of an introductory book. It must suffice to cover only the areas in which there is substantial agreement. First, it is useful, if not essential, to employ the term *personality* in an inclusive way. Personality includes *all* of the traits and characteristics which make up the person, his physical traits like eye color and height, his overt habits such as laziness or golf playing or smoking, his attitudes like attraction for blonde women or prejudices against Chinese, his mentality, his conception of himself, and any or all other things about him which can be observed by him or by another person. For beginner's purposes, then, we may formally define personality as the *sum total of the observed or observable characteristics of a person.* All characteristics, "good" and "bad," physical and mental, overt and covert, are parts of the personality. It should be clear, then, that in the discussion of the original nature, the socialization of the person, and the unique experience, we have really been discussing the process of personality formation and development. The term *personality trait* is commonly used to refer to some one aspect of the personality much the same as the term *trait* is used in connection with culture.

As with all concepts, personality is an arbitrarily chosen word, but it has come into common usage among behavior scientists. Until he gets accustomed to this usage the student may find it necessary to be quite cautious when he encounters the word in his reading of behavior science literature or when he uses the term himself. This use of the word *personality* should not be confused with the term as employed popularly. Speakers or musicians or teachers who are particularly successful and well-liked are sometimes referred to as people "with a personality." Having a personality, however, is of no distinction, because every one has a personality. One person differs from another, that is, their personalities are different in many respects, but they all have personalities.

### *Evaluative Adjectives*

Other popular phrases which sometimes cause beginning students confusion are "good personality" and "bad personality." When such terms are used, the speaker or writer ordinarily intends to convey the idea that the person under discussion has certain personality traits which meet with approval or disapproval. Perhaps the subject is friendly, affable, or honest. Since in our culture such characteristics are sought after and admired, it is easy to understand why the evaluative word *good* is employed. The error lies in the lack of qualification of the expression "good personality." The person may have many other traits of his personality which are not good according to customary standards of value. He may be lazy, a drunkard, and a thief and yet at the same time be generous, affable, and kind. When one has in mind one set of characteristics he might use the adjective *good*, but when he has in mind the other he might use the adjective *bad* to designate the same person. To avoid this confusion the behavior scientist does not use vague and confusing phrases like good and bad personality. Instead he describes the personality trait as objectively as he can. For example, "John is very intelligent and is usually cheerful" or still better, if he has the necessary facts, "John has an intelligence quotient of 131 and is regarded by most of his associates as a cheerful man." That way it is clear exactly what one means and on what evidence the statement is based. The listener may make his own evaluations as to the goodness and badness of the subject in the way the facts are meaningful to him.

### *The Importance of Context in Evaluation*

Another difficulty in the use of *good* and *bad* and other evaluative terms, is that goodness and badness are usually valid only in some particular context. Suppose, for example, that a man is "a dreamer." Is that good or bad? It would seem to depend upon what the man did with his dreaming. In certain occupations the ability to dream may be a valuable asset. In others it might constitute a handicap. Few personality traits are inherently good or bad. They acquire their evaluation according to the definitions and requirements prevailing in the culture and/or the judgments of the person who is appraising them.

This is very well illustrated by a character sketch entitled "The Sculptor's Funeral." The setting is a funeral held in a small town where the body of a promising young sculptor has been brought home for burial. The reader is informed that the young sculptor was regarded as almost a genius by the men in his field because he possessed such rare traits of artistry. But then one also hears another evaluation of the deceased man. This time the farmers who knew him as a boy are speaking. They too are evaluating his personality. But they are evaluating it in terms of their culture and their experiences with him. It soon becomes clear that they do not hold this man in very high respect. It seems that he was a queer boy with such impractical ideas, and he did such thoughtless things. And soon one recognizes that the traits which probably contributed to his fame as a sculptor contributed to his low status in the community of his origin. One might possibly say that he had a bad personality for rural agricultural society but he had a good personality for the profession of sculpture.

It is not to be assumed from this illustration that success in different occupations necessarily requires such diametrically opposite personality traits as the sculptor's funeral account implied. But, as far as it goes, the illustration is valid and the principle true: personality traits are not inherently good or bad. They secure their goodness or badness from the evaluation they receive by people. This evaluation usually embodies the prejudices involved in the folkways and mores of the evaluator's culture.

The next four chapters will take up a number of phases of personality in some detail. The student is not to assume that the areas thus emphasized are necessarily regarded as more important than any others. They are, instead, the areas of personality which the sociologist (and social psychologist) has studied more thoroughly because they fall into his professional province, human social interaction. Other specialists have studied other phrases of the personality in such specialized fields of study as physiology and psychology. It is not intended to imply that attitudes and values, for example, as treated in the next chapter, are any more or any less important than the circulatory system as studied in physiology or the nervous system and intelligence as studied by psychologists. It is simply a convenient division of labor to concentrate on the topics which one knows best on the basis of empiric study.

### SUMMARY

In the first part of this chapter attention was focused on the ways in which the unique experience of a person affects what he acquires from his environment. It was stressed that the subjective facts, however erroneous, which a person secures from his environment are the real facts so far as he is concerned, and that many times conflicts between persons and groups arise as a result of each one having a different definition of the situation. Objectively, if it could be determined, all might be incorrect. But correctness is so often only a matter of how one interprets the item under consideration. "The imaginations which people have of one another are the solid facts of human life."

A factor in the environment has no significance to a human being until it is experienced by him, the environment containing almost always many more potentials than any human being ever experiences. Different persons experience different things in the same environment because of individual physical differences in their sense organs, differences in the previous education through which their environment is interpreted, emotional blocks to participation in the environment, the inescapably specialized nature of participation in the larger culture due to one's social class, age, sex, religion and other group affiliations, and certain superimposed hindrances to participation even in one's immediate group such as overprotective parents or inferiority feelings.

Personality is here defined as the sum total of the observed or observable characteristics of a person. The student is cautioned about popular usages of this term which tend to confuse him. It was stressed that it is necessary to avoid sweeping evaluating terms like *good* and *bad* when speaking of personality, because the same personality usually includes traits which would be approved and traits which would be disapproved by the same judge. Evaluative terms are meaningless without reference to standards of judgment which are highly variable.

## SUGGESTED READINGS

BONNEY, M. E., "Parents as the Makers of Social Deviants," *Social Forces*, XX, pp. 77-87. **B**

Analyzes a group of cases of extreme deviants, and interprets the etiology of each with special reference to their family rôles. Also summarizes the results of several other studies of similar scope.

BROWN, L. G., *Social Pathology* (New York, F. S. Crofts and Co., 1942). **A B**

The most consistent and express use of the unique experience factor in socialization to be found in modern sociological literature. The introductory chapters contain the theoretical formulation of this concept. Some sociologists are of the opinion that Brown may overstate the unique experience factor somewhat, but none would deny that it is a very significant one or that it needs a more prominent place in social-psychological study than it has often gotten from sociologists and anthropologists who tend to see socio-cultural norms more clearly than they see individualized deviations therefrom.

LaPiere, Richard and Farnsworth, Paul, *Social Psychology* (New York, McGraw-Hill Book Co., 1936), Chapter XIII, "Individuality." **A B**

A very useful and clear treatment of personality traits, their classification, and such personality constructs as dominance, submission, introversion, and extraversion.

Young, Kimball, *Sociology: A Study of Society and Culture* (New York, American Book Co., 1942), Chapter XV, "Personality." **B**

A summary chapter on personality by one of America's most widely-known social psychologists. Contains a great deal of material and many definitions and concepts. The treatment is thorough and scholarly.

## STUDY QUESTIONS

1. How is the concept "unique" experience relative? To what is it relative? What is its connotation as used in this book?
2. Why would "the same experience" not have a similar effect upon any two individuals?
3. How may uniqueness in a person's behavior result from "typical" experiences? How may "ordinary" family life, and the "typical" play group be sources of unique experiences?
4. Which is the more important to an individual, subjective reality or objective reality? Why? Illustrate.
5. How does the acceptance of subjective reality instead of objective reality often result in conflict?
6. How does subjective reality color the acceptance and influence of objective reality?
7. Why is any factor in the environment of no consequence to a person unless it is experienced? Illustrate.
8. How is one limited in his experience of factors in "his" environment? Illustrate.
9. Why do we have difficulty understanding the "problems" of others? Do we ever "understand" others' problems completely? Why?
10. Can the "experience" and the "interpretation of the experience" by a person be separated by him?
11. What is the difference between "personality" as used by the behavior scientist and the "personality" or popular usage?
12. Why do we say that "every one has a personality?"
13. What determines the use of *good* or *bad* when applied to personality? Why are these unscientific, ambiguous terms?

# Chapter XI

## ATTITUDES

Preceding chapters have already pointed out that human beings are motivated (prompted to act), by their basic organic drives which express themselves in a variety of ways depending upon the manner in which they have been conditioned by the culture and by the unique experience of the person. Human motivation is one of the most important and yet difficult aspects of the study of man. Why and how do people develop the likes and dislikes, the attractions and repulsions, the interests and apathies toward other persons, situations and things?

### ATTITUDES

#### *Definition*

Few, if any, concepts of behavior science have caused more difficulty than the concept *attitude.* It is beyond the scope of an introductory book to go into an involved analysis of these somewhat technical questions, and it must, therefore, be sufficient for our purposes to be concerned only with the areas of professional agreement on the subject of attitudes. An attitude is, first, an orientation or a "tendency to act" in some way toward some person or situation or object or idea. Stated crudely, attitudes amount to likes and dislikes, attractions and repulsions, interests and apathies.

#### *Attitudes and Overt Behavior*

The attitude should always be distinguished from the overt behavior related to it. A teacher, for example, may dislike some student intensely but because she has a code of professional ethics which frowns upon such discriminations, the teacher "leans over backwards" to be kind, considerate and helpful to this student. Thus the teacher really conceals her attitude by acting overtly as if her attitude were different from what it really is. In fact she may "act the part" so well as to deceive the student and other people who observe her. But the negative attitude toward the student is still there. It is an ever-present potentiality for overt behavior and may be expressed in the form of overt behavior at any time, perhaps when the teacher is a bit "off guard" or the situation extremely provocative. One of the chief errors made in appraising attitudes is the confusion of attitudes, which are abstract tendencies, with overt behavior which is a more readily observable and objective fact.

One must be careful not to assume, however, that attitudes and overt behavior are distinct phenomena; they are really intimately related and it is very doubtful whether they are ever entirely inconsistent. Let us return to the illustration in which the teacher disliked the student. There were really several attitudes operative in the teacher, her dislike for the student and also her desire to live up to the code of professional ethics which stipulates that she should be fair to all students regardless of personal preferences. Her kind treatment of the student is, thus, an overt response which is quite consistent with her professional attitude. It seems more in line with the facts to interpret this situation as one in which two (if not more) attitude-response patterns were in conflict, her dislike of the student and the desire to behave professionally. The latter attitude was presumably more dominant, and thus she really treated the child with consideration most of the time. Upon the occasions in which she did otherwise, her attitude toward the child predominated over her attitudes of proper professional conduct. Exigencies of living present to all persons at almost all times the same type of conflict which faced the teacher in our illustration. Standards of morality and etiquette confront the expression of our more basic attitudes pertaining to immediate appetitive satisfactions like food and sex. Thus we see that while overt behavior is shaped by attitudes, several attitudes may be operative simultaneously, and some of them may be inconsistent with others. Whatever overt behavior actually occurs, some other overt behavior related to the other attitude or attitudes involved must remain unexpressed or inhibited.

### ATTITUDES ARE LEARNED

There is no way whereby attitudes can arise in a person except by learning them. Even those tendencies to act which are associated with the organic drives of food and sex still have to be learned *in the specific form* in which they exist. A man may have an organic need for sex expression, but that does not mean that all women regardless of age, color, appearance, character, or relationship to him would be equally acceptable as sex partners. Quite to the contrary. On the basis of his learned preferences there would be numerous women who would be defined as non-acceptable even though they would be quite satisfactory to meet the physical requirements of the drive. They would not conform to the man's standards of acceptability as defined by his values. The values, like attitudes, are learned through social participation.

#### *Origins May Be Obscured*

Often when laymen try to be introspective and seek the origin of some attitude, they cannot recall any particular instance or occasion upon which the attitude was learned. Moreover, the attitude seems so fundamentally a part of their behavior that they cannot conceive of their behavior ever having been or being other than it is. Thus, they often refer to the attitude as "natural" or "instinctive" as if it were inherently a part of their original nature. Very few persons, even among those partially trained in behavior science, are sufficiently objective analysts of their own behavior that they can recall when, where, and how they acquired a certain attitude. Seldom, also, can they appreciate fully the degree to which long-standing, emotionally ingrained attitudes can create the illusion of being inherently a part of one.

#### *Attitudes May Grow Gradually*

It is a common mistake, also, to assume that some one experience or occasion is the sole source from which one acquires a given attitude. While it is possible to acquire an attitude as a result of one unit of experience, most attitudes are built up gradually over relatively long periods of time, and are derived from and through many different kinds of experience. A basic attitude toward the members of another race is a case in point.

## PERSONAL VARIATIONS AND SIMILARITIES IN ATTITUDES

### *Standardization of Attitudes Through Group Affiliations*

Group affiliations and participations tend to standardize attitudes for the members of the group. We have already pointed out that in the course of growing up in a group with a common culture, a person tends to acquire the attitudes which prevail in that culture. Ethnocentrism (Ch. V) is perhaps the cardinal illustration of this principle. Through membership in some group whose culture defines a situation in a certain way, a person often has no real opportunity to reach fundamental conclusions which run counter to the prevailing notions of the group. As soon as he shows signs of deviation he becomes the subject of criticism and correction. In short, he is "under pressure" to react in the way in which he is supposed to. To be sure, his conformity may be more conspicuous in his overt behavior than in his subjective attitudes, but it would be easy to overexaggerate the probability of wide discrepancies between them. A glance at one's own group associates readily reveals the great extent to which similarities in attitude and related overt behavior exist. The things we think "important," what we consider "beautiful," what we define as "wrong," what we consider "practical," what we consider "valuable" are very similar from one person to another in the same group, and in many cases are virtually identical. Among persons participating in other cultures comparable unanimity of attitude is equally conspicuous. One tends to attain attitudes consistent with those of his associates not only because of pressure to conform, but because it usually never occurs to him that there is really any other normal or intelligent way of looking at a given situation.

*Attitudes within a group vary, but usually not radically.* One should not lose sight of a companion principle, namely, that there may be individual variation, sometimes appreciable, in the formation of individual attitudes within a group. One will readily observe that many of the differences between persons' attitudes are really only relatively minor variations of the general attitude which is predominant. An excellent illustration of this is provided every four years when presidential elections are held in the United States. The campaigns call forth arguments concerning the relative merits of the party platforms and the expressed views of the candidates. But as one analyzes the contents of the party platforms and the stated views of the candidates, he can invariably find many more points of agreement than of disagreement. No major candidate for the presidency in recent years has ever officially expressed attitudes at variance with the fundamental concept of democracy, the customary freedoms, the capitalistic system, or the American Constitution. That is not to deny that one could find persons at variance with any or all of these values.

As a further illustration of the fact of attitude variation, the following study of the expressed attitudes of five hundred students on the *ideal* number of years which a man *should* serve as President of the United States was made. (1) Seventy per cent of the students thought the present system was right without any amendment. (2) The remaining 30 per cent split almost evenly as to whether a longer or shorter period would be desirable. (3) Very few persons, about 4 per cent, wanted a presidential term shorter than two years or longer than six. (4) Lastly, no one wanted a permanent or an indefinite term of office. Not all issues which one could formulate would, of course, show results of this sort. On questions such as the moral rightness of birth control, the same group tended to divide into opposite camps, some favoring, some opposing. It is noteworthy here, however, that the birth control issue is one of the points of sharp disagreement between Catholic and non-Catholic culture in America. If one then took either group alone and studied attitudinal variations, he would find the same sort of a result as in our illustration about the attitudes toward the length of presidential term.

### *Ambivalence*

Thus far it has been implied that a person has only one attitude toward a given thing or person or situation at a given time. Such is not always, of course, the case. It often occurs that the same person's attitudes toward the same subject are inconsistent with one another. Such a condition is termed *ambivalence*. Most people find that certain occasions arise in which they feel opposite attitudes toward the same persons or things, particularly where strong emotional feelings are involved. Studies reveal that parents are not infrequently ambivalent toward children, especially unwanted children.

> We had not planned to have a child until we had sufficient funds to give the child and ourselves a decent standard of living. But sometimes the best laid plans run amiss and ours certainly did. Junior is now two years old, and to be perfectly frank with you, I don't know whether I love him or hate him—or really I guess I both love and hate him. I love him because he is, like any little child, dependent and lovable. Besides he is mine; he is physically and otherwise a part of my very being. But I hate him too, because very often when I look at him I realize that even though he couldn't help it, he has been the cause of the greatest tragedy which I shall ever know. As a result of his coming my husband had to give up school and before he gave it up he tried to support the child and me and go to school too. As a result of this impossible task he so ruined his health that he is destined not to live much longer. What might have been a gloriously happy future for Junior's father and me turns out to be pretty bleak. And regardless of how objective I try to be, at times I find it almost impossible not to think of Junior as the cause of it all. I know he can't help it but that doesn't change the fact that his existence caused it. . . . Of course I would never tell this to anyone else who could possibly know us, because it would sound so utterly immoral. But it is true, so I have to say it.

This is by no means an unusual case. Any person with wide counseling experience or who has otherwise had the confidence of many persons will recall numerous instances of ambivalence. Sometimes the person both loves and hates a mate or an occupation or a colleague or his parents. This ambivalence is often so carefully suppressed that it is concealed from the person's associates, and sometimes he does not even realize it very clearly himself.

*Personal attitudes and social norms.* Frequently ambivalence springs from the conflicts between the attitudes a person actually acquires through his unique experience and the attitudes he is supposed to have acquired according to the norms of his culture. Parents, for example, sometimes conduct themselves in such a way that they lose the respect of their children, but the children also have learned that they should "honor" their fathers and mothers. But how can one honor someone whom he does not respect or, more bluntly, how can one honor someone who is not honorable? Most persons resolve the conflict in some measure by behaving overtly in the manner in which they are expected and reserving their disapproving attitudes to themselves. This does not entirely solve the problem, of course, because some people are sensitive to being "hypocrites" and may have mental conflicts resulting from such "insincerities." The chief point to be noted here, however, is the normality and inevitability of ambivalence for many persons in many situations.

### STEREOTYPES

One of the most significant ways in which participation in culture standardizes attitudes is through the indoctrination of persons with *stereotypes.* Stereotypes may be regarded as caricatures of persons or situations or things. Newspaper cartoons (not comic strips) serve as a convenient illustration. Here, characteristically, we see Uncle Sam with his striped trousers, tall stately poise, and kindly face. We also see the Russian Bear and the British Lion and the anemic, bespectacled college professor in cap and gown clutching a college diploma. The politician, always of more than adequate girth, is smoking an oversized cigar. And, of course, there is the tax-payer, bewildered and exploited. No one, of course, points out that the United States is not a benevolent looking man or that the business man, the politician, and the college professor are all tax-payers too, because it is not the purpose to present the whole truth—the graphic fragment is enough. Another common source for observing stereotypes is the stage, screen, and radio where the Jew is usually a clothing merchant with a mixed Brooklyn and Russian accent, and where the Negro is either a servant or a somewhat cheerful, though lazy, person with a flair for music and loud clothes. Other sources of stereotyped oversimplifications are found in the stock jokes and anecdotes, in which the overthrifty man is always portrayed as a Scotchman, the "lady's man" is a traveling salesman, and the naïve girl is the farmer's daughter. Some of the conventional stereotypes are complimentary to persons in the category to which the stereotype pertains, others are defamatory, but they are all incorrect. They are incorrect not because it is impossible to find some instances which conform to the stereotype, but because *most of the persons in the class to which the stereotype pertains do not conform to the stereotype.*

If stereotypes are as inaccurate as the above paragraph would imply, why then, do they exist? No one knows exactly why they exist, but it seems to be a reasonable inference from our knowledge about culture and human behavior, that they are a result of ethnocentrism combined with the desire for brevity, generality, and simplicity. There is a certain mental economy in the use of stereotypes. Newspaper editors know that they can usually get across a much more vivid impression to many more people through suggestive stereotyped cartoons than through a brilliant editorial. The stereotype is a kind of mental shorthand through which vivid images are presented to people so simply and so often that the illusion of their accuracy is finally almost completely indoctrinated.

Much of the misinformation which is current takes the form of widely circulated stereotypes concerning the habits of peoples of foreign nations, remote parts of one's own country or other social classes with which one is not completely familiar.

Stereotypes are very significant sociologically for at least two basic reasons. (1) Stereotypes represent *institutionalized misinformation, distorted information,* and *caricatured ideas* of places, peoples, and things, and (2) *stereotypes have profound influence on the formation of attitudes pertaining to these areas of experience.*

One of the early students of stereotypes defined them as "preconceptions" of persons, situations and things "which are dominant over our perceptions" of these things. The key words in this definition are *conception* and *perception.* A *conception* is an idea which has no special time or place reference, and which may be difficult to formulate precisely in objective form. The idea suggested by the word *dog* is a case in point. Every one knows what dog means, but is it a St. Bernard or a Chihuahua, black or white, long-haired or short-haired, gentle or vicious, male or female? Obviously being a concept, it embraces all of these antitheses. It is thus a generalized abstraction, based upon a great many objective instances, but often cannot be defined in purely objective terms by the persons who are familiar with the concept. *Perception,* on the other hand, refers to a specific experience. It refers to the physical stimulation which enables one to see, smell, or feel a stimulus, plus the meanings through which he "understands" the experience. Thus one can perceive a man but only conceive mankind, he can perceive this book, but only conceive books.

Returning to the definition of stereotypes, it will be recalled that according to the definition, the significance of the stereotype to human experience is that through stereotypes prior conceptions are predominant over actual perceptions. That means that the actual experiences one has with a person or a thing may be overshadowed by the previous conceptions he has had of that same thing. The following case in which a person relates his experience with teachers constitutes an excellent illustration of this point.

> Before I went to school I was thoroughly enlightened, so it seems, on the subject of teachers. My playmates, my parents, and my friends all passed hints or related anecdotes which led to the conclusion that school would be an unhappy experience, chiefly because the schoolroom would be presided over by a personality called a teacher. Vaguely I got the idea that the teacher was female, but it was also clear that she did not have the feminine attributes of kindness, sympathy and affection which Mother did. Instead the teacher was a disciplinarian who made people stand in corners and stay after school. Moreover these punishments were not just punishments, but were unfairly meted out by the arbitrary whim of this teacher. . . . I remember upon my return home from my first day at school of telling my mother that I had had a pretty good time of it but had not yet met the teacher. I was noticeably shocked to discover that Miss ——— in whose charge I had been all day was really the teacher. She punished no one, she was friendly and kind and even looked, surprisingly enough, much like Mother. . . . Looking back over my entire school experience I can recall only one case of a teacher who fits the stereotype. Yet whenever the words *school teacher* are mentioned, they call up to me in a vivid image of a middle-aged, grouchy, meticulously but outmodishly attired old maid, wearing horn-rimmed spectacles and using very pedantic but obviously correct, language.

Here we have a splendid illustration of the way stereotypes operate in socialization. Prior to the actual experience with a thing or person or situation, there is usually verbally transmitted information *about* the person, situation or thing to be experienced. Through this vicarious experience the person learns how the anticipated experience is supposed to be defined, that is, what may presumably be expected. Then, when the experience is actually encountered one tends to read into it the meanings with which he has previously been indoctrinated. Thus, for example, since people from the Latin countries are supposedly "temperamental," when one observes an Italian or a Frenchman in an outburst of anger, he reacts, "That is just like a Latin—they're very temperamental." Rarely does one pause to try to recollect carefully whether he has really observed a larger proportion of Latin people exhibit such traits than he has persons from other regions. Nor does he usually stop to think whether the situation he has observed is actually a fair test of the hypothesis at all. As a matter of fact, to most persons there is no hypothesis involved; it is a *fact* that the Scotch are penurious, Italians temperamental, and English slow of wit. The fact that the evidence may be contrary to most of these stereotypes is not known to most people.

A subsequent chapter on Race will discuss a number of common stereotyped conceptions of Negroes widely held by whites in America, on which sufficient research has already been made so that it can be stated beyond reasonable doubt that the stereotypes are utter fictions. But the stereotypes still persist, and constitute one of the most knotty handicaps to the treatment of contemporary problems in race relations. The same principle operates with respect to different classes and regions within the United States.

*Vicarious and Real Experience*

It has sometimes been said that humans "secure their attitudes from their experiences." This generalization is fairly accurate but only if the vicarious experience which comes to the person through indoctrination with stereotypes is included. Unless the contacts with stereotypes is included as "experience," it would be impossible to account for persons having attitudes so utterly contrary to the real experiences which they have had. How, on the basis of his actual experiences with school teachers, could the man whose case was cited above, come to the conclusion he did relative to school teachers? A woman also reports in her case history that all of her relationships with Jews have shown them to be strictly honest, but that every time she thinks of a business deal with a Jew she expects to be cheated. These are by no means unusual instances. They illustrate the predominance of vicarious early experience over subsequent real experience especially where stereotypes are involved.

## THE MEASUREMENT OF ATTITUDES

One of the persistent problems facing the behavior scientist is the discovery and measurement of attitudes. On the surface it might seem relatively easy to determine a person's attitude simply by asking him. Experiments, however, have shown (1) that persons are frequently unwilling to indicate their attitudes, particularly if the attitudes are at variance with those which they think are expected of them in the situation. Thus mothers will not admit having attitudes of dislike for their children, or a sadistic surgeon will not admit that he likes to perform surgery because he likes to see people suffer. It is always easier to talk as if one agrees with the customary conventional notions. (2) Even if they are quite willing to admit the truth, persons do not always know what their attitudes are. Most people, in fact, find it difficult to put attitudes into words, even when they feel reasonably sure that they understand what their attitudes are. Limitations of language are serious enough even for the experts who have long and involved schooling and have learned many of the more precise forms of expression. When interrogated regarding his attitudes toward something, the laymen often cannot say anything more exact than that he "likes" or "dislikes" it, and perhaps that he likes or dislikes it more or less than something else. But attitudes vary from person to person in *intensity* as well as in direction. Also there are many middle-of-the-road positions between categorical likes or dislikes. One may like certain things about the Fair Employment Practices Act and dislike other things. And so on. (3) Also when a person tries to put his attitude into words the language may seem clear enough to him, but he cannot be certain that it will have the same meaning to the person who reads or hears his statements.

This problem of language is especially pertinent when one is requested to state his attitudes in terms of "Yes" or "No" answers to questions in a questionnaire. There is experimental evidence to show that many persons often do not understand what the questioner is asking or find that they cannot accurately state their own positions through the choices allowed on the questionnaire. The techniques for better questionnaire construction are gradually being refined, but even under the most expert study, questionnaire results are not to be regarded as entirely valid.

The root of the problem is that *one really does not study attitudes directly; instead the behavior scientist is forced to infer attitudes from some other behavior* which he considers relevant. It must be realized that answering questionnaires constitutes behavior. The assumptions regarding the connection between the observed behavior and the actual attitude are as likely to be wrong here as in any other kind of behavior. It has been suggested by some scholars that a sharp distinction be drawn between *opinions* and *attitudes,* opinions being merely the verbal statements which are presumed to reflect the attitudes, but may not do so in fact, for reasons we have already discussed.

Even when one observes the direct behavior of the subject he still is in no position to be certain what attitudes the behavior reveals. As we have already seen, several persons may perform the same overt act and be motivated by entirely different attitudes. The persons may be deliberately trying to conceal their real attitudes or may wish to suggest attitudes differing from those which they know they have. The observer, moreover, must be careful not to infer attitudes too freely from observation of overt behavior.

In spite of all the problems inherent in attitude study, attitudes are of the essence where human behavior is concerned. Although it is readily admitted that it is difficult to prove the connection conclusively, most authorities feel that overt acts result from, that is, follow, the attitudes which people have. Thus, for example, if a man refuses to move into a neighborhood where foreign-speaking people live, it seems reasonable to assume that it is either because he has attitudes which define that situation as undesirable or because he believes that other people in whose estimation he wishes to remain high, have negative attitudes toward living in foreign-speaking neighborhoods. Either way the attitude precedes the choice and presumably tends to control it. The idea that attitudes cause behavior, of course, may not stand the test of further research and knowledge. Perhaps we only *think* that attitudes come first and overt acts follow. We may some day learn that some other sequence is the correct one.

### ATTITUDES CHANGE

Attitudes are habits. Like all habits, they tend to persist; to act in the habitual way is always more easy than to act in a new way. Certain attitudes which are deeply entrenched during childhood may give the direction to long standing adult patterns of behavior. Other attitudes may be modified as the person has new experiences and some attitudes may be remade entirely. The whole volume of evidence on attitudes, however, would seem to justify the statement that it is the exception rather than the rule for fundamental attitudes to change radically for adults. That is not to deny the existence of numerous cases of radical attitude reformation in adults, but simply that such cases are not common. When such cases do occur it will usually be found that a somewhat unusual circumstance has been operative, or that there is something else unusual in the personality involved.

The tendency for attitudes to resist change has frequently been seized upon by conservatives as "scientific evidence" that new forms of behavior or new social systems are impossible of attainment. The evidence does not support such an extreme view. There have been numerous instances of radical changes in behavior patterns and in the structure of whole societies which have been lasting. Usually, however, in these instances there has slowly been built up over a preceding period of time a reservoir of unexpressed attitudes sometimes called a "behavior reserve," favorable to the change. These latent attitudes are released when the opportunity for the change is presented. The New Deal in the United States represents such an historical fact. Throughout the 1920's in college classrooms, in liberal magazines and books, the governmental and social reforms of the New Deal were widely discussed and many attitudes were formed which resulted in the tremendous popular acceptance of many of the reforms of the New Deal. Most observers would be doubtful whether these reforms would have been instituted, however, had it not been for the serious depression of the early thirties. Much more will be said concerning the factors involved in specific social changes in subsequent parts of this book. It is sufficient to point out here that *the fact that attitudes are habitual does not preclude radical social change or even revolution* from occurring, although it is clear that *habituated attitudes tend to deter change*. It is equally true, however, that *other attitudes tend to foster change*. It should not be overlooked that change itself is a basic value which may be defined either as desirable or undesirable by the culture. There are those people who think that we are coming into an era in which change will be more rapid and more radical than anything mankind has ever known. If this forecast proves correct, we shall probably see a somewhat new pattern of attitudes with respect to the acceptance of social change.

## ATTITUDES CAN BE INFLUENCED THROUGH THE CONTROL OF THE AGENCIES OF MASS COMMUNICATION

Nazi German culture, now in the process of being systematically disintegrated, provides perhaps the best illustration of the formation of new attitudes in a relatively short time. Under modern conditions of mass communication, where a man can literally place his voice in almost every home of the nation, anyone who gets a complete—or even near complete—control of radio and of the press for any substantial period, can exert a tremendous influence upon the attitudes of the society served by that radio and press. That is precisely what Hitler did in Germany. By employing the best and most effective techniques of the advertising and publicity business, it took a relatively short time to eliminate opposing attitudes—at least so far as overt behavior was concerned—and get almost everyone mouthing the simple clichés which officialdom wanted them to believe, even though very recently the prevailing attitudes were contradictory to some of them. The Allied Nations are only now learning how very successful the Nazis were in indoctrinating the German people with attitudes conducive to the Nazi philosophy. The eventual de-Nazification of Germany is probably inevitable, but whether we shall be able to de-Nazify the Germans as quickly or as thoroughly as the Hitler group were able to Nazify them is yet to be determined.

The United States, however, is by no means immune to minority control of the radio and press and the resultant reformation of mass attitudes along lines desired by those who secure the control of such agencies. At this writing no serious dangers are evidenced and a code of relative freedom of expression for opposing factions obtains, at least in radio. There is nothing to prevent some future control by a small group from shaping up, however. Of course, some change in the legal rights of the press, and especially of radio, would be necessary but it could very conceivably, be accomplished. That is what many people have in mind when they voice a fear that "America may become Fascist"; they do not necessarily mean that Hitler's or Mussolini's brands of social organization will be transplanted here. They mean that it is quite possible for some group to secure such a strong hold on the agencies of mass communication that the ideas and attitudes of America can be fashioned in a relatively short period so that we will come to favor some forms of culture and society which are now regarded as undesirable. The experience of some other nations lends support to such fears. In a highly centralized society such as the American, there is an ever-present danger that these fears may be well founded.

## SUMMARY

Attitudes are among the most difficult aspects of socialization to understand, and yet seem to be among the most important products of socialization which behavior scientists study. The existence and nature of attitudes must always be inferred from verbal and other kinds of behavior, and the problems of drawing accurate inferences are great. Attitudes are learned from experience, but one must be careful to include stereotypes and other kinds of vicarious learning, if he is to understand the similarity in the attitude outcomes found among persons within a given group.

Attitudes permit a paradoxical generalization, which applies, of course, to most cultural products, namely, they are habituated and hence resist change but still do change nevertheless. The changes may be gradual and unconscious, or they may be the result of someone's or some group's deliberate planning which can be made effective through the control of newspapers, radio, and other media of mass information.

## SUGGESTED READINGS

BAIN, Read, "Verbal Stereotypes and Social Control," *Sociology and Social Research,* XXIII, pp. 431-46. **AB**

A novel study of stereotyped verbalisms among a group of 133 college freshmen, showing that stereotypes also function on a verbation level as well as on the pictorial level through which they are so often portrayed. Bain's interpretations are especially important.

CUBER, John and PELL, Betty, "Method for Studying Moral Judgments Relating to the Family," *American Journal of Sociology,* XLVII, pp. 12-23. **A**

Advances a criticism of studying attitudes through the opinion poll procedure and devises a presumably better technique. Presents the results of a study employing the new device and evaluates the instrument.

DAY, Daniel, "Methods in Attitude Research," *American Sociological Review,* V, pp. 395-411. **A**

An examination of the main methods utilized for attitude study. Has an extensive bibliography.

MCCORMICK, T. C. and SCHMID, R. C., "A System of Attitude Experiments," *Social Forces,* XIX, pp. 351-356. **A**

This is a report on a somewhat novel method of attitude measurement which seems to have utility. Not only the method but the set of data secured by using it are included.

Nettler, Gwynne, "The Relation Between Attitude and Information Concerning the Japanese in America." *American Sociological Review,* XI, pp. 177-192. **A B**

Shows that attitudes are not entirely or usually modified by exposure to "contrary" facts, although there is some tendency for facts to change attitudes pertaining thereto. The author suggests that the non-rational basis for attitudes is a fundamental factor to be borne in mind.

Newcomb, Theodore, "Community Rôles in Attitude Formation," *American Sociological Review,* VII, pp. 621-31. **A B**

This study may be taken as representative of a great many which show that social position is of the essence where attitudes are concerned. Later we shall see the effect of social class upon voting and other behavior and in various ways demonstrate the social relevance of attitudes. Specifically, Newcomb shows by objective methods that the rôle which a person plays in his society seems to make a significant impact on the attitudes he has. While somewhat technical statistical knowledge is required to fathom all of the implications of the study, a general reading will prove enlightening.

## STUDY QUESTIONS

1. Why does one have inconsistent attitudes?
2. Why must attitudes be learned? Illustrate.
3. Why are some attitudes believed to be "natural" or "instinctive?"
4. What is the connection between attitudes and knowledge?
5. Why do our attitudes *tend* to be consistent with those of our associates?
6. Why do attitudes vary within a group as well as from group to group?
7. Why may a person have inconsistent attitudes toward the same subject?
8. Of what value are stereotypes to the propagandist?
9. How do stereotypes influence the attitudes that we acquire from an experience?
10. How are stereotypes "inaccurate generalizations?"
11. How does vicarious experience as well as real experience determine attitudes?
12. Why is it difficult to measure attitudes? Why must we measure attitudes indirectly?
13. What three major difficulties are involved in the measurement of attitudes.
14. Why do attitudes often tend to resist change?
15. How may some attitudes tend to foster social change?
16. What is the significance of the press and radio in the formation of attitudes.

# *Chapter XII*

## WISHES AND THEIR FRUSTRATION

### THE NATURE OF WISHES

Much of the behavior of human beings is oriented toward the future. Many of the satisfactions of life consist of the pleasure one secures out of the belief that the actions of today are contributing in some way to the outcomes of tomorrow. People save money, pursue tedious and difficult courses of study, and endure painful medical or dental therapy because these things presumably contribute toward the realization of some goal which is cherished. Thus man lives much of his life in the future, so to speak. For our purposes we may define a wish as a pattern of behavior which involves (*a*) an anticipated future satisfaction (*b*) which the person believes is reasonably likely of attainment and (*c*) toward which he usually relates some of his present behavior. In other words the components of a wish are the acceptance of a goal, faith in the probability of its attainment, and the modification of present behavior to facilitate the realization of the goal.

Human behavior scientists have come to use the concept *wish* as a useful analytical tool to facilitate the study of human behavior. *Wish* as used by the behavior scientist subsumes such popular ideas as "desires," "hopes," "aims," "ambitions," "goals," and "plans." In short we use the general concept *wish* to designate what might be called "anticipatory behavior."

Suppose a man desires to be a physician. In our society the realization of such a goal requires the successful completion of a course of study in an accepted medical school and the passing of examinations held by the state government. After he has attained these preliminaries successfully, a man may reasonably expect to be successful in his undertaking. He can never be certain, of course, because wherever there is future involved, there is always the possibility that unforeseen circumstances may alter the entire course of events. He would have relative assurance, however, that his goal could be attained provided he is able to accomplish the preliminary achievements.

*Subjectivity of Wishes*

It must be borne in mind that the *reasonableness or the strength of the probability that a wish goal can be realized is a subjectively determined fact.* The person may be entirely in error concerning, for example, his personal fitness for the attainment of requirements preliminary to the attainment of his goal. He may have been ill-advised about his competence. He may not be prepared to accomplish some of the indirectly related obligations. In short, he *might be entirely irrational* in his choice of goal or in his assumptions concerning what will be required of him and of the external situation in order to achieve the goal. Under the stress of wishful thinking many persons have manifested notorious errors in judgment in their attempts to anticipate the future. In the business field alone, for example, during normal business periods it is reported that two hundred business establishments fail each week in the United States. Hundreds of students fail in college for one reason or another every year. Thousands of marriages end in divorce every year in the United States. Many of these business ventures, college entrances, and marriages are very probably ill-advised and should never have been attempted, but the wisdom of the judgment as seen by the outsider is of no consequence whatsoever to the person involved in the effort. To him the goal seemed attainable or he would not have made the attempt. That does not mean that he thought he was absolutely certain that the venture would have a successful outcome, but merely that he was sufficiently certain that he felt justified in risking the possibilities of failure which practically every one realizes are always remotely present. Merely because some third party considered a marriage ill-advised does not reduce the hurt of the person whose marriage has failed. The college student who fails because he was not a good college prospect suffers no less because he was in error concerning his own abilities. Whether wishes, then, are based on good judgment or bad judgment, sound reasoning or faulty reasoning, they are equally real to the person having them, and the failure to attain them no less difficult to endure.

It is important to note also that in many instances wish realizations are blocked due to factors largely or entirely outside of anyone's power to anticipate. Frequently all indications point to the likelihood and reasonableness of a given goal and yet it may never be attained.

### *Logic Involved in Wishes Reflects Cultural Patterns*

Noteworthy also is the fact that in the formation of a wish-pattern people frequently make cause and effect connections between their present behavior and the attainment of the goal which are faulty. There is the case of a woman who sought to insure the health of her unborn child by "being very careful about my diet, my moral behavior and reading my Bible every day. If I do these things my child will not only be healthy of body and mind but will also have an unimpeachable character." To anyone familiar with the most elementary biological and psychological knowledge, this woman's reasoning is utter nonsense. Her child might be a moron, he might grow up to be a criminal or might be a malformed human being, regardless of this woman's safeguards against such outcomes. But so far as her behavior is concerned, she believed that there was some connection between the realization of her goal and these overt acts which she performed so dutifully. Less extreme instances can be observed in the behavior of a great many people. Many women spend time, money, and energy upon a varied assortment of special foods, cosmetics, and drugs upon the mistaken assumption that these things will have some connection with their future beauty. These mistaken assumptions are part and parcel of their beauty wishes. They constitute the present behaviors which these women perform because they believe that they will have significant influence on the realization of their desire to be beautiful in the future. Many of these mistaken inferences connecting present acts with future outcomes receive their authority from the definitions and explanations provided by the culture. There are many folkways "due to false inference" such as those mentioned above. In this way culture contributes not only to the formation of wishes but also to the almost inevitable disappointments and consequent suffering of people who perform the required acts but do not secure the presumed benefits. It almost taxes one's credulity when he observes the countless ages through which men and women have meticulously observed many folkways based on false inference.

The goals of wishes are, of course, largely defined but not entirely dominated by the attitudes, values, stereotypes, and other definitions of the prevailing culture of the person. The behaviors which presumably conduce to the attainment of the goals include almost every act of which the human being is capable. The observance of taboos or positive acts, overt or covert behavior are all involved in some wish patterns.

### *Wish Goals Significant in Present Behavior*

It cannot be emphasized too strongly that the wish should not be regarded as only of future significance. True, the goal is in the future, but the behavior presumed to relate to the goal is in the present. The dominance of current behavior by future expectations can readily be appreciated by anyone who will pause to analyze the activities which make up a typical day in his life. Why does the student do his work? Because the work is related to the eventual achievement of a college diploma. Thus the student foregoes, for example, an evening at the movie which he thinks he might enjoy not only because he will save the cost of admission which he may need to purchase other things, but also because the time spent at the movie might be sufficient to master the lesson in physics. It always makes an interesting academic argument whether the student would "really" enjoy the movie more or whether he "really" enjoys studying the physics lesson, in spite of the onerousness of the latter task. If one takes the position that he would enjoy the physics lesson more, the source of his enjoyment is probably in the greater feeling of security which he is able to enjoy as he makes his day-to-day progress toward the ultimate attainment of his goal. So predominant is the concern with future goal satisfaction that it strains one's imaginative powers even to try to conceive of life in which no one assumed that it would be possible to control his future satisfactions by his present behavior, that is, where only immediate satisfactions would be possible.

While considering this point it might be well also to observe that some philosophers of human behavior have raised the interesting speculation whether the pleasure of anticipating the realization of goals might not even be more satisfying than the actual, eventual attainment of the goal itself. It is not necessary to attempt to answer such a question in order to appreciate the fact that human beings are capable of vicarious satisfactions through imagining the pleasures which they will achieve when some cherished goal is realized. These musings are pleasurable only so long, of course, as the person is able to believe that the goal is reasonably certain of attainment at some determinable future time.

### *Hierarchy of Wishes*

At any given time a given person usually has not only one, but many, wishes. These wishes differ in the importance attached to the various goals and in the amount of effort which goes into seeking their attainment. The relative importance of different wishes in the total pattern may vary greatly from time to time. Thus, making money may be a more important wish when one has a child who needs costly medical care than when no such crisis is imminent. It should also be noted that the various wishes of a person are related to each other. It is the wish to save the child's life which prompts the wish to have the money with which to purchase the medical service. Under such conditions the man's wish to see his favorite baseball team play would probably not seem very important to him. The relative importance placed upon different goals is accounted for in the same way as is the existence of the goal, namely through the interaction of the organic needs (original nature), the culture, and the unique experience of the person. Any one of these three factors may account for differences as well as for similarities among persons.

## FRUSTRATION

*Frustration* is the term used by behavior scientists to designate a condition in which a person's wish goal has been blocked, or more accurately when he realizes that it has been blocked or is unattainable in the form in which it has been held. Thus, when a student is informed that he has failed a course or when one learns that his mate has died or when he discovers that his business has failed, he is said to have encountered a frustration. Not all frustrations, of course, are related to such important matters as these. One also encounters frustrations of a more minor sort when he misses a train, cannot get tickets for a football game, or breaks his watch. Since wishes differ markedly in their importance, so frustrations differ in theirs.

### *The Effects of Frustration*

Some of the more apparent effects of frustration are readily observable in one's own behavior or in the behavior of his fellows. Everyone has seen people weep, lose their tempers, or become hysterical when frustrations have occurred. Some of the long-run effects of frustration, however, may not be so apparent to casual observation and frequently escape detection altogether by the layman. It is these long standing and more subtle effects of frustration with which the student should become somewhat familiar. There are several recurring or typical patterns of adjustment which the person makes to the fact of frustration. These adjustment patterns have come to be known by more or less standardized terms which we shall now introduce, explain, and illustrate.

1. *Rationalization.* This is an adjustment to frustration which is popularly called the "sour grapes" reaction. If it is impossible to attain a goal, the person unconsciously explains the situation to himself by denying that he ever wanted to attain the goal anyway. Sometimes rationalization takes the form of explaining the frustration to others in such a way as to "save face." Thus the man who has been frustrated in his desire to secure a college education concludes that college is all nonsense anyway, that it is a waste of time, that many men have succeeded in life without it, and he can learn much more from "life" than from books. There is just enough truth in such explanations to make them appear plausible, particularly if one *wants* to interpret the situation in that way. If one cannot secure membership in a certain club, he denies that he really wants to get into the club. Since he does not want to be in the club, the fact of his being out of it cannot possibly be construed by anyone as failure on his part. One cannot lose a race he does not choose to run.

It is necessary to distinguish clearly between rationalization and the deliberate, conscious offering of alibis and excuses. The latter is not rationalization as the term is used by behavior scientists, although the thinking process underlying it is much the same: the person attempts to justify himself by formulating interpretations which present his ideas and acts in a favorable light. The basic difference between rationalization and excuse-giving is that *rationalization is unconscious and excuse-giving is conscious.* The two are often interrelated, however.

Many of the stock rationalizations used to take the "sting" out of frustration are provided by the folklore of the culture. "If you are about to be fired, then quit." "If you are about to be jilted, jump the gun and do the jilting." And so on. "Luck" or "fate" also make excellent scapegoats. The influence of uncontrollable factors occurs just often enough to be an ever-present plausible explanation for frustration. Then, too, one can always "change his mind" and go out of business voluntarily, just ahead of bankruptcy. Or one can explain that he failed the examination because he held such "high principles"; the rest of the class cheated, but he was so honest that he chose to fail rather than to compromise his character. The opportunities are legion and, like ready-made clothes, unless one's tastes are unusually unique, he can usually find something available which fits fairly well, both for his own comfort and to satisfy the judgment of others.

It has been fashionable to decry the human propensity to rationalize as a means of escaping from the responsibility of facing the consequences of one's acts. There is little doubt that in numerous cases the habit of offering alibis is a personal weakness. The chronic excuse-giver has in some way learned that he can "get by" through offering excuses and alibis when he is inadequate to the situation. While from an ideal point of view such behavior may constitute weakness, it may be the only way in which an inadequate person can get along in his social world. When it comes to the major frustrations of life, moreover, the ability to rationalize can save a person from having to face too realistically some of the bitter facts of frustration. If a woman never gets an opportunity to marry, her rejection may be less painful to bear if she can convince herself that her life can be fuller outside of marriage, and that she was really fortunate not to have fallen into the snare of matrimony. And perhaps even the student who fails in college because he has not enough ability may be permitted, even on moral grounds, the right to enjoy whatever consolation he may find in the belief that he failed "because he had to work" his way through school.

Religion has traditionally offered people some of the most satisfying rationalizations for life's greatest frustrations. According to the point of view of traditional theology, loved ones do not die; they are "taken" or are "relieved of earthly burdens" and "go to their rest" where they will ultimately be met again in the after life. Poverty represents no serious failure because wealth, while not exactly wicked in itself, provides temptations to wickedness. "Blessed are the meek for they shall inherit the earth," and the rest of the Beatitudes have offered consolation to countless generations of believers during the times of their frustration.

2. *Ambivalence.* Rationalization is sometimes incomplete or the person finds it difficult to believe the rationalization all of the time. He then vacillates back and forth between his original definition of the goal and his rationalization of the frustration. Such a condition is called *ambivalence.* Ambivalence is characterized, as we have noted in the previous chapter on attitudes, by coexistent or intermittent opposite definitions and emotional feelings. It is not infrequent to hear a divorced person confess that he both loves and hates his former mate. He probably would like to continue in the love relationship, but since he was rejected he finds it easy at times to hate the person who caused him the unhappiness. But he also remembers the happiness he had in the earlier state of love. And so he swings from emotional feelings characterized by the word *love* to their antitheses of *hate.*

Sometimes ambivalence results from differing reactions resulting from differing parts of a total frustration experience. Many men define their military experience in such a way. They are unhappy about having been drafted and having to lay aside their civilian plans for several years, but they can also recall some phases of their army experience which they are glad they had. Thus one moment they speak of "hating the army" and the next moment assert with ill-concealed pride "the army made a man of me."

3. *Compensation.* This involves a sort of substitution of goals. But, of course, there can be no true substitution, because the goals were of unequal value to the person before the frustration. One common form of compensating adjustment involves taking over some second-best wish and throwing oneself so wholeheartedly into

its attainment and enjoyment, that it may actually yield more satisfactions than were originally anticipated from the first goal. The classic and overused instance of the boy who wanted to play football but was physically unable and thus forced into the world of books and ideas in which he later distinguished himself is a valid, even if trite, illustration. The various service and humanitarian occupations frequently attract men and women who turned to benevolent work as a means of escape from the frustration of the ordinary wishes of the ordinary people of their time. The woman disappointed in love may compensate by devoting her life to the care of orphaned children not because she was interested in orphaned children in the first place, but because this activity is somehow satisfying nevertheless. It is not infrequent that the person may discover in a compensatory readjustment that he has attained satisfactions even greater than he might have attained had his original wish been realized according to schedule.

On the other hand many of the "objectionable" traits which people find in the behavior of their associates are also often traceable to compensations. The "henpecked husband" may find compensations through being very tyrannical in the treatment of subordinates at the office or, conversely, the man who is frustrated in his desire for power in his professional field may compensate by asserting undue domination over his family. It is thought by some authorities that the avid participation of many people in sports and hobbies through which they achieve distinction may be compensations for the frustrations of their more ordinary personality needs and wishes. One is, of course, not to assume that all sports and hobby participation are to be explained in this way, although some probably can be.

4. *Fantasy*. "You can't stop me from dreaming," is a line taken from a recently popular song hit. The idea embodies a common adjustment to frustration. Even though the actual realization of the goal is blocked, in the realm of one's imagination the goal can be realized over and over again. The process is clearly illustrated in the imaginary playmates and imaginary worlds of children, although it is by no means clear that children's make-believe worlds are entirely due to their frustrations. Adults, having more inhibitions than children as a rule, are more careful to conceal their imaginary playmates and their worlds of fantastic wish fulfillment. It is not at all

uncommon, however, to find adults with sufficient insight into their own behavior who will frankly admit that through their daydreams they vicariously participate in the realization of their frustrated wishes. Here, then, is another sort of psychological "safety valve" which human beings use to reduce, even if only momentarily, some of the more bitter pangs of frustration.

5. *Identification.* Another adjustment to frustration is that of living through the lives of others, by participating vicariously in the successful attainment of goals by other people. It may well be that for many people the greatest satisfactions of parenthood are the result of identification. Thus, it does not matter so much whether one is poor or in bad health, so long as one's child can have financial security and better health. Many parents are frank to admit that they receive greater satisfactions out of their children's successes than out of their own, particularly in those areas of life in which the parents have been most seriously frustrated. It is not to be assumed, however, that this is true of all parents or that all of the satisfactions of parenthood arise from this source. Many tensions which arise between parents and children, however, are due to some parents' attempt to regulate the children's lives too closely. The parents make a too-close identification of their wishes with their children's lives. If the children's wishes coincide with those of their parents no tensions may result, but this is not always possible. Other forms of satisfying identification are found through conversation, reading, and movie or theatre attendance. Through these media a person participates in a vicarious, but often very real, substitute social world, unconsciously identifying himself with other persons and sharing their wish realizations. Particularly novels and plays of the stereotyped sort, where the hero and heroine can always be depended upon eventually to secure the realization of their goals, may have their popularity explained in no small measure by the needs of many people to identify themselves with other people, even though fictitious, who are almost certain eventually to triumph over adversity.

6. *Conversion.* A somewhat different type of adjustment to frustration is found in conversion. Conversion is usually defined as the substitution of a physical maladjustment for the psychic pain which attends or follows frustration. Thus instead of "just feeling unhappy" about the loss of a loved one, one may actually become ill,

having very real physical symptoms such as pain, nausea, paralysis, or any other physical symptom of which the human organism is capable. Not as much is known about conversion as it would be desirable to know, but it seems reasonably clear from the evidence that through some unconscious process the psychic anguish becomes translated into physical illness. While this is an oversimplified statement of the matter it will do for our purpose. The following illustration may assist in understanding a case of conversion. It occurred ten years ago.

> Joe was driving with one arm, the other was occupied appropriately with his fiancé. Due, no doubt to his divided attention, an accident occurred in which both Joe and the girl were pinned for thirty minutes beneath the wreckage of the automobile. Joe was almost completely unhurt, but the girl was mortally injured and bleeding profusely. By the time help arrived she was dead.... Joe realized full well for several hours after the accident that he was solely to blame for what had occurred, that if he had been normally cautious and attentive to his driving, his fiancé would still be alive.... The day before her funeral Joe's family noticed that he used his left arm very slightly and within a few hours was unable to control it at all.... He was taken from physician to physician, clinic to clinic and no one could discover anything physically wrong with Joe's arm.... Gradually Joe verbalized an explanation for the accident. The accident occurred, he said, because he lost control of the use of his left arm—certainly no one could blame him for that.... For several months his arm hung limp at his side until eventually a psychiatrist became interested in the case. Joe responded to treatment and in a very short time recovered the complete use of his arm.

Many even more striking cases are found in the records of the army and navy medical corps during the recent war.

Extreme cases of conversion of the above sort are very graphic and interesting but are, of course, not very common. Many conversions take minor forms like chronic head aches and pains or paralyses. These are often called "neurotic symptoms" since they are frequently associated with the larger pattern of psychoneurosis. Many cases frequently dismissed by the physician as "notional" or "hypochondria," because he can find no physical basis for them, are conversion symptoms which frequently, though probably not always, have grown out of frustration.

These forms of adjustment to frustration—rationalization, compensation, fantasy, identification, and conversion—are only a few of the many types of more or less lasting personality change which grow out of frustration. They have been discussed here because of their prevalence, and because they serve as useful illustrations of the typical forms of adjustment to frustration in our culture.

*Several cautions shall be observed by the beginning student in thinking about these processes of adjustment to wish frustrations.* Specifically, the following should be noted.

1. Diagnosis of frustration symptoms in most cases is best reserved to the professional psychotherapist. A little knowledge in this area, as in many others, is often a dangerous thing.

2. All persons do not react in the same way to frustration. One may adjust by fantasy, another by rationalization, a third through conversion.

3. Rarely is a person's adjustment limited to any one type of adjustment. Usually there are combinations of adjustments. Even in the illustrations cited here, traces of one type can be observed in a case illustrating another type.

4. Not all persons show the same degree of change as a result of frustration. This may be due to several factors. Frustration like any other part of experience has to be defined by the person having it, and is therefore subject to all of the variations involved in any unique experience. Moreover there is no way of knowing actually whether one person's frustration is as "severe" as another's, although some idea of relative severity may perhaps be inferred from the severity of the symptoms. The layman is much more apt to talk about severity than the specialist is.

5. The layman also is apt to speak glibly about "weak" and "strong" persons so far as apparent resistance to extreme frustration symptoms is concerned. The expert knows better than to use such notions, for he has techniques which enable him to see beyond the obvious. He has seen too many cases of "strong minds" who allegedly can "take it" so admirably, who later come or are brought to him as advanced and serious cases.

6. Finally, the student should not assume that all maladjustments of personality are the results of frustration even though frustration is a very important factor in personality maladjustment. There may also be "good" results from frustration, that is, personalities may take on attributes as a result of frustration which are generally approved, although such is not commonly true.

It is extremely difficult to present a scientifically satisfactory classification of the causes of frustration because *any occurrence can cause a frustration for some one*. Schools cause frustration by failing people, also by passing people, and also by informing people about the nature of the universe. Success for one person may cause frustration to another. Hobbies, games, rivalries, loves, may all cause frustration to someone in some way at some time. About all that can be reliably stated is that the *sources of frustration are inherent in the interaction of human beings*, and possibly, also, that when there is any marked disturbance of customary modes of living such as wars, depressions, or other catastrophies, the opportunities for frustration are greatly multiplied.

There are several professions which have arisen, such as psychiatry, counseling, and psychoanalysis, which are designed to assist those people whose frustrations become severe. Obviously these professions touch only a small proportion of the existing cases and only the more severe ones. These fields will be discussed, however, more fully in a subsequent chapter.

## SUMMARY

Persons acquire, through their socialization, certain goals which they desire to attain in the future, and tend to behave in such a manner as seems to them likely to result in the attainment of these goals. This pattern of anticipated goals and current behavior designed to achieve the goals, is termed the *wish*. Wishes are strongly influenced by the values prevalent in the culture, but are always modified somewhat by the unique experiences of the person.

Frequently the attainment of wishes is blocked and the person becomes frustrated. The frustration of major wishes often constitutes a severe and lasting modification of the personality. Some of the recurring readjustments to frustration are rationalization, ambivalence, fantasy, compensation, identification and conversion. These may be found in various combinations and in varying degrees in many, if not most, people.

Frustration inheres in the fact of human living together. Almost every occurence brings frustration to some one. Frustration, therefore, cannot be eliminated, but some of its effects can in some measure be reduced. Not all of the effects, of course, are harmful, but frustration constitutes an ever-present and at least annoying aspect of human life.

## SUGGESTED READINGS

DOLLARD, John, *Frustration and Aggression* (New Haven, Conn., Yale University Press, 1939). **A**

This is an intensive study of the relation between the frustrations of the person and his manifestation of aggression. While the work has met with some criticism for its alleged overstatement of the relationship, it remains a very valuable treatment of an immensely important problem in human behavior.

FOLSOM, J. K., *Social Psychology* (New York, Harper and Bros., 1931), Chapter V, "Wish Frustration and Personality Adjustment." **B**

A clear, effective, and accurate presentation of the nature of wishes, their rôle in human behavior, and the forms of adjustment to frustration. A fuller treatment than is included in this book.

GRINKER, Roy and SPIEGEL, John, *Men Under Stress* (Philadelphia, The Blakiston Co., 1945). **A B**

A volume describing the nature and treatment of the frustrations behind the "combat neuroses" as encountered by the Army Air Forces Medical Corps both in the combat areas and later. The chapter on "The Return Home" (Chapter 8) is an especially vivid description of the behavior of the combat fatigue man when he finds himself in the midst of non-service people. The authors are AAF psychiatrists.

HORNEY, Karen, *The Neurotic Personality of Our Time* (New York, W. W. Norton and Co., 1937). **A B**

A well-known and highly regarded volume written by a prominent psychiatrist who also writes a great deal for the lay reader. This is an attempt to explain personality in terms of the neurotic manifestations resulting from frustration or at least working out through frustrations.

PRATT, George, *Soldier to Civilian* (New York, Whittlesey House, 1944). **A B**

As the title indicates this is a study of the effects of the change of rôle from military to civilian. The author is a psychiatrist with wide experience with the subject. The book is not technical.

## STUDY QUESTIONS

1. What are the characteristics of wishes? Illustrate.
2. How do wishes for future attainment influence present human behavior? Illustrate.
3. Are there "universal" wishes? Why and why not?
4. Why are some wishes "wishful thinking?" Illustrate.
5. What is the relation of cultural values to individual wishes? Illustrate.
6. How do wishes often give satisfaction before they are achieved?
7. Why do wishes vary in importance? How does this difference in importance vary from time to time?
8. Why do a person's wishes usually form a related pattern? Illustrate.
9. How is the importance of a frustration related to the importance of the wish? What unconscious and non-logical factors may alter the relationship?

10. How does religion aid people to adjust to frustrations? How does it create frustration?
11. How is the person who "tells a lie so often that he believes it himself" an example of rationalization?
12. How are the presence of love and hate attitudes toward the same person possible? Illustrate with some cases of ambivalence with which you are familiar.
13. How may adjustment by compensation result in greater satisfaction to the individual than if the original wish had been realized? How may it produce "objectionable" behavior?
14. How is day-dreaming a means of adjustment to frustration?
15. How may symptoms of physical ailments actually be symptoms of frustration? Illustrate.
16. How may the same situation cause frustration to one individual and not to another?
17. How may any normal event in life be a source of frustration to some one? Illustrate.

# Chapter XIII

## THE SELF AND SOCIAL RÔLES

Among the numerous attitudes which every person has is a group which refer to himself. Very early in his life each person learns that certain attributes of his own personality are important to him through the effect which they have upon other people and, therefore, upon other people's treatment of him. A very young infant soon learns that when he cries certain consequences follow in the form of changed adult behavior toward him. Perhaps he will be picked up, perhaps fed, or talked to. In this simple way a fundamental fact of socialization is brought home to him at a very early age, namely, that what he does affects how he is treated by others.

On the adult level, of course, the operation of attitudes about one's own personality are exceedingly numerous and much more complicated. They are evidenced in common speech by many recurring phrases with which almost every one is familiar and probably uses, "I lost control of myself"; "I hated myself"; "He loves himself"; "She was ashamed of herself"; and so on. What is the significance of the reflexive word *self* which recurs so frequently and so consistently in the everyday language of people? It seems to be tacit evidence of the existence of a pattern of attitudes which each person has concerning his own personality. This *pattern of reflexive attitudes* has come to be called *the self.* Most of this chapter will be devoted to the consideration of how self-attitudes and feelings develop, how they become organized and how they affect and are affected by other behavior.

Perhaps the fundamental understanding necessary to appreciate the nature of the self is to recognize that *each person through his imagination takes a position as if he were outside of his own personality and from this assumed position observes his personality as if he were someone else.* The recurrent phrases "as if" are significant; no one really leaves his own personality in any objective sense. He merely exercises his imagination in such a way that it has the effect upon him of taking a detached position for the purpose of self-observation and appraisal. Actually, of course, the person is really not necessarily any more objective when his self-attitudes are operating than when any other attitudes are involved. He does not really "see himself as others see him"; he only thinks he does. His observations of himself may be as erroneous as his observations of anything else. His attempts to evaluate experiences may be confused by stereotypes, faulty observation, and misjudgment. It is, then, a sort of illusion that one has that he is looking at himself the way others would, but he never really knows exactly how others do regard him.

It is essential to note also that *attitudes toward himself are frequently not easily verbalized* by the person. One may, in fact, be largely or completely unconscious of how his attitudes toward himself would look to him if he saw them present in someone else, or how they would sound to him if they were actually stated as they exist. Thus, it is not at all uncommon to hear an egotistical person express disapproval of someone else because "he is so egotistical." The egotistical person may not know that he is regarded as egotistical himself. Probably no one has sufficient insight into his own behavior to be conscious of the existence of all of his own attitudes toward himself, and even more certainly not of the objective accuracy of these attitudes.

*Are the person's attitudes toward himself his own attitudes or a reflection of others' toward him?* This way of stating the question sets up a false distinction. A person's attitudes are, of course, uniquely his own, but at the same time they are derived from the attitudes of others toward him as he has observed them. This is not to deny that it is possible for the person to have different attitudes toward himself than those which other people have toward him. The point is that his attitudes result from interaction with other people. In short, self-attitudes, like all attitudes, are learned through socialization and are strongly influenced by the culture norms of valuation as well as by his unique experience. There may be uniquenesses in self-attitudes just as there may be uniquenesses in the way in which a person writes or speaks, but it is no more correct to ignore the influence of other people on the formation of self-attitudes than it is to deny the significance of other people in the formation of one's language patterns. Self-attitudes are a social product.

### THE "LOOKING GLASS SELF"

The nature of the self may perhaps be more clear if it is described in the manner in which C. H. Cooley conceived of it when he coined the phrase, the *looking glass self*. He explained that there is an ever recurring thinking process going on in each person's mind and is characterized by three separable phases.

1. *The imagination of how "I" appear to others,* that is, simply what they see or perceive when they interact with the "I." Strictly speaking, of course, no one can ever know what anyone else experiences when the two interact. All that he can ever know is what he thinks or assumes or has reason to believe they perceive. As a matter of fact "they" may not even see him at all, and yet he may think that they do. Thus the first stage of the looking glass process is *the person's imagination of what other persons perceive about his personality*. If he wears a blue suit he assumes that they see a blue suit. If he is tall, he assumes that they perceive tallness. If he lies to deceive them, he assumes that they believe what he has told them.

2. Once the person believes he knows what others perceive of him, the second phase of the process occurs, namely *how do they interpret what they see?* Or how do they *evaluate* what they have seen? If the person has a "black eye," he assumes not only that others see the black eye, but he is also aware of the ways in which people characteristically interpret a black eye. They may assume, perhaps, that he has gotten the worse of a fight, whereas, he actually acquired the black eye in an auto accident. Since having the black eye is not usually a virtue, he probably concludes that others are evaluating him negatively in that respect. Actually, of course, no one may have noticed the black eye, but since the person knows from past experience that people usually interpret black eyes in certain well-known stereotyped ways, he will probably assume that his black eye has been interpreted characteristically. In other words,

the person not only imagines that his behavior is visible to others, but he also imagines, as best he can, how that behavior will be evaluated by them. As has repeatedly been pointed out, his estimates of others' evaluations of him may actually be incorrect, but because he knows or thinks he knows what the standards and definitions and criteria of the group are, he feels that he knows how they will be applied to him.

3. On the basis of the above two processes the person derives *feelings about himself*, such as pride, embarrassment, of chagrin, depending upon how he thinks the evaluation was made. It should be clear, of course, that *it is the evaluations by others and not the behavior being evaluated which determines the kind of emotion called up*. Let us suppose that a man is among a group of men who are telling risqué stories. He tells one which he considers to be appropriate and the laughter is intense. He probably would judge that his behavior has been evaluated favorably and would be proud of himself. Just at this moment he notices that his mother has overheard the story. It is the same story which the men heard, but he knows that, being a woman and having the kind of standards his mother does, she will strongly disapprove of his conduct. Instead of being proud, he is now ashamed of the identical act from which he derived pride a moment earlier. Thus, it can be seen that the feelings derived when one's behavior is being judged are not determined so much by the behavior per se as by the way in which one thinks the behavior is defined by other people.

## INDIVIDUALITY AND SOCIAL ACCEPTANCE

Frequently one hears the protest that he should not be "dominated" so completely by what other people think. He should "make up his own mind," "be himself," and "assert his own individuality." Such a view is altogether natural and understandable, particularly after one has experienced pain as a result of others' evaluations. But the advice is largely meaningless. So many of the satisfactions of human life result from the approval of oneself by other people that it is impossible to escape very long from the knowledge that *what others think is important*, not only abstractly but also in *many practical ways*. Rewards and punishment are meted out on the basis of others' evaluations. "No man liveth unto himself."

A person learns by trial and error, by joys and pains, through the operation of the self, not only the importance of others' evaluations but also how to secure favorable evaluations. This is essential to him, not merely for the abstract value of "being well thought of," but also for the inescapably practical requirements of successful living. On the basis of other people's judgment of one's personality he is given rewards and punishment, promotions and demotions, satisfactions and frustrations in myriads of practical matters from day to day. Small wonder that virtually everyone is interested in "how to make friends and influence people." Most people know how to do it passably well; most would like to do it much better than they do.

*Asocial Behavior*

It often appears that one knows persons who seem largely to ignore what other people think, who by words and deeds antagonize people at every turn and seem, in fact, to enjoy securing negative evaluations of their conduct from other people. At first thought such persons might seem to constitute an exception to the principle under discussion in this chapter. When they are observed more closely, however, it usually becomes apparent that such persons do not really constitute an exception. Sometimes they have experienced uniquenesses in their socialization as a result of which they are spared some of the disprivileges normally resulting from social disapproval. Not infrequently such persons have enjoyed relatively secure positions in their social worlds. This is well illustrated by the case of a man who was the son of "the wealthiest man in town." He was so secure as far as financial and social prestige were concerned, that he was accepted by everyone because "no one would dare to offend his father. No one really liked the boy's temper tantrums, his snobbishness, or his boorishness, but no one dared to register disapproval of these behavior patterns because of the fear of incurring the disapproval of the boy's father." When the boy became a man, he did eventually learn through a very bitter experience that he really was held in very low esteem, a fact from which he had been sheltered. He would have very probably learned it normally and gradually if he had been an ordinary child. It would have early been impressed upon him that other persons are usually in a position eventually to make their evaluations felt in some way or another, and that, therefore, one must accede to their judgments. Sometimes, also, the apparent disregard of other people's evaluations can be explained by the poor judgment of the subject, due to low intelligence rather than to unusual socialization.

*Diverse Group Norms*

Finally, it should be noted that the man or woman who seems "out of step with the passing procession" may really be marching "in step with the cadence of another drummer." The person, for example, who was willing to go to prison rather than register for Selective Service is a case in point. Such persons were often members of some organized religious sect against whose principles it was to coöperate in any war. To such a person it was more important to adhere to the principles of his faith and to remain in the high esteem of the people in that faith than to secure the approval of the larger and more impersonal group outside. Many other kinds of non-conformists are like that.

In a somewhat less conspicuous sense, most persons are like that. They recognize that different standards for evaluating conduct exist in different groups, and do not expect approval by persons in whose system of values their own behavior is not rated highly. The devout Christian student who excuses himself from a New Year's Eve party just before midnight in order to go to a sanctuary where he may usher in the New Year with prayer, constitutes a pertinent instance. Such a person would not expect approval of this conduct among a conventional group of New Year's Eve merry makers. He might even be ridiculed by this group, but in the evaluation of another group the student knows that his behavior will be recognized as correct and, in fact, virtuous. From these examples it will readily be seen that persons who appear not to desire the approval of their behavior in the eyes of others actually do. Not to do so with respect to *some* group would leave a person hopelessly, not to say helplessly, isolated from human beings, a condition preferred by only an insignificantly minor fraction of any people.

*Social Judgment May Be Faulty*

A person's estimation of how his behavior is being evaluated by other people may, as has already been pointed out, be distorted or even completely wrong due to inaccuracies or ineptnesses in his judgment. It should also be noted that another factor contributes to the existence of discrepancies between the evaluation of one's behavior by others and his own estimate of their judgment. Not infrequently persons, because they wish to be tactful or because they are cowed by the real or assumed prestige of another person, may feign approval when they really disapprove certain behavior. Some of the bad manners, for example, of very wealthy or otherwise socially prominent persons, may receive tacit approval because no one quite dares openly to voice disapproval of such a high personage. "The King can do no harm." The practical problem, of course, is not so much involved with royalty but the principle is the same. Indulgent parents have not infrequently treated their children as if the child's defects of character were virtues, and thus have contributed to a defective self-appraisal pattern in the mind of the child.

## INFERIORITY AND SUPERIORITY FEELINGS

It is a matter of common observation to the layman that some persons realize quite accurately how they "rate" in the evaluations of others. But some people are "egotistical," that is, regard themselves more highly than others generally do. Others have "inferiorities," that is, regard themselves less highly than other people do. Sometimes, also, superiority feelings are feigned to compensate for more basic inferiority feelings. Thus, the very talkative and assertive person who seems to be so overconfident may be behaving in this manner as a camouflage for his fundamental feelings of inferiority. This may be either a conscious or an unconscious adjustment.

Both the person characterized by inferiority feelings and the person characterized by superiority feelings represents a somewhat distorted self-appraisal. The nature of one's socialization has a great deal to do with the origin or intensification of distorted notions of oneself.

So long as I can remember my parents and my brothers and sisters never permitted me to do very many things on my own initiative. They seemed not to trust my judgment. Someone always accompanied me when I went away from home, as if I were unable to find my way back. Whenever I was sent to the store to buy something, I was always given the exact change as if I would not know what the correct change was. Meanwhile it was not uncommon to be told I lacked "responsibility." For a while I seemed to resent the injustice of the situation.... Of course, I did lack initiative; I never got the chance to exercise it. I was like the person who couldn't swim because he never got the chance to try.... Eventually though, I fell in line with the pattern laid out for me. But I do recall feeling upon many occasions that I really did have the ability to do the things which I was always being told I did not have the ability to do. Once in a while by accident a situation would arise in which there was some opportunity to exercise responsibility, initiative or judgment, but when those situations arose I was so bewildered by my lack of experience in acting on my own, that I would hold back a little, preferring to follow rather than to lead. As I see it now, I had learned so well the fallacy that I lacked responsibility, that I would not even exercise initiative when I did have the chance.... Now as an adult, even though I understand the situation, I still rarely take on any kind of leadership or do any kind of pioneering whatsoever. Time and again I know I have the necessary ability and have seen persons of less ability get along very well. But from force of habit I still hold back. I still think of myself in the way I had learned to think of myself—lacking responsibility, having to be taken by the hand like a child. Even though my friends keep telling me that I can do all sorts of untried things I still cannot get over my lifelong habit of thinking of myself as not equal to the demands of the situation.

Here is a case which illustrates how a person can develop a lack of confidence in the appropriateness or adequacy of his own behavior as a result of the way in which his behavior has been defined by others. He has come to think of himself, and particularly of his abilities, as being less good than objectively they are. The reverse can be equally true. The following case is taken from a longer interview with a man who had recently been discharged from a position which had originally been given to him on the basis of his falsified statement that he had had the necessary technical training which the job required.

*Question*: But why did you try this work knowing as you must have that it required technical knowledge which you did not have? Was it because you needed a job so desperately?

*Reply*: No, I quit a job to take this one. Of course, I knew the job required what you call "technical knowledge." That is why I lied about my education. I've never found anything yet I couldn't do. [His record showed that he had been five times discharged for not being able to do his work]. I could have bluffed this thing through if I hadn't gotten a bad break. I've always been smart—not in school, just in general.

Further insight into this case came from the young man's mother whose interview revealed much more than she apparently intended.

He has always been such a smart boy. When he was eleven years old he fixed my vacuum cleaner. He has always been handy. He always knows what to do. Of course, he makes a lot of mistakes. He spoiled the alarm clock trying to fix it and almost ruined the car when he repaired it, but I've never held these things against him. You know a child always has to be encouraged or you are apt to break their [sic] spirit. I think it is horribly unfair that he has been discharged—they'll be sorry they let so promising a man go.

Thus it appears that his mother's treatment of him and her appraisal of his abilities may have been the reason for his failure to get a balanced view of his abilities and his disabilities. Perhaps he received deserved praise for repairing the vacuum cleaner, but he was never made also to understand, apparently, that his failures revealed the limitations of his ability. He therefore did not have to pay for failures—his failures were made to look like successes. Small wonder, then, that at twenty-one he thought he could do "anything" successfully!

### A PERSON HAS MANY SELVES

We have already seen that the nucleus of attitudes which we call "the self," arise out of the estimates of one's personality which he acquires from his associates. In other words, self-attitudes consist of one's beliefs concerning his evaluation by others. Each person, however, participates in numerous groups intermittently. Persons in different groups judge him by different standards. In fact they may even judge him by opposite standards. Since the person is aware of the multiplicity of criteria through which he is being judged, his attitudes toward himself vary from group to group and from time to time. His feelings and behaviors which are based on these notions of high and low prestige also vary. A man may be timid and "self-conscious" in a classroom where he is asked to make a speech before sixteen other students, but the same man may be aggressive and self-confident when he is playing football in a stadium packed with 50,000 onlookers who intermittently acclaim and jeer him. One can say with accuracy neither that this man is timid and self-conscious nor that he is aggressive and self-confident, because he is really both, each, to be sure, in a different situation. It is not difficult to understand why the young man would show such diametrically opposite personality traits in the two situations. Although there may be several other factors involved, the difference may be accounted for by the fact that he knows approximately how he is being evaluated in the two situations. His evaluation in the classroom, as a speaker on an academic question, is made in terms of standards quite different from his evaluation by the football fans. He is probably correct in his judgments that he is superior as compared to his observers in the one situation, but inferior in the other. He measures up to standards of approval very differently, and his attitudes of self-esteem are correspondingly different. The case just discussed, while a true one, is not altogether typical. The contradictions in this case are perhaps more extreme than would be the case for most persons, but the principle is the same, namely that a person's self-attitudes reflect the appraisals of the group in which he is participating.

### ADJUSTMENTS TO LOW PRESTIGE

There are various adjustments which a person may make to the fact that he believes he has low esteem in certain groups. Low esteem is a type of dissatisfaction, since a person usually prefers high esteem. Thus any of the adjustments to frustration discussed in the preceding chapter could be utilized as defensive measures. A simpler solution, of course, is that of avoidance of the persons or groups by the standards of which he knows he does not rate. This solution is not always a ready one, however, because he may find that his participation in the group is essential. Compulsory school attendance for the child who does poorly in school is an obvious case in point. He has no choice except to go. One's family may present almost the same problem. Personality difficulties can sometimes be traced to a person's low estimate by those in his family circle.

In my profession as you know, I enjoy a very high status. My colleagues regard me as a leader and frequently refer their most difficult cases to me. You know, also, that I have received many honors for my work....

But at home it's all different. There I am just another male who compares somewhat unfavorably with the plumber, for the plumber can accomplish something which is tangible and valuable but I can't. Although the source of the difficulty is probably with my wife, my greatest humiliation comes from the way the children, influenced of course by her, think of me. They treat me fairly decently as far as the formal amenities are concerned, but it is always made clear to me in dozens of subtle but unmistakable ways, that I am not as useful to anybody in the family as somebody else's husband is to his. This is the reason I have considered a divorce. But, as you know, I can not drive myself to carry it out. There are too many ties and pulls to my family. That will probably result in my enduring the humiliation of rejection. I would rather rate high in the eyes of my two children than in the eyes of all the world. Instead I have the acclaim of the world and the amused condescending tolerance of my family.

There may be good reasons which would account for this husband's low prestige in his family. But that fact is outside the point under discussion. The case illustrates clearly why persons may continue to participate in group situations which continually aggravate the unpleasant feelings of rejection. Sometimes one's occupation presents a comparable problem; he knows he does not have the respect of his colleagues in his occupation, but he cannot leave the group because he is not trained in any other occupation.

### GROUP AFFILIATIONS AND SELF-FEELINGS

One may also derive self-feelings of inferiority or superiority from the position of the group with which he is identified. Groups as well as individuals enjoy high and low prestige in the evaluations of the larger society or community.

> I guess I'll never feel well adjusted in any complete sense. Now and then there are times when I feel that people see me as I am and judge me strictly on the basis of how I measure up. But most of the time people never get around to see me as I am. They see, instead, the label and that label is anything but complimentary. They don't see me as a gentleman or as a student or as a football fan or as a physicist. They see instead that I am a Jew. I was born of Jewish parents and that one fact, over which I had no control, stands in the way of my ever being really seen *as a person* by many of the people in my society.

Comparable cases could be found from the autobiographical accounts of Negroes, immigrants, American-born Japanese, and those of many other group affiliations. Group membership, however, works also in the other direction.

> I almost feel a little guilty about it, but everywhere I go I am accorded deference and treated with the greatest respect because I was a member of the —— Division. Actually I had very little to do with the heroic deeds of that outfit. But just because I was *in* it, I find myself not only decorated with hardware, but given all kinds of prestige which any guy likes if he's human.

What, then, can one conclude about the aggregate self, made up of all of the separate prestiges and statuses which a person is accorded by his several groups? Is there such a thing as a "total self" made up of all the selves from all the groups in which one participates? The answer to this question is largely a matter of how one wishes to state it. It should be obvious from the foregoing that the aggregate of one's selves contains a considerable variety of differing prestiges and very probably some downright contradictions from group to group. One could not regard the person, however, as merely an average of these varied selves, because they are not all coördinate with one another. In the case of the football player discussed above, his low status in the classroom was not of much concern to him because his football rating was so conspicuous that it completely overshadowed what he knew to be very low status in the classroom. Thus high or low status in some one group, or of a few groups to which the person attaches greater importance, may fashion his personality with but little important modification by other group evaluations. This can, of course, work both ways. The man who was accorded such low status by his family in the preceding illustration, came gradually to be a more and more generally insecure man whose inferiority feelings gradually spread to his professional life. His family evaluation was so important to him that it eventually overshadowed all of the others. For all of these reasons, then, it is difficult to determine in any general sense whether one may accurately speak of a total self, except in a purely academic and abstract sense. One can, with much greater certainty, however, speak of the multiplicity of selves, of the contrast and contradictions among the several selves, and of the way in which certain selves became predominate or subordinate in the total life-pattern of the person.

## RÔLES

It has been said that all the world is a stage and men and women merely the actors of the drama of life, speaking their parts and enacting their rôles. While this analogy is not accurate, it does contain a near-truth. In each society the standards of the prevailing culture or cultures contain patterns of behavior which are expected or required of persons in the various social positions. Thus, in our society, the man is expected to work and earn a living for his family, expected to do the physically heavier kinds of work in the home, expected to be more stoic than a woman, and expected to show deference in many "little ways" toward women in general and in special ways toward women in various relationships to him. Not all of these requirements are regarded as of equal importance. Anyone living in contemporary American society cannot avoid the expectation that he will observe the required behavior norms. Taken together they constitute a pattern of requirements, which Shakespeare probably had in mind when he likened human beings to actors in a play. These societal standards of behavior do show interesting similarities to the parts of a play. The persons carrying them out usually have little if anything to do with the original formulation of the rôles they are expected to play. True, one may take liberties with the rôle, but if he takes too many liberties he runs the risk of making interaction with other people difficult for all concerned, and also runs the risk of being regarded as "queer" or definitely immoral.

The various social rôles as we have noted earlier, fit together. The rôles of husband and wife, for example, are reciprocal. Each of the obligations imposed upon the man also impose reciprocal obligations on the woman, and when the two rôles function together there results a fairly smooth organization of activities called "family life." When the customary rôles are not followed, interaction becomes difficult because others have no way of understanding or evaluating behavior contrary to the rôle, except to conclude that it is wrong, indiscreet or, at least, eccentric.

But the analogy suggested by Shakespeare overstates the matter. He fails to point out that human beings are not mere automatons, that they fashion the rôle somewhat even while they are playing it. Each time, moreover, that the rôle passes to the next actor it has already become a difficult rôle from what it was the preceding time it passed from one person to another.

We may, then, define a *social rôle* as the *culturally defined pattern of behavior expected or required of persons in specific social positions.* It should be borne in mind that the term *behavior* as used in this definition includes, as always, both overt acts and covert behavior such as attitudes, values, and ideas. When persons in different rôles think about a given matter, their thinking may and often does differ widely. Rôles, then, provide also different "points of view."

*Ascribed and achieved rôles.* It is helpful to distinguish between two types of social rôles—*ascribed rôles* and *achieved rôles.* Some rôles are "ascribed," that is, they are assigned to a person more or less automatically by the culture of a society on the basis of his age, sex, his race or some other category into which he falls. The double standard of sex morality, for example, in which certain behavior is considered right for men but not right for women is a case in point. The person has absolutely no choice where ascribed rôles are concerned. The fact that he is male or that he is eighteen or that he is Negro automatically gives him certain rôle assignments requiring certain behavior of him and tabooing other behavior. Other rôles are "acquired," that is, the individual has some measure of choice in the matter. The rôles of husband and wife serve to illustrate this type of rôle. Presumably, a person in American society is usually not required to marry, but if he or she chooses to marry, the obligations of the husband or wife rôle immediately come into operation. With parenthood a new rôle is added. Occupational rôles also are of this type. Although it is easier to illustrate the requirements of occupational rôles in such occupations as the ministry or teaching, the same principle holds true for most occupations; aside from the actual discharge of the work duties, other auxiliary and often non-essential behavior requirements are imposed on the person such as, for example, union membership, the kind of clothes he wears, where in the community he may or may not live, and to some extent his language usages.

It is important to note, however, that the difference between ascribed and acquired rôles is not clear-cut. The assumption of choice in achieved rôles is only partially valid, because of the many societal and other factors which we know limit choice. It is highly questionable, for example, whether we are justified in saying that people who marry really choose to marry or whether they become so conditioned to marriage through living in the society, that they cannot choose not to marry. Thus, the ascription aspect of rôles is the predominant factor to be kept in mind.

Each *person participates, as a rule, in a number of different rôles,* perhaps as many different rôles *as he has group affiliations.* Thus a more or less typical man in American society plays the following rôles in the course of an ordinary week in his life: husband, father, church member, chairman of a committee to buy flowers for a sick lodge brother, member of the draft board, foreman at the plant, county golf champion, and usher at the church. Each rôle requires somewhat different behavior and each rôle carries more or less well understood privileges, obligations, and taboos. Sometimes the rôles get into each others' way. As an active church member the man is expected to attend church on Sunday morning, but as golf champion he is expected to defend his golf championship on the same Sunday morning. This could easily be further complicated by the fact that his church frowns on Sunday golf playing and his golf associates scorn churches. Or, again, even more closely related rôles may present difficulties because they require different things. Many married women with children report difficulty in managing their activities so that their husbands will regard them as good wives and their neighbors regard them as good mothers. Their husbands regard them as good wives if, for example, they go out together in the evening, but a good mother should not leave her children. So what to do?

A given person's rôles change from time to time, of course, and many persons find difficulty in learning or submitting to the requirements of their changing rôles. Many of the stock jokes in our and other societies center around the ludicrous things which people do when they are new in their rôles. The newly-weds, the newly-rich, parents with their first child, the young man on his first job, the rookie in the army, are all funny or tragic depending upon how one looks at it, but at least are conspicuous because they are having some difficulty in getting accustomed to the requirements of the rôle.

Persons do not always find it equally easy to fulfill the requirements of their various rôles. If the rôles are of the achieved type, it is sometimes possible to escape from the obligations of continued fulfillment of the rôle. But even this is not always possible in a practical sense. Some persons have found their personalities not well suited to many of the requirements of marriage and parenthood but find other aspects of marriage and parenthood quite to their liking. One can rarely choose only part of a rôle. He usually has to accept all or none. And in the case of ascribed rôles he has no choice at all. A woman may not like the behavior norms expected of her because she is a woman, but she is left no choice. One may, moreover, sometimes regret the rôle he has chosen, but often there is no escaping from the choice after it is made. In the following chapter we shall be concerned with some of the personality problems which are directly related to the inescapable necessity of playing some of the common rôles in American society.

The significance of rôles in determining the way in which people behave toward each other may perhaps be appreciated more fully through an illustration. Suppose that two men are playing as team mates on a fraternity baseball team. Here their relationship is one of more or less equality, since the positions they play are almost identical. One of the players is a physician, the other is a lawyer. Suppose that the lawyer gets injured while playing ball and for that reason becomes the physician's patient. Each then has new obligations to the other. The patient must take orders from the doctor and the doctor is responsible for the patient's health. Their status positions and resulting behavior are now entirely different because they are in different rôles. The sudden way in which events sometimes reverse rôles makes, often, for difficulties in the interaction of persons who formerly had different rôle relationships. A professor's bright pupil became his superior. Both men confessed serious discomfort in the situation, because the relationship seemed awkward, especially at first. The transition from civilian life to army life, and then back again from army life to civilian life required many extreme rôle changes in very short periods of time. While there was much joking comment about the day when one's commanding officer might have a job washing the private's car, there is also a very serious aspect to this situation. Many persons are finding and will continue to find it extremely difficult to adjust to new rôles thrust upon them by unforeseeable or uncontrollable circumstances.

*Rôles standardize behavior* in two ways: (1) by habituating the person to the requirements of the rôle as we have already seen, and (2) by selecting certain personality types for certain rôles. Sometimes it is the selection factor rather than the modification of the person's behavior which is the more important influence making for the similarities one observes among persons in the same rôle. If it is true, for example, that lawyers are more facile with verbal language, that is "smoother talkers" than scientists, one should not assume that being lawyers made them smoother talkers. They may have been attracted into the legal profession because they already were smoother talkers. Also very probably the two factors of selection and modification may work to reinforce each other, and in that way accentuate the similarities among persons in the same or similar rôles.

## SUMMARY

Each person acquires a set of attitudes concerning himself based upon the evaluations which he has reason to believe other people make of him and of his behavior. Each group contact results in a different set of evaluations and may result in very different self attitudes and feelings. These group evaluations are important factors in feelings of happiness and security.

Each society imposes upon the individual patterns of obligation which he is required to observe. These are called his social rôles. Each person normally plays many different roles intermittently and in succession, and each rôle may require different behavior of him. This presents difficulties in social adjustment. The problem is often further complicated by the enforced changing of rôles partly as a consequence of the person's choices and partly due to factors entirely beyond his control.

## SUGGESTED READINGS

Cooley, C. H., *Human Nature and The Social Order* (New York, Charles Scribner's Sons, 1902). **A**

This is the classic work regarding the self. As early as 1902 Cooley explained the nature and social genesis of the self in terms not markedly different from our understandings today.

Cooley, C. H., Angell, R. C. and Carr, L. J., *Introductory Sociology* (New York, Charles Scribner's Sons, 1933), Chapter IX. **B**

This is essentially the Cooley conception of the self somewhat simplified for textbook presentation by the junior authors.

Mead, G. H., *Mind, Self, and Society* (Chicago, University of Chicago Press, 1934). **A**

This is a splendid, though somewhat technical, treatment of the self in relation to society. Generally considered to be the outstanding contemporary work on the self (Cooley belongs to an earlier period).

Waller, Willard, *The Family: A Dynamic Interpretation* (New York, Dryden Press, 1938). **A B**

Waller's distinct contributions to the field of the family lie in his portrayal of the family rôle patterns and his emphasis upon the family as the group-genesis of the self.

Young, Kimball, *Sociology: A Study of Society and Culture* (New York, American Book Co., 1942), pp. 378-394. **B**

A good textbook statement of the leading ideas relating to the self. Summarizes Cooley, Mead, and others.

## STUDY QUESTIONS

1. Why do people have attitudes concerning their own personality?
2. Why is it difficult to be wholly objective in observing one's own personality?
3. How are self-attitudes "a social product?"
4. How do interpretations of other person's judgments influence self-attitudes? Illustrate.
5. Why are most individuals concerned over the evaluation of their personality by other people?
6. Why do a few individuals *apparently* disregard the evaluation of their personality by other people? Why may this be more apparent than actual? How does evaluation by others vary in different kinds of groups?
7. How are diverse loyalties often the cause of "eccentric" conduct?
8. How may faulty interpretations of the reactions of other people influence behavior?
9. Some people have inferiority feelings while others have superiority feelings. How do both relate to self-attitude formation? Illustrate.
10. Why do people develop different, and often antithetical, patterns of self-attitudes in different social situations?
11. Why is it often difficult to adjust to low prestige?
12. How are self-feelings of inferiority or superiority related to the position of the group with which one is identified?
13. What is the relation of inferiority and superiority feelings to one another?
14. Why is the person not merely an "average" of his selves?
15. Why is there often conflict between the different rôles of the same individual?
16. Why do people sometimes have difficulty in fulfilling the requirements of their rôles?
17. How do rôles tend to standardize behavior?

# *Chapter XIV*

## INDIVIDUALITY: TALENT AND INADEQUACY

A great deal of popular comment as well as scientific effort centers around persons who possess such extremes of behavior that they are conspicuously set apart from the run-of-the-mill or "normal" folk. Genius or talent, on the one hand, and delinquency or insanity on the other, represent marked variations in personality traits and behavior. Some of the basic understandings concerning social variants constitute the material of this chapter.

### DEVIATION

There was a time when behavior scientists used the term *abnormal* to designate the more extreme personalities and types of behavior found among persons in any society. But the word *abnormal* has taken on a secondary meaning implying disapproval and immorality in the minds of many people and is, therefore, not neutral enough to be used as a scientific term, except, perhaps, by the person who is quite familiar with the difficulties. The term *deviation* is, therefore, coming increasingly into use. Deviation means, simply, that the person or act being described varies noticeably or markedly from the ordinary norms characterizing persons in the society.

#### *Continuum of Personal Attributes*

Deviation really constitutes either more or less of some attribute or behavior in question as compared with the norm or with some other person. Since the vast majority of persons have an intelligence quotient somewhere between 90 and 110, we speak of the highly intelligent person (for example, intelligence quotient 140) or the very dull person (for example, intelligence quotient 78) both as "deviants" since both vary noticeably from the average. Almost every kind of behavior can be observed and conceived in terms of more or less of some measured attribute, when comparing the person in question to an average. Height, weight, and health are obvious illustrations. Morality, character, or prestige lend themselves quite as readily to such a conceptualization. "There is a little bad in the best of us and a little good in the worst of us" runs the adage. Obviously the difference between the best and worst is not a categorical difference, like black and white, but a difference of degree, like varying shades of gray distributed along a continuum from black to white. Psychological differences like intelligence, inferiority-superiority, moodiness, intellectual attributes like objectivity, knowledge attained or facility with language all illustrate the statistical nature of human trait variations. In regard to most attributes human beings range along a series of continuums, each one designed to measure some one attribute of the personality which is under observation.

The extremes of the continuum, of course, contain the persons and acts which attract the greatest attention because they are so conspicuously different from the rank and file. There is a mistaken tendency to think, therefore, of the extremes as being categorically different from all the rest of the group. The error lies in not recognizing that there are differences all along the line and that it is almost impossible to draw the line between adjacent persons along the continuum. The line between the "just passing" and "just barely failing" student in a class is often very hard to draw just as is the line between the just barely acceptable and just barely rejected man at the army induction station, because the differences are often negligible. But the requirements for satisfactory functioning whether in college or in the army require at least certain minimum competencies and the line is arbitrarily drawn somewhere between the acceptable and the rejected often on the basis of a "hair's breadth."

### STATISTICAL DEVIATION IS CULTURALLY DEFINED

It has recurrently been pointed out that it is the nature of culture and society to define all phenomena which humans can experience.

And so the fact of personality deviation comes to be defined in the value system of the culture of each group. The standards or criteria of evaluation are always arbitrary as seen from the outside, but easy to rationalize ethnocentrically. Deviations may be roughly grouped into those regarded as desirable and those regarded as undesirable. In general the desirable ones enhance the prestige of a person who has them and the undesirable ones lower his prestige. There is, of course, no way outside of the prejudice system of a given culture for determining which behavior items or personality characteristics are to be highly or lowly valued. In the chapter on cultural variability, as well as elsewhere, it has been repeatedly pointed out that extreme differences exist in the definitions of the same acts or of the same traits in different cultures. In some societies, for example, insane people are regarded as sacred.

The beginning student must, therefore, be extremely cautious that he *does not confuse the fact of deviation with the definition of deviation.* An admittedly extreme illustration may help to sharpen the distinction. Jesus Christ was certainly a deviant by his own claims, by the kinds of values he embodied in his daily living, and also by the records of the acts he performed. But was his deviancy good or bad, undesirable or desirable, valued highly or lowly? Obviously, it depends entirely upon whom you ask, either among his contemporaries or among yours. Hitler provides another illustration. His deviancy is obvious to almost everyone. If Germany had won the war and succeeded in diffusing its culture into the rest of the Western world, in time he would have gone down in history as one of the greatest of men. Whatever the real traits of George Washington's personality, the personal evaluation of him both by his contemporaries and by posterity was determined by the success of the American Revolution. Had it failed he probably would have been shot for the crime of treason.

In the ordinary acts of ordinary people the same principle is involved, only less dramatically. In the illustration of the sculptor's funeral discussed in a previous chapter, it was pointed out that the same traits of the same man were valued highly and lowly by the two principal groups in which he participated. By one set of standards he was a failure and by another he was a success. The same would hold true for most of the personal attributes and behaviors of almost anyone.

### DEVIATION DEVELOPS THROUGH SOCIALIZATION

Deviant behaviors and characteristics develop through socialization in the same way that conventional behaviors develop. The basic ingredients are one's original nature, his culture, and his unique experience, although, of course, the specific content of each is different from person to person. Case studies of deviant persons as well as seemingly "normal" persons reveal very clearly the large amount of accident, chance, and coincidence which have had a vital influence upon the formation of personality. It is not intended to imply that every person begins life with an original nature equally capable of normality, distinction, or failure. Basic factors like differences in intelligence and physical health, as well as many others, certainly influence the formation of personality as we have already seen. But there are always alternatives; both the original nature and the environment are multipotential, and there is no ready device for predicting the outcome precisely.

This principle may be illustrated by the following case.[1]

Old Black Point, Conn., where Willie Colepaugh was born and raised, was an "exclusive" Long Island Sound summer resort, which meant that it had a high gate at its entrance with a sign reading, "PRIVATE BEACH. NO TRESPASSING." Willie lived just outside the gate.

Inside the gate, in their sprawling mansions, lived the summer residents, carefully protected from all people whom their Old Black Point Association considered "not acceptable." The men were stockbrokers who made the three-hour trip from New York every weekend. The women were socialites who gave cocktail parties. The children were scions who were tutored all summer long.

Willie Colepaugh had a different background. His grandparents had worked as servants for Mr. Black, of the New York jewelry firm of Black, Starr and Frost. With his help they bought two summer hotels on the Point, which is 10 miles from New London, and ran them successfully. Willie's father helped around the hotels and later married one of the waitresses. When Willie's grandparents died, the hotels were sold. After that Willie's father sold fish and pottered about as an electrician but never made very much money. Then one year he died of cancer, leaving his wife, his son Willie, and his daughter Louise with a small income from the sale of the hotels. The Colepaughs were very careful with it. Willie's sister worked as a nurse. Willie raked the Old Black Point bathing beach and mowed lawns there. Most of the summer, while the other boys were playing together, Willie worked by himself. In the fall, when there was no work to be done out on the Point, he was free to play. But by then everybody else was gone.

A lot of the time Willie was lonely. So when the first summer boys started to filter back to the Point, Willie would usually look them up. He already

[1] A. B. C. Whipple, "The Education of Willie," *Life*, 18:11-12 (Jan. 22, 1945).

knew the reception he would get, but he looked them up anyway. The boys were Willie's age but they seemed older. They had a clean, well-scrubbed look. Willie was sallow and his hair was never cut right. They were educated to speak impeccable English. Willie, who had a nasal twang, said "ain't" and "gonna." They were taught to stick out their chins and say what they thought. Willie had a weak chin and his eyes seemed shifty when he talked. A few of the boys were warm and friendly to Willie but found him a dull, unattractive companion. To all the summer boys, who never thought to call him "Bill," Willie was the perfect definition of today's term: "meatball."

In the late summer afternoons the summer boys would taper off the day's activities with a game of croquet. It was usually then that Willie would appear, pick up a mallet and make aimless shots about the wickets, waiting to be invited into the game. He rarely was. After a while he went away. At the bathing beach, when Willie flopped down in the sand beside the boys, they decided to swim out to the raft. If he went along they kept swimming until he got the idea.

So Willie went back to his solitary adventures, exploring the islands around the Point and poking into abandoned fishermen's cabins. If he rowed out to Griswold's Island, the boys' favorite picnic spot, and heard noises, he knew he would not be welcome. So he would turn around, row back to the creek, tie up his boat and go home.

After a few summers of the "silent treatment" Willie kept to himself. People who had houses on the waterfront would see him in the early morning or late evening, quietly rowing his boat or picking his way over the rocks, going in no special direction and in no special hurry. Moonlight swimmers would see Willie seated on the "Big Rocks" at the bathing beach, as still as if he were a part of the stone mass. People began to say that Willie was "a little queer," that he "wasn't healthy mentally." But when the time came for the summer boys to go off to Andover and Taft and Hotchkiss, Willie's mother managed to get him into Admiral Farragut Academy on Toms River, N. J.

At the academy Willie buckled down to work. He wanted to get into Annapolis. Although the work came hard for him, he managed to keep his grades just above average. But when his schoolmates greeted him sociably and called him Bill, they found him pretty dull. He kept out of athletics. He was never in on the bull sessions or Coke parties. When he graduated, his yearbook referred to him as the "little obscure gentleman with big castles in the air."

Willie didn't get into Annapolis, but he did get into the Massachusetts Institute of Technology. At M.I.T. he even got a bid to join a fraternity and made a fresh start. But the grind was too tough for him. His marks flopped badly. Twice he was dismissed, went back to Farragut and studied some more. Both times he got back into M.I.T. But his marks stayed low. His social life was even worse. The boys at Phi Delta Theta began to see their mistake and Willie was never actually initiated in the fraternity. He began to drink too much. He became openly surly and violently anti-Semitic. He grumbled at being gypped out of his Annapolis education. Finally, in his loneliness, he went back to the seashore.

Along the waterfront of Boston Harbor, Willie wandered over the wharves and watched the ships come and go. Then one night as an adventure he visited an interned German ship. Soon he was taking candy, gum and cigarets to the crews and listening to them talk about "beautiful Germany" and the Third Reich and Adolf Hitler. Among the homesick German sailors Willie was warmly accepted. Here, suddenly for the first time, he became one of the boys. Willie's education was now complete. When he came back to the fraternity house at M.I.T. he repeated things about "beautiful Germany," and said it was an "outrage" the way the interned sailors were treated. He was expelled from M.I.T. in February of 1941.

The rest of Willie Colepaugh's history was documented by the Federal Bureau of Investigation on New Year's Day. It told how Willie drifted to Philadelphia, was arrested on a draft charge but was allowed to enter the Navy, was discharged from the Navy after four months' service because of his anti-American attitude. After that Willie shipped as a messboy to Lisbon, ducked ashore and volunteered his services to the Nazi government. In the middle of the night 55 days ago Willie came back to the U. S. in a German submarine and landed on a Maine shore very much like his lonely haunts at Old Black Point. Within 33 days he was in federal prison, faced with a military trial as a traitor to his country. Back in the town of Niantic, four miles from old Black Point, the name of Apprentice Seaman William C. Colepaugh has been rubbed from the World War II honor roll. But in his mother's deserted house, just outside the gate at Old Black Point, there is still a raveling service flag, imprinted with one star and the legend, "SERVING OUR COUNTRY."

The thoughtful person will probably note several crucial points in this case history at which the outcome could just as well have been opposite from what it was. Suppose the father had not died, suppose the family had moved away, suppose he had "made the grade" at Massachusetts Institute of Technology? Since he had to learn the attitudes, values, and rôle of being a Nazi spy, any influence which could have filled his life with a substitute interest, anywhere along the line, would have altered the final outcome radically.

The same principle holds for persons of distinction. In common parlance, they "got the breaks." Our purpose is not to enter into the age-old argument whether the "breaks" make the most of the man or whether the man makes the most of the "breaks." It is sufficient to note that most of the factors affecting a person's distinction constitute factors over which the man has no more control than Willie did over the factors which shaped his destiny. The ordinary success story well illustrates this fact. Whether the boy goes to school or borrows the books from a friend he still gets access to the books which are not of his making. If the culture did not contain the books he would never see them. Eventually our hero gets a job through which he is rewarded, but unless the society contained the job or could be induced to provide the job, our hero would have no position and achieve no distinction.

It seems unfortunate that the folklore of American society has resulted in the cultural entrenchment of numerous myths about success which simply do not square with the facts as they have been observed by students of the process. The chief error seems to lie in the neglect of the socialization factor in the development of the personality which attains the distinction or disapproval. Many people erroneously seem to assume that the behavior in question sprang full-grown from the original nature or from some one item in the total experience of the person. On the contrary, we have found that the human personality is an on-going process and learnings are built upon learnings. Every experience outcome has a potential "other" outcome if circumstances were different anywhere along the line. This does not ignore the factor of inherited differences in the original nature, but even a defective original nature has alternative potential modes of expression in actual behavior depending on the kind of culture and the kind of unique experience such a person has had.

It is well also to note that so-called "good" hereditary factors like high intelligence or physical vigor have frequently become factors in the eventual acquisition of personality deviation of a sort which is disapproved by the norms of the society.

> School was always easy for me. By just sitting around and listening to what happened I could always learn enough to pass the examinations pretty well. I never bought a textbook and never studied one single lesson throughout high school. My grades were never high but I never failed a course and my grades averaged more than satisfactory. . . . I also learned quite young that if one is smart he can outwit the ordinary suckers who are really pretty dull. Only dopes work for a living. I've never really done a day's work in my life and I don't intend to. I have always found it possible to work out some kind of a racket and you can always be sure to find some sucker who will do the work for half the gain. I live on the other half. . . . I am now 40 years old and in this scrape which will probably land me in jail. I just overstepped a little—didn't cover up too well. My lawyer tells me I won't get over four years and I may be out in two and a half for good behavior. You can bet that my behavior will be —— —— good. And the guys who sent me up will be working for me yet.

This man is certainly a deviant in several senses of the word. He is not only a criminal but he possesses basic attitudes not typical of the small city in which he lived. The testimony recorded above is part of a psychiatric interview in connection with his trial on the charge of manufacturing and selling counterfeit gasoline ration coupons during the war when gasoline was rationed. The man had made a small fortune in this and other activities which were clearly illegal, or very close to the border. His case history showed that he had a phenomenally high intelligence, that he was liked by his teachers and fellow students, and came from a respected middle-class professional family in a mid-western city. It was the consensus of opinion of the behavior scientists who worked on his case that one of the major factors in the gradual unfolding of his deviant career was his high intelligence, not that the intelligence alone would account for his becoming a criminal, but rather that his high intelligence gave him an opportunity to "get by" easily. The rest of the more normal people about him were readily fooled by his superior wit. Finally, he had developed a mode of life based upon exploitation, and even while being tried for one offense he was already making plans for his next "racket" which he planned to launch when he finished serving the penitentiary sentence for this one. It may be interesting to note that while the man's case was pending, much persuasion and some pressure was brought upon the court by several prominent and respectable people who expressed the view that "this fine man could not possibly have been involved" in such criminal practices as those for which he was being tried. He had been intelligent enough to handle his "public relations" very well.

*There is no trait or group of traits in the original nature and no social situation which one can be certain will result in any particular outcome for an individual person.* There is evidence, to be sure, that certain kinds of situations have *greater probability* of producing deviants than others, but there is *no certainty in the individual case.* It can not be determined in advance precisely how original nature traits, culture, and unique experience will interact to fashion the particular human being.

## WHAT MAKES FOR DISTINCTION?

### *The Factor of Intelligence*

One of the factors frequently involved in the approved forms of deviancy called talent, genius, greatness, and distinction is high general intelligence which, of course, is original nature. The possession of high intelligence as we have seen in the above discussion does not by any means insure success. However intelligent a person may be, he still must learn what the culture requires him to know and to do, and usually before the talented person is able to demonstrate any unusual competence he must undergo a great deal of preliminary learning.

There are many reasons why a *person of high intelligence may fail to achieve distinction.* His health may be impaired so that he does not feel well enough to learn at a rate which maintains his interest and feelings of success. This is especially important in the group type of learning which we find in the public school, where once a person "gets behind" it may be almost impossible for him every really to "catch up." One's "spirit may break" under the strain. The potentially talented person, moreover, may achieve no eventual distinction at all because he does not have opportunity to participate in the culture which might train his intelligence to the place where it could be useful. Poverty of one's family is a case in point. Lack of interest or realization of the child's potentials for greatness by parents may also have the same eventual effect. Many potentially talented children are often misguided by parents, teachers, and friends so that the wrong kind of education is attempted, then fails, and both the child and the interested adults conclude that he does not have ability, when actually he does have ability but of a different kind than was presumed. Lack of interest in training one's intelligence is another factor. Emotional complications such as unhappy relationships with teachers or fellow students may discourage an able person from training his abilities.

### *Special Aptitudes*

Lay people tend to exaggerate the extent to which special kinds of achievement really exist. Psychological research has clearly indicated that most of what pass as "special inherited abilities" are not really inherited at all, but rather are the result of special interests which the person acquires in the course of his socialization and then cultivates and develops in ways which ordinarily escape notice. The basic general intelligence which is biologically "given" is capable of a vast variety of uses. When persons of superior intelligence say that they have "never been good at mathematics" or "cannot learn history" they really are giving voice not so much to their biological mental deficiency for these learnings, but rather to other factors like interest and unique experience which created a dislike for history and mathematics, and a consequent cumulative decline in learning results in these areas.

*Motivation*

It is also clear that average or only slightly superior native intelligence may enable a person to achieve distinction if he is strongly motivated along certain lines. Concentration of effort, so far as the apparent results are concerned, can easily be mistaken for unusual intelligence. Particularly when the task is not especially involved, that is, does not involve the use of varied and profound mental operation, a person may achieve somewhat conspicuous success merely by long and concentrated effort. Sometimes an extremely stimulating situation may contribute to such concentration, such as strong rivalries between persons. Thus there may easily be an illusion of high talent when the real factors are merely minuteness of specialization and/or unusual effort.

*Specialized Culture Norms*

Sometimes "talent" requires no unusual mental endowment at all. Often a person attains distinction merely because of some current faddish exaggeration on some specific attribute which his personality includes. Thus at least one woman, for example, has attained national distinction primarily because she possesses a shapely body and apparently has no serious objections to disrobing in public, if the professional fees for so doing are large enough. Box offices have collected millions on the basis of her "personal" appeal. Another one secured comparable fame through a dance in which she was "attired" in nothing but a fan. Similarly, certain "artists," musicians, and other entertainers may derive their distinction almost solely from some very specialized ability which happens to catch the public fancy but requires no outstanding intelligence to exercise it successfully.

*The Factor of Timing*

Much greatness also is a result simply of a fortunate coincidence between the "man and the moment." There are particularly ripe periods for the appearance of some ability which results in a person's attaining fame. Had he or someone else possessed the same trait or created the same object a few years earlier or a few years later, either mediocre success or complete failure would probably be the result. For example, a politician with the ideas of President Roosevelt could not possibly have gotten a chance to put his ideas into effect ten years earlier, because a man openly expressing President Roosevelt's ideas ten years earlier could not have been elected president. Some tried and were hopelessly defeated. Greatness is very often relative to the happy combination—almost accidental—of a particular period of time and a particular personal attribute or ability. Greater persons at other times, so far as the traits in question are concerned, pass unnoticed.

It is not to be assumed from the foregoing discussion that the person involved is merely a passive agent waiting docilely for "the moment" to carry him to heights of societal approval. The person of distinction, while he cannot make the moment ripe for the acceptance for his contribution, can influence the moment to some extent and may need considerable ability to know when the right moment has arrived. These abilities which influence acceptance and the judgment as to when to seize opportunities are themselves, of course, subject to the various principles pertaining to learning which we have already discussed. Much trial and error is involved, the successful person being the one whose trials were rightly timed. The failures are seldom recalled.

## DISAPPROVED DEVIANCY

### *Personal Responsibility*

Many persons fail to measure up to the minimum standards required by the society and are, therefore, more or less conspicuous for their limitations. The criminal, the poor, the mentally defective, the insane, the sick and physically handicapped, the eccentric, and the "unpopular" are all obvious cases in point. In common parlance, some of the inadequacies are presumed to be the person's "faults," like crime, while others are presumed not to be the person's fault, like illness. Objective examination of the facts, however, readily reveals that in numerous instances these assumptions completely break down. Some criminals may commit criminal acts as a result of a chain of circumstances over which they have had no real opportunities to exert control. Likewise persons who are ill or physically handicapped may have become so because of their "willful disregard" for health and safety rules which they understood but "chose" to violate. The better acquainted one becomes with the environmental forces which operate through culture and unique experience, the less inclined he is to speak glibly about a person's "responsibility" for either his inadequacies or his distinctions.

It is not meant to deny that humans are not in some measure responsible for their acts but rather that there are many factors which so operate as to turn what are wise choices at one time, into unwise choices as events develop. Moreover, in the operation of choice a person can only use the knowledges which have come to him through the culture he has contacted, and these knowledges may quite as easily be incorrect as correct. For example, less than two hundred years ago juries sat in American courts and passed judgments indicating that certain of their neighbors were "bewitched" and some persons were put to death or imprisoned for the crime of witchcraft. Yet these persons, both the witches and the jurors, had no real opportunity to choose to behave on the basis of any knowledge other than the knowledge they had. (It appears probable, incidentally, that the persons charged with "witchery" would today be considered as simply "mentally ill" and would be regarded as fit subjects for hospitalization, not for penitentiaries.)

*Cultural Limitations on Knowledge of Causes*

One does not need to go far back into history to find illustrations of this principle. In the ordinary day-to-day choices of ordinary persons, it will readily be observed that they make "unwise" choices not because they wish to do so but because they reason incorrectly or have never been exposed to more correct knowledge pertaining to the choice in question. Frequently, also, there is no clear-cut issue of correctness and incorrectness, the choice being made on the basis of a point of view, or of a principle, which is not capable of objective testing. Yet on that choice may possibly hinge the whole future rôle and status of the person. By and large, it is best not to make assumptions as to the controllability of a deviant act or pattern of behavior, because one really seldom can be certain that the person involved actually had any real opportunity to control the outcome. It is, of course, a favorite pastime of people to gossip about the errors and the wisdoms of their acquaintances as they work out their lives. Rarely is it possible for the layman to know enough about the facts that are involved to arrive at much more than a crude guess as to what "caused" what, to what extent the person actually had any *real* opportunity to make a choice other than the choice he made, or to alter the course of events which subsequently unfolded.

## TYPES OF PERSONAL INADEQUACY

In the past behavior scientists have been more interested than they are at present in working out general classifications of personal inadequacy. "Defectives, dependents, and delinquents" was a threefold classification frequently found in the early books. *Dependents* were defined as those persons unable to care for themselves, such as unmarried mothers or the unemployed. *Delinquents* were the wrong-doers, who behaved counter to the laws and other mores of the society, such as criminals, prostitutes, or truants from school. *Defectives* were defined as those persons who were inadequate because they inherited or acquired some physical or mental inability which presumably made it impossible to make a living by their own efforts. Persons of low intelligence, the insane, and the crippled were put into this classification. Although there was an element of soundness in the "dependent–delinquent–defective" classification, it contributed to too many misunderstandings about the nature of inadequate people. For example, many delinquents and defectives are quite as dependent as those defined as dependent. The delinquent are often delinquent because they are defective or dependent. In other words, this classification suggested distinctions that are not wholly useful and in addition are conducive to faulty thinking about inadequate persons.

### *"Seriousness"*

Classifications on the basis of *seriousness* might also seem useful. Thus one might speak on inadequacies which were completely "incapacitating," requiring the person to be supported by someone else. Others might be termed "limiting or impeding," these being less severe cases in which the person's inadequacy constitutes a serious handicap but with a little assistance he is able to "get along."

The mild alcoholic is sometimes such a case. Finally, there is a still less serious group which does not "measure up" to social standards, but yet does not constitute as serious a problem as the two foregoing. So far as seriousness is concerned, of course, there is no satisfactory classification, because the cases differ from each other *in all degrees along a continuum* rather than falling into types, and estimates of seriousness vary by time, place, and social standards.

### *By Cause*

Classification by "cause" has long constituted a snare in which the ill-informed seem particularly insistent on becoming entangled. In the crudest form, one hears references to "born criminals," "born great," and "insane due to heredity." No person was ever born a criminal nor is any act necessarily criminal unless it is performed in a society which taboos it. No person can be born great; his greatness always depends on how he uses his original nature and how his greatness is evaluated by his fellow men. A small, in fact negligible, part of insanity is now regarded by authorities in the field to be inherited or inheritable.

A second common error in classification by cause, is the tendency to overemphasize one cause when there really are many. While it is entirely possible that some one cause may be more prominent than another or some one cause may be singled out for reasons of emphasis such as has been done in this book for instructional purposes, most careful diagnosis of inadequate persons reveal that there are *many* factors which interact to produce the outcome, not just one.

A listing of causes frequently depends entirely upon the point of view from which the case is being observed.

> Joe had been irregularly employed for eight years prior to 1932. He was not the best worker in the department nor was he the poorest. When it was necessary to lay off two or three men he was always one of those laid off.... He drank quite a little, although he never came to work drunk. He did sometimes come with a hangover which reduced his efficiency for a day or so.... Then came the depression and he was laid off in 1931 and was on public relief off and on, until the war boom. Since 1940 he has been employed full time and has earned an average of $350 a month for the past five years.

Is Joe an inadequate personality or not? Apparently he is able to make a living when the demand for labor is high but not when the demand is low. What is the cause of the limitations he has? On the basis of the evidence of this fragmentary account, one could say that he was unable to make a living for a number of years simply because he was not a good enough workman in comparison to the other men in his department. The moralist would be quick to point out that his drinking might be the cause of this low efficiency. His low efficiency may also have "driven him to drink." Finally one could conclude that the general economic condition caused him to be inadequate, because during periods of high labor demand he was able to make a liberal living. This illustrates the difficulty of classifying inadequacy by cause.

Thus there is no really satisfactory classification for personal inadequacy. For certain purposes, however, the specialist may find it useful to employ certain classificatory systems, but these are to be regarded as technical tools of the scientist, not readily usable, and possibly even dangerous, in the hands of the layman.

### SPECIFIC BEHAVIOR OR TRAITS OF ADEQUATE PERSONS MAY BE INADEQUATE

One's personality is made up of a large number of traits and behavior patterns. Everyone is deviant in some respects. A man known to the author is abnormally short, abnormally good in singing ability, has more than average capacity for lying, is over-sexed, is undernourished, and is allergic to camel hair. In all of these repects he is markedly deviant, but is a successful, in fact prominent, business man with an enviable reputation. It is obvious that several of the deviations mentioned above are handicaps to him occupationally, but they do not handicap him sufficiently to limit seriously his success. In his personal life, however, some of these deviations are somewhat more important, and probably are also related to his unpopularity on strictly personal grounds. The man's wealth and reputation, however, are such as to protect him somewhat from serious social consequences of these inadequacies.

Most persons are a unique combination of deviations from the average, some good and some bad, as judged by the standards of society. Most of them are usually not very extreme and therefore do not detract greatly from overall adequacy. Some persons are adequate to the demands of some situations, but not to others. A man may be an excellent husband and father but inadequate as a business man. Another man may reverse the two. Moreover, the *same personality traits which contribute to a person's success, in one area of his life may also contribute to his inadequacy in another area* where the demands are quite different. This is illustrated, for example, by the cases of men who made conspicuous successes in civilian life but made mediocre successes or failed completely in the army. Or, conversely, there were men who made conspicuous success in the army and poor adjustment to civilian life. It is almost inevitable that such cases would occur because of the great differences in the duties and privileges of military and civilian life. The standards for judging adequacy are certainly markedly different in many basic ways. Originality, for example, might be more readily appreciated by the boss than by the top sergeant!

Every person, then, has a number of variations in his personality, some of which facilitate and some of which impede successful group adjustment. Since the demands of groups upon the individual differ greatly, traits which are an asset in one situation may be a liability in another. The ultimate factor consists of the demands which some situation places upon one.

### PERSONAL INADEQUACY AND SOCIETAL DEMANDS

*The increasing standards of minimum competency.* It is generally held by students of human behavior that as society becomes more complex, the proportion of persons who are inadequate is increasing. This seems true in spite of our improved methods of education and our better treatment of the persons who have "broken down." This apparent increase in personal inadequacy is probably due to the increases in the kinds and number of demands which society places on a person. The standards of minimum competence are constantly being raised. Persons who could "get along" passably well as illiterates in a simple rural society of a generation ago, would be woefully helpless in the complex urban society of today, where one needs to be reasonably literate merely to move around safely in a community, not to mention being able to sell his services to an employer. The minimum standards for admission into the various professions and occupations are constantly being raised. The average housewife operates more precise machinery in an average day than a skilled workman would have access to a generation or two ago. Thus, numerous persons break down physically and mentally as well as morally in their attempts to live up to the demands placed upon them by their society. This is not entirely a modern phenomenon, of course. There probably have always been in all cultures and at all times, persons who have not found it possible or who have not wanted to fulfill the requirements set forth for them. Some

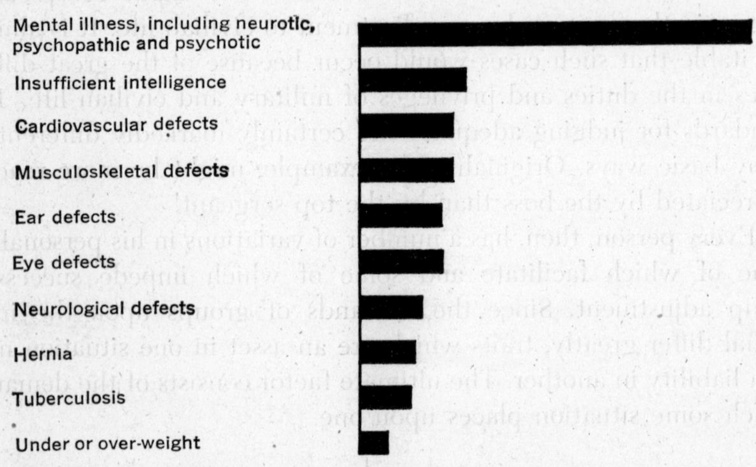


CAUSES FOR REJECTION OF 18-YEAR OLD SELECTEES, UNITED STATES, FEBRUARY-MARCH, 1944

Special Report of the Selective Service Headquarters, February-March, 1944. These figures may be taken as roughly typical of the whole period. The months taken were not abnormal ones.

persons now, as always, find that they are more able than others are to "make the grade." But the proportion seems now to be greater.

*American society is, therefore, organizing to reduce personal inadequacy.* Since everyone is affected in one way or another by the inadequacy of other persons, and never really knows when he may be inadequate himself due to factors beyond his control, there have arisen many organizations in the United States and elsewhere, to cope with personal inadequacy. Some are set up to operate on a *preventive* basis and others on a *corrective* or on an *ameliorative* basis. Hospitals and public health programs were early recognized as necessary to prevent and treat personal inadequacy due to health factors. The public school system was designed to bring the advantages of both general and vocational training to more persons than were able to afford it under the earlier system of private education. Later public education was made compulsory because it was found necessary to have a larger proportion of the total population capable of at least the minimum standards of literacy. The

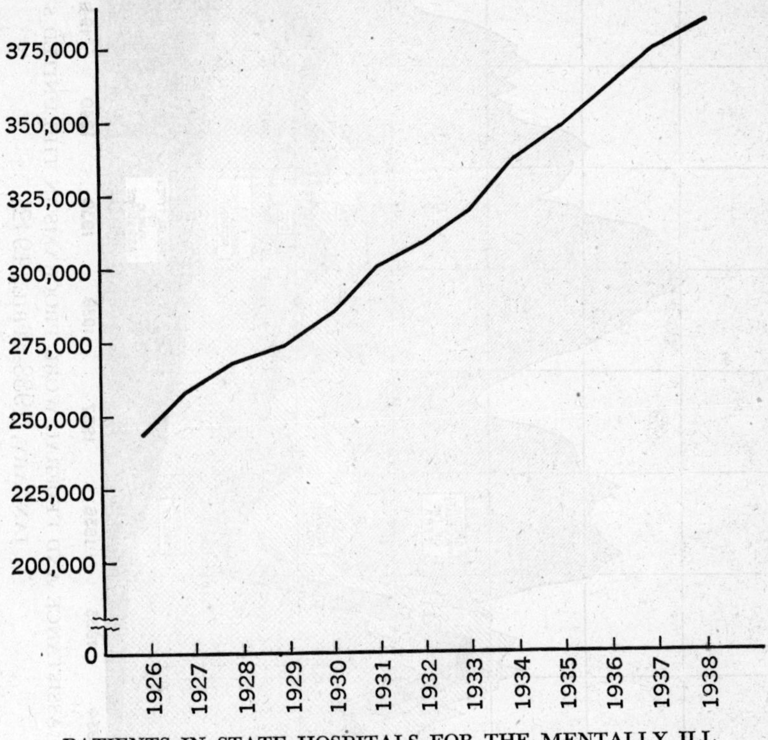


**PATIENTS IN STATE HOSPITALS FOR THE MENTALLY ILL, 1926-1939**

Taken from *Patients in Hospitals of Mental Disease*, 1937, United States Department of Commerce, Bureau of the Census, Washington, D. C., 1939. The 1938 data are probably too low. They are actually the number of cases as of December 31, 1937.

great depression of the 1930's brought to public attention the great need for setting up national programs either for reducing the instances of inadequacy or at least for reducing some of the harmful effects of inadequacy. Thus we have the Social Security system which provides insurance against unemployment and old age. Currently the Veterans' Administration has been set up and functions throughout the nation for the purpose of assisting veterans and their families in a wide variety of ways so as to prevent, if possible, their becoming inadequate or to assist them again to become ade-

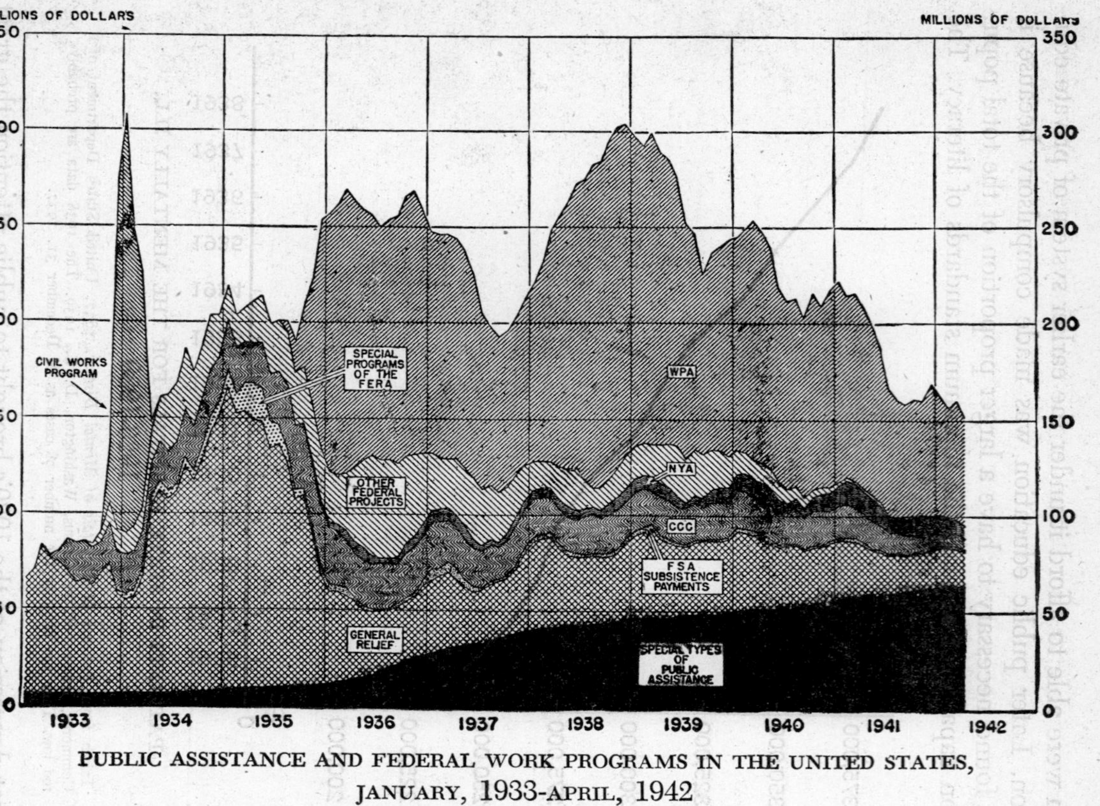


PUBLIC ASSISTANCE AND FEDERAL WORK PROGRAMS IN THE UNITED STATES, JANUARY, 1933-APRIL, 1942

*Social Security Bulletin*, Vol. 5, No. 6 (June, 1942).

quate to the demands placed upon them. For some veterans this means getting an education, for others a job, for others financial assistance, for others psychiatric service and for some medical service. In all these and many more ways, both through the government and through voluntary group action, there is being organized an impressive and growing social structure consisting of thousands of agencies designed to protect persons against influences which will lower their ability to function successfully or to correct the inadequacies after they have occurred. Even with this impressive array of organizations and professionally trained personnel, there are many cases which need assistance and do not get it. It appears that inadequate persons are being created even more rapidly than the existing agencies can reconstruct them.

*Considerable opposition has arisen* particularly against the government's entrance into this field. It is frequently argued that "so and so" achieved success or solved his problems without the assistance of any agencies and organizations. What is overlooked frequently is that "so and so" may not have needed the hospital because he did not become ill but perhaps his brother did. It was fortunate for his brother, however, that the hospital was there to serve him when he needed it. And so the critic of, say, the public supported mental illness program may not realize how soon he may himself need the services of the agency which he is now opposing. This condition is, of course, a normal one in regard to cultural change: present developments tend to be appraised by many persons through the use of criteria derived from their own limited personal experience or from a previous age during which the needs were different.

It is probable that many of the critics of expanding public agencies in the area of personal guidance and care, base their objections on some of the errors made by agencies doing such work. Mistakes are probable, if not inevitable, especially whenever a new undertaking is launched. We lack the techniques necessary to do the job more effectively. In the original stages of any new public project, error may therefore be regarded as normal. But techniques may be expected to improve as experience accumulates.

Those who *favor the expansion of governmental efforts* into this field of preventing and treating personal inadequacy, base their reasoning in part at least, on the ground of practical economy in the long run. Frequently it is possible to discover a case of personal inadequacy before it reaches a stage so crucial that greater public expenditure will follow. If, for example, a case of mild mental illness comes to the attention of the proper agency, the man may be treated and his family given a little care until the husband gets well. If the case is ignored it may not only get worse and probably take longer to treat, but may create additional difficulties to the wife and children resulting in an almost endless number of possible consequences ranging from malnutrition to juvenile delinquency. It is the modern implementation of the adage about the ounce of prevention being worth the pound of cure, or better perhaps the "stitch in time."

### SOCIAL REFORM AND PERSONAL INADEQUACY

There is, of course, another entirely different approach to solving problems of personal inadequacy. If appreciable numbers of persons are made inadequate by some social condition it might be possible to eliminate or change the condition in some way. On the surface such an approach seems relatively easy, but is actually exceedingly difficult to carry into effect. Some conditions have long been known to have important bearing on a number of different kinds of inadequacies. Slums, for example, make for bad health, juvenile delinquency, and higher death rates. But the elimination of slums cannot be done by the stroke of a pen; the problem is much more involved. It is complicated also because there are influential persons and groups in the community who, while giving lip service to programs for the elimination of slums, are not willing to make the financial sacrifices necessary to accomplish the objective.

Sometimes also the same conditions which create inadequacy also create other conditions or results which are valuable according to the prevailing standards. The big city is a case in point. Certainly the vice, crime, filth, and crowding found in the working class sections of many American cities must impair the adequacy of many personalities. But large cities also create many benefits which we are apparently unable to secure without also incurring the liabilities. And thus the cities remain.

One of the most inscrutable theoretical issues concerns the ever-present proposals for social reforms designed to increase human efficiency and/or happiness. On almost every hand some group has a program designed to change some aspect of society for the purpose of aiding some people. Opponents of such schemes are as numerous and as belligerent as are the devotees. One group sees the solution in terms of this or that piecemeal social reform which can be achieved by the passage of a law or two, requiring or prohibiting something. Another group sees the complete modification of the entire society as the only really workable and lasting adjustment. Some wish to achieve this objective by slow means, others think that only a quick and sweeping revolution can accomplish any worthy results. In the bedlam of claim and counterclaim, the voice of the objective scientist of human behavior is largely lost. If heard it is not at all clear that the social scientists' advice would be either valued or worthy. We do not know objectively, as yet, very much concerning what kind of personal attributes would grow out of some basically different social system from the one which now exists. Indictment of the inadequacy-provoking conditions of contemporary society is easy enough, and this can be done, often, with considerable objectivity. But comparable objectivity can not be attained on the precise evaluation of some allegedly "better" systems of human living.

## SUMMARY

Norms of human behavior are a fundamental part of every society. Different persons attain or observe the norms in varying degree. Thus everyone is to some extent a deviant. Deviancy is of two basic sorts; (*a*) variation from norms in the direction of superior public approval or distinction and (*b*) deviancy in the direction of disapproval or inadequacy to meet minimum social requirements.

Deviation is always defined. A given act may have high or low evaluation, depending solely on the standards of judgment of the culture at the time.

Deviation develops through socialization, through substantially the same processes as does normality or approved conduct. No trait of personality and no situation per se causes deviancy; it is always a matter of the interaction of many factors with the outcome unpredictable in the individual case.

Deviation which is favored is popularly explained by many fallacious ideas. It can be said with assurance that not all kinds of distinction require high intelligence, that high intelligence does not necessarily result in distinction, that general intelligence is a far more significant factor than the assumed special talents which people presumably inherit, and that greatness is a time matter, its ingredients lying in the moment quite as much as in the man. Personal attributes other than intelligence may contribute to "success."

The same general principles which apply to approved deviancy apply also to disapproved deviancy or inadequacy. It should be emphasized that many popular notions concerning both the causes and types of inadequacy are not tenable in the light of our scientific knowledge. Persons who are generally adequate may be inadequate in certain parts of their personality and vice versa.

It cannot be stressed too greatly that the extent and nature of personal inadequacy is largely determined by the number and kinds of demands which society places on the person. The assumed increase in the amount of personal inadequacy in present society is thus a result not of any "degeneracy" in the human being per se, but rather of an increase in the demands both physical and mental which are imposed on the person by the society.

The alarming increase in personal inadequacy in present day America is being attacked by two kinds of approaches. One approach emphasizes the individual and seeks to guide him by education and other means so as to prevent inadequacies from arising, and treating inadequacies if they do arise. This is a tremendous task and the need may be greater than our collective ability to meet it. The other approach through general social reform to remove the causes of inadequacy is a major controversy in America and has not been extensively treated in this chapter. Later chapters will be devoted to its consideration.

## SUGGESTED READINGS

BARNES, H. E., *Society in Transition* (New York, Prentice-Hall, Inc., 1939), Chapter 19, "Mental Diseases, Mental Defects, and the Rise of Mental Hygiene." **B**

A semi-popular, but essentially accurate, treatment of the subject of psychopathology. Very readable, although a bit too full of nomenclature, which is introduced and then not used.

CRISPELL, R. S., "The Bearing of Nervous and Mental Diseases on the Conservation of Marriage and the Family," *Social Forces*, XVIII, pp. 71-76. **A B**

A clear discussion of the "two-way bearing" of mental illness on the family. The family is both the cause of mental illness and one of the areas of life most vitally affected by mental illness.

DUNHAM, H. W. and FARIS, R. E. L., *Mental Disorders in Urban Areas* (Chicago, University of Chicago Press, 1939). **A B**

A study of the distribution of various kinds of severe mental illness in the urban community. The authors find that different kinds of urban areas have different kinds of mental illness patterns which characterize them. Some sociologists feel that this study does not draw the right conclusions from the facts, but for the facts at least, the study should be read.

FARIS, R. E. L., "Sociological Causes of Genius," *American Sociological Review,* V, pp. 689-700. **A B**

An examination of the phenomenon of "genius" in the light of the evidence from many sources. Conclusions support those found in this book.

LEMERT, Edwin, "Legal Commitment and Social Control," *Sociology and Social Research,* XXX, pp. 370-378. **A B**

A study of the commitment of psychotic deviants. Shows that the factors which make for commitment are not the kind or the severity of the maladjustment of the subject, but the specific social situation in which the person lives. An important contribution to the diffusion of the "real patterns" of institutionalization of mentally ill.

ROTH, W. F. and LUTON, F. H., "The Mental Health Program in Tennessee," *American Journal of Psychiatry,* Vol. 99, pp. 662-75. **A**

A study of the psychiatric "case rate" for Williamson County, Tennessee. Gives an excellent (although somewhat inadequate) conception of the frequency of "serious" mental illness and deficiency in a rural county.

## STUDY QUESTIONS

1. Why is personality deviation a relative term? Illustrate.
2. How does personality deviation depend upon the culture of a society?
3. How is the development of deviant behavior similar to the development of conventional behavior?
4. Why does man have no control over most of the factors affecting personality development?
5. Why is it impossible to predict with any high degree of certainty what kind of personality will result from a given original nature and a given social situation?
6. Why does the possession of "high" general intelligence not guarantee the achievement of distinction?
7. What part do "special inherited abilities" play in the successful attainment of goals?
8. How is motivation a factor in success? Why can it often be confused with intelligence?
9. How do "time and circumstance" often determine success or failure? Illustrate.
10. In what sense is it inaccurate to hold a person "responsible" for his behavior?

11. Why is it difficult to determine the cause, or causes, of any specific pattern of behavior?
12. What problems arise when we attempt to classify personal-inadequacy types?
13. Why is "cause" an unsatisfactory basis for the classification of personal inadequacy?
14. Why may the adequate person possess inadequate traits and still be considered a success?
15. What is the relation between the increasing complexity of society and the increasing proportion of persons who are inadequate? What difficulties are there in interpreting this causally?
16. Why and how are we attempting to reduce personal inadequacy in our society? On what basis do some people oppose collective action of this nature?
17. Why would prevention rather than alleviation and reduction of personal inadequacy be more desirable? Why is it difficult to agree upon a program of prevention?

# *Part IV*

# SOME GROUPS AND AGGREGATIONS IN MODERN SOCIETY

# Chapter XV

## GROUPS AND GROUPING

### WHAT IS A GROUP?

The term *group* is the pivotal concept of sociology. Since the word is loosely and variously used in popular language and in the language of other sciences, it is necessary to define somewhat precisely what it means in the technical nomenclature of sociology. Stated tersely, *a group is any number of human beings in reciprocal communication.* It may be well to emphasize certain aspects and implications of this short definition which beginning students, as well as some sociologists themselves, frequently overlook or do not appreciate fully. First, a group refers only to persons *in communication.* Mere physical closeness, if there is no communication, does not make a group. The communication creates the group, not the mere fact of spatial proximity of physical contact. Second, a group may be of any size from two persons to, theoretically and potentially, the entire population of the world. Third, communication need not be face-to-face or by "word of mouth"; it may be indirect through writing or at long range through such instruments as the telegraph. Persons need not "know each other personally" in order to be in communication; they merely need to contact one another via language, oral or written or gestural. Finally, the persons in a group influence each other reciprocally; one-way communication does not form a group. This, of course, does not mean that the various persons in a group influence each other equally, but merely that they influence each other. This concept of the group will perhaps become more clear when we have distinguished two other kinds of human pluralities—aggregations and categories.

*The category.* A category is a number of persons who are *thought of* together, whether they are in communication or not. Morons are a category. So also are the males 40 to 44 years of age in the population of the United States, or all the women in the United States who have failed in college. None of these are groups, as we have defined the term, because *they are not in intercommunication.*

*The aggregation.* An aggregation is a collectivity of persons who are held together in a physical sense by some factor other than intercommunication. The populations of a county or of the world are cases in point. Aggregations may, of course, be groups also, but all aggregations are not groups because the people involved may not be in interaction.

## WHY GROUPING?

Wherever humans are found, they are living in groups. The universality of human grouping has attracted attention, and several false notions have arisen claiming to explain the "reason" for groups. These errors have become so widely diffused that it seems necessary to examine them critically at the outset.

### 1. *Instinct or Learning?*

Perhaps the chief fallacy is the widespread explanation of human grouping in terms of an *inherited* "need" or "urge" or "instinct" for group activity. Evidence for this explanation is lacking. Stated tersely, modern sociology finds that grouping is practically a necessity for most people—a necessity because through their socialization they have acquired, that is, learned, wants which can be satisfied effectively only by group participation. Each person has become so dependent in so many different ways upon other people, that permanent and consistent living outside of groups is virtually unthinkable and impossible. From the birth cry to his burial, the desires of the human being are ministered to by other humans. While at times interaction with other people may not be wholly pleasant, the overall experience of his life is characterized by dependence upon other people.

2. *"Common Interest"*

A second popular fallacy pertaining to groups is the "common interest" cliché. Men are said to be found everywhere functioning in groups because they have common interests, and through group participation the common interests are satisfied. Undeniably *some* of man's interests are common, but others are individualized or specialized, while some are openly antagonistic. Observe, for example, the large number of groups found in the modern community which grow out of men's conflicts with one another. Courts, strike mediation boards, and legislative bodies are only a few of the many groups which come into existence because of conflicts among men. Other groups are made possible only by the fact of divergent, but not necessarily antagonistic, interests. The market-place, stores, banks, and schools come into being because different members of the society have different needs which can often be satisfied through interaction among persons whose interests are reciprocal. Thus, the seller and the buyer form a brief group which fulfills the need of the seller to sell and the buyer to buy. The bank provides a medium through which people who have money to lend for interest may make contact with persons having a desire to borrow money and are willing to pay interest for the privilege. Schools arise because there is a category and perhaps also a group of people (teachers) who have talents which they are willing to sell and which the pupils directly or indirectly buy. The teachers' interests are to sell their services and the students' to buy them. Thus it is readily demonstrated that the common generalization to the effect that groups are based on common interest is an oversimplification, or an exaggeration, of one factor which accounts only for the existence of *some* groups. A great many groups, possibly a majority, are based on divergent interests or antagonistic ones.

## THE PERSON AND "HIS" GROUPS

### *Group Participations Are Rôles*

In preceding chapters it has been pointed out that a major part of each personality consists of patterns of behavior called *rôles.* A person's rôles are usually numerous in modern society, and vary greatly, as a rule, from one another. Through these rôles a person's participation in groups is carried on. A personality can be conceived as a collection of group-related rôles. While some of each person's behavior may not be obviously related to any distinguishable group, most of his behavior is group oriented. Segments of John Doe's personality consist of his behavior in the rôle of Mrs. Doe's husband, first clarinet player in a dance orchestra, member of the bowling team, Chairman of the Board of Trustees of the First Congregational Church, and Mrs. Doe Sr.'s son, to mention only a few. These various group participations are, of course, not equally important to Mr. Doe, nor does he devote an equal amount of time to each of them. It is well to note also that Mr. Doe need not be actually present in a group situation in order to be participating in group-related behavior. Thus when he is practicing on his clarinet he may be quite alone, but this behavior is still related to his functioning in the rôle of first clarinet player in the orchestra.

It will also be recalled from earlier chapters that group affiliations are important in making John Doe the kind of man he is. It is likewise clear that he chooses his group affiliations, in part at least, on the basis of their congeniality with his personality. Once he begins to participate in a group, his experiences in that group become influences further affecting his personality. One should be cautious lest he lose sight of either of these processes. Both are important to a balanced understanding of the relationship of the person to his group. Persons choose to function in groups in terms of their values and needs, and once participating in a given group that group in turn influences the person's values and needs.

*Behavior Varies with Group Situations*

The visible part of John Doe's personality, that is, his overt behavior, is not the same in all of his groups. His "bowling personality" is very probably not the same as his husband personality, and both may be quite different from his church personality. This is an altogether natural outcome of his playing different rôles in each of the different instances. Somewhat distinct behavior is expected of him in each situation, and if he wishes to be favorably received by his fellows, or if he wishes to have adequate self definition, he must behave somewhere near the rôle norms prevailing in each group.

This fact of variable personality traits under varying group conditions has attracted the attention of moralists for a long time.

It has been fashionable to point out the inconsistencies in the behavior of a person from group to group, and to decry the fact that the behavior in one group does not "come up to" the standards present in another group. Thus, it is common to hear a devout churchman called a "hypocrite" when he manifests behavior in another group which differs from his behavior in church. It is not our purpose either to condone or to condemn this fact, but rather to explain why it so frequently occurs that people behave very differently from one group to another. The rôle requirements which the person encounters in each group are, simply, different.

## CLASSIFICATION OF GROUPS

Sociologists have devoted a great deal of effort to the difficult problem of classifying groups into types. At first thought this would seem easy to do, but perhaps after further reflection it will be found to present numerous difficulties. These difficulties are so great, in fact, that at present we have no overall systematic classification of groups which is entirely acceptable to all sociological scholars. That is not to deny, however, that considerable understanding of the nature of groups cannot be derived from a study of some of the attributes or characteristics of groups which might be useful in forming classifications.

### 1. *Size*

Groups vary along a continuum, one pole of which is the human pair (the smallest possible group) and the other might conceivably include all of the human inhabitants of the earth as soon as some medium for their intercommunication is devised. In other words there is no real limit to the size to which human groups may eventually reach.

### 2. *Choice*

Some group participations are compulsory. The inmate of the penitentiary, the child in school, or for that matter in his family, all represent group participations, over which no choice exists. Participation is thus said to be *non-optional* in such groups. Other group participations are seemingly matters of choice, although as has been pointed out previously, there always exist numerous *limi-*

*tations* upon a person's unrestrained or free choice of anything. Still other group participations fall somewhere between choice and outright compulsion. Thus we speak of "pressure" to belong to certain groups. Actually, then, there is a *continuum of compulsion.* At one extreme are the groups over which one has no choice at all, at the other extreme are the groups which he is free to choose or reject, and there are all gradations in between the two extremes.

3. *Duration*

Some group participations last for long periods, sometimes covering an entire lifetime. Other group participations are so temporary that one scarcely thinks of them as "group" behaviors at all.

4. *Primary and Secondary Groups*

One important distinction which sociologists have found very useful is that between "primary" and "secondary" groups.[1]

> By primary groups I mean those characterized by intimate face-to-face association and coöperation. They are primary in several senses, but chiefly in that they are fundamental in forming the social nature and ideals of the individual. The result of intimate association, psychologically, is a certain fusion of individualities in a common whole, so that one's very self, for many purposes at least, is the common life and purpose of the group. Perhaps the simplest way of describing this wholeness is by saying that it is a "we"; it involves the sort of sympathy and mutual identification for which "we" is the natural expression. One lives in the feeling of the whole and finds the chief aim of his will in that feeling.
>
> It is not to be supposed that the unity of the primary group is one of mere harmony and love. It is always a differentiated and usually a competitive unity, admitting of self-assertion and various appropriative passions; but these passions are socialized by sympathy, and come, or tend to come, under the discipline of a common spirit. The individual will be ambitious, but the chief object of his ambition will be some desired place in the thought of the others, and he will feel allegiance to common standards of service and fair play. So the boy will dispute with his fellows a place on the team, but above such disputes will place the common glory of his class and school.
>
> The most important spheres of this intimate association and coöperation—though by no means the only ones—are the family, the play-group of children, and the neighborhood or community group of elders. These are practically universal, belonging to all times and all stages of development; and are accordingly a chief basis of what is universal in human nature and human ideals.

Non-primary groups or "secondary" groups consist of forms of participation in sharp contrast to the primary groups—imperma-

[1] C. H. Cooley, *Social Organization* (New York, Charles Scribner's Sons, 1915), pp. 23-24.

nence, casualness of contact, and fewer ties of deep sentiment among the members. Primary and secondary groups are not to be thought of as two distinct categories, into one of which each and every group could be pigeon-holed. Here again we have a *continuum with poles of primariness and secondariness,* groups differing from one another not categorically, but in the *degree* to which the interacting behavior of the participants is characterized by the attributes of primariness as discussed above.

### 5. *Vertical and Horizontal Groups*

Some groups are made up of members or participants who are alike in their relation to the class system of a society. Thus a union made up of meat cutters or railroad engineers represents a relatively uniform group, the members of which have approximately the same income and approximately the same general prestige rating. Such a group would be considered *horizontal* since, as the word suggests, the persons in the group are about "on the same level" of the society. Of course the use of a geometrical term like *horizontal* to describe a societal phenomenon like class position, is not strictly apt. The license for using such a word arises from the common language usage implied in such expressions as "higher" and "lower class," people "on the same level," and so forth. *Vertical* groups, on the other hand, are groups whose members or participants include persons from a variety of different social classes. The church would be a case in point; well-to-do and poor, people of high status and low, may all be members of the church. In the vertical-horizontal distinction, as in the preceding ones, there will always occur numerous difficulties in classifying some individual group. The difficulty will disappear if one will think of the group attribute of horizontalness and verticalness as defined, and then use these concepts for comparative purposes. Thus, while the C.I.O. type of union organization is a vertical kind of union organization, the A.F.L. craft union organization is more horizontal. Both, however, are more horizontal than the Lutheran Church.

### *Groups Have Many Attributes*

Each actual group, whether a husband-wife group, the neighborhood card club, or the Republican party, could be classified somewhere along each of the above continuums. It is not of importance to determine whether the card club is a primary group *or* an optional group *or* a horizontal group. It may be all three. Moreover, it is also a relatively temporary group, and a relatively small group. The card club could, however, be compared with the Republican party in respect to each of these and other attributes. It might, then, be described as more temporary, smaller, more primary, more horizontal, and possibly more optional. And so for any comparison of any other two or more groups which one might care to make.

### *The Importance of Nomenclature*

The student should become acquainted with this nomenclature regarding groups for at least two reasons. First, each of these terms facilitates understanding of the nature of groups, because it calls attention to one or more group attributes, like primariness, permanence, verticalness, and so forth. Second, like all vocabulary, this nomenclature provides one with an economy of effort in communication. Reading and writing about sociological phenomenon is made more easy and more meaningful when the persons communicating with one another have the common understandings on which the common language is based. This is true, of course, of technical concepts in general, and the same point has also been made elsewhere in this book. It is repeated here so that the student may be reminded that the technical nomenclature just introduced is not arbitrary or "merely academic," but is functionally justifiable.

## SOME CURRENT TRENDS IN AMERICAN GROUPS

Before discussing specific groups, it is possible to take an overall view of the general group composition of American society for the purpose of considering some of the outstanding trends in group organization and personal participation in groups.

### 1. *The Decline of Primary Groups*

While there are, of course, numerous primary groups still to be found in American society, more and more of the groups in which a person functions are of the secondary type. More important, perhaps, is the decreased amount of time being spent in primary groups and a corresponding increase in secondary types of participation.

Although this trend is more apparent in urban society, it is true throughout most of the United States in some degree.

Various interpretations are placed upon this transition. There are those who decry the trend as one having unfortunate consequences to the personality. Primary groups, it is thought, foster the virtues of loyalty to high ethical standards, devotion to common purposes, and the "we feeling." No one has ever successfully demonstrated, however, that these attributes are indispensable to human happiness or efficiency. True, life is *different* when there is less primary group participation, but is it necessarily *inferior*? All that can be objectively determined is that American society is changing in that more and more groups are becoming secondary in nature. Much of the assumed indispensability of primary groups seems to be simply conservative reaction to change. When the kind of human relationship to which one has become accustomed, and from which, therefore, he has derived much pleasure, seems to be declining, it is quite understandable that he would feel a sense of personal loss at the change. But to assert that, therefore, human life is "deteriorating" seems to be going decidedly beyond the objective facts and into subjective valuation. The evaluation of social change is an entirely legitimate function, but it should not be confused with the objective reporting of the facts. Social change normally brings with it numerous discomforts for persons who have been habituated to, and therefore prefer, the old system. Particularly during a period of transition, some persons are conspicuously aware of their own personal loss and discomforts due to the change. But one must be cautious not to assert that dire consequences for persons in general will result, merely because he has observed that he and some people encounter difficulty in their efforts to function in the new way of life. While it is quite possible that the decline of primary groups constitutes a distinct loss of irretrievable human values, at this time social science lacks the evidence to assert such as fact.

### 2. *Increasing Casualness of Group Contact*

In modern life, especially in the larger cities, a person is really not known *as a person* by the other participants in many, if not most, of his groups. Only a fragment, and often a very small fragment, of his personality is known and reacted to by his associates. One neither knows nor needs to know anything more about the man who sells him a suit or drives the bus or serves as his boss or runs the movie projector in his favorite theatre, save the one objective fact that this person does his job sufficiently well to meet the others' wishes or needs. One neither knows nor needs to know anything more about him. Numerous persons in one's group experience, then, associate merely as *functionaries,* not as persons. The word *functionary* is employed because it seems to suggest that the only matter of consequence to the participants in many secondary groups is how well the functions which the other person is supposed to carry out are actually carried out by him. Perhaps the bus driver neglects his wife, causes trouble among his in-laws, and has "stupid views" on politics. In a vague sense, perhaps, one might prefer that the bus driver was a different person, but he would probably not refuse to ride on the bus because of a dislike for these aspects of the driver's personality. It is sufficient that the man drive his bus, arrive on time, and make change correctly; his personal life is usually not known and even if known, is not regarded as of much consequence to the bus riders. The same applies to the bus riders as viewed by the driver.

Other secondary group contacts, though less casual than the one just discussed, still illustrate the same characteristic. Thus teachers are gradually finding it more and more possible to secure employment on the basis of their merits *as teachers* with less and less attention to the other aspects of their lives not directly related to their functioning as teachers. There was a time, for example, when a divorced woman or a person of radical political views could not possibly secure employment as a teacher, if these facts were known. In pointing out the change, it is not being overlooked that such factors as marital status and political views might be significant to the teacher's functioning as a teacher. The point is that in modern secondary society we are becoming more concerned with her ability as a teacher per se. And so with the other persons with whom one associates. We are usually in no position any longer to secure all, or even many, of the facts of the person's other group participations, and increasingly people take the position that they are irrelevant anyway. It should be borne in mind that it is still not difficult to find exceptions to this trend, especially in rural communities, in other more primary group types of society, or even in some of the more primary group aspects of urban society. The point to be noted is that these instances are becoming less and less prevalent, and thus do not in any way contradict the trend. Moreover, it must be recalled here, as in many other places in this book, that we are describing what is true; not what our personal wishes would like to have true. Thus, we are not advocating the increase of mere functionary participation in contemporary groups; we are reporting that it has occurred and that it appears still to be increasing.

### 3. *Groups Are Becoming More Specialized*

Not only individuals but groups also are becoming increasingly devoted to specific purposes and functions, and are limiting their activities primarily, if not exclusively, to these purposes. Few persons who live in a metropolitan city of minimum size (100,000) could probably designate by name one-tenth of the organized groups which are to be found in their city. This figure (10 per cent) is not entirely an estimate, but was derived from a study in which approximately 700 people were asked to name as many organized groups in their community as they could. This was checked against the list of organized groups having telephones listed in the directory of that city. Only one person came even near to 10 per cent, the majority fell far below 5 per cent. Most of them were familiar with the existence of some of the large groups or of some of the groups in which nearly everyone participated, such as his family group, school group, or those specialized groups with which he came in contact. But he was almost entirely unaware of the great mass of specialized groups permanently organized and functioning in his own community.

### 4. *Transfer of Functions from Existing Primary Groups*

These specialized groups have not all grown up because of new or even basically changed needs of people living under modern urban conditions. Many have arisen as specialized agencies concentrating on functions formerly carried on by primary groups. Thus, the family at one time supplied many of the needs of its members for which now there exist such various specialized groups as nursery schools, bakeries, laundries, diaper services, and even organized groups of "baby sitters," to mention but a few. Likewise, the functions formerly performed by the "family doctor" are now divided up among dozens of specialized kinds of medical groups working in hospitals, laboratories, and special clinics for almost every organ in the body, each organization having some specialized sort of function for meeting the health needs of the person. It is probable, of course, that the opportunity is thus provided for better health for many people, but the kind of group interaction characterized by the family doctor and his patients is slowly but surely declining, and in its place are arising these specialized groups in which a person participates more or less "as a number," participates perhaps a few times in a lifetime or maybe not at all. The same principle operates in almost every area of a person's life, and is one of the inescapable facts about modern society.

5. *Increasing Complexity of Overall Community Structure*

With the ever increasing numbers and specializations of groups, comes an almost inevitable complexity of the total group structure of one's social world. One may properly inquire, in fact, what particular pattern of groups really constitutes "his" social world. Surely not all the groups in a city are participated in by anyone, and almost certainly no one participates in as much as a majority of them. But the groups, groups within groups, groups serving groups, and groups opposing groups, constitute a veritable maze of human activity. It strains almost anyone's imaginative faculties to conceive of the whole process.

There are those observers who believe that much of the apparent increase in personal inadequacy discussed in Chapter XIV is a rather direct result of the strain placed upon many persons who try to work out their life patterns in this intricate and changing maze. While one cannot be certain that this assumed causal connection is sound, it appears altogether probable that the complexity of modern living, for some people at least, has introduced a strain which they are unable to withstand successfully. Inefficiency, physical impairment, or mental inadequacy in some form seems to be a concomitant of this complexity. It may well be, however, that the observed instances of personal inadequacy which appear to be associated with group complexity are the result not so much of group complexity per se as of a period of early adjustment to a less complex and changing group structure. So many persons now living in urban areas have had rural origins, and the problem may merely be one of disorientation.

### 6. *Institutionalization*

Sociologists have coined the term *institutionalization* to describe the process of formalizing group interaction. There is a tendency for participation in most groups to become habituated and formalized into increasingly rigid rôles. Each person's behavior becomes laid out for him in specified ways, and elaborate rules and regulations exist prescribing the proper procedure for everything from securing a position to building a house. The employer-employee relationship, for example, was on a primary group basis originally. The terms of each man's employment, like wages, hours, the amount and kind of work to be done, were arrived at by direct negotiation, no one being very much concerned if each detail was not worked out precisely. Now the majority of employees in industrial establishments in America never even see their employers. They belong to unions and are represented at wage conferences by officers of the union, who in all probability they do not know personally either. The employer is likewise represented by some functionary. Eventually an elaborate wage contract is worked out, carrying numerous details stipulating the obligations and privileges, the duties and proper functions of employer and employees, which contract would require the services of a competent attorney to understand it completely.

Institutionalization is also illustrated in the organization of any typical American university. When the student presents himself for admission he must be prepared to offer numerous proofs of his qualifications to do college work. No one, it seems, takes his word for anything. He then goes, or his papers are sent, from functionary to functionary. Each term or semester he enrolls for further work he again goes through a more or less routinized procedure of deans, department heads, advisors, cashiers, and all of the various assistants which each of these various functionaries have. When he nears graduation, again the formalities come into the fore. Has he the right number of courses, hours, the right "sequences," the prescribed grades, in majors, minors, and electives, and so on and on? To the average student the whole procedure must seem both arbitrary and bewildering, and yet it appears to be necessary. Most of the rules are there for good and sufficient reasons, although sometimes even those who are supposed to know, find difficulties in understanding the rules; much less are they able to justify them. The complexity is a result of an attempt to secure efficiency of operation so that students do not get lost in the complex and specialized maze of sub-groups in the university. Under the old primary group kind of education, a student could not avoid securing some form of guidance, in case he needed it. He got it continuously and informally in the course of association with the teacher. Now he gets learning from the teacher, guidance from a guidance officer, academic guidance from the academic dean, personal guidance from the personnel dean, and occupational guidance from the occupational information officer. Each person's rôle is formally set down for him so that he and others all may know what is expected, not only of them but of the other people as well. Who occupies a given rôle does not make much difference so long as the rôle incumbent, whoever he is, is competent and discharges the functions of the rôle more or less as prescribed. The rôles are often more lasting than the specific incumbents who fill them.

Perhaps the Army and Navy carry institutionalization of rôles to the most extreme form. In military organization every one almost invariably knows precisely where he belongs in the hierarchy of rank, and knows exactly what his rights and duties are in relation to everyone with whom he could possibly come in contact. The person, then, is a Captain first and John Doe secondarily. A glance at another man's insignia is all that is needed in order to know exactly the way he ought to be addressed, as well as many other things relating to the interaction with him. There is a "chain of command" perfected so that under almost any possible condition it can be determined who is in the position of authority and what his rights and limitations are. The difference between military and civilian group structure is, however, not as great as one might at first think. Many civilian groups such as large-scale industry may be institutionalized to an extent which is more than a little suggestive of the more extreme forms to be observed in the military. Likewise the group organization of the Catholic church is institutionalized quite thoroughly with a carefully worked out rôle pattern. There seems to be objective basis for concluding that one of the basic trends in American groups is the extension of formal organization into groups which traditionally have been much more loosely and informally integrated.

### 7. *The Rise and Dominance of Pressure Groups*

One of the specialized types of groups which is very prominent in modern society exists for the purpose of influencing or controlling the conduct of other persons and other groups. Many groups in modern society, for example, have desires and vested interests which they try to further by influencing governmental decisions in their favor. Labor, industry, agriculture, and the professional groups each have the desire from time to time to secure governmental action or public support for or against some measure or proposal. Some management groups in industry, for example, would like to have labor's right to strike either curtailed or eliminated, while labor, on the other hand, would like to extend its power to secure greater control over the management of industry. Thus each group "puts on the pressure," so to speak, to try to secure enough public support for its point of view so that the elected government officials will have no choice but to side with them. The techniques for managing publicity campaigns are involved and costly. Billions of dollars are spent every year in paid advertising, printing of hand bills, circulars, booklets, salaries of lobbyists who try to influence government officials in various ways, speakers touring the country, and radio programs. These are only a few of the devices through which pressure groups exert their influence.

A representative type of democracy like the United States lends itself particularly well to the existence of pressure groups. Since public officials are either elected or appointed by those who are elected, they recognize that they can stay in power only so long as the "public" is satisfied or not too dissatisfied, with their decisions and actions. Thus, pressure groups strive to inflame public opinion on some issue, thus virtually forcing the officials to act in accordance with what is or appears to be "public opinion," or run the risk of defeat at the next election.

Some of the propaganda techniques of pressure groups have periodically been found by courts to be illegal, and a great many more are of dubious legality. Every trick known to the propagandist is utilized to bring about the kind of public opinion he wants. Thus, the citizen is deluged with "information," advice and assertion, claims and counter claims. Everyone's case is made to seem "convincing," and the conscientious citizen who tries to take an impartial point of view in the interest of the whole society, instead of some special group, finds it almost impossible to get the whole truth or to know what to do after he gets it. He is often in a difficult position to exert any effective influence unless he "joins up" with one side or another. Pressure groups in connection with government will be discussed in a subsequent chapter. This brief treatment has been introduced at this point, because pressure groups constitute so prominent a part of the general group structure of modern American society. Pressure groups are, thus, the instrumentalities or the agencies through which the larger groups they represent strive to win supporters for their points of view.

## SUMMARY

Groups are universal aspects of human life. Each person needs group participation because he has grown up in groups and has thus acquired wants, most of which can only be satisfied, directly or indirectly, by other persons.

Some groups are based on common interest among the participating persons, but other groups are based on the divergent interests of their members or even on antagonistic ones.

Each person participates in a variety of groups which differ in importance and predominance in his total behavior. These participations are rôles, and constitute significant segments of one's personality. Groups likewise consist of segments of the behavior of each of the participants. Behavior can therefore be conceived as readily from the point of view of the group as of the individual. Both are equally "real."

Groups may be classified on the basis of any of their attributes—size, the extent to which the participation is voluntary, the duration of the participation, the extent to which the group is "primary" and "vertical."

Several current trends in the structure of American groups were discussed, such as the decline of primary groups, the increasing casualness of group participation, functionary interaction, specialization, complexity of groups, and institutionalization. The nature and significance of pressure groups was also briefly treated, but will be discussed at greater length in the chapter on government.

Most of the rest of the book will be devoted to a somewhat more detailed analysis of each of the principal groups and group patterns making up American society.

## SUGGESTED READINGS

ANGELL, R. C., *The Integration of American Society* (New York, McGraw-Hill Book Co., 1941). **A B**

A statement of the relations between groups and the integration of a society. While Chapter III is entitled "Groups," the whole book discusses various types of groups in relation to social integration. The book should be read as a whole, however, since it is oriented around a theory of social integration which one might miss if he read only parts of the book.

BUSHEE, F. A., "Social Organizations in a Small City," *American Journal of Sociology*, LI, pp. 217-27. **B**

A study of Boulder, Colorado, for the purpose of determining the number of social organizations existing in the city and the extent of participation in them. Twenty-nine per cent of the adults belong to no group among the 268 social organizations catering to adults. Women exceed men in memberships by a ratio of 3 to 2.

COOLEY, C. H., *Social Organization* (New York, Charles Scribner's Sons, 1909), Chapters III, IV, and V. **A B**

The original statement of the primary group concept by its founder.

EUBANK, E. E., *The Concepts of Sociology* (New York, D. C. Heath, 1932), especially pp. 135-156. **A**

A careful statement of the nature of groups ("human plurels") and the problems of classification.

LUNDBERG, G. A., *Foundations of Sociology* (New York, The Macmillan Co., 1939), Chapter IX. **A**

A classification of groups by objective methods of study. Lundberg is one of the leading exponents of the use of natural science methods for studying social data. His treatment of groups is, therefore, especially important, since in the nature of the case, groups are "troublesome" matters to conceptualize. The first five pages of Lundberg's treatment are very important.

## STUDY QUESTIONS

1. Why are human groups "necessary" for most people?
2. Why is the "common interest" only a partial explanation for groups?
3. Why does a person in our society have numerous and varied roles?
4. Why would it be difficult to classify all groups into either optional or non-optional?
5. How could club membership be either primary or secondary group contact? How is this a matter of degree?
6. Are American Legion Posts vertical or horizontal groups? Why?
7. What criteria should we use in determining when the use of technical nomenclature is necessary and desirable?
8. How do sociologists interpret the "decline" of primary groups?

9. Why has there been a growth in casualness of group contacts in our society?
10. How does our present society foster the growth of specialized groups?
11. What is a possible relationship between personal inadequacy and group complexity?
12. Why has there been an increase of institutionalization in our society?
13. How are some civilian group participations similar to military institutionalization?
14. What is the function of pressure groups? Why have they developed in our society? What objectionable features do they have?
15. What is the purpose of classifying groups? What are the dangers? Illustrate.

# *Chapter XVI*

## RACE RELATIONS IN THE UNITED STATES

Race relations in the United States present an excellent example of at least two basic principles of human behavior, both of which have already been discussed and need, therefore, merely to be restated. (1) *Mistaken ideas are as real* to the person who believes them *as accurate ones are.* In other words, the firmness with which one believes something is no criterion whatsoever of its accuracy or validity. History has shown countless examples of men's willingness even to die for some idea which was based on a fundamental untruth. The belief in a "super-race" among Nazi Germans, for example, is only one of many cases in point. Much similar nonsense about race is believed very firmly by millions of Americans. (2) A second fundamental principle which is basic to understanding problems of race is the *inability and/or unwillingness of persons to be equally or comparably scientific about different aspects of the universe.* Thus we find numerous instances in which persons can be scientific and intellectually honest in the realms of chemistry, medicine, or agriculture, but utterly unscientific—if not anti-scientific—when thinking about and acting in the realms of race relations or other phases of human behavior. It is difficult to overemphasize the importance of this. Evidence of competence, or even brilliance, of a person in some scientific realm gives no assurance whatsoever that that person will show similar objective thinking ability in another realm. It is common to find persons of distinction in various fields of modern scientific endeavor who show evidence at the same time of the most unscientific ideas concerning race and race relations. A large part of the difficulty in the interaction of the races in the

United States is a direct result of the mistaken pre-scientific ideas about race which have become deeply ingrained in American culture.

In view of the foregoing it is necessary to discuss at least three separate aspects of race and race relations in the United States.

1. The latest *scientific evidence* regarding race as discovered by modern researches in the fields of biology, psychology, sociology, and anthropology.

2. The *beliefs characteristic of the non-scientific but still often quite influential Americans* on the same subjects. These beliefs are, of course, survivals from a period before scientific research on man himself was common. They represent largely pre-scientific or folk thinking.

3. The *result of the discrepancies between scientific evidence and popular belief* on the interaction of persons in the various races.

The enlightened student of race relations needs always to keep clearly in mind that the *beliefs about race* and the *facts about race* are often as opposite as the poles. Moreover, it is to be noted that the possessors of the scientific knowledge about race are relatively few in number, because the acquisition of expert knowledge in this field, as in others, is a result of careful specialized study for which many persons lack the ability, the interest, or the time necessary to enable them to master the existing facts. Meanwhile the rank and file rely on the folk "wisdom," the stereotypes, and other non-rational sources of "information" which prevail in the culture. An excellent illustration of science *versus* folklore in respect to race was brought to the fore during World War II when "blood banks" were being built up for the purpose of supplying blood plasma to injured men in the service. Negroes as well as whites volunteered to give blood for this purpose. An issue was raised by persons who feared that some of the blood contributed by Negroes might be used for wounded whites. Medical authorities testified that there was actually no difference between Negro and white blood of the same blood "type," but public pressure remained so great that the Red Cross was forced to keep the two identical bloods separate in order to appease an incensed but ignorant lay group. This example shows clearly how deep-seated prejudice patterns can result in the rejection of conflicting (but accurate) scientific knowledge and force expensive and inefficient courses of action to protect prejudice.

## RESEARCH EVIDENCE PERTAINING TO RACE

### *Race Itself*

Probably the basic popular illusion lies in the conception of race. On the basis of "common sense" observation it would appear, for example, that since Negroes are dark (often mistakenly called "black") and whites light (not really white) that a great chasm of difference separates the two groups. Actually, of course, in the sum total of physical traits of the two races, differences are negligible both in number and in extent. All of the races overlap in all of their traits, that is, one can find persons of another race who will possess traits ordinarily characteristic of some given race. For example, some whites can be found with darker skin coloring than some Negroes, and some whites can be found with higher cheek bones than some Mongoloids. What is more important is, however, the fact that careful analyses of the physical makeup of the various races show that they are virtually identical. The blood plasma, for example, of a Negro cannot be distinguished from that of a white of the same blood type. If an internal organ is taken into a laboratory for observation the physiologist has absolutely no way of determining with certainty whether the organ came from a Negro, a Mongoloid, or a white.

These facts are not in the least surprising when one recognizes the fact that there is *no pure race*, that historical and anthropological research has demonstrated that from time immemorial racial inbreeding (though not necessarily intermarriage) has occurred in most parts of the world. Moreover, there are *differences in the physical structure of the sub-groups within a given race*. Although the American Negro originally came from Africa, for example, he is no longer, on the average, like the African Negroes physically. The differences are accounted for by several facts. First there has been considerable race mixture in the United States, although very little intermarriage. This began in slave days and has extended to the present time. Some "Negroes" are so light in color that they pass for whites. They probably have more white ancestors than Negro ancestors. Moreover, the American Negro has been isolated from the diverse African Negro stocks from which he descended for a sufficient number of generations that differences are probably appearing because isolation and inbreeding are creating a somewhat different type. Irrespective of the reasons, however, the fact is clear that American Negroes and the various kinds of African Negroes are not the same. Comparable illustrations could be found among other races. The American Indians, for example, are clearly Mongoloid, but they are quite distinguishable from the Chinese, Japanese, and other Mongoloids.

Students of race history have now rather well agreed that races probably originated as a result of *mutation, isolation,* and *inbreeding.* The student will recall from his biology that a "mutation" is a somewhat markedly different specimen which appears in a species for no apparent reason, and then passes on his somewhat unusual characteristic to his offspring through heredity. In the million years or so during which man has been on the earth there has been ample opportunity for numerous mutations to have appeared. Then through isolation, due either to geographical factors or to man's self-imposed separateness from others, inbreeding among the offspring of the mutation would tend to perpetuate and magnify the original uniqueness. Differences would also come about through ordinary variation and become intensified by inbreeding. Thus, in time, the original uniqueness of the mutation or the variant could become a commonplace trait of the group. It is possible, moreover, that certain factors in the climate might have had an indirect effect upon the modification of traits since certain traits have greater survival value in certain climates. Scientists are less sure about this geographical factor than they were at one time, however.

Thus the history of each race is one of isolation and inbreeding on the one hand, and contact and outcrossing on the other. Consequently, there is small wonder that most careful scholars in recent times who have tried to discover one valid criterion for the classification of races have concluded that there is *no satisfactory single criterion for the classification of races,* because there are no pure races and because the races are so basically similar in the first place.

### *Mental Differences*

One important modern finding on race pertains to intelligence. The idea has been common in America, for example, that Negroes, as a whole, are inferior in intelligence to whites, as a whole. Superficially, it appears to many that such a conclusion is true because of the high incidence of illiteracy among Negro groups and the small number of Negroes who have attained educational and scientific distinction. A somewhat more careful analysis, however, would reveal that the problem is complicated by several important factors. First, the American Negro lives in a society dominated by whites, and has not been given an equal educational opportunity with whites. Even yet his opportunities for education are limited throughout most of the United States. Since, then, Negroes are not given the same opportunities to develop their abilities that whites are, how can we determine whether or not they have comparable inborn capacity for learning, that is, comparable intelligence? There is, basically, only one way to answer this vital question. A group of Negroes and a group of whites must be given the same opportunities for learning and then at intervals both groups can be tested. If differences appear, it may be assumed that those differences are inherited differences and presumably reflect the difference between the two race groups. Even this is not as easy to do as might be at first thought. It is not easy to find, for example, a community which has *really* given Negro children the same opportunity to develop their intelligence as white children have been given. So far as the school alone is concerned there are numerous communities with approximately equal school facilities for Negroes and whites, but it has long been known to educational experts that the pre-school and the out-of-school experience of a child has a great deal to do with the amount and kind of learning which the child acquires in school. The child, for example, who has grown up in a family which speaks precise English has a much better opportunity to learn the language arts in school than does the child in whose home there is illiteracy and the spoken language is made up of colloquialisms. In spite of the difficulty of equalizing the out-of-school experience of children of Negro and white parentage, satisfactory samples of Negroes and whites of comparable social position have been selected for research purposes. Numerous tests of such equalized groups have been made and they have *shown conclusively that there are no significant native intelligence differences between Negroes and whites when both have approximately the same opportunities to learn the kind of material found in the test*. Early studies, incidentally, which did seem to reveal differences in favor of the whites have now been entirely discredited, because the researches had usually made the error of using samples of Negro and white children whose learning experience had not been truly comparable. In recent years there have been large enough and sufficiently numerous valid tests to demonstrate conclusively the absence of differences in mental ability between Negroes and whites and also between whites and Mongolians.

*Race Prejudice*

It is undeniably true that persons of each race possess characteristic attitudes of distinctness from, if not also antagonism toward, members of other races, in short, that race prejudice exists. Although persons vary in the degree to which race prejudice is manifest, there is no denying that race prejudice is a very widespread phenomenon.

One of the significant things about race prejudice found by persons who have studied it, is that *it is not directed toward a race in general, but rather consists of a number of separate evaluations of specific social relationships.* Many persons in the North, for example, do not object to their children attending the same school with Negro children, but do object to having Negroes living in their own neighborhood. Others would accept Negro neighbors, but would object to having their children "date" Negro children. Some persons do not object to working with Negroes or having Negro servants in the home, but would bar Negroes from membership in their lodges or churches. It is significant that race prejudice, in the United States at least, does not so much object to the physical proximity of the other race. There could hardly be a closer physical relationship, for example, than that of having a colored servant, and yet such relationships are very widely practiced and are, in fact, status-enhancing practices. This fact has given rise to a useful concept in understanding human relationships. It is not limited to race, but is certainly pertinent to race. The concept is *social distance.*

*Social Distance*

Social distance refers to the attitudes of closeness or farness, acceptance or rejection, which persons have toward each other. Social distance can be measured, approximately, through an opinion scale. Such a scale might consist of a series of questions as follows:

1. Would you live in the same city with a Chinese?
2. Would you hire a Chinese as a gardener?

3. Would you hire a Chinese as a cook?
4. Would you permit your children to attend the same university which Chinese attended?
5. Would you work in an organization which employs Chinese at jobs comparable to your own?
6. Would you live in the same apartment house with a Chinese family?
7. Would you permit your son to play on an athletic team with a Chinese?
8. Would you object to your children playing with Chinese children?
9. Would you object to your children dating Chinese children?
10. Would you marry a Chinese?

Here then, is a series of questions beginning with a relationship permitting great social distance, namely, living in the same city. Succeeding questions are then roughly graduated in degree of reduced social distance, ending with what is probably regarded as the most intimate relationship, marriage. It is not to be assumed that, for example, Question 4 implies *necessarily* less social distance than Question 5 does, if both were answered "Yes." The point is that taken *as a whole* this social distance scale moves in the direction of reduced social distance. When scales of this sort are given to large numbers of people the results usually show: (1) considerable individual difference in social distance felt by various persons toward the members of some race; (2) regional-cultural differences such as those between Northern and Southern whites on Negro evaluation; and (3) approval or disapproval of races or relationships on the basis of current stereotypes, rather than on the basis of actual personal experience. In one study, for example, numerous persons indicated unwillingness to permit members of a certain race to join the churches to which they belong, and yet admitted further along in the questionnaire that they had never seen or had direct personal experience with persons of the race which they would thus ostracize.

### *Source of Race Prejudice*

A common error in thinking about race prejudice is the expressed or implied notion that it is inherited, that one "instinctively prefers his own kind" and recoils from other races. This view is clearly false according to the accumulated evidence which is now available. In the first place, there is no evidence whatsoever that an attitude pattern, like race prejudice, can come to a person through the germ plasm. Patterns of evaluation, like other attitudinal phenomena, are learned through the real and vicarious experience of the person. Moreover, specific researches have revealed such facts as the following which certainly contradict the idea of innateness of race prejudice.

1. Children—especially very young children—do not show race prejudice. Their likes and dislikes for other children are based upon criteria other than physical appearance. As children get older, of course, and learn more of the adult evaluations they take on the characteristic race prejudices of their group.

2. Different cultures have radically different patterns of race attitudes. Many American servicemen, for example, who were recently stationed in England and France, expressed great surprise that Negro men were accepted socially by the "respectable" white women of these societies. Such behavior would be rare indeed in the United States. Apparently in those cultures persons had learned radically different patterns for evaluating Negroes. Even within the United States, of course, there are considerable regional differences in the nature and extent of race prejudice. In the South where race prejudice is regarded as most categorical, it has always been a sign of distinction and high status for white families to employ Negro house servants, even trusting to them such intimate matters as the preparation of food and care of babies. Surely if there were an innate basis for race prejudice such intimate physical contact could hardly be tolerated by these genteel people.

How, then, is race prejudice explained by scholars who have studied it? First, it should be noted that race prejudice consists of a pattern of evaluation which is ingrained in the culture. Like all ideological patterns, race prejudice has a history. It can never be understood independently of its cultural history. Thus the differences by which Northerners and Southerners in the United States have traditionally evaluated Negroes cannot be separated from the differential facts of history of these two regions, including such factors as slavery, the Civil War, the Reconstruction period, and the Underground Railway. Moreover, race evaluations are not the same among all the social classes in a community. To the employer, sometimes, the Negro represents cheaper unorganized labor which may help him in the competitive struggle to produce lower cost goods. But to the white workman who must compete for jobs with the Negro, a very different evaluation of the Negro may be characteristic. He sees the Negro as a potential source of lowered wages. Yet the Negro does not prefer to work for lowered wages any more than the white man does, but is usually forced to accept inferior wages or working conditions because it has become traditional for him so to do. As this is being written the United States Senate is practically inactivated by a filibuster of Southern senators against the "Fair Employment Practices" legislation which would in some measure give equal rights to colored and white workmen doing the same work. These political leaders of the South apparently consider that a great principle is at stake, and have announced their intention of monopolizing the debate indefinitely until the fair employment legislation is withdrawn. They apparently realize that if the bill came to a vote it would pass and have, therefore, taken to the filibuster technique to prevent democratic procedure from operating. From this and many other examples, one can secure some idea of the relative importance of "keeping the Negro in his place" as compared to such other pressing American problems as the current wave of unprecedented strikes, food shortages, and a very critical housing problem.

Race prejudice, then, is accounted for like any other prejudice—tradition, false "facts" and inferences from these "facts," and rationalization all interrelated into a web of evaluations with which the person is indoctrinated in the course of his socialization. The person has no real opportunity for viewing the matter objectively, because the pressures toward conformity all tend to operate so as to keep him in line with the "right way of looking at the situation." In the next section, we shall discuss the ways in which the prejudice pattern still remains a potent factor in a society whose objective scholarship has now demonstrated that the basic assumptions underlying race prejudice are false.

## WHAT IS BELIEVED ABOUT RACE

In the foregoing section it has been shown that the various races have all been interbred at various times in man's history, and that, therefore, no race is pure, or for that matter even distinct, from any other. It was shown, moreover, that there are no inherent intelligence differences between the groups which are commonly designated as "races." Finally, the race prejudice phenomenon has been demonstrated not to be innate, but rather entirely a matter of indoctrination. *Popular belief runs contrary to all three of these demonstrable truths about race and race relations.* The phrase "popular belief" in the above sentence may easily be underestimated. As used here, it refers not merely to the less literate, obscure people in the society, but to the whole hierarchy from rich to poor, from moron to genius, with the exception only of the relatively small group familiar with modern research findings on race. Probably less than one-tenth of one per cent of the people of the United States have even had any *real opportunity to know the facts* about race. But even when these facts are presented, the great majority refuse to accept them in any practical manner. How is this unwillingness to accept the facts to be explained?

*Popular Race Prejudice Has A "Logic"*

It is not, of course, scientific logic, but it is a convincing logic. It is based upon a number of assumptions, some true, some false. It uses scientific knowledge when that knowledge seems to support the prejudice pattern, and rejects any scientific knowledge which would weaken the pattern. Such is the nature of folk "wisdom" in general, of course.

First, there is the fact that Negroes came into America as slaves. They seemed ignorant and illiterate, and by our standards they were. But they were ignorant and illiterate only because they had been *socialized in another culture* of which the controlling American whites were really ignorant. Since the whites were in a position of control, however, only one deduction was ethnocentrically possible —Negroes were an inferior people. History, moreover, records that the whites controlled the activities of Negroes in such a way as to keep them inferior. Whether white control was so intended cannot be determined, but it did have the effect of keeping the Negro an underprivileged class. In slave days, practically no Negroes were made literate and were kept working at the most menial kinds of work. They were also required to live under conditions which were certainly not conducive to high standards of cleanliness, taste, and refinement, not to mention morality. Then came the Civil War and emancipation. Since the South had fought a costly and bloody war for the principle of state's rights (mostly concerned, however, with the state's "right" to legalize slavery) it could hardly be expected to look with favor upon free Negroes. Like any persons encountering a frustration, they worked out substitutes for slavery and rationalizations for their plight. The Negroes were as unprepared for emancipation as the whites were. It is reliably recorded that some of them actually preferred to remain as slave laborers, because they had had no experience being free men. They had never played that rôle. Under unscrupulous and opportunistic "carpet bag" guidance of adventurous Northerners, Negroes were rushed into positions of government and other leadership for which they were unprepared and in which they made, and were led to make, numerous colossal mistakes. That this carpet bag régime would only serve to establish more deeply the white prejudice against the Negro was probably inevitable. There is no denying that at the time of emancipation many Negroes were ignorant, were immoral, and were lacking in the skills and techniques then characterizing the behavior of free white men as a class. Thus it was easy for the basic white rationalizations pertaining to Negroes to be made to appear very plausible. Negroes were ignorant, therefore they were incapable of learning. Few apparently inquired into the matter of opportunity, that is, whether the Negro had been given the same opportunity to learn the white man's rôles as the white man had. It was easy to use the Negro's many errors as prima facie evidence that he was an inferior species. Certainly by the end of the reconstruction period, if not before, the "Negro problem" had caused the controlling whites so much trouble that it would be only natural to assume that prejudice against Negroes was instinctive. And, thus, briefly and approximately, the basic assumptions regarding the nature of the Negroes and of the white man's relation to them became established in the South at least.

It remains now to show how these prejudice patterns became institutionalized in the American value system, how they diffused regionally and to succeeding generations.

First, it should be noted that the patterns of race prejudice just described seemed entirely "logical" and "true" to the pre-scientific folk knowledge, not only of a few decades ago, but also today. It requires a somewhat superior level of intellectual ability, for example, to understand that the lower level of performance of Negroes as a category, when compared to whites, is meaningless as a test of innate ability unless and until educational opportunities are equalized. Even when some persons grasp this general idea, they still seem unable to recognize that since both Negroes and whites "have schools" there is still a great difference in their *real* opportunities. It is difficult to understand the significance of radically poorer schools and teachers for Negro children and the effects of characteristic Negro living conditions on the total educational experiences of the Negro child. It is so much simpler to "reason" from the fact of Negro (average) inferiority to the "inherent" Negro incapacity to match the white. Besides, it is ego satisfying to be numbered among the most competent of human kind!

*Prejudice patterns come to the person by way of many channels not ordinarily recognized as related to the formation or intensification of race prejudice.* Stereotypes operate through plays, movies, jokes, and "art" in insidious ways, which, while probably not intended to create race prejudice, really do create or perpetuate race prejudice. Literature, from the child's *Black Sambo* book to his father's "Amos 'n Andy" radio program, appears to have a significant influence in the subtle but reiterated portrayal of the "fact" that Negroes are really "different people." The significant factor may lie, also, in the fact that their "differences" are usually portrayed as inferiorities as judged by current white standards of behavior, judgment, and correct English usage. The Negro is portrayed on the stage and in fiction largely as happy-go-lucky, poor, unwise in his judgments, somewhat lazy, and grossly superstitious. Even *Green Pastures* does little to suggest that Negroes are "like other people." When the Negro is portrayed as a "good Negro" he is shown in stereotyped Negro occupational rôles—cook, porter, or similar servant occupation. It should be noted that for many millions of Americans the first or at least the most intimate contact with Negroes is often the contact through such vicarious experiences as movies, reading, or "stories." One should not assume that it is necessarily any person's intent to use these media for creating race prejudice, but rather that they are perpetuated by their own momentum, so to speak, and have the effect regardless of intent, of creating and intensifying prejudice.

In time the person forgets to question—even if he at one time did—whether the stereotyped portrayals of Negroes are correct or not. Should he have doubts, he finds as he looks about him that there are clear evidences that the stereotypes are "true" because, for example, he knows "a Negro just like Andy" of the "Amos 'n Andy" radio team. He could find whites like Andy too, but he does not think of that. The powerful influence of stereotypes is in creating the unconscious impression that all, or most, or even many, Negroes are really like the stereotype. Having been indoctrinated with the stereotype one's later experience with the Negro is defined or conditioned for him. He sees what he has been conditioned to see in a complex situation, and does not see the contrary evidence because he has not been trained so to do.

### *Ambivalence*

The folk wisdom and prejudice about races which we have described is still very much in evidence, but is becoming harder for many whites to sustain. Increasingly there is evidence among whites, even among Southern whites, that there is growing awareness and sensitivity to some of the *facts* about race. Many are finding it more and more difficult to rationalize race discrimination with democratic and Christian ideals.

But, of course, there are also those to whose interest it would be to keep the existing prejudice patterns intact as long as possible. So long as Negroes are "kept in their place," Negro wages will be lower, Negroes will be less intelligent and urgent in the demands they make of their city governments, their service institutions, or as consumers. Thus the issue is perpetuated—one group working to reduce the number and intensity of conflict-evoking prejudices and other groups working, deliberately or unconsciously, to perpetuate if not intensify the antagonisms. We now turn to some of the specific issues and tensions in contemporary American race relations.

## ISSUES IN RACE RELATIONS

### *Democracy and Discrimination*

Tensions between the races in the United States and elsewhere center around a relatively few basic issues. At the risk of oversimplification, these issues may all be regarded as ramifications of the minority races' desire for democracy, for the same political, social, and economic rights and duties which whites have. One is not to assume, of course, that white society is entirely democratic. The point to be emphasized is simply that the basic issue in race relations consists of colored peoples' desire to be treated in the same way as is a white person of the same ability, the same wealth, the same education, and other comparable traits. The dominant white group has of course, already granted the Negro some measure of democracy. In many parts of the country, the Negro may vote and may even hold office. In many Northern white cities, Negro and white children attend the same schools and play on the same athletic teams. In fewer cities, they are permitted to attend the same movies and play on the same playgrounds. This democracy is, of course, very irregular and incomplete. It varies, for example, from city to city in the North. Frequently the democracy is more apparent than

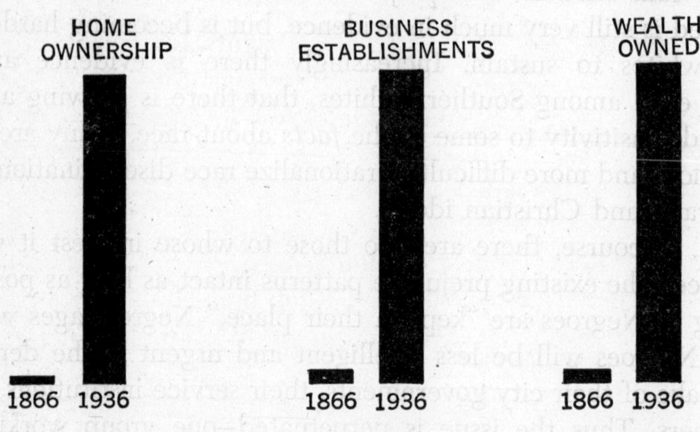


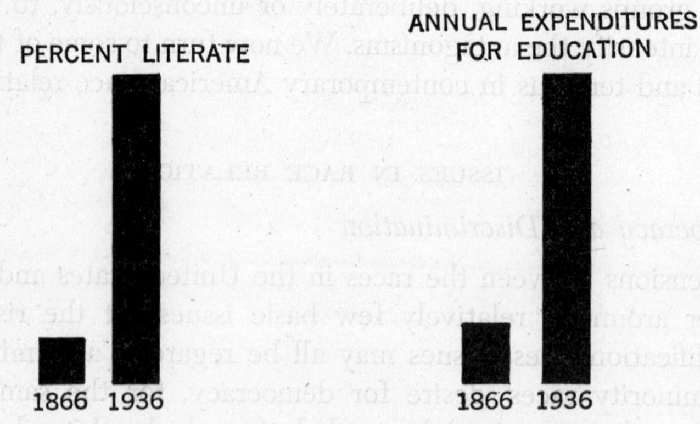


MEASURABLE PROGRESS OF THE AMERICAN NEGRO, 1886-1936

*Negro Yearbook*, 1937-38, pp. 1, 93, 210. Published at Tuskegee, Alabama.

real, that is, it appears to be democratic so long as one does not examine the facts too closely. In one city, for example, which has a large Negro population, Negro players are usually found on the high school athletic teams, but in many subtle ways pressure is brought upon the coach to keep the number of Negroes down to one or two per team even though, perhaps, there are enough Negroes who excel in the sport so that the team might even have a majority of Negro players. Thus while Negroes are not categorically rejected, they still do not have equal rights to secure recognition on the basis solely of their merit.

*Economic Aspects*

The struggle to secure comparable rights for Negroes has an important economic foundation. Negroes constitute competition for whites in whatever jobs the Negroes are permitted to enter. If the Negroes can be kept out of a given job, some whites have argued, the whites could not only be more secure in that job, but also command better wages. Whether they are right or wrong in this contention is beside the point; the significant fact is that they think so and have frequently opposed opening job opportunities for Negroes on the basis of this "logic." Employers have often thought it desirable to keep Negroes out of "white jobs" so that Negroes could be employed more cheaply at other jobs. Here again, the point of view may be sound or unsound economically, but it is widely held.

*"Fair Employment Practices"*

There are advocates, on the other hand, of granting approximately equal rights to Negroes. These persons base their argument either on moral grounds or on the "practical" ground of thereby reducing conflict in race relations. The issue has been sharpened both during the war and at present in the form of legislation under the name of "Fair Employment Practices." There is a current attempt being made to secure federal legislation requiring employers who hire large numbers of workmen to employ Negroes or other racial groups in approximate proportion to their numbers in the total population of the community from which the industry draws its employees. Moreover, the legislation would require employers to pay Negroes the same wages which are paid to whites *for the same kind and amount of work.* As this is being written it appears that the federal Fair Employment Practices legislation will be defeated without a vote due to the filibuster of some Southern senators. It will, however, almost inevitably come up again and again, and may eventually become federal law. New York State, however, already has a Fair Employment Practices law. It remains to be seen how well these state and federal laws will be enforced, what their effects on race relations will be, and whether or not they will be retained.

It should not be assumed, however, that Fair Employment Practices necessarily solve the problem of Negro job and wage discrimination. Many Negroes reside in parts of the country where public opinion would not support such federal laws even if they were enacted. Furthermore, numerous Negroes work in occupations or establishments which are not covered by Fair Employment Practice laws. Even where Fair Employment Practice laws are effective, it is still virtually impossible to override the deep-seated prejudice against Negro workmen on the part of fellow-workers and supervisors. These prejudices result in many subtle and largely uncontrollable forms of discrimination. Moreover, the Negro professional person frequently encounters difficulties which legislation can hardly correct. Negro lawyers, for example, have complained of the practical impossibility of exercising their theoretical rights to practice in court because of the widespread prejudice against them on the part of the jury, judge, and legal colleagues. They complain that Negroes patronize white lawyers because by so doing they feel they can get better "breaks" in the courts. Negro physicians, moreover, have reported difficulty in getting coöperation in securing specialist consultations, ambulance services and hospitalization for their patients. They also report that many Negroes select white physicians in order that they may have better access to these specialized services if they should need them.

*Legislation as a Means*

It remains an unanswered question whether more rapid democratic privileges for Negroes in America will be secured by approaching the matter through legislation. Some advocate legislation because it gets results more quickly. It forces everyone covered by the law to do what the law requires them to do. These people argue that if the nation waited for the slow change in attitude, decades or centuries might elapse before a more equitable solution could be worked out. The opponents argue, on the other hand, that laws are effective only in so far as there is a public opinion which will support them, and that if legislation moves too far ahead of popular thinking, ways or means of evading the law will become common and enforcement, therefore, almost impossible. These also point out that attempting to bring about social change by force may engender a great deal of ill-will against Negroes by whites who might, if given time, come around to a more democratic conception of race relations. Finally, Fair Employment Practice legislation is said to be undesirable because it tends to build up false hopes among Negroes for a quick and complete settlement of problems through law when there really is no quick and complete solution possible. The result, then, is disillusionment among Negroes and an embittered antagonism among white opponents of Fair Employment Practices. Both sides of the issue present arguments which are in some measure sound. It is exceedingly difficult to determine which point of view is correct, because not enough is known about the factors involved to enable one to assert with confidence that the legislative method is the best method. All that can be said is that under conditions of modern life more and more dependence is being placed upon legislation as a means of handling major social problems, and perhaps that this is the reason why the advocates of Fair Employment Practices have so many supporters.

### *Segregation*

But jobs and wages are not the entire issue in American race relations. The second large area of conflict concerns segregation, the requirement that Negroes live in areas set aside partly by law and mostly by illegal and unconstitutional tradition as "Negro areas." The first objection frequently raised is that the Negroes are forced to live in their segregated areas, but whites are not bound by any such requirements. Chiefly, however, the issue centers around the *kind* of living conditions prevalent in the segregated Negro areas. The lowest paid Negroes probably have living conditions somewhat comparable to the lowest paid whites, but as one ascends the scale into the income groups of the better paid, the Negro professional or business man, it becomes virtually impossible in most American cities to find the kind of comfortable housing which a family of such income wants and can afford to buy. Moreover, it is common to find poorer facilities—police protection, fire protection, parks and playgrounds—in the Negro segregated areas. Another common Negro complaint is that many of the "public" buildings, parks, and cultural centers are virtually closed to Negroes. The same holds true of the better theatres, the better restaurants, and other places of wholesome recreation.

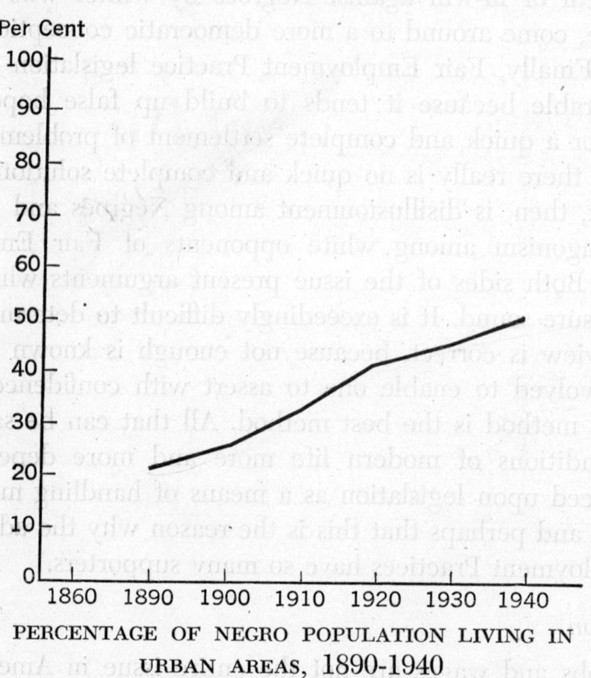


PERCENTAGE OF NEGRO POPULATION LIVING IN URBAN AREAS, 1890-1940

Data compiled from Bureau of the Census reports.

There is also a political aspect to segregation in those places where Negroes are permitted to vote and hold office. Frequently segregation works in such a way that in each voting district whites outnumber Negroes so that it becomes very difficult if not impossible for a Negro to hold an elective office. The result is that the Negro is largely unrepresented in city government or greatly underrepresented in proportion to his actual numbers in the total city population.

There is one aspect of segregation which is frequently overlooked and which has an important practical angle. Very often there is unbelievable crowding in segregated Negro areas of cities as a direct result of segregation. Perhaps at the time when the segregation pattern was started in a city, there was somewhere near ample room for the Negro population *at that time*. Meanwhile, as the Negro population increased due to large-scale migration, the boundaries of the segregated area have not been changed. Thus the same area is forced to house two or three times the number of

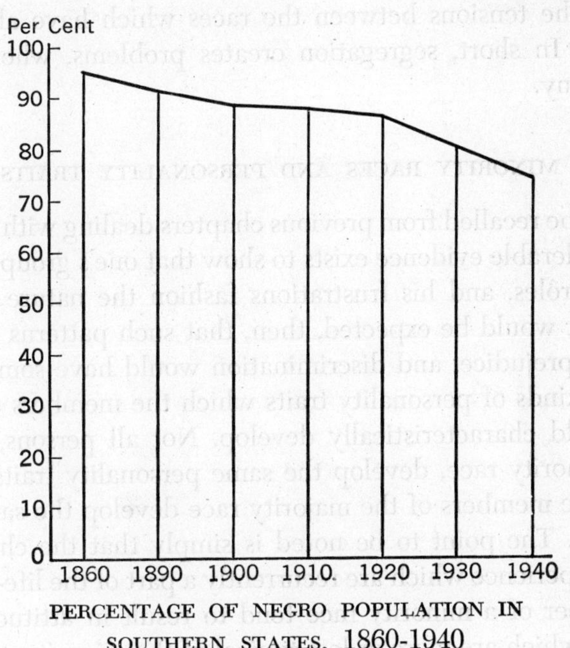


PERCENTAGE OF NEGRO POPULATION IN SOUTHERN STATES, 1860-1940

Based upon Bureau of the Census data.

persons for whom it was originally designed. Race riots in at least three large cities during the last few years have been related to this problem of inadequate room in the segregated area. There has often been a refusal or inability on the part of the city to provide for additional space to house the growing Negro population. Crowding of any population, Negro or white, is a serious condition and is closely related to many social problems varying from disease to crime.

The view is commonly held that segregation is necessary in order to reduce violence and other undesirable forms of race tension which might otherwise break out intermittently. We do not have the necessary facts to determine whether this assumption is correct or incorrect. It is probable that the pattern of segregation is sufficiently entrenched in the American way of handling race relations that any radical change from this pattern is exceedingly unlikely to be tried for some time to come. It should be clear, however, that the fact of segregation has a great deal to do with the perpetuation of many aspects of the mythology about race, and is the source of many of the tensions between the races which have already been discussed. In short, segregation creates problems, whether or not it solves any.

## MINORITY RACES AND PERSONALITY TRAITS

It will be recalled from previous chapters dealing with personality that considerable evidence exists to show that one's group affiliations, his social rôles, and his frustrations fashion the nature of his personality. It would be expected, then, that such patterns as segregation, race prejudice, and discrimination would have some influence upon the kinds of personality traits which the members of minority races would characteristically develop. Not all persons, of course, in any minority race, develop the same personality traits any more than all the members of the majority race develop the same personality traits. The point to be noted is simply that the characteristic kinds of experience which are recurrently a part of the life-experience of a member of a minority race tend to result in attitudes, values, and ideas which are more or less typical of the minority race person. Some of these recurrent personality patterns will now be discussed.

### 1. *Oppression Psychosis*

The term *oppression psychosis* aptly phrases one very common minority class reaction. It applies not only to races, but also to other minority groups such as immigrants. Once a class recognizes that it is being oppressed, that is, being discriminated against, it comes gradually to take discrimination more or less for granted. As a member of a minority class, the person expects to be discriminated against and exploited because he has had repeated experience with both. He soon learns that he is not highly regarded by the larger community and unless he is very cautious he will be "taken advantage of" in many subtle as well as obvious ways. But he *over-*

*learns the principle,* that is, *he learns to expect discrimination and oppression; even when it is really not present, he experiences it anyway.* Whites who have tried to be personally friendly with Negroes or who have tried to do generous things for Negro communities have often been met with distrust and suspicion. The Negroes have become so accustomed to being exploited that they have interpreted even good intentions and good deeds as concealed exploitation. The existence of this oppression psychosis has sometimes made it difficult if not impossible for well-meaning whites to assist colored groups or individual members of colored or other minority groups.

2. *Exaggerated Aggression*

Another characteristic personality pattern is the exaggerated militant one, characterized by such phrases as, "They won't shove *me* around," "The best defense is an offense," "I follow the Golden Rule, but I'll do it to them first," "You've got to fight for your rights." Here again, as with the oppression psychosis, it is relatively clear how such patterns can develop in a minority class. It is aware of hostile feelings from the outside, has also learned that in order to secure privileges one must fight for them, and that concessions are usually granted grudgingly and sometimes only because of a show of force. Even if no tangible results follow, many persons receive a personal satisfaction from having made a show of force, or even from only having contemplated one. Some superficial white observers of Negroes have pointed out that Negroes are "touchy" and that they seem overwilling to "make an issue." These traits are illustrative of the kind of reaction here discussed.

3. *Cowed Subservience*

There are also those in the minority group position who are quite willing to accept the inferiority assigned them, and to accept rather literally the biblical admonition not to "kick against the pricks." Thus many Negroes approach whites with undisguised and unfeigned deference, or even in a spirit of genuine humility. It is difficult to determine whether this adjustment to the bi-racial situation results from having been so often and so long "beaten down" or whether such persons are of a mild and unaggressive temperament, irrespective of the racial situation. In any event it is not difficult to find numerous instances of minority class members who appear at least to be quite willing to accept the assigned rôle without serious objection or outward evidence of resentment. In some minority groups, there have even developed a number of folkways and folklores rationalizing the disprivilege as an advantage in disguise. Among these people often it is a sign of indiscretion, if not immorality, to aspire to those privileges or behaviors or possessions which are characteristically denied to the minority but common among whites.

### OTHER ASPECTS OF RACE RELATIONS

Thus far attention has been devoted almost entirely to race relations in the United States and even then mostly to Negro-white relations, almost to the exclusion of Mongolian-white and Mongolian-Negro relations in America and to race relations throughout the vast areas of the world. The emphasis upon Negro-white relations in the United States can be justified by the numerical preponderance of Negroes over any or all of the other colored races. The principles involved, however, such as race prejudice, the false inferences about race which are commonly drawn, and the economic problems resulting are very similar in the Mongoloid-white relations (including Indian-white relations). There are, of course, notable differences, too. First, the history of each race is somewhat different. Aside from the American Indians, Mongoloids came to the United States more recently than did Negroes, and were brought or attracted here as free men, not as slaves. Orientals have, of course, also been segregated and the same general form of prejudice and the same general kinds of response to discrimination are patent. There is another historical factor which is notably different in the case of Japanese and American-born Japanese, namely, the additional problems and hatreds brought about by World War II in which Japan was one of the enemy nations. Because of the fears (largely unfounded) that among these Japanese-Americans there might be numerous Japanese secret agents, the Japanese and Japanese-born Americans living on or near the West coast were forced to leave these areas and take up temporary residence in "relocation" areas under strict supervision. Opinions have differed and still differ widely as to whether such treatment of American citizens by American citizens was either morally right or necessary. Many informed persons believe that the move to force residents into relocation centers was prompted more by hysteria than by established facts pertaining to the conduct of these people. It is at present too early to determine what the long-run effects of the relocation experience may be.

Relations between the American Indian and whites are familiar to most students of American history in some measure at least. During the earliest period of Colonial America, relations with the Indians were on the whole friendly but with a considerable amount of economic exploitation by the whites. Indian "troubles" in Colonial America were not as common or as bloody as some of the writers of juvenile history books have made them appear. With the growth of the white population and the movement westward more warfare occurred and on a larger scale. Much sentimental pity for the Indians and exaggerated accounts of the virtues of the westward-moving whites have left an historical mythology consisting of an admixture of truth and fiction from which it is difficult to extract the true account. Certainly the stereotyped portrayals of the western movie thrillers are grossly inaccurate, but probably very influential in formulating characteristic white attitudes toward Indians. Ultimately, of course, the American Indians were given certain territorial rights to the ownership of large areas of land called "reservations" where they were somewhat supervised but permitted to retain much of their original culture, taking on gradually certain of the material and non-material culture of the white man. This paternalism of the whites, plus the fact that the American Indians neither moved to the cities nor took up agriculture on any appreciable scale, has worked in the direction of reducing potential conflict between whites and Indians on anything approaching the magnitude of Negro-white conflict.

In these differences among Negro-white, Indian-white, and Oriental-white relations in the United States one finds abundant evidence of the basic principle that *it is not so much the fact of race contact but the conditions surrounding the contact which make for tensions and conflict.*

Especially when one surveys the relations among the races on a world-wide scale, it becomes even increasingly obvious that the manner in which individuals of the various races interact, the kind of cultural traditions through which they interact, are the significant factors making for peace or conflict. The mere fact of a bi- or multiracial situation in itself is of little significance. In general, as we shall see in Chapter XVII, white men from western European countries have dominated the colored peoples of the rest of the world and have exploited in varying degrees the labor of these people and the resources of the areas in which they live. For a time this exploitation was little protested, but a condition has now arisen in which the colored races are aware of the ways and the extent to which they have been exploited and are threatening in one way or another to force a "new deal." It is difficult to determine at this time to what extent these protests will be effective, or when and in what measure the white minorities who control other races will relinquish their control in time to avoid even more disastrous outbreaks of violence than have thus far occurred.

## SUMMARY

The relations among peoples of the various races constitute one of the leading social problems of this generation. This is true not only in the United States, but throughout the world. The problem is more complicated than it needs to be because of the widespread existence of false ideas on the subject of race in general and with respect to the specific races involved. Several of the more important fallacies have been discussed, and the abundant and conclusive scientific evidence against them has been reviewed. Specifically it has been shown that the basic assumption of racial uniqueness is a fallacy, that races are all interbred, that the traits of persons in each race overlap markedly with those of persons of other races, and that a few physical characteristics like skin color, have become exaggerated out of all proportion to their true significance. It was demonstrated further that race differences in mental ability (intelligence) are largely non-existent. It has also been explained why it required so long a time to discover this basic fact.

Race prejudice has been treated most fully in connection with Negro-white relations in the United States. It was shown that race prejudice is not innate, but like most attitudes is learned from experience. It was emphasized, moreover, that vicarious experience through the learning of stereotypes and the insidious influence of folklore, humor, and similar devices dominates the socialization of the person so that he eventually unconsciously conforms to the prejudice patterns of the group with which he is identified.

Race tensions in the United States center chiefly around the problem of extending the same measure of democracy to Negro groups which is ordinarily accorded to whites with the same personal, economic, and class attributes. This involves not only economic opportunities for comparable jobs and wages for Negroes, but also social democracy now largely denied through the enforced segregation of Negroes. Efforts are being made to solve these problems in various ways and sharp difference of opinion exists as to whether the more direct frontal attack through legislation is the best method or not.

Very cursory treatment of Oriental-white relations in other parts of the world concluded the chapter.

Several basic principles of race relations should be apparent from this treatment.

1. There is nothing necessarily inherent in the fact that two or more races which are in contact need necessarily be, therefore, in conflict also. Conflict or the absence of it, results from the manner in which the persons of the races involved interact, the kind of definitions they have of each other, and the kind of traditions which exist.

2. Race relations, like all human relationships change with the passing of time. Just as slavery had its day and its twilight, so also the particular forms of race relations now present, like segregation, will also probably pass out of existence eventually.

3. Race relations will be influenced for better or for worse by the kinds of policies which the two groups, but especially the dominant group, formulate and carry out. There are wise and unwise methods of handling the problem, but they are not wise or unwise per se. They can only be judged in the light of the values which one tries to attain. Thus if one wants democracy in race relations, then something perhaps along the line of Fair Employment Practices is indicated. But if one wishes to perpetuate, or institutionalize, a rigid caste-like subservient colored group, that too may be possible, in which case Fair Employment Practices is clearly "undesirable." A problem is posed, however, by those who would advocate this latter objective, namely: Is it possible for a nation to retain democratic

ideals in more than mere name, if it categorically denies democracy to one out of ten of its population?

## SUGGESTED READINGS

DOLLARD, John, *Caste and Class in a Southern Town* (New Haven, Conn., Yale University Press, 1937). **A**

A "depth study" of the class and caste system of an anonymous Southern town. The author attempts to get at the psychological rudiments of the caste system by the intensive life-history technique. Very interesting and illuminating statement of both his research methods and his findings.

EMBREE, E. R., *Brown Americans: The Story of a Tenth of the Nation* (New York, Viking Press, 1943). **A B**

A well-written "story" of the "progress" of the American Negro during recent years in terms of such criteria as increase in college enrollments, more aggressive use of citizenship rights, increase in union membership, and growth of political power. Also treats the difficulties of the Negro position in view of such conditions as segregation, educational disprivilege, and institutionalized prejudice in general.

HUMPHREY, N. D., "American Race Relations and the Caste System," *Psychiatry*, VIII, pp. 379-81. **A B**

An interpretation of American race relations in terms of the *caste* concept "because, as a scientific concept, it encompasses and contains these socio-cultural data more adequately than any other."

JOHNSON, Charles, *Growing Up in the Blackbelt*. (See bibliographic note, p. 100.)

KLINEBERG, Otto, *Race Differences* (New York, Harper and Bros., 1935). **A B**

An important volume by the man who has probably spent more time on refining the techniques for studying race differences realistically than any one else. This book should be read and pondered well by the person who thinks that there are innate differences in racial mentality!

LAING, James T., "Social Status Among Migrant Negroes," *Social Forces*, XVI, pp. 562-568. **A B**

A well-illustrated discussion of class differentiation among Negro migrant coal miners in West Virginia mining fields.

MYRDAL, Gunnar, and others, *An American Dilemma: The Negro Problem and Modern Democracy* (New York, Harper and Bros., 1944). Two volumes. **A B**

This is generally regarded as the outstanding book on race relations in the United States. It collects data from many sources and analyzes the inter-racial problem from many points of view. The author is himself not an American; thus he may be presumed to approach the problem with the prejudices of neither a Southerner nor a Northerner. Should be read by every student of America, whether interested specifically in race or not.

Reid, Ira DeA., *In a Minor Key*, American Council on Education, Washington, D. C., 1940. **B**

Abundance of accurate facts pertaining to Negroes—birth rates, death rates, crime, relief, literacy, job competition, et cetera. Compact and readable.

## STUDY QUESTIONS

1. Why are some people scientific in regard to some things but unscientific in regard to human behavior?
2. Why are there few people with scientific knowledge about race?
3. Why are there no pure races?
4. Why is it difficult to determine if there are differences in mental capacities between Negroes and whites?
5. Demonstrate that race prejudice is not directed toward "a race in general?" Show how racial prejudice consists of attitudes toward *specific* social relationships?
6. Why do people often seem "inconsistent" in regard to social distance? Is this *really* inconsistency?
7. Why is race prejudice not inherited? What proof do we have of this?
8. Do "equal" school systems for whites and Negroes guarantee equal educational opportunities? Why or why not?
9. How are stereotypes a factor in race prejudice? Illustrate.
10. What is the basic issue in race relations?
11. How is racial "democracy" often more apparent than real? Illustrate.
12. Why do whites often oppose equal job opportunities for Negroes? How do some employers use this to their advantage?
13. What special difficulties does the Negro professional person encounter?
14. How would a Fair Employment Practices Law help to eliminate racial discrimination? How might it increase prejudice?
15. Why is segregation undemocratic? How does it tend to cause racial conflict?
16. How are segregation, race prejudice, and discrimination factors in the development of personality traits? Illustrate.
17. How did World War II intensify racial antagonism between white Americans and Japanese-Americans? Was it merely the war? Explain.

# Chapter XVII

## POPULATION TRENDS AND PROBLEMS

### POPULATION AND THE FACTORS WHICH AFFECT IT

*Population and Land*

There are approximately two billion people in the world. No one knows exactly how many human beings inhabit the earth, because over large areas no census has ever been taken and we must rely, therefore, on estimates. These two billion people represent the largest population the world has ever had, so far as can now be determined. Increase has been most marked during modern times, particularly since the Industrial Revolution and the development of scientific agriculture have made it possible to support large populations on a given amount of land.

At any one time, the absolute size of the population of the world is limited by the ability of the earth at the given time to produce enough food to sustain life. In the United States, where food is normally very abundant and surpluses are the usual problem, one has little conception of the extent to which the stark reality of insufficient food is the major factor determining the number of people who may live. In many parts of Asia, notably China and India, famines occur from time to time as a result of which millions of people die from starvation. Millions more die from day to day from malnourishment and attract no more attention than those in our population who die of heart disease or pneumonia, because these causes of death are widespread and common. There is insufficient land to support the existing population in many parts of the world under the conditions of land use and modes of agriculture used there.

### *Technology*

There are several reasons why the population of some nations such as the United States is so far removed from starvation. First, the American culture possesses an elaborate technological development which enables the society to utilize many natural resources which the people of simpler cultures cannot use. Moreover, our scientific knowledge enables us to utilize the resources we have in such a way as to yield much greater results. Scientific farming is a case in point. In many crops, an acre of land can produce several times the yield of a hundred years ago. For all practical purposes, a technological culture can almost "create" land, through the drainage of swamps and the irrigation of deserts. Thus land which would ordinarily be waste land becomes capable of yielding food for human sustenance. The same principle applies in industry as in agriculture. Through man's technical knowledge, he can discover sources of energy like coal and oil to replace human effort in the production of the necessities of life.

### *Birth Control*

A second factor which enables the American population to remain far above the starvation point is the deliberate limitation of our population through the practice of birth control. Studies show that large numbers of persons practice limitation of the number of children in one way or another and with varying degrees of success. The usual reason for so doing is to enable the parents and the children they have to enjoy what is usually called "a higher standard of living." In other words, our culture contains values which result in the voluntary control of population. One is the high valuation placed upon non-essentials in the pattern of living. Strictly speaking, of course, all of the elements of a high standard of living may not be really "non-essentials." Certainly better balanced diets, better preparation of foods, better medical care, more education, could not be regarded as non-essentials by our standards. But they are non-essentials in the sense that some sort of life *could* be sustained without them, that is, a few more of us might die earlier without these protections, but the vast majority of the peoples of the world "get along" quite well without them. Most of the items in the American so-called "high standard of living," however, have not the remotest relation to physical health or longevity. Fur coats, big automobiles, expensive amusements, costly but by no means nourishing items of diet, and expensive personal adornment are cases in point. Several Chinese families could be supported on their standard of living by the money spent by the average middle class American family on its automobile alone. But this American standard of living, as anyone knows, is very highly valued. It is so highly valued in fact, that it supersedes another value, also highly held, namely, that of early and more frequent parenthood. It is very difficult to state the situation entirely accurately, however, because most people regard the limitation of the number of children as a device for securing a high standard of living for those fewer children whom they do have. In other words, quality rather than quantity of children seems to have become the greater value. To what extent this is all a common rationalization to permit a higher level of living for the parents themselves, cannot be determined and perhaps need not be for our purposes. It is sufficient to note that the deliberate reduction in the number of children born keeps the numbers of the total population somewhat reduced, and enables those who are living to have a greater share in the available necessities, comforts, and luxuries which the natural resources and the technical knowledge of the culture can produce.

### *The Factors in the Population Balance*

No one knows how large a total population the world can eventually support. That number depends upon three factors, none of which can be precisely computed but can be studied mathematically nevertheless. These factors have already been mentioned but should be analyzed further.

1. *The amount of available land.* Offhand one might think that the amount of available land could be readily determined. But man is always making land, practically speaking, by the irrigation of deserts, the drainage of swamps, and even more important, by the discovery of means whereby a given area can produce many times what it formerly did. Man is, thus, really creating land through his agricultural and engineering arts. At this time, there seems to be no discernible limit to the extent to which man can go in this extension of the resources which can be derived from the earth's surface.

2. *Knowledge concerning the use of land or "the state of the arts"* of production, as it has been termed, makes it almost impossible to determine how much sustenance can eventually be derived from existing land or the land yet to be brought under cultivation or other usage. There seems now no limit to how far man's technical knowledge can ultimately go. It cannot be stressed too strongly, however, that *at any given time both the amount of land and the state of the arts set absolute limits to the number of people who can be supported on a given area or for the entire world.* Many parts of the Orient as well as areas inhabited by primitive people with minimal standards of living represent concrete instances of these absolute limits on the size of the population.

3. *The "level of living."* Since man has learned the techniques necessary to enable him to limit his offspring, he has found it possible to enjoy a higher level of living under the existing conditions of the arts and of available land. It would be an error to conclude that, therefore, any area of the world could have a high level of living if the prevailing culture contained the knowledge and would otherwise permit the voluntary limitation of reproduction. A time element is involved. It is clear that there could, *after a reasonably short* period, exist a *higher* level of living than now prevails. Even a stationary population can secure a higher level of living in time, because the ever expanding technical knowledge creates more, better, or cheaper materials with which to increase the level of living. This gain would in fact increase the level of living if the population remained constant.

*The Three Factors Interact: Man's Fundamental Choice*

Thus we see that these three factors, the amount of available land, the state of the productive arts both in agriculture and in industry, and the level of living interact with population in a variety of ways. The interaction may be explained in this way: The available land and the state of the arts set up the available sum total of want-satisfying materials. If the population becomes larger, the level of living must be lower because the available goods and services must be divided among more people. If the population becomes smaller, the level of living can be higher. Over a longer period, of course, the existence of aspirations for a higher level of living may, as we have seen, operate in such a way as to reduce the population, and thus the available goods and services available to each person becomes greater. Much of the phenomenal advance of man's ability to produce food and other goods during the last century has been taken up by great increases in the population, but not so great as to prevent higher levels of living for much of Western civilization from also occurring. The significant fact to be noted is that man has a choice, so to speak, of what he will do with the gain in sustenance which his advancing technological arts provide him. (1) He may increase his numbers, holding his level of living the same; (2) he may increase his level of living, holding his numbers constant; or (3) he may divide the gain some way between increased numbers and increased level of living. But increased numbers or increased level of living can only come from increased sources of sustenance.

*The Individual Case: Distribution of Goods*

Thus far we have spoken largely in broad theoretical terms. Actually, the level of living enjoyed by a given person in a society is not so simply determined. According to our reasoning thus far, Henry Ford would have the same level of living as your garbage collector because both are part of the same society. The factor omitted from our discussion, then, is the factor of *individual and class distribution of the total goods and services which the total society produces.* All of the numerous factors involved in distribution make the subject an involved one and quite beyond the scope of this book. One basic fact, however, can be briefly stated: Each society through the value system of its culture contains a set of standards or criteria on the basis of which the available goods and services are distributed among the social classes and among individuals. Capitalism has one system, communism another. The system worked out for distributing the profits of the joint efforts of capital, management and labor has changed considerably with the coming of labor unions, and more recently with their increased power in determining labor's share of the total product. The prevailing class system of a society, as we shall see in a later chapter, has a great deal to do with how the share of the goods and services which make up a level of living is determined for different persons. But it must be borne in mind that no system of distribution can distribute more goods and services than the society can secure, although history records numerous examples of the coexistence of fabulously high levels of living for one class and pitifully low levels for another. But these conditions are determined by the value system and not by the population problem per se.

### *Density and Population Pressure*

Differences in population density, the number of persons per square mile, are frequently used as evidence of the overcrowding of some peoples. Density figures are frequently misleading unless one knows at least (*a*) how the population derives its sustenance, (*b*) how much of the area of the nation consists of tillable soil and how fertile the soil is, (*c*) whether the climate is favorable or unfavorable to high production, (*d*) the degree of technological progress, and (*e*) the extent to which the resident population is being exploited by absentee populations. Thus, for example, India has a population density of 195 persons per square mile while England and Wales have a population of 680 persons per square mile. Yet living conditions in most of India are almost unbelievably difficult, and famines are common. Meanwhile the English level of living is among the highest of the world. England can support the high population density which she does, because she has largely a skilled manufacturing and trading economy, this enabling the English citizen actually to draw sustenance indirectly from the land of the entire world, including India. The population of India on the other hand is forced largely to subsist on its own land, much of which is not especially fertile under the kinds of tillage and agricultural knowledge practiced by the Indian farmer. Other examples of the same principle can readily be found. Comparative density figures are valid only when climatic factors, the state of the arts, the natural resources, and the trade relations of the two societies are comparable. Otherwise they are confusing and misleading.

It should be pointed out, however, that very probably *in the long run* the advantages of certain people due to their greater scientific knowledge will tend to decline if not to disappear, because under modern conditions of communication scientific and technological secrets are hard to keep. This means, among other implications, that nations in western Europe and America are likely to find greater and greater difficulty in trying to maintain their present higher living standards in the future. Asia is "getting wise."

### POPULATION DISTRIBUTION: GEOGRAPHICAL

The two billion people which inhabit the earth are distributed very unevenly. Over one half of all of the people of the world live in Asia alone; the remainder is distributed among the other four continents. At first thought, one might conclude that the Asiatic continent must have either a wealth of food producing resources or a highly advanced technological culture to enable it to support so large a proportion of the world's people. Actually neither is the case. The chief factor enabling this fabulous population to exist is the low standard of living which prevails for practically all of the population of that continent.

WORLD POPULATION BY CONTINENTS
(Total Population, 2,095,000,000)

From *Foreign Commerce Year Book,* Bureau of Foreign and Domestic Commerce, 1937, pp. 367-368.

The areas of the world with a high level of living are not the most populous. It is probably objectively true that the United States and Canada now have the highest average level of living to be found in the world, and yet these two nations together contain less than 10 per cent of the population of the world. To say that their high level of living is due to any one factor would be to oversimplify what is a complex series of cause and effect relationships. Surely the level of living can be higher if the population is kept down by the practice of birth control, but that is not the whole story. The population of the United States and Canada is favored by a recent history of relative abundance of land in proportion to the number of people on it, and also by a recent period of history during which scientific knowledge and technology has been increasing at a phenomenal rate. Added to these factors is another one, somewhat less easy to grasp, but certainly important. The nations of the world with the more advanced technology are always in an advantaged trade position with the rest of the world which has a simpler economy. The more advanced society can sell its manufactured goods to the simpler society in exchange for raw materials. This has the effect of expanding the land area from which the people of the complex society may draw a wider variety of raw materials. The people of the complex society really exchange their labor and their knowledge for the raw materials of another part of the world. Through trade the American, then, may utilize in his day-to-day living, materials which come literally from every quarter of the earth. All of these factors are involved and together largely account for the high level of living prevalent in such societies as the United States and Canada.

To a considerable extent, the same principles hold for northwestern Europe, but with a few modifications. The Europeans began their technological advance and world trade earlier. They began with a larger relative population, and probably practiced less birth control. They also began with a traditional kind of distribution which approved great distinctions in income levels for different segments of the society. Finally, modern wars have destroyed and disrupted European economy several times. These factors together largely account for the somewhat lower average level of living in northwestern Europe, although as compared with the Orient the European's level of living is relatively high.

## DISTRIBUTION: RACIAL

### *Relative Numerical Strength and Location of the Major Races*

The several races are unevenly distributed in the world population. For convenience, we may distinguish three races, although as we have seen, racial classification is somewhat difficult: the Caucasoid, or "white" race; the Negroid or "black" race; and the Mongoloid, or "yellow" race. Since it has already been shown that the Orient comprises half of the population, it follows that the Mongoloid race is the most numerous, inhabiting continental Asia, many of the surrounding islands such as Japan, and parts of the East Indies. The native Indian populations of North and South America are also Mongoloid and are not, as is popularly believed, a separate race. The white race, inhabiting primarily Europe, North America, South America, Australia, and Asia Minor with numerically small settlements in scattered parts of the world, comes numerically second with approximately one-third of the world population. The remaining sixth is Negroid and native chiefly to Africa. There are also thirteen to fourteen millions of Negroes in the United States who have descended from the Negroes who were brought here originally as slaves. Negroid peoples are also found, like other races, in smaller societies in scattered parts of the world.

*Numbers* versus *Power*

It is significant that the entire world is virtually under the economic and political control of the white race, although in areas such as China the control is not especially evident to the unsophisticated observer. It is sometimes assumed that this prestige and power out of all proportion to its numerical strength, is an outgrowth of the superior intelligence of the white race as a race. This is entirely erroneous. It has now been clearly demonstrated that inherent differences in the general intelligence of races does not exist. The dominance of the white race in the world is explained *at this time* by the unique and probably temporary *historical advantage* of having invented a set of effective cultural techniques and the desire for world control. The development of Europe and later of America as a manufacturing and trading economy gave the white race the prestige and the power to enforce its position over the other peoples. In order to protect trade relations, guarantee markets, and sources of supply, gigantic navies and later armies were built up to hold the advantages gained and to "protect" the higher level of living which a trading and manufacturing economy made possible.

How long the ascendancy of the white race will continue is a matter of judgment. No one who is familiar with the facts, however, thinks the white race can hold this position of advantage forever. There are already unmistakable signs, particularly in the Orient, that the colored peoples realize the potential power of their numbers and resent their inferior position in the world. There seems little doubt that this factor was *one* of those involved in the recent war with Japan. It is fortunate for the continued domination of the whites that Japan also had a war with China, and thus the yellow peoples were divided among themselves. There is little doubt also that the white race is still far enough ahead in the technical implements of war at least, so that the Allies could have won a decisive military victory over Japan even if she had not been at war with China. It is impossible at this time to determine whether the Allies will also have "won the peace," by which phrase is meant whether they will be able to manage the victory in such a way as not to further inflame the existing hatreds of the Japanese and other Orientals to the point where there will be sown the seed of other warfare.

It would be a mistake to assume that warfare is the only or even the major way in which the struggle for power between races and nations takes place. In dozens of ways in economic, political, and other relations among nations, the struggle for power is constantly going on. The struggle breaks out in warfare only after an impasse in other means of struggle has been reached. Thus the struggle between the white race and the yellow race for control of the Orient is by no means ended by the victory over Japan. The same sort of resentment against whites' domination, one must remember, has occurred in China and in India and other parts of Asia which happened to be aligned with England and the United States in the last war. Throughout Asia there are very strong feelings against the white man, not only because of the power he has had over the yellow peoples but, also because of the way in which he has used that power. The existence of these attitudes, of course, does not mean that war in the Orient is either inevitable or necessary. It means simply that one must be realistic and face the facts that the white man's position of power in the world out of all proportion to his numbers, is probably only a passing phase in history. Perhaps if the white peoples recognize this fact in time and retire gracefully to a world position comparable to their numerical strength, no serious international difficulties need be encountered. On the other hand, it seems likely that the white race will attempt to maintain its power at all costs—even of another war, if necessary. Should this prove to be the case, the outcome is not pleasant to anticipate. Processes like these, of course, may take long periods to work themselves out, and therefore it is altogether possible that persons now living might live out their lives while the white man still dominates the Orient.

## THE POPULATION OF THE UNITED STATES

The United States contains between 6 and 7 per cent of the world's population. There are several items of information about the American population which are significant and not generally known. They are important because of their influence upon American society both now and in the immediate future.

### 1. *Negro Population*

One out of ten persons in the United States is a Negro. This varies, of course, from community to community, there being sections of the South in which Negroes outnumber whites and areas in the Middle West farming regions where Negroes are almost wholly absent. There is a popular belief to the effect that Negroes are increasing more rapidly than whites and that this increase poses a serious social problem. The facts are to the contrary. The Negro population of the United States is not increasing any more rapidly than is the white population. Certain communities, of course, show a recent increase in the number of Negroes, because of the migration of Negroes into industrial regions where wages are somewhat higher than they are in the Southern and agricultural regions. This has been especially true during the war years when Negroes were encouraged to take industrial jobs to meet a serious shortage of man power in many fields. But, for the nation as a whole, the Negro population is not increasing. It remains about one out of ten.

### 2. *Declining Birth Rate*

In common with most countries with the western European type of culture and society, the long-run American birth rate is declining. It cannot be determined whether this decline is due entirely to the practice of birth control or to the fact that modern living results in the involuntary infertility of more men and women. Population research experts seem inclined to attribute much if not most of the decline to the deliberate limitation of families. It requires approximately three children per married pair on the average to maintain a stationary population, two to replace the two parents and the third one to take the place of those who do not marry and those who die before they reproduce. (For statistics on the extent of the decline in the American birth rate see pp. 392-393.)

### 3. *The Differential Birth Rate*

Particularly among the so-called "middle classes" of America, there are large numbers of couples who have no children or only one child. While the total number of children being born in the United States is sufficient to exceed the total number of deaths which are now occurring, the failure of the upper middle class to have sufficient children means that *as a class* they are not reproducing themselves. This condition is called a "differential birth rate." The extent of the differential birth rate is rather striking. Here is one way of putting it.

> High school and college graduates are having about one and three-fourths children on the average, while persons with less than seven years of schooling are having four children. To put it another way, college trained men and women are failing to reproduce themselves by 26 per cent, while men and women who have not reached the seventh grade are over-reproducing themselves by 39 per cent.

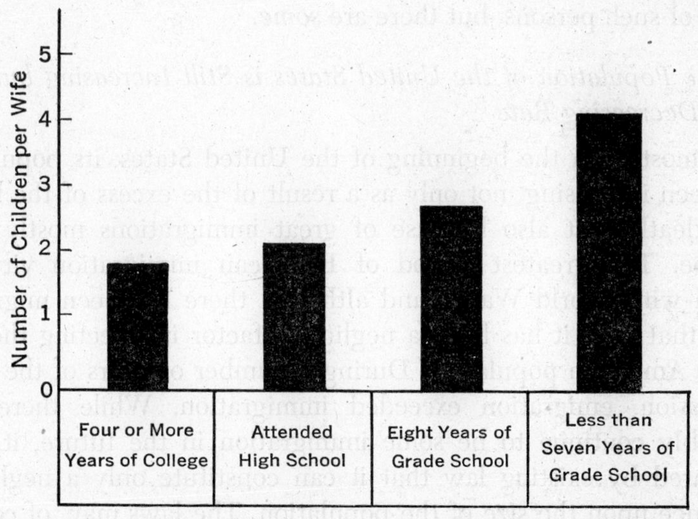


EDUCATION AND THE BIRTH RATE

P. K. Whelpton and Kizer, Milbank Memorial Fund *Quarterly*, July, 1943. Data are for women 40-44 years of age in a sample population.

What do the facts mean? The hasty conclusion has been drawn by some people that the differential birth rate is a very serious condition because it tends to deplete the storehouse of ability from which society can draw. Before this position can be established, however, one must prove that the persons in the upper middle classes have more innate ability than persons in the lower classes. The word *innate* in the preceding sentence is a crucial one. Because of a lack of educational opportunity, there is an appreciable reservoir of persons with high intelligence in the lower classes who are able to acquire, if given the opportunity, sufficient education to fill the society's needs for skilled personnel. This is not just "opinion," but is supported by extensive intelligence tests which have been given to the children of lower class people in the United States. There has been a differential birth rate in cultures like ours for many generations, and there has been no lack of competent people to handle the responsibilities of the positions which the society has had open. This is not to be taken as a flat denial of the *eventual possibility* of depleting our reservoir of talent by the differential birth rate. It is, however, clear that *for the time being at least*, there is an ample reservoir of potential talent in the lower classes for the present and immediately forseeable future. There are relatively fewer of such persons, but there are *some.*

### 4. *The Population of the United States is Still Increasing but at a Decreasing Rate*

Almost from the beginning of the United States, its population has been increasing, not only as a result of the excess of the births over deaths but also because of great immigrations mostly from Europe. The greatest period of European immigration virtually ended with World War I, and although there has been migration since that time it has been a negligible factor in affecting the size of the American population. During a number of years of the great depression, emigration exceeded immigration. While there will probably continue to be some immigration in the future, it is so regulated by existing law that it can constitute only a negligible influence upon the size of the population. The laws may, of course, be changed, but there is now no evidence that any change is imminent.

Any change which occurs in the size of the American population, then, must come from what is called natural increase, that is, the excess of births over deaths during the same period. American birth rates still exceed death rates so that the American population continues to grow. *But the rate of growth has gone down more or*

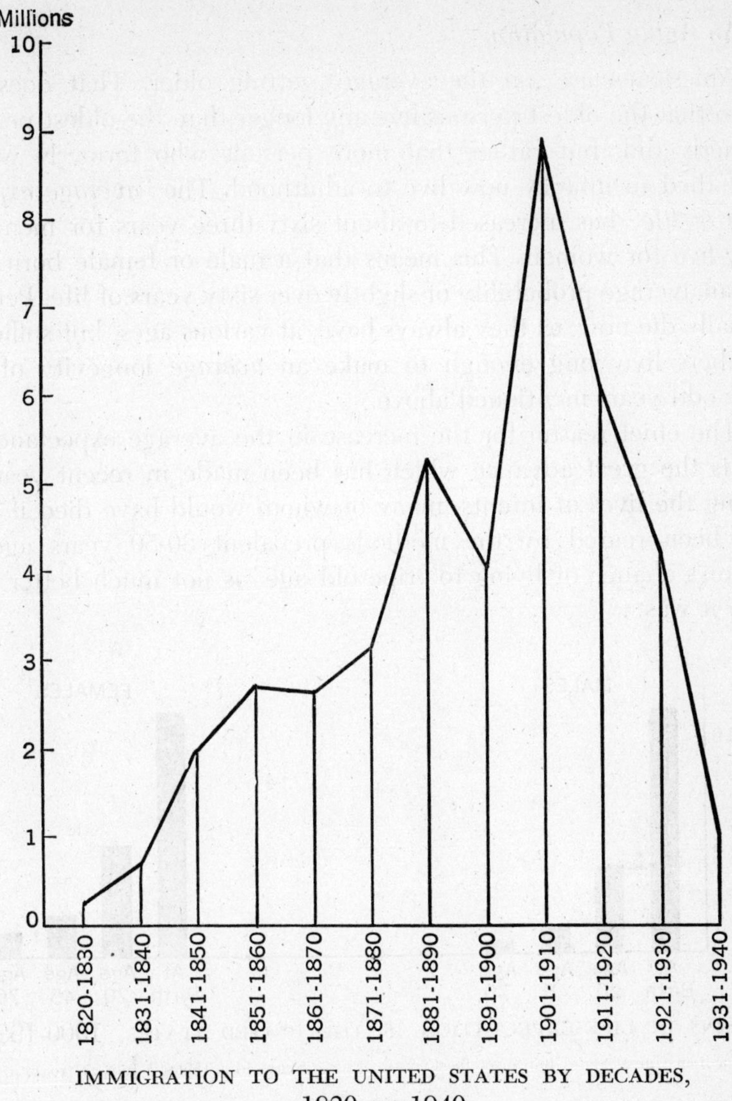


IMMIGRATION TO THE UNITED STATES BY DECADES, 1820 TO 1940

Based upon data compiled and published by the *World Almanac.*

*less consistently for several decades. In other words births do not exceed deaths in the same degree as they formerly did.* Moreover, as we shall see in the next few pages, the population of the United States is already failing to reproduce itself, but that fact is temporarily concealed.

### 5. *An Aging Population*

Americans are, on the average, getting older. That does not mean that the oldest persons live any longer than the oldest persons formerly did, but rather that more persons who formerly would have died in infancy now live to adulthood. The *"average expectancy of life"* has increased to about sixty-three years for men and sixty-five for women. This means that a male or female born now has an average probability of slightly over sixty years of life. Persons actually die now, as they always have, at various ages, but sufficient numbers live long enough to make an *average* longevity of the sixty-odd years mentioned above.

The chief reason for the increase in the average expectancy of life is the great advance which has been made in recent years in saving the lives of infants, many of whom would have died if they had been reared by the methods prevalent 30-50 years ago. A person's chance of living to "ripe old age" is not much better now than it was.

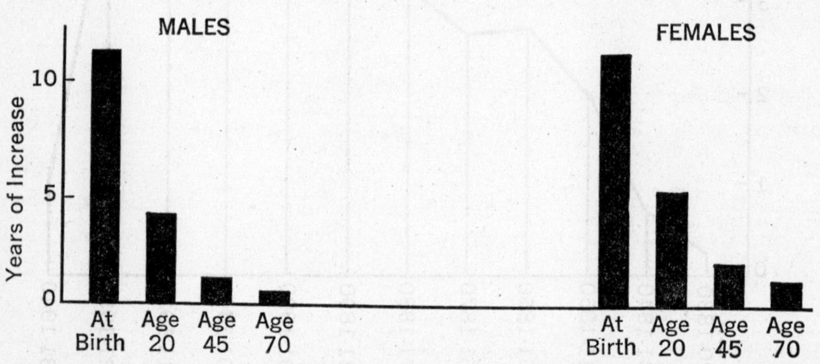


GAINS IN LIFE-EXPECTATION IN THE UNITED STATES, 1900-1939

Data from United States Bureau of the Census, "United States Life Tables," July 21, 1941, p. 1.

An aging population will necessitate some changes in the values and organization of the society. Bluntly, it means that there will be fewer persons in the relatively young age-groups, who must support not only themselves and their children but an increasing number of older people as well. This does not refer simply to their own relatives who may perhaps be able to support themselves through savings or some other way, but to the overall national burden of persons who have to be supported in some way by some one, either through private charity or tax supported relief of some sort.

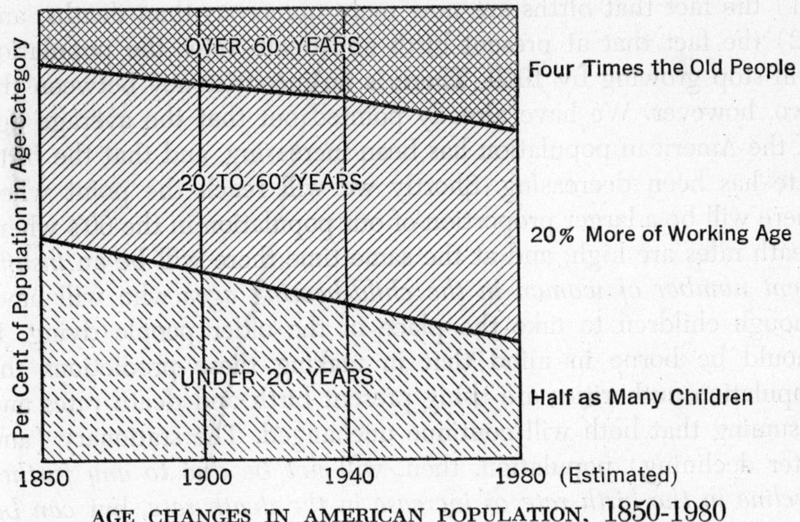


AGE CHANGES IN AMERICAN POPULATION, 1850-1980

Figure redrawn. From George Atteberry and others, *Introduction to Social Science* (New York, The Macmillan Co., 1945), p. 243.

Several devices may be employed to reduce the severity of this problem. It may be necessary to employ persons on into later life than is now customary. To what extent it will be possible to do this in industry, for example, is a very real concern to many. The Social Security system will also probably help to meet the problem, although not as much as might at first be thought. The payments to the aged still have to be paid out of the productive activity of the whole society at the time at which payments are made, and the building up of social security payments by the workers' contributions cannot constitute as much security, say the finance experts, as one might be inclined to expect. While the aging of the population is probably by no means America's "number 1" future social problem, it is still a problem which must be met in one way or another.

### 6. *Probability of a Stationary Population Size*

Population experts have clearly shown that at present rates of increase, that is, present birth rates, present death rates, and present immigration and emigration rates, the American population will stop growing somewhere between 1960-70. If birth rates go down, as they may, the stationary population could occur even earlier. Many persons are perplexed by the seeming inconsistency between (1) the fact that births are now more numerous than deaths, and (2) the fact that at present birth and death rates the population will stop growing by 1960. There is no inconsistency between the two, however. We have already pointed out that the average age of the American population has been increasing, and that the birth rate has been decreasing. Shortly we will reach the point when there will be a larger proportion of our population in the 60's where death rates are high, and at the same time there will be an *insufficient number of women in the child-bearing ages* who will have enough children to take the place of the older people dying. It should be borne in mind that in making these predictions the population authorities are using present birth and death rates and assuming that both will continue unchanged. The stationary (and later declining) population, then, will *not be due to any further decline in the birth rate or increase in the death rate,* but *can be accounted for solely by the aging* of the population due to the *past decline in the birth rate.*

## SUMMARY

The world population of two billions is very unequally distributed over the earth. The pressure of population upon the means of subsistence depends upon the state of the productive arts and the level of living, not simply upon the available land. Different parts of the world have different kinds of population problems depending upon how these factors interact to affect them. Moreover, some measure of relief from the population problem can be found through one or another of four possible approaches: control of numbers, expansion of the land area from which sustenance is derived, decline in the level of living, and improvement in the efficiency of the agricultural and manufacturing arts.

The distribution of a society's want-satisfying goods and services is a somewhat different problem. It depends upon the kind of prevailing ideas concerning who shall have how much of the joint product of the society. There may be, and certainly has been, terrible poverty where the overall potentialities of the society could be more than ample if the distribution system were different. The distribution problem, however, should not be confused with the basic population problem.

The various races share in the world population picture also very unequally, and this condition introduces some interesting paradoxes as well as overwhelming world problems. The most numerous race, the yellow race, has the least economic and political power, while a minority race, the white race, virtually dominates the affairs of the world. The dominance of the white race should be understood for what it is, an accident of history, and not as a demonstration of any inherent superior abilities of white people. Just as there were times in the past when the culture of white people was markedly inferior, so it is entirely possible that again the leadership, prestige, and power may pass to another race. The Orient particularly poses the problem for the future. Resentments against continued white domination are real and deeply held. How long the white race can hold the position of dominance in the world will probably depend on how skilfully the forthcoming problems are handled as they arise.

The population of the United States, consisting of 6 or 7 per cent of the world's population, is showing some significant trends. The ratio of about one Negro to nine whites is not changing appreciably, but since the Negro population is unequally distributed the racial composition of specific local communities may vary greatly from one another and vary appreciably from time to time. While the population of the United States is still increasing, the rate of increase is declining so that a stationary population in the 1960's seems probable as does also a declining population thereafter. The increased expectancy of life made possible during recent years, plus past declines in the birth rate, are the factors responsible for the main population problems we face.

The differential birth rate is a condition of long standing in western European society, and the dire consequences so often predicted as a result of it have not occurred because of the tremendous reservoir of unused intelligence in the less privileged social and economic groups. This reservoir may not be limitless and, therefore, the differential birth rate should probably not be brushed lightly aside, even though for the immediate forseeable future there seems little to worry about.

## SUGGESTED READINGS

BURCH, G. I. and PENDELL, E., *Population Roads to War and Peace,* Population Reference Bureau, Washington, D. C., 1945. **B**

An attempt to relate the facts regarding population to the problems of peace and war. Also evaluates various proposals and programs relating to population.

GRABILL, W. H., "Effect of the War on the Birth Rate and Postwar Fertility Prospects," *American Journal of Sociology,* L, pp. 107-111. **A**

A statistician from the United States Bureau of the Census presents the facts regarding birth rates and natural increase. "The recent upsurge in the birth rate should not lull us with a false sense that the problem of a declining birth rate has been solved."

LANDIS, Paul H., *Population Problems* (New York, American Book Co., 1943). **A B**

A treatise on population problems written from the thesis that population and other biological behavior of man can only be realistically comprehended in terms of the culture patterns in which the phenomena occur. This is a commonplace idea among most professional sociologists, but needs to be said again and again for others!

THOMPSON, W. S., *Population and Peace in the Pacific* (Chicago, University of Chicago Press, 1946). **A B**

An analysis of the Asiatic population problem in relation to war and peace. Written by the author of the well-known *Danger Spots in World Population.* He calls for the end of the Colonial system as we know it, and for the industrialization of the Orient as the only security from more and more serious "trouble" in the Pacific.

THOMPSON, W. S., *Population Problems* (New York, McGraw-Hill Book Co., 1935), Chapter XV. **A B**

Chapter XV, "The Future Growth of Population in the United States and its Consequences," is an excellent short treatment of the methods used by population experts to predict population, a practice which is very accurate. Also contains the various population estimates for the United States for future decades.

THOMPSON, W. S., *ibid.* This entire book is useful. **A B**

It is a standard textbook on population problems. While the census data are incomplete in that they do not contain the 1940 census data, the theory and trends are essentially correct.

VANCE, Rupert, and others, *All These People* (Chapel Hill, N. C., University of North Carolina Press, 1945). **A B**

An excellent study of population trends and problems with special reference to the position of the South in the national economy.

## STUDY QUESTIONS

1. What limits the size of the population of the world at a given time? Why is the phrase "at a given time" important?
2. How do advances in technology permit an increase in population *or* an increase in the available food per person?

3. Why do many American families practice birth control?
4. What are the three major factors that determine the total population the world can support? How is each a factor?
5. What three choices does man have when there is an increase in sustenance?
6. What determines the level of living of a given person?
7. What information besides density of population is necessary to determine if a country has an overcrowded population? Why?
8. Why do the people of the United States and Canada have an average higher level of living than the people of the rest of the world?
9. How does the white race compare in numerical strength with the other races?
10. Why has the white race been able to acquire and maintain political and economic dominance of the world?
11. Why do some people believe that the Negroes are increasing more rapidly than the whites?
12. To what factors is the decline in the American birth rate attributed?
13. Why are some people needlessly alarmed over our differential birth rate?
14. What two factors entered into the early increase in population of the United States? Why has there been a decrease in the rate of increase?
15. Why has there been an increase in the average expectancy of life?
16. What problems may be created by an aging population?
17. Why is a stationary population predicted for some time between 1960 and 1970?

# *Chapter XVIII*

## THE ECOLOGY OF THE CITY AND THE REGION

### ECOLOGY

#### *Biological Ecology*

Modern biologists have discovered that important new light could be thrown on the older knowledge about many species of plants and animals through the study of plant and animal "communities." The several plant and animal species living in a given area depend on one another for their sustenance. This interrelationship between different kinds of organisms living in the same environment is a very complex one. One such obvious dependence relationship among organisms is that of parasitism. In other instances, one form of life lives on or near another without in any way injuring it, and may in fact indirectly assist it in its struggle for survival. Some kinds of birds, for example, feed on the excrement of mammals. This in no way harms the mammal and may, in fact, be an indirect benefit as a sanitation factor. Other animals secure their food as scavengers. The possibilities of interdependence are many. *These various kinds of sustenance interrelationships* found in the plant and animal communities have been collectively termed *symbiosis.*

The symbiotic relations of plants and animals constitute a complex "web of life," and "balance of nature," each species being dependent upon other species while still others are dependent upon it. Darwin pointed out, in jest, of course, that the number of old maids in a community had an effect upon the abundance of the clover crop. This was his reasoning. The larger the number of old maids, the larger the cat population (this is, of course, a stereotyped connection which research might or might not bear out). The larger the cat population, the greater will be the ravages of the cats on the field mouse population. Since field mice feed on the larvae of bumblebees, the bees would increase in number as a result of the smaller mouse population. With a larger bee population there will be a larger clover yield, because the clover plant (of some varieties, at least) lacks the power to pollinate itself, its pollination relying on the activity of bumblebees. Thus, he concluded in part, the greater the population of old maids, the greater the clover yield! This humorous illustration does show the important fact of intricate and vital interdependence of plant and animal species in any area. Some of those interrelationships are so involved that the findings of ecologists make some of the most fascinating reading in biological literature. Every species, including man, depends for sustenance upon other species and itself provides the basis for the existence of additional species in an endless chain or "web of life" or symbiotic interrelationship.

### *Human Ecology*

Sociologists have found the concept *symbiosis* to be applicable also to the human community. The sociologist, of course, studies *intra*-species symbiosis while the biologist studies (mainly but not exclusively) *inter*-species symbiosis. In other words, the interdependence which the sociologist studies is the interdependence of humans with other humans. The cardinal concept in studying human symbiosis is *division of labor*. Human division of labor forms an intricate and complex web of interdependence between persons, groups, nations, and continents which becomes more and more intricate and complex as modern society develops.

Just as the population of grazing animals in a natural state is limited by the amount of edible foliage, so the number of persons in any given occupational specialty is limited by the size of the human population of the community in question. The number of dentists, filling stations, or lawn-mower sharpeners who can make a living in a given community is limited. Additional ones simply divide up the available work among themselves, until such a time as some are forced to drop out because they cannot secure enough work to make a living. Human beings can, of course, change occupations or move to another area, and thus mobility or economic failure rather than starvation tends to be the result of the oversupply of any of the specialties in the symbiotic pattern.

The abundance of the subsistence which a given individual of the species can enjoy, whether plant, animal, or human, is determined by the abundance of the source of supply and the individual differences in ability to compete. Thus, if there are too many dentists in a community all of them will not suffer equally by the oversupply of dentists. Some will continue to secure more work than the others do, and very probably those who secure the least work will be forced to drop out. It is probable, however, that when this or any other occupation is overcrowded, many of the persons in it will find their incomes reduced somewhat, but by no means equally. In many other ways the analogy of the symbiotic interdependence of the plant and animal community and the intra-species symbiosis of the human community may be made to appear exceedingly similar. But pointing out such similarities should by no means imply that they are identical. The differences are at least equally important.

*Basic Differences Between Human and Sub-human Ecology*

The chief difference between human and sub-human symbiotic relationship lies in the fact that for the sub-human species the relationships are *purely biological while for human beings the factor of culture intervenes.* Thus the whole symbiotic process becomes materially altered. For example, in our society we do not permit the persons who are unable to make a living to die; those who are able to make more than a minimum for their own subsistence help to carry the others along in some way or other. What may be even more important, humans exert control on many occupations so as to keep the number of persons in those occupations sufficiently low, and thus virtually guarantee not only subsistence but a very liberal supply of it. Furthermore, culture is constantly creating new occupations while related established occupations become obsolete. Sometimes what appears to be overcrowding in an occupation may simply be the result of the occupation becoming obsolete due to social change. There are other differences between the symbiotic processes in human and sub-human communities, but probably enough has been said to indicate that real and fundamental differences exist. So long as the student recognizes the difference between occupational symbiosis and species symbiosis he will probably find that many of the biological concepts pertaining to symbiosis can be fruitfully employed in studying the human community. A very real error arises, however, when the differences are overlooked. Even human ecologists themselves have sometimes overlooked or minimized the cultural factor. We shall treat this problem, however, more fully in a later part of the chapter.

### *The Spatial Pattern*

As a result of the symbiotic interdependence of species, certain well-known plant and animal location relationships can readily be observed. Certain kinds of grass cannot grow under trees because of the shade. Other plants require specific soil types. Animals, too have their habitats, determined by such factors as climate, sources of food, and the abundance of animals of prey. Because of these spatial regularities it is possible to map many forms of biological life. These spatial patterns, then, arise out of the symbiotic relationships and, therefore, are strikingly similar for the same and related species from community to community in the same general type of geographical and climatic area.

Human communities also have a characteristic spatial patterning. It is based partly on symbiotic relationships, but is by no means solely determined by them. Probably almost every one has observed the similarity among American cities in the location of the various industries, service establishments, and living arrangements. This is no accident; it is a direct result of the interdependence of human beings in various separate but interrelated occupational specialties. So standardized is this spatial pattern that a stranger in a city for the first time has little serious difficulty in finding any of the usual services he might want, even without making special inquiry.

### *Human Ecology Defined*

Summarizing the foregoing paragraphs, we may now define ecology as *the study of the symbiotic relationships and the resulting spatial patterning of human beings and human institutions in the community.* While sociology is not the only study of man which treats ecology, sociologists during recent years have built up a considerable body of knowledge on human ecology. We now turn to some of these knowledge areas.

### THE SPATIAL PATTERN OF THE MODERN CITY

The interdependence of the persons and institutions which make up the modern urban community have been found to result in the formation of a recurring overall configuration called *the urban pattern.* The urban pattern may best be represented by a series of concentric circles, thus.

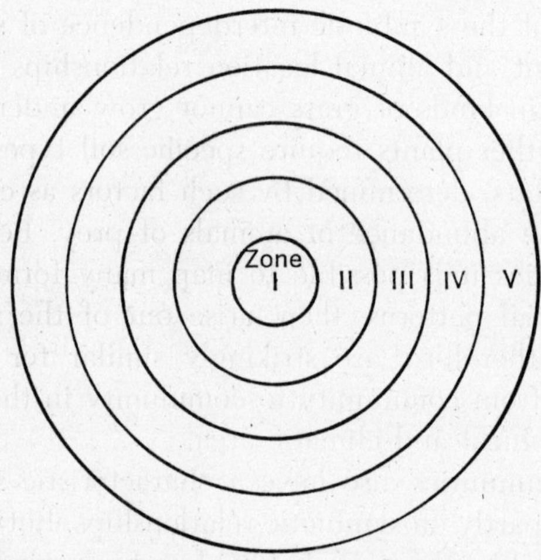


THE URBAN PATTERN

From Park, Robert, Burgess, E. W., and McKenzie, R. D., *The City* (Chicago, University of Chicago Press, 1925), p. 51.

### *Zone I*

Approximately in the center of the city is a well-known *central business* district containing retail stores, eating establishments, movie houses and, on upper floors, the offices of the more important business organizations and professional persons. The central business district is an area of dense population during the working part of the day, yet almost no one lives there, except for the transients who occupy the hotels. It is the place where people converge for specific commercial or recreational purposes. It seems to be convenient and efficient to concentrate activities in this way. The central business district, often called Zone I, is in the center of the schematic diagram (above) through which the modern city is now characteristically represented.

*Zone II*

Zone II, also called the *zone in transition,* is in the area surrounding the central business district. Conspicuous buildings in this area are a number of large, made-over private dwellings, now usually used for offices of persons and business which cannot afford the high rental values of the central business district. This is also the area of rooming houses and cheaper hotels. Because it is somewhat centrally located and yet not as costly an area in which to live or to maintain a business as compared with the central business district, the zone of transition attracts such establishments as pawn brokers and second-hand stores, restaurants and taverns catering to a less discriminating clientèle. Very often wholesale business establishments are also located here.

The zone of transition is usually the area of the city in which occurs the greatest concentration of crime and criminals, houses of prostitution, gambling establishments, and similar activities which the ideal culture patterns of the society frown upon, but which enjoy a considerable clientèle nevertheless. The resident population of the zone of transition is predominantly male and relatively transient. This area is called the zone of transition because it usually represents an area which, during bygone days when the city was smaller, contained the pretentious homes of the city's most wealthy and prominent people. This was before the day of the automobile when it was fashionable for the city's wealthy and élite class to live in the conspicuous houses which now are largely remodeled into inferior office buildings and interspersed with new commercial structures. Thus the area is "in transition" from a residential area of the upper class to the kind of area just described. The transition is relatively complete so far as the function and personnel of the area are concerned, but architectural survivals of the past age are present, although becoming less and less predominant as time goes on.

Also in the zone in transition is the area of the poorer workingman's homes. This area usually contains the city's "slums," the poorer Negro colonies, and the neighborhoods occupied by immigrants who are not yet assimilated into the American culture. Most of these persons live here not by preference, but because rents are lower and transportation costs to work are likely to be less. The level of living of this area is, of course, low. The area is usually relatively congested. This is an area of large families, but not as large as one might at first think as he travels the streets because, almost literally, the children have no other place to go, either in their own homes or out of doors. In times of unemployment, this area contains much of the community's relief load, because of the narrow margin of financial reserve which the persons in this area can accumulate.

*Zone III*

Zone III is also an area of workingmen's homes and usually "shades off" from Zone II very gradually. In general the housing is slightly better, although still clearly below average for the whole city. Frequently, in smaller cities especially, Zones II and III virtually run together.

*Zone IV*

As one goes out further from the center of the city, the housing becomes more modern and less crowded. It becomes apparent that although still a workingman's area, it is definitely better by the accustomed standards for measuring the desirability of housing. Hence it gets its name "area of better workingmen's homes" or "middle class family area." As compared to Zone III, Zone IV is characterized by more space, fewer children, larger incomes, and better housing.

*Zone V*

The gradual increase in the quality of the housing is apparent as one moves even further out from the center of the city, ending in the fashionable suburbs with the fetching names—the "heights," the "monts," the "brooks," and "parks." This is the area where there is economic abundance and security. On a whole, it is the area where the city's most prominent and successful business and professional leaders live. Here there is relative cleanliness and modernity. During recent years in a number of cities, better working-class housing has developed in and around some of the formerly exclusive suburban areas. Trailer camps can now be found in some cities within reasonable access of some of the more exclusive suburbs. A number of the suburban communities have their own schools, churches, and retail shopping areas. Often they also have their own local government, separately incorporated from that of the central city.

*Rurban Areas*

Outside Zone V there has more recently developed a conglomerate area with some of the characteristics of the zone in transition, some aspects resembling the area of poorer workingmen's homes, and some phases manifest rural life as well. Home building outside the city is usually unrestricted and uninspected. Side by side may be found the city "gentleman farmer's" combination farm and estate and a tar-paper shack, while across the road may be anything from a small airplane landing field to a night club, a filling station, or a truck farm. Here is a land area which is neither rural nor urban, and the uses to which land may be put are not yet established. There is much trial and error and changes occur frequently and unpredictably. This is almost a second "zone in transition."

*The Superimposed Radial Pattern*

The coming of the automobile introduced several modifications of the urban pattern as we have already seen. Noteworthy, however, is its influence upon the land-use pattern along the main roads entering the city. Filling stations, eating establishments, and entertainment facilities have developed along these major radii of the city. There is almost an uninterrupted business development for miles along the highways branching out from most cities. Behind these commercial areas are usually found the "middle-class" suburban dweller's subdivisions, interspersed with areas still under cultivation as farms.

*Individual Variations*

It should be borne in mind that we have just described the general ecological pattern of the modern American city. No city conforms exactly to a series of concentric circles. The point to be emphasized is that *most* cities *tend* to approach, and some conform very closely to, such a pattern. Geographical features are frequently responsible for distorting this basic pattern of concentric circular areas. This is most noticeable in the cities located on the banks of large lakes, the sea coast, in narrow river valleys, or on some other site where the geographical features make it difficult if not impossible to follow a circular pattern. Cleveland and Chicago are excellent examples of cities built on lake shores and having an urban pattern made up, therefore, not of a series of concentric circles, but a series of concentric semicircles. New York and New Orleans are illustrative of a group of cities which are distorted from the general pattern not only because of geographical factors but also probably because of somewhat unusual historical influences.

So long as the student recognizes that the urban spatial pattern we have just outlined is a general concept and not a photographic picture of some specific city, he should find it useful in understanding a number of principles about human living in the modern city.

*Social Gradations in the Urban Pattern*

The urban pattern permits a number of striking generalizations which may not be immediately apparent, but are important nevertheless. For example, beginning with Zone III, as one goes out from the center of the city he finds higher incomes (even though they may be earned in the same factory), smaller families (even though one might think that the economic pressure to have the smallest families would exist in the lowest income areas), greater education, smaller relief loads, and lower infant death rates. The student will readily observe, of course, that most if not all of these differences are closely related to occupation and income. The size and modernity of the home, the length of the wheelbase of the family automobile, the cost of "milady's" dresses, the quality and amount of the families' medical care, are all largely the result of the breadwinner's ability to pay for them.

Of course, there are exceptions to each of the above generalizations regarding the factors associated with the urban pattern. It is sometimes possible to find a slum on the outskirts of the city or a fashionable suburb fairly close in. Some families in the zones of workingmen's homes may actually have more money than some of the families who live in "the heights." But the point is that these *are* exceptions and must be understood as such. The general picture is as we have indicated. It may also be important to point out that what appear to be "exceptions" in human behavior at some given time may be the points of origin of new forms of living which in the future may be the normal phenomena.

### *Why This Particular Urban Pattern Rather Than Some Other?*

Students of the ecology of the city tend, at the present, to offer two quite different answers to this question. According to the first and older point of view the urban pattern is a *direct* and *inherent* result of the symbiotic relationships of individuals and groups in the society. The proponents of this point of view, claim that economic factors underly and determine the spatial distribution of the city. The business district is in the center of the city because that is the most efficient place for it to be located. The time and distance "costs" of getting there are, on the average, lower than would be the cost for any other location. The retail establishments which have the highest rent-paying ability occupy the pivotal, convenient locations, while wholesale establishments, which do not depend on large numbers of customers each day, may locate just outside the central shopping district at rent and other cost advantage to themselves. Persons who cannot afford the higher rent and home ownership costs and greater daily transportation costs of the outlying areas, locate in the lower housing areas closer to the center of the city. Restaurants and theatres locate near shopping districts and hotels for the advertising advantage of direct appeal to large numbers of daily passersby, and also because of the convenience to public transportation routes which have been developed largely to serve the retail shopping trade and service establishments located in the central business district. Drug stores tend to locate on corners because they can afford to pay a higher rental for this more advantageous position. Likewise, other commercial establishments which can afford to pay the highest rents get the choicest locations, like corners and first floors, while those with lower rent-paying capacity have to take upstairs locations, center block locations, or side street locations. The proponents of this "struggle for position" explanation tend to see human activity as a basically, if not solely, competitive process with individuals and groups striving for the economically desirable situations, and then using these situations for still more effective competition.

More recently a considerable modification of this point of view has developed. These critics center criticism upon the *fact of culture* as an important influence both in forming the symbiotic pattern and in influencing the particular space arrangement which the symbiotic interdependence creates. The proponents of this second point of view do not disagree necessarily with the basic explanations of the spatial pattern as stated in the preceding paragraph. They *center their objections upon the implication that the particular kind of symbiotic and spatial patterns which one finds in American and similar societies is dictated by man's nature as man.* To put it bluntly, this newer group of scholars charges the preceding group with being ethnocentric, that is, with assuming that the symbiotic relations and the spatial order found in their own society is necessarily inherent in the scheme of things. This group emphasizes some of the principles contained in Part II of this book concerning culture. They point out that ours is a highly competitive culture with emphasis upon financial matters and particularly with the status or class system based upon money. Furthermore, money in our society is a means to power in a much greater degree than in other societies. They point out further that the spatial pattern based upon the rent-paying ability of land is vitally affected by such cultural practices as private ownership of land and especially absentee ownership of land and buildings. It is important to note that even with our existing highly competitive and pecuniary culture, several factors about the spatial plan of the American city are not wholly explainable. Take, for example, the tendency to move out from the center of the city. Obviously, it costs more to live on the periphery and work at the center, because of the cost of transportation alone. It also takes much time to commute. Why, then, do people live in such an inefficient way? Why, for example, does a man who lives five miles from his work consent to travel 3000 miles a year just going to and from his place of employment? Certainly he would be a more efficient competing agent if he lived near his work, thus saving the time and cost of traveling the 3000 miles a year to and from work. The obvious answer is the correct one: he lives in the more expensive and exclusive part of the city instead of in Zone II near his factory, because he lives in a society the culture of which defines it as "better" to live in the suburb or at least somewhere else than in Zone II or III. In other words, such factors as having "more room," the "proper" neighbors and half an acre of lawn to mow are "good" simply because they are defined as good by the culture. They not only have prestige value, but the average person is sure in his own mind that they are worth the extra 3000 miles he has to travel. Let us take another example: the enforced segregation of Negroes and other minority groups by legal means as well as by informal pressures. Why is this done? It is done simply because of the way in which Negroes are defined by the white culture, and made possible because the whites have both the economic and political power to enforce their views upon this minority. There is little which is strictly economic about segregation, because the more wealthy, educated and, socially prominent Negroes are segregated along with all of the rest. The basic factor would seem to be the cultural definition of Negroes and no strictly symbiotic matter at all.

The discrepancy between these two schools of thought is a fundamental one. In this book, written as it is for the beginning student, few of the professional issues among sociologists have been introduced because it was thought best to confine the book to the discoveries, explanations, and other knowledges upon which there is agreement by leading scholars. An exception was made in the case of this ecological issue because of its currency, importance, and the lack of agreement among ecologists.

## DOMINANCE

### *Prominence of Pecuniary Valuation in American Society*

It has been pointed out in a number of places in this book, and doubtless suggested also by many of the students' own experiences, that ours is a highly pecuniary society. According to our cultural standards, money is important not only because with it one can buy most, if not all, of the necessities and comforts of life (including even life itself, since medical care has also to be purchased in much the same way as bread or shoes) but also because money has great prestige value, even though one does not use it directly to buy goods and services. There is scarcely anything in the society which is not measured in terms of money. Even in the realm of religion, where one would expect to find wholly non-pecuniary considerations if he found them anywhere, much emphasis upon money can readily be observed. Church organizations, like individuals, build far more extensive and far more luxuriant edifices than they can possibly justify by their needs for comfortable housing. Clergymen receive rewards for work well done in financial terms such as salary increases. This is not said by way of criticism, but rather by way of explanation of the preponderant significance of economic valuation in our society. Thus individuals are tied together, organizations are integrated, and whole areas held together by the web of economic relationships from which no one can escape.

*The Rise of Regional Organization of American and World Society*

Prior to the rise of the present American society, this nation was organized along territorial lines—states, counties, townships, cities, wards—with boundary lines delimiting one from the other. With the rise of large-scale financial and industrial organization, better transportation and communication, and more specialization and interdependence of persons and areas, a new form of territorial organization of people came into existence. The various parts of modern society are now primarily held together not by locality ties but by the vital needs of securing raw materials, labor, and selling finished products. Not only individuals specialize, but industries specialize, and so even do cities. A given factory or a given city provides certain materials or services for very large areas. Thus New York is virtually the financial center of America, while Chicago is the livestock and meat processing center, and Detroit the automobile center. Recreation production becomes similarly specialized with movie manufacture in Hollywood, the horse-racing industry in Kentucky, and winter resorting in Florida and Southern California. These specialized centers and areas provide the services for the whole continent and some may even be worldwide in scope, such as the women's fashion designing industry in Paris, at least prior to World War II.

Under the impact of this new large-scale economic organization, political boundaries like those of the several American states have become less and less significant except as descriptive terms like street names. States and counties still continue to exist of course, as convenient (and sometimes very inconvenient) administrative units of government such as for highway construction, school maintenance, and policing. But so far as the economic organization of the nation is concerned, state lines are more to be regarded as nuisances. The people in one state may find themselves more vitally concerned with what happens in a remote part of the nation or in some far corner of the world than by the happenings of their local community. A change in women's fashions may create a depression in some industry or a boom in another.

*Cities Are the Dominance Points of Regions*

Large cities are, of course, the focal points of the regional organization of the modern world. The converging of all of the railroad, highway, and air lines on Chicago or New York or New Orleans is symbolic of the *dominance* of these cities over their *hinterlands*. Out over the surrounding area each day are spread fabulous numbers of copies of the big city newspapers, while its radio stations broadcast into the homes of persons far removed from the city. The goods people buy are distributed from the great cities to smaller ones and so on down to the tiniest hamlet.

It is not to be assumed that it is only the large cities like Chicago or New York which exert dominance. All cities exert dominance, but over different aspects of life. In fact it is because it exerts dominance that a given city may live. Agricultural villages have dominance, too. They secure their dominance because they contain the stores, banks, professional offices, churches, schools, post offices, and all of the service institutions which people use to meet their wants. But the local village does not exert dominance over clothing design, supplying refrigerators, college education, or radio entertainment. For these services the centers of dominance are elsewhere and may be widely dispersed.

*Declining Dominance of Rural Areas*

One of the relatively new features in American life is the great dominance of urban centers for the organization and control of the society. Although some manufacturing is done in smaller cities, the chief function of small cities is that of distributing goods and services which have been created for the most part in far-away places. The overall direction of modern industry comes from a few very large cities. This relegation of small and especially rural communities to "service station" functions is decried by many people, but seems to have become, nevertheless, already an accomplished fact. The major decisions affecting the pattern of life of the nation, or at least of great areas of it, are made in the large cities and tend therefore, to reflect urban needs, urban interests, and urban values.

## SUMMARY

A branch of sociology called "human ecology" has arisen in recent years for the purpose of emphasizing the study of the symbiotic interrelationships and the resulting spatial pattern of human living. Although many of the concepts employed, like "the web of life," "symbiosis," "spatial pattern," are also employed in the study of plant and animal communities, the student should bear in mind that the factor of culture makes symbiotic relationship among humans fundamentally different from that of plant and animal communities. In the sub-human community the individual must adjust to his environment purely on a physical basis and the inability to adjust means death. Through the medium of culture humans, however, modify their environment and alter the conditions of survival in various other ways. The important thing to note, however, is that the intra-species symbiosis resulting from division of labor among humans does make the general ecological approach a fruitful one through which to study certain aspects of collective human life. The ecological approach should be employed with caution.

One of the most important and fundamental spatial patterns in American life is found in the typical structure of the city which divides itself rather clearly, as a rule, into five more or less distinct areas now conventionally described by a series of concentric circles. In the approximate center is the central business district, then the zone of transition, then the zone of low income dwelling units, then the middle class residential area, and finally the commuters' and suburban area. While not every city conforms to the concentric circle pattern, and every community presents some exceptions to it, the overwhelming prominence of this pattern of urban living is impressive.

Two schools of thought among ecologists seek to explain the reason for this particular spatial pattern. The earlier group of ecologists tend to conceive of the spatial pattern as inherent or "subcultural," as if man had nothing to do with its making, except to carry out the immutable laws of nature. The other school of thought emphasizes the factor of culture in producing the underlying values, such as our current emphasis upon efficiency, competition, and pecuniary valuation, the preponderance of which *in our culture* would tend to result in some such pattern as we actually find. Moreover, some of the ecological changes in recent years, like the suburban movement, cannot be sufficiently explained simply in terms of sub-cultural symbiosis.

In the western European-American type of industrial civilization, cities are the centers of dominance from which societal influences radiate. There are differing degrees and kinds of dominance, varying from New York city to the cross-roads country store, but it is to the large cities that leadership for culture control and culture change has almost completely shifted. The basic ingredients of social life, both material and non-material, are fashioned in the offices, factories, laboratories, and studios of a very few great urban centers. In this regional organization around a few super-dominant cities, state and local boundaries mean little. The interdependence and specialization of cities like the specialization of individuals and of industries is a fundamental part of modern life.

## SUGGESTED READINGS

Harris, C. D., "Suburbs," *American Journal of Sociology*, XLIX, pp. 1-13. **A B**

Analysis of the growth and trends of the suburbs of the 140 metropolitan districts reported in the 1940 census. Suggests an interesting classification of suburban types.

Hollingshead, A. B., in Park, editor, *An Outline of the Principles of Sociology*, (New York, Barnes and Noble, Inc., 1939), Part II. **A B**

A brief but inclusive statement of the main ideas and concepts of human ecology. Contains much more detail than is to be found in this volume.

McKenzie, R. D., "The Scope of Human Ecology," in Burgess, E. W., *The Urban Community* (Chicago, University of Chicago Press, 1926). **A**

The original statement of the University of Chicago "school" of human ecology by one of the leading ecologists in the United States. May be taken as representative of the first of the two conceptions of ecology discussed in this chapter.

McKenzie, R. D., "The Rise of Metropolitan Communities," in *Recent Social Trends in the United States* (New York, McGraw-Hill Book Co., 1933). Vol. I, pp. 443-496. **A B**

This is a synopsis of the more complete study reported in full in the monograph, *The Metropolitan Community* (McGraw Hill Book Co., 1933). A pioneer study on the metropolitan city. Many data with a minimum of "theorizing."

Mauldin, W. P., "Selective Migration from Small Towns," *American Sociological Review*, V, pp. 748-59. **A B**

Attempt to determine by statistical means whether the more or the less intelligent persons tend to migrate from the small town to the city. Also comparative data for males and females. Main conclusion is that the superior persons migrate in greater proportions to their numbers, thus sustaining the "drain of talent" theory. See also the following article in the same issue of the *American Sociological Review* which gives data from another study but which leads to the same conclusion.

RHODE, C. Von, "The Suburban Mind," *Harper's*, 192, pp. 289-99. **B**

A semi-popular discussion of the growth of suburbs and an evaluation of the suburban "way of life." Critical of the isolationism of suburban dwellers.

## STUDY QUESTIONS

1. What links of the "endless chain" are missing in the old-maid-clover-crop illustration of symbiotic interrelationship?
2. On what factors does the number of profitable shoe repair shops in a community depend?
3. Why do some trades and professions use various devices to limit the number of people entering their field of endeavor? Illustrate.
4. How do human and sub-human ecology differ?
5. Why do American cities tend to have similar spatial patterning?
6. What are the characteristics of the central business district of a city? Why?
7. Why are there "zones in transition" in most cities?
8. Why is it often difficult to distinguish between the Zone II type of area and the Zone III type?
9. Why do some people believe that it is more desirable to live in a Zone IV type of neighborhood than in a Zone III or II type?
10. On what does living in a Zone V type section of a city depend?
11. Why does no city exactly conform to the general pattern of concentric circles?
12. How do the economic and cultural explanations of urban development differ? How are they similar?
13. How does our culture tend to be a "money culture?"
14. How is economic relationship the integrating factor in human "webs of life?" Illustrate.
15. How do cities dominate their hinterlands?
16. What is the significance of the increase in urban dominance?

# *Chapter XIX*

## URBANIZATION AND URBANISM AS A WAY OF LIFE

### THE FACTS OF URBANIZATION

Large cities are a conspicuous characteristic of modern life. While cities have existed in Western civilization, for several centuries, there are at least two phases of modern urbanization which are products of the last half-century: (1) the great size of the largest cities; and (2) the proportion of the total population living in or adjacent to cities.

*The Growth of Large Cities*

The so-called "large cities" of medieval and modern Europe would scarcely be considered cities at all in terms of our modern conceptions. In the fifteenth century, for example, London had a population of 40,000. All other English cities were under 15,000 and such German cities as Cologne, Frankfurt, and Nuremberg each had less than 20,000 people. In comparison to present cities whose populations are measured in the millions, the European cities before the Industrial Revolution seem almost inconsequential. Fifteenth-century London, for example, contained less than 1 per cent of the present inhabitants of New York. The 1940 population of New York City numbered seven and one-half millions in the city proper and including the immediate adjacent populations in northern New Jersey and New York State, the aggregate urban unit of "greater" New York City contains around 15,000,000 people. In the last one hundred years New York has grown almost 1900 per cent. The population of the five leading American cities, New York, Chicago, Philadelphia, Detroit, and Los Angeles, including their suburban areas amounts to about 20 per cent of the entire American population. In other words one American out of five is part of these five giant American metropolises.

*Urbanization in the United States*

These figures give only a slight indication, however, of the extent to which the United States is urbanized. In about a hundred years America has shifted from a predominantly rural to a predominantly urban nation. Only slightly over 40 per cent of the American population is now classified as "rural" according to the census system of classifying persons living in population units of less than 2500 as "rural." Only about half of these persons (22.9 per cent of the total population, to be exact) are persons gainfully employed in agriculture. Almost as large a number, then, are living in rural areas, but do not derive their livelihood from agriculture. These include persons in the service occupations in the small villages and suburban dwellers who live in the open country on the periphery of cities, but who really belong to the city so far as their ecological relationships are concerned. In 1870, on the other hand, 53 per cent of American workers were gainfully employed in agriculture, or almost two and one-half times as many proportionately as in 1940.

*Urban Access*

By 1930 the *majority of Americans,* regardless of occupation, were living *within daily access of metropolitan American cities.* Metropolitan cities were defined by the census in 1930 as cities with a total population of 100,000 or more, including all persons who lived in the contiguous minor political areas with a density of 150 per square mile or more. Thus, cities with populations of 50,000 in the central city plus a sufficiently large suburban development could total 100,000 and be regarded as "metropolitan." There were 96 such metropolitan cities by 1930. The majority of the American people in 1930 lived close enough to these 96 metropolitan cities so that they could conveniently use these cities as their place of work or as shopping and recreation centers, traveling to and from the central city daily.

Thus we see that within the memory of many persons now living America has evolved from a primarily rural to a primarily urban population, and from a nation predominantly made up of farmers to a nation of predominantly non-farmers.

*United States Not the Most Urbanized Modern Nation*

It should not be assumed, however, that the United States is the most urbanized nation in the world. Both England and Germany, for example, were urbanized by 1930 to a considerably greater extent than the United States was. In England and Wales almost 80 per cent of the population lived in population units of 2000 or more and in 1933 Germany had 67 per cent of its population classed as urban by the same method of defining urban. At about the same time only 56 per cent of the American population was urban, using the census definition of urban as population units of 2500 or more.

*Declining Rate of Growth of America's Largest Cities*

The 1940 census of the United States revealed a noticeable decrease in the *rate* of growth of the largest cities. Metropolitan cities which grew 23 per cent between 1920 and 1930 grew only 5 per cent, as a whole, between 1930 and 1940. A somewhat greater growth was shown during the same years by cities of medium size. Places between 10,000 and 25,000 increased by approximately 9 per cent. Thus we see that the urban trend continued during the 1930's, but not at as great a rate as during the previous decade.

Much speculation has resulted as to the reason for this decline in the rate of growth of American cities. The great depression of the 1930's may have been a significant factor in this decline. Not only did the migration from farm to city cease, but there was a considerable "back to the farm" movement as well. Perhaps if we had census figures for each separate year between 1930-1940 we would have a better idea as to the exact influence of the depression. It may be well, however, not to attach too much significance to the mere fact of a decline in the rate of growth during this period, since a net growth still occurred in urban areas. Even the metropolitan cities grew more rapidly during the decade than did the entire population of the nation. By 1950 we may have more reliable information on the long-run trend since by that time the dislocations resulting from the war may have become stabilized again.

*Reasons for Urban Growth*

The facts of urban growth, as we have seen, are reasonably clear. To determine why the growth has occurred is not as easy a task as might be thought. Sometimes it is held that people have moved from farms to cities because they like city life or because of the attractiveness of the real or imagined higher wages paid in the city. This seems not to be the whole truth, however, because during the years of great urban growth there had also been occurring an unprecedented depression in American agriculture. Therefore, we do not know whether the migration to the cities was due to the greater attractiveness of the cities or because rural living had become so economically unattractive that many people were left no real choice. Probably both factors reinforced one another. Assuming that the migrants preferred to move to the city, we still do not know whether they preferred the urban mode of living or were merely willing to endure it for the sake of the somewhat higher wages which they would receive, or thought they would receive, in the cities.

*Ecological Factors*

It is possible to approach the reasons for the growth of cities from a less personal angle. Cities grew because there was a sufficient demand for labor in the cities to enable people to make a living there. That fact is fundamental, although one must not assume that everyone who lives in the city actually makes a living there. Numerous persons in the city are supported in whole or in part by philanthropy, not only in depression periods but in normal times as well. The point, however, is that the city must be economically able to support not only those gainfully employed there, but also those who are directly or indirectly supported by the gainfully employed. Cities have been able to support their large populations because of the presence of the great basic employing units—factories. It would be a mistake to assume, however, that the production of goods is the sole or even major type of urban employment. Cities are also the centers of the great service institutions: colleges and universities, hospitals, banks, insurance companies, and recreational services of all kinds, to mention a few of the more obvious ones. The affairs of government, moreover, are employing a greater and greater proportion of the population, particularly since the services of government are constantly expanding. These centers of government are, of course, all located in urban centers. In short, our society has produced a culture which emphasizes the kind of values and activities which we seem to best carry out when functioning in these large, sometimes tremendous, population units called cities.

*Urban Growth Not Necessarily Eternal*

It should not be assumed that cities will necessarily continue to grow, or that the largest cities will not show a decline in the years to come. There is nothing inevitable about these particular arrangements any more than there was about feudalism. They have simply arisen because they seemed to work, and whenever any other system of living arises which promises to work any better, it will in all probability supersede the present one. Such changes, of course, do not occur overnight, partly at least because of the habit patterns which are built up around the current arrangement. Nevertheless, the same inevitable principle of change in human affairs which brought the rise of the city, especially the great city, may also bring its decline.

*Some Long-Run Trends*

Forecasting is always fraught with difficulties, but some aspects of the future of cities in the United States seem now to be rather clearly shaping up and can, therefore, be anticipated. It seems highly probable, for example, that fewer persons will be engaged in agriculture in the immediate future than are now engaged in that industry. Labor-saving devices already invented, but not yet in wide usage, plus a decline in the export trade of agricultural goods as soon as Europe recovers from the ravages of war, will both probably operate in the direction of lowering the amount of human employment in American agriculture. There may be more living in the open country by persons engaged in non-agricultural activity, however. As transportation becomes better it is becoming possible for persons to live farther and farther from their work, should they have any preference so to do. There is also evidence that some industries are deliberately planning to decentralize their manufacturing units and scatter them among a larger number of small cities and even agricultural villages. Some industrial experts are of the opinion that the disadvantages of congestion in the largest cities may outweigh the advantages of large factory units and have advised their concerns to set up smaller manufacturing units in the smaller cities. If this decentralization principle is a sound one economically, and it seems to be, it may contribute to a marked change in the distribution of the city population. The greatest cities may then show declines in population and the moderate cities increases. The 1940 census figures, as we have already seen, would seem to suggest that this movement may already be under way. Like all social change this one, if it comes, will probably be strongly influenced by factors not now readily forseeable. But so far as we can now determine, these are the probable immediate developments.

## IS THERE A UNIQUE URBAN PERSONALITY TYPE?

Anyone who has lived in both rural and urban communities or who has become even indirectly acquainted with these two modes of living, is clearly aware of the contrasts between the "typical" persons one encounters in these two societies. The faster tempo of the city, the more precise scheduling of activities, the emphasis upon secondary group contacts, the transiency and general instability of friendship and group associations, crowding, noise, anonymity, and the contrasts of wealth and poverty, luxury and squalor, are a few of the striking differences from rural life about which much has been written. Obviously, therefore, the behavior of people who live in urban areas, especially the large urban centers, would be expected to be different in order to enable the person to function effectively in this utterly different type of community. But is the difference only in the superficial details of human personality, or is it more basic? In short does urban living either create or select a fundamentally different kind of human being? Students of this problem have not fully agreed concerning the answer to the question. A few subordinate phases of the problem, however, seem clear enough. Urban life is a specialized kind of existence for the human being. From the collective point of view, it may be characterized as *heterogeneous*. Hence a person may develop highly individualized behavior patterns in the city, which in rural areas would not be tolerated by the mores, not necessarily because the mores are so different, but rather because more of the person's behavior is conspicuous in a small and primary group society. With the *anonymity* of the city and the large population from which one may choose his associates, it is possible for the person to indulge his idiosyncrasies and eccentricities by finding congenial persons like himself if he wants to. The "Greenwich Village" personalities apparently succeed in finding congenial associates among the large and diversified population aggregate of the great city. In the small town the same behavior would result in ridicule if not ostracism, and if the person in question wanted social acceptance he would have no choice but to conform. In the city, on the other hand, through the wider selection of specialized associations, and then by the reinforcement of his conventional behavior and values through association within the special groups, *personality specialization* may be fostered. Thus, the city population may come to be characterized by greater individual differences as compared to rural areas. Its groups offer a congenial environment for the individualist who wishes to escape from the watchful eye of local mores.

It is thought by some students of the crime problem, for example, that the prevalence of crime and criminals in the large city is largely explainable in terms of the principle here being discussed. In the large city primary contacts can be largely escaped if one so wishes, and anonymity be made virtually complete. The large population, the mobility, and the anonymity multiplies the *opportunities* for behaving in criminal ways, and particularly offers better opportunities for escaping detection and apprehension by the law enforcing officials. Thus, a sort of anti-social society comes eventually to be organized. The paradoxical phrase "anti-social society" means, of course, that the criminal society is based on values which are contrary to those of the larger society, but the criminal society is a society in itself.

For the "ordinary person," however, who lives and works in the large city, urban living means merely that he must learn a number of specialized techniques required for successful urban living, like learning the folkways of subway travel, being more cautious about exploitation, learning the more formal and superficial "line" of casual conversation, and other folkways all of which make no fundamental difference in the important affairs of life anyway. The dwellers of cities have largely been recruited from the rural areas in the United States, which areas have always created a surplus of population from which city dwellers come. On the whole these persons of rural origin adjust soon and easily to the new demands of urban life. They tend to retain, of course, certain values and habits from their rural antecedents, but these personality traits seem not to interfere seriously with the person's successful functioning as an urban citizen. It seems that so far as our present knowledge goes, the chief significance of the city lies in the *greater opportunities* for participation *in the more specialized and individualistic groups if one so desires.* These participations are, however, not universal for urban dwellers, the majority of whom share many of the basic sentiments and values characteristic of the overall culture of American society. Persons reared in the large city learn city ways by the same processes of socialization that rural children learn rural ways, but, as we have seen, their out-of-home participation is characterized by more secondary group contacts. They encounter urban ways and learn urban ways. There is no reliable evidence that the resultant urban and rural personality "types" are necessarily unique.

### *The "Communality"* [1]

In the history of the United States the "community" has served as a center of man's concerns. From Main Street of the cross-roads village tc Broadway of the City of New York, men have tended to identify themselves with their communities and to defend them with boasts of their advantages and superiorities. In an earlier day the community was a definite social unit with a *locale* whose boundaries were co-terminous with the homes of the people who used its services. People, land, interests, services were essential elements. Residence within the named area was a means of personal identification. Status and prestige were the guerdons which the community bestowed upon its "worthy" citizens. Competition within the area whetted the individual desire "to stand well" in the eyes of his compatriots. Acquaintance was widespread; neighbors "depended" upon one another. They played together, worked together, worshipped together, and shared common hopes and dreams not only for themselves personally but also for their home community.

. . . Above all, the active participation of the citizens in local affairs has been, at least traditionally, the bulwark of the type of democracy peculiar to the United States of America, and, historically, has established a pattern of social behavior expected of the local resident, of the man "who belonged."

With new methods of transportation, with changes in types and forms of industry and of industrial organization, and with the domination of a money economy, man has tended to become increasingly detached from the earlier

[1] B. A. McClenahan, "The Communality: The Urban Substitute for the Traditional Community," *Sociology and Social Research,* XXX, pp. 264-71.

"home community" both physically and psychologically. This current social detachment has significant results for individual personality patterns, for local democratic activity and organization, and for community autonomy.

In the city hundreds of thousands of people are renters. They have little or no stake in the *place* in which they live except that involved in the month-to-month purchase of living space and conveniences. Many of them live in "furnished" rooms and apartments and have few *impedimenta*, except suitcases or trunks. They travel "light." They move easily. They have no roots in locality. Even the owners are restless and frequently eye covetously newly opened subdivisions with "newer" homes and up-to-the-minute "improvements." Witness the recurrent "for sale" signs. Automobiles have widened the territorial range of people and both stimulated and satisfied their urge for adventure. There are sheer pleasures in the swift motion of the automobile and a sense of power in its manipulation. No wonder people spend much of their leisure in their cars, "going places" and "doing things." "Neighboring," especially in the city, has almost become a lost art.

Who lives next door? Why should anyone be concerned unless the nigh-dweller gets too noisy or the children or dogs get into a fight? Today, the local resident is rarely socially dependent upon his neighbors; in fact, he frequently prefers *not* to know them. He chooses friends and associates, not because they happen to live near by, but because they enjoy doing the same things or because their work interests bring them together in a mutual association to protect and advance both their social and economic welfare. A few people may be politically inclined, and they are the ones who serve perennially on precinct and ward committees, especially on the election boards on voting day. Local residents as a whole vote casually or not at all. National elections are lodestones to the voting booths. School board elections tend to be the least interesting and compelling.

The general decline of interest in local affairs does not necessarily mean that people lack social contacts and activities. Within contiguous communities people inevitably gravitate together into congenial groups. If they have common interests they will get together, the only limitation being time and means of transportation. The place need have no special relation to their place of residence, but is determined only by its convenience as a meeting place. It is this type of association which may be called "a communality."

The communality is an interest-circle characterized by the social nearness of members whose places of residence may be widely separated. It may be a formal or an informal group, as close-knit as a fraternity, as fluid as a public dance hall crowd. Its members belong, not because they share a place of common residence or are identified with the same community, but simply because they share like interests, ranging from the ephemeral to the relatively permanent. They meet together whenever they find it convenient. . . .

Communalities are as varied as the interests of people. They form a kind of shifting, shimmering overlay above the more stable, earth-bound community. They are territorially detached social groupings, and their activities run the gamut of social, economic, political, and religious concerns. They provide for the socially popular, as well as for the so-called social misfit. Their varied type and makeup permit the crossing of many social boundary lines. As a consequence, they provide opportunities for the expansion of personality in the easy give-and-take of social interaction.

## IS URBAN LIVING HARMFUL?

### *The Anti-urban Bias*

That urban life is *different* is obvious enough, but is it, therefore, a *less desirable* mode of life as compared to rural? It has become somewhat fashionable—a sort of intellectualized fad—to decry the "terrible conditions" under which people are forced to live in cities. Such provincial judgment and beliefs are understandable enough when they are voiced by rural people whose ethnocentrism would be expected to cause them to come to a negative conclusion about a mode of life foreign to them. Somewhat more surprising, however, is the same evaluation coming from some city dwellers themselves. The notion is prevalent both among urban and rural evaluators that urban life is an inferior mode of existence. The indictment is probably familiar to most persons, so we need review it only briefly.

### *The Indictment*

Cities are noisy, crowded, dirt and disease laden. Life is monotonous in many specialized occupations, working conditions in numerous factories are not conducive to health and longevity. Activities are so rigidly scheduled as to make the person a mere robot. People are said to be "unfriendly, aloof, casual, too-reserved, too superficial, and not always trustworthy." Poverty and wasteful luxury abound almost side by side. The "moral tone" is said to be low, with gambling and prostitution prevalent, and the "sex theme" is much overplayed and commercialized not only in recreational matters but on every hand. Moreover, urban dwellers are said to be a "parasitic" people because their birth rates are so low as to make it necessary for cities to draw recruits from rural areas in order to maintain even a stationary population. The rural areas rear and educate these migrants at considerable expense and when it is time for them to make a contribution to their communities, they migrate to the city.

These facts are all true enough. Suppose, however, we analyze the indictment further to determine more precisely what it means and how significant it really is. Is it based upon objective facts? Are the inferences which are drawn from the facts reasonable inferences or do they go beyond the data?

### *Remediable and Inherent Conditions in Urban Life*

First, the characteristics of city life can be divided into those which are remediable, that is, can be eliminated or greatly reduced when there is the will to do so, and those which are inherent in the city as a form of spatial grouping. Among the remediable characteristics are noise, dirt, disease, bad working conditions, excessive speed, and traffic congestion.

Already great strides have been made in many cities toward reduction and elimination of many of these dangers and nuisances. They are no more inherent in the nature of city life than outdoor toilets and folk superstitions are inherent in rural life. Both merely happen to be present at the time, and can be eliminated when there is sufficient knowledge and determination so to do. We do not mean, however, to oversimplify a complex problem when we make this point. Many of the city's difficulties such as traffic fatalities and congestion or smoke nuisances are still very knotty problems. But there is tangible evidence from numerous cities that there are solutions to these problems within the reach of many urban areas, whenever the citizens organize or otherwise coöperate to reduce the severity of such conditions.

### *The Problem of Evaluation of the Inherent Characteristics*

Other characteristics of urban life such as low birth rates, the secondary group nature of social interaction, and the more emancipated morality seem to be more inherent in the nature of urban living. But are these really disadvantages? Or do they only seem to be disadvantages when observed through the prejudices of rural culture? The low birth rate of urban populations is characteristic, but is a low birth rate an undesirable condition? There are those who certainly would argue the reverse. Many of the great strides which have been made in the standard of living for millions of American children have been made possible because there were fewer in the family unit, thus enabling the father's limited income to provide more of the necessities and comforts for those who were present. In other words whether a higher birth rate is desirable or undesirable is an "open question." So long, therefore, as it remains an open question, we cannot objectively take the position that urban living is bad in that it is conducive to a lower birth rate.

It is also true that the city presents appalling contrasts between the luxury of some persons and the tortuous poverty of others. The condition, however, is not unique to cities. It is a characteristic of our entire system of distribution through which we reward people with extreme differences of income. Furthermore, it is quite possible that the greatest extremes of poverty in America are not found among urban dwellers at all, but in rural society with its sharecroppers and migrant agricultural workers. Instead of regarding the city as the cause of some workers' poverty, one should secure the correct perspective through which both the city and the poverty are the results of the other more basic conditions. Moreover, as agricultural industry becomes more mechanized and capitalistic, it is showing some of the same characteristics as typical urban industry.

The moral tone of cities is also different. But when broad evaluative terms such as "low" or "degraded" or "degenerate" are employed, they reveal that the facts are being subjectively interpreted. All one can objectively say is that *some* of the moral standards of *some* city dwellers are different from *some* of the morals of *some* of the rural dwellers. Not unimportant either is the fact that as rural people are securing more and better access to urban communities, houses of prostitution, gambling dens, and sex exploiting night clubs, are securing many and willing customers who live in the quaint and picturesque country side!

Social contacts in the city are brief, many of them superficial, and functionary relationships (see p. 274) are carried to the extreme. But, again, can one prove objectively that these things are necessarily harmful or undesirable? It is true that we have reasonable assurance that healthy personalities require some intimate contacts with other people through which they secure their apparently needed feelings of sympathy, dependence upon others, and a sense of being important to others. But most of these things are provided primarily by one's family and close friendship associations both of which are available in urban life, although somewhat modified by the conditions of urban living.

### *Advantages of Urban Life*

Over against the indictment of urban life—or rather whatever elements of the indictment still remain—should also be placed a series of advantages which can be somewhat objectively evaluated. Urban life permits a great deal of specialization, thus enabling the society better to utilize the diversified talents and interests of people. Cities, moreover, have taken the lead in providing better water and food inspection, traffic control, specialized medical and hospital facilities, better schools for children and supervised out-of-school and recreational facilities for children. Cities have largely been the centers for research, education, and scientific development, many of the benefits of which have been extended to rural areas to reduce some of their own more undesirable characteristics.

It is not being contended here that urban living is necessarily better or necessarily worse than rural living but simply that urban living is different. Some of these differences are obviously undesirable according to existing standards of health and comfort. But most of these are being remedied, and some of them at a rapid rate. Other attributes of urban living are difficult to appraise if one is truly objective in his analysis. Finally, urban life presents certain advantages which few could deny to be advantages on the basis of almost unanimously accepted standards of evaluation.

### *Anti-urban Bias May Be Reduced in Time*

Much of the prejudice against urban life is due to the lack of knowledge on the part of the rank-and-file citizens as to how they may exert effective collective control to eliminate many of the undesirable conditions of urban living. But the city is apparently here to stay, although the biggest cities may become somewhat decentralized. No one seriously claims that urban living does not present problems, but sweeping depreciation of urbanism as a mode of existence seems to be largely wasted effort unless it contributes to the eventual improvement of at least the improvable aspects of city life. City dwellers need no longer take for granted that they must forever accept all of the nuisances and dangers present in the city. Many of these have come down from the recent past and are the result largely of giving free rein to the industrial and commercial interests which largely planned the city on the basis of criteria of financial gain, leaving the economically less favored persons to endure the squalor, while those who planned it now usually live with their families in the more costly and attractive suburbs. The point is not that industrial and commercial leaders deliberately planned the less desirable aspects of city life, but that they were permitted a free hand in laying out the city primarily for the convenience of industry and commerce with practically no concern for the housing and recreational interest of the great mass of citizens of moderate means who have to live in the city because they work there. Nor should the commercial and industrial interests necessarily be blamed for doing what they were permitted to do under the existing laws and customs prevailing at the time when present American cities were being built.

There is growing evidence that enlightened groups of citizens are becoming more aware of their democratic rights to assert themselves on what kind of city they want and then force the government to bring about the needed changes. Progress in the past has been slow, because there were always convenient excuses. A new park would cost too much money. If there were laws requiring industry to reduce the smoke nuisance, industries would move out of the city to other places where the citizens were less exacting in their demands for a clean city. High traffic fatalities resulted from "poor driving," not from narrow streets, insufficient policing, and poor lighting! In time citizens have become enlightened not only concerning their rights under the law and the right to make new law, but also have "seen through" much of the propaganda of vested interests who placed the immediate economic welfare over the eventual public good. In several cities great and sweeping improvements have already been planned and the legal barriers have been crossed, with the result that the next decade will probably see appreciable improvements in the livability of many cities. It is unfortunate that persons of the different social classes will share unequally in the coming benefits, but in a society organized around pecuniary valuation, greater power goes with greater wealth, and those who do not share too prominently in the distribution of income, share comparably in social privileges.

## LARGE-INDUSTRY AND SMALL-INDUSTRY CITIES

Traditionally cities have been compared in terms of size and no doubt many important differences in the mode of life are the result of differences in size. There are other factors than size, however, which affect the quality of life in the city. One of these factors, although not the only one or even necessarily the most important one, is the nature of the predominant industry. Specifically, does the city dominated by large business make a better or a worse place to live as compared with the city of small business establishments? In what ways is the difference manifest? The following is a resumé of a recent study prepared for a sub-committee of the United States Senate for the purpose of securing an answer to the question of whether a big-industry or a small-industry city is better in terms of civic welfare.

### SMALL BUSINESS AND CIVIC WELFARE [2]

A few gigantic corporations are now responsible for the bulk of America's entire industrial production and employment. In 1944, 2 per cent of the manufacturing concerns in the United States employed 60 per cent of the industrial workers.

How does this concentration of economic power affect the general welfare of our cities and their inhabitants? This is one aspect of the concentration problem which has received little attention, despite its obvious importance. Does economic concentration tend to raise or depress the levels of civic welfare? . . .

This exploratory report is designed to shed light on the effects of economic concentration on civic welfare. It is based on a study of six American cities. They were selected in such a way as to provide contrasts in industrial organization and to make possible an evaluation of the effects of big and small business on city life. . . .

At first glance, civic welfare may appear to be a highly difficult topic to measure or even to discuss objectively. Yet, there does exist a considerable amount of concrete, factual data bearing directly on the subject. Thus it was found that the chance that a baby would die within 1 year after birth was considerably greater in big than in small-business cities; in fact, the chance was almost twice as great in one big-business city than in the comparable small-business city. Public expenditures on libraries (per capita) were 10 times greater and on education (per student) were 20 per cent greater in one of the small-business cities studied than in the comparable big-business city; slums were more prevalent—in one case nearly 3 times more prevalent—in big than in small-business cities.

These facts are cited here merely to indicate the nature of the standards employed. The broad conclusions suggested by the study are that—

1. The small-business cities provided for their residents a considerably more balanced economic life than did big-business cities;

[2] "Small Business And Civic Welfare," Document No. 135, 79th Congress, Second Session, Senate, Report of the Smaller War Plants Corporation To The Special Committee to Study Problems of American Small Business, United States Senate, United States Government Printing Office, Washington, D. C., 1946, pp. 1-4. This investigation was made by Dr. C. Wright Mills, Sociologist, and Melville J. Ulmer, Economist.

2. The general level of civic welfare was appreciably higher in the small-business cities;
3. These differences between city life in big- and small-business cities were in the cases studied due largely to differences in industrial organization—that is, specifically to the dominance of big business on the one hand and the prevalence of small business on the other.

The more "balanced" economic life provided in small-business cities was noted in several ways. First of all, industrial stability was much more pronounced. In small-business cities employment was more diversified; not only did a relatively large number of industrial firms operate in a number of different manufacturing lines, but a much greater proportion of workers were engaged in wholesale, retail, and other distributive pursuits. On the other hand, the entire pay roll of big-business cities was largely dominated by one or a few great industrial firms.

This economic dominance of a few big absentee-owned corporations in the big-business cities studied resulted in relative insecurity and instability. The mere decision of one corporation to move its local plant to some other area would be sufficient for economic collapse in a big-business city. Moreover, it has been contended by some economists that production and employment are typically less stable in monopolistic or quasi-monopolistic industries. In any event, it was found that in the big business cities studied, fluctuations in employment, wages, and even in the number of business enterprises were considerably greater, on the average, than in the small-business cities.

Second, it was found that retail facilities were more satisfactory in small-business cities. They were more abundant, more efficiently managed, and offered greater variety. In the big-business cities, it was discovered, retailers hesitated to make substantial investments because of the business hazards incident to the economic instability referred to above. Thus, the residents of big-business cities often had to go elsewhere to buy.

Third, the gap between the incomes of the few very rich and those of the poor appeared to be greater in big-business cities, although available evidence on this point is not conclusive. In small-business cities it appeared that a larger proportion of the population earned medium or high incomes.

The final and most important test applied to big- and small-business cities was the measurement of the general level of civic welfare. The measure employed was that developed by an eminent social scientist. It gives weight to most of the important measurable factors which bear on the welfare of a city's residents, including, for example, numerous items relating to health, housing, sanitation, incomes, education, and recreation among others. A few of these factors—for example, infant mortality and slums—were cited above. The overall measure of civic welfare, summarizing all of these figures, showed that in each case the small-business city studied rated materially higher than did the comparable big-business city.

In the concluding chapter of this report certain tentative reasons are advanced for the generally higher level of civic welfare found in the small-business cities. It was found that in these cities, civic spirit was more pronounced, more widely shared, and more active. The economically independent middle class was more abundant in the small-business cities. For several reasons cited later, it was the independent middle class which usually took the lead in the voluntary management of civic enterprises. In the small-business cities they operated with the relatively widespread coöperation of labor groups.

In the big-business cities, on the other hand, the independent middle class was not only small but for the most part was not truly independent. In these cities the giant corporations were the real powers. Local executives of these corporations had little interest in civic enterprises as such, except insofar as such enterprises might impinge upon the profit opportunities of the corporation. The nominally independent middle class in these cities—directly or indirectly—was compelled to follow the dictates of the corporation executives. Whatever civic activities were undertaken by labor in these cities were instituted not in coöperation with other groups in the city but usually in conflict with them.

In short, in small-business cities the environment was favorable to the development and growth of civic spirit. The interests of the potential leaders of civic enterprise were generally mutual and locally rooted. In big-business cities, civic spirit was stunted or distorted. The potential leaders of civic enterprise were either powerless to act or were motivated by interests outside the city—particularly the home office of the giant corporation. These differences were reflected in the contrasting levels of general civic welfare found in big- and small-business cities. . . .

For purposes of this report a big-business city is defined as one in which (*a*) a few large firms employ all or most of the workers; (*b*) ownership of most of the industrial facilities lies outside the city; (*c*) business activity is concentrated in one or a very few industrial lines. Conversely, a small-business city is one in which (*a*) most of the workers are employed by a large number of small firms; (*b*) the bulk of the industrial facilities are locally owned; (*c*) business activity is diversified in several different industrial lines.

In accordance with these definitions three pairs of cities in the United States were selected for study in this report. The members of each pair were so selected that they had several basic factors in common—general geographical location, population size, percentage of foreign-born and Negroes in the population, etc. In the case of two of these pairs, however, the members differ sharply in one important respect. One of each pair is clearly a big-business city; the other is distinctly a small-business city. In the case of the third pair, there is also a differentiation with respect to big- and small-business industrial organization, but is not as sharp as in the case of the other two, and thus they constitute an intermediate check.

To these cities were applied standards of evaluation generally recognized by sociologists as suitable for the purpose. The figures used to measure the levels of civic life were obtained from official Government sources, from authoritative sociological studies, and from direct field investigation of the cities selected by a sociologist. Also obtained in the field by the sociologist was a considerable amount of information concerning non-quantitative factors in city life, such as the attitudes of civic leaders, the rôle in city life played by executives of the great absentee-owned industrial plants, and so forth.

Finally, it should be noted that the big-business cities studied here were chosen to represent the local manifestations of a national trend—the trend toward industrial concentration, absentee ownership, the dominance of giant corporations. Similarly, the small-business cities were selected to represent the typical community of small, locally owned, competitive enterprises.

It is obviously impossible to state whether or not the conclusions derived in this report are applicable to all big-business and all small-business cities in the United States. An answer to this question would require a field study covering most of the cities in this country. Among big-business cities as well as among small-business cities, there must be many deviations from the patterns found in this survey. It is left for studies of the future to show just how important and how frequent these deviations are.

## SUMMARY

The rise of large cities is a relatively recent development in the United States. It is the result of the Industrial Revolution which created job opportunities and of the revolution in agricultural production. The rate of growth of cities in the 1920's slowed somewhat during the 1930's, but growth still occurred.

Urban life seems to necessitate different behavior patterns than rural life but evidence is lacking that there is a uniquely different urban personality type. Cities are, however, heterogeneous population units and thereby permit persons of marked deviation from behavior norms to form their own special groupings.

City living, and especially metropolitan city living, is often held to be undesirable if not harmful to the inhabitants. When one examines the evidence somewhat more closely, however, much of the indictment seems difficult to substantiate. It seems to be largely anti-urban prejudice, probably the result of the recency of urban development and the tendency for older thought habit-patterns to persist. Many of the things about urban life which are said to be harmful are merely irksome. Others are dangerous merely because we have not learned techniques for conducting ourselves and controlling certain groups in the city in the interest of the general safety and convenience. This applies to the noise, smoke nuisances, auto traffic, and similar urban conditions. It is now scientifically possible virtually to eliminate smoke, appreciably to reduce the inconvenience and dangers of auto traffic, and radically to reduce noise. Usually the continued endurance of these nuisances and dangers are the result of the unwillingness on the part of the cities' citizens to force the utilization of available scientific knowledge upon those in a position to bring about the improvements. Those who derive the benefits of urban living in the form of profits and wages may, however, have to be forced to assume the obligations for removing the undesirable aspects of urban life. There is evidence that considerable additional improvement in urban life along some of these lines may soon be expected. Perhaps eventually the idea may become more widely diffused that many of the inconveniences of urban life are reducible or can be entirely eliminated through attention to the problems instead of the supine resignation to their inevitability.

Other aspects of urban life like anonymity, rigid scheduling and the increased tempo of life may eventually be seen for what they are—simply different modes of behavior neither inherently good nor bad—just different. It should be clear from the foregoing that it is not being contended that urban living is necessarily better or that it is necessarily worse than rural life. It can be factually demonstrated that urban life is different, that it is changing, and that many of its characteristics cannot be objectively evaluated as either good or bad per se, because the judgments depend upon the prejudices of the observer.

Cities differ markedly from one another in many important aspects of the mode of life. The study of social differences between large-industry and small-industry cities quoted at length in this chapter, while not final and conclusive, suggests that the quality of living varies in favor of the small-industry city in terms of the criteria of civic welfare used by the study.

## SELECTED READINGS

ANGELL, R. C., "The Social Integration of Selected American Cities," *American Journal of Sociology,* XLVII, pp. 575-92. **A**

An attempt to show the relation of certain criteria of "good living," such as low income disparity, and non-employment of mothers, to the crime index. Shows a negative correlation between these factors in twenty out of the twenty-eight cities studied.

BLUMENTHAL, Albert, *Small Town Stuff.* (See bibliographic note on page 79.)

HARMS, Ernest, "Rural Attitudes in Modern Urban Life," *Social Forces,* XVII, pp. 486-89. **B**

Shows that urban dwellers both consciously and unconsciously seek to attain rural values in their mode of life. May not prove his hypothesis conclusively, but certainly makes an interesting case for it. The thesis may be sounder than some of the detailed illustrations contained in the article.

LYND, R. S. and LYND, H. M., *Middletown in Transition* (New York, Harcourt, Brace and Co., 1937). **A B**

This is a follow-up of the Lynds' famous study of the culture and social life of Muncie, Indiana, ("Middletown") and covers the period containing the prosperity boom of the twenties and the great depression of the thirties. Considered the most significant study of its kind. Covers almost every conceivable aspect of life in a Midwestern city. Objective, yet dramatic.

Marshall, D. G., "Hamlets and Villages in the United States; Their Place in the American Way of Life," *American Sociological Review,* XI, pp. 159-166. **A B**

Considers the question of the relative rôle of non-agricultural rural population units and cities in America. Explains why hamlets and villages persist in a big-city dominated society and what they contribute to it.

Muntz, E. E., *Urban Sociology* (New York, The Macmillan Co., 1938). **A B**

An encyclopedic textbook on the city. Contains exhaustive treatment of such varied subjects as commercial recreation and sewage disposal problems. Emphasizes social control of the social problems of the city. Contains an abundance of factual materials.

## STUDY QUESTIONS

1. Why were the "large cities" before the Industrial Revolution so small in comparison to modern cities?
2. What changes are taking place in the distribution of American urban population?
3. Compare the long-run and the short-run trends in American urbanization.
4. Why is it difficult to determine the reasons for urban growth? Make what you consider to be the best possible objective statement of the case.
5. Is there a unique urban personality type? Discuss *pro* and *con.*
6. What is meant by the "communality?" Why is it an "adjustment to urbanization?"
7. Is urban life better or worse than rural life? To what extent is the answer to this question an exercise in ethnocentrism?
8. Distinguish remediable and inherent problems of urban living.
9. What do we mean by the anti-urban bias?
10. Summarize the study of small business and civic welfare quoted in this chapter. Criticize the study for possible bias.
11. What is "rural urbanization?" Compare it to urbanization.
12. Is the suburban dweller primarily urban or rural? Explain.
13. What aspects of urbanism are involved in the "corporation farming" pattern?

# *Chapter XX*

## SOCIAL STRATIFICATION: CASTE AND CLASS

In all human societies from the most primitive to the most modern, persons are accorded *differential status.* Prestige, esteem, honor, and power tend to be unequally divided among persons in different age-groups, between the sexes, and among those of different occupation, education, and lineage. Most modern societies have institutionalized (see p. 277 for definition of "institutionalization") some aspects of differential status: persons are placed into categories forming a hierarchy of rank usually called a "class system" or, somewhat preferably, "social stratification." The word *stratification* seems appropriate since the different statuses accorded to persons carry with them definitions of "higher" and "lower" value as compared to other categories of persons. In common language we speak of successful persons as "rising" or "coming up," and refer to "higher" and "lower" social classes. The valuation implied in these language usages is clear. The people of the society regard certain persons and groups *as if* they were more important or more valuable than other persons and groups. Much formal lip service is paid to the democratic ideal in America which pretends that there are no classes and that "every one is equal to every one else," but a more realistic examination of actual behavior makes it quite clear that people characteristically think and act in terms of conceptions of higher and lower social position.

### SOCIAL CLASSES DEFINED

A social class may be somewhat variously conceived, and the conception may be phrased in a number of different ways. While no definition is wholly acceptable to all scholars, the following one contains the essential core of meaning upon which there is a substantial agreement.

A social class or stratum of a society is a major segment or category of the population, in which persons have about the same status or rank. The essence of the rank position is prestige. Prestige may result from special talent, or from the possession of wealth or other prestige goods, or from education, or from family line, or from some combination of these, or from some other valued attribute or supposed attribute of the person. Class systems are, of course, value systems and have the same non-rational basis as many other aspects of human life. A given class system may appear logical or illogical depending on the point of view from which one evaluates it. Thus, most contemporary Americans tend to interpret the class systems of feudalistic Europe as "unfair" to the serfs who were bound to the soil and also point out that the nobility enjoyed superior privileges but did nothing personally, as a rule, to warrant such preferential treatment. The same evaluator, however, is less likely to see that the distribution of privilege in contemporary American society is also very unequal, if not also inequitable, with many persons "bound" by the conditions of their birth to permanently humble social position, while others "inherit" a high prestige which is in no way related to their own efforts or abilities. To be sure, the *legal* position of the serf was less free, but his *actual* ability to participate in the benefits of the society may be comparable to that of many Americans, both urban and rural. Moreover, the evaluator is usually more likely to "see" class inequalities and their non-rational aspects, if he views the system from the less privileged than from the more favored social stratum. It is easy, on the other hand, to rationalize high class position.

It is necessary to distinguish, however, between the fact of differential status and a class system. In a class system the group affiliations of a person, not his own intrinsic traits or behavior, are largely the basis for his stature. Whenever a person is *accorded status on the basis of the group to which he belongs,* then the first aspect of class is manifest. Thus, for example, in a pecuniary society persons of greater wealth and income are able to purchase more status-giving goods such as better homes, more expensive automobiles, better clothes, and superior medical care. The possession of these things gives prestige, privilege, and more or less power over other people.

It is sometimes held that the "society rewards talent" and that, therefore, the possession of status-goods through higher wealth and income is not really a class manifestation, but simply reflects difference in personal ability. This point of view would probably be true enough, let us say, for a man who is the first in his family line to attain somewhat greater wealth and income than has been characteristic for his group. But he alone does not enjoy the wealth and income which he has presumably "earned" or the superior prestige which those possessions give him. His wife and children also have the superior advantages of his income, yet very probably they have done nothing significant which would warrant the receiving of the superior social and economic advantages which they get. They receive their superior social privilege by the good fortune or the historical accident that they happen to be associated with the somewhat exceptional man in our illustration. Carrying the point somewhat further, it is apparent that this man's children in addition to enjoying advantages because of their father's success, have superior opportunity to be successful themselves. The chances of their having superior education are good; they have financial "backing" and "social standing." All of these factors tend to give these children an advantage, and sometimes a great advantage, over other children for achieving either monetary or intangible status. Thus, *differential status tends to become formalized or institutionalized into a system of differential privilege and opportunity accorded to the person on the basis of his family and other group affiliations.*

This principle is sometimes misconstrued as prima facie evidence that persons in the United States, for example, do not "deserve" their high class position since they get it by the fortunes of inheritance or the accidents of their group affiliations. While such may sometimes be the case, this conception constitutes an exaggeration which goes beyond the facts. The point is not one of whether the person in superior class position "deserves" or "earns" the privilege, but rather that having originated in a given class he has had superior opportunities to achieve the skills and abilities for which he may later be only justly rewarded. For example, it probably could not with accuracy be contended that Henry Ford II does not have the required skills and abilities to fill his rôle as head of one of the nation's most gigantic industrial enterprises. The point is that his position as grandson of Henry Ford I gave him superior opportunities to develop his talents along the lines necessary to discharge this rôle effectively. Also, being directly in the line of inheritance from Henry Ford I, he probably did not have to be much concerned about competition from very many other Americans who might possibly fill the job as well or better than he does, because such persons probably would not be given the opportunity to try it. It would be difficult to contend that this man and many other leaders whose power positions are great do not actually possess the ability necessary to hold their power positions. The significance of class goes beyond this fact into the *differential opportunities for achieving and developing talent, and differential opportunities actually to demonstrate whether one has talent or not.*

It is important to emphasize that the possession of wealth and income which figure so prominently in American social stratification are not the bases of stratification in all societies. Among European royal families, for example, wealth has been a relatively unimportant factor, lineage being much more significant. In other societies education or occupation, irrespective of the income received, are the bases on which differential class position is determined. "Race" is sometimes the determining factor. In short, valuation is of the essence, and whatever the society has chosen to value highly may be the basis for affording differential status.

Wealth and income are, of course, not the sole determinants of class position in the United States, although they are prominent features of class. Education and occupation loom large. There are numerous cases of persons of great wealth and income who are not "accepted" by persons of higher class groups because they lack the necessary requisites of education and the "right occupation." Professional people, for example, are not among the most highly-paid groups in the United States, but usually are quite acceptable in higher class society because they have other high status, prestige-providing attributes. In most local communities, family background and length of residence are also factors affecting the person's class position.

One's class position in a society consists of a set of privileges and disprivileges, freedoms and restrictions, opportunities and limitations. A person of low class position in American society would probably find it impossible to secure an audience with the President of the United States even should he have good cause so to do. But a prominent leader in industry, finance, the professions, or the entertainment world would not find it difficult to confer with the President whether he had any good reason to do it or not. The hypothetical interview with the President, of course, is not of vital intrinsic importance, but it serves as a useful illustration of the way in which differential status carries with it differential privilege. Of greater concern are such differential privileges as the exclusion of Negroes from white schools, or the refusal to admit Jewish persons as students in some American professional colleges, or the ostracism of some persons from social and professional groups because they do not come from the "right" families.

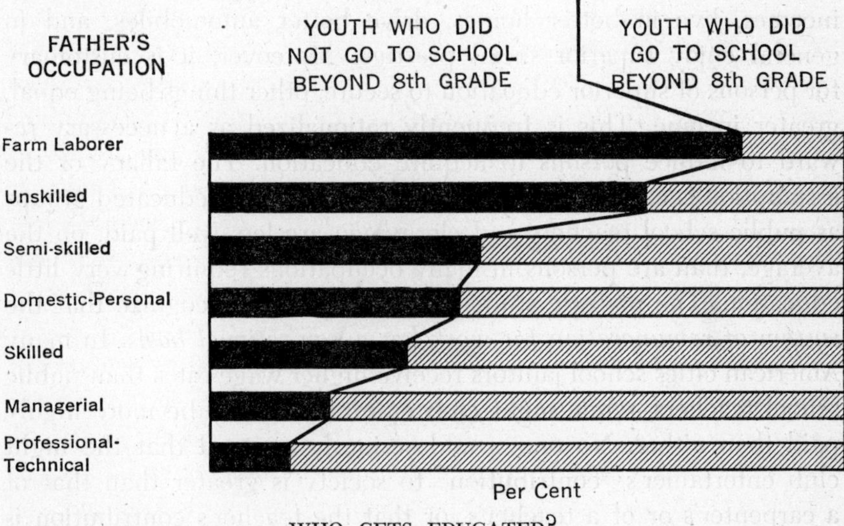


WHO GETS EDUCATED?

Adapted from Howard Bell, *Youth Tell Their Story,* American Youth Commission, American Council on Education, Washington, D. C., 1938, p. 59.

Law enforcement is likewise affected by the differential status of the accused. From juvenile court to criminal court, there is evidence of the advantage of wealth and social position in the determination of guilt or innocence and in the imposition of punishment. It is not simply that "justice is bought," but that superior economic status gives such differential opportunities as securing more competent legal counsel, securing bond, as well as the more intangible factor of securing better "consideration" because of one's higher social position. In myriads of other ways tangibly and intangibly, status position impinges upon the every day activities of persons.

*Division of Labor and the Class System*

As we have noted repeatedly, one of the cardinal sociological facts is the division of labor. It has sometimes been said that the class system is simply an outgrowth of this basic factor. The division of labor per se, however, does not make for any particular class arrangement. In all modern industrial societies, for example, some persons do managerial work, some skilled manual work, and some relatively unskilled work. This is a basic division of labor, but there is nothing in the fact of the division of labor which necessarily requires that the executive and managerial class should secure higher incomes, live in better homes, drive better automobiles, and in general enjoy superior social prestige. Moreover, it is customary for persons of superior education to secure, other things being equal, greater income. This is frequently rationalized as a necessary reward to induce persons to acquire education. The fallacy of the assumption is easily seen when one notes that such educated groups as public school teachers and clergymen are less well paid, on the average, than are persons in many occupations requiring very little education. The realistic student of society must recognize that the *system of remuneration for work has a non-rational basis.* In many American cities school janitors receive higher wage rates than public school teachers, while night club entertainers may be more highly paid than either. No one would seriously contend that the night club entertainer's "contribution" to society is greater than that of a carpenter's or of a teacher's, or that the teacher's contribution is inherently any more or less valuable than the carpenter's. The wages paid for different kinds of work are more or less arbitrarily arrived at, and custom tends to perpetuate the established wage system. Within occupations, however, wage differentials may often be explained in terms of differences in the quality or quantity of the work done, but between occupations no just basis of comparison can be formulated. and differentials remain largely arbitrary. One can best "understand" a class system. like a wage scale, in terms of the underlying values of the society. There are *many* "logical" systems.

## FORMS OF SOCIAL STRATIFICATION

Taking a broad view of all societies, past and present, it is possible to distinguish certain forms or types of social stratification.

### *Caste*

The most rigid form of social stratification is the *caste*. Membership in a caste is determined by birth. One inherits a caste position from which, with few exceptions, he cannot rise or cannot fall. In some instances membership may be acquired in a caste through marriage or adoption, but such instances are clearly exceptional. Caste is, therefore, a permanent basis of stratification for the person. It cannot be overemphasized that placement in a caste system is not determined by one's personal qualities, whether good or bad, or by the talents or wishes of the person.

No modern Western nation is characterized by a caste system, although there are certain caste-like attributes to be found in several. The position of Negroes in the United States, for example, has certain attributes of caste. Negroes and whites are forbidden by law to intermarry in thirty American states, and by strong custom in most of the rest. Many of the jobs are closed by law or custom to Negroes. Segregation in some degree is practically universal. In spite of these facts, however, the position of the Negro in the United States is probably not truly one of caste. Segregation is not complete. Many occupations are shared by Negroes and whites, and the two races are not set apart by different dress or insignia of rank or the possession of exclusive caste goods. Furthermore within the Negro group there is social stratification based upon the same general kind of valuation that one finds in white society.

Caste stratification consists of rigid hereditary placement of the person irrespective of personal attributes or desires. Caste is often characterized also by endogamy, occupational prohibitions and requirements, segregation, distinguishing caste attire and possessions, rigid requirements for eating and other intimate associations, or some combination of these.

### *Estates*

The estate system is somewhat less rigid than the caste system. Persons in each stratum have their rights, privileges, and responsibilities fixed by law and, therefore, somewhat subject to rational modification. European feudalism constitutes an excellent illustration of the estate system. The duties and privileges of nobles, freemen, and serfs were clearly set forth in written and common law. The estate, while relatively permanent and largely a hereditary basis for determining status, is less rigid than the caste system. Thus in medieval Europe sometimes serfs could become freemen under certain stipulated conditions, but not many actually did or could. The position of the titled nobility in Europe during more recent years, and even to some extent today, has many of the characteristics of an estate. Estate systems leave open some theoretical and occasionally utilized channels through which a person may change his class position. Workmen may, through education or political activity, rise sometimes to notable prestigial heights. At least one British prime minister in recent decades has risen from the ranks of labor. Such instances are, of course, the exception, not the rule, but the fact that they can and do occur, however infrequently, is significant.

### *Open Class*

Open classes are distinguished largely in terms of the degree of ease and the frequency with which persons change class position. An open-class system may be defined as a class system which does not place categorical limitations on the person with respect to his class position. This means that admission to another class is not denied to a person for any reason other than that he does not possess the necessary skills pertinent to the rôle of the class to which he aspires, whether higher or lower in the hierarchy. So long, for example, as persons are barred from occupations because of color, creed, family background, or similar considerations, an open-class system cannot be said to exist. The open-class system may also be conceived as a "democratic" system, that is, a person's status is accorded strictly on the basis of his own fitness for the rôles which a given class position requires.

### *American White Society Often Cited as an Open-Class System*

It is a matter of common knowledge that many persons reared among humble people have risen, and are still rising, to higher and sometimes topmost social and economic position in many different aspects of American society—religion, business, entertainment, or the professions. It is part of the American mythology, however, to *exaggerate the frequency with which this occurs* and to *minimize the many influences which impede the process.* Probably because of our democratic ideas, Americans are sensitive to the existence of non-democratic forces, and console themselves somewhat by minimizing or overlooking or denying that they exist. Many astute observers feel that there is sufficient evidence that American social stratification was once close to open class, but is now moving away from it. They cite as evidence the "fact" that fewer and fewer persons are able to change class position regardless of the amount of ability which they happen to have. It is extremely difficult to test such an hypothesis objectively, and until some technique is devised for so doing, we must rely upon judgments which are, of course, somewhat varied.

### *A Continuum of Class Systems*

The various forms of social stratification, caste, estate, and open class, may be thought of as *positions along a continuum.* Caste and open class represent the extremes, with estates as a midpoint along the scale. Probably no perfect caste system or open system has ever existed, although some actual societies have come quite close to each. Thinking in terms of this continuum will tend to emphasize the fact that actual societies distribute themselves along the continuum, varying from one another *in the degree to which the individual secures his class position by virtue of his own traits, and the corresponding ease with which he may change his class position if he has the requisite personality to meet the requirements of another stratum.* Stated in another way, societies vary along the continuum on the basis of the degree to which they impose categorical limitations on a person's social status and/or assign permanent position to persons on the basis of inheritance.

Thinking in terms of a continuum will also assist the student to comprehend the important fact that systems of social stratification like all socio-cultural phenomena are *constantly changing.* A given society may move either in the direction of caste-like tendencies, or open-class tendencies, or it may move for a time in one direction and then reverse itself. These sudden reversals have often taken the form of revolutions, like the Russian Revolution or the French Revolution, as a result of which the whole stratification system has been radically altered in a very short space of time. Like all social change, modifications of stratification may occur either through slow evolutionary development or through sudden revolution.

### WHAT IS THE URBAN AMERICAN SOCIAL CLASS SYSTEM?

While the facts of differential status, privilege, and power are obvious enough even to the untrained observer, it becomes exceedingly difficult to determine the precise system or pattern of stratification which makes up American society. Traditionally we have loosely referred to upper, lower, and middle classes, but how can one determine objectively that there are three classes rather than four, five, or seventeen? Furthermore, assuming for the moment that there are really three classes, to which of the three does the public school teacher belong? Measured by income she might conceivably be in the lowest of the three classes, and yet she usually enjoys the privilege of participating socially in many ways with members of the upper class. Furthermore, is the class system of an Iowa county seat town comparable in any realistic sense with the class system of an Atlantic sea coast metropolitan city? From these and other questions which could readily be formulated, it becomes apparent that it is no easy task to determine the class structure of the United States, even though one has lived in it all of his life.

The Lynds, in their famous *Middletown* books which are classic and penetrating analyses of a middle-sized American city and more or less typical of much of Middle-West America, have made extensive use of a rough two-class conception of stratification which they term simply "the working class and the business class." The terms hardly need definition. "Business class" is used loosely to include not only persons engaged in commerce and the management of industry, but also in the rôles ordinarily called the professions. While professional persons are not concerned strictly with business, some of them like lawyers, veterinarians, and many physicians are essentially highly trained persons who sell services rather than goods, but who come very close to the business class because of the size of their income and because of their general social acceptance by business class people. When issues are drawn between business and working class interests, professional persons have, in the past at least, almost invariably "lined up" with the business class point of view. One should not assume that all business class persons necessarily receive higher incomes than working class persons, for such is not the case. *On the average,* however, business class persons do receive superior incomes, but their community position does not depend entirely upon how much money they receive.

The business class-working class dichotomy is an oversimplification. So also is the capital-labor classification. Others speak of lower, middle, and upper classes. Obviously, any such simple and clear-cut categorization does not adequately portray the multiplicity of differences in rank which actually exist. The chief difficulty in accurately describing the class system lies in the fact that there are classes within classes, and unless one is quite familiar with the value patterns of the groups in question, he can easily err in his judgment as to where in the status hierarchy a given person or family really "belongs." Class differences are most easily appreciated when the observer is comparing persons of wide class discrepancy, and is not so clear when the rank difference is slight. *The fact that the class system cannot be neatly pictured should not, however, obscure the tremendously important nature of class difference and the largely non-rational aspect of it.* Class differences are very real—possibly even the cardinal modern social reality.

Class position is dependent upon two related subjective factors—*identification* and *acceptance*. To a greater extent than is sometimes realized, some persons may identify themselves with either of two or more classes depending upon where they *feel* or *think* they belong. There are, of course, numerous limitations imposed upon a person's "choice" of class identification. For example, the corner peanut vendor might consider himself a member of the business class, but would probably not be accepted by that class. But, on the other hand, large groups of persons, for example, public school teachers, farmers, and "white collar" clerical workers, may identify themselves either with the working class or with the business class. They would be more or less acceptable among either group. There is one group of American teachers, for example, which is organized into a union affiliated with the American Federation of Labor and presumably, therefore, feels loyal to the interests and point of view of working class people. Other teachers adopt a rôle, sometimes exceedingly difficult to maintain on their incomes, which rather clearly indicates that they choose to think of themselves as affiliated with the business class, and in most communities are more or less accepted in that category if they so choose.

It is important, however, not to overdraw the element of choice in class position in America. Probably for the vast majority of people there is no choice at all. Identification with the working class is the only allegiance possible. The same would hold true for persons of the business class.

The so-called "superior advantage" of membership in the business class also has its limitations for many persons. Privilege tends to carry also responsibility. Much of the difficulty of "keeping up with the Joneses" which many young people of the business classes feel so acutely, becomes a problem because of the virtual necessity of participating in activities and making expenditures which the persons themselves often would not prefer. But the obligations of class position are virtually dictatorial. This obligation may apply to dress, housing, entertaining, to recreational patterns, in fact to the whole pattern of living.

Acceptance of persons in the class system of the American community, thus, rests not only upon financial considerations like wealth, income, and possessions but also upon education, possession of titles (which presumably imply some sort of distinction), or the possession of some unusual talent which is valued highly. It is sometimes difficult to determine the relative importance of pecuniary and non-pecuniary bases for class position in American society. About all that can be said with assurance is that financial factors loom large, but are by no means the exclusive determinants of one's class acceptance.

## POWER AND THE CLASS STRUGGLE IN THE UNITED STATES

Class systems are not static. History records a long series of bitter struggles between class strata in many societies. These struggles have usually centered around the revision of the system of social stratification or some part of it. Probably the most significant single factor in the class struggle is the matter of power. Whatever the class differentials in standard of living or the security of income and employment, the differential power to exert control over the society seems to be the ultimate factor over which classes have traditionally struggled.

By the sheer force of numbers, of course, the working classes have a vague, potential sort of power. It would seem, in a democracy particularly, that this would be a significant factor giving to the working class the opportunity virtually to dominate the society in any manner which it chose. In practice this assumption has not proved accurate, because persons in the working class have not until very recently, and perhaps not even now, regarded themselves as *a* class. Consequently there have been divisions and rivalries within the working class which have largely prevented any sort of effective, unified, and concerted action at the polls. It is thought by many observers that the situation is now changing, and that beginning with the introduction of the New Deal, a working class consciousness has become manifest in American political and economic life. It is too early to determine objectively whether this interpretation is accurate, although there seems considerable evidence to support it.

*The numerically smaller business class, however, has tremendously important sources of power* which in the past have been sufficient to keep it in a dominant position in American life, and probably will continue so to do for some considerable time into the future. First, the business class has control, and largely ownership, of the great aggregates of capital in the form of factories, mines, railroads, public utilities, banks, insurance companies, upon which the working class is vitally dependent for the opportunity to make a living. The financial resources of persons in the business class are *on the average* superior to those of working class people, so that any "showdown" for power such as a strike or boycott can be personally weathered much more easily and for a longer period by the business class than by the working class.

Probably more important, however, is the *control which the business class has over the media of mass communication* such as the radio, newspaper, the movies, and to a considerable extent education also. This makes it possible for the "public relations" representatives of the business class so to present the business class "case" that many persons whose class position is uncertain use their political influence on the side of the business class. In other words, whether or not their true interests are on the side of the business class, they give their allegiance to the cause of the business class. While there is theoretical, and to a considerable extent actual, freedom of speech for spokesmen of either the business or the working class, *in the practical situation the person who can pay for time on the air, pay for newspaper space, and pay for the service of propaganda experts, can have his "say" much more effectively* than can one who cannot afford to purchase these media for winning "friends" to his cause.

While the above mentioned factors may not in themselves constitute the entire explanation for the superior power position of the numerically smaller group in American society, they constitute at least a significant part of the whole explanation.

As we shall see in the following chapters, especially those dealing with economic groups and government, there are sharp issues in contemporary American society regarding a number of class related problems. Wages, regulation of industry and labor, control of prices, freedom of education, Fair Employment Practices, more adequate representation for formerly underrepresented or unrepresented groups, and the improvement of the conditions of urban living for the underprivileged are a few examples. Some observers interpret "the trend of the times" as moving toward sharper and more frequent class issues. Regardless of whether this interpretation is the correct one or not, it is certainly clear that interclass issues are fundamental factors in the changing American society.

## SUMMARY

Differential status is a universal aspect of all societies past and present, primitive and modern. In most societies differential status becomes formally organized or institutionalized into systems of social stratification such as caste, estates, and open-class arrangements. The essential difference among these forms of stratification is the extent to which the individual person is permitted to achieve his class status on the basis of his personal merit, irrespective of categorical placement or categorical limitations on placement.

A social class may be defined as a group within a society, the members of which have essentially the same rank in the hierarchy of status. Difference in function does not in itself determine the relative rank which a class or a person is permitted by the society. Rank is the result of the value system and the whole cultural tradition of the society. Systems of rank are highly variable like all other aspects of society and essentially non-rational.

Placement in the American class system is the result of a number of factors, some obviously economic like wealth and income, others indirectly economic like possessions and education, while still others may or may not be related to economic matters, such as family background or the possession of a special talent. It is difficult to determine the relative importance of these factors. While the primacy of pecuniary valuation is clear, it is not the sole or even the determining factor.

It is exceedingly difficult to outline the structure of the American class system. Throughout most of our discussion we have employed the business class-working class dichotomy formulated and popularized by the authors of the *Middletown* studies. The formulation seems useful enough for elementary purposes in studying the class system of the urban community, but obviously does not apply to rural society nor does it give insight into the many substrata within each of the two groups. The American class system presents the seeming paradox of superior power in the hands of the numerically smaller group. This would be understandable enough in an authoritarian society, but in a democratic society it requires explanation. A part of the explanation, at least, can be made on the basis of the control which the management rôle gives to the business class. Through this medium most of the agencies of public control are at its command as a result of its superior ability to pay for and, therefore, to receive the loyalty of newspapers, the radio industry, and education. Meanwhile, the working class has up to the present time not realized much of the potential power of its great numbers, because of internal differences and in general a lack of consciousness of common interest. Moreover, the business class has traditionally enjoyed the allegiance of many persons and groups like professional persons, the church, and politicians who have tended to place their loyalty primarily with the business class. There is some evidence that a change in this respect is occurring and, therefore, many observers anticipate some rather marked changes in the power structure of American society in the not distant future.

## SUGGESTED READINGS

FORM, William, "Status Stratification in a Planned Community," *American Sociological Review,* X, pp. 605-613. **A B**

A study of the differential status system in an "artificial" "community" (Greenbelt, Maryland, built in 1937). The community is made up of persons migrating from areas of different class systems. Despite the effort made to create an ideal and class-less community, a local class structure exists, but it is a somewhat different one from that of less planned communities of similar "suburban" culture.

LYND, R. S., and LYND, H. M., *Middletown in Transition.* (See bibliographic notes page 365.) **A B**

Chapter III, "The X Family: A Pattern of Business Class Control," is an interesting and graphic account of the ways and means whereby upper class families dominate the social organization of the city whether they intend so to do or not.

NORTH, C. C., *Social Differentiation* (Chapel Hill, N. C., University of North Carolina Press, 1926). **A**

A monograph on social structure. Gives an historical and systematic account of social stratification in formal terms.

PARSONS, Talcott, "The Professions and Social Structure," *Social Forces,* XVII, pp. 457-67. **A**

An excellent evaluation of the rôle of the professional person in the class system.

SAENGER, G. H., "Social Status and Political Behavior," *American Journal of Sociology,* LI, pp. 103-113. **A B**

A statistical study which seems to indicate that the voting and other aspects of the political behavior of the persons studied are more clearly related to their class position than to "personal experience" or exposure to propaganda. Sample cited is in New York City.

SUTHERLAND, E. H., "White Collar Criminality," *American Sociological Review,* V, pp. 1-12. **A B**

An epochal research on crime. Shows conclusively that our official concepts of crime are class-biased. Contains abundant official evidence to prove his revolutionary thesis regarding criminal behavior. Should be familiar to every informed citizen!

VEBLEN, Thorstein, *The Theory of the Leisure Class* (New York, Huebsch, 1919). **A B**

This is a classic. It advances the theory that class position is affected, if not determined, by "conspicuous consumption" and the obvious use of leisure. Vigorously written.

WARNER, W. L., and LUNT, Paul, *The Social Life of a Modern Community* New Haven, Conn., Yale University Press, 1941). **A**

A well-known and somewhat controversial formulation of the American class system based on actual study of the value system of a specific community. Advances a sixfold classification of society. Of interest also will be Mills' criticism in *American Sociological Review,* VII, 263-271.

WEST, James, *Plainville, U. S. A.,* Chapter III. (See bibliographic note p. 101). **B**

## STUDY QUESTIONS

1. What is meant by "social stratification"? Why is this concept a figure of speech?
2. Distinguish between differential status and a class system? Illustrate
3. Discuss the *pros* and *cons* of the question whether persons in superior position deserve their privileges.
4. Is there anything inconsistent about a class system and democratic ideals? How is it necessary to qualify one's answer to this question?
5. Evaluate *pro* and *con*: "The class system is a result of the division of labor."
6. Explain: "The system of remuneration for work is a non-rational aspect of culture."
7. Is the above quotation more accurate within or between occupations in the United States?
8. What aspects of caste are found in the position of the American Negro?
9. Why is it difficult to determine whether America is moving in the direction of an estate system or of an open-class system?
10. Criticize the "working class-business class" dichotomy.
11. Why is a class system difficult to define? Illustrate.
12. What evidence is there of a class struggle in America?
13. How can a numerically smaller class maintain superior power in a democracy?

## *Part V*

# MAJOR AMERICAN SOCIAL INSTITUTIONS

# INTRODUCTORY NOTE: INSTITUTIONS IN GENERAL

Little of the technical nomenclature of social science has given scholars as much difficulty as has the concept *institution*. The difficulty has stemmed largely from the fact that the word had an established core of meaning in the layman's language before the social scientists began to use it. That core of meaning, variously stated, was to the effect that certain basic values and the activities which embody them are important and relatively permanent aspects of each society. Thus the family, government, and other major segments of the society are usually referred to as "institutions." But a great many other phenomena, for example, capitalism, liberty, and some particular university or mental hospital, are also called "institutions." Hence the confusion.

The first essential to bear in mind is that the *term* institution *is an abstraction*, such as the abstraction involved in such generic nouns as government, man, life, or behavior. One cannot *perceive* any of these things. He can see *a* man, can observe *a* government, can observe *a* life or some *one* behavior. He cannot possibly see all men past and present. Therefore, we say, that one must *conceive* an abstraction, like "man," though he may *perceive* some specific instances which approximate the abstraction conceived. So it is with an institution, such as the family, education, or religion. The words stand for ideas which are derived not from any one government or one religion, but from many governments and many religions, past and present, embracing both their similarities and their differences.

What are the *characteristics* or attributes of institutions? Angell says: [1]

> Institutions are *systems of social relationships* to which people feel loyal because these systems are judged to *embody the ultimate values that these people have in common*. . . . Their acceptance need not be rational or conscious; it is often traditional or emotional. This is obviously true of such long established institutions as the family.
>
> Societal institutions . . . are institutions expressive of so broadly shared an orientation that they *become the focuses around which the life of a society revolves*. There may be a few in the population who are indifferent or even hostile; but they are regarded as queer, and they are powerless to prevent the reception of the institutions by the next generation.
>
> Institutions are *accepted not merely by all who actually participate in them but by all who share the common orientation*. For example, a bachelor can accept the institution of the family and believe it conducive to the realization of the highest values he cherishes. . . . Though the individual is within the structure he does not feel it as constraining. A father plays his rôle in the family loyalty, not from fear of legal sanctions if he does not, but from a *sense of the importance of* the family in the scheme of things that he values. . . .

The observable organizations, groups, or "associations" which one finds in any society, tend to exemplify the values of the abstract institutions, or some parts thereof. Thus, the First Congregational Church of Middletown or of Plainville, U.S.A. is a specific grouping of people which manifests a number of values and activities characteristic of the institution of Protestant Christian religion in the United States. But this group of people also embodies other aspects of life such as providing opportunities for some people to assert power over other persons through church positions and providing a market for coal dealers who sell fuel to the church.

It is important to note this *distinction between the institution, which is an abstract nucleus of values* centering around some segment of human life, *and the specific organizations and groups through which institutions are actually expressed*. For example, it is probably true that no two existing families in the United States are exactly alike in the manner in which they are organized, the purposes which they fulfill, or the activities which they carry out. In fact striking contrasts exist. Moreover, a growing number of families are broken up due to divorce. Yet the institution of a permanent monogamous family is part and parcel of the culture of

[1] R. C. Angell, *The Integration of American Society* (New York, McGraw-Hill Book Co., 1941), pp. 25-27 (italics ours).

this society, and any deviations or variations from monogamy or permanence, even though they are numerous, are usually viewed as unfortunate occurrences and often regarded as morally wrong. In a very real sense a divorced family illustrates the institutional principle of permanent monogamy quite as well as does a conventionally unified family. The divorced family had to secure legal permission to be dissolved, and had to show cause before it would be possible under law for the courts to grant the couple the right to an exception to the institutional rule of abiding monogamy.

In many other ways the *close relation of institutions* and associations or groups could be illustrated. The essential point is that *groups tend to embody institutions when viewed as a whole, but specific groups may embody institutions very imperfectly.* Therefore, one cannot infer the institutions in a society merely from the observation of one or a few groups, because he may find in the groups he chooses, important variations or downright exceptions to the institutional pattern. One can only *infer* institutions from a broad and extensive, as well as deep and intensive study, of a great many existing groups, associations, or organizations of a society.

Sociologists generally regard the family, government, religion, the economic system, and education as the basic, important institutions of a society. We now turn to an examination of some of the major characteristics and developments occurring in these aspects of American life.

# Chapter XXI

## THE FAMILY

In previous chapters we have discussed several significant aspects of the family, and have advanced several basic principles pertaining to the family.

1. The family is a universal social grouping found in broad outline in every society.
2. Family makeup is highly variable including such divergent forms as polygyny, polyandry, and group marriage, as well as the monogamous form with which Americans are, of course, familiar.
3. The requirements of the rôles of husband, single adult, married adult, parent, and child are likewise radically variable. What is characteristically male behavior in one society may be typically female behavior in the other. Authority for governing the family may be vested solely or largely in the husband, solely or largely in the wife, or may be a combination of these two. A person may be required to be sexually indulgent before marriage is permitted, or permanent chastity may be expected. And so on through all the almost innumerable behavior variations from society to society and from time to time.
4. The family, like all social forms, changes. The rate and direction of change has varied considerably at various times and among the various societies, but the fact of change has never been successfully resisted by any people which social scientists have been able to study. Considerable effort is often put into contriving ways and means of preventing family change through law, church dogma, and informal public pressures, but at best these devices serve only to reduce the speed of change (if they even achieve that) but they cannot prevent it.
5. Not only do the norms of family life vary, but so also do the individual families vary from the norms characteristic of the larger society of which the given family is a part. Thus in any society one can find individual cases of marked variation from the general family pattern. Numerous married women in our society, for example, are employed outside the home. Some couples are deliberately childless, and in some families greater authority is held by the wife. Moreover, it is common knowledge that there is widespread variation in the standards of sex morals to which different people adhere.

6. The family is affected markedly by happenings in other areas of the society. War, depressions, and prosperity all exert a marked influence upon a characteristic form of family living. The family does not live unto itself, anymore than the individual human being does. Constantly there are influences impinging on this group and thus modifying its form and function.

With these background principles in mind, we now turn to a somewhat more specific treatment of the contemporary American family.

## SOME LONG-RUN TRENDS

### 1. *Declining Male Dominance*

The antecedent European and early American family was patriarchal. Gradually women have gained more freedom and power legally, politically, educationally, and economically. Although all of the differentials between male and female prerogatives have not disappeared, they have been sufficiently reduced so that today men and women stand more nearly on an equal footing with respect to the freedom and power which they hold. Thus today it is not at all unusual to find married pairs in which the women are more educated than their husbands or who hold positions which are superior to those of their husbands in salary, status, or both. Certainly at least one of the factors in the high divorce rate of this generation is the unwillingness of women to tolerate unhappy matings which formerly many women were forced to tolerate because they lacked the economic and social status necessary to make a fresh start toward another marriage or toward a single life. There is a less sharp line now between men's and women's jobs, men's and women's recreational patterns, and even men's and women's dress for many occasions. While the equality is not complete the trend in the direction of equality continues.

### 2. *Increasing Impermanence*

Ours is an era of declining permanence in most human relationships. Persons and families move freely from community to community and from region to region. Frequently they have no real choice to do otherwise. Fewer and fewer people live out their lives in one community and with the same circle of relatives, friends, and working associates. Moreover, as everyone knows, there is a high divorce rate. This means that impermanence is extending also to the husband-wife relation. A larger proportion of the entire married population has been married more than once. For the last eighteen months (1945-46) many of the large metropolitan American cities have recorded approximately as many applications for divorces as applications for marriage, and the divorce rate is still rising. No one knows how far this trend may go or whether or when there will be a reaction. Post-war periods normally are periods

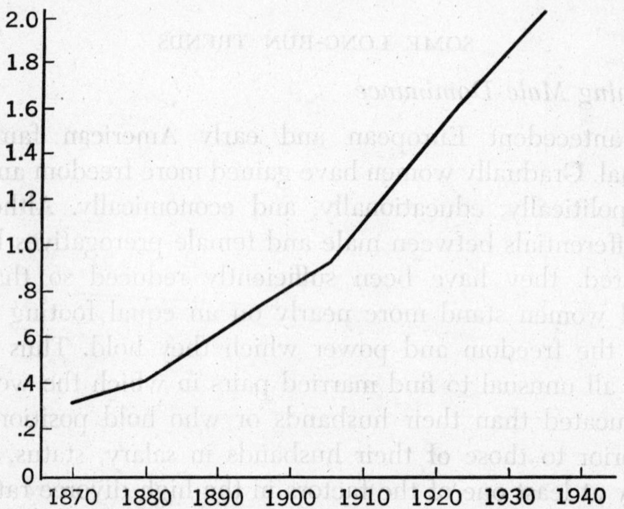


TREND OF DIVORCES IN THE UNITED STATES: DIVORCES PER 1,000 OF THE TOTAL POPULATION, 1870-1940

Based on data from Bureau of the Census, *Statistical Abstract of the United States,* 1943, p. 92.

of high divorce rate, and, therefore, the extremely high rates of the present will probably decline somewhat. It may be significant to note, however, that at least since 1900 there has been a long-time rise in the American divorce rate. While short periods have shown more rapid rises and some declines, such as during the depressions of the early 30's, the overall trend has been upward. Divorce rates are higher for married pairs without children, but the number as well as the proportion of children who have experienced four or more parents is appreciable.

3. *Decreasing Family Size*

It is common knowledge that the American birth rate has been declining. The average American family in 1940 was about three and three-fourths persons, a decline of around 30 per cent since 1850. This decline has not been uniform for all social classes and all regions of the nation. Lowest birth rates are found in the higher middle class urban groups. Higher birth rates are found among populations in agricultural areas, but even among these groups the trend toward a lower birth rate is becoming apparent. The lower birth rate is ordinarily attributed to the practice of contraception, but one should not overlook the possible existence of an appreciable

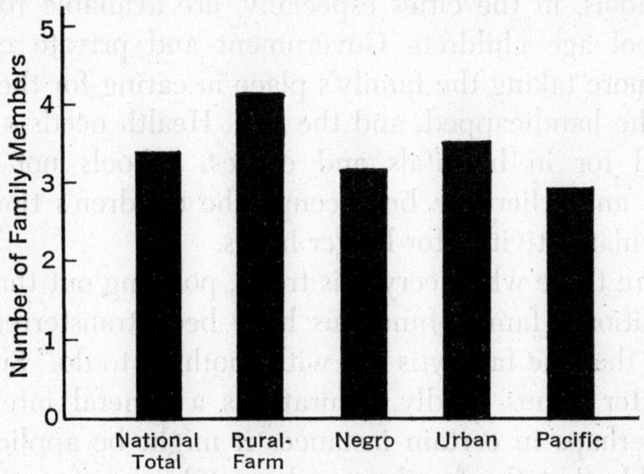


MEDIAN FAMILY SIZE OF VARIOUS CLASSES AND REGIONS IN THE UNITED STATES

Data taken from the 1930 *Census.*

amount of involuntary sterility especially among urban people. It is impossible to determine how much the birth rate is affected by the practice of birth control and how much by involuntary childlessness, but most students of the problem express the opinion that birth control is the primary factor.

4. *Loss of Traditional Family Functions*

The European and early American family of the nineteenth century performed a larger number of functions for its members than the present family does. In addition to rearing somewhat larger average families than are reared today, the home was to a considerable extent a small manufacturing unit for making clothing, canning and other food processing, and often, even, the growing of food. Moreover, much of the recreational activity of the people was centered in the home and neighborhood primary groups. The early family also performed numerous welfare functions such as the care of the aged, the sick, and destitute relatives.

It is evident that in each of the respects mentioned above, the American family's functions have declined or been transferred to other groups. A whole host of service institutions from bakeries and delicatessens to beauty salons and diaper services have grown up to do work formerly done by the family members for themselves and each other. Public schools take children at an earlier age, and nursery schools, in the cities especially, are available for the care of pre-school age children. Government and private charity are more and more taking the family's place in caring for the aged, the destitute, the handicapped, and the sick. Health needs are increasingly cared for in hospitals and clinics. Schools not only take children at an earlier age but occupy the children's time through extra curricular activities for longer hours.

There are those who decry this trend, pointing out that so many of the traditional family functions have been transferred to other institutions that the family is left with "nothing to do." Such a view of the matter seems hardly accurate as a general interpretation, although perhaps in certain instances it might be applicable. It is quite possible that the family may have taken on functions which are less conspicuous than those it has lost, but possibly more important. For example, the standards of child rearing have certainly risen during the last fifty years. This applies not only to the physical requirements of feeding, clothing, and health provision, but also to psychological services to the child of which increasing numbers of parents are becoming conscious. Perhaps the time formerly spent in baking bread and making children's clothes may now be spent in studying children's nutritional needs and in supervising and planning the child's recreation. Moreover, there is some evidence to indicate that husband-wife companionship may be greater when less time must be devoted to the economic aspects of the family. There is no assurance, of course, that such will be the case always, the point being that to many couples companionship with one another and recreational activities in common are important values, and values which can be attained only if there is available time for such activity. No one can determine, of course, the answers to such imponderable questions as whether the "old-fashioned" family" was, on the whole, "better" or, on the whole, "not so good" as the present family. All that can be said is that the present family's functions and activities are *different* and that the difference is such as to provide the *possibility* for what are commonly regarded as improvements in the quality of child rearing and husband-wife companionship.

5. *Changed Morality*

Morality, too, is new and different. Opinions differ widely concerning the extent of moral change and the desirability of it. The sociologist usually does not become as excited about changes in morality as some persons do, because of his familiarity with the facts of moral variability in past times and in other cultures. Objectively it can be shown through sample studies that in various ways moral standards have changed during the past generation or two. The change has been most apparent with respect to women. The facts are sufficiently well known that they need not be rehearsed here. Suffice it to say, that there is increasing approval of the propriety of women's smoking, drinking alcoholic beverages, and being pre-maritally unchaste. There is also greater approval of birth control and divorce, and an increasing toleration of some kinds of extra-marital freedom on the part of married persons. These changes have come very unequally in different regions, different social classes, and different religious groups. The change is more apparent in the "real" behavior of persons than in the "ideal" culture patterns. (See pages 112 to 113.) There is evidence to show, for example, that *when asked,* persons will assert that certain moral conduct is wrong categorically, but will admit to such acts themselves and to the approval of such acts among their friends. The inconsistency, if it be inconsistent, is rationalized by the "logic" that it is good for other people, or for children, or for appearances, to give lip service to higher standards of morality than are actually observed in one's own personal conduct. Whether such a view is correct or incorrect, desirable or undesirable, is probably not for the social scientist to pass judgment upon; in the interest of accuracy it is necessary, however, to report such facts as these, since they are significant factors in human behavior. (The student should be cautious in the use of the cases with which he is familiar as a basis for reaching conclusions regarding moral conduct. His sample may be atypical without his realizing it.)

WORLD WAR II

In addition to the long-run trends which we have just discussed, there are some more recent effects which may be traced to the war period from which American society is just now emerging. These effects may be lasting or very temporary, and they vary widely from person to person. Certainly for large numbers of persons, many of the experiences occurring during World War II for both civilians

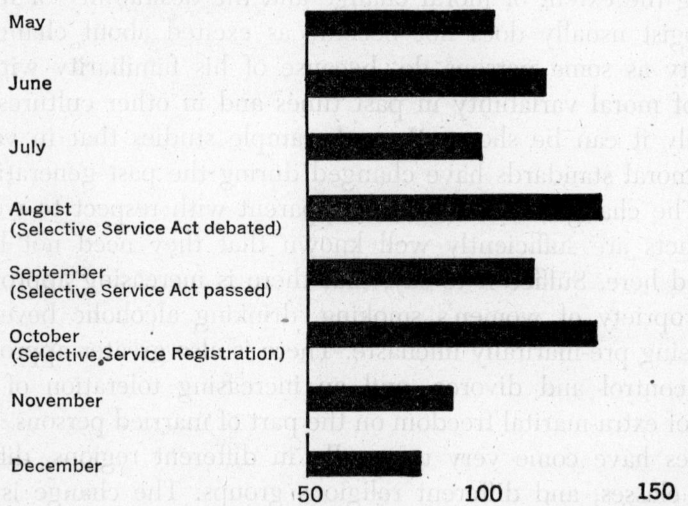


MARRIAGE RATE (26 STATES), MAY TO DECEMBER, 1940
(Expressed as a percentage of the rate for corresponding months of the preceding year)

Taken from W. F. Ogburn, "Marriages, Births and Divorces," *Annals of the American Academy of Political and Social Science*, 229, p. 25.

and service personnel were new. People, for example, who in normal times would receive mediocre incomes, were often suddenly receiving incomes and enjoying standards of living to which they were previously unaccustomed, and to which, in the long run they will likely be unable to adhere. Will such persons further limit their family size in an attempt to retain the advantages of a higher standard of living which was "tasted" for a time when incomes were abnormally high? Many couples were separated for substantial periods due to the man's military service. Some persons remained celibate during this period, but infidelity among both men and women was by no means uncommon. Will this factor make for a

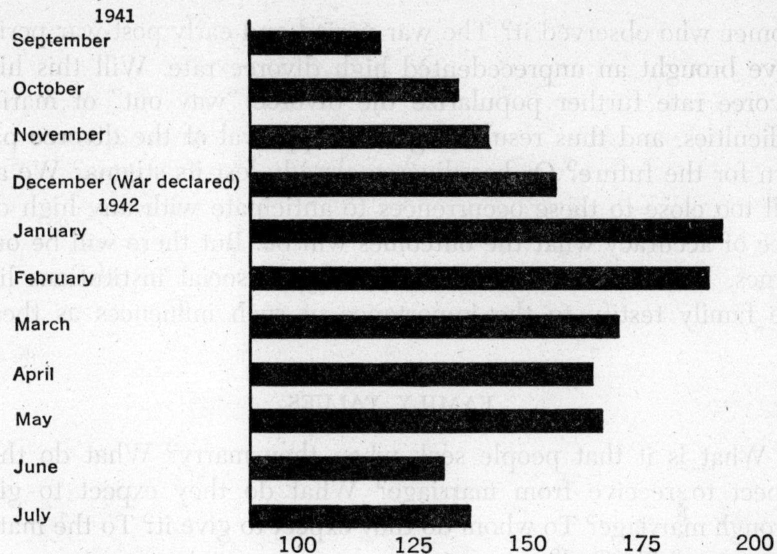


MARRIAGE RATE (8 STATES), SEPTEMBER, 1941 TO JULY, 1942
(Expressed as a percentage of the rates for corresponding months of 1939)

From W. F. Ogburn, "Marriages, Births and Divorces," *Annals of the American Academy of Political and Social Science,* 229, p. 25.

freer or less exclusive kind of husband-wife relationship than has traditionally existed in America? Furthermore, will the influence of the different moral codes to which the overseas personnel was exposed result in changing the personal morality of the men and

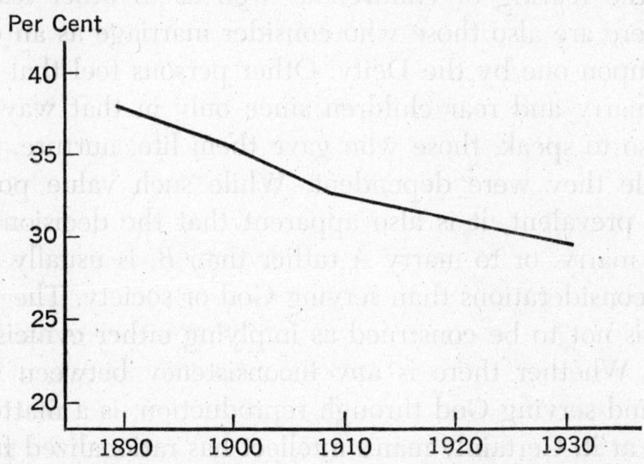


PERCENTAGE OF TOTAL POPULATION 15 YEARS OF AGE OR OVER WHICH HAS NEVER BEEN MARRIED, UNITED STATES, 1890-1930

*Fifteenth Census of the United States,* 1930, Population, II. Chapter on marital condition.

women who observed it? The war period and early post-war period have brought an unprecedented high divorce rate. Will this high divorce rate further popularize the divorce "way out" of marital difficulties, and thus result in greater approval of the divorce pattern for the future? Or has divorce already lost its stigma? We are still too close to these occurrences to anticipate with any high degree of accuracy what the outcomes will be. But there will be outcomes, because the facts of the history of social institutions like the family testify to the importance of such influences as these.

## FAMILY VALUES

What is it that people seek when they marry? What do they expect to receive from marriage? What do they expect to give through marriage? To whom do they expect to give it? To the mate? To society? To God?

Whenever questions such as these are discussed it becomes apparent that there is great difference among persons in American society concerning the basic values involved. Perhaps the chief value issue centers around the *purpose of marriage*. Is it primarily a source of satisfaction to the mates, or is marriage an obligation to someone else? There are those who believe that the basic purpose underlying marriage is to serve what is vaguely called "society" through the rearing of children as well as in other less obvious ways. There are also those who consider marriage as an obligation imposed upon one by the Deity. Other persons feel that it is their duty to marry and rear children since only in that way can they "repay," so to speak, those who gave them life, nurture, and guidance while they were dependent. While such value positions as these are prevalent, it is also apparent that the decision to marry or not to marry, or to marry *A* rather than *B*, is usually prompted by other considerations than serving God or society. The preceding sentence is not to be construed as implying either cynicism or disapproval. Whether there is any inconsistency between sexual attraction and serving God through reproduction, is a matter of how one looks at it. Certainly man's intellect has rationalized far greater inconsistencies than these. It may well be, however, that the high and lofty motivations for marriage so often espoused in public may be, like other broad moral, or ethical pronouncements, the idealized moral precepts which the culture of a people holds up as noble and worthy. Meanwhile there is a tacit understanding that most of the time most of the people are really thinking of something else, and being guided by other values.

A realistic examination of reasons for marriage and personal conduct after marriage on the part of most couples seems to indicate that marriages are made, maintained, and broken by far more mundane considerations, such as being in love, wanting to "settle down," wanting to legitimatize sex relationships, and, in general, wanting to acquire the socially approved status of "being married." While there are undoubtedly people who have children out of the feeling of duty, the preponderant value among those who deliberately plan to have children, is that they simply like to or want to have children. Others do not want children and remain childless if they can. Some couples have children because they cannot avoid it, but, of course, since such motives are not highly regarded, they must not admit of such "base" values to others, and often not even to themselves. Thus, they go through the conventional rôles of devoted parents, very often playing the rôle so well as to be indistinguishable from those who originally wanted children. It cannot be overemphasized that the ideal culture patterns of Americans as revealed in the trite and glib comments which people make concerning their reasons for marrying or for having children or for getting divorces, should not be taken at face value. They represent so often what persons think they *ought* to say to meet with social approval or what they have *unconsciously* come to believe they ought to believe, in spite of their actual motivations to the contrary.

There are increasing numbers of persons who will candidly admit that they do not accept any moral obligation to marry, or to have children, or to stay married. These persons say simply that the criteria for making their decisions are individually fashioned. If they think they will be happier married than single, they marry. And if they think that the satisfactions of having the children will outweigh the inconveniences, they try to have children. Likewise if one thinks he will be happier married to someone else than to his present mate, giving varying degrees of consideration to the justice of such a decision to the mate, he will seek a divorce. While it would be impossible to document the conclusion with formal empiric researches, it seems justifiable to conclude that increasingly, and perhaps in a majority of cases, the basic values involved in marriage, children, and divorce center in the personality needs and desires of the persons involved, and not in broad moral obligations pertaining to these things. Whether such values are better or worse is again not usually regarded as the proper province of the social scientist as he conceives of his rôle.

### LEGAL CONTROL OF THE FAMILY

In the past, and usually in primitive societies, societal controls upon the family were largely *informal.* What has been facetiously but aptly phrased as "the strong voice of Mrs. Grundy over the back fence," was usually enough to keep most people approximately in line with the behavior required of them by the social codes. Informal public opinion is effective enough as a guide so long as society is largely primary-group oriented. But with the rise of large cities, secularized thinking, a great deal of movement from place to place, and with increasing impersonality of behavior, informal controls have become largely superseded by *legal controls.* In many more ways than most persons realize the modern American family is regulated by law.

*Each of the forty-eight states has its own set of laws pertaining to the family.* While there is a basic uniformity requiring monogamy, great variations occur from state to state. One student of family law recently pointed out, for example, that the same person without as much as moving from the driver's seat of his automobile could by traveling fifty miles pass through three states under the laws of which he would be variously a single man, a married man, and a bigamist! Numerous other similar legal entanglements are easily found. Many persons are of the opinion that this radical variation from state to state is undesirable, and attempts have been made to secure federal legislation and/or constitutional amendment in order to unify state laws. It now appears doubtful that any such reforms will occur soon.

*State laws prohibit marriage* to certain categories of persons such as the feeble-minded, the insane, and the epileptic. All states set minimum age limits at which persons may legally marry. These age limits, however, vary several years among states. In some states divorcees may not marry until a specified time has elapsed. In some states cousins may not marry. No couple can marry without securing *permission* from the state in the form of a "marriage license," and the license is often granted only after other conditions such as a blood test have been met.

*Once a couple is married, their relationships to each other and to any children which may be born to them are also somewhat regulated by the law.* The husband is required to support his wife and children, and failure to do so may result in fine, imprisonment, or both. Adultery or "fornication" or "illegal cohabitation" are serious crimes in many states. The state laws stipulate which of the parents, or both, are the legal guardians, and set forth the kind and extent of legal responsibility which parents have for the conduct of their children. State laws usually require children of certain ages to attend school and sometimes require parents of children who have communicable diseases to be quarantined for stipulated periods. Several states have sweeping laws providing severe penalties for adults, including parents, who in any way "contribute to the delinquency of minors." Moreover, the laws set various requirements pertaining to the inheritance right of adults and children either under terms of a will or in the absence of a will. In a few states it is illegal even for physicians to give contraceptive information to their patients and in numerous other states contraceptive information and materials cannot be bought and sold legally except under physicians' prescription.

*Each state has the right to regulate divorce* as well as marriage. In one state, South Carolina, divorce is unobtainable for any reason whatsoever. In New York State a divorce may be granted only if the court possesses evidence of adultery, whereas in other states as many as ten to eighteen different grounds for divorce are provided in the statutes. The right to a divorce, contrary to much popular belief, is a prerogative of the state, not of the individual. "Giving" a spouse a divorce is often spoken of glibly, as if it were in the power of a mate to give his spouse a divorce in the same sense as he could give his spouse money or property. Divorces can be given only by courts, and even then the courts are limited by the laws of the states within which they have jurisdiction.

*The enforcement of all of these laws is, of course, highly variable.* Persons falsify their age, and get married contrary to the law. Public officials are sometimes negligent, and persons to whom marriage is theoretically denied are permitted to marry anyway. Some of the laws pertaining to marriage and particularly to sex conduct are openly violated and prosecution is practically negligible. Perjury and collusion, especially in divorce cases, are almost the rule rather than the exception. Taken as a whole, the laws of marriage and of divorce represent one of the most confused areas of legal practice found in the United States. Perhaps the chief factor in this confusion is the discrepancy between the requirements of the law and the wishes and desires of the people who theoretically, but not actually, make the law.

In spite of the above condition it should not be overlooked that the "rights" of persons in regard to marriage, parenthood, childhood, inheritance, and divorce are only such rights as the laws stipulate. While it is true, as we have seen, that the laws and the values of the people may be at variance, this condition should not obscure the basic fact that marriage is a legal status made possible by the law, and the rights and duties related to it are protected by the law. In the long run, perhaps, the law tends to approximate the values of "the people," but values are so variable, traditional ideal mores loom so large in many persons' thinking, and legislative inertia is so great, that contradictions such as we have noted seem "normal."

### INFORMAL CONTROL OF THE FAMILY

There are some areas of family life which the laws leave largely untouched. Broad "leeway" is allowed parents with respect to how much and what kind of discipline is imposed upon their children, and husbands and wives are subjected to little, if any, legal interference in working out whatever kind of rôle-pattern they wish. Married persons are not under legal obligation to have children nor is a man under any legal obligation to make any financial provision for his family in the event of his death. Yet, as we have seen, persons are under "social pressure," so to speak, to behave in certain approved ways, nevertheless. Mates who dominate each other unduly, parents who discipline their children too severely or not severely enough, are under more or less well-known social influence to conformity, exerted informally if not unconsciously by their associates. "For the sake of appearances," if for no other reason, persons believe that they must fall approximately "in line" with the prevailing folkways. Usually, of course, one is quite willing to follow convention, because being a member of the society which contains the norms, he probably considers these norms as the right or the proper or the decent or the only ways to behave anyway. Fear of gossip, of "what the neighbors will think," of how one will appear to his associates, are still significant factors in keeping some persons and some families somewhat consistent with the societal norms. Moreover, many of the efforts of school, church, and of one's own childhood experience serve to reinforce one another in the direction of conformity to customary family norms.

## THE PERSON AND THE CHANGING FAMILY PATTERN

### *Mental Hygiene Problems*

We have already seen that in numerous ways the traditional American family is being modified. These changes have been described largely in objective language, in terms of such factual statements as the decline of male authority, the increasing outside employment of married women, the changing moral code, the decline in the size of the family, and the increase in divorce. Describing these conditions in such objective language tends to minimize the seriousness of the personal problems encountered by the person who tries to adjust his ideas and conduct relating to family life during a period of change. It is easy to describe, for example, the increase in the out-of-home employment of married women and to point out the objective fact that there is nothing inherently or necessarily permanent about the traditional rôle of women in the home. But to the man whose ideals and values of family life were learned from participation in the older family type, it may be exceedingly difficult to *accept* this change even though he can *understand* it in a purely rational way. To him, "family" means a wife in the home and not a second "bread-winner." To him "family" means a single family dwelling, a white picket fence, and children, not a penthouse apartment with maid service, a nursery school, and most of the meals in a restaurant. Rationally, of course, he can understand that his wife has as much "right" to a career as he does, and usually he does not wish to deprive her of the things she wants. But he still cannot escape from the fact that the values he holds and the conceptions of family life which are meaningful to him are products, not of rational judgments and considerations of justice, but are the unconscious, non-rational images, and sentiments which are the results of his socialization. He cannot escape from these, often, even though he might like to. To many thousands of men in the United States the outside employment of their wives constitutes a fundamental and persistent frustration of their basic wishes. Many persons do not have sufficient insight to recognize this condition as frustration, because it may be largely unconscious, but its effect upon happiness and feelings of security is often very evident to the professional analyst of human behavior.

It is not only the man who finds personal problems resulting from this change in the family pattern. On the surface it would seem that the woman has had the advantage of securing her "freedom." But frequently there are complications for her too. First, she is likely to possess some of the same traditional family habits and values of traditional home making and accepts them as a woman's proper activity. But she cannot do these things and work outside the home without encountering difficulties. The difficulties may take the form of overwork due to attempting two jobs at once. In some cases husbands have been known to expect too much domestic activity on the part of an employed wife, not because they consciously wish to be unreasonable, but because unconsciously they think in terms of woman's traditional rôle in the home. Sometimes health problems for the woman result from the attempt at doing double duty. In these and many other ways, social change may bring additional personal problems to those persons upon whose lives the social change impinges.

While the illustration of employment of married women has been used here, it is not to be assumed that this is the only or even major problem brought about by social change in the family. Changes in morality have often created tortuous problems for both husbands and wives. Persons of radically different moral codes, without realizing it, may fall in love or even marry. Under such conditions tensions are almost inescapable. Under the emotional stress of being in love or of devotion to the mate, persons have often behaved in ways which have resulted in serious "guilt complexes." Likewise, the transfer of functions from the family has ostensibly freed women from much household drudgery, but only to leave many of them confused and bewildered because they have too much time on their hands and do not know how to use it to advantage. Illustrations could be multiplied almost indefinitely. Together they reinforce the important generalization that change in the family pattern creates problems for many persons. Husbands and wives frequently have had different value-backgrounds which seemed unimportant before or at the time of marriage. After marriage they have discovered that their basic conceptions of what family life ought to be were different. These values are often not only markedly different, but sometimes basically incompatible. This factor is an important one in numerous cases of divorce or of domestic discord, and has caused intense personal unhappiness.

*It is not to be assumed from the foregoing discussion that change in the family pattern is to be disapproved merely because it has brought unhappiness to some people.* In the first place, whether one disapproves of change or not, change will inevitably occur. No useful purpose is therefore achieved by decrying it. Moreover, many of the changes which bring personal unhappiness and disorganization to individuals during the period of transition, may bring important benefits to many generations thereafter. The decline of male dominance may have been a frustrating experience to many males. But this change made possible the emergence of a freer personality for women. It could be justified not only on moral grounds, but also in that it probably resulted in objective benefits in the long run for men also.

There has been an unfortunate tendency in the recent past for some students of human behavior to oppose change and especially rapid change on the ground that it disorganized and frustrated the persons whose values had been fashioned by the older régime. It is true enough that social change is confusing, but since it is also inevitable, and since it can be demonstrated that many of the benefits of modern living were made possible only by the effects of change, it seems both useless and ill-considered to oppose change per se. Better it would seem to seek to understand the change and to adjust as rationally as possible to it.

### *Evaluation of Change*

It does not follow, either, that merely because change is inevitable that all specific changes are necessarily inevitable or that all changes are to be equally approved. It appears that we have arrived at a stage in social development, in America at least, in which it is possible somewhat rationally to decide what kind of a social system we want, and then use our influence to get it. Merely because past attempts to control social change have frequently been unsuccessful, is no assurance that they will always be doomed to failure. Democracy failed many times before it succeeded, but it did eventually succeed. The same logic can be applied to the family. Although it is undeniably true that most persons cannot think objectively about the family in such fundamental respects as evaluating monogamy itself, it is also true that recent generations have seen societal approval of basic modifications in the family system such as the increased use of divorce, of birth control, and of a somewhat more scientific rearing of children. It is not being asserted here that these changes are desirable or undesirable in themselves, but rather that they illustrate how the family can be modified even during relatively short periods. It is a debatable question, of course, whether these changes were the result of deliberate planning or the unconscious result of impersonal forces making for change, which merely happened to work out in these ways. Certainly, however, if a given couple decides to limit the number or the time of birth of their children, they must have a desire so to do. Or if a woman wishes to have a career as well as marriage, one must presume that she wants a career. When sufficient numbers of people do these things, the family pattern has been changed. It seems reasonable to conclude that the change represents deliberate choice on the part of at least some of the people of the society in which the change has occurred. In formulating this interpretation we have not overlooked the fact that underlying a person's desire to change from the traditional way of behaving, there are other influences over which he perhaps has no control. Yet when a significant number of persons desire to have a somewhat different kind of life than has traditionally existed, and choose to implement their desires by action to bring about what they want, it would seem justifiable to regard these changes as rational and deliberate.

## GUIDANCE FOR FAMILY LIVING

It is common knowledge that many persons meet with great unhappiness in family life. Not only are divorces numerous, but many couples who do not seek divorces are exceedingly unhappy in their marital state. Not only adults but children as well, are frequently severely frustrated by the family situation in which they find themselves. While conclusive evidence does not exist to prove the assumption, it is commonly held by persons familiar with the facts that personal unhappiness in connection with family living is on the increase. Certainly a consciousness of unhappiness is widely felt.

It seems probable, moreover, that there is more domestic maladjustment than there needs to be, that many of the tensions grow either out of ignorance of the mates or out of ill-advised matings in the first place. Accordingly there has arisen a movement to educate people more fully pertaining to various areas of marriage, varying from sex behavior to budgeting. Books have been written and courses in college and even in high schools have been introduced for the purpose of acquainting as many people as possible with as much knowledge as is available concerning marriage. This is a new movement. Prior to World War I it was practically impossible for a person, even if he wanted to, to get any reliable guidance of a scientific nature regarding marriage. All that was available was the folk wisdom, the homespun philosophy, and the platitudinous advice of friends and relatives and of a few intuitive poets and moral leaders. Gradually it has occurred to more and more people that the scientific method could be applied to the discovery of the basic principles and facts involved in marriage. While there is much yet to be learned, considerable progress has already been made along at least three lines: (1) prediction of success and failure in marriage; (2) courses in preparation for marriage; and (3) counseling techniques applied in individual cases by experts in human behavior for the purpose of treating difficulties that have arisen and disposing of them or adjusting to them, before too-serious results have occurred. We shall now discuss each of these three forms of education and guidance.

### 1. *Marriage Prediction*

There are now two important studies which form the factual basis for the prediction of success or failure in marriage: the Burgess and Cottrell study conducted by two sociologists and the Terman study conducted by a psychologist. These studies though somewhat different in method and results, are much the same. Both provide a factual basis for determining in advance the probabilities that a given person will have high, low, or average marital adjustment. The originators of these predictive instruments have been careful not to claim too much for them, but the experience of numerous persons who have used them extensively for actual predictions has indicated that they are quite reliable and accurate. The technique is not difficult. On the basis of a number of questions about a person's background, a score is secured. Then this score is compared with the results of the original study summarized in a table. Thus, the person contemplating marriage may be informed that persons whose marital prediction scores are like his, have shown a certain percentage of very successful marriages, a certain percentage of less successful marriages, and so on through five categories of success and failure. The test cannot predict with certainty that a given marriage will succeed or fail any more than the results of a physical examination would necessarily guarantee how long a person will live. Like the physical examination, the marriage prediction results can show a person approximately what the probabilities are, on the basis of numerous other cases that have been examined.

Up to the present, of course, marriage predictions have been made for only a negligible proportion of the total marrying population. Sometimes even when the results are available the persons involved may not use them; some couples may marry even though the prediction indicates that the marriage is not advisable. There seems some reason to believe, however, that in the future greater use will be made of marriage prediction as a basis for determining who is suitable to marriage and who is not, and also perhaps at what time marriage is indicated for a given pair.

Some persons mistakenly assume that the chief value of marriage prediction lies in the prevention of divorce. Of far greater significance, however, would seem to be the insight which a marriage prediction can give a couple concerning the degree of adjustment which they may expect, between high happiness on the one extreme and just barely avoiding divorce on the other. As the availability of marriage prediction becomes more popularized and more trusted, and as the prediction techniques are improved, probably greater use of these promising devices may be made.

### 2. *Marriage Courses*

Practically every college and university now has one or more courses designed to inform students on the subject of marriage, or at least on some aspects of it. These courses vary a great deal in content, popularity, and probable effectiveness. Many are of limited value, if not useless, because of the strict censorship concerning the discussion of sex and other important aspects of the problem. Others are weakened materially because they are oriented too obviously around a desire to indoctrinate the students, rather than to inform them honestly on such subjects as sex, birth control, and divorce. Some courses are not effective because they are taught by persons whose intentions are good but whose scientific knowledge is not up to date in the several fields of knowledge which such courses should include. In spite of these criticisms numerous scientifically valid courses are to be found and it is usually reported that such courses are popular with students. Gradually better textbooks are being written and better trained teachers for such courses are becoming available.

There are, however, numerous unsolved problems in marriage education. First, there is no evidence to prove that such courses really result in better matings and happier marriages. There is evidence from other areas of education that the successful completion of courses is no indication whatsoever that the knowledge contained in the courses will be successfully applied by the students who have taken the courses. In other words the possession of accurate knowledge about sex or budget-making gives no assurance that the person who has the knowledge will be able to *use it successfully* in his own life. Studies now in progress may supply reliable answers to the question of effectiveness of marriage education. All that we possess now is the faith and the hope that marriage education may in practice help persons to achieve more success and happiness in marriage.

In the second place there is no complete agreement as to who should be responsible for guiding marriage education. It is often held that the person's home and family should be the source of this instruction in regard to marriage and family, but it is obvious that numerous families are unwilling or unable to offer much reliable guidance, even though they are themselves successful. Others, moreover, have failed themselves and hence often do not have the confidence of their children. Some think that the church should assume the responsibility for marriage education. But a large proportion of the population is not actively interested in organized religion, and a large proportion of the churches are neither interested in nor competent in this area. This leaves the task to the school which in spite of its shortcomings may be the only agency which could possibly be effective in marriage education.

At the present time marriage education is largely limited to the college level. This eliminates probably nine-tenths of the marrying pairs categorically, because they do not attend college. And even among the one-tenth who attend college, only a small proportion take marriage preparation courses.

It is possible that the most effective marriage education for the masses of people is presented by the movies, the radio, and popular fiction. Almost every movie and every work of fiction has a man-woman theme. Thus, over a period of years the average person sees enacted before him a few hundred family sequences which are almost certain to influence him in some way in the formation of the values and conduct of his personal life. There is a prevailing notion that this movie and fiction influence is an undesirable one, but evidence is lacking which would enable us to determine even what the influences of movie and fiction are, much less to evaluate the worth of such influences.

3. *Marriage Counseling*

Another significant development which shows some promise in assisting persons to adjust more successfully in their family rôles, is the rise of marriage or domestic relations counseling. Counseling is done by a variety of persons who are by no means equally well trained for this technical work. Marriage counseling of a sort has been done in the past by the clergyman and by the family physician. Both of these functionaries have enjoyed a great deal of respect, and have generally been regarded as proper persons in whom to confide concerning matters of relative intimacy such as those pertaining to family problems. For their time the clergyman and the family doctor probably represented the best kind of sympathetic listener and advice-giver that was available. But neither of these functionaries is a marriage counselor in the professional sense of the word, because neither has been trained very extensively in the science of human behavior. More recently there has developed a professional field of marriage counseling staffed by psychologists, social workers, psychiatrists, and sociologists. Some physicians, ministers, and lawyers also are becoming competent in this practice.

It is not our purpose here to discuss the professional training necessary or the techniques used by marriage counselors. It must suffice to point out that such a professional service exists, but is largely limited to the larger cities, and that this service is being used increasingly by persons who are unable to solve their marriage problems themselves. Since this field is a new one and not subject to much legal control, there also exist numerous charlatans and quacks who pose as competent counselors, extorting sizable fees from persons in trouble who do not know how to choose an ethical and competent counselor when they need one. The quack counselor, like the quack doctor, does the profession a great deal of harm and causes his clients serious harm. Legal control of the quack counselor is even more difficult than that of the quack doctor, because counselors are not yet licensed, and thus the state has little control over them. Perhaps before many years have passed minimum standards of competence for counselors will be agreed upon so that counselors can be licensed and only properly trained persons permitted to practice.

As in the case of marriage education, it is difficult to determine objectively how effective counselors really are. One never can determine what the conditions would be if the counselor had not been consulted. There is some reasonably objective evidence, however, which seems to indicate that many of the persons who use the service of counselors feel that they have been helped by counselors and sometimes markedly so.

## WHAT VALUES SHOULD THE FAMILY FOSTER?

Perhaps the fundamental problem underlying all considerations of the desirability of trends in the American family is the pivotal question: For what does the family exist? American culture contains more than one answer to this question. Because there is more than one answer, there are bound to be different evaluations of the desirability of this or that specific change and of this or that specific solution to problems. If the chief function of the family is to reproduce the human race in the largest possible numbers, then the practice of contraception, employment of married women outside of the home, and the delaying of marriage for any reason whatsoever, must be regarded as undesirable because each of these results in smaller families. On the other hand, if the purpose of marriage and the family is to make people more happy, then such trends as the above may be desirable. If the purpose of marriage is to facilitate human happiness, then the somewhat mismated pair might find it desirable to secure a divorce and try a second mating in which they might be happier. But if human happiness is regarded as less important than subservience to such dogma as the sinfulness of divorce per se, then obviously divorce can be viewed only as something bad. Since there are many value systems current in American culture, there are many defensible interpretations of the desirability of recent changes in the family and many different points of view concerning what, if anything, should or can be done about these conditions. There are those who regard this value variability as a weakness in American society because it makes for confusion and ill-will. But there are others who would defend value variability on the ground that it is consistent with democracy, that it is, in fact, democracy to permit a person to exercise choice over which of several values he prefers.

## SUMMARY

The family, like all other social groupings, is constantly in a process of change. Some of the leading long-run trends present in the American family pattern are the declining dominance of male authority, the decline in family size, the increasing impermanence of family relationships, the transfer of many of the traditional family functions to other groups in the society, and changed morality. Some of the more recent effects like those of the war cannot be appraised with as much accuracy as the foregoing, but may be quite as significant in the long run.

Family values, like other societal values, are difficult to discover, because so much discussion is on the level of idealized and platitudinous verbal statements which are not the true basis upon which many people really behave.

Society exerts control over marriage and the family not only by numerous legal devices but also in various informal ways.

When family patterns are in a state of change the individual's problems of adjustment are multiplied. This is due to the discrepancies which may exist between the values which the person has learned. Or his values may not be compatible with the standards of conduct required of him later on. Or mates' values may be incompatible. Difficulties in personal adjustment are, however, not products of change per se, and should not be construed as categorical liabilities of change in general or, for that matter, even of any specific changes.

Marriage education and domestic relations counseling represent recent societal attempts to assist people with the many difficulties involved in modern family living. These techniques are so new and affect so small a fraction of the total population, that it is impossible at this time to determine their effectiveness.

Basically all evaluation of the desirability of change in the family and all evaluation of proposals for counteracting or fostering change, depend upon the values which underlie the interpretations. Since there are many and diverse conceptions of the purposes of the family, it is inevitable that there will be varying interpretations concerning the desirability of programs affecting the family. Is this variability in basic values a source of good or evil in the American family?

## SUGGESTED READINGS

BROMLEY, Dorothy and BRITTON, Florence, *Youth and Sex* (New York, Harper and Bros., 1938). **A B**

A well-written report on a study of over 1300 college and university students with special reference to their affectional and erotic behavior. Suggests an interesting sixfold classification of both men and women, and also indicates how many persons among those studied fall into each class. This is, however, no "dry" presentation of statistical facts. It is a moving, dramatic, and sympathetic study of a generation groping for a *modus operandi.*

BURGESS, E. W., and COTTRELL, L. S., *Prediction of Success and Failure in Marriage* (New York, Prentice-Hall, Inc., 1939). **A**

One of the two leading scientific bases for prediction of success and failure in marriage on the basis of the background and social characteristics of the prospective spouses. The book contains the history of the study and discusses in some detail the values and limitations of the techniques. Technical treatment, requiring some rather advanced knowledge of statistical procedures. For more recent developments of the prediction technique see the following reference.

Burgess, E. W., and Locke, Harvey, *The Family: From Institution to Companionship* (New York, American Book Co., 1946). **A B**

This is a combined textbook and treatise. It contains the usual data and information found in the better textbooks on the family and in addition some original materials and interpretations.

Cuber, John, "Functions of the Marriage Counselor," *Marriage And Family Living*, VII, pp. 3-5. **A B**

A description of the functions of the marriage counselor in very abbreviated form. Suggests a fourfold classification of case "types" which the counselor serves. Numerous illustrations.

Glick, Paul, "Family Trends in the United States, 1890 to 1940," *American Sociological Review,* VII, pp. 505-516. **A B**

An analysis of census data on the family—number of children, family size, distribution by region and race, rural-urban differences, etc. Angell's "comment" immediately following (pp. 515-16) raises a number of important "theoretical" issues pertinent to interpreting the empiric facts of studies such as this one.

Mangold, G. B., "The Changing Size of the Family Unit," *Sociology and Social Research,* XXV, pp. 150-157. **B**

Presents data based on a sample of 400 persons who gave information on the size of their own and their parents' families. Shows simply and graphically the extent of the decline in the number of children per family among those "middle class" families which are represented by present college students. The technique lends itself to class use very well.

Symposium, "The American Family in World War II," *Annals of the American Academy of Political and Social Science,* Vol. 229, September, 1943. **A B**

A symposium volume by various American sociologists. Treats such phases of the war period as statistics on marriages, births and divorces, women in the services, and changing courtship customs. Scholarship is uneven, and so is the writing, but symposia tend to "be like that."

Waller, Willard, *War and the Family* (New York, Dryden Press, 1940). **A B**

This little fifty-page booklet is a frank and moving description of the effects of war on the family. It discusses with candor and accuracy a great many aspects of the situation which tend to escape treatment among many less courageous writers.

## STUDY QUESTIONS

1. Why do individual families vary from the norms of their own society?
2. Why do happenings in other areas of society affect the family?
3. What are the indications that impermanence is becoming a family characteristic?
4. To what factors do we attribute the decrease in size of families? Why is it inaccurate to state that contraception is the cause of family decline?
5. How do the functions of the present American family differ from those of the early nineteenth-century family?

6. Illustrate several ways in which the real family patterns differ from the ideal patterns.
7. What areas of family life are still left to informal control?
8. In what ways may changing family patterns be sources of frustrations? In what ways may changes remove or reduce frustration?
9. What is the importance of similar value backgrounds to successful marriage?
10. Why are some changes in family patterns inevitable and others rational and deliberate?
11. Why is there more domestic maladjustment than "necessary?"
12. What type of marriage guidance was available prior to 1920?
13. How may we apply the scientific method to the study of marriage?
14. Of what value are the techniques of predicting success or failure in marriage?
15. Why are marriage courses offered in schools? What are the limitations of these courses?
16. What are the limitations of marriage counseling?
17. Why are real family values difficult to discover?

# Chapter XXII

# ECONOMIC GROUPS AND IDEOLOGIES

## BASIC CHARACTERISTICS OF MODERN ECONOMIC ORGANIZATION

### *Division of Labor and Interdependence*

In every society there is a division of labor in the production of the goods and services which the people consume. Sometimes the division of labor is very simple, and may be overlooked by the casual observer. But even in the most primitive society there is division of labor between sexes and among the various groups and classes. At least a few specialized functionaries like warriors, agriculturalists, and religious mediators are usually found. In other societies the division of labor becomes more complex, culminating in such intricate specialization as characterizes modern economic organization in the United States. Division of labor results, of course, in the interdependence of the specializing persons. This applies on all levels of specialization from the simplest society to the most complex.

Societies organize their division of labor and mutual dependence into what is often called an "economic system." The word *system* may not be the best word to characterize economic culture and organization, because system implies a more carefully planned and smoothly working pattern of interrelationship than often exists. Perhaps the phrase "economic organization," therefore, is a better one. Regardless of terminology, the basic fact is that the process of producing and distributing goods and services requires some sort of working arrangements through which the various specialized persons and groups exchange the products of their labors for the goods and services which they utilize.

*Barter and Money Economy*

Like all aspects of human life, the details of economic organization vary greatly from society to society and from time to time. But there is at least one *fundamental function* which division of labor and interdependence require. The farmers' auction and the New York Stock Exchange, however different they seem on the surface, both supply the same basic need as a corner grocery store,

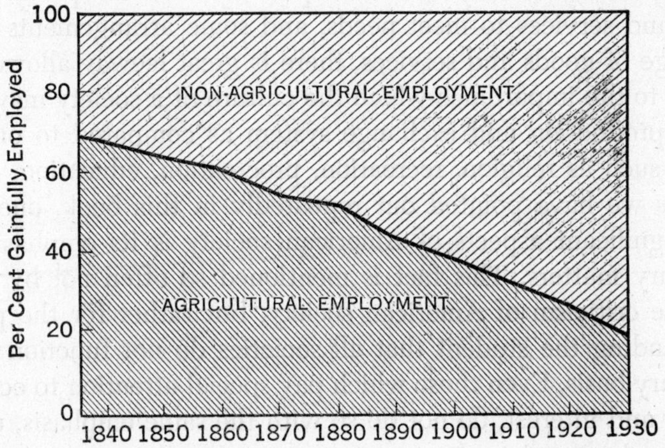


100 YEARS OF OCCUPATIONAL CHANGE IN THE UNITED STATES

Data compiled by Warren Thompson from various sources. See his *Population Problems* (New York, McGraw-Hill Book Co., 1935), p. 302.

namely, providing an organization through which different functionaries may get together for the purpose of *exchanging* the items of value which they produce for the items of value which they consume, or at least exchanging the items of value which they do not want for those which they do want.

In our society, and in most others, this basic exchange of goods and services is somewhat obscured by the fact that we exchange money for the things we buy and receive money for the things we sell. This includes wages which are paid us in exchange for our skill, time, and energy. But money is only the intermediary. Actually, all exchange in goods and services is based on barter. But since barter is cumbersome in a society where the division of labor is complex, the use of money has arisen as a convenience. It should be recognized as a convenience and not regarded as in any sense a contradiction of the fact that barter is the basis of exchange. Thus, societies vary greatly in the form and in the indirectness with which the barter system operates through the medium of money instead of direct barter "in kind."

### *Economic or Pecuniary Valuation*

Another basic difference among societies is the importance or value attached to economic activity in comparison to other activity. Although every society has some provision for the production of goods and services to meet needs, and some arrangements for the exchange of goods and services, there is great leeway allowed with respect to the importance which the culture of a society may attach to the production and exchange system as compared to other activities such as religion, recreation, procreation, education, or warfare. As we have pointed out repeatedly in this book, one of the most significant aspects of American society is its emphasis upon pecuniary matters. This fact is mentioned so often not by way of negative criticism of American society, but rather for the purpose of reminding the student that all societies do not function on this pecuniary basis. Even those which pay special attention to economic activity and interest, do not do so with the same emphasis, usually, that American society does.

### *Formal and Informal Control of Economic Activity*

In each society there are rules and regulations pertaining to the proper conduct of persons and groups in carrying out their producing and exchanging functions. Sometimes these rules are largely informal, being formulated and enforced through the tacit control of public opinion. The violators of the customary rules are punished by informal means as effectively, if not even more effectively, than they could be by law. As societies become more complex, however, informal controls tend to be superseded by formal legal controls. It would be difficult indeed, for example, for each user of electricity in the city to make his own wage contract with the public utility workers and with the capital owners who together supply the electric current. Instead, the consumer makes a formal contract with the electric power company, which in turn makes contracts with workmen and others. In addition, the basic rates for electric power cannot be left to the informal source of "supply and demand," because the supplying of electric power is a monopoly industry. Therefore, the government through public utility control agencies fixes and enforces what seem to be fair rates for water supply, electric current, gas, sewer operation, and telephone service.

*Government Control Is Expanding*

As society has become more complex, more and more economic activity has come under governmental control. This has been done usually at the request of some special groups, sometimes consumers, sometimes labor, sometimes agriculture, and sometimes industry. Some economic group is constantly asking that the government serve in the rôle of establishing and enforcing "fair" rules and practices for some phase of the barter system where informal customary control is no longer effective. Thus, over a half-century ago the federal government of the United States assumed control over the railroad system through the Interstate Commerce Commission, and also established a Federal Trade Commission to control the monopolistic practices of "big business." Long before that, however, the federal government, and every other government, had set up court systems, much of the activity of which consists of arbitrating disputes arising out of the exchange of goods and services.

Gradually, and during some periods rapidly, the legal structure set up to control economic activity has developed into an intricate and gigantic web of formal control. This is especially distasteful to many Americans because of the American traditions of laissez faire (the idea that government should avoid regulating economic activity or regulate it only at the very minimum). Often, of course, the persons and groups most vocal in opposition to governmental control are those whose abuse of power or other "objectionable" behavior brought about the control. Usually if there is no abuse of power, no one agitates to have the power curtailed, because there is no necessity for so doing. The phrase "abuse of power" means, of course, "different things to different groups." It should be noted, also, that opposition to increased control over economic activity is usually centered around some *specific* control by some *specific* group. Thus, a corporation is not likely to object to "the interference of government in the private affairs of citizens" when the government is forcing persons to pay their debts to the corporation or in other ways protecting the corporation's property or interests. Moreover, business interests have traditionally urged the government to establish tariffs in order to prevent industry from having to compete with foreign goods. Industry, likewise, seems not to object to laws which would outlaw strikes, although objections to the legal recognition of the right to strike are commonly voiced. Thus, while the ideal pattern of laissez faire is commonly verbalized, no one seems wholly or really to mean it.

### *Group Values and Control*

It seems no longer a question in America whether there shall be a laissez faire or a controlled economic system; the only remaining question is *whose wishes* are incorporated into law and *whose values* will take precedence over others' values. Thus, in America it is a question at the time of this writing, whether labor will be given more or less freedom to strike under the law. If labor is given less freedom, it means simply that the wishes of management have succeeded in securing government support for the kind of control over labor which management wants. On the other hand, if labor wins out, it will mean neither necessarily more nor less control, but rather the kind of control which labor wants. In short, the issue has ceased to be one of laissez faire *versus* control; it is now a question largely of whose brand of control, that is, whose values, will be incorporated in the control system.

### *The "Public Interest": Consumers*

It is not to be assumed from the foregoing that there are only two parties to the issue of the amount and kind of control which the government imposes upon the economic processes. There is at least a third interest, namely, that of the consumer. While in general, labor's interests favor high wages, short hours, and "good working conditions" and industry's interests favor lower wages and somewhat longer hours, the consumer's interest is in lower prices for a given quality of goods and an uninterrupted flow of goods. In the past, the consumer has been largely a "forgotten man" in the struggles between labor and management. Consumers have tended to take sides on the basis of whether they were primarily affiliated with labor or primarily affiliated with capital or management. Gradually there is a growing consciousness of the distinct interest of the consumer, even though most consumers are also probably dependent on the economic system in the rôle of laborers or as the owners of capital or as the managers of industry.

In the past, the consumer's interest, insofar as it has been expressed in formal pressures for government control, has taken the form of securing fair weights, accurate labeling of products, fair advertising, and protection against adulteration of goods. The setting of prices and the division of profit between management, capital, and labor has been regarded traditionally as outside the scope of the consumer's legitimate concern. There is some evidence of a growing awareness that the consumer does have a legitimate interest in the nature and kinds of control which the government imposes over labor and management, because the nature of these controls affects the cost of goods, the quality of goods, and particularly the uninterrupted flow of goods to the consumer. It remains to be seen whether consumers organize and become effective in forcing government control to protect their more fundamental interests to the same extent to which industry and later labor have secured government support for control of the sort they wanted.

## MODERN ECONOMIC SYSTEMS

Modern economic systems can be classified in several ways. Because each system has many attributes, there are many possible classifications. Thus, economic systems can be classified on the basis of the amount of government control, on the basis of the importance attached to economic activity, on the basis of complexity, or on almost any other basis. An exhaustive treatment of classifications would involve a series of books. Within the brief scope of this book it will be possible to focus major attention on only one of these differences, namely, the relation between economic activity and government control. Five types stand out in this classification: capitalism, regulated capitalism, socialism, fascism, and communism.

### 1. *Capitalism*

Capitalism is an economic system which grew up in Europe in the eighteenth century. It spread to America and flourished during the nineteenth and the beginning of the twentieth centuries. It is questionable whether or not capitalism may still be said to exist in the United States for reasons which shall shortly be pointed out. One might assume, as many do, that capitalism means simply the private ownership of property. But all economic systems have some private ownership of property. One of the important distinctions between them is the *amount and kind* of private property which the system permits, and the *degree of absoluteness* of private control over the property held.

*a. Producer's and consumer's property.* There are at least two basic kinds of property to which a person may hold title. The first is "consumer's property," or goods which are directly utilized by the person for the satisfaction of his wants. This includes such things as his home, his automobile, clothing, jewelry, and any other items which are used by him to satisfy his wants. The other class of property may be called "producer's property." This represents ownership of goods which are designed to produce other goods for sale or exchange. Thus, the farmer's land on which he produces food to sell or exchange for other goods, is production property in the form of land. While the electric refrigerator in the farmer's home is consumers' property, the refrigeration system in the building in which he stores the milk prior to sale, is producers' capital because he uses it in the production of goods which are sold on the market and not consumed by him. Thus, factories, stores, trains and buses, mines, farms, hotels and apartment houses, all represent producers' property. Private automobiles, private dwellings, "victory gardens," and household equipment, when these things are used directly by the persons who own them, represent consumers' property.

This distinction between producers' and consumers' property is an important one for understanding economic systems, because a very significant difference between modern economic systems of the world centers around the ownership and control of producers' property. In all societies, including even Russia, persons are permitted to own some private property. It is private ownership of producers' goods which under communism is not permitted. Capitalism, of course, especially in its early forms, permitted almost unlimited private ownership of producers' property and almost unlimited private control of producers' property owned.

*b. Ownership and control of property.* Ownership of property rights is always conditional. Phrases like "unlimited freedom of ownership," "completely owned private property" are misleading and inaccurate, because no society permits anyone the unconditional use of any property right. Some of the common limitations require the payment of taxes and the requirement not to use the property in such ways as would interfere with other people's rights or privileges. Thus, a person who owns an automobile is permitted to use it only so long as he pays the taxes required and uses it in accordance with the provisions of the law. The same principles hold true in the ownership of a home, or of a herd of swine, or of a radio.

One of the conditions of modern living—especially of urban living—has been the increase in the number of controls and limitations imposed upon the owner of property. Building codes require the observance of many regulations before one is permitted to construct a house on his own lot, and one can be prohibited from playing his radio if it interferes unduly with his neighbor's sleep. Examples could be multiplied to an impressive total, but the legal principle is probably clear, namely, that there are no absolute property rights in ownership, and that for the public good or the protection of other people, even those property rights which have been traditional are becoming increasingly abridged by law. This applies both to the use of consumer goods and to the use of producer goods.

Capitalism has traditionally been a system which permits very great, although not unlimited, freedom to the owner of producers' goods. Early in the history of the United States, for example, if a man had money enough he could build a noisy, unsightly, and unhygienic factory in the heart of the residential area of a city. If he owned the land, he could do with it as he wished. Gradually there has been established, although not without great struggle, the legal principle that the interest of others in the use of private property is a legitimate and constitutional one. But what are "legitimate interests" of other people in the use of one's private property? Does the ownership of a factory carry with it the right to dump refuse into the river, endangering the health and property of those who live downstream? There was a time when American courts upheld the legality of such action. Does the ownership of a railroad give the right to pollute the city with smoke in the vicinity of railroad yards and terminals, or does the collective interest justify forcing the railroads to use electric locomotives within the city limits? Some laws to that effect are now in operation. Does the ownership of an industrial establishment carry with it the right to refuse to employ workmen who are affiliated with a union? According to existing law, the management of no large industry has such a right, but in the past such rights did exist. Thus, it can readily be seen that the amount and kind of control and the values underlying the control are, like all societal phenomena, highly relative to the prevailing values.

*c. Public properties.* Capitalistic societies for over a hundred years have recognized that certain property rights should not be permitted to be privately owned. Roadways, rivers, harbors, and the postal system are cases in point. There were times in American history when certain improved roadways, called "turnpikes," were privately owned, and the persons who used them were required to pay rental in the form of "tolls." This arrangement was not permitted indefinitely. A comparable condition still occurs occasionally in the case of toll bridges and a few toll roads in the United States, but these are either state owned or almost completely controlled by the government. There is usually provision for the ultimate restoration of these facilities to complete public ownership. The logic underlying the prevention of private ownership of these properties is simply that they are limited in number and constitute "natural monopolies." It is usually considered that the private ownership of natural monopolies would not be consistent with the public interest. It would give too much power to the owners of these properties.

The extension of this logic to such public utilities as electric light and power, telephone, gas, and water is at present a controversial one. There is a rising tide of belief that these privately-owned public utilities should in some way or other be transferred to public ownership and operation. It is often concluded that these systems should be operated at cost or else that the profits should go into the government treasury. Public utilities are now, however, governmentally regulated in many respects, but the profits from most of these industries still accrue to the owners of stock. A few cities own some of their public utilities in the form of electric light systems, street railways, and often water supply systems.

## 2. *Regulated Capitalism*

Several times in the discussion of capitalism it has been pointed out that more and more regulation is being exerted over the use of private property in the form of producers' goods, on the theory that the public interest requires it. These controls have now become so numerous and so extensive that many observers believe that private capitalism can no longer be said to be in existence. By the gradual process of increasing control, capitalism has become transformed into a quasi-capitalism or regulated capitalism. This new system still has some of the attributes of the old capitalism, but also has many new features as we have seen. This is true not only in the United States but also in most of Europe as well. Other interpreters argue that so long as there is *any* private ownership of producers' goods with as much freedom as still exists, that capitalism is still in existence. Regardless of the terminological argument, the facts are clear, namely, that the laissez faire capitalism identified with the nineteenth century has now passed from the American scene.

## 3. *Socialism*

Although there are many different varieties and definitions of socialism, there is a common core of meaning which the term has. Socialism is an economic system which permits private ownership of private property in consumers' goods and in a few small industrial enterprises as well, but the major industries are regarded as publicly owned enterprises, much as school systems and the United States Post Office now are. Industry as a whole is supervised by the government in the public interest, not primarily in the private interest of the owner alone. Production is said to be primarily "for use" and not primarily for profit.

It will be recalled that American industry during World War II slightly resembled socialism. While the owners of capital were permitted to make profits, they had to produce only such goods, charge only such prices, and operate only under such conditions as were conducive to the public interest in winning the war. The status of American industry during the war, however, was *unlike* socialism in that the major interest was winning the war, not serving the consumer needs of people as would be the case in a peace-time economy. Moreover, a larger percentage of profit was allowed during the war, as an incentive to greater production, than would be allowed probably during a peace-time socialistic economy. The belief, both on the part of industry and on the part of government, that the war-time controls were temporary also made the period not truly a socialistic one. It is difficult to determine at precisely what point controlled capitalism becomes socialistic, just as it is difficult to determine at what point capitalism becomes controlled capitalism.

### 4. *Fascism*

During the last twenty years a mixed form of controlled capitalism and socialism arose in Europe, especially in Spain, Italy, and Germany, known as *fascism*. Under fascism the economic system comes under rigid governmental regulation, even domination. On the surface, this might seem to be like socialism. The distinction, however, lies in the *purpose* of the control, that is, control in whose interests? Whereas under socialism the control is designed to be in the interests of the whole society as nearly as possible, under fascism a relatively small group of wealthy persons, governmental and army functionaries are served, almost to the exclusion of everyone else. Lip service may be paid to objectives which sound socialistic, but the evidence is clear that the interests of this small class, not the interests of the rank and file, are regarded as paramount.

### 5. *Communism*

Communism represents the complete or "logical extreme" of both government ownership and government control of producers' goods. It differs from socialism in that no private ownership of producers' goods is permitted. "The wealth belongs to the people." Incomes may, however, be unequal. Communism as an economic system, however, should not be confused with the economic system found in present day Russia and popularly called "communistic." Russia represents a specific form of economic system which is a combination of socialism as here defined and also of communism, just as United States represents an admixture of capitalism, socialism, and regulated capitalism. American capitalism has unique features which make it different from that of France or Chile or

China. Particularly in agriculture, there is some private and group ownership of land in Russia, which is not, strictly speaking, communistic.

The modern world has had less experience (if any) with pure communism than with any of the foregoing economic forms. It is believed by some that there is a world-wide trend in the direction of a more communistic-like society. This reasoning is based upon a number of facts, but represents a mode of analysis which goes considerably beyond the facts. The trend from capitalism to regulated capitalism and possibly to socialism is a rather clear trend as we have seen. But to assume that the trend toward increasing government ownership and control of producers' goods will become as complete as that of communism, represents either a hope or a fear, depending on one's values, but not a fact.

### GOVERNMENT REGULATION A BASIC ECONOMIC ISSUE

The trend toward increasing government regulation of economic matters is probably the predominant social-economic issue of the twentieth century. Interpretations and evaluations of both the necessity and desirability of this trend vary radically. One school of thought regards the change as simply a normal and natural adjustment to modern economic conditions. Large-scale industry, rapid fluctuations in the business cycle, monopoly, large-scale union organization, international organization of business, are merely a few of the conditions which seem to require governmental regulation. Individuals and groups must be regulated so that their arbitrary acts do not unduly jeopardize the public interest. This school of thought regards the government as a necessary arbiter to mediate the large-scale struggles between capital and labor, between powerful business or labor union competitors, as the representative of the public interest. There has been a tendency for both management and labor to work toward the solution of economic problems on the assumption that only the views of these two groups are important. Meanwhile the general public and its interest tends to be overlooked. Government should, it is argued, oversee the whole system.

The opposing school of thought recurrently orients its thinking to the "good old days" when the government was virtually impotent so far as the operation of industry or the struggles of capital and labor were concerned. The group opposing increased government control speaks loudly and often about the "sacrifice of freedom" which government control brings. Every new regulation of business by government is interpreted as an infringement on free enterprise. Private property, moreover, tends to be interpreted by these persons in a rather literal sense. Whatever use the owner of capital wishes to follow, is regarded as "his own business." If it is more profitable, for example, to produce motors for pleasure yachts than for farm tractors, then the manufacturer should be perfectly free to produce the motors for the yachts. The fact that we need tractors desperately is a "sentimental" consideration of no importance. Prices, moreover, should not be controlled, because if the person who has the money is willing to pay the price, that is prima facie evidence that the price is "fair." Supply and demand, it is said, will always result in a fair price in the long run.

The two schools of thought represent *two basically different philosophies* concerning the use of producers' capital. One regards producers' capital in the same strict sense as consumers' capital is regarded. If, for example, the owner of an automobile wishes to run it with insufficient oil and wear it out quickly, that is regarded as his own business. But if, instead, the private property represents capital goods used in production, the matter assumes greater social significance. The users of capital goods produce materials for the use of the general public. They employ labor and thus many persons come to be dependent directly or indirectly upon what the owner or manager of the capital goods does with it. It is small comfort to the workman or consumer, after the company on which he is dependent has gone bankrupt, to learn that the owners or managers of the plant had "just misjudged the market." It is more as if the factory or railroad or mine is in some degree like a public utility. They can exist only because the public buys the goods produced and because the government protects the properties used in manufacturing these goods. This point of view is often sharply challenged as socialistic, which it undoubtedly is. But calling it a name, even though an unpopular name, hardly meets the argument. Growing numbers of persons are taking this point of view, at least regarding the larger units of capital goods. Basic social implications like wages and working conditions, prices, and the kinds of commodities produced, are regarded as having a public interest of greater importance than the personal freedom of the owner of the capital goods to do with it as he pleases.

It does not follow automatically, of course, that government regulation means regulation in the public interest. *If the government regulates economic activity, the effect of that regulation depends upon who controls the government.* Government control of industry can be in the public interest only if and when the public is really in control of its government. Nominally, in a democracy this would seem to be easy. With every adult having the right to vote, one might assume that the mass of people will have voice in government. But, as will be discussed at greater length in the next chapter, the public is not always sufficiently informed to know where its best interests lie. People are misled by the propaganda or misrepresentation of persons with axes to grind. Both sides of every issue try to win public support by making their side *seem* to be in the public interest. Moreover, there are numerous examples of incompetence and unscrupulousness among the public officials who represent the government in the actual administration or regulation of industry or unions or agriculture. Not infrequently men have posed as representatives of the whole people for the purpose of getting elected or appointed to office, when they really intended to serve some special group or themselves.

On the other hand, numerous government regulatory bodies have had a long and reputable record for both competence and honor. They have represented the public interest capably, and with effective resistance against powerful and well organized attempts to harass them. The Interstate Commerce Commission has for over half a century handled the intricate problems of American railroads and more recently of trucks and buses. The Federal Trade Commission, Bureau of Standards, and some state public utility commissions are also noteworthy examples. Many more could readily be mentioned. When one considers the strong and not always ethical practices of many pressure groups to get special favors either under the law or by circumventing it, the record of these regulatory bodies becomes even more impressive.

*The essence of the entire issue is again one of values. Which, for example, is more important, making large profits and high wages or serving some other generally accepted general social purpose?* It has been argued that there is nothing inconsistent between high profits and/or high wages and the attainment of legitimate social utility. This argument represents a common rationalization for laissez faire. It is undoubtedly true that in the past our having granted freedom to the owners and managers of capital resulted in great social benefits, but it is also true that many great social injustices and problems have resulted. Low cost goods, for example, seem to be a public "benefit," but often they have been produced at low cost because the industry manufacturing them employed child labor, exploited workers, or cut prices to crowd out competitors in order to create an eventual monopoly. Quite conceivably the general interest could better be served by, perhaps, somewhat higher prices with more humane employment practices and higher ethical standards.

The "public interest" is an exceedingly difficult phrase to implement. It is not difficult to determine who the public is, but one encounters unanticipated and baffling inconsistencies when he seeks to discover the "common interest." Society is divided into groups with greatly different rôles and functions and with varied power. Not all persons can be served equally by giving them the same theoretical freedom. For many years before the general recognition of labor unions was taken for granted as it is today, the argument was frequently advanced that collective bargaining was really unnecessary, if not evil, because the employer and employee should have "equal rights" in working out the terms of the work and wages contract. The fallacy lay, of course, in the fact that in a given industry there might be thousands of workmen but only one employer. Theoretically, both were free to bargain, but actually the freedom was largely in the hands of the employer, particularly in the one-industry towns and in the very large industries.

Another illustration of the diversified nature of the so-called public interest was presented during World War II and the postwar period. Price regulations under the direction of the Office of Price Administration were in effect on almost all commodities. Many persons opposed this regulation on the ground that if some commodities were scarce, the prices should be permitted to go higher so that the persons who needed them more and would pay more could get them. But is this in the interest of the person of limited means who could, therefore, secure only very little of the higher priced articles or probably be unable to afford any of them?

Whether the early abolition of price ceilings would be good or bad would depend on one's position in the income range of the nation, and also very probably upon whether he saw the price ceiling from the point of view of the seller or of the buyer. The same applies in labor relations. Whether labor should have more or less power, higher or lower wages, more or less participation in management, depends upon whether one sees the issue from the point of view of a worker or of manager-owner.

It has been said that government regulation "stifles initiative," and thus cuts down on the number of new products and the rate of improvement of old products on the market. Assuming that the above causal connection is true, which it may or may not be, different values appear again with respect to whether it is in the general interest to have rapid changes in the kind of goods manufactured and sold. A study of automobile models between 1930 and 1940, for example, reveals numerous changes in appearance, but many of these changes had no relation whatsoever to the mechanical operation of the automobile, its safety, or riding comfort. Many changes were made by the industry for the sole purpose of making cars obsolete or at least out of date long before they were really worn out. This, it is said to be believed by the industry, would be better for the industry and would result in larger profits (and probably larger pay rolls). But was it in the public interest to create artificial obsolescence of such a major commodity as an automobile?

Many of the highly lauded "rises" in the American standard of living have been of the sort just discussed. The later model is probably slightly better than the one it is supposed to supersede, or at least it is made to appear to be better. Sometimes at staggering advertising costs, eventually paid by the consumer, he is convinced that he is better off, whether he actually is or not. It is conceivable that if such costly goods as automobiles, radios, and expensive household equipment change designs less radically, or over longer periods, that these commodities could then be used until they wore out, yielding a net saving to the consumer which could be used for satisfying other wants and needs, and probably contributing in that way to a net increase of the real standard of living.

These are only a very few of the basic considerations involved in the issue of increased government control over the owner and manager of producers' capital. For exhaustive treatment of the economic subtleties involved, the student is referred, naturally, to courses in economics. Unfortunately, perhaps, much of the economic philosophy and basic viewpoint which persons acquire result from the acquisition of the outworn mythology about economic matters which have been derived from the folk "wisdom" of another era. This folk "wisdom" is as out of date in many respects as is the medical knowledge or the mechanical knowledge of two generations ago. The formulation of realistic values pertaining to the "freedom of enterprise" issue is further complicated by the deliberate circulation of facts, ideas, and points of view by persons or groups with an axe to grind. Each seeks to make his interest appear to be the public interest, and hires the most clever, skilled, and persuasive persons he can to make the unsuspecting person see it that way, too. Thus, the rank-and-file member of society finds it exceedingly difficult to secure realistic ideas on the issue. Perhaps, also, the realist is the person who recognizes that the issue is not one of freedom *versus* dictation, but rather who is free to do what, and who ought to be restrained from doing what.

## TECHNOLOGY AND THE ECONOMIC SYSTEM

Thinking about the economic aspect of society is often needlessly beclouded by failure to distinguish between technology and the economic organization or the value system. *Technology consists of the culture objects and the skills which make it possible to produce the goods and services.* Early technological improvements consisted of such elementary accomplishments as the discovery and control of fire, the principle of the wheel, and the lever. Modern man has, of course, gone beyond these elementary technologies. Present technological improvement is so elaborate as almost to defy description. The intricacies of an automobile plant or the accounting system for a giant corporation illustrate the elaborateness with which modern man's culture has developed intricate processes for producing and distributing goods.

The *economic system,* on the other hand, *consists of a set of values concerning how and by whom the technological knowledge and materials are to be owned and controlled.* As we have already seen, man has invented numerous economic systems as radically different from one another as laissez faire and communism. The cardinal fact to be borne in mind by the beginning student, is that economic systems of all kinds *are value systems* and subject to the same *time and space variations to which all value systems are subject.* No economic system has proved permanent any more than any moral code has lasted forever. Because each person becomes habituated to some particular economic system, he tends, as a rule, to regard that system as the embodiment of the eternal or inherent or indispensable good, and often finds it almost incomprehensible to think in terms of any other system. It is probably as difficult for the average capitalist to think in a communist frame of reference as it would be for the average communist to think in terms of the capitalist's economic values.

The same principle is illustrated within our own culture as it is changing from a laissez faire to a more controlled type of capitalism. Much of the nostalgia for the "good old days" of economic freedom is simply a reflection of the fact that for many persons it is exceedingly difficult to modify the values with which they have previously been indoctrinated. Any judgment concerning the worth or desirability of a change in economic culture always resolves itself into a consideration of values. Should the government control prices? To whose interest would price control be? Who should have the greater influence over the determination of prices? Are we willing to give up certain other values in order to attain the value of more stable prices? Answers to these and similar questions can only be formulated in terms of other values and, therefore, dependent upon the point of view from which the evaluator considers the issue.

A great deal of serious confusion often results from the failure to distinguish between technology and the value system. The United States, for example, has a highly developed technology of industrial production. According to some observers this efficient production system is a direct result of unregulated capitalistic enterprise. The evidence for this cause-and-effect assumption usually consists of pointing out that during the period of capitalistic enterprise the great technological changes occurred. No one knows, however, whether comparable or perhaps even greater technological change might not have occurred under a different economic value system. Modern Russia, for example, has become industrialized very recently and has developed impressive production skills in a very short time under an economic system radically different from that of the United States. It is true, of course, that much of this change in Russia has been brought about through diffusion of technological skill from other societies. But all of Russia's modernity has not consisted of merely copying the older capitalistic technology. Modern Russia also has laboratories staffed with skilled and inventive technicians, and her factory system is, like ours, in the hands of industrial engineers who also show inventive genius along technological lines. It is not to be inferred from what has just been stated that all economic systems produce technological change equally rapidly or that different economic systems would necessarily make the same technological changes. The point is simply that it is necessary to *keep the technology and the value system distinct* in one's thinking. There are modern factories in Russia as well as under capitalism, and there is "backward," non-efficient production under either system.

### INTERDEPENDENCE AND PERSONAL INSECURITY

Practically no one in modern society produces very much for his own consumption. The policeman, the banker, and the president of the United States along with infants, the ill, and the aged must depend for their daily needs upon the labor and skill of countless other people, most of them personally unknown to the ultimate consumer of their goods and services. Even modern farmers are becoming increasingly dependent upon other functionaries for machinery, oil, fuel, seed, fertilizer, technological knowledges pertaining to agriculture, and even much of the food which they consume from day to day.

Division of rôles has become more intricate and more interdependence has occurred. Meanwhile the *personal insecurity of each person has grown phenomenally.* The employment and wages of a New England textile worker are much more dependent upon what happens in the textile industry of the South or of some foreign nation than upon his own ability and activities as a workman. A change in government policy, which may be necessary for the public interest, may close whole industries or seriously impoverish others. This may occur *independently of the skill or integrity of the persons affected.* Technological changes render certain occupations practically obsolete. Changes in consumer habits, and even whims, may bring poverty or bankruptcy to the managers and workmen which supply some consumer good or service. Business cycles of prosperity and depression bring waves of poverty and plenty which to the average man are both unknown and unpredictable, but before

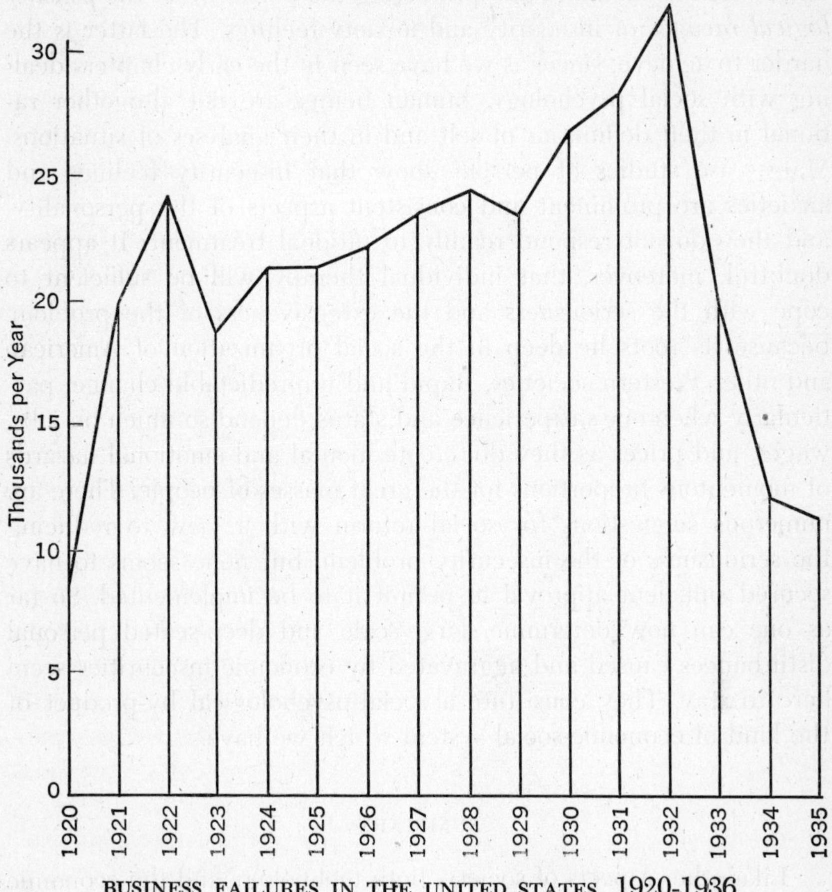


**BUSINESS FAILURES IN THE UNITED STATES, 1920-1936**

From the *Statistical Abstract of the United States*, 1937, p. 291.

which forces he is largely powerless. It is easy enough for the poets to write inspiring lines about men who are "masters of their fate" and "captains of their souls," but in such "clutches of circumstance" as depressions, wars, and changing technology, few individual persons can shape their destinies in fact!

One of the most baffling public problems is that of discovering ways and *means of protecting persons from the more severe ravages of insecurity.* Two aspects of the problem stand out as distinct: (1) protecting the person from some of the obvious *physical effects* of insecurity by providing him with such varied assistance as unemployment insurance, liberalized credit in times of crises, and direct relief when needed and (2) protecting the person from the *psychological ravages* of insecurity and anxiety feelings. The latter is the harder to achieve, since, as we have seen in the early chapters dealing with social psychology, human beings are not altogether rational in their definitions of self and in their analyses of situations. Many case studies of persons show that insecurity feelings and anxieties are prominent and consistent aspects of the personality, and they do not respond readily to rational treatment. It appears doubtful, moreover, that individual therapy will be sufficient to cope with the seriousness and the extensiveness of the problem, because its roots lie deep in the social organization of American and other Western societies. Rapid and unpredictable change, particularly when one's experience and status depend so much on jobs, wages, and prices as they do, create mental and emotional hazards of momentous proportions for the great masses of people. There are numerous suggestions for social reform with a view to reducing the seriousness of the insecurity problem, but none seems to have secured sufficient approval to permit it to be implemented. So far as one can now determine, large-scale and deep-seated personal disturbances caused and aggravated by economic insecurities seem here to stay. They constitute a social-psychological by-product of the kind of economic-social system which we have.

## SUMMARY

Like other aspects of society, both technology and the economic system vary greatly from time to time and from place to place. Moreover, the existing value system and technology are constantly changing and, during modern times at least, are changing at rates so rapid that many persons are bewildered. Even many of those who recognize and understand the processes somewhat clearly, find it difficult to change their older values in conformity to the new scheme.

Although almost any abstract discussion of economic systems is somewhat arbitrary, it is also essential in order that one may secure some perspective on the processes of change which are taking place in his own society. Thus, we have distinguished capitalism, controlled capitalism, socialism, fascism, and communism. The distinction among these centers largely on the control and ownership of *capital* goods as distinct from the private ownership of *personal* goods. A basic consideration in evaluating these five systems is the determination of what constitutes the public concern in respect to economic activity, and how far that public interest can and should be extended over the freedom of action of persons and small groups seeking their own gain.

Perhaps the cardinal economic change, in America at least, has been the increasing control of government over economic activities and organization, which began nearly three-quarters of a century ago, although, of course, government is inescapably concerned in all societies and all times with such matters as the control of property rights and the settlement of issues between persons concerning property rights.

The distinction between technology and the economic system is an important one. The technological system consists of the knowledges and skills necessary to the production of goods and services used in the level of living. The economic system is a value system concerning the importance of economic activity in comparison to other activity, basic considerations concerning the public interest, and the goals which the technological culture is supposed to serve. Designation of the groups which ought to be in predominant controlling position in the economic system is also part of this value system. Generally speaking, however, almost any technological system can serve with almost any economic system and vice versa. The historical coincidence of the capitalistic system and modern large-scale and high-speed technology should be seen as coincidental and somewhat related, but the myth should not be perpetuated that either is indispensable to the other.

Perhaps the most fundamental economic-related psychological problem of modern time is that of personal insecurity. Both the magnitude and seriousness of the problem are astounding, particularly since we have no ready solution for it. There are those students of the problem who believe that it is the most serious economic-related matter and that it threatens the continued existence of the economic system as we now know it. Are they right?

## SUGGESTED READINGS

Arnold, Thurman, *The Folklore of Capitalism.* (See bibliographic note page 100). **A B**

This entire book is useful in connection with the topic under discussion here. A very significant book.

Berle, A. A., and Means, G. W., *The Modern Corporation and Private Property* (New York, The Macmillan Co., 1933). **B**

This is a classic study of the realisms involved in modern business organization in the United States. Contains both theoretical and empiric materials.

Davis, Jerome, *Capitalism and Its Culture* (New York, Farrar and Rinehart, Inc., 1935). **A B**

Essentially an evaluation of capitalism, defined as the economic system of the United States prior to 1935. While the work is not wholly unbiased, it is a splendid antidote to the mythology regarding economic philosophy and business organization which are current. Shows how capitalism affects the non-economic aspects of culture and society, such as education. Also contains a history of the evolution of capitalism.

Epstein, Abraham, *Insecurity: A Challenge of America* (New York, Random House, Inc., 1936), Revised Edition. Especially Chapter I, "The Spectre of Insecurity." **B**

A convincing and essentially accurate description of the meaning and extent of personal insecurity in the modern world.

Lorwin, L. L., *Time for Planning* (New York, Harper and Bros., 1945). **A B**

A timely work on the subject of planning. Contains a history of the planning ideology. Discusses planning from the point of view of labor, "democracy," and includes a treatment of the international aspects.

Symposium, "Recent Social Trends in the Soviet Union," *American Sociological Review,* IX, No. 3, 1944. **A**

A special issue of the official organ of the American Sociological Society devoted to a discussion of various aspects of Russian life and culture. Treats population, ecology, social stratification, the main social institutions, and values. Evaluation is irregular showing varying degrees of objectivity.

Vincent, Melvin, "Labor Under Review," *Sociology and Social Research,* XXX, pp. 353-365. **A B**

A detailed factual review of changes in law, strikes, policy formation and modification among unions and industry, from July, 1944 to December, 1945. Also attempts an interpretation of the trends.

## STUDY QUESTIONS

1. Why do we find a division of labor in every society?
2. How does the culture of a society determine the relative importance or value attached to economic activity in comparison to other activity?

3. Why does the control of economic activities tend to become formalized as societies become more complex?
4. Why do we have disagreement in regard to the extent and kind of government control over economic activities?
5. How does the consumer tend to become the "forgotten man" in the struggles between labor and capital?
6. In what ways do we not have capitalism in the United States today?
7. Why is it incorrect to say simply that we now operate under a system of "free enterprise?"
8. How do producers' property and consumers' property differ?
9. How has the relationship between the ownership and control of property changed?
10. Why do we have public ownership of certain types of property?
11. To what extent do we have socialism in the United States?
12. How do capitalism, controlled capitalism, socialism, fascism, and communism differ? How are they similar?
13. Why is it difficult to determine the "public interest?" Why do some groups claim that government regulation "stifles initiative?" How may this stifling of initiative possibly benefit the "public interest?"
14. Why do groups often attempt to make their own selfish interests appear to be the "public" interests?
15. What changes in our economic system have contributed to the growth of personal insecurity?
16. Why are we a nation of increasing insecure and dependent people and also the "richest nation on earth?"
17. What should be the basic consideration in evaluating an economic system? Discuss fully.

# *Chapter XXIII*

## GOVERNMENT AND THE STATE

Several phases of government have already been discussed in connection with economic activity and the family. But there are numerous aspects of government to which more pointed attention should be given. First, we shall distinguish a group of concepts pertaining to government which are sometimes used so loosely that confusion results. Popular writers and speakers often confuse the concepts *government, state, nationality, nation,* and *language-group.*

### THE STATE AND ITS GOVERNMENT

1. *The State*

The state is a fundamental territorial grouping. The concept *state* often gives the American student difficulty, because we designate the subdivision of the nation-state by the word *state.* Thus we are accustomed to using *state* when referring to Ohio, Michigan, or North Dakota. This usage should not be confused with the more fundamental one which we are here describing. The student will be able to distinguish the two usages from the contexts in which they occur.

The state may contain persons and areas alike in culture, language, or race, but many states contain very diverse cultural units. In the United States, for example, there are substantial numbers of persons representing each of the three major "races" of the world. Almost every nationality and language native to Europe can be found in the United States. Cultures as diverse as those of metropolitan New York and the hill people of the Ozarks make up this nation. While the United States is in this respect probably not typical of most states, it serves as a useful example to illustrate the fact that states are not necessarily made up of "like" cultural elements. Most states are highly heterogeneous.

The state is, however, held together by a number of *symbiotic* and *cultural ties* which we have already discussed. *Force*, however, is basic. In the Roman Empire or the German state under Hitler, the unity seemed to be based largely on force. Most enduring modern nations have been built up by a combination of overt force and peaceful penetration of power. It is frequently difficult to determine the relative importance of arbitrary power and informal consensus in holding together the diverse sub-groups which make up a modern state. The case for the large rôle of power can easily be made. The Civil War period in the United States may serve as a convenient illustration. The Confederate States seceded from the rest of the nation, but the secession was forcibly challenged through the Civil War, and was nullified by the eventual destruction of the armies of the Confederate States of America. While it is not frequently brought to our attention, the fact is nevertheless clear that the part of the United States of America south of the Mason-Dixon line is today a part of this nation-state because its attempt at secession was denied by force of arms.

Moreover, American history contains other illustrations of the element of force in building and holding a state together. Largely, though not exclusively, by force the original inhabitants of this continent, the Indians, have been incorporated into the present nation-state. Similarly the American Negro has descended from persons forcibly brought to this country as slaves. Other territorial units have been added to the territorial control of the United States as a result of successful participation in wars. Both the Spanish American and Mexican wars resulted in the addition of territorial possessions (under various legal statuses) to the United States of America.

For the ordinary citizens of a nation the real or potential force of the government is the factor which secures the payment of taxes and the observance of many other laws. There seems ample evidence that much of the "loyalty" which it is claimed people give their governments is prompted by the tacit force which the government possesses. While it is true that in such extreme circumstances as war many people voluntarily offer their personal services and their property to the government, it is overwhelmingly evident that the government is usually required to force most persons to subordinate their personal wishes to the needs of the state by an elaborate legal network of profit-control, price-control, black market control, control of trading with the enemy, as well as a system of conscription and manpower control. Behind all these measures is the force of the government. In peace-time a large and elaborate organization is required to force people to pay taxes and observe the laws which their elected representatives have made.

It would be a mistake, however, to assume that force is the exclusive element in the building and maintenance of states. The history of modern states has shown that common cultural ties of unity are important also, and in many instances fundamental to the territorial organization of power which we have just discussed. Difficulties usually result from attempting to keep too-diverse cultural groups integrated into one nation. Modern European history contains numerous illustrations of this. Even in the United States a few cultural differences between North and South almost divided the nation in 1861, even though the cultures of North and South were in other ways similar. Among the common cultural ties which tend to knit people and groups into an integrated and relatively permanent state are language, race, religion, and economic ideologies. It should be clear, however, that while these factors *tend* to make for national unity, they do not guarantee it. Thus, for example, the English-speaking peoples of the world are not in the same state, nor are the Catholic peoples, nor is the Mongolian race, nor are the capitalistic peoples. Each of these factors interact with other factors. The cohesion of the groups making up a modern state may well be conceived as the result of a *series of forces* and pressures interacting with one another, some making for unity and others for disunity at the same time. Whether a state becomes stronger or weaker, larger or smaller, with the passing of time depends on the subtle interplay of these many forces.

Thus far we have considered the growth and decline of states in terms of the territory over which the government of the nation has control. Nations also increase or decrease in size and influence as a result of migration. The United States represents an outstanding example of a nation which grew phenomenally in numbers and power as a result of great emigrations from Europe. More than enough persons came from Europe to the United States within a period of seventy-five years ending in approximately 1915, to make up the present populations of a small modern European nation, or of several present-day states within the United States. This migration took place peacefully and slowly, although in the peak year approximately one million immigrants came to America. Brazil is now showing a similar rapid migrational growth.

The character of a nation-state may also change over a period of time through the gradual disappearance of cultural differences among the groups which make it up. Thus the immigrants from a dozen European nations with at least twice as many language traditions have come to the United States, gradually have become assimilated into American culture, have intermarried, and now are practically indistinguishable from one another. This "assimilation" process will be discussed more fully in a subsequent chapter.

Summarizing this discussion of the state, we may formally define it as *a territorially delimited aggregation of people under the control of one central government, usually but not always consisting of groups alike or similar in culture, particularly in language, religion, and economic philosophy.* The state, like all aspects of human life, constantly changes. Change may occur through addition or loss of territory by war or by peaceful acquisition. Changes also occur within the state through the assimilation of diverse peoples into the common culture, as well as through the rise of diverse groups and classes.

2. *Government*

Government is the power organization which has supreme control in the state. This power organization is ever changing. History records numerous examples of radical modifications of government in many modern states in recent times. England changed from an absolute monarchy to a limited monarchy to a democracy. France, through the French revolution, changed suddenly from a monarchy to a democracy. Germany, prior to World War I, was essentially a monarchy, was a republic for a time, became a dictatorship under Adolph Hitler, and at present its government is difficult to determine because the control of that nation lies almost entirely with the Allied victors in World War II.

Not all changes in the source of power in government have occurred by revolution. Some have been brought about by gradual, often called "evolutionary," methods. From 1789 to the present, numerous changes in American government have occurred such as granting voting rights to all citizens instead of only to property owners, popular election of United States Senators instead of by choice of state legislatures, and the enfranchisement of women. These and many other changes over a period of 150 years have resulted in a greater degree of popular control of the federal governmental power. This trend is usually interpreted as a trend toward greater democracy, because the voice of the "common man" seems to have more influence than it formerly did.

*"Consent of the governed."* It has frequently been said that all governments, regardless of form, derive their power from "the people governed" and may, therefore, be regarded as the kind of government which the governed people "want." Proponents of this view show that history is replete with illustrations of revolutions and gradual government changes which resulted from popular dissatisfaction with existing government, and point out that potentially any people can change its government if and when it so wishes. There is much sophistry in this view. (1) The existing government has the advantage of continuing control by virtue of sheer tradition. This is illustrated by the steadfastness with which the British have clung to the traditions of monarchy. Thus, while England is a democracy, the prime minister and his party elected by the people are still called "His Majesty's Government," and the British people, apparently, willingly tolerate a titled nobility in conformity with ancient custom. A somewhat similar situation is found in the United States where numerous obsolete traditions are perpetuated sometimes at great cost because they have the sanction of age. Many inefficiencies in American rural and local government are perpetuated at great cost and loss of efficiency. The electoral college in the federal government is another illustration of the retention of archaic custom. One could hardly say that the American people really *want* the electoral college, because a majority of them at least, do not know what it is, how it works, or why it exists.

(2) In addition to the force of tradition, the existing pattern of government has a second advantage favoring its continued existence. The existing government exerts a considerable influence on

the way in which people "think." Perhaps the extreme instance is found in Hitler Germany where the propaganda ministry held almost complete control over education, radio, newspapers, the utterances of public speakers, in short, over all communication. Under such conditions the government could virtually force the people to "want" and to "think" whatever the government wished them to want and think. Even in much less tyrannical governments than that of Hitler Germany, the same principle holds true: the power position of the existing government can have a great influence in causing a people to wish it continued.

(3) A third fallacy in the "all governments rest on the consent of the governed" notion arises from the fact that "the people" is a catch phrase of very many meanings. As we have seen in previous chapters, there are many diverse interest groups in a society and frequently some one of these groups is best served, or thinks it is, by a form or action of government which another group finds not to its interest or liking. Thus opposing factions all claim to represent "the people," meanwhile, incidentally, using all the forms of influence and propaganda available with a view to convincing as many people as possible that what that group wants is really in the interest of all. Thus the "Divine Right" king in medieval Europe represented not only "the people," but also the "Will of God." Hitler claimed to represent the people; in short, the prevailing government and the challenging group may often both claim with logic to represent the people. But in reality both only represent *some* people.

Governments in power frequently rely on the apathy and the ignorance of substantial numbers of people for their continued power position. Studies of the public affairs knowledge of rank-and-file eligible voters in the United States have revealed that misinformation, lack of information, and gross inaccuracies in thinking are prevalent. Thus it seems hardly justifiable to claim that a given form of government is "a people's choice" when in some cases the majority of them do not even know what it is that they have chosen! Perhaps the relationship between the people and the controlling government can be more accurately stated negatively. One can presume, perhaps, that a people cannot be too acutely dissatisfied with a government, if they permit its continued existence without challenge. But even this statement of the matter overlooks the fact that a people may remain subservient to a government which they oppose, because they fear the consequences of opposing it either openly or even by subterfuge. A sufficiently ruthless government may retain power by naked force, and by other means we have mentioned, for long periods of time.

### IDEAL AND REAL PATTERNS IN AMERICAN GOVERNMENT

At several points throughout this book we have emphasized the nature and importance of the distinction between real and ideal culture patterns. The study of government presents another striking example. Suppose, for example, someone wholly unfamiliar with American government were to read the American Constitution and all of its amendments for the purpose of understanding how Americans are governed. While he would no doubt learn something about the form of American government, he would receive a very unrealistic, not to say downright inaccurate, impression concerning the actual working of the American federal government. First, there is no mention of political parties or lobbies or pressure groups, yet these are of the very essence of the American mode of government. Also he would read in the Constitution that every four years the American people go to the polls to select a group of officials called "electors," who later meet to deliberate upon and to choose some man to serve as president for the next four years. Nothing is said of political parties holding nominating conventions, candidates representing each party traveling over the land trying to convince voters, nothing about party workmen who exchange support of the party for promise of appointment to office if the party wins, and nothing is said in the Constitution which will lead its reader to understand that usually before midnight of election day it is common knowledge who is elected president, even though the electors do not meet for some weeks thereafter.

It is imperative that the student understand that the *formal legal structure of government is only a part of the actual organization and working of government. Customs and traditions are built up over the years which supplement and sometimes contravene the formal legal Constitution.* Thus, while the amendments to the Constitution of the United States permit Negroes to vote and enjoy the same civil and economic rights as whites, it is common knowledge that in the large areas of the nation voting rights are denied Negroes, and almost everywhere Negroes are somewhat disprivileged with respect to the civil liberties which they enjoy. These are only a few ways in which informal patterns of government supersede the formal ones.

*Representation*

Theoretically the people in each territorial unit, county, city, ward, or state, periodically elect persons who sit in legislative bodies to pass the laws by which the people are governed. In theory these representatives are the official spokesmen for all the people who live in the territorial unit from which the legislator is elected. Evidence is overwhelming that this theory of representation contains much myth. First, as we have seen in previous discussions, *the people of each territorial unit are divided into interest groups* such as farmers, workmen, business men, prohibitionists, Protestants, parents, pacifists, and so on. It would be impossible, even should the legislator wish so to do, to represent all of these divergent and opposing interest groups. As it works in practice, most legislators tend to sense and to serve certain group interests rather than others. The groups which tend to be served are not necessarily the groups which contain the largest number of potential votes, but rather are the groups which seem to possess sufficient power to dethrone the politician through indirect means of influencing voters. Thus, powerful business interests, strong labor unions, owners of newspapers and radio stations, leaders of well-organized religious groups "have to be catered to," because even though they represent minorities, they possess sufficient power to threaten the security of the legislator at subsequent elections.

Under the American system *large minorities and sometimes majorities are actually not represented.* If a clear issue is drawn in the election, the side that wins even by a bare margin tends to regard its victory as a "mandate from the people" to put into effect the policies which it espoused in the campaign. Possibly election constitutes a mandate from *some* of the people, but certainly not from all of the people. While there are of course, numerous exceptions, the tendency is all too prevalent for law makers to serve those interest groups which they personally represent and toward which they, therefore, have loyalties, and those groups which they believe have enough power in the community to facilitate reëlection in the future. The recurrent scandals which have been revealed through the years in both of the major parties present rather telling testimony of the behind-the-scenes dealings which are made by candidates for public office. Campaign funds, editorial support, and votes are all too frequently bought—not bought in the sense that a contract for sale is drawn up—but "bought" in the sense that a tacit gentlemen's agreement is made to the effect that if a party or a candidate is supported he will, if elected, serve the wishes and objectives of those who assisted his election or who contributed funds, time, or influence to his support.

It should be noted, also, that under the American electoral system several Presidents of the United States have been elected by less than a majority of the votes cast, and that in many elections a majority of the eligible voters do not vote or are not permitted to vote. In certain areas of the South where there are large populations which are disfranchised by one unconstitutional means or another, men have been elected to the United States Senate by less than 10 per cent of the eligible voters of the state!

*Whether this realistic conception of representation is desirable or undesirable is, of course, a matter of value judgment* upon which there is room for sharp disagreement. Without entering into the evaluation unduly far, it may be pointed out that the crux of the issue seems to be clear: *If law makers are merely the creatures of special interest groups who want this or that favor through law, is there not danger that the common unity apparently necessary to a strong nation may be jeopardized while the law makers busy themselves paying their political debts to their supporters?* On the other hand, *how else can the wishes of special groups be incorporated into law than by the threat of removing the law maker from office if he does not support the wishes of the group or groups who put him into office?*

Fortunately, the issue is not as categorical as the above two questions might imply. An excellent illustration is presented by the World War II period in American government. Once the war began, many special interests were subordinated to the collective goal of winning the war, because the collective welfare seemed to require such concerted action. But even during this crisis period, there was ample evidence of this or that group trying to secure whatever advantage it could for itself, even when it was clear that such advantage was not in the public interest. And as soon as the war was over the former struggle for more favorable legal position between labor and management, producer and consumer, farmer and city dweller, again became apparent. The correct inference may be that in times when national existence is dramatically endangered, such as during a great war, special interests may be at least somewhat subordinated to the collective good. But as soon as the crisis passes, self-interest of special groups again seems to occupy the central value position.

*Propaganda*

It has repeatedly been pointed out that special interest groups try to strengthen their position by securing as many converts to their point of view as possible. Thus, for example, during the period in American history when it was considered to the advantage of industry to secure high tariffs, much energy was devoted by special business groups to convincing workmen and farmers that their interests also would be served by a high tariff policy. Organized labor, in more recent years has tried to "sell" as many people as possible on the philosophy that high wages benefit not only the workmen who receive the high wages but others as well, because the expenditure of high wages would constitute a stimulus to prosperity. It is outside the province of this book to evaluate the soundness or fallacy of any of these economic arguments. Our concern is rather with the examination of the ways and means through which special interest groups try to win adherents among persons not directly a part of the interest group, but useful as political power allies.

Almost every large organized group in America sponsors under one name or another a *public relations* department. It is the duty of this public relations department to sponsor the cause of the interest group through supplying information to newspapers, bringing "pressure" on legislatures, providing speakers, and in any way possible gaining favor for the program and policies of that particular interest group. These public relations officers often organize and sponsor what are called "pressure groups" whose name well describes their purpose, namely to exert influence either directly upon legislators or indirectly through voters for the purpose of winning favor for their cause.

Frequently the possessors of the largest funds ultimately succeed in winning the most adherents. This is not necessarily due to an unethical use of money such as bribery, but rather due to the fact that the *group which possesses the funds can purchase the services of skilled persons to represent the cause and can purchase organized means of reaching the public such as newspaper space, time on the radio, and skilled personnel, called lobbyists, to convince legislators or coerce legislators into giving ear to the wishes of the group represented.* It then becomes the duty for the hirelings of the pressure group so to present the case of the group to "the public" that it will really believe that it is serving its own interest rather than the interest of the propaganda group. It is, of course, possible that the interest of some group and that of the public might be wholly compatible, but in numerous and obvious instances the propaganda can easily be demonstrated not to be in the public interest at all.

Although there are many devices used by propaganda experts, propaganda resolves itself into a process of so rationalizing some group's wish as to make it appear to be in the "best interest" of someone else. Moreover, it is to the propagandist's advantage usually to conceal his real motive. Thus it would be difficult if not impossible to go before the American people with a frank and outright request by farmers, for example, for higher prices so that they, the farmers, would enjoy a higher standard of living. Such an appeal might win support from some altruistic people, but would largely be ignored. Instead the propagandists would make it appear that great public danger would lurk in the failure to provide farmers with higher prices. He would not necessarily *falsify* the facts, but would *select* the facts which would serve the purpose and make the cause of higher farm prices appear to be necessary to the national defense, the public welfare, or the struggle against communism.

Not only does a propagandist strive to rationalize the real objective which he serves but also usually finds it useful to use *catch phrases to which the public is already conditioned,* and then in some way to *attach the catch phrase to the cause favored or the cause opposed.* Thus it is usually safe in America to make an opposed program appear to be "communistic," without troubling oneself to define communism, or really to determine whether the matter in question has any connection with communism or not. The propagandist has learned that most people are unwilling or unable to think effectively on the more involved public issues, and that they tend to rely on sweeping and loosely-used concepts. These concepts usually have a more precise meaning, but in order to understand that meaning more knowledge is required than most people have. Currently *inflation* is a bogey word. Diametrically opposite programs are being "sold" to the American people by interest groups in the name of curbs to inflation. Obviously someone is rationalizing, perhaps unconsciously, for certainly it cannot be objectively true that both the retention of the Office of Price Administration and the abolition of the Office of Price Administration would curb inflation!

Propaganda, then, seems to be an inherent part of the realistic operation of American government, not because the government itself necessarily conducts or authorizes the propaganda, but because the decisions of the men who constitute the government and the decisions of the voters are so largely influenced by the public relations and pressure tactics of special interest groups. These groups strive to gain support for their program by making them appear to be laden with virtue and the public interest, while those of their opponents are, of course, fraught with grievous dangers and are contrary to the American way of life, the sanctity of the American home, if not also the will of God!

*Patronage*

Americans tend to think of office holders as persons who secure their position by election. While the more prominent public officials such as the President, the Senators, and members of the House of Representatives are elected by the people, vastly more persons who administer the affairs of government are appointed. This is not only true of minor officials, but applies to such important office-holders as the President's Cabinet, the United States Supreme Court, Ambassadors to foreign nations, and representatives to the United Nations. The tradition has become established in American government that the appointees of the numerous offices from Secretary of State to the Postmaster at the cross-roads general store, receive their appointments in part as a reward for political service to some elected officer who either makes the appointment or arranges for the appointment. The phrase, "the spoils system," may perhaps overdramatize the matter, but it is essentially correct: to the winner of the election belongs the "spoils" of appointing to numerous offices those persons who helped him get elected. While the Civil Service system has placed certain limitations upon the cruder operation of the spoils system, it has by no means eliminated it. Most of the really important policy making, administrative, and judicial positions are outside the scope of Civil Service control.

The *elected official* who is responsible for the appointments to office is, of course, *not entirely free* to pass out political offices on the basis of his personal wishes. Appointive officers are in the public eye almost as much as elected ones, and the elected official who chooses too many unpopular appointive subordinates may find his popularity jeopardized by his misjudgment or favoritism. At least, then, one may say that the appointive official must present a minimum degree of competence for the position as well as claiming the favor of his appointer. Probably public officials vary greatly in the extent to which their decisions concerning appointees are dominated by the desire to render the best possible public service over against the desire to pay their political debts.

In many other ways the informal organization of government shows striking deviations from the publicity proclaimed and formally stated ideal principles. We have limited this discussion to some of the realities involved in representation, propaganda, and patronage.

## SOME LONG-RUN TRENDS IN AMERICAN GOVERNMENT

### 1. *More Government*

Almost any way of measuring the magnitude of government shows a long-run increase throughout the nation's history, throughout the administrations of all political parties. The number of persons employed in government, the cost of government, the functions of government, the number of laws, the number of separate controls over the person, are all indices of the steady growth of this aspect of society. It is fashionable for the party out of power to decry this continued growth of "bureaucracy," and increase in taxes, and point out the dire consequences which face the nation if the conspiracy fostered by the party in power is permitted to endure for another four years. This argument would perhaps be more convincing if, when the parties changed places, the incoming party would show any marked evidence of reducing the functions or costs of government. This, of course, does not happen, largely for the reason that most of the increasing duties of government are necessary, if not indispensable, to the smooth functioning of modern society.

There is, of course, a second reason why parties coming to power do not abolish offices: more patronage can be handed out if there are more office holders to be replaced. It seems clear, however, that the principal factor is that of need for more governmental control. Large-scale organization of business and labor requires more governmental regulation. The closer relationships with other nations throughout the world require more persons to carry out the work incident to these relationships. The public, or certain segments of it, has turned to the federal government as the most appropriate agency for handling certain specialized duties in the public interest, such as the administration of unemployment insurance funds, old age security systems, pure food and drug enforcement, and more recently health protection and insurance. Most of these functions were highly controversial issues at the time they were first proposed and were usually branded by their opponents as "un-American," "impractical and unworkable," "too costly," and "subversive." These have become cliché reactions to changes in the traditional conception of what a government ought to do in a society. Opponents of the government's entry into these areas were undoubtedly correct in their repeated assertions that some alternative to government *could* have been found to serve these functions. There are always alternatives. But one must choose, from among the available alternatives, some one which, balancing advantages and disadvantages, seems best to meet the need. Increasingly the federal government is being chosen as the agency of society in which persons and groups are placing increasing responsibility for meeting needs and serving purposes which cannot be reliably served by other agencies.

### 2. *Centralization of Functions in the Federal Government*

The last half-century, at least, has been characterized by a gradual, and at times rapid, transfer of government functions from the states to the federal government and the addition of new functions previously carried on by no governmental unit. This gradual relative decline of the importance of state and local government has been the object of considerable concern among many people. It has been feared that concentration of power in the federal government would result in the eventual loss of local and state authority over matters which are of special importance to the local area. Some acts of federal officials and some federal legislation have given justification for this fear. In the attempt to work out an overall policy for the entire nation, the federal government has sometimes introduced changes contrary to the cultural traditions of the local areas, or has moved more rapidly than regional public opinion has been willing to accept.

Whether this condition is desirable or undesirable is, of course, a matter of evaluation which almost inevitably defies objective analysis. Is it, for example, desirable or undesirable that the federal government outlaw child labor in some areas in which child labor is still legal by state law? Was it desirable or undesirable that the federal government during the war required that "Fair Employment Practices" be observed in states and cities in which previously Negro employment had been sharply segregated? Is it desirable or undesirable that the Social Security Act of 1935 provided for old age security through wage deductions of workmen in parts of the country which still clung to the older philosophy that it was not a legitimate function of government to concern itself with the financial security of old people? If one approves of these newer philosophies, he would probably tend to favor these changes since they would result in a more rapid incorporation of the philosophy into practice. On the other hand, the superimposition of a program or a function of the federal government might tend to antagonize many persons who through a more gradual introduction to the program might come eventually to favor it.

One of the major factors making for centralization of federal authority has been the *need for uniformity and standardization of practice*. In a day when people move freely from state to state, hardly conscious of crossing state lines, great confusion and much injustice can be done when the states vary radically in the nature and kinds of services which they provide for the individual. During the depression, for example, when unemployment was rife and destitution common, many persons faced virtual starvation because they were not yet legal residents of the states in which they were actually living. They were not, therefore, eligible for any assistance, but were too poor or otherwise unable to move back to the state in which they were legal residents. Since they had not yet lived the required year or two or six months necessary to establish legal residence in a second state, there seemed little solution other than the quick introduction of a federal system of relief administration or employment. This is only one of a great many instances which could be cited whereby state-to-state variation has worked serious hardship on many people.

*Difficulties of legal enforcement within single states* has sometimes led to federal expansion into functions formerly handled by individual states. War-time rationing, price control, pure food and drug standards, disease control, and other government services would be virtually impossible, if one could escape the requirements of the law simply by moving across the state line.

Sometimes federal control has been necessary because *the group to be controlled has been so powerful that no individual state authority could or would exert effective control in the public interest.* State regulation of large-scale business, railroads, and other enterprises which transcend several state boundaries would be virtually impossible without federal jurisdiction.

### 3. *"Bureaucratic"* versus *"Due Process" Regulation*

A fundamental problem in governmental control is that of enforcing the laws. According to the traditional American legal procedure, the accused violator of a law is tried in court to determine whether the accusation against him be true, and if so, what the penalty shall be within the somewhat varied limits which the law usually provides. Moreover, it has usually been the responsibility of the courts to determine whether a given law passed by the Congress was a law which, within the legal framework of the Constitution, the Congress had the right to pass. In short, the courts must determine whether the law is legal. Under modern conditions, however, more and more law enforcement has been placed in the hands of boards, bureaus, commissions and administrative officers set up by law for the special purpose of enforcing special laws. These agencies have the same purpose as courts, but do not follow the same procedure as courts.

The usual justification for this change is that traditional legal machinery is so slow—even in the case of clear violation of law—that great public loss may result while the legal machinery is being put into motion. By way of illustration, let us suppose that all of the merchants of a city deliberately violated the "price ceilings" set by the government during the war and refused to abide by the "point rationing" system. By the time that traditional legal procedures for indictment and trial, and a series of appeals challenging the law itself, could reach the Supreme Court, the war might be over and the attendant public loss and confusion be great. Even though the court eventually upheld the law, the effect of the law would actually be nullified during the critical period when it was most needed. Thus the federal government has devised numerous bodies with *quick authority*, most of them, however, *subject to eventual review by the courts.*

From the point of view of older American legal traditions, such "government by bureaus" seems to be a radical departure from the time-honored mode of procedure. But from the practical point of view, namely of getting things done in an emergency or preventing some group from jeopardizing the public interest on pure legal technicality, government by bureaus is considered by many to be not only desirable but essential so that the public interest may better be served. There seems little doubt that sometimes the decisions of administrative boards, commissions, and bureaus have been ill-advised, but whether, when the whole truth is known, their record will be any more impeachable than that of the courts is a question which cannot now be authoritatively answered. So long as events move as rapidly and as unpredictably as they now do, government must have some means of protecting the public interest which is so often jeopardized while selfish and sometimes conflicting factions of the society follow their own interest, too frequently in total disregard of the larger and more fundamental general public interest.

Current dissatisfaction with government by bureaus is so great and the pressure groups working against it are so insistent and powerful, that it is quite probable that a major issue will be made of this matter in the near future. Although it is relatively easy to point out defects in government through bureaus, it is quite another matter to find a substitute which will be flexible enough to meet the needs of a dynamic social world. Insistent pleas for a return to the "traditional American system" which was devised to meet a situation which we do not now have, are too often used to conceal a real desire by some pressure group to get rid of controls and thereby reopen opportunities for the exercise of selfish freedom. This is the very evil which originally gave rise to bureaucratic government, and merely to repeal bureaucratic government is by no means a solution to the problem of making government control in the public interest flexible enough to meet the public interest in time to avoid serious injustice, if not catastrophe.

## INTERNATIONAL ORGANIZATION

Nation-states, like individuals and special interest groups have selfish desires, and tend to interpret "justice" in varying ways to suit their own purposes. This gives rise to international issues sometimes ending in warfare. Accordingly there have been several attempts to set up governing or quasi-governing bodies with the hope that they will be effective in reducing conflict and making for a more orderly and equitable international scene. All of these attempts prior to the present one have failed, but only in the sense that each has been eventually discontinued in favor of some new organization. The last one to have "failed" was the League of Nations, organized immediately after World War I and rendered largely ineffective by the onset of World War II. The League of Nations failed to prevent World War II, but may have served a useful purpose in several other respects. For example, the League of Nations may have delayed the outbreak of hostilities so that the world might enjoy a longer period of peace before the next war. It probably contributed to a better exchange of views among nations. Even more important, perhaps, the efforts of the League of Nations provided an opportunity to test various procedures so that when it came time to organize its successor, the United Nations, a better organization could be formulated.

Opinions vary sharply concerning the value and effectiveness of the present United Nations. It is still too near its infancy to permit one to evaluate it objectively. All that can be reported is that after each modern major war an attempt has been made to avert the next one.

The chief stumbling block to all international organizations has been, of course, the tradition of *state sovereignty,* that is, no major nation-state has been willing to acknowledge any authority superior to itself. Each nation clings to the traditional idea that it must remain completely sovereign with no really effective delegation of authority to the international government, if the United Nations can be called a government. It is entirely possible, of course, that the turning point in international organization may now have been reached, and that the current attempt may achieve the success which its predecessors have failed to achieve.

## SUMMARY

The *state* as a sovereign territorial grouping of people should be distinguished from the *government* which is only the power organization which is dominant in the state at a given time. Governments are of many forms, which may be regarded as varying along a continuum with one-man rule at one extreme and complete democracy at the other. There has probably been no actual example of either extreme on this continuum. The most absolute monarchs in the past secured advice and guidance and were somewhat influenced by at least a few other people, and thus were somewhat limited. Moreover, no complete democracy exists. In the United States, for example, there are relatively disprivileged races and social classes who are not permitted to share equally in the affairs of government with other races and other classes.

All major nation-states in the world have been characterized by change not only in their composition, but also by marked change in their government. Sometimes changes have been gradual and at other times revolutionary. Groups which have important power positions at one time in the history of a state may have their power sharply reduced or removed entirely by the change of events.

The realistic study of government provides numerous illustrations of the discrepancies which may and do exist between the formal, verbal *ideals* regarding government and the *actual* ways in which government works. This has been discussed in some detail concerning the theory and practice of representation in the American government, the use of propaganda by power groups, and the system of patronage.

American government is characterized by certain long-run

trends, prominent among which are the increase in the size and functions of government, the centralization of function and power of the federal government, and the replacing of "due process" control by "bureaucratic" control in some areas of government administration.

It is doubtful whether one may accurately refer to world government. There is, however, a world organization which has at least some of the functions of government. World organization lacks the one essential ingredient, however—sovereignty. It is difficult to anticipate the eventual success or failure of the United Nations so long as absolute sovereignty of the major nations is insisted upon.

## SUGGESTED READINGS

Bain, Read, "Sociopathy and World Organization," *American Sociological Review,* IX, pp. 127-138. **A**

An interpretation of war as "psychotic sociopathy" accompanied by much "neurotic behavior." "Two sociopathic social structures are the main obstacles" to world organization—the military system and the economic system. Sees the only hope in the United Nations.

Cottrell, W. F., "Cultural Growth of Internationalism," *American Sociological Review,* X, pp. 586-95. **A B**

Chronicles the historical development of international ideas in Western culture. The "process is slow and undramatic" but "perhaps some dramatic episode will serve to mark its official emergence as the dominant form of political organization, but to proclaim it now is premature and will serve only to delay the event."

Harding, T. S., "Uncle Sam Unwhiskered," *American Journal of Sociology,* L, pp. 305-310. **A**

A sophisticated treatment of the "real" patterns of bureaucracy and how they must be learned by "liberals and reformers" who are not experienced with the "liturgy and ritual" which have developed "to cloak subterfuge and allay opposition."

Lee, A. M., "An Analysis of Propaganda: A Clinical Summary," *American Journal of Sociology,* LI, pp. 126-135. **A B**

A splendid and terse summary of propaganda techniques viewed from several different angles. Written by the executive director of the late Institute for Propaganda Analysis.

Lumley, F. E., *The Propaganda Menace* (New York, D. Appleton-Century Co., 1933). **A B**

A well-known book on propaganda. Tries to give the term a somewhat scientific meaning and to define it in terms of purpose or intent on the part of the user of propaganda. Contains a wealth of illustrative materials. **A B**

Young, Kimball, "Society and the State," *American Sociological Review,* XI, pp. 137-146. **B**

A review of the trend toward increasing federal governmental control over the individual and society. He points out the need for more data and better interpretations of this trend and speculates on some of its "deeper" implications.

## STUDY QUESTIONS

1. What problems often arise in states that are made up of diverse cultural units? Illustrate with respect to the United States.
2. What is the relation between state and government? Illustrate.
3. What is the basic function of government?
4. Why is the statement "all governments derive their power from the people" fallacious?
5. How does American "ideal" government differ from its "real" government? Illustrate.
6. Why are "empty" customs and traditions a part of government?
7. In what ways do pressure groups exert "more than their share" of influence in shaping governmental policy?
8. In America why are large minorities and even majorities often not represented?
9. How do special interest groups use propaganda to attain their objectives?
10. For what purposes does a political party use patronage? What limits the use of patronage?
11. What is meant by the statement "less government in business and more business in government?"
12. Why has there been an increase in the size and functions of our government?
13. Why has there been an increase in control by the federal government at the expense of the state governments?
14. Why is there opposition to government regulations by bureaus and commissions?
15. Why is a world organization more necessary now than formerly? What is the chief obstacle to effective international organization?
16. What major change will be necessary as a prerequisite to effective world government?

# *Chapter XXIV*

## EDUCATION IN AMERICAN SOCIETY

Most persons think of education as being synonymous with the school. This leads to numerous faulty interpretations and unreasonable hopes. It is doubtful if one should assume that the school is even the chief educational agency in modern society. The teaching-learning process, whether so intended or not, is a continual process resulting in the socialization of the person literally from the cradle to the grave. Only a small part of the total education time of even the most learned person is spent in school, and learning occurs continuously through a wide variety of media outside of school, from movies, radio, the church, political speeches, newspapers, magazines, books, informal association with other persons, and from myriads of other sources.

As an institution, on the other hand, education is chiefly the function of the societally sponsored school system from the nursery school to the post-graduate college. While such agencies as the movies, the play group, or the pool room undoubtedly have educational influence, they do not exist primarily for that purpose. Their educational functions are incidental to other functions. In the broadest sense, education as a process is synonymous with the socialization of the person; in its more strict sense, education as an institution consists of the programs of the formal educational organizations of the society and the effects of these programs on the persons influenced by the organizations.

It would be an error to overlook either of these two aspects of education. Education, in the broad sense of socialization, has already been discussed at numerous points in this book, notably in the sections on social psychology and in some of the chapters on culture. A few additional aspects of informal, non-school education in the United States will be discussed before we turn to our primary concern, which is an examination of formal, institutional education in America.

## SOME NON-SCHOOL EDUCATIONAL INFLUENCES

### 1. *The Family*

The first and basic learnings of the child take place in the family. For the first few years, the family is almost the entire world of experience for a child. Even though he may attend nursery school for a few hours a day for a few weeks a year, and may spend some time playing with other children or with adults not related to his family, these experiences constitute a small part of his total exposure to people from which experiences he acquires his basic personality patterns. The trend of research findings in the fields of psychiatry and social psychology during recent years has increasingly emphasized the paramount importance of this pre-school learning period. All later learnings and personality changes, from whatever source they may come, are conditioned and modified by the preëxisting traits and characteristics of the person which he acquired in his early childhood. As we have seen in previous chapters, these early family experiences may be such as to create desirable traits of behavior as defined by the current cultural values, or they may result in the child's learning patterns of conduct and acquiring values which are disapproved by the larger pattern. Family conditioning may cause a child to be socially rejected, or accepted in ways which imply lower status than he would like. Whatever the outcome, of course, in terms of normality or abnormality, the influence of the family in the formulation of the person's behavior can hardly be overemphasized.

Reasons for the importance of the family as a socializing agency are not hard to find. In the first place the family is the only educative agency which really starts with a "clean slate" in molding the person's behavior. By the time the school assumes control of the child's learning, he is already a person whose previous experiences have resulted in the formation of attitudes, values, and overt behavior patterns. Upon this preëxisting structure the school can only build or try to make modifications, if the child's personality is not acceptable to the standards held by the school. Not only does the family have a head start on all other educational agencies, but it has the advantage of continuous influence. Moreover, the family may influence the child through several very effective media, very important among which is the unconscious teaching through example. The child does not merely "study" morality so much as he "sees" morality in operation in his family group. Unfortunately, sometimes, the discrepancy between real and ideal morality is made too effective. The child frequently observes more than is intended from the overt behavior of his parents and family group. It appears that children are influenced more by suggestion and by their own observations than by their parents' verbal teachings. For these and other reasons the family is "the cradle of the human personality."

2. *The Play Group*

As the child becomes older he spends an increasing proportion of his time in association with other children in large and small, supervised and unsupervised play groups. These play groups give the child usually his first opportunity to test his status among others without the artificial protection and sheltering of parents or teacher. In the play group the child must fend for himself. Many children learn the "rules" of social living through the forthright and sometimes brutal interaction with other children. Here he begins to see himself the way outsiders really see him. He does not have to guess about his status, for children in play groups usually let each other know in no uncertain terms what they think of each other. There is much less tempering of true feelings, less inhibition of impulses due to the social graces, than the person is likely to meet in other areas of his experience. Through trial and error in the play situation the child learns how to lead or how to follow. He learns how to control other people, and how to be controlled by them. He learns the rules of games and also how to violate the rules and "get by with it." He learns individual differences among his associates too. He learns that some of his playmates can be "pushed around" and others cannot. He discovers that he "rates" with some people and not with others. In short, he learns social rôles and acquires basic definitions of himself in relation to other people.

Characteristic types of personality like the "bully," the

"sissy," the "tom boy," the "eager beaver," and the "gold brick" are frequently learned at this early age. The person learns these rôles and habituates them by repetition, if he is successful. If he meets frustration, he makes adjustments (Ch. XII). As he encounters new situations in later life, he falls back upon the rôles he has previously learned and found successful. Life-history studies present ample evidence of the enduring nature of childhood basic behavior patterns.

3. *The Radio*

Radio functions twenty-four hours a day. By a flip of the wrist an adult or a child can make instantaneous contact with a variety of outside "worlds." Music, drama, sports, news, and advertising, all expertly produced, crowd upon his consciousness. Radio programs are designed to be the most vivid listener-experiences possible. They are planned and produced by some of the ablest people of the land, and they utilize every psychological device known to capture attention and hold interest. With the advent of radio a semi-literate can be fairly well informed about a great many things, and can participate vicariously in places, activities, and ideas which would otherwise be closed to him. Not as much is known concerning the precise influence of radio upon personality as would be desired, but studies of the listening habits of both children and adults indicate that a great deal of time is spent with radio. One may presume, therefore, that the influence is considerable even though we do not know exactly what it is.

There are those who decry many of the apparent influences of radio, such as the extremely melodramatic, trite, and trivial content of the well-known daily "soap operas." Judged by accepted standards of sophisticated dramatic production, these programs are undoubtedly of inferior calibre. But it does not follow that the persons who listen to them would participate in any "higher" level of dramatic production if the "soap operas" were not on the air. In other words, the defendants of the allegedly mediocre type of radio production point out that by offering a wide variety of programs, the persons with mediocre taste may participate in mediocre program content, while persons of more discriminating tastes are also offered grand opera and better drama. This sort of an explanation smacks of rationalization in at least two ways. First, mediocre or definitely inferior programs greatly outnumber the more substantial ones, often giving the listener no real choice. More important perhaps, through the continuous presentation of trivial material, tastes for trivial material may be heightened. This would apply as much to music as to dramatic presentation, and to reading material as well as to radio.

There is another significant aspect of radio—news coverages, both in the form of news broadcasts and the well-known "commentaries" or interpretations of the news. There is evidence that more persons listen to news commentators than read newspaper editorials and columns which contain substantially the same kind of material. It has never been determined, however, whether radio commentators are influential in formulating political attitudes or influencing political conduct. But it seems reasonable to assume that they have influence. The "on the spot" news coverages add an element of the dramatic to world happenings and may result in more persons listening to radio than would take the time to read about these same happenings in newspapers or magazines.

It has been suggested that one of the long-run educational influences of radio may be an improvement in the quality of spoken English since, in the main, the diction, pronunciation, and sentence structure of commercial as well as other programs represent a high level of correct English usage. Through the continuous suggestion of hearing better-than-average oral language, it is argued, the child and perhaps even the adult may unconsciously acquire more correct speaking habits.

In many other ways, no doubt, the radio is an educational influence on both children and adults. Perhaps some of the influences are more acceptable than others in the light of standards of perfection in such matters which our culture contains. Regardless of one's evaluation, however, the fact of appreciable influence seems probable.

### 4. *Movies*

Much of the same holds true for movies as for radio. The chief differences are in the almost continuous influence of radio, while movie attendance even for the more ardent fan, is only intermittent. Moreover, it is clear that a larger part of movie time is intended to provide entertainment. But entertainment is also educational, that is, while being "entertained" a person is being exposed to vicarious social experiences. Through this vicarious social experience he is formulating attitudes and acquiring or modifying values continuously. Even though the observer is fully aware that the segment of life presented to him on the screen is "fictional," the vividness with which it is presented creates such an effective illusion of reality that the person often responds *as if* the persons and situations were real. Movie characters, like characters of fiction, are socially real in that they have the same influence and provide the same function for the person as living personalities do. This may be more true for children, but it applies also to adults.

It is perhaps unfortunate that the movies make as great use as they do of stereotyped personalities and situations which unwittingly conduce to the establishment or entrenchment of false ideas about persons of minority races, certain occupation groups, certain parts of the country, and certain so-called "personality types." It is highly doubtful, however, that movies are any more serious offenders of reality than newspaper cartoons and many fiction writers.

5. *The Church*

It will be noted in the following chapter on religion that churches support an extensive program of education, not only through the traditional Sunday Schools and other religious education for children, but through adult classes of various sorts and through church school teacher training courses. Moreover, the traditional public worship service is itself an educational experience. Sermons are intended to inform as well as to exhort people toward the observance of Christian standards of thought and action. Prayers, communion, the reading of Scriptures, and singing of hymns are all learning experiences, and the repeating of these experiences probably has a conditioning influence on the out-of-church behavior of church people. Moreover, most church denominational headquarters publish numerous periodicals and books designed also to inform and to guide personal conduct.

6. *Magazines and Books*

It is probably obvious enough that books and magazines constitute an educational influence through the vicarious experiences which readers secure from them. Over 11,000 new books are published in the United States each year, many of the better-known ones selling thousands of copies. In addition, numerous copies of books published in preceding years are also sold. The circulation of library books of non-school and non-college libraries is truly impressive. For several years the book circulation of the public libraries of such cities as Chicago and Los Angeles totaled over ten million per year, and greater New York City alone exceeds twenty millions. The per capita circulation of books in leading American cities varies from ten books per person per year for Cleveland, Ohio, to one and one-half for Philadelphia. In addition newspaper and magazine subscriptions amount to over one-half billion dollars per year.[1] It is difficult to interpret the significance of these statistics, however, because it cannot be determined how many times a given book or magazine is read, how much of it is read, and most important of all, with what results. One may assume, however, that if the American people spent 5 per cent of the national income on magazines, newspapers, and books each year, that they are read and that their influence is appreciable.

### 7. *Social Interaction and Learning*

Finally, the greatest educational influence of all consists of living and associating with other people. In this manner the person acquires and continually modifies his personality. He reads, he talks to people, he achieves success and he meets with failures, he observes behavior and its results in the lives of other people, meanwhile somewhat integrating the whole kaleidoscopic total of experiences for himself. Whenever we separate any one item of educational experience from the total, we do a certain violence to reality. It is necessary for purposes of analysis, to separate a single part of the total educational experience like the school or the radio in order to concentrate upon it more fully, but whenever such isolation of one factor is made, one should be cautious lest he overlook the great importance of the other educational experiences which also play upon the person. Most of the materials found in Part III of this book were designed to sharpen understanding of the processes by which the human personality is formed through association with others and is continually modified by this interaction.

[1] These statistics are taken from the *World Almanac* and are to be regarded as approximate only.

## WHAT ARE THE FUNCTIONS OF INSTITUTIONAL EDUCATION?

### 1. *The Universal Function of Education*

Education of the young is a universal process found in all human societies. Everywhere and at all times man has found it necessary to bring up his young by indoctrinating them with the culture of his society. Part of that indoctrination he does deliberately through formal teachings either through the family or through organized education or religion. Some societies, however, do very little formal educating of their young. For example, the Manus people of New Guinea do not have schools, books, teachers, or even an alphabet. Yet the Manus child learns the Manus language, the religion, the morals, and the etiquette required in order to function successfully in the Manus society. Much of this learning is, of course, informal and unconscious. The child learns by imitation and by the suggestion and examples of his associates. In short, the Manus child, like the American child or the child of any other society, learns the skills, the ideas, and the values which he needs to know in order to be able to function in his society. This we may term "the universal function of education." Stated tersely it consists of the *conditioning of the plastic and growing human being so that he will be able to function in a society made up of similarly conditioned people*. This every society needs to do for a substantial number, though not necessarily all, of its members in order to remain intact. If it fails to achieve this objective, the nature of the society changes or it may go out of existence as a society entirely. In a sense, the ultimate requirement for the continuity of any society is the ability successfully to perpetuate itself by indoctrinating its offspring with the folkways and mores which enable it to exist. The preservation of the cultural heritage is indispensable to the continuity of any society.

As we have previously noted, of course, no society reproduces itself identically in successive generations. This is simply another way of saying that the indoctrination of the young has always been incomplete, or that once indoctrinated, the people do not remain indoctrinated. This fact of social change, however, should not obscure the fundamental fact that even in the most revolutionary society there is much that is old in the post-revolutionary social order. Living with other people would be incomprehensible unless there were a fundamental basis of understanding, a common heritage of language, and some agreement upon values. Without these common denominators a society would simply fall apart, or perhaps to put it more accurately, there would be no society at all. Not only, then, is the indoctrination of the young with the prevailing culture a universal educational process, it is also an indispensable one.

### 2. *The Variable Functions of Education*

After the universal, indispensable societal need is met, there remains considerable choice as to the form, content, and purposes which a society may incorporate in its educational efforts. Education may be formal or informal, it may be dominated by the family, by the government, by organized religion, by a semi-independent agency such as the school in America, or by some combination of these. Education may be extended to both sexes or limited to one. The sexes may be segregated during some or all of their formal education, or they may be educated together. The culture of the society may condone or encourage almost universal education, or may limit education to certain social classes. Education may be concerned with training people for vocations, or it may be limited to liberal or spiritual or aesthetic matters. It may be the purpose of education to mold people along a single basic pattern as closely as possible, or it may be considered desirable to encourage individuality and individual differences in greater or lesser degree. The educational system may exist for the purpose of indoctrinating or for encouraging "free thinking" along certain lines. In short, there is almost no end to the differences which can be found in the educational systems and philosophies now existing or that have existed in the known past.

### *Education a Function of the Total Society*

Once the indispensable function of basic indoctrination is met, there seems almost no theoretical limit to the alternatives which the educational process may follow. There is, of course, the practical *limitation imposed by the values of the prevailing society* which the educational system serves. The educational system is a creature of the society, although it is sometimes so constituted that instead of serving the purposes of the society, it may modify or possibly even destroy it. There are those who think that the contemporary American educational system is doing precisely that. It was originally established and supported by a capitalistic and somewhat democratic society. It was given freedom under the law to formulate in some measure its own policies and objectives, but that freedom is by no means complete. This American educational system then became "liberal," that is, it chose to examine and to criticize many aspects of the government and society which created it and supported it. It succeeded in creating critical, usually called "liberal," attitudes on the part of its products, the pupils, many of whom not only became liberal but radical, and used their educational knowledge for the purpose of changing the larger society.

It is entirely possible that the pressure for change may become so great that the entire basic structure of American society may be changed. Should this occur, as appears not unlikely, other forces than the educational system, of course, probably will be found to have shared in the process. But certainly the school system, especially the university system, appears to have exerted an appreciable influence toward liberal social change in America. It is desirable, therefore, that the educational system of America be examined for the purpose of determining (1) what influences other institutions exert upon the system of education, (2) what values and philosophies are involved in the educational system, and (3) what main lines of evaluation of these values, philosophies, and proposals are current in the present American culture.

## THE INSTITUTIONAL EDUCATIONAL SYSTEM OF THE UNITED STATES

### 1. *"Liberal" Education*

The phrase "liberal education" is used in somewhat different ways by different persons, but it has one core of meaning in common acceptance. Liberal education stands in contrast to indoctrination. It is the philosophy that a person should be made familiar not only with the values and ideas and precepts of his own culture, but also with other cultures both past and contemporary. It holds, for example, that even though a man is Protestant he should be familiar with the history of Catholicism and the ideas of the great Catholic thinkers. Thus a liberally educated person will probably have read Hitler's *Mein Kampf*. But why spend time reading a book written by the leader of an enemy nation? Hitler is dead, as probably also is much of Germany's Naziism. A liberally educated man, however, would want to be familiar with the content of *Mein Kampf*, not because he wishes necessarily to accept any of its preachments, but simply because it has been an influential book in fashioning or at least in representing one of the great movements in modern Europe. The same logic would hold for studying the *Communist Manifesto* or the works of St. Thomas Aquinas. The liberal would study science also, not necessarily because he wishes to become a scientist or otherwise put his scientific knowledge to "practical" use, but rather because science is a significant part of modern culture, and the scientific mode of thinking is an important one. Liberal education, of course, does not neglect the study of one's own culture, but tries to get the student to *see his own culture within the perspective of the larger stream of ideas, men, and events which antedated and surround it.*

Liberal education, however, also has its *opponents.* In recent years it has been attacked because of the "moral relativism" which the liberally educated tend to develop. Moral relativism means the recognition that there are many different moral-ethical-religious-political systems, each of which has its own logic and justification, none representing a corner on the whole or sole "truth." It is easy for the liberally educated person to become a moral relativist. Having familiarized himself with other ideas and philosophies, with others' attempts to rationalize different thought systems than his own, he may tend to lose at least some of his cruder ethnocentrism. During the early period of World War II, the complaint was commonly heard that America's educated young men, because they could "see" both sides more clearly than the ignorant, would not have sufficient enthusiasm to fight for their own nation's side, since they could see virtue and fault in both sides. The implication of these critics was to the effect, then, that ignorance of other cultures would be an asset because one could feel more secure in the all-sufficiency and perfection of his own!

Another criticism of liberal education is that it is "impractical," by which is usually meant that it does not necessarily fit one for a special job, with the possible exception of such professions as journalism, ministry, politics, and perhaps teaching. This criticism really is beside the point, of course, because liberal education was never claimed by its opponents to be vocational education. No one claimed that knowledge about American history or the Magna Charta would per se make a better filling-station attendant or a more effective salesman. The values of liberal education are those of better citizenship, broad understanding of the universe, and a perspective on change.

2. *Vocational Education*

Another emphasis in American formal education, and to a considerable extent a reaction to liberal education, has been the rise of an emphasis on special training for specific jobs. Emphasis on vocational education extends from the post-graduate schools of the great universities down to the junior high school. Most metropolitan cities have one or more high schools, often called "vocational high schools," which specialize in training children for such jobs as stenography, agriculture, printing, carpentry, and machine shop work. The theory underlying this movement is obvious enough. (1) The trained person does better work, receives better pay, and more rapid advancement, as a rule, than the less well trained. (2) There has, however, been a second factor in the rise of vocational high schools. Many boys and girls, either because they lacked ability or because they lacked interest, were found not to be well adjusted in the conventional academic high school. Since compulsory school attendance laws, and laws prohibiting the employment of children, existed in most states, these persons who were not well adjusted to the conventional high school had to be placed somewhere. The vocational high school seemed to be a logical place. (3) There were also those people who favored the vocational high school on the ground that many people could not afford the time or the money for the "luxury" of a liberal education. They could make their time count for more in dollars and cents by using their school time to train them for some job. This philosophy has a strong appeal in a society in which pecuniary values are as prominent as they are in the United States.

The critics of vocational education have taken the position, first, that much time is wasted in vocational education. Not very many children know what occupation they wish to follow when they are in junior or senior high school. Even if they did know, it would be possible to learn the necessary skills in a much shorter time and with much better results, if training were received directly as apprentices in the training departments of large corporations, or in specialized trade schools for adults. Critics have also contended that often the standards of work in vocational schools have been low and technically obsolescent, and that they have tended to encourage vocational school courses for students capable of attaining advanced educational objectives.

The vocational *versus* liberal education quarrel has also entered into colleges and universities where, however, it takes a somewhat different form. Colleges on the whole do not give training in manual skills such as vocational high schools do. Vocational training offered by colleges and universities is largely limited to the major professions such as medicine, law, ministry, teaching, social work, engineering, and more recently the various branches of business administration and agriculture. No one denies that each of these fields requires a specialized type of training on the college and university level of quality. The issue centers around *how much of the total education* of a veterinarian, or an architect, or of an accountant should be liberal education and how much should be strictly vocational. It is especially important that college-trained professional people have a background in liberal education because they tend to be the leaders in the political and economic life of their communities. It may not make too much difference, it is sometimes argued, whether a skilled laborer in a factory is very well informed about the United Nations organization, since he is rarely in the position to do much about it or to influence other people concerning it. But a minister, for example, ought to know as much as possible about such matters, because in his pulpit work he wields a considerable influence over the attitudes of other people. He should, therefore, possess an accurate background of facts and interpretation, lest he use his position of prestige and leadership unwittingly to mislead or misinform his parishioners. The same logic would hold true for the teacher and somewhat less clearly for other professional persons.

But the issue still persists. *How much* of the seven or eight years which a physician or a lawyer or a university professor spends in preparation for his profession should be devoted to a liberal education, and how much to the pursuit of the specialty by which he earns his living and serves his constituency? Traditionally the bachelors' degree, the first four years, has been presumed to be largely liberal. The technical content of the various fields of knowledge have grown through research, and deeper and deeper inroads into the liberal program of the undergraduate have been made. Usually there are numerous prescribed "prerequisites" to admission into the professional schools. Sometimes the prerequisites almost crowd out the liberal courses. Many educational leaders feel that the movement has already gone too far in the direction of professionalizing college education. The social, political, and economic illiteracy of professional men and women is said to be appalling. The day when the physician, the clergyman, or the teacher represented the community's best informed and generally learned men is said to have largely passed. So much of the period of college training goes into specialized instruction for the coming profession that the professional man is sometimes only slightly if any better informed along liberal lines than the person who did not go to college at all.

The above criticisms of over-professionalization have brought some results, mostly in the form of increasing the total time for professional training so as to include opportunities for the choice of liberal electives during the undergraduate years. This means, of course, that the total cost of education for the professions has been increased through the greater total time required to complete the longer curriculum. It seems to many, however, that it is fortunate that at least some recognition is being given by at least some of the graduate schools to the responsibility of training somewhat more competent citizens and leaders, as well as simply more competent professional personnel.

### 3. *Progressive Education*

Perhaps the most controversial issue in all American education centers around the program and philosophy which goes by the title "progressive education." Progressive education arose as a protest movement against what were thought to be evils and imperfections in the traditional school system. It was felt that there was a great deal of needless and meaningless curriculum content in the elementary school and high school, and that much of the teaching was being done by methods which did not result in desirable learning experiences for the children. The teaching of such traditional subjects as Latin and mathematics was sharply challenged. It is said that a negligible proportion of the great mass of children who go to high school ever make any practical use of these subjects, nor can they be well defended as liberal subjects. Why not devote this time to the study of subjects which will have some relation to the kinds of problems and needs which the children will encounter in their later lives? Moreover, the traditional educational system is said not to be well balanced, that it emphasizes academic matters to the neglect or omission of such other important aspects of the personality as health, recreation, and citizenship. Traditional teaching methods also are criticized. Instead of merely reading and discussing topics which were frequently unreal to the child, it would be better to place the child in practical situations where he could observe directly or even participate in the things being studied. Instead of reading about city government, for example, the child could be taken to meetings of the city council, visit the health department, and talk to the park commissioners. Finally, the older curriculum is said to be "too rigid," not allowing sufficiently for the individual needs of particular students.

On the positive side, progressive education emphasizes teacher-pupil planning of curricular activities, not teacher domination of the classroom situation. It urges individualized instruction and flexible curricula. It makes great use of extra-curricular activities, even giving academic "credit" for participating in them. It emphasizes physical and health training, and guidance along recreational lines. Parents are urged to take greater interest in the school and many evening activities are planned to encourage such greater integration of school and home. Extensive use of visual and other more effective teaching aids are advocated, such as movies and field trips.

Progressive education has not "taken" equally thoroughly, or equally quickly in all parts of the nation, in all types of communities, or among all educators. Some schools and some communities seem to have been almost unaffected by the movement while other represented the epitome of the progressive educational philosophy and program.

Progressive education has had its critics—and many of them are exceedingly vigorous in their opposition. Progressive education is said to be a fad—to have "run a good idea into the ground." Academic standards are said to have been lowered, and the neglect of formal training in such basic subjects as reading, writing, spelling, and arithmetic has "given us a generation of educated illiterates, who can tell you all about how the nation should be run, but cannot locate the nation's capital on a map, and cannot spell the names of half the cities in the state correctly. They can talk glibly about the national budget but cannot accurately add up the figures on the grocery bill." And so on.

On the surface, the criticisms of progressive education sound plausible enough, but have not stood up well under the scrutiny of research. A study was recently made of the college records of a sample of progressive high school graduates and a comparable sample of graduates from the traditional high schools.[1] Not only academic success but the extra-curricular activities, and almost all other measurable phases of college participation were included. The claims of the critics of progressive education were found to have been largely erroneous. Apparently many of the "logical" arguments and a priori assumptions concerning the educational experiences of children were mistaken. Many of the criticisms and attacks on progressive education continue, of course, largely unimpressed or ignorant of such factual data as those found in the study cited above. In this issue as in so many others, facts are not necessarily accepted, or even known, by the proponents and opponents of "pet" ideas and programs. The mythologies believed about progressive education will probably endure for many years after the facts about progressive education are common knowledge among experts in the field of education.

4. *"Streamlined G.I. Education"*

World War II necessitated a large number of somewhat highly trained men to fill various military rôles which demanded specialized training varying from navigation to foreign language proficiency. When the relatively small number of already trained men was utilized, the armed services were left with no alternative but to train the required number of men themselves. But there was insufficient time to accomplish this objective by the methods commonly employed in civilian education. Some quicker way had to be found. Accordingly, the armed services recruited some outstanding civilian educational leaders (and some not so outstanding ones,

[1] C. P. Chamberlain, and others, *Did They Succeed in College?* (New York, Harper and Bros., 1942).

also) and made them responsible for the organization of curricula by which to teach the men the required materials in a fraction of the time which would be required by civilian schools for the "same" training. Fortunately, the services did not require general education; training in a very specific set of materials was sufficient for most purposes. And so traditional curricula and sequences were radically cut, and material of non-military significance was omitted. As a result the impression was sometimes created that a whole college education was being secured in twenty weeks! The facts, however, were that twenty weeks or so of material were sorted out from the curriculum and instruction in these selected items given. It is probable, however, that due to the high motivation of many of the soldier-students, and the pressure under which they worked, there resulted more thorough effort than most civilian students would ordinarily put forth in a comparable period of time. Finally, the personnel selected for such training was probably superior to the average mental ability found in the high schools and even college classrooms. The services employed rigid selection of their "students," whereas civilian educational institutions neither can nor desire to practice such selection.

It was thought by some observers that the G.I. educational experiments would bring about radical modification of post-war college and high school educational practice. Such may prove yet to be the case, but at this writing (one year after the end of the war) no very marked influences can be seen. There are probably several reasons for the failure of civilian education to follow the policies of military education. First, the *objectives are different.* The purpose of military education is to win a war. It is unimportant, for example, what a mathematics course contributes to the liberal education of a pilot. In a war situation, it is sufficient that he learn how to fly a plane well. Only such items are included in his training as seem likely to contribute to the flying objective. But in a civilian mathematics course there are other objectives than the immediately practical ones. Moreover, many of the topics and subjects omitted entirely from the military educational program constitute the very essence of civilian education. Liberal subjects such as philosophy, literature, and economics are of the very essence of a liberal education. It appears doubtful whether fields of knowledge of this type can be abbreviated, taught under pressure, and objectively tested in the manner in which military-oriented materials can. American education still largely adheres to the idea that it is training citizens for a democracy, that this responsibility requires gradual development—most certainly not indoctrination—of the personality of the student, and that it is as interested in his development as a citizen as in his vocational success.

There may, however, remain some lasting influence from wartime education. Course contents in many fields are currently being somewhat carefully scrutinized for the purpose of determining what non-essentials or relatively unimportant materials can be omitted. Many students have already announced their intention of attending school eleven months a year instead of eight as they traditionally had. Whether these changes will be lasting, of course, cannot now be determined.

### IS AMERICAN EDUCATION REALLY FREE OR IS IT SUBSERVIENT TO OTHER INSTITUTIONS?

It is commonly held that the United States has a "free" educational system. The word *free* is intended to connote that schools, although they are largely supported by the government, are free from political and religious domination. There is growing doubt, however, that the American system of public education is as free as it appears to be on the surface.

The formal organization of schools would imply that education is not dominated by government or religion. Local schools are under the control usually of boards of education elected by the real-estate property owners in some states and by all citizens in others. These school boards appoint the chief executive officer of the system, who in the large cities is usually called a "superintendent" or "commissioner." Presumably he runs the educational system as he thinks best, and presumably he is appointed because he is a capable professional man whose training and experience qualify him for the office. Both of these assumptions are, in many cases, not borne out by the facts. Many school administrators are not really permitted to operate the school systems in the manner which they deem wise, nor are they chosen always strictly on the basis of their professional competence. In one way or another, there is recurrent meddling and dictating to school administrators by the various and sundry pressure groups of the community. During recent years there have been startling revelations, for example, concerning the choice of textbooks. Books have been discarded, not on the basis of their merit, but rather because they have been too accurate in revealing certain truths about American history or some aspect or other of the economic system. Presumably, someone does not want the truth taught in our free public schools!

There are, of course, great variations from community to community with respect to the degree of freedom permitted. Paradoxical as it may seem, one of the chief and recurrent problems of public school administration in America is the *struggle to maintain the freedom in fact which is granted in name.* There seems little doubt that there are still substantial groups of persons in the United States who conceive of the function of education as being largely that of the indoctrination of children with some one set of ethnocentric values to the exclusion of all others. Not infrequently school boards have made it an express policy to appoint only such administrators as will be "safe" (which means conservative about innovation in either the methods or the contents of teaching) and have required that the same policy be enforced in the selection and promotion of the teaching personnel. Some observers believe that this condition is growing worse, and some that it is growing better, but the facts, of course, are difficult to secure.

Colleges and universities face the same basic problem, although they are not as subject to direct local community censorship as are the more elementary schools. The tradition has somehow been established that higher education may pursue the truth much further in those instances in which the truth lies along lines contrary to the values of the power groups of the community. But the difference between colleges and elementary schools is only in degree. Basically, colleges and universities must depend for their support (1) on public funds which are controlled by state legislatures, (2) by city boards of education, or (3) on the voluntary endowments and gifts of philanthropic persons or institutions. Thus the universities are really only as free as the holders of these "purse strings" permit them to be. College and university administrators and professors alike hold tenure always subject to the wishes of those who pay their salaries. This fact is made obvious periodically when some state legislature, philanthropist, or pressure group conducts an investigation, stages a "red hunt," or demands the dismissal of some officer or teacher. But the latent power is there all the time, and the consciousness among teachers that it exists, probably constitutes an important limitation on the kinds of research undertaken, the publication of research findings, and the kinds of materials presented in the classrooms. There are undoubtedly persons in educational rôles who disregard, overlook, or deliberately challenge the pressure groups which scrutinize public education, but it seems probable that such persons are clearly in the minority. It could hardly be otherwise.

It is probably inevitable that there would exist some discrepancy between the values held by certain groups in the community and those held by the scientist and scholar. The scientist and scholar is a seeker after the truth, and his worth is usually judged by professional standards in which originality, creativeness, and discovery are very prominent. The scholar is a pioneer, ever pushing out on the periphery of human ignorance. But each new discovery runs the risk of antagonizing persons and groups who have vested interests in the previous untruth, or who conceive of their function as that of perpetuating the old, not because they wish to be "backward" but because they may believe sincerely that their old values are the right ones. Thus, when certain branches of organized religion rose up to quell the teaching of the theory of evolution in the universities, they did so either because they refused to accept the scientist's findings or because they believed that general knowledge of this fact would destroy the authority of the Bible and of the church. Similarly, when many conservative people opposed the study of Russia in American colleges and universities during the 1920's and 1930's, they did so because they believed that such knowledge about another economic culture would weaken the loyalty and faith of American youth in their own economic system. Regardless of the motives, the *fact* of pressure groups and their constant influence upon American higher education should not be overlooked.

Probably one of the distinct attributes of American culture has been the existence of the semi-autonomous educational system, which in spite of its control is still the freest mass educational system with which man has had experience in his whole history. There are those who believe that out of this fact grows much of the distinctiveness of American culture. When one considers the fundamental problems of ethnocentrism, the significant fact seems not to be that education is inhibited, but rather that it is as free as it is.

## SUMMARY

Education as a process is synonymous with socialization. Wherever there is learning, whenever there is modification of behavior, there the teacher-learner process is operating. From cradle to grave education is occurring. Every group with which one is in contact is an educational influence, although, of course, there are great differences between groups as educational agencies. Aside from the school system, and quite as important as the school system, are the family, the play group, the radio, the movies, the church, newspapers, magazines, and books.

Education, as an institution, consists of the organized program of teaching. The universal function of formal education is one of indoctrination of the infant and growing person into the culture of his society. This may be done in a startling variety of ways and for very different purposes, and therefore there are many variable functions of education.

The educational system of the United States is currently characterized by numerous clashes among different schools of thought concerning the advisability and the relative importance of such emphases as liberal education, vocational education, progressive education, "streamlined" education, and others. The main arguments for and against each of these have been summarized.

According to our idealized culture patterns, American education is and ought to be free, that is, not influenced by other institutions such as church, state, or economic groups. While American education is probably the freest educational system in the world, there are many ways in which various pressure groups exert effective control over both public and private education in the United States. In many respects colleges and universities are more free from some of the cruder aspects of this control, but they are by no means immune to it.

Conflict between education and other aspects of the society is probably inevitable because of the difference in the rôles of the scholar and most of the rest of society. The scholar is an innovator, a searcher for new truth, while many of the other agencies of society, for one reason or another, are the perpetuators of old traditions. It is quite understandable that the custodians of the old would find themselves in conflict with the diffusion of new discoveries and would seek to control if not prevent the diffusion of such knowledge as is either misunderstood or contrary to the preëxisting values. Authoritarian societies have solved the problem by sharply limiting or entirely prohibiting the activities of scholars, at least so far as the diffusion of their findings is concerned. One of the significant earmarks of democracy is its attempt at least to maintain a semi-autonomous community of scholars and learners called a "free educational system." If democracy is not to be reduced and eventually lost, many scholars of education warn, constant effort must be directed at the groups and forces which are ever seeking to subordinate education to other societal interests.

## SUGGESTED READINGS

BLUMER, Herbert, *Movies and Conduct* (New York, The Macmillan Co., 1933). **A**

A careful examination of the evidence on a very difficult problem, namely, the relation between movie "education" and overt conduct. A splendid antidote to the person with "all the answers" based upon armchair speculation!

CHAMBERLAIN, C. D., and others, *Did They Succeed in College?* (New York, Harper and Bros., 1942). **A**

A volume in the series designed to evaluate the progressive high school program. As explained in the text, this study tends to show that by whatever criterion of college success one uses, the progressively educated students did well as compared with the graduates of the more traditional high schools.

COOK, L. A., *Community Backgrounds of Education* (New York, McGraw-Hill Book Co., 1938), Chapter XVIII, "Who Controls the School?" **B**

A summary of the evidence regarding the important question of the freedom of American education. The book also contains excellent discussions of such topics as movies, employment of children, race in relation to education, and the influence of the family on the child.

JUDD, C. H., "Education," in *Recent Social Trends in the United States* (New York, McGraw-Hill Book Co., 1933). **A B**

This is a study of American education for the well-known President's Committee on Recent Social Trends in the United States. Presents a good short history of formal education and points some of the problems. The author is a distinguished authority on education.

SYMPOSIUM, Education and Society, *American Journal of Sociology,* XLVIII, No. 6, May 1943. **A**

Treats education in other societies, such as Guatemala, Pan-Africa, and among the Bushmen. Also the education among selected minority groups such as the Jews, the Brazilian Negro, and others. Contains several theoretical articles such as "Education and Cultural Crisis" and "Education and Cultural Dynamics."

WALLER, Willard, "The Teacher's Rôles," in Roucek, J., and others, *Sociological Foundations of Education* (New York, The Thomas Y. Crowell Co., 1942), pp. 204-225. **B**

A very readable account of teacher rôles by the author of the well-known original work, *The Sociology of Teaching* (New York, John Wiley and Sons, 1932). Discusses the teacher in both her stereotyped and actual rôles, both in the classroom and in the community.

WARNER, W. L., HAVIGHURST, J., and LOEB, M., *Who Shall Be Educated?* New York, Harper and Bros., 1944). **A B**

This is one of the volumes of the well-known "Yankee City Series." It uses the six-level class system and attempts to relate various aspects and problems of education to the class structure. While the theory of classes used here may be faulty, the materials regarding the class bias of the school system are accurate and useful for granting insight into a neglected aspect of the American school system.

## STUDY QUESTIONS

1. Distinguish between education and the school system. Why is this distinction important in American society?
2. Why is it difficult to determine the educational significance of radio and movies?
3. What reason is there to believe that the influence of movies is not as great as is commonly assumed?
4. What is the "universal function" of education, and why is it universal?
5. What are the "variable functions" of education, and why may they be variable?
6. Explain: "Education is a function of the *total* society."
7. Define and evaluate "liberal" education. To what extent is your evaluation biased by your social class position and aspirations?
8. Evaluate "progressive" education. How do you account for its unpopularity among many persons?
9. Why are the methods and objectives of "G.I." education not applicable to general civilian education?
10. Is American education free? What qualifications does one need to make in his answer to this question?
11. What do you consider to be the chief problems facing American education today?
12. "Education is the acquisition of culture." Criticize.
13. Are literacy statistics a fair index to the educational level of a nation or of a region? Why?

# Chapter XXV

## RELIGION AND RELIGIOUS ACTIVITY

### WHAT IS RELIGION?

To define religion in formal terms is difficult, both for the person doing the defining and for the person trying to understand the definition. Part of the difficulty arises from the wide variety of more or less accepted conceptions of "religion," and partly from the ethnocentrism regarding religion which dominates many people. It is difficult, for example, for a contemporary American Christian to understand that such behaviors as erotic dancing, body mutilation, alcoholic drinking, or prostitution can be religious rites in some societies. As we have seen in the chapter on cultural variability, *practically every phenomenon in the universe is or has been regarded as supernatural by the logic of one or more cultures, and practically every act of which the human being is capable has somewhere or sometime had a sacred significance.* It is necessary, therefore, to formulate a conception of religion which will include its universal aspects and its variable ones as well.

Religion is a part of every known culture. This does not mean that the Christian conception of God or the Christian form of worship is, however, any more normal or natural than any other. It only seems that way to the person who has been accustomed to the kind of religious experience which organized Christianity has set up for him. The fact that many people feel very dependent upon the Christian religion, and that it seems so natural, merely illustrates that both the need and the satisfaction of the need for this kind of religious experience has become so indelibly fixed in the personalities of many Americans that the illusions of naturalness, inherency, and necessity persist. One must recognize that religious ideas and practices are among the most highly emotionalized human experiences, and that religion is an aspect of culture about which many people are most thoroughly and extremely ethnocentric. It is necessary, particularly for the beginning student, if he is going to understand religion *objectively*, to strive to take a somewhat detached view of his own beliefs.

Although there are numerous ways of objectively defining religion, we may state it this way. Religion is a pattern of behavior made up of (*a*) sacred beliefs, (*b*) emotional feelings accompanying the beliefs, and (*c*) overt conduct presumably implementing the beliefs and feelings.

These three aspects are closely interrelated, but may be separated from one another for the purpose of analysis.

1. *Belief*

Fundamental to all religions are ideas, that is, beliefs concerning the nature of the universe or of some part of it. In the thought patterns of each culture, it is usually possible to make a rough division between two spheres or orders of knowledge. One knowledge area consists of phenomena which the people regard as natural, earthy, mundane, and satisfactorily understood on a matter-of-fact basis. There is an additional group of phenomena which are regarded as sacred, understandable and explained by modes of logic not usually objectively verifiable. These sacred beliefs are values which derive their validity from various sources and through various logics. Thus the universe tends to be divided into what we may call the *natural* and the *sacred*. Any particular item, of course, may fall into the natural or the sacred category on the basis of how the culture of the group in question happens to define it. Thus, for example, thunder and lightning may be regarded as a mere meteorological phenomenon brought about by natural causes, or thunder and lightning may be regarded as an arbitrary phenomenon reflecting the will of some non-natural force or power or person. Epidemics and catastrophes have been defined also in both of these ways. So with practically every item of the universe.

*Science and religion.* This explains in some measure the perennial quarrel between science and religion. As science makes each new stride in the understanding of some phase of the universe, its matter-of-fact or "natural" explanation may come into conflict with the sacred (and usually supernatural) explanation held by religious dogma. Organized religion frequently strives in one way or another to rationalize its pre-scientific conceptions, because only by so doing can it retain its prestige and its reputation for being correct. It should be noted, of course, that all scientific discoveries do not run counter to religious belief, but only such scientific explanations as challenge the preëxisting religious conception. Thus, for example, the theory of evolution challenged the Christian notion that man was a special creation, brought forth in the Garden of Eden precisely as he exists today. But the findings of biochemical research concerning vitamins or the endocrine glands encounters no violent religious opposition, because there have been no religious teachings about them which the research findings have called into question.

It is not only in highly scientific cultures such as our own that religious beliefs and scientific knowledge are in conflict. Incidents have been revealed by anthropological researches which show that even among primitive peoples there have occurred discoveries of natural causes of phenomena which came to the attention of the people, and thus challenged the current religious beliefs.

Those religious beliefs having to do with proper conduct, such as the Golden Rule are, of course, not readily susceptible of any scientific examination, because they are not based upon any assumptions of cause and effect. If one should be charitable, then being charitable is a virtue by its own definition, and science can neither approve nor disapprove of charitable acts. On the other hand, if one were admonished to be charitable in order that he live longer, then it could be scientifically determined whether the persons who performed more charitable acts or greater charitable acts did actually live longer. If, of course, the rewards come in Heaven, then the scientist is again stymied, because he is not privileged to go there and check the original hypothesis.

*Extra-scientific nature of many religious beliefs.* It is probably already clear from the foregoing that religious beliefs are usually neither scientific nor unscientific, but rather tend to be *extra-scientific.* They constitute explanations concerning phenomena about which science has not secured or cannot secure empiric data. They are values which are accepted because they seem right or important.

It is, of course, possible for religious belief to be scientific, if the sacred is in line with scientific truth, or unscientific, if it asserts explanations or causes which science in the same culture has already discovered to be false. But much current religious belief in contemporary America is extra-scientific rather than demonstrably scientific, unscientific, or anti-scientific.

Most religious beliefs (values) secure their validity by authority or logic or tradition and not by scientific proof. Thus in the Christian conception, God is supposed to have inspired the writing of the Bible. God being the Supreme Authority, the Bible must represent the ultimate in authoritarian belief. "Thus saith the Lord" then becomes an order which takes precedence over kings or emperors. Other religions, likewise, have their authorities who claim their right to reveal ultimate truth either categorically, like Jesus' assertion that He is the Son of God, or by the supposed self-evident logic of the truths which they proclaim.

*The alleged "need" for religious belief.* It has been suggested that man is so psychologically constituted that it is necessary for him to "believe in" some sacred, if not also supernatural, force or forces which are "on his side" in order that he feel secure. On the surface, it would seem that the universality of religion would tend to establish the validity of this principle. It seems more likely, however, that there is a subtle cycle of self-perpetuation which may better explain religion than any assumption about the inherent need to believe in the supernatural. If people are taught, particularly in early childhood, that they are being protected by a Supreme Being who knows all, sees all, and forgives, it is only natural that they build up patterns of dependence upon this unfailing benefactor. Then, throughout life, repeated assurances of the continued protection of the Supreme Being, and repeated affirmation that He is on the side of the right, are comforting. The loss of these beliefs would be frustrating, and the person would probably feel insecure if he were bereft of them. The same explanation would hold for any other pattern of dependence taken from any other religion.

## 2. *Emotionalized Feelings*

Sacred beliefs usually have strong emotional accompaniments of awe, fear, reverence, love, humility, hate, in fact of every emotion of which man is capable. This results in part from the manner in which religious beliefs are taught, and also because of the great importance which is attached to the beliefs and the values which they represent. Again, one should be very cautious about his ethnocentrism. The emotional feeling-tone characteristic of Christian religion is by no means universal. Worship, for example, as Americans know it, and the sentiments and emotions of "love" as Christians are taught these sentiments, are merely variable instances in the great panorama of religious experience. It is, in fact, very difficult to determine what the religious "feelings" of another religion really are. It is quite probable that they are so different that our concepts such as love, fear, or hate, familiar enough in American culture, do not even have a counterpart in many other religions. We really do not know how the Bushman or the Hottentot or the Toda "feels" about his religious concepts. We know merely that they do feel intensely, because their behavior, like ours, shows evidence of strong emotions.

3. *Propitiation*

In the logic of each religion there is a set of behaviors which constitute proper religious conduct. These acts are called *propitiation*. In the Christian tradition, for example, observance of the Christian moral code, prayer, tithes and offerings for the support of organized religion, deeds of charity, church attendance, and formal ceremonies like baptism, confession, and communion illustrate these devices. If one inquires as to why these things are done, he is told that they "are pleasing to God" or that they have some connection or other with the disposition of one's soul after death. In short, there are cause-and-effect relationships between what one does and how the universe will treat him.

Propitiatory devices include practically every act of which the human being is capable. Antitheses of every religious act can be found in the propitiatory practices of some other culture. Thus by the logic of one religion, fasting is acceptable in the eyes of the supernatural, while feasting is so regarded in the next. Kindness and gentleness are virtues in one religious system, while brutality is approved in the next. Public assemblage is the form of religious participation in one society, while the mores of another require that all religious activity be done in solitary confinement. One people sacrifices in the name of religion, and another is acquisitive in the name of religion. Dancing is a religious rite in one society, and is regarded as the work of Satan in the next. Sexual behavior, of course, comes in for its share of propitiatory definition. One set of religious mores defines sexual behavior as something disapproved by the deities, with the possible exception of procreation, while in other societies sex orgies and religious prostitution become the means of appeasing the gods. Truly man's capacity for contriving devious religious ways seems almost boundless.

*Magic and taboo.* Propitiatory devices have been divided into two classes to which some anthropologists have attached the terms *magic* and *taboo.* Taboo represents propitiatory devices of a negative sort, that is, the person should abstain from certain acts which are presumably inimical to the desires of the gods. Thus, the abstinence from certain foods on certain days, or the refusal to indulge in certain pleasing behaviors are regarded as virtues, and presumably result in keeping one in the good graces of the gods. Propitiation also works affirmatively. Sometimes the gods are said to be pleased by positive acts. Sacrifices, good deeds, and religious observances illustrate this form of propitiation.

It is perhaps somewhat confusing that the word *magic* has been used to stand for this positive type of propitiation. To many persons the word *magic* suggests the sleight-of-hand artist and the humbuggery of the carnival, and therefore, offense is sometimes taken when the word is used to describe so sacred a phenomenon as one's religious rites. This, however, is a problem of language usage and is by no means the only case in which the same word stands for radically different things. Perhaps a better word could be found, but none has yet come into common usage. The point is that one cannot prove in any scientific way that the assumed connection between the propitiatory act and the favorable consideration of it by the Deity really exist. The only way one can accept the authoritative character of propitiatory acts is on faith. Apparently for the great mass of human kind, faith is not difficult to attain.

Having thus separated religious belief, "feelings," and propitiation for purposes of discussion, it might have been suggested that these three aspects of religion are more separate and separable than they really are. Actually, of course, all three are bound together into a more or less logical whole. None is meaningful apart from the other two. One has deep emotional feelings because he has certain religious beliefs, and having those beliefs he observes whatever taboos seem appropriate and participates in the pertinent magic as a means of implementing his emotions and beliefs about religious matters. It is quite possible, of course, that one's sacred beliefs may not require intense feelings or formal propitiatory behavior, but taking the religions of man as a whole, the pattern outlined is overwhelmingly present.

It should perhaps be emphasized that religion, like all other aspects of culture, is not participated in equally by all of the members of a society. This variation in participation may either be provided under the "rules and regulations" of the prevailing religion which may exclude certain classes of people from its "fold," or it may result simply from a lack of interest in formal participation in religion itself by some individuals. It is not equally probable that all persons will have the same amount and kind of interest in the religious segment of culture. This is no more difficult to understand than any other sort of nonconformity, disinterest, or opposition to some part of culture which a person has participated in.

## ORGANIZED RELIGION IN THE UNITED STATES

While the American constitution expressly guarantees "religious freedom" to each person, and one hears and reads much about the "private and personal" character of religion, there exists in the United States an imposing and powerful organization of formal religious bodies designed each to teach and otherwise promote its own brand of religious belief and practice. The property assets of these religious bodies measure into the billions of dollars, and the professional functionaries which staff the organizations run into at least hundreds of thousands. Although it is difficult to measure the political power of organized religion, it is probable that such power would be impressive if accurately known.

### *Statistics on Religious Affiliation and Participation*

Statistics on a number of persons who are affiliated with these organized religious groups are difficult to secure, and even more difficult to interpret accurately. Since 1906 the United States Census Bureau has conducted a census of Religious Bodies every ten years for the entire nation, and this compilation of information on membership, assets, contributions, and property, has provided at least an approximate basis for surveying the measurable aspects of organized religion. The latest census of Religious Bodies available at this writing was conducted in 1936. We are forced, then, to utilize the 1936 figures as the best approximate indication of the numerical significance of organized religions. The 1936 census of Religious Bodies showed that nearly fifty-six millions of Americans were members of some religious body—almost twenty million of whom were Roman Catholic and four and one-half millions were Jews, leaving the remaining thirty-two millions distributed among the 254 Protestant groups.

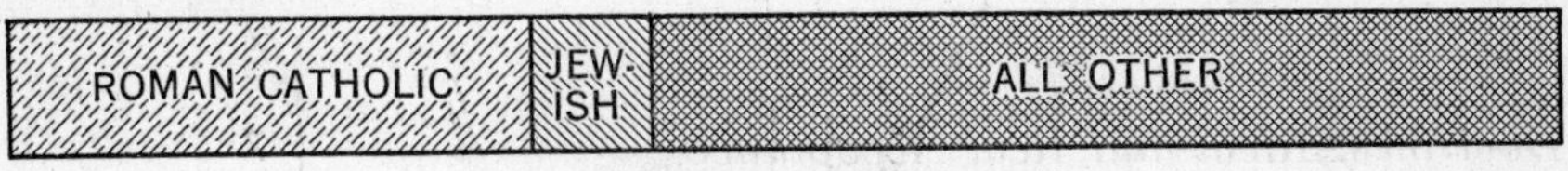

| ROMAN CATHOLIC | JEWISH | ALL OTHER |
| --- | --- | --- |

Total Membership 56,000,000

CHURCH MEMBERSHIP IN THE UNITED STATES

Data from *Summary and Detailed Tables, Religious Bodies:* 1936, Vol. I, Government Printing Office, 1941.

This would indicate that in 1936, less than half of all persons in the United States were members of some organized religious group. But how significant is membership? One can be a church member, because he joined when he was eighteen years of age, and has never been in church for the rest of his life. Cases of this sort are by no means exceptional. Several studies have been made for the purposes of determining what proportion of the persons on the membership rolls of churches attend these churches with some degree of regularity. Roughly it has been found that about half of the nominal church membership is in some measure active in the programs sponsored by the church. If the results of these studies are typical, one may conclude that not over one out of four or five Americans are actively participating in the activities of the churches of their communities.

### *Is There a Decline or an Increase in Religious Participation?*

No evidence exists for determining whether church *attendance* for the nation as a whole is on the decline, on the increase, or is remaining approximately constant. Claims of all sorts are made by various churches and denominations but many of these claims have proved quite inaccurate whether they were so intended or not.

While some individual churches are undoubtedly gaining in membership and attendance, others are undoubtedly losing. While a given church may show an appreciable gain during a two- to three-year period, that same church may show an equally impressive loss during the next period. It appears probable that the above approximate estimate of one active church attendant out of every four persons in the total population is a liberal estimate.

*Rural-urban differences in participation.* Church membership and attendance varies in the United States from region to region, but the most outstanding difference is between rural and urban. A larger proportion of rural people belong to churches, and the attendance record of members is somewhat higher than for urban populations.

### *Doctrines: Ideal and Real Acceptance*

Each organized religious group has a set of principles or a creed or a group of doctrines which form the basis for its teachings, its organization, and its policies. Earlier in the history of the United States, these doctrinal differences were considered to be important, but in more recent years there has been a declining emphasis, at least within urban Protestantism, upon these beliefs. A study conducted in 1934-35 based upon a sizable sample of the Protestant church population in one of America's largest cities showed that a majority of church participants either were not familiar with the religious teachings of their respective denominations or did not agree with these teachings if they were familiar with them. A smaller sample of clergymen showed substantially the same condition, except that the clergymen were somewhat more likely to know where their churches stood on doctrinal matters, but a majority of them still did not agree with the doctrinal stands taken by their own denominations.

Accurate information concerning such matters as those mentioned above is very difficult to secure. The already familiar distinction between ideal and real behavior patterns shows prominently in almost every study designed to test the allegiance of Americans to their churches. Much comment is heard concerning the alleged "hypocritical" nature of persons who attend church but do not subscribe to the principles for which the church stands. Parents who require their children to attend Sunday school, but do not themselves attend church, are frequently subject to criticism. Whether such conduct is "right" or "wrong" is not for the scientist to say, but the presence of such behavior patterns is indicative of the difficulties involved in appraising the extent and kind of influence, or dominance, which organized religion exerts in the United States. On the one hand, there is the fact that nominal membership overestimates the extent of active allegiance to the principles espoused by organized religion. On the other hand, it is equally evident that there are many persons outside of organized religion who adhere substantially to the same beliefs for which the church stands. It is important to note that no one really knows what the situation is, even though hopes, fears, guesses, and assertions are abundant.

## TRENDS IN ORGANIZED RELIGION IN THE UNITED STATES

Like all organized aspects of American society, churches are going through periods of change. These changes include modifications of doctrine, as well as changes in the programs of churches.

### *Doctrinal Change*

Perhaps the chief doctrinal change manifested by organized religion in the United States, especially among Protestant groups, is the decline in the emphasis upon supernatural beliefs and supernatural sanctions for behavior. Under the impact of a growing acquaintance with scientific findings, increasing numbers of persons have come to distrust many of the old supernatural explanations of historical facts and of biological and physical phenomena. The informed leadership of churches is aware of this change, and has attempted to retain the allegiance of members by deëmphasizing supernaturalism. Particularly in urban centers, liberal churches have developed with liberal clergy directing them. Although the word *liberal* is a term of varied meaning, it tends to mean (when applied to religion) that supernaturalism is being deëmphasized in favor of some other program and teaching. Sermon topics of "liberal" churches show increasing concern and interest in problems of personal living. Many of the sermons sound more like mental hygiene lectures than like the "Hell-fire and brimstone" preachings of an older day. Some clergymen have taken up family counseling, and church leaders are sponsoring Boy Scout troops and in similar other ways attempting to serve the personal needs of their members. These modifications vary, of course, greatly from church to church and from region to region in the United States.

A second doctrinal change is the attempt to incorporate into the church's system of teachings a set of beliefs which have come to be called the *social gospel*. The roots of the social gospel lie far back in the Jewish and Christian traditions. The emphasis here is upon the practical application of principles of justice and tolerance to broad social conditions. The social gospel advocates argue that for centuries the church has been emphasizing individual sin and individual salvation while corruption, injustice, and intolerance in the whole society have been permitted to go unnoticed and unchallenged. The church is said to have been willing to convict the individual sinner of the wrong of stealing a loaf of bread, while powerful business interests have in one way or other stolen billions. Moreover, it has been emphasized that "the church has sat idly by and tolerated gross social injustices like racial intolerance, the exploitation of children, which conditions are as clearly inconsistent with Christian principles as any individual sin might be." Finally, it is pointed out, individual salvation is made difficult, if not impossible, when the individual must live in a social system which implements so little of Christian virtue.

The social gospel has, of course, encountered *strong opposition* from many sources. Conservative persons have argued that it is not the church's concern what kind of conditions prevail in the general society, that its function is to "minister to the individual souls of individual people." Other "practical minded" persons have pointed out that when the church "takes sides" on social questions, it is bound to alienate certain persons or groups who have a vested interest in continuing some form of exploitation or some condition which the church has condemned. This stand would cost the church membership, and perhaps even more significant, financial support. It was pointed out that there are other agencies for social reform besides religion, and that the church should content itself with the traditional job of individual *guidance within the social system as it is.*

Different churches have moved at unequal rates and with varied results in the direction of integrating social gospel thinking into their teachings. In general, the larger denominational organizations have gone further in this respect than have the individual local churches, probably because the local churches are subject to more pressures and oppositions. If specific churches become aggressive in attempting to remedy local conditions, they may greatly antagonize those of their members who have vested interests in some condition which the church brands as incompatible with Christian doctrine. It is relatively easy, for example, for a local clergyman to preach against the "evils of child labor" if there is little or no child labor in his community. But if the chairman of his Board of Trustees operates an industry which employs children, then it may require more courage than the clergyman has to take issue with the local child-labor conditions. The social gospel has probably been retarded by the tendency for churches to compromise in order to retain members and financial support. Nevertheless, there is evidence of more concern for conditions in "this world" than earlier in the history of American Christianity. The social gospel in its most extreme forms has not been integrated into the teaching program of the church, but neither is it being entirely overlooked. Various denominations show marked differences in this respect.

### *Church Programs*

Not only has the doctrinal aspect of churches undergone change in recent years, but the program of activities has also been altered. The average number of worship services per week has declined until now most Protestant churches, in urban areas at least, have only one service per week. Sunday evening services and mid-week services remain mostly in rural areas and among some of the smaller cults. Urban churches have taken on a large program of recreational activities, such as sponsoring athletic teams, Boy Scout troops and Camp Fire Girl units, and summer camps. Increasing numbers of ministers have taken up the study of marriage counseling with a view to serving the growing need for trained persons to assist families whose tensions and conflicts cannot be solved by the family's own ingenuity. Theological seminaries are paying increasing attention to the training of ministers for this work and numerous ministers are supplementing their training by taking post-graduate courses designed better to equip them for counseling work. Some Protestant churches have attempted to formalize their worship services through the increase of ritual, and through a greater use of symbolism; even the architecture of some churches has been affected by this trend back toward medieval formalism.

*Dominance*

Thus it can be seen that the church, like all social institutions, has gone through and is still making changes in its thinking and in its overt activities. Whether the overall importance of religion has changed is a matter upon which it is far more difficult to reach agreement. It is extremely difficult to determine whether religion is becoming more or less important to church members on the average. Moreover, there are several schools of thought on the question whether the church is more or less effectively meeting the competition of other kinds of activity which clamor for people's attention and loyalty. There seems little doubt that a generation or two ago it was easier for the church to secure the attendance and loyalty of its membership, because it did not have to compete for people's attention with so many and so engaging an array of other activities. The automobile changed the Sunday habits of people, and so also did the radio. Commercialized amusements, especially in cities, are now available almost literally around the clock and throughout the week. Under the pressure of competition from other available activities, it may be that church attendance and church activity require an even greater devotion to the "cause" now than during past periods when there was not much else to do with one's time.

## THE CHURCH AND OTHER INSTITUTIONS

Organized religion in the United States offers an excellent illustration of the way in which change in one institution of a society affects others. We have already seen how the high incidence of divorce and family breakdown has resulted in the church's entry into family counseling service. Other relationships of this sort can readily be found. The rise of science and the increasing average level of education have no doubt been important factors in forcing churches to moderate their more extreme supernaturalistic dogmas and doctrines. Competition from commercial amusements has turned the church's attention toward providing amusement itself, not only because by so doing the church would retain a somewhat greater hold on the individual, but because the church could also, in that way, exert some influence on the kind of recreation in which its members participated. The higher standards of teaching competence in the public schools may have been the factor influencing the churches to try to improve their standards of educational practice. Churches dropped Sunday evening services in the main, not because they wished to and certainly not because they did not consider these services important. They were virtually forced to discontinue Sunday evening services because growing numbers of people found other things which they preferred to do on Sunday evenings. With the decline of some of the supernatural sanctions for engaging in religious activity, church-going can now not be induced by fear of offending God, and consequently church attendance can be less taken for granted. People have to be attracted to church instead of coerced into church. Not many people believe any longer that they will pay penalties in the after life if they play golf on Sunday morning instead of going to church, and even fewer consider it in any way sinful to attend a movie or listen to a radio on Sunday evening.

It is more difficult to discover influences of the church upon other institutions. Although the church makes certain pronouncements concerning the kinds of business relations which should exist and the kind of laws which ought or ought not to be passed, it is difficult to determine how effective the church's influence upon government and the economic system really is. Perhaps, moreover, the church's influence is indirect, that is, it helps to formulate the attitudes and values which its members have, and in that way influences their political ideas and perhaps their conduct also.

## WHAT ARE THE DIFFERENCES BETWEEN CHURCH AND NON-CHURCH PEOPLE?

On the surface it might seem that since the church deals with moral guidance and often speaks, so far as its members are concerned, with Divine sanction, that there would be fundamental differences between the moral and ethical standards of church and non-church personalities. At the outset one must admit that the evidence is not very conclusive, because not enough careful studies have been made comparing the real behavior patterns of church members with those of non-members. Marriage prediction studies show that church-connected people have somewhat higher happiness ratings in their marriages, while studies of character traits of Sunday School and non-Sunday School children reveal little difference between the two. Attitude tests have shown that on numerous questions of moral standards and ethical values, no appreciable difference appears between church members and non-members so far as their actual conduct is concerned, although differences in verbal response were noted.

It should not be inferred from these data, however, that the church does not influence conduct. It is quite possible that the church exerts control not only over its members but also over the moral standards of the entire community, including non-members and non-attendants. In at least one study of the religious attitudes of several hundred university students, it was revealed that non-members and non-attenders showed many of the same moral ideas and ethical principles which churches characteristically proclaim. Apparently these persons receive the moral and ethical training of churches somehow indirectly in the course of their socialization, but they do apparently receive it. It is also quite possible, of course, that church affiliates and non-affiliates both learn moral and ethical values from some source outside the church.

Some students of human behavior are of the opinion that the church attracts certain personality "types" more than others, although evidence is lacking to support these possibly accurate hypotheses. Studies of samples of church attendance have almost invariably shown that Protestant churches claim the allegiance of more women than men, and more of middle-aged and old people than young people. There is insufficient evidence, however, to permit any sweeping conclusions concerning the influence of the church upon personality or of the personality attributes which attract some persons to churches but not others.

## SUMMARY AND CONCLUSION

Although religion may be variously defined, it seems helpful to conceive of it in terms of belief, emotional concomitants of belief, and propitiatory devices, including both magic and taboo. Thus defined, religion exists in every culture although the specific beliefs and propitiatory practices vary radically from society to society.

Organized religion in the United States has the allegiance of somewhat less than half of the population and the active participation of about half of this membership. There is a widespread impression that membership and attendance are on the decline, but there is no conclusive proof that such is the case.

Organized religion manifests change. Doctrinal changes during recent years have centered around the liberalization of traditional supernatural beliefs and some incorporation of the social gospel philosophy into the teachings and organization of many churches. Church programs also show significant change in the direction of a reduction in the number of worship services, expansion of the church's activities into the realm of recreation, counseling service, and a more professionalized religious education program. Most of these changes have been adaptations to changed conditions. Important inventions like the automobile and the radio, and the diffusion of scientific knowledge and liberal education, have made their influence felt in many ways. Changes in institutions like the family have also affected religion, and certainly the rise of large cities has modified the function of organized religion. Although the church undoubtedly exerts influence upon other institutions, such influences are not as evident as are the influences of other institutions upon the church. This may be due to the indirect nature of religious influence, or to the ineffectiveness of organized religion to exert sufficient power to make its verbal pronouncements effective in controlling such powerful segments of the society as government and the economic system.

Not much is known scientifically about the degree to which churches really affect the moral conduct and ethical practice of their members. Fragmentary research data have cast at least some doubt upon the common popular assumption that church people as a whole show markedly different moral and ethical conduct than non-church people. This is sometimes taken to mean that churches are not very effective as social control agencies, but such an interpretation may overlook the fact that non-church people manifest many of the ethical and moral values espoused by the churches. Apparently, then, the influence of churches extends in some way to persons not in the direct membership and attending constituency.

It cannot be emphasized too strongly that our knowledge concerning the dominance of religion in the modern world is very limited. Assertions of all sorts are common. Religious enthusiasts frequently make claims as misleading as are the counterclaims of the opponents of organized religion. In the absence of truly reliable evidence no one knows what the facts are.

Religion and organized religion should not be confused. There is an appreciable number of persons, especially among the more educated, who remain outside of organized religion, if not also hostile to it. A large proportion of these people are religious and essentially Christian in their beliefs and practices. Their quarrel is not with religion, but with *organized* religion or some part of it. While it cannot be determined how large this number is, it is probable that such persons are numerous and certain that many are prominent and able people. Their absence from the ranks of organized religion undoubtedly weakens organized religion. The fact that these non-members are largely unorganized does not mean that they are inarticulate. They may possibly form a nucleus for the development of some new form or forms of religious life in America, or they may in time be reassimilated into the older established religious organizations. Or, again, they may remain a miscellaneous collection of somewhat individualistic people whose religious ideas and practices are not radically dissimilar, but also do not square with those upheld by the formal religious bodies.

## SUGGESTED READINGS

Commission on Appraisal, *Re-Thinking Missions, A Layman's Inquiry after One Hundred Years* (New York, Harper and Bros., 1932). **A B**

This is the famous study appraising the missionary movement. It was a somewhat controversial volume when it first appeared, but more rational appraisal indicates that it is the most accurate summary volume on the nature and effectiveness of the missionary aspect of American churches.

Cuber, John, "Marginal Church Participants," *Sociology and Social Research*, XXV, pp. 57-62. **A B**

A summary of part of a study of religious organization and participation in a sample of 300 Protestant Churches in Greater Detroit, Michigan, 1934-35. This article discusses some of the implications of the large "marginal" church constituency as well as summarizing statistical data which measure marginality.

Douglass, H. P., and Brunner, E. de S., *The Protestant Church as a Social Institution* (New York, Harper and Bros., 1935). **A B**

An attempt to appraise the nature of the Protestant church in America. This is one of a series of studies sponsored by the late Institute for Social and Religious Research. These books are realistic and objective studies of an aspect of life about which many people are unwilling or unable to think objectively. The chief criticism of the Douglass series is that the authors strive so consistently to be objective in the statistical sense that they omit discussion of some of the less measurable but possibly more significant aspects of the problems.

LYND, R. S., and LYND, H. M., *Middletown in Transition* (New York, Harcourt, Brace and Co., 1937), pp. 295-318. **A B**

With the characteristic insight of the Lynds, the religious life of "Middletown" is described in a vivid and accurate manner.

RAUSCHENBUSCH, Walter, *Christianity and the Social Crisis* (New York, The Macmillan Co., 1908). **A B**

It is of interest to note that the "social crisis" referred to in the title of this book is that of the pre-World War I period of American History. The book is written by the first major American exponent of the "Social Gospel" theology. This book may be taken as essentially the modern formulation of the doctrine.

## STUDY QUESTIONS

1. Why is it difficult to formulate a universal definition of religion?
2. Why are most people intensely ethnocentric in their ideas and attitudes about religion?
3. How does culture determine which phenomena are natural and which supernatural?
4. What determines a society's specific religious forms?
5. Why is there often conflict between science and religion? Why is this not always true? Illustrate.
6. What is the basic difference between science and religion?
7. How may the sudden loss of an absolute belief in a Supreme Being create mental ill-health?
8. Why may religion be regarded as rational? What is the criterion of rationality?
9. Why are propitiatory devices not the same in all societies? Why are they not the same in all religions in the same society?
10. How are magic and taboo complementary types of propitiation?
11. Why do all members of society not participate equally in religion?
12. How could organized religion exert a powerful influence upon most phases of American life? Why does it not exert a direct influence comparable to its great membership?
13. What determines church membership? How does this vary among Catholic, Protestant, and Jewish groups?
14. Why is it difficult to estimate the kind and amount of influence which organized religion exerts upon American life?
15. What is the "logical" basis for churches teaching the social gospel? Why do some people oppose this type of teaching?
16. Why would it be difficult scientifically to evaluate the influence of the church upon the conduct and moral standards of an entire community?
17. Why are many of the moral ideas and ethical principles of non-church members very similar to those of church members?

of the Christian ... and ... readings ... to ... is ... Protestant ... of the ... problems.

Lynd, Robert S., and Helen M. Lynd, *Middletown in Transition* (New York: Harcourt, Brace and Co., 1937), pp. 295–318.

... the religious life of Middletown ... in a ... manner.

Rauschenbusch, Walter, *Christianizing the Social Order* (New York: The Macmillan Co., 1912).

Of ... interest ... the ... religious ... period of American History. The book is written by the ... exponent of the "social gospel" theology. This book may be taken as ... formulation of the doctrine.

## STUDY QUESTIONS

1. Why is it difficult to formulate a universal definition of religion?
2. Why are most people somewhat ethnocentric in their ideas and attitudes about religion?
3. How does culture determine which phenomena are natural and which supernatural?
4. What determines a society's specific religious forms?
5. Why is there often conflict between science and religion? Why is this not always true? Illustrate.
6. What is the basic difference between science and religion?
7. How may the sudden loss of an absolute belief in a Supreme Being create mental ill health?
8. Why may religion be regarded as rational? What is the criterion of rationality?
9. Why are propitiatory devices not the same in all societies? Why are they not the same in all religions in the same society?
10. How are magic and religion complementary types of procedure?
11. Why do all members of society not participate equally in religion?
12. How could organized religions exert a powerful influence upon most phases of American life? Why does it not exert a direct influence comparable to its great membership?
13. What factors explain church membership? How does this vary among Catholic, Protestant, and Jewish groups?
14. Why is it difficult to estimate the kind and amount of influence which organized religion exerts upon American life?
15. What is the logical basis for churches teaching the social gospel? Why do some people oppose this type of teaching?
16. Why would it be difficult scientifically to evaluate the influence of the church upon the conduct and moral standards of an entire community?
17. Why are many of the moral ideas and ethical principles of non-church members very similar to those of church members?

# *Part VI*

# SOCIAL ORGANIZATION, SOCIAL CHANGE, and SOCIAL PROBLEMS

# Chapter XXVI

# THE ORGANIZATION AND INTEGRATION OF SOCIETY

## THE ORGANIZATION AND INTEGRATION OF SOCIETY

It is a matter of common observation that the persons and groups making up a society are "somehow held together." The purpose of this chapter is to present a more adequate conception of some of the ways and reasons for this social cohesion. This is the part of sociology which is usually called *social organization.*

## THE BASIS OF SOCIAL ORGANIZATION

### *Interdependence of Persons and Groups*

It is probably unnecessary to elaborate the basic societal fact of interdependence. Previous chapters have contained numerous data pertaining to this condition. Perhaps the cardinal process throughout human evolution from primeval man to modern man has been the extension of interdependence. With each elaboration of the division of labor, the helplessness of the individual human being and the group becomes more manifest. Man is inherently helpless and dependent upon others in the infant stage, but modern man has magnified this dependence upon others to include the entire life span. This fact of interdependence has both symbiotic and non-symbiotic phases.

(The student will probably do well to review our previous treatment of symbiosis, pp. 330-334; division of labor, p. 372; groups, pp. 265-269; and institutions, pp. 387-389.)

### *Symbiotic Interdependence*

In the chapters dealing with human ecology, it was stressed that the intricate system of division of labor which characterizes modern life, necessitates a somewhat elaborate social organization simply for the purpose of coördinating the efforts and activities of the specializing persons and groups. It has been suggested that a person could receive a graphic appreciation of the extent of his symbiotic dependence by tracing the items appearing on his breakfast table back to their origins. Such an effort would show vividly how dozens, if not hundreds, of specialized functionaries have contributed energies and talents to the production, transportation, and fabrication of the simplest tableware and the most fundamental items of diet. At almost innumerable points the activities of each functionary or group must be coördinated with others, or the entire web of interdependence breaks down. Thus, one aspect of the organization of society, the symbiotic one, can be appreciated.

Railroads, aeroplane lines, telephone and telegraph systems are the mechanical media through which much social organization is carried out. If modern man is to draw his sustenance from widespread geographical areas, he must not only transport raw materials and fabricated items from their production points to their consumption points, but must also maintain a system of communication through which he can regulate the whole structure of symbiotic relationships. Much of the rivalry among modern nations stems from their competition for access to the desirable sources of raw materials and the protection or construction of trade channels, such as that of the British Empire which has aptly come to be called its "lifeline."

### *Non-Symbiotic Bases of Interdependence and Social Organization*

Sustenance considerations are by no means the only forces which hold societies together. Cultural factors such as common religion, national loyalties, and common language, are value-patterns which form another type of sociological tie. It is futile to argue whether the symbiotic ties *or* the cultural ties are more "important" or more "fundamental" in the maintenance of social organization. Both are important and both are fundamental. Raising such an issue as this seems almost like a modern version of the trite and meaningless question whether man's "physical or mental" nature is the more important. The issue is meaningless, because human life, whether for an individual or for a society, is an inextricable unity of both the biological and the ideological aspects. Each person is born into a society with one or more cultures. In the course of his socialization he acquires numerous needs, some of them appetitive, like his food wants, his standard of living, or his sex wishes. These learnings which formulate much of his behavior result from his organic biological needs and from the specific forms which these needs are given by the folkways which he learns. Usually he is unaware that there are really any alternative ways of meeting the problem of human existence. If he grew up in American society, "food" means three meals a day consisting of certain folkways like desserts and *hors d'œuvres,* white bread with butter, sitting at the table, and so on. Likewise sex needs are oriented to married heterosexuality, influenced by the prevailing standards of beauty and prestige, and more or less related to monogamy. Thus, almost inescapably he learns that these objectives are attainable only from and through the behaviors of other people. In short, he learns his rôles and statuses which are links in the chains of mutual interdependence with other people. Except in an abstract academic sense, the value-unity of the people of a society is largely inseparable from their symbiotic unity. Thus, the average American's emphasis on pecuniary values has a symbiotic aspect, since it is related to his sustenance needs, but it also has a sentimental aspect, since many phases of it have no discernible connection with symbiotic needs at all. Long wheel-base automobiles, fur coats, and other aspects of "conspicuous consumption" can be adequately understood only in terms of their status value. In many other ways the subtle interplay of symbiotic and ideological factors could be demonstrated, although it seems hardly necessary to press the matter further.

In summary, social organization results from both the symbiotic needs and the common values which the person learns through socialization. Social systems are perpetuated as each new generation in a society is reared and taught the prevailing values and folkways concerning these things. In short, social organization lies in the habit systems of the persons of the society quite as much as in the formal laws, rules, and customs of the groups through which the organization is implemented. Social organization should be studied both as individual rôles and as overall structure.

## REVIEW OF PREVIOUS TREATMENT OF SOCIAL ORGANIZATION

Without so labeling it, previous chapters have treated a number of aspects of social organization. It seems well to review these materials before proceeding further into this subject.

1. It was pointed out that all societies show a few major and basic divisions of human activity, such as the family, government, economic organization, systems of social stratification, and religious activity.

2. While these major divisions are universal, or practically so, the *specific content* of each of the divisions is *highly variable,* that is, while the family system is universal, the family systems of specific societies contain such radical differences as monogamy and polygyny, matriarchate and patriarchate. It has also been shown that these major societal divisions of human behavior vary from society to society in the degree to which they are separated from one another and in the degree to which they are formally organized. Thus, for example, it was shown that while every society has some ways and means of educating its youth to conform to the culture of the society, some societies may accomplish this objective by informal means without the use of writing, books, teachers, or schools, whereas, on the other hand, societies like ours have an elaborate system of formal education.

3. In the chapters dealing with socialization, the reciprocal relations of person and group have been emphasized. It was shown that while a group may be conceived as being made up of the behavior of the persons in it, so also a person's behavior may be conceived as a series of group-relevant rôles. This reciprocal relationship of person and group applies to the whole social complex. Societal organization can be seen quite as much through the overall analysis of the behavior of persons in the society as in the overall formal structure of the society. Social psychologists have demonstrated, for example, that almost an entire society can be reconstructed from a careful and lengthy life history of one person.

4. Laymen, and to some extent experts also, have spent a great deal of time arguing the question whether social organization determines the nature of the person through its socialization of him, or whether the person, especially the so-called "great man," determines social organization through the influence which he is able

to exert upon it. Like many other particularistic arguments, neither extreme view is wholly right nor is either wholly wrong. As we have seen in the treatment of society and the person, while social experience significantly molds the person, it does not entirely make an automaton of him. The recurring solution of new problems which the person meets results in the modification of culture. This not only applies to the influence of the great man who seems sometimes to have altered the basic makeup of societies, but applies none the less surely, even though less dramatically, to the everyday influence of obscure and humble people.

5. These various main divisions of society like family, government, and religion are not isolated from one another. Instead they influence each other in many significant ways. For example, depressions and prosperity are really aspects of the economic phase of society, but numerous researches have shown that the recurring waves of prosperity and depression have profound influence upon marriage rates, divorce rates, and birth rates, which are certainly aspects of the family. More recently we have seen that there is a close relationship between government and economic activity, or science-education and religious beliefs. In almost innumerable other ways, reciprocal influence can readily be shown.

*a. Changes in dominance.* Although it is difficult to prove by formal statistical means, most professional students of society agree that one of the chief differences among societies is the relative preponderance or "dominance" of some one of the major divisions over all or some of the others. Thus in medieval Europe the Roman Catholic church was dominant over formal education, much economic activity, and exerted considerable power over government as well. Much less of such dominance exists today either in Europe or America. This does not mean, of course, that the church, Catholic and Protestant, is without any influence on education, government, or economic organization, but simply that whatever influence exists is more indirect and seems to most qualified observers to be demonstrably weaker. The reverse could be said of the economic segment of society. In medieval Europe economic activities and interests were subordinated to Church and government to a considerable extent. Money lending for interest, for example, was defined by the Church as "usurious" and was prohibited to Christians. Such a pronouncement today by organized religion would hardly be likely to close the banking, insurance, and other industries which depend for their existence upon lending and borrowing money for interest. Many observers are also of the opinion, and are able to cite considerable supporting evidence, that instead of government really controlling industry and labor, industry and labor control government through legal and extra-legal devices, to some of which we have given attention in preceding chapters. Without necessarily going the whole way in accepting this point of view, it is certainly evident that economic interests and economic activities predominate in the overt behavior and in the thinking of American people more than was true in the society of medieval Europe from which much American culture originally came. In still other societies the family system predominates over industry, religion, and government. Up until very recently, and probably to some extent still, many parts of the Orient show this strong familial dominance which was common, of course, among such ancient peoples as the Hebrews.

*b. Transfer of functions.* In the chapter on the family it was pointed out that one of the most significant changes which has occurred in the American family system since the latter part of the last century, has been the large number of traditional family functions which have been transferred to other groups in the society. Many of the activities and functions which were a normal part of everyday existence for the nineteenth-century family are today performed by schools, recreational organizations, bakeries, laundries, and welfare agencies. A study of other characteristic social groupings reveals the same process of transference of functions among groups. Higher education was once largely the function of the church, but now in America, at least, higher education has been taken over by government-supported colleges and universities, or by privately-supported but non-sectarian institutions of higher education. Formerly the welfare needs of the inadequate members of the American society were taken care of by the individual's family, neighbors, and friends. Today these functions, especially in urban centers, are taken over by other organizations, prominent among which is the government. Illustrations could be multiplied indefinitely.

When one attempts to analyze the processes through which this transfer of functions takes place he encounters more serious difficulties than might at first be expected. Why, for example, has the processing of food, which was formerly done almost exclusively by the family itself, been transferred to bakeries, canneries, delicatessen stores, and restaurants? Is it because these tasks were so onerous that there arose a public demand for the rise of these commercial agencies? The social historians of this period of our history have certainly not recorded any objective evidence of the existence of such a demand. Perhaps, then, the changes occurred because industries arose offering the services, advertising the advantages to the person of commercializing this aspect of family life. If so, did the industry create the demand or did it capitalize on the potential unexpressed desire for these services? To what extent did scientific advance affect the change? Did education have any influence? Thus, one might go on almost indefinitely raising questions which are pertinent, but either unanswerable or difficult to answer in the light of existing knowledge. About all that can be said, with objective evidence to support the point of view, is that apparently many factors were operative such as those implied in the above questions. The overall process seems to have occurred so gradually that few if any persons were aware of the change taking place or of the profound influence which the change was having both upon the family and upon industrial society. Even the persons who lived through the period and whose lives have been radically altered by the change, seem usually unable to recall just what factors brought about the changes in their own lives or just why they decided to "accept" the change.

The same principle could be illustrated in many other ways. The significant point is that social change involving the transfer of functions among the major segments of society is (*a*) the result of interplay of many factors, some encouraging and some discouraging the particular change. (*b*) Most transfers of functions have occurred unconsciously and gradually and the persons whose lives manifest the change are often largely unaware that they are participating in a major and basic social change.

## THE INTEGRATION OF SOCIETY

*Societies vary in the degree to which the various parts—institutions and groups—are integrated into an overall pattern which is consistent within itself.* It has become fashionable for many students of American society, both laymen and professional, to decry the "lack of integration," the "disunity," the "inconsistency," and the general "absence of a unifying feature" in contemporary America.

On every side one sees glaring inconsistencies among the values which seem to be implicit in group life. The church proclaims Christian principles regarding men being each other's "brothers" and "keepers" and the all-importance of the Golden Rule, meanwhile accepting membership and contributions from persons and groups who obviously conduct themselves contrary to the values which organized religion espouses. Self-interest in economic matters does seem to be a common value or objective, but it seems doubtful to many whether such values are not more divisive than integrating. During the war, to be sure, self-interest was somewhat subordinated to the common interest but the extent to which this was done voluntarily and without subterfuge could very easily be exaggerated.

What are the basic values which give America unity? Other modern nations seem to have basic loyalties to common purposes. In ancient and medieval times religious loyalties and national patriotism were values which transcended self-interest and unified the society. It is interesting and probably significant that those modern nations which have had a clearly integrated value system have been, like Germany, Japan, and Italy, trouble makers in the community of nations. This may serve to indicate that devotion to common societal values, if they are values not compatible with those held by the controlling world powers, may actually hasten the disintegration of the society through aggression and war, rather than keep it integrated at all. There may, however, be a basic illusion in all this. It may be that we are more conscious of the integrated value system of aggressive nations like pre-war Germany and Japan because they embodied values which are different from those which our society embodies.

Finally, it should not be overlooked that the *theory that a society must or ought to be consistent and integrated around common transcendent values may be an incorrect one*. In other words, perhaps symbiotic relationships among individuals and groups may be sufficient to keep a society sufficiently well organized and enable it to continue to secure the advantages of division of labor and exchange of goods. Perhaps the so-called "deeper loyalties" to traditional values like nationalism or some religion or ethical system may not really be necessary to the continuous practical working together of a great modern society. In other words, a secularized society may be held together on a basis of rationality and expediency, no longer requiring sacred or semi-sacred loyalties to enforce cohesion.

These are among the unsolved theoretical problems which sociology recognizes. They are unsolved problems because sociologists are unable to agree on the basic interpretations, and some even refuse to consider such problems as within the domain of competence of the social scientist.

### DELIBERATE AND UNCONSCIOUS FORMATION OF SOCIAL ORGANIZATION

The organization of a society *may* be planned, but it is more common to find contemporary societies which have simply "grown up" over the years and the centuries, with no person or group having either the ability or the power to plan the overall development.

On the other hand, *certain aspects of societies are the result of deliberate, purposive planning* by some person or group or perhaps by the entire society. A revolution, for example, would be possible only if some person or group planned it, however imperfectly the plan may have been formulated. The deliberations of legislative bodies, moreover, out of which laws affecting social organization are formulated, certainly result in the purposive modification of social structure. Therefore, while it would be an error to assume that society as it exists is the product of rational planning, it would be an equally serious error to assume or conclude that society, and more especially modern society, is entirely devoid of the rational element.

It appears that with the passing of time, *more and more rational control is entering into social organization.* More and more there is evidence that individuals and groups are asking fundamental questions about the nature of their society, and as a result of these analyses, it is frequently decided that something in the makeup of the society is not as it should and could be, and thus change is introduced. It is also important to note that the *absence of change, quite as much as change, may be evidence of rational influence* on social organization, because a group which gives thought to the evaluation of some existing aspect of the society, and then concludes that things are better as they are, reflects rational choice just as much as would a decision to introduce some change. Summarizing our discussion of rational and unconscious factors in the emergence of social organization, (1) the overall organization of few societies, if any, are entirely the result of deliberate or rational planning, and (2) modern societies are more affected by rational control than past, and especially primitive, societies are and have been.

### CHANGING SOCIAL ORGANIZATION AND THE PERSON

Throughout this book, it has been emphasized that all systems of human relationship are constantly changing, and that the rate of change as well as the direction of change are variable. In the chapters dealing with such societal segments as the family, education, and government, specific changes have been discussed and to some extent evaluated. The point has been repeatedly made that negative reactions to change are common, and that *many persons in the society tend unconsciously to think of some given form of social organization as indispensable or inherent in the scheme of things.* Such notions are uncompromisingly fallacious. Their *fallacy lies in their disregard of the facts of intersocietal variability* and *in their tendency to overlook the large rôle of habit in human affairs.* One becomes habituated to a specific social system. From early childhood on, he learns to become dependent upon some particular form of organization. Not only the satisfaction of his needs are secured by the accustomed scheme, but his wants are themselves created by the society to which he has become habituated. Much of this process is, of course, unconscious, especially to the layman who must secure what little insight he has from the crude common-sense procedures of observation of himself and of the social processes of which he is a part. In short, it is almost impossible to escape being ethnocentric. In the overall organization social scientists cannot find any such phenomenon as a "best" social system. Any one of a *wide variety of social organizations meet human needs. They meet human needs because they create human needs.* Much popular evaluation is therefore largely an exercise in ethnocentrism. It does not, however, need to be such for those persons who have learned how to objectify their thinking about social conditions.

## SUMMARY

Societies are held together by symbiotic interdependence and by common value orientation. Neither of these can be asserted as primary or more fundamental. The human being becomes habituated both to the symbiotic aspect and to the value aspect in the course of his socialization. Social organization, through socialization, creates the person's social needs and wants. It also provides him with rationalizations, which are more or less consistent with the existing social structure. Thus, social organization lies both in the behavior patterns of the persons of the society and in the formal organization of the society through the rules, laws and other written paraphernalia of organization.

Symbiotic interdependence and common value orientation are implemented largely through groups and institutions. Institutions are manifest through groups or associations, but are themselves essentially abstract. They provide the basic values which the individual groups embody, although groups may embody non-institutional values.

Social organization may result either from deliberate, purposive formation or from unconscious formation. Modern societies differ from ancient and primitive societies in that organization of modern society is somewhat more rationally controlled. It is unlikely that we have yet discovered the full extent to which society can be effectively controlled by deliberate planning.

The major institutional segments of society, such as the family, government, the economic "system," and religion, all undergo change. Many of the changes consist of shifts in dominance among them and of the transfer of functions from one to another.

Value disunity and conflict within a society has been frequently interpreted as evidence of a lack of societal integration and construed to forebode ill. Such a thesis is difficult either to defend or to attack conclusively. The difficulty may lie in the fact that symbiotic unity is difficult to appraise as a unifying force. Perhaps, also the kinds of common value unity which seem to be passing from American society were only an aspect of a transitory period of history, and have been erroneously construed as an indispensable aspect of society per se. Such considerations as this, notwithstanding their importance, are in the domain of the not-yet-agreed-upon areas of sociological theory.

## SUGGESTED READINGS

Angell, R. C., *The Integration of American Society.* (See bibliographic note p. 281.) **A**

Chapter II, "The Integration of a Society," is a formulation of the value-unity thesis as the basis for social organization. A clear statement of the point of view.

Barnes, H. E., *Social Institutions* (New York, Prentice-Hall, Inc., 1942), Part I. **B**

This is good description, but does not contain any new or elaborate theoretical formulation. It is intended as an elementary textbook and is useful for that purpose.

Lynd, R. S., and Lynd, H. M., *Middletown in Transition.* (See bibliographic note page 365.) **AB**

Chapter XII, "The Middletown Spirit," is an effective handling of a very difficult phase of the social organization of Middletown. The authors attempt to verbalize the values which Middletown "holds." Should be read thoughtfully as an index to the Middletown, and also American, "mind." The concluding chapter, "Middletown Faces Both Ways," is also useful for the same purpose.

MacIver, R. M., *Society: A Textbook of Sociology* (New York, Farrar and Rhinehart, 1937), Chapters XIII to XVII. **A**

Parallels the treatment in this chapter to some extent, but introduces some new concepts and ideas.

Ogburn, William, and Nimkoff, M. F., *Sociology* (New York, Houghton Mifflin Co., 1946), Chapters 23 and 26. **B**

The treatment of the "interrelationships" among institutions is especially useful (pp. 740-775). Chapter 26, "The Social Effects of Inventions" is also important as a careful discussion of this phase of the problem of comprehending social organization in a dynamic sense.

## STUDY QUESTIONS

1. Distinguish between symbiotic and non-symbiotic kinds of interdependence. Illustrate.
2. Why is it preferable to think in terms of "symbiotic" and "non-symbiotic" interdependence rather than in terms of "symbiotic" and "cultural"?
3. What is universal and what is variable about social organization among the various societies?
4. What do we mean by "changes in the dominance" of an institution? Illustrate.
5. Give some illustrations of transfer of group functions. Strictly speaking, are the functions transferred?

6. Define and illustrate "institutions." What do we mean when we say that institutions can be "conceived but not perceived?"
7. What does Angell mean by saying that an institution "may be in any degree abstract?" Illustrate.
8. What is the connection between institutions and groups? Illustrate.
9. Illustrate non-institutional aspects of groups.
10. What do we mean by the integration of a society? What problems arise in attempting to determine integration objectively?
11. Why is it incorrect to say that changing social organization causes individual mental hygiene problems?
12. Is it correct to say that social change is unrelated to mental hygiene? Explain.
13. What is correct and what is incorrect in saying that "Institutions compete with one another?"

# *Chapter XXVII*

## SOCIAL DISORGANIZATION AND SOCIAL CHANGE

Traditionally sociologists and other writers and thinkers about social conditions have been interested in a recurring societal condition which they call *social disorganization.* Modern research and thinking has raised serious questions concerning this concept. In fact, the criticisms have become so basic and their implications so profound, that it now appears doubtful that the concept *social disorganization* can be retained as a valid one to the person who desires to think realistically about human behavior and society. This chapter is organized around three basic problems. (1) How has the idea of "social disorganization" grown up and what utility has it had? (2) Why is the use of this concept in need of fundamental rethinking? (3) What more acceptable interpretation can be placed upon some of the conditions which formerly had been conceived as social disorganization?

### WHAT HAS THE TERM "SOCIAL DISORGANIZATION" MEANT?

We have seen in an earlier chapter that the persons and groups making up societies are organized, not only by the fact of symbiotic interdependence, but also by such cultural ties as sentiment, convenience, and tradition. It has been observed by many students of society that from time to time this organization seems to break down, the mechanism of organization seems to "go to pieces," and unexpected, unusual, or abnormal behavior then occurs. Since such conditions as these seemed to be the opposite of organization, it appeared logical to call them "*dis*organization."

*Disorganization Illustrated*

To take an extremely simple illustration, suppose that there is a baseball game in progress. The players of both teams are playing by the rules as the rules are interpreted and enforced through the decisions of the umpires. The spectators, although they possess loyalties to one team or another, abide by the decisions of the umpires, because it is considered "good taste" or "good sportsmanship" to do so. Occasionally the umpires make a decision which seems to many to be unfair, or perhaps an obvious error has been made. Ordinarily such incidents are mildly protested by players or managers arguing with umpires, and by groups of spectators shouting or "booing" their disapproval of the umpire's decisions. Although the ideal culture patterns of the game as found in the rule books make no express provision for behavior of this sort, the real pattern of baseball, as it is actually enacted by players, umpires, and spectators, clearly shows that such behavior is more or less normal, understood, and expected. Moreover, if persons perform some act which is at variance with these generally recognized norms of conduct, the *modus operandi* also provides for their treatment. A discourteous player may be reprimanded by the umpire, may be removed from the game, or may be fined. An uncoöperative spectator may be removed from the park, and an incompetent or unjust umpire will probably be removed from his position at least in time. The "organization" provides for all of these regulatory practices.

Now let us suppose, further, that at some baseball game the players refuse to abide by the decisions of the umpire, fights between players ensue, and groups of spectators leave the stands and rush on to the field to participate in a "battle royal." Now the game is clearly disorganized. The kind of behavior taking place is not provided for in the rules and regulations or may even be wholly disapproved by the rules and regulations, but the violations are so numerous and the entire situation so uncontrollable, that the rules are virtually inoperative for the time being. The game may later become organized again, after this period of confusion, or the confusion may last so long and become so involved that the game is never resumed. In either case the condition just described would be considered disorganization.

The student will probably already have noted that the disorganization is not caused merely by the fact of physical conflict. That is purely incidental. The disorganization would be manifest by the fact that persons were behaving in ways not consistent with the approved manner in which they were supposed to behave while playing their respective rôles. The players are expected and/or required to play baseball, not to fight. The spectators are supposed to watch the game from their seats in the stands, and not participate in player-umpire discussions. If the contest had been a boxing match instead of a baseball game, then, of course, fistic combat of the sort prescribed by the rules in boxing would be normal for the competitors, and if some person or factor should prevent such behavior, then the more pacific situation would constitute disorganization. The essence of disorganization is that the *customary and approved ways of behavior no longer prevail.* This tends to cause or reflect confusion. The persons who are expected to be subordinate may not abide by their rôle, and numerous other kinds of unexpected or "abnormal" behavior would be in evidence.

Our illustration of the baseball game was, of course, a greatly simplified one and not a very important incident in the organization of the society. Rarely do sociologists become concerned with such a phenomenon per se, but it serves as a useful illustration of a more basic principle. Comparable situations arise in the larger and more significant groups in the society. *The symptoms of disorganization, however, are essentially the same: persons do not abide by the traditionally recognized patterns of behavior pertaining to the rôles in which they are presumably functioning.*

### *The Family*

Thus, some students of the family have suggested that the modern American family is disorganized, because many persons secure divorces, some couples deliberately do not have any children, some women have careers outside their homes instead of devoting their time and energies to home making, and various kinds of new and strange moralities can be observed in the actual lives of many married men and women. Since the traditional rôles of husband and wife presume permanent monogamous marriage, reproduction, and women in the rôle of home makers and child bearers, these new patterns of behavior which are appearing on a large scale constitute evidence of the fact that many people are not playing the rôles which have been traditional. Thus, the modern American family is said by some observers to be "disorganized."

*Economic Activities*

Disorganization is also alleged in the economic sphere. Until relatively recently, as we have seen, our capitalistic culture has been organized around the concepts of private property in capital goods and free enterprise. The owner of capital goods had the right to hire and fire labor as he chose. He had the right to make any kind of product he wanted and market it in any way he chose, with only a few limitations imposed upon him in the case of extremely harmful goods or extremely untruthful advertising or labeling. He had the right to set both the wages and conditions of employment with no interference either from government or from organized labor. If the worker did not like the conditions of employment, he could, of course, quit. Gradually, as we have seen, each of the above mentioned rôle-prerogatives of the owners and managers of capital goods, and also of labor, have been modified by changes in law or custom. In large industries, especially, the employer no longer has the exclusive right to fire or hire a specific man without cause. Certainly it is now not legal to discharge a man because he belongs to a labor union as was once the case. During the World War II period, moreover, certain commodities could not be manufactured and other commodities could be manufactured only in the numbers and in the ways which the government permitted. To some extent these regulations are still in force. Moreover, the seller of some kinds of merchandise is no longer permitted to charge any price which he can get; the maximum prices of many products are fixed by the Office of Price Administration under terms of laws passed by Congress. It is common to hear numerous and vigorous complaints that the new practices and policies are "ruining" business and there is much yearning for the "good old days."

There is no denying that there is an element of truth in the complaints of many persons who allege that they are confused or even wronged by the new patterns of economic activity. Although it is difficult to get precise facts, it appears that many persons are refusing to abide even by the new laws, and some are finding legal, as well as illegal, ways of circumventing the operation of the laws.

In short, there is uncertainty, because the rôles have changed, and because significant numbers of persons are unwilling or unable to follow the new rôles. Some are hoping that by large-scale violations, the new rôle requirements may be altered or repealed completely. Other persons, on the other hand, are quite satisfied with the "new order." They approve of greater rights for labor, lower margins of profit, and government regulation of the kinds and amounts of goods which should be sold. They regard these war-time modifications of the economic *modus operandi* as worthy of permanent incorporation into the American economic system. As this is being written the outcome cannot be foretold with certainty, although it appears that the extreme forms of public control of manufacturing and distribution which were introduced during the war period will be repealed or at least modified appreciably. It seems not likely that all regulation will be repealed or that we shall go back to quite as "free" an economy as obtained before the war.

Regardless of the specific outcome, however, it seems to some that there is justification for referring to the present economic aspect of American society as being disorganized. New and strange practices are common. New forms of large-scale violation called "black markets" are widespread. Business policies which many ethical concerns would once have frowned upon seem now to have become everyday practices. Strikes of labor and strikes of capital are daily recorded in the newspapers. Everywhere, it seems, there is confusion and uncertainty. No one seems quite to know what to take for granted in the behavior of his fellows. He does not even know what kind of behavior he himself should observe in order to meet his own needs and enhance his own interests. In fact he often does not even know in which direction or with which group his ultimate best interests lie. This, indeed, seems to be disorganization.

*Religion*

Contemporary religion presents a comparable panorama of change and confusion. Church doctrines, as we say in the chapter on religion, clash with one another on fundamental issues. Some churches are following programs and teachings which are largely new, and there is much confusion concerning the wisdom of these new philosophies and policies. Criticisms of the church are heard both from within and from the outside of this age-old institution.

Confusion, experimentation, large-scale and open violation of time-honored taboos, all give evidence that the traditional rôle pattern has broken down, no generally accepted new ones seem yet formulated, and disorganization is said to exist.

### DO THESE CONDITIONS TRULY DENOTE DISORGANIZATION?

It will probably appear to the person who has just read the foregoing paragraphs, that the term *disorganization* is indeed an apt one to describe such conditions as were there discussed. It usually seems quite clear that formerly there was organization and now the organization has "somehow broken down." Why not call this condition, then, disorganization? Perhaps the reason for sociologists' growing reluctance to do so may best be shown by a more careful consideration of the symptoms and of the criteria which supposedly indicate disorganization.

From our discussion of the allegedly disorganized aspects of American society, it will probably be clear that the criteria employed for judging disorganization consist of such conditions as the "breakdown of social controls over the behavior of the individual," changes in the social rôles, experimentation with new rôles, and confusion among the persons behaving. On the surface it might appear, moreover, that such conditions as these, are obvious enough and can easily be seen or even measured. Why do they, then, not denote social disorganization?

The crux of the problem lies in the *inability to distinguish between the breakdown of a traditional rôle and the appearance of a new rôle.* It is certainly an obvious conclusion from the many facts and interpretations contained in this book that man is the kind of being who can live and be happy under a wide variety of social conditions. This does not necessarily mean that a *given* man necessarily can, but that man *as a whole* not only can but does. A given man might find it very difficult to live in a radically different society or follow radically different behavior patterns than those to which he has become accustomed, due to his habituation to the ideas and overt behavior standards of his particular society at his particular time. Since, for example, many millions of modern men are living under communism and under modified capitalism, one cannot but conclude that both of these systems are workable, even though quite different from one another, and both quite different from laissez faire capitalism.

It will also be recalled that attention has been repeatedly drawn to the fact of ceaseless social change. Since, then, change is always occurring and new rôles or rôle requirements are constantly appearing while others are disappearing, how can we be sure that the conditions which we called disorganization are not merely the emerging new organization for the coming societal mode? *They only seem to be disorganization because we are familiar with the rôles which have come out of the past, but we are unfamiliar with the rôles which are shaping up for the society of tomorrow.* For example, when the Negro slaves of the South were made free men, the rôles of the Negroes as well as of their former owners were abolished—or radically altered, whichever way one prefers to state it. In either event, the customary folkways and thoughtways were destroyed or at least rendered inoperative in the new scheme. There was experimentation and confusion, but the experiment and confusion were really the process of trial and error in the development of new rôles for Negroes and whites such as are now quite familiar. Suppose that there had been a group of sociologists describing the Negro-white situation in the South at that time. They would very probably have concluded that conditions were disorganized, because they were new and strange and would probably have been more or less nostalgic for the good old days when everything was under control, because everyone knew what to expect in the behavior of everyone else.

Let us suppose, further, that some of the sociologists observing the conditions following emancipation were former Northern Abolitionists, while others were former Southern slave holders. How could each group, then, tend to interpret the condition? It seems rather obvious that the *points of view would be radically different because the person's vested interests had been different.* The former slave owner, being familiar with the rôle of slave owner and its advantages both to him and to the slave, would probably see little which was good in the new situation, and probably be very unhappy and pessimistic about the outcome. The Northern Abolitionist, on the other hand, having had first-hand experience with a free society, would probably consider that the pending confusion was nothing to be alarmed about since it was, in fact, worth the confusion in order to secure a society in which no man could hold another man as his slave. In short, the Southerner would probably decry the new condition because he did not approve of it, but the Northerner would probably approve because it was consistent with the kind of values which he held. These *factors of value disagreement, and evaluation from the points of view of different vested interests are important considerations. They make objective description of disorganization very difficult, if not impossible.*

Let us now go back over the conditions which were formerly described as denoting disorganization in the family, the economic sphere, and religion in contemporary United States. Let us, then, see whether the conditions described denote disorganization in social rôles or whether they simply describe the appearance of new social rôles or new rôle characteristics. It may be that we tend not to approve of these innovations because they are new or because they run contrary to the value and prejudice patterns which have resulted from our having been conditioned to the culture of the preceding society. Perhaps we shall find that the conditions which looked like disorganization of the old social rôles are simply the appearance of new rôles which herald the shape of things to come. Instead of decrying the appearance of these new patterns of behavior and waxing eloquent about the good old days when things were different, one might then find it more advantageous to use his energies to understand better the nature of the new social world which is being formulated.

*The Changing Family*

The wide variation in types and forms of family life seem to constitute an adjustment to the variations in the conditions of human life in the United States—rural and urban, working class and business class, various occupational specialization, and different educational backgrounds. Probably for many educated women it seems neither desirable nor necessary to spend their time and energies doing many of the menial tasks ordinarily associated with traditional home making. It seems a more "sensible" adjustment to utilize their own talents in some skilled occupation and hire domestic service in the home. It can be argued that this is merely carrying on the logic of division of labor anyway. Such arrangements not only conduce to the happiness and ego-satisfaction of the woman concerned, but may also add something to the overall efficiency of the whole society if greater use can be made of special talent and training. The same may hold true even for reproduction. Most married persons want to have children, although they seem to wish to exercise some control over the time of their appearance and the numbers involved. But should some person either desire not to marry or to marry and not have children, such a decision could be justified both by the logic of democracy and of further division of labor. There are those, of course, who view such conditions in terms of prejudice patterns such as one's "duty" to marry or his "obligation" to have children or of the "sinfulness" of artificial control of the timing and number of children. When people do not behave consistently with these prejudice patterns, the observers often regard the condition as disorganization or as reflecting a lack of adjustment. Actually the behavior in question may itself constitute an adjustment. Similarly with divorce. Is the high divorce rate evidence of social disorganization in the family or simply of an increased use of a legal instrument through which unfortunate matings may be dissolved and the mates secure a second chance to find happiness through legal and socially approved means? To be sure each divorce dissolves a particular family, but is that disorganization of *the* family? It seems not. Is a freer sex code evidence of disorganization and confusion, or of the fact that more people have found avenues of sex expression which constitute better adjustment to the conditions of life than the previous more inhibited patterns did?

*Mental hygiene problems may be severe to the person changing rôles and values.* In stating the above alternatives so casually, it is not intended to imply that the transition from the customary to the innovation is an easy or "good" one. Actually it may be very difficult and many persons have become confused and hurt in the process. Sometimes the problem has arisen from the conflict between the individual and the tendency for the society to superimpose outmoded types of control upon him. In other cases, the problems inhere in the person. He struggles in the throes of indecision and ambivalence. He sees "good" both in the old and in the new, and cannot make up his mind between them. Or he does make up his mind, only to find that the more emotional aspect of his personality will not follow the course set by his intellectual processes. Thus, the woman who foregoes traditional home making in favor of a career may find it relatively easy to rationalize her choice, but finds conflicts resulting from her early conditioning. She often finds that she has been emotionally fashioned to want and to need the kind of rôle which she has rationally decided to forego. Mental ill-health in some degree is an almost inevitable result. However tragic this may be to the individual caught in the changing situation, it should not obscure the fact that the basic condition is change. Persons have from time immemorial often found it difficult to integrate the old and the new in their own lives. But many very desirable social changes have come out of such periods. There is no evidence, in fact, to prove that such conditions are other than normal. *Adjustment to change is a wholly normal fact of human existence.* That some persons find it difficult or impossible, or the fact that they are "lost" altogether, is unfortunate of course, but it is nevertheless unavoidable. Possibly the person who understands the process of social change may be somewhat better able to shape his own mental hygiene processes, but perhaps, also, the non-logical character of social valuation may be so deeply ingrained in the personality that a veneer of intellectualized education makes little real difference or even aggravates the difficulty. We are unable at present to be any more definite about the relation between intellectual knowledge and personal adjustment to changing social norms.

### *Religion*

Perhaps religion, like the family, may be not so much disorganized, as merely different. The religious ideas of one period in the development of a given culture may seem as incomprehensible and "superstitious" when seen in the prejudice patterns of another period as if they had come from another continent. Similarly religious practices change radically—even though usually they change slowly. Thus, for example, the great diversity of religious belief and practice in contemporary United States may be merely the emergence of a number of new and somewhat specialized multiplicity of religious thoughtways and folkways, each satisfying and functional to the personality and social rôle configuration of some specialized segment of society. What may be regarded as "irreligious," "pagan," or "eccentric" by the person who is evaluating it from the point of view of traditional theology and practice, may be commonplace theology and practice in a short time. If one be inclined to doubt the truth of the foregoing statement, a review of the evolution of Christian doctrines and practices will provide abundant factual materials to support it. Birth control was once almost universally regarded as sinful, and now some churches provide birth control services for their communities. Examples are abundant.

As in the case of the family, mental hygiene problems accompanying the changes in religious beliefs and practices are many and sometimes very severe. Religion both causes and heals mentally disturbed persons. Liberal religion both causes and heals troubled minds. Conservative religion both creates mental ill-health for some people and assists others in developing feelings of security and adjustment in a changing world of frustration. Religion has sometimes been falsely "sold" as a mental cure-all and irreligion falsely interpreted as the result of mental inadequacy or confusion. The falsity springs from over-generalization. *For some persons,* religion provides solace from frustration, but for others it has been the source of the anxiety-producing frustration or of the conflict which caused the person to suffer. Particularly in a period of rapidly changing religious norms, mental hygiene problems are numerous. With the emergence of new forms and norms of religious ideology and practice, however, there may have come quite as much adjustment as maladjustment. While one cannot assert with confidence that such is the case, he certainly cannot deny the possibility or even the probability thereof.

### *Economic Organization*

In the realm of economic phenomena, we encounter the same problem which we did in considering the changing family and the changing religious organization, namely, the inability to determine objectively whether conditions are disorganized or merely changing. Viewed by conventional criteria, for example, a strike wave may appear to constitute economic disorganization, but the strike may also have become a normal form for the periodic adjustment of wages and other employment conditions. To be sure, for the duration of the strike there is confusion for others, but the strike itself may be a recognized mode of economic functioning. Similarly, depressions are usually regarded as disorganized economic conditions, and yet economists explain that depressions are almost inevitable

intermittent results of the kind of economic order we have. The depression, however serious to the mental and physical health of many persons, is a phase of the process of change in economic culture, and is quite as much the result of known forces as prosperity is. Many of the current confusions of an expanding governmental control over business and agriculture may be the process of adjustment to the kind of coming economy, the confusion being due to the learning of new rôles both in industry and in government. When these emerging rôles have been learned, they, too, will have to be unlearned and new ones learned in adaptation to new conditions or new values.

## SUMMARY

From the illustrations and interpretations contained in the foregoing paragraphs it should be clear that much of what has been traditionally called "disorganization" is objectively indistinguishable from normal social change. The confusion and experimentation which allegedly are symptomatic of disorganization are quite as clearly indicative of adjustment to the demands and requirements of new rôles.

Much erroneous thinking, moreover, has been introduced into the literature on social change as a result of the use of the word *disorganization*. Disorganization carries an implication of disapproval and abnormality and suggests that it is an unfortunate and temporary condition, whereas social change is a quite normal condition and quite as likely to bring about better as worse social conditions. In fact, both desirable and undersirable social change is characterized by new social rôles, and in their early stages are difficult for many persons to master, resulting in confusion and diverse evaluation. Such is, however, the normal pattern of change in human affairs. Therefore, social disorganization is becoming less useful as an objective concept in the vocabulary of the sociologist.

It should not be concluded, however, that there is no utility in the concept *disorganization*. The concept is useful certainly to describe conditions such as riots, earthquakes, and similar disruptions of accustomed social organization. These conditions may truly present *disorganization* because of their *relatively short duration* and the strong probability that after the period of confusion, order will return on approximately the same pattern as existed prior to the interruption. In the case of larger social organization, however, one does not have the same degree of certainty that the confusion will be short or that a return to the former pattern will almost certainly come along the accustomed lines. In other words, the Smith family may be disorganized by the illness of Mrs. Smith. Presumably when she recovers her health the family will become reorganized along habitual lines. In the case of *the* American family, however, we have no comparable basis of alleging disorganization or anticipating reorganization. Thus, also, the dislocation of social organization and individual life-patterns necessitated by the war can hardly be regarded simply as social disorganization, since the likelihood of return to the identical pre-war forms of behavior and social organization is very slight, the post-war social order and the post-war mode of life for the person are not the same as the pre-war ones. There is no real going back; the "duration" was also an on-going social process, shaping the new order and the new person as it evolved.

## SUGGESTED READINGS

Cuber, John, "Some Aspects of Institutional Disorganization," *American Sociological Review,* V, pp. 483-488. **A**

A summary of social disorganization thinking, and an attempt to refine some aspects of it. This is not to be taken as representative of the author's present thinking, but may have historical interest in tracing the social disorganization idea.

Elliott, M. A., and Merrill, F. E., *Social Disorganization* (New York, Harper and Bros., 1934). **B**

This book may be taken as approximately representative of the social disorganization approach to social problems and social change. The theoretical formulation found early in the book seems not to be as well or as consistently used as might be expected.

Schilder, Paul, "The Relation Between Social and Personal Disorganization," *American Journal of Sociology,* Vol. 42, pp. 832-839. **A**

An attempt to relate conditions termed "social disorganization" to certain kinds of personal inadequacy. The theoretical formulations are quite unlike those found in this book, but a comparison may be useful in grasping the difficulty in using disorganization concepts.

Sutherland, R. E., and Woodward, J. W., *Introductory Sociology* (Philadelphia, J. B. Lippincott Co., 1940). **B**

A short textbook discussion of social disorganization will be found in Chapter 28.

## STUDY QUESTIONS

1. What has "social disorganization" traditionally meant?
2. Why is it difficult to be objective in describing and interpreting social disorganization? Illustrate.
3. How is social change related to what has been called social disorganization?
4. Evaluate: "A strike is an example of social disorganization."
5. Why can disorganization frequently be approached through a study of rôles?
6. What do a person's vested interests have to do with his evaluation of social change? Illustrate.
7. Why are the severe mental hygiene problems of persons experiencing social change not an adequate criterion for judging the desirability of the change?
8. Why is it often impossible to distinguish change and disorganization in society?
9. What criterion does this chapter suggest as valid for distinguishing disorganization from change per se?
10. State the case for considering present economic conditions in the United States as "disorganized."
11. Criticise your reply to Question 10.
12. Why can we not determine objectively whether the American family is disorganized or not? Illustrate.
13. What would be lost if the social scientist dropped the phrase, "social disorganization" from his vocabulary? Might the concept live on anyway? Why?

# Chapter XXVIII

## SOCIAL INTERACTION: COÖPERATION AND COMPETITION

Persons and groups are almost continuously in a process of reciprocal stimulation and response, called "interaction." The classroom, the market-place, the night club, the ball game, or the factory, functions through the diverse behaviors of people whose interrelated rôles are worked out in conjunction with one another. Interaction usually follows, of course, the patterns provided by the culture of the society. As we have seen repeatedly throughout this book, human behavior patterns are largely standardized and routinized. Moreover, the behavior of different persons, or of the same persons at different times, tends to be integrated and organized into larger patterns of behavior. The various interrelated social rôles culminate, finally, in the overall organization of the society.

The interaction of groups and of individuals tends to follow a relatively few basic types or forms. Their existence apparently has been obvious enough to have attracted the interest of the layman, because his language patterns contain standard words and precepts which reveal a more or less accurate conception of some of these basic forms of interaction. *Competition* and *coöperation* are perhaps the best known. These concepts are well enough understood by almost everyone, so that formal definition seems to be largely unnecessary. We shall turn now to a somewhat more detailed treatment of competition and coöperation as important basic forms of social interaction. Probably in all societies both coöperation and competition have existed side by side in the daily behavior of the people, but the folklore relating to them shows serious misunderstandings.

## COMPETITION

The basic factor underlying competition is that there is a limited quantity of many items of value which groups or persons strive to secure. If the item of value exists in such abundance that there is enough for everyone's needs, then no competition takes place, regardless of how precious the items might be. Thus, under normal conditions people do not compete for air and water, even though these two materials are essential for the continuation of life. But under occasional artificial conditions of scarcity of air and water, competition for these commodities can and has been extremely acute.

Many of the objectives for which human beings compete do not derive their values from the sustenance needs of the human organism, but rather from the non-rational value patterns of the culture. Men and women compete for such goals as golf championships and political offices, not because these things have any discernable connection with the quality or quantity of their physical existence, but simply because these quite artificial distinctions reflect superior status upon their possessors.

### *Status Competition for Intangibles Is Often Basic*

It may already be apparent that some of the most intense competitions in which people engage have as their objective the attainment of intangible items of value. This is not only true in modern societies such as ours, but has also been found among primitive peoples and among culture types quite different from ours. At the risk of oversimplification, it may be said that the intangible objects for which people compete are rationalized as worth the severe competitive effort, because the successful attainment of the objective reflects superior status on the person who is successful in the competition. This is always contingent, of course, upon the fact that the particular rivalry in question, and also the goal, are approved by the value system of the society in which the person is desirous of securing the higher prestige rating.

### *Forms of Competition*

There are several sub-types of competition which ought to be distinguished from one another. In some forms of rivalrous interaction, the competition is defined in such a way that only one person can normally claim to have become the successful partisan or the victor. Championships are for the most part of that sort. There is only one winner of the Kentucky Derby or of the world championship baseball pennant. There is only one President of the United States at a time. All other competitors must have been eliminated before anyone can claim success. Other competitions are simply *matters of degree*. People compete for money, prestige, and fame. But no one expects to attain all of the money or all of the prestige or all of the fame. He realizes when he begins the competition, that he probably can never aspire to even the top fifty per cent, but he competes anyway, striving to secure as much as possible of whatever items of value he desires to acquire.

Competition may also be classified as *personal* and *impersonal*. In personalized competition the competitors strive with one another, each consciously trying to defeat his rivals at the polls, on the golf course, in court, or at love. Each competing person is aware of the existence of his competitors and recognizes that in some way or another the competitor must be eliminated before he can attain his objective. Other competitions are largely de-personalized. In the present competition between labor and management over wages, for example, there is no necessary personal focus for the rivalry. While it is true that each side bargains through specially designated representatives, everyone knows that these representatives are only functionaries or spokesmen and that they could be replaced by other functionaries or spokesmen without in any way altering the outcome. The rivalry of various industrial concerns which produce competitive products may constitute an even better illustration of impersonalized competition. Each is courting public favor through advertising, attempting to build a superior product, or provide better service for his customers. But the customers and the managers of the enterprise never meet and do not know each other, nor do the competing managers usually regard themselves as competitors in the personal sense.

### *Competition Is Seldom "Pure"*

Competition is usually accompanied by some joint or coöperative effort. When two athletic teams or two industries compete, it can easily be overlooked that a great deal of coöperation among the persons within the group is necessary in order to achieve a more effective organization as a competing unit. Moreover, in many forms of competition there is evidence of coöperation among the rivals. They coöperate in abiding by the rules of the "game" as recognized by the culture, and in many other ways also. It is true, of course, that in these instances mentioned, the coöperative effort is subordinate to the competitive purpose, but it seems important to note that the competition in order to be effective seems often to require considerable coöperative effort both within and between the competing units.

### *The Importance of Culture*

There is a prevailing tendency to overlook the large rôle played by culture in group or individual competitions. Many persons tend to think and talk about competition as if they believed that the competitive process was inherent in the original nature of the person without any significant molding through cultural experience. While we are not here denying that rivalry may be rooted in original nature, it is necessary to emphasize the basic cultural learning superimposed upon and built into the person as a result of living in a specific culture at a specific time.

We may roughly classify cultures along a continuum on the basis of the importance which each culture attaches to competitive interaction. Some cultures are highly competitive, and attach great prestige to the person who is successful at competitive effort. Other cultures devalue competition, and sharply reduce the number and importance of personal prestiges which result from it. Ours is a highly competitive culture, and there is a pronounced ethnocentric tendency to assume that the values and behaviors approved in our culture are somehow inherent in the scheme of things. Actually, of course, such is not the case.

In addition to the overall emphasis upon competition, culture defines this form of interaction in numerous basic ways. (*a*) The values of the culture determine the basic items which are regarded as desirable. Wealth, for example, may or may not be defined as a worthy personal attainment. The same with education or with physical attractiveness or with romantic love. (*b*) Culture, moreover, defines the propriety or impropriety of attempting to attain given values by competitive effort. The religious and ethical systems of many peoples, for example, disapprove of rivalrous means of attaining certain values. "Covetousness" along specified lines is very frequently frowned upon. In our society, on the other hand, it is considered altogether proper that the several men who desire a given woman as their wife should compete with one another for the purpose of "winning" her. There are other cultures, however, in which this method of securing a mate would be considered inappropriate, if not indecent. (*c*) The culture of a people defines who may and who may not compete for a given item of value. This is most pronounced, as we have seen, in caste and in estate societies, where it is regarded as inappropriate and therefore virtually impossible for a person of one caste to compete with a person of another caste for the same item of value. Abundant illustrations of this principle can be found in the United States pertaining to white and colored persons. Many jobs, areas of residence, and educational opportunities from which Negroes are categorically excluded illustrate the way in which the culture defines who may or who may not compete for the attainment of a given value. (*d*) Finally, culture formulates and enforces more or less recognized rules for competitive effort. Competition is almost never unrestrained. The epithet *cheat* has wide currency in the thoughtways of almost every people. The cheat is not necessarily the person who has violated some carefully worded law or rule or regulation. He is more often the person who does not follow the informal customs which are supposed to regulate the rivalry and keep the competition "clean." The cleanliness of competition, of course, is entirely a matter of definition. Whether the rivals for the affections of a given girl who fight it out in the alley are playing the game "clean" or "dirty" depends upon the unwritten rules of the game of courtship among the group in question. In one community such behavior would be regarded as altogether fair, but in another group it would be defined as contrary to the standards of "decency" which ought to obtain among courting rivals. At one time in the United States a man who was insulted by another man could defend his honor successfully only by challenging the other to a duel. The culture of that time condoned such behavior, but our society would not. In at least these four ways, then, the prevailing culture of a people institutionalizes the competitive process. Like all forms of culture these approval-disapproval patterns are highly variable in time and space.

### *Competition as a Real and as an Ideal Pattern in American Economic Life*

The folklore and mythology of American business extol the virtue of competition. Competition is said to be the "life of trade" and the basis of the "American way." If a person were naïve, he might reach the conclusion that this reverence for competition is the outgrowth of American experience with it, and that our economic life implements competition wherever possible.

The more sophisticated observer of the economic sphere, however, will note that practice departs very radically, and at many points, from these idealizations of competition. The student will recall from his study of American history that one of the most recurrent problems which America has faced has been that of large scale coöperation between supposedly competing businesses. Device after device has been invented by the management of industry for concealing the extent and kind of coöperative effort among supposedly competing business enterprises. Time and again when competitive bids have been opened for the construction of a public building, road, or bridge, identical bids have been made by all the competitors. Obviously such unanimous agreement is not the result of chance. There have also been "gentlemen's agreements," conclusively proved in court, whereby competing concerns have agreed on certain prices and have agreed not to change prices without consulting each other. Other "gentlemen's agreements" have concerned wage rates and agreements not to compete in certain areas. These and other techniques of avoiding competition have now become public knowledge. Labor, more recently, has followed the pattern set by industry. Individual workmen do not really compete with one another in large union-dominated industries. In fact the workman who does too much work is penalized by his fellow union members and promotions and discharges are forced by union contract to follow seniority and not individual differences based upon competition.

Thus, the economic sphere in America presents an interesting paradox, or at least inconsistency, between the ideal and real practice of competition. Competition is said to be the basis of economic life, and yet at almost every opportunity to eliminate competition and establish monopoly, competition has been reduced or eliminated entirely. The realistic observer of the whole process is left with no choice but to conclude that in practice free competition apparently does not work as well as it is alleged to work.

*Is Intense Competition "Good" or "Bad?"*

Competition is said, by the folklore, to be good for the person and for society in that through a competitive type of interaction the person will exert himself more than he will in a situation in which he has less to gain by his efforts. Thus, it is argued, if we encourage the competitive type of interaction, each person will try to "outdo" the other, and as a result of this rivalry a greater total expenditure of effort will have been made. This is said to constitute a net gain to the society in that more work will thus be accomplished. The fallacies in this point of view are manifold. Many intense forms of competition which require a tremendous expenditure of human effort, result in no collective or individual social good whatsoever. In other cases there may be some social benefits derived from intense competition, but the mountain of effort expended brings forth an anthill of result. Also some intense rivalries may be harmful to the competitors both physically and mentally as judged by the prevailing standards of this society.

To illustrate the foregoing, let us consider the competitions involved in the American system of electing people to public office. There is no denying that the competitive effort is intense. But practically anyone familiar with the process will readily observe, first, that much of the competition is socially harmful in that ill-will, even criminal activity, has been known to occur. Frequently, the competition is worked out on the basis of skills and talents wholly unrelated to the problems of government in which the successful competitor will be expected to show proficiency. The candidate with the best vote-getting strength, not the best governmental judgment, is the one who wins. (It is a happy coincidence that at least some of the time the better vote-getter is also the better statesman.) Moreover, much time and energy is spent in creating differences when there are no real differences present, and of advertising candidates' virtues which have no discernible connection with the skills of good government.

A serious mental hygiene problem is created and seriously accentuated by highly competitive interaction. Although we possess no easy devices for the accurate measurement of such a phenomenon, it is quite probable that there is an appalling loss in social efficiency which results from the frustration of the many defeated persons in a competitive struggle. Moreover, the intensity of the competition may make for anxieties, fears, and phobias which further reduce the efficiency of large numbers of persons.

Some phases of competition, however, do lend themselves to careful observation and research. Experiments show, for example, that in such specific motor activities as running or typewriting, a person placed in a competitive situation will usually exert more effort and get better results than he will in isolation or where no stimulation by others' efforts is present. It should be noted, however, that the experimental evidence is based on a very few and relatively minor kinds of activity. We do not know whether intense rivalry results in better art, more scientific progress, or clearer human insight. There are good reasons to doubt that such is the case.

Thus far we have stressed the negative aspects of competition. This seems desirable as an antidote to the uncritical apologetics for competition which have such wide currency in popular thinking. What we have said should not be construed to mean that all competition is undesirable or that there now exists some radically different orientation around which present society could function. After all, even though our society emphasizes competition, there is a great deal of non-competitive interaction to be found. Very possibly both the individual and the society as a whole could better attain many of the values which we hold, if the more extreme forms and the less socially beneficial forms of competition were gradually to be deëmphasized. Even if this adjustment were not made, it is certainly desirable that a truly informed citizen should secure a more balanced appraisal of the *pros* and *cons* of competitive interaction than he gets from the conventional folklore and mythology which circulates so widely and so uncritically.

## COÖPERATION

In some ways, but not in all, coöperation may be regarded as the antithesis of competition. The interaction is oriented toward joint achievement of a goal. It will be recalled that in the above discussion of competition, it was pointed out that competition and coöperation may coexist in a situation, such as in the behavior of the members on an athletic team who coöperate with one another for the purpose of competing more effectively with the other team.

### *Coöperation and Self-Interest*

It is often held that coöperative activity is difficult to achieve because "individuals are basically selfish" and that their alleged selfishness makes it difficult, if not impossible, to subordinate their individual wills to the collective enterprise. The chief factor overlooked in such a conception of the matter is that there is no necessary discrepancy or conflict between selfishness and coöperation. A person may be seeking to further his self-interests by competitive activity, by coöperative activity, or by both. Competition and coöperation are merely two somewhat distinct means of attaining either self-interests or self-subordination as objectives. Either objective can be served by either means or by some combination of the two. Probably the reason for the close linking of self-interest and competition is a result of the coexistence of these two values in American culture. In short, it is an ethnocentric view of the matter.

### *The Rôle of Culture*

Culture is the determining factor in defining the propriety or impropriety of coöperative effort, very much the same as we observed in the case of competition. The particular culture defines certain goals as most appropriately attainable through coöperation. Thus, members of a family are supposed to coöperate with one another in the attainment of joint values, and members of an organization such as a church or labor union or board of directors are supposed to be characterized by behavior patterns reflecting coöperation. There is no inherent reason, in most cases, why the opposite form of interaction might not be quite as workable. Yet because one has been indoctrinated with one view rather than another, the way in which his thinking has been fashioned usually seems to him to be more natural or more logical.

Just as some societies tend to emphasize competition as the preferred overall form of interaction, so other societies place coöperation in a preferred value position. It is to be noted, of course, that no society is entirely and consistently competitive nor is any society entirely and consistently coöperative. In each society there will be found elements of both forms of interaction, but the relative predominance of one or the other in the total pattern of behavior constitutes whatever justification there may be for such phrases as "competitive society" or "coöperative society."

### *Kinds of Coöperation*

It has already been shown that there are several kinds of competition. Coöperation, likewise, is of several forms. (*a*) The most obvious form of coöperation consists of behavior which results from loyalty to the same objective. In that sense, the citizens of a community coöperate for the purpose of building a school or lynching someone. In that same sense, we may say that the diverse groups making up the United States recently coöperated for the purpose of winning the war. (*b*) Coöperation may also be of a form frequently called "antagonistic coöperation." This paradoxical expression seems to be a rather apt one. Frequently persons coöperate for no reason other than for the purpose of organizing their basically opposing desires or interests. When employer and employee agree to a conference for the purpose of arriving at a wage settlement, they are, in a sense, coöperating, but they are coöperating as a means of attaining a set of objectives fundamentally at variance with one another. The employee wants high wages and the employer low wages. Each side realizes that it is vitally dependent upon the other and that there is no alternative but to work out some sort of an arrangement coöperatively. (*c*) Other coöperation is the result of *mutual dependence* of two or more persons and groups. The interest may not be the same nor yet clearly antagonistic. The overall organization of society through the division of labor is a largely unconscious form of coöperation due to economic interdependence. (*d*) We have already seen that it is often necessary that the members of a group coöperate in order that they may compete more successfully with some other group. (*e*) Finally, coöperation may result from the superior power of a group with which one must coöperate, because there is no real alternative. In this sense many individuals and groups in Germany and in Japan coöperated with the Allied armies of occupation after the war. Obviously these people would prefer not to be held under the absolute authority of a conquering power, but since they have been vanquished in war, they cannot escape this domination. Hence, they elect to coöperate in order that they may secure better treatment than they would if they resisted.

*The Evaluation of Coöperation*

Coöperation, like competition, is neither inherently a part of original nature nor contrary to it. Coöperation is a culturally defined matter. Like competition it has to be learned and rationalized by the thoughtways of the society. It may have a high valuation or a low one. It may be considered superior or inferior to competition. It may be regarded as evidence of strength in a person, or it may be deemed to reflect weakness.

Obviously, therefore, we can find no objective basis for categorically approving or disapproving of coöperation as a form of interaction. Such evaluation depends largely, if not solely, on the values which the evaluating person holds. As a rule, to persons in contemporary American society competition seems to be the more virtuous basic orientation to human interaction. As we have repeatedly pointed out, this superior valuation is altogether natural since our society is one in which, in theory at least, competition is the more approved method of behavior. Obviously competition will seem more normal and natural than coöperation for exactly the same reason as English will seem more normal and natural than Chinese and that Christianity will seem a more normal and natural religion than Shintoism. This may be understandable enough in view of the relation between cultural and individual behavior. It may not be so obvious, however, that because of the American preoccupation with competition, much actual coöperation which occurs passes unnoticed or inadequately appraised. The somewhat more enlightened person who has secured a measure of insight into at least some of the subtleties of human behavior and society should not make such errors.

## SUMMARY

The interaction of persons and groups takes on a few basic forms or types. This chapter has been concerned with the discussion of two somewhat antithetical forms of interaction—competition and coöperation.

An objective evaluation of competition and coöperation is very difficult for most persons because of cultural bias. The prevailing folkways and thoughtways of one's own culture create a barrier of prejudice which is exceedingly difficult to cross over, even for purposes of theoretical analysis. The characteristic American reverence for competition usually makes it very difficult for Americans to understand that many of the objectives which we attain through competitive effort are attained in other societies through coöperative effort. This applies as much to material matters as to psychological satisfactions such as prestige or status.

The prevailing culture of a society defines such fundamental considerations as whether competition or coöperation is the superior virtue, what objectives of life may be properly regarded as attainable by competition and what ones by coöperation, who may and who may not compete or coöperate, what the rules and regulations for the various competitions are to be, as well as many other basic considerations.

It cannot be stressed too emphatically that in each society there are elements both of competition and of coöperation in the makeup of the total pattern of interaction. No society is entirely coöperative or entirely competitive. Differences are matters of degree.

In the long run each society may, perhaps, have something of a choice concerning whether it will move in the direction of channeling more or less of its vital activities through competitive behavior. This is especially true of the more rational types of societies, such as ours, in which social change is more the result of deliberate planning. There is some evidence to suggest that some Americans, at least, are attempting to evaluate the existing forms of behavior somewhat objectively in an attempt to determine whether the individual and public "good" will be fostered more by the continuation of the present emphasis on competition or by a gradual deemphasis in favor of more coöperative interaction. It remains to be seen what the eventual influence of such thinking shall be, and how long it will take to make an appreciable modification of the present *modus operandi*.

## SUGGESTED READINGS

BROOKS, Lee, and EATON, M. A., "The Concept of Co-operation in Textbooks of Introductory Sociology," *Social Forces*, XX, pp. 46-53. **A**

An examination of current textbooks in sociology reveals that while there is some treatment of coöperative interaction, the treatment seems not to be proportional to the amount or importance of coöperative behavior in the society. It may be that sociologists have fallen under the influence of the competitive ideology of American society to such an extent that they unwittingly neglect the phenomenon of coöperation even when it is conspicuous.

*Coöperatives in the United States—A Balance Sheet*, Public Affairs Pamphlets, Public Affairs Committee, Inc., New York, 1939. **B**

A simple and clear review of the extent of organized coöperatives as social groups in the United States.

KROPOTKIN, P. A., *Mutual Aid, A Factor of Evolution* (New York, Alfred Knopf, Inc., 1922). A B

This small book was written as an antidote to the overemphasis upon competition as a factor in life, which has been current since the appearance of Darwin's *Origin of Species*. It is Kropotkin's thesis that mutual aid is a significant form of behavior not only on the human level but also in many sub-human forms of life. A significant book.

MAY, M. A., and DOOB, L. W., *Competition and Coöperation*, Social Science Research Council, New York, 1937. A

A sophisticated treatment of coöperation and competition. Summarizes the many materials on these subjects and attempts an overall interpretation and theoretical formulation.

MEAD, Margaret, editor, *Competition and Coöperation Among Primitive Peoples* (New York, McGraw-Hill Book Co., 1937). A

A number of students of primitive societies contribute their observations on the competitive and coöperative processes among the peoples whom they have studied. An authoritative work.

## STUDY QUESTIONS

1. How does our society foster competition?
2. Why do people compete for intangible "items" of value?
3. Why are some competitions "only a matter of degree?"
4. How can advertising be an indication of personal or impersonal competition?
5. Why does coöperation often accompany competition?
6. How does the type and degree of competition within a society depend upon its culture?
7. How is competition related to cultural values?
8. Why do men of different races usually not compete for the affections of the same girl?
9. What determines whether a given kind of competitive interaction is "clean" or "dirty?"
10. Why is the theory of competition in present American economic life more of an ideal than a real pattern?
11. How is competition "a waste of human effort?"
12. How may competition result in impaired physical and mental health?
13. Why does competition often not create social benefits?

14. Is coöperation the antithesis of competition? Can this be an "illusion" due to our ethnocentrism?
15. Why is it possible to achieve the same goal by competition, coöperation, or a combination of the two?
16. Why are some goals attained by coöperation while others are attained by competition?
17. How does a society determine the relative values of competition and coöperation?

# *Chapter XXIX*

# CONFLICT, ACCOMMODATION, AND ASSIMILATION

## CONFLICT

Some of the rivalrous interaction among the persons and groups in a society takes place within the more or less culturally approved channels of competition. But there are other rivalries which are less controlled, less within the recognized and accepted "rules." In the absence of agreed-upon standards for carrying out the rivalry, crude hostility and more intense forms of struggle become common. Rivalry of this sort is less easy to define than is competition, but tends to be called *conflict* by students of social interaction. We shall not attempt a formal definition of conflict but shall note merely that some rivalries are carried out in a society with the relative absence of established rules and characterized by hostility and intense struggle. Rivalries of the sort just described are usually called conflict to set them apart from the more orderly type which we have defined in the preceding chapter as competition.

### *Violence Not the Essence of Conflict*

It should be noted that the distinction between competition and conflict lies in the regulation of the rivalry by the society, and does not lie in the degree of violence which accompanies the interaction. Many physically violent kinds of interaction with even lethal results may be approved by the culture under the competitive rules. Dueling and feuding in the societies which approve them are cases in point. Non-violent interactive behavior is conflict behavior, whenever it consists of acts which are regarded as "out of bounds" by the societal norms. "Whispering campaigns," slander, and espionage are well-known instances.

*Competition and Conflict Frequently Difficult to Distinguish*

There are numerous cases in which rivalrous behavior has some aspects of competition and some aspects of conflict according to the definitions which we have advanced. There are numerous rivalries in American society, for example, which it is difficult to classify either as conflict or as competition, because the rivalries have attributes both of being worked out within rules and also outside of rules. Capital-labor rivalries, interracial rivalries and business-government rivalries are of this sort. Suppose we illustrate with business-government rivalry. Frequently we have pointed out that one of the basic social trends in America is the increasing control of business by government, presumably in the "public interest." Some, but not necessarily all, of this control has been opposed by business interests. Propaganda campaigns have been launched, both by business groups and those groups which have favored more government control, such as some consumer groups and some labor groups. In these propaganda campaigns there has been much misrepresentation of facts, if not downright falsification. Moreover, very clever techniques have been used often through conventional advertising channels, but which appear to have been designed to be deceptive. Instances of bribery and intimidation of public officials are by no means infrequent. Do these behaviors constitute competition or conflict? They have some aspects of competition in that there are *some* rules, some standards of decency, which can still be observed. As compared to the way Fascist groups operated in Germany, for example, the American modes of intimidation and bribery are indeed genteel. Whether this is due to the presence of ethical standards on the part of these groups or due to fear of court action and other kinds of public censorship cannot, of course, be determined. It is clear, however, that there is some observance of rules by both sides. On the other hand, there are aspects of conflict in the situation. It seems difficult, indeed, to rationalize the deliberate deception by propaganda as other than "cheating" for the purpose of winning adherents in a debate. Similarly, some of the actions of pressure groups in influencing legislators constitute more nearly the tactics of the racketeer than those of responsible citizenship. And yet it is entirely possible that these ethically reprehensible practices may have become so widely practical and accepted that they already constitute competitive practices, rather than conflict techniques.

The same difficulty is presented by other large-scale rivalries in American life. The conflict between liberal and traditional religion, and between some of the large religious bodies show the same combination of competitive and conflict rivalry. Certainly the interaction between the races falls into this same borderline zone between competition and conflict. It should be borne in mind, however, that the distinction between conflict and competition is a very real and valid one for the purpose of understanding rivalrous interaction, even though we must candidly admit that in numerous specific instances the interactions have aspects of both types of rivalry. There are numerous other rivalries which are much more clearly either competition or conflict.

## ACCOMMODATION

Competition and conflict frequently become so intense or so wasteful or so time-consuming that they are terminated. In their place are substituted other kinds of non-rivalrous relationships between persons and groups. As this is being written, for example, the nation is almost paralyzed by a strike of bituminous coal miners. Although strikes are now a more or less recognized means utilized in the settlement of labor disputes, this particular strike has caused more than the accustomed amount of inconvenience and danger to the public welfare. While the strike is not yet settled, a *truce* has been arranged by the two parties under terms of which the miners have agreed to return to work for two weeks so that enough coal might be mined to meet the most pressing health and welfare needs. Another form of accommodation which is well known and probably requires no comment is the *compromise.* A third is the designation of some presumably disinterested party or group to serve in the capacity of *arbitrator,* both sides agreeing or being bound to abide by the arbitrator's decision. Courts for the handling of civil cases are an illustration of this form of adjustment. Perhaps now we are ready for the terse definition of accommodation. *Accommodation is a permanent or temporary termination of rivalrous interaction which, while not necessarily settling the issue involved in the rivalry, permits the rivalrous parties to function coöperatively in at least some respects.*

*Forms of Accommodation*

It is neither possible nor necessary to present an exhaustive list of the specific forms of accommodation which one finds in a society. Since these forms are social expedients for reducing or resolving rivalries, inventions occur from time to time so that even a complete list at one time might be outmoded before it is published. We shall limit ourselves, therefore, to brief comment on a few of the recognized and long-established forms of accommodation. (*a*) The *truce* is found in almost every society in some form or other. It consists merely of the cessation of rivalry for a definite or indefinite period with the issues in no sense settled. (*b*) The *compromise,* each party agreeing to certain concessions, but still retaining the right and the power to engage in further rivalry, is also an old and well-established practice found in such dissimilar social situations as legislatures and families. (*c*) Temporary *subordination-superordination* arrangements are also widespread. Under this form of accommodation, one or the other of the rivalrous parties secures a partial advantage or "upper hand." This is recognized by both sides and there is devised, more or less tacitly, some sort of working arrangement which gives the subordinate person or group something less than victory but something more than defeat. This is somewhat similar to compromise, of course, the difference being in the fact that under compromise there is an assumption of approximate equality in the strength of the rivaling parties, whereas under subordination-superordination arrangements it is unmistakably clear that one group is dominant over the other, but not completely so.

The armistice with Japan illustrates subordination-superordination arrangements rather clearly. In return for permitting the Allies to land peacefully in Japan, the Japanese were promised better treatment than they would have received if the Allies had landed forcibly. It had been recognized by both sides that Japan was defeated, the only questions remaining were two: how soon and how conclusively was Japan already defeated? Thus, the Japanese pacifically subordinated themselves in return for some concessions. The basic conflict between Japan and the occidental nations is not settled in any final sense; it is only accommodated for the time being under these arrangements. (*d*) *Arbitration* provides for the termination of a rivalry on the basis of a decision reached, and possibly also enforced, by some third party. Courts constitute a conspicuous example of arbitration, but in the everyday affairs of ordinary people there are innumerable occasions in which third parties intervene in rivalries, and terminate them at least temporarily. (*e*) *Toleration* represents a form of accommodation of which there is abundant evidence. Frequently there is no formal truce, no agreed upon arrangements for terminating the rivalry, no arbitrator, but by informal procedures each party to the rivalry agrees to "put up with" the existence of the other rather than to assume the effort, inconvenience, or expense of further rivalry. Sometimes there is an ethical principle involved, such as we find in the democratic ideal, in which it is generally granted that persons of dissimilar views and behaviors also have the "moral right" to exist and "be free." So long as all sides to the rivalry recognize and accept this principle, some conflicts can be subordinated if not, in time, eliminated entirely. The various forms of accommodation may be lasting or very temporary.

### *The Significance of Culture*

It may appear tedious to the student, but it is a fact not to be overlooked, that cultural standards play a significant rôle in working out accommodations. The forms of accommodation are themselves, of course, culture; they are men's inventions for handling the problem of rivalrous interaction. Moreover, culture also defines which rivalries are or are not accommodatable. To attempt to accommodate certain rivalries is regarded as inappropriate, and a person or group which consents to terminate such rivalries may lose "honor" or "face" or prestige by so doing. Perhaps the cardinal illustration in modern times is presented by those European nations which accommodated themselves to the Nazi régime in Germany. Through the forms of accommodation worked out with Germany, conventionally called the "appeasement" of Germany, these nations were able to avoid armed conflict or to reduce the severity of armed conflict with Germany. But many persons both within the appeasing nations and outside of them take the position that such appeasement, however practical or impractical it might have been, was dishonorable and should not have been attempted. The same principle is involved in more personal interaction. Suppose a husband discovers that another man is showing inappropriate attentions to his wife. Being a peace-loving and democratic gentleman, he decides to do nothing about the situation. He decides to practice the philosophy of "live and let live." In such a situation most persons would condemn the husband almost as much as the wife, since rivalries of this sort are regarded as "dishonorable." The issue must be sharply drawn and settled promptly, if the husband is to "save face" and maintain his status in the eyes of many conventional people.

The society also establishes and enforces organized means of accommodation for the purpose of settling certain types of rivalries which are regarded as undesirable, dangerous, or unnecessary. The court system, as we have seen, has this as one of its purposes. In more recent times the court system has been supplemented by other kinds of deliberative bodies such as strike mediation boards, price control panels, and various other federal and state boards and commissions. Less formally enforced societal pressures impinge upon the conflicts of ordinary people in the ordinary daily affairs of life. Thus, if two gentlemen disagree upon some basic matter and a rivalry develops, it is often considered "good form" not to gossip about it, to refrain from making an overt issue of it, and most assuredly not to enter into fistic combat concerning it. One may find himself in a rivalrous relationship with his neighbors because of the inconveniences involved in the perennial fights between the neighbor's dog and his own. Obviously, both have loyalties and both may have deeply injured pride, but the standards of etiquette are such that probably neither of the two men involved would want to make "too much" of an issue of these incidents. Each tolerates the intolerable situation because there is nothing else to do about it—if one wishes to remain a "gentleman."

The thoughtways of the culture also provide numerous *rationalizations* to support the ego of the person who has accommodated a rivalry. He would not "stoop" to such behavior as that of his opponent. It is "better to be a gentleman than to win" the issue. One must "see first things first" and "not jeopardize larger values to attain more minor ones." One should "live and let live." One has to "give and take." And so on and on.

## ASSIMILATION

Some competitions and conflicts tend, in time, to disappear. They may disappear because one side becomes overwhelmingly stronger than the others, and there is no longer any basis for effective rivalry. Or the persons and groups which make up one faction may decline in numbers, move away, or change their minds. The rivalries between native populations and immigrant groups frequently show a cycle of conflict resulting in the eventual disappearance of the basis for conflict, because in time, the differences which were the basis for conflict have disappeared. A third generation Pole or Swede or Slovac is no longer a Pole or Swede or a Slovac; he is an "American." He talks, acts, and thinks along the same lines as the native. Most people are no longer conscious of the matter of origins, and even the tell-tale names come to be almost wholly ignored.

It should be emphasized that all group distinctions do not disappear so soon or so completely. Some may even be accentuated with the passing of time. Thus, a third-generation German or Russian tends to be readily accepted in American society as an American—provided he is not also a Jew. In the latter case his Jewish group affiliation tends to persist, but for no really inherent reason. Groups merely fix on certain facts of difference, and this fixation tends to perpetuate certain differences while others shortly disappear. The long-run tendencies, of course, are for group differences within a society to be reduced through the diffusion of one group's traits into the other's, until eventually the differences have largely disappeared. Some religious differences seem to be among the most difficult to assimilate; the categories Protestant, Catholic and Jew are among our most persistent group antagonisms.

Assimilation may be defined, then, as the *gradual process whereby group and personal differences and rivalries tend to disappear*. Obviously some differences and rivalries disappear more slowly than others, and some may even be accentuated with the passing of time.

### *Forms of Assimilation*

It is possible to distinguish different kinds of assimilation. A person who has been socialized in one culture may later come in contact with another culture. Through interaction with people in the second culture, he gradually, but seldom wholly, becomes assimilated into it. If the cultures are not too dissimilar and the prejudice patterns not too sharp, this may be accomplished in a relatively short period. But otherwise an entire lifetime may pass with the personality still "marginal," that is, having traits and characteristics from both of the cultures, sometimes in marked conflict with one another.

Two cultures may merge into a third culture which has aspects of both, but is still somewhat distinct. At one time in the United States rural and urban societies were rather radically different in a number of respects. Such factors as isolation, the nature of the farming industry, and of rural institutions made for a personality type rather conspicuously different from that of the more cosmopolitan and secular urbanite. These differences have now largely disappeared in many parts of the United States. Farm homes contain the same paraphernalia as city homes. Farm and urban people participate in the same recreational patterns, and many close friendships cut cross the old somewhat sharp rural-urban lines. While the differences have not been entirely eliminated, they have certainly been remarkably reduced.

Assimilation may occur, also, in small groups—even the pair group consisting of mates. Dissimilar patterns of overt behavior and ideas often tend in time to disappear. As the persons interact, each becomes acquainted with the other's behavior and consciously or unconsciously often tends to conform more closely to the other. This does not preclude, of course, the appearance of new differences which may appear simultaneously in the new interaction.

*The Marginal Man*

The assimilation of a person into a culture other than the one in which he was originally socialized requires considerable time and may, in fact, never be completed within an individual's lifetime. For a considerable period the person's behavior is usually an admixture of the two cultures to which he has been exposed. He is thus said to be a *marginal man.* This condition of marginality has received the attention of sociologists and social psychologists for some time. The marginal man, because he has been partially socialized by each of two cultures, does not fit very well into either culture. The extent and seriousness of his idiosyncracies depend in part, of course, upon the particular kind of cultures involved. If the ideologies and overt behavior patterns of the two are greatly dissimilar or in direct conflict with one another, his problems of adjustment would tend to be more severe. If, on the other hand, the cultures in question differ only in superficial details, the fact of marginality may present no serious problems of adjustment.

The marginal man experiences *two kinds of difficulties.* One group of problems are *subjective.* He frequently finds it difficult to reconcile the opposing ideas and contradictory ways of the two cultures. One student of the process writes at length about how the marginal man is "poised in psychological uncertainty" between two cultures, not knowing which one is to be followed at the points where the two conflict. His condition is further complicated by the *objective problems of social rejection.* Neither group feels that the person quite "belongs" to it. The result is that the marginal man loses his security in the original group from which he has grown away and has not yet secured acceptance and security in the new group whose culture he has perhaps not yet fully mastered, understood, or accepted. Large numbers of marginal men are found among (1) the second-generation immigrant group, (2) American-born and American-reared Japanese, and (3) Jews who do not observe the traditions of the traditional Jewish religion. To a lesser extent the person of rural origins who moves to the city as an adult, or the native urban dweller who takes up residence in a rural community, represent mild forms of marginality. Similarly the person of humble family background who marries into a wealthy social group or for some other reason makes a radical change in his position in the social hierarchy also illustrates marginality. Thus, we see that there are all degrees of marginality found in a society such as ours in which there are numerous somewhat distinct cultural streams.

## SUMMARY

Differences in the needs and values of the persons and groups which make up a society frequently give rise to a form of rivalrous interaction which is less well controlled by the society than is competition. This relatively unrestrained rivalry is called conflict. Numerous rivalries in society have characteristics both of competition and of conflict and are, therefore, somewhat difficult to classify categorically. This should not becloud the fact that there are still two quite distinct rivalrous interaction patterns; the one which is worked out more or less clearly within rules and the other which is expressed outside such regulation. At the present time in American society it would be difficult to classify the rivalries between capital and labor, business and government, white and colored peoples, traditional and liberal religion, as either competitions or conflicts, because they have attributes of both.

Some rivalries eventually become accommodated, that is, rivalrous interaction ceases for the time being, either because some person or group has secured the "upper hand" but has not won a clear-cut victory, or because the rivals conclude that the rivalry is too destructive, unnecessary, or for some other reason should be terminated. This gives rise to a number of forms of accommodation such as truces, compromises, temporary subordination-superordination arrangements, arbitration, or toleration, as well as other forms which we have not discussed here. The prevailing ideologies exert a great influence upon the extent and kind of accommodation which the persons and groups in a society will utilize. Cultural values also largely determine which rivalries are accommodatable without losing face or honor. Sometimes the society sets up and enforces adherence to such accommodation agencies as courts, arbitration boards, and the like. Also the thoughtways and language clichés of the society assist the accommodating groups to rationalize the cessation of a rivalry.

Some differences among persons and groups tend to disappear in time and are said to have become assimilated. Other rivalries persist over long periods. During the period before which assimilation becomes complete, the person being assimilated may go through a period of marginality during which time he belongs wholly to neither culture, either by his own acceptance or by the acceptance of him in the groups concerned. Thus, the marginal man has both subjective and objective difficulties. Marginality may last for the major part of a lifetime, and in some cases persons belonging to minority groups may go through several generations of marginality before assimilation becomes final.

It is well for the student to bear in mind that terms like *compe-*

*tition, coöperation, assimilation,* and *accommodation* are, after all, highly abstract language usages. As ideas or concepts they have validity and utility for the analysis of the interaction of human beings and groups. But the generality of these terms tends to minimize the actual variations found in the interactions which one observes in specific situations. For example "competition" for grades in a college course, "competition" in a football game and "competition" in winning a court case may all seem to be "the same" in an abstract sense, but the actual behavior involved in each individual instance may be greatly dissimilar. It should be recalled that under each of these interaction types we have discussed a number of subtypes. Even these are somewhat generalized concepts, but are much more realistic and specific than the four major types which have been treated in this and the preceding chapter. It is well for the student who has not yet become accustomed to thinking about human behavior in such abstract terms, to strive to keep the general type and specific sub-type as distinct as possible in his thinking. At best, the study of social interaction requires a high level of abstract thinking. It is nevertheless an important aspect of the study of human behavior.

## SUGGESTED READINGS

DANHOF, Ralph, "The Accommodation and Integration of Conflicting Cultures in a Newly Established Community," *American Journal of Sociology,* XLIX, pp. 14-23. **AB**

A study of Boulder City, Nevada, a community formed in consequence of the Boulder Dam Project. The hypothesis suggests that conflict patterns may not so much tend to disappear as to become institutionalized as time passes.

NISBET, R. A., "The Coming Problem of Assimilation," *American Journal of Sociology,* L, pp. 261-270. **AB**

Pointed comment on the "strain of transition from the Army to civilian life." The author expects the adjustment to be most difficult for those who entered the services "during adolescence." A good statement of the cultural contrasts of Army and civilian rôle.

PARK, R. E., "Human Migration and the Marginal Man," *American Journal of Sociology,* Vol. 38, pp. 891-893. **A**

Discusses the relationship between mobility and the personality "type" of the secularized marginal man. Suggests the hypothesis that marginality is a psychological by-product of migration.

RAPPORT, V. A., "Conflict in a New England College Town." *Social Forces,* XVII, pp. 527-32. **AB**

Patterns of intergroup conflict in terms of (1) group self-consciousness, (2) hyper-organization, (3) propaganda and rumor, and (4) the confusion of actual and assigned reasons for the conflict.

STONEQUIST, E. H., *The Marginal Man* (New York, Charles Scribner's Sons, 1937). **A**

A well-known volume dealing with the historical and social-psychological aspects of the persons with multi-cultural participations.

## STUDY QUESTIONS

1. How may conflict grow out of competition? *Vice versa*?
2. Why is violence "not the essence of conflict?" Illustrate.
3. Why is it often difficult to distinguish between competition and conflict? Illustrate.
4. Why may accommodation be regarded as a form of coöperation?
5. Describe five common forms of accommodation? How does the problem situation involved determine the form of accommodation? Will this vary from society to society? What, then, do you conclude from this?
6. How does the culture of a society determine the forms of accommodation usually adopted? Give examples.
7. How do assimilation and accommodation differ?
8. What conditions are necessary before assimilation occurs?
9. How is diffusion similar to assimilation? Illustrate.
10. How is the "marginal man" a result of incomplete assimilation? Explain.
11. Why does the marginal man have both subjective and objective problems? Illustrate.
12. Why do some kinds of marginal men take longer to assimilate than others? Explain and illustrate.
13. Give some examples of accommodations which "broke down" and gave rise to renewed conflict?
14. Is there any real limit to the duration of a given accommodation?

# Chapter XXX

## SOCIAL PROBLEMS AND SOCIAL VALUATION

Certain societal conditions such as crime, poverty, juvenile delinquency, prostitution, the high auto accident rate, and unemployment are usually regarded as undesirable and are usually termed loosely as "societal problems" or "social problems." From superficial observation it seems obvious to many that these conditions are problems of "society" because the solution of them is often beyond the control of any one person or group. Either prevention or amelioration of these conditions seems to require some sort of collective societal action. But as one delves further into these social problem phenomena, he encounters numerous fundamental theoretical as well as practical difficulties which seem rarely if ever to have occurred to many observers and commentators.

### WHAT IS A SOCIAL PROBLEM?

*Undesirability Depends on Values*

Suppose we begin with the elementary supposition that a social problem is an undesirable social condition. What makes it undesirable? If it is undesirable because it is harmful, what are the criteria of harmfulness? Immediately one finds himself in the realm of values. Under a democratic value system, for example, the caste-like position of the segregated and underprivileged American Negro is often regarded as harmful or at least undesirable, because it runs contrary to the democratic ideal of "equality regardless of color, race, or creed." In a caste society, on the other hand, segregation and discrimination constitute quite normal and equitable aspects of society, not problems at all.

Moreover, it is important to note that a given societal condition *may be harmful to one class or group, but have no direct or discernible harmful effect on another class* of people. For a period of twenty years following World War I, for example, American agriculture and the people dependent directly upon agriculture experienced a long depression as a result of the disparity between agricultural and non-agricultural prices. This meant that farmers were, in effect, being discriminated against. They had to sell the goods they produced largely in a free market, whereas they had to buy goods on a tariff-protected and otherwise artificially-controlled market. Agricultural economists disagreed only slightly as to the *extent* of this differential, all agreed that it was considerable and that it was grossly unfair. The great mass of urban dwellers, however, seemed not to recognize during these years that there was any agricultural problem, other than having to listen to the recurrent protest of farm groups. Urban dwellers did not define the condition as harmful to the general welfare, and seemed quite willing to continue indefinitely to enjoy the benefits of abnormally low agricultural prices. One might properly doubt whether the agricultural price condition just described was a social problem at all to the rank and file of Americans, however much discrimination and poverty it caused for agricultural people. Many other societal conditions present the same difficulty; they affect certain groups in the society adversely, but the rest of the society either do not know about the condition or do not regard it as a problem condition either to themselves or to others.

### *Rationalization*

Harmfulness of societal conditions alone seems not to constitute a social problem condition. Sometimes *harmful conditions are rationalized as inevitable or as indirectly beneficial.* "The poor you shall always have with you," has frequently been quoted in a context suggesting that society not concern itself unduly with the poor, because poverty is presumably inevitable anyway. In the past perhaps more than at present, theologians have frequently rationalized painful or harmful conditions as punishment meted out by a just and angry Deity for people's wilful infractions of Divine decree.

Human suffering has, moreover, often been rationalized as indirectly "good for the people, because it builds character, fortitude, and appreciation of spiritual values."

From these illustrations it becomes apparent that a clear-cut definition of social problems in terms of harmfulness is exceedingly difficult. It seems necessary, then, to consider some other formulations of social problems theory. Not only will such an effort serve better to define the varying conceptions of social problems, but should add appreciably to one's understanding of the social problems themselves.

### *Social Problems Have Been Defined in Terms of a Clash of Values Within a Society*

The history of human kind provides innumerable illustrations of harmful and even deplorable conditions which have been accepted by persons living under them either as inevitable aspects of human life or even as desirable. Slavery, poverty, death from preventable causes, famine, racial discrimination, caste exploitation of the underprivileged, and war have for most of man's history constituted quite acceptable forms and products of human living. In our generation, however, each of these conditions is under discussion, not to say attack. They are no longer accepted either as inevitable or defensible by many people. Much attention is centered around the prevention and treatment of these and other similar conditions. In short, the conditions mentioned above are "problems" in this era of man's history, because *man has now acquired values and ideas which are contrary to such conditions.*

Perhaps the chief value which modern man espouses is the *ideology of rational control of society.* Man has traditionally tended to accept the inevitability of his social world as he found it, but modern man, in Western civilization at least, has rebelled against such complete acquiescence to the tyranny of custom. He possesses what has been called "the planning ideology." The generic use of such expressions as "modern man" is not, of course, wholly accurate. *Some* modern men in Western civilization possess the planning ideology, and there are enough of such to make a concerted and consistent impact of effort in the direction of rational modification of many parts of the social structure. Thus, in America we have groups working to remove racial discrimination, if not also racial

prejudice. In most of the modern nations there are groups working in the direction of eliminating war. And so with our conditions which are called the "problem areas" of modern social life. In fact, it is the efforts of these groups and the counter efforts of their opponents which make certain areas of modern life problem areas. Probably no condition, however intolerable one might think it is, is a self-evident social problem; the problem aspect inheres in the fact of value conflict, not in the deplorable condition per se.

*Value conflict may center around several different phases of a social problem.* (1) Sometimes the clash of values relates to the issue *whether or not a problem really exists.* During the period of Northern agitation against slavery in the South, many Southern spokesmen repeatedly insisted that slavery constituted no problem either to the slave or to the free white in the South, but that instead a problem was rapidly being created by the "agitation" of Northern reformers. At this stage the issue was one of disagreement over whether or not the condition of slavery was a harmful condition and, if so, to whom was it detrimental? Most social problems go through this stage of definition or formulation before any consideration of what ought to be done about the condition can, of course, be considered.

(2) Once a consensus (not necessarily a majority view) that an undesirable condition exists has emerged, the value clash shifts to a consideration of *which of several alternative solutions is the most desirable course of action.* Not infrequently persons and groups take the position that "of course" some social condition is harmful, but that nothing can be done about it effectively because the problem is "too big" or it "inheres in human nature" or it would "be made worse" by efforts to attack it directly. Sometimes the proponents of this view are, of course, sincerely of the opinion stated, but there is also evidence that the difficulties of successful attack on some social problems have been exaggerated by certain persons and groups in order to discourage or delay efforts to improve the conditions. Owners of real estate in slum areas, for example, have been known to exaggerate the difficulties of constructing better housing, because some of them, at least, have considered it to their financial interest to keep the slums. In other words, if the argument could be shifted from discussion of the seriousness of the problem to the magnification of the difficulties of solving the problem, the

same end would be attained, namely inaction. Thus the opponent of reform would remain, in the eyes of some people at least, as a person who is not insensitive to the plight of the slum dweller. Such insincerity is not uncommon.

But even among those who sincerely wish the problem attacked and solved, sharp disagreement concerning means of attaining this objective are possible, in fact, probable. Frequently, this involves values, too. Many persons will admit, for example, that the large-scale consumption of alcoholic beverages particularly by the "heavy drinker" is an undesirable condition. It can easily be demonstrated, for example, that health problems, child support problems, auto accidents, work inefficiency, and similar results affecting other people follow excessive drinking. There would, moreover, be little disagreement that these conditions were harmful. But what should be done? Is a return of prohibition warranted? Some think so. Should there be restrictions on the hours and quantities of alcoholic beverages which should be sold in public places? Some people think that the only real solution is one of "education." Whatever social problem one chooses to consider, disagreements concerning ways and means are numerous, and much discussion is usually required before there develops a sufficient consensus so that some one course of action can be launched.

### *Solutions Also Need Evaluation*

It should not be overlooked that so-called solutions to social problems also constitute or bring about conditions other than those which they are supposed to remedy. For example, it has been suggested that the auto accident rate could be materially reduced by requiring each automobile to be equipped with a governor which would prevent the car from being driven faster than forty-five miles per hour. Assuming for the moment that this would materially reduce casualties from auto accidents, it is clear also that such a policy would make basic alterations and inconveniences in the personal habits of many people. The time consumed, on long trips especially, would be appreciably increased. For high-salaried persons whose time is valuable, this would constitute a material economic loss. Moreover, the automobile industry for many years has been concentrating on the production of more speedy automobiles. If a maximum speed of forty-five miles per hour were put into effect, the "progress" of many years of research and engineering would be wasted and competing industries in the automobile field would be obliged to find new bases for competition. Moreover, speed has an intangible psychological value to some people. Living as we do in a rapid moving cultural configuration, time saving has become a value in itself. Many persons would feel greatly deprived if forced to travel at reduced auto speeds. It is not intended in raising these questions either to favor or to oppose the speed limitation proposal, but rather to point out that there are always by-products to solutions to undesirable conditions. This fact serves often as a deterrent to the introduction of some specific solution and, of course, multiplies the possibilities for value disagreement among the advocates of the several alternatives designed to solve or ameliorate the social problem.

### *Amelioration* versus *Elimination*

There is room, also, for sharp value disagreement concerning whether an undesirable condition should or can be eliminated completely or whether its harmful effects should or can only be ameliorated somewhat. Thus while many persons and groups oppose slum clearance projects to provide reasonably modern housing for low-income groups, these same persons may favor assisting individual slum dwellers who have personal problems which arise from poor housing. Thus, some persons will approve and even contribute to free clinics for the treatment of the health needs of slum dwelling people, but will oppose the abolition of the slums which produce the bad health through crowding, lack of sanitation facilities, bad ventilation, and the other unfortunate concomitants of life in the slum areas.

The emphasis upon amelioration rather than upon basic solution of causative conditions has been justified on the ground that amelioration is immediate, whereas fundamental solutions usually require considerable time to be worked out. This logic is no doubt valid, as stated, but the history of purposive social change in America at least shows that ameliorative programs instead of being used only as temporary expedients *may* often become permanent programs instead. Thus, the sources of undesirable social conditions may remain unmodified long after it is possible to control or eliminate them.

### *Causes of Social Problems Often Unknown or Uncontrollable*

It should not be inferred from the foregoing that all of what are popularly called "causes" of social problems are either known or, at the existing state of our knowledge, controllable. Careful students of social problems tend not to think in terms of "causes" the way popular writers and laymen so often do. *Cause* is a slippery concept when used in regard to social phenomena, and even the most careful students of social problems have made serious errors in cause-and-effect thinking. The difficulties arise from several facts. First, what are called "causes" are themselves effects of other causes, and thus one must go far back of a given condition to understand its *chain of cause and effect.* Control, moreover, is not easy even if causes be known, because the *given cause usually has numerous effects,* some desirable and others undesirable. Finally, most social problems are the result, so far as can now be determined, of *many causes, not of one.* To single out some one or a few from among the multiple causes, is a common and serious error.

### *Should Social Problems Be Determined by the Sociologist or by Society?*

We have just discussed one conception of social problems, namely, the idea that the social problems of a society originate from the value clashes of the various groups in the society. This conception of the matter is not the only one current among sociologists. Some regard social problems as those conditions which are defined as problems by the expert in social analysis, the social scientist, whether economist, political scientist, or sociologist. The logic of this point of view is, however, better than its practicality. Proponents of this view make a good case by analogy. They argue that, for example, one takes the advice of the physician, not the garbage collector, when questions of health are at stake. When one wants legal advice he secures the counsel of an attorney, not a baseball player. He has his automobile checked and repaired, if necessary, by a specialist in auto mechanics, not by a pharmacist. Why not then, be consistent, and utilize the social scientist similarly? Why not give him the responsibility for determining what social conditions are healthful and beneficial, which ones are to be regarded as pathological, and therefore, requiring special attention? On the surface this logic seems convincing but the analogy, like so many analogies, does not stand the test of more careful scrutiny. The physician, for example, is the authority on health matters, *but his authoritative position does not result directly from his competence. It exists rather from his acceptance as an authority.* The people of no society appear as yet to be willing to entrust to any group of experts the sole or even major responsibility for determining *in the social realm* what is good and bad, and what is to be done about it. It is possible that the time may come when the expert social scientist may be permitted to exercise his competence in this way, but at present that time seems remote. The prevailing position taken by people with respect to social problems is that they know what they want, their major difficulty being that of convincing others to accept their point of view, and finding capable leadership to implement that point of view. Only to a limited extent is the social scientist's counsel sought and even when it is, his advice rarely goes beyond some very circumscribed project.

Considerable use is, of course, currently being made of the service of social scientists by the federal and state governments. Opposition to this practice is prevalent and strong. Not many persons and groups appear really to want an objective appraisal of social conditions from the point of view of the *general welfare.* What they appear to want instead is partisanship, that is, representatives in government who will champion a specific point of view as if it were self-evident that the point of view espoused were the only sound one. Thus the determination of fair wage rates is certainly a social problem, however one wishes to define social problems, but neither labor groups nor employer groups appear *really* to want, or to respect the judgment or even the findings of a *disinterested* expert who sees the wage problem from the point of view of the general public interest of which both workers and employers are a part. Instead both sides use their power positions directly or indirectly in an effort to solve the problem in whatever way they regard as most conducive to their own interests. And so it is with other social problems. Public thinking has not yet, and may never, accept the point of view that the expert analyst of social problems is to have the responsibility for determining what the problems are, or for charting the course of action which should be taken to correct or ameliorate the objectionable conditions.

The foregoing is not to be construed as meaning that social science experts are entirely ineffectual in the practical treatment of social problems. There are probably practical effects which result from their research and judgment, but these effects are largely *indirect*. Most social scientists are affiliated with the teaching staffs of the leading American colleges and universities. In the exercise of their normal duties they teach classes dealing with social problems varying from the care of the physically handicapped to the control of public utilities. They also write articles and books and are in considerable demand as lecturers and consultants to various practical action projects. Thus, the students in their classes formulate attitudes and values under the guidance of the professional students of society. Meanwhile the findings and judgments of social scientists also get into the general stream of public discussion through their writings and speeches. It is impossible to determine precisely how effective these indirect influences are, but it appears probable that they have at least some influence both upon public consciousness of social problems and popular consideration of possible solutions. But the influence cannot be calculated precisely.

Probably the most serious weakness of the social problems expert is also his greatest strength. Most careful scholars studying social problems follow the dictates of scientific inquiry, namely objectivity, caution in reaching conclusions, and the critical retesting of facts before final conclusions are reached. However important these attributes may be from the scientific point of view, they constitute impediments in the practical situation. The findings of social scientists are usually not partisan enough to capture any group's enthusiasm; they are usually not dogmatic enough to give quick conclusions and simple recipes for action, nor are they usually dramatic enough to capture the popular mind. Thus the charlatans, or the pseudo-scientists, or the opportunitistic politicians with their simple clichés and dramatic oversimplifications of the facts usually have an initial advantage in winning popular support or popular antagonism to some program or proposal which serves the interest of some special group. The initial advantage, however, in the long run especially, can not always be retained. The expert in his usually cautious, undramatic, and objective manner does convince some people, and the various competing and extremist quacks sometimes neutralize each other, thus providing the opportunity for the findings and recommendations of the expert to receive consideration and sometimes, even, to become the basis for action.

*The Two Views of Social Problems Are Not Inconsistent*

It may already be apparent from the foregoing discussion that there is much truth both in the notion that social problems are defined by the society and in the notion that they are defined by the expert. Neither view appears in the actual situation to be wholly correct or wholly incorrect. Fundamentally, of course, there can be no problem until there is an awareness that a certain condition is undesirable. Nor is there likely to be a problem for long if there is complete agreement on the values involved. The essence of the problem condition is conflict or clash of different groups with different values, out of which conflict may result solutions or attempted solutions or inactivity. Thus far, then, we may appear to have accepted the school of thought which defines social problems from the clash of social values. But one of the interest groups whose values appear in the total situation is the group of social science experts who possess certain power and influence by virtue of their positions as teachers, writers, speakers, and consultants. Although they cannot dominate the discussion or the conclusion, they can and have sometimes significantly influenced it. The immediate issue which seems to face democratic societies like America is not whether we are to turn over the analysis and treatment of the social problems to the social problems experts, but rather whether the findings and the judgments of the social problems experts are to be given a more or a less prominent place in the whole discussion of social problems. The experts will have some influence so long as American education remains at least partially free, but in the immediate future the amount and kind of audience which will be given to the expert is problematical. Some would have the expert politely, or impolitely, ignored, leaving the evaluation and solution of social problems largely to the partisans representing this or that special interest group and each with, therefore, his special axe to grind. Other persons, however, are becoming increasingly conscious of the existence of a "general interest" or "the public good" or the "general welfare," and seem increasingly to be insisting that public councils should include the best informed and objective as well as the least informed and most partisan persons.

## SOME BASIC UNDERSTANDINGS CONCERNING SOCIAL PROBLEMS

While it is not the purpose of this chapter to enter into a discussion of specific social problems such as crime or unemployment or the housing shortage, it is still possible to present certain discoveries and observations concerning social problems in general. Some of these understandings have already been explained in this and other chapters and need, therefore, only to be reviewed.

### 1. *Social Problems Result from Differences in Value Judgment*

A given condition is a "problem" only when it has come to be regarded as a problem. Before it is defined, no matter how demonstrably harmful it may be, it is not a problem to the persons who have not yet become aware of it. Others may think it a problem but that fact, unless and until diffused to the persons involved, does not make it a problem *to them.* To illustrate. Many authorities on human behavior are currently concerned with what they call a "mental hygiene problem" in the United States. It is evidenced by such conditions as the high Selective Service rejections of young men with various kinds of mental-emotional personality deviations, and the large number of army discharges for the same reasons. At one time early in the war, before the American armies had encountered any appreciable amount of combat on a large scale, medical discharges from the army for mental hygiene reasons alone ran over 30,000 men per month. Selective Service rejections in addition, of course, ran much higher than this. Furthermore, it should be noted, that men above and below draft age and all women are excluded from these figures. It is impossible and probably unnecessary to review all of the evidence here, but the fact of an appalling amount of human unhappiness and inefficiency due to mental-emotional disturbances is obvious. It is obvious, that is, to the person acquainted with the facts. It appears not to be obvious to the rank and file of American people in whose hands the decision ultimately rests whether or not anything effective is done to reduce this appalling waste and toll of human efficiency and happiness. It appears doubtful whether one may yet say that this condition is "a problem" in the minds of the rank and file in the same sense that housing, the auto accident rate, or the cancer death rate is a problem to them. On the basis of the evidence we now have, the actual danger of harmful effects to the average person may be greater from the mental hygiene problem than from the auto accident problem, the cancer problem, or the housing problem. So long as present apathy remains it is doubtful whether practical, effective treatment of this mental hygiene condition can be expected. In the realistic sense, then, there is a condition which a few informed people know to be deplorable, but it is no "problem" to the majority.

2. *A Given Social Problem Usually Has Many Causes, Not Only One*

Since this point has been previously made, we shall limit ourselves to a brief illustration. The mental hygiene condition just mentioned springs from many known causes and probably from some which are not yet known. The nature of family life, certain school procedures, employment practices, uncorrected physical defects, are only a few of the many known causes. Likewise, the auto accident rate which currently results in around 40,000 deaths in the United States per year results from many causes, such as high speed, poor driving habits, poor roadways, mechanical defects in automobiles, intoxication, confused traffic laws, inadequate policing, to mention but a few. In formulating practical reforms it is sometimes necessary largely to concentrate on *certain* causes and disregard others in order to get started on *some* course of action. The danger lies, however, in the unconscious overlooking of the principle of *multifactor causation* and proceding as if the matter were entirely in hand, when in reality only one small part actually is.

3. *Solutions Have Multiple Effects*

Rarely can solutions to social problems be restricted so that they affect only the condition for which they were designed. Instead they ramify in many subtle and sometimes exasperating ways. When America tried the prohibition experiment just after World War I, few persons, even the opponents of prohibition, realized that this "noble experiment" would give rise to the large and powerful pattern of organized criminal practice which it did. Nor could many have envisaged the extent to which this organized system of law violation would infiltrate into the ranks of law enforcement officers, thus bringing about one of the most scandalous and degenerate periods of law enforcement in American history.

This principle of multiple effects of social action has sometimes been misused by the opponents of some social reform. It has become a common opposition technique to exaggerate the detrimental by-products of the proposal for change. There exists, of course, always the inescapable problem of balancing benefits against detriments in appraising any social condition or proposal for change. Fundamentally, this again involves values. In fact, judgments of benefits themselves are values, and are subject to the same wide variations among persons and groups which we have so often discussed in previous chapters. This inescapable problem of evaluation even further complicates the practical treatment of problems.

4. *Social Problems Are Closely Interrelated with Social Change*

It has sometimes been alleged simply that "social problems grow out of social change." While this is undoubtedly somewhat true, it is an oversimplification of a much more complex relationship. While problems do grow out of social change, they also create social change. This is most readily illustrated when one considers that modern society often "does something" about its social problems. These *solutions constitute social change.* When the Congress passes a law for the purpose of correcting some undesirable social condition, the provisions of that law eventually become part of the organization and structure of the society, and change the society from what it was before the law was passed. Social change also may terminate or reduce social problems while at the same time creating new ones.

5. *Social Problems Affect a Society Differentially*

The so-called "harmful" effects of a social problem do not always, or even often, affect all of the people in a society in the same way. Earlier in the chapter mention was made of the price disparity suffered by American agricultural people at least since the end of World War I. While this condition was obviously harmful to farmers as an income group, and was probably unjust on ethical grounds, it served as a temporary benefit to the urban buyers of agricultural produce who enjoyed the privilege of somewhat lower prices than would have obtained if farm prices had been on a parity with non-farm prices. Modern society, moreover, contains numerous examples of *exploitation,* of which child labor is a case in point. Since in general children's wage rates are lower than adult's wage rates for the same quality and quantity of work done, the employer of child labor has an advantage over the employer of adult labor with whom he has to compete. If the prices of the two industries are the same, then the employer of child labor has a greater margin of profit. If the employer of child labor sells at a lower price, he will secure a larger share of the market, and will probably eventually force the employer of adult labor to reduce his price and, therefore, his profit. Whatever condition finally results, the employer of child labor profits unduly from the practice as compared to his competitors who do not employ children. The same principle holds true for the employment of women and the employment of Negroes, the wage rates of both being somewhat below the wage rates for white men doing the same quality and quantity of work. Moreover, the problem of unemployment is a far more stark reality to working-class members than to business-class members of the society. True, in time of depression, members of the executive, managerial, and professional groups usually have their incomes sharply curtailed, and may in some cases be completely unemployed, *but on the whole*, they are still well above the subsistence level in income, and even if completely unemployed very probably have access to reserves built up during better times. There are, of course, individual exceptions, but taken as a group the above generalizations are applicable. Housing currently presents another example of the same phenomenon. As this is being written the nation is experiencing a critical housing shortage. Yet there are thousands of houses being offered for sale. These, however, can be bought only by the person who can afford to pay for them. The housing shortage does not affect everyone equally; it affects people differentially, the persons of little or limited means really being the ones "unable" to find a home. Many other examples of class and group differences in social problem effects can easily be observed. This condition is related, of course, to the unwillingness, often, of certain groups to permit problems to be attacked and the efforts of some groups to delay action on social problems as long as possible.

### 6. *Social Problems Are Usually Interrelated with One Another*

Social problems do not exist in the air-tight compartments in which they are frequently discussed, especially by laymen. Many times a given condition can quite as logically be regarded as an aspect of one social problem as of another. For example, is the problem of child labor an aspect of the "labor problem," of the "home problem," of the "school problem," of the "youth problem"? Obviously it is related to all four and possibly also to others. Moreover, social problems sometimes reinforce the effects of one another. For example, divorce is frequently regarded as a social problem. (This way of looking at divorce may or may not be realistic, but we shall assume for the sake of discussion that divorce is a social problem.) The high divorce rate is a result of many conditions, among them the emancipation of women from many traditional home duties, careers and outside employment for married women, and the decline of the patriarchal authority. Each of these conditions also has other problem aspects as we have already seen in the chapter on the family. Moreover, divorce creates still other problems such as that of providing a somewhat near normal family life for the children of divorced parents.

### 7. *Social Problems May Arise from or Be Increased by Generally Desirable Social Change*

Most persons would grant that the emergence of women as persons with comparable freedom to men has constituted a desirable social change. Women are now free to acquire an education, provide for their own livelihood, follow careers of their own choosing, and participate in many recreational practices formerly tabooed to them. But the emancipation of women has also created problems, such as the inequities between men's and women's wage rates and tensions between husbands and wives resulting from differing conceptions of the nature, extent, and implications of women's emancipation. Many women are attempting both marriage and a career, and not a few are failing in the double duty of careerist and parent. The children of some employed women are receiving sub-standard family life and their first introduction to juvenile delinquency. Mechanical inventions such as the automobile have also brought "mixed blessings." While the auto has made it easier for the family to spend a pleasant week-end in the country, it has also made it possible for criminals better to elude the law enforcement officers because of the quick and anonymous character of auto transportation.

### 8. *Individual Persons Often Cannot by Their Own Efforts Escape the Influence of Some Social Problems*

The effects of certain social problems are among the chief risks or hazards of modern societal living. However wealthy or virtuous the separate human being may be, he is still practically powerless to protect himself or his children from all of the impacts of the many social problems such as auto accidents, epidemics of disease, and the changing social rôles of women or children, to mention only a few. Whether he realizes it or not, and regardless of whether he approves of it, the fact remains that the modern human is so interdependent with others that it is practically impossible to insulate himself, so to speak, from social influences or to protect himself from many of the collective hazards. This is one of the most convincing arguments for collective control of social problems.

## ARE WE HYPERCONSCIOUS OF SOCIAL PROBLEMS?

It has been suggested that contemporary America is "hypersensitive" concerning its social problems. Many of the conditions which are currently being decried and for which large-scale solutions are being sought, are said to be problems which have always existed. "After all, some men have always been unemployed, some families always broken, some people always poor, some children always born out of wedlock, someone always violating law, and someone always being in some way disprivileged, exploited, or discriminated against." "All that is new and different," say the complacent ones, "is the form which these personal misfortunes take and the big play which they are given by the sentimentalists."

It is altogether possible that part of the difference between past and present may lie in the changed consciousness of social trouble areas. At present many persons are less willing than their ancestors were to accept human suffering or inefficiency or discrimination as inevitable. Gradually man has learned that he need not accept the inevitability of any particular social system or any part of it. Particularly in a democratic society, there is a growing consciousness of power on the part of many disprivileged persons and groups, and they propose to use this latent power in an effort to remove or at least to ameliorate those conditions which seem not conducive to their welfare. Thus, perhaps there may be some truth in the hyperconsciousness thesis.

But the modern world is to a considerable extent a new world. The web of interdependence has become almost a maze instead. As we have seen in the chapter on personal inadequacy, many persons get lost in the maze. The modern world is also new in its impersonality. Some of the prototypes of modern social problems did exist in the past, but their effects were somewhat ameliorated by the mutual aid practices of the primary group society of that time. With the decline of primary groups, one is forced to utilize secondary groups with their impersonal power tactics in his struggle for existence. "Less than a living wage" means something very different to the man in modern society where the relations between employer and employee are impersonal and where almost every item of life has a pecuniary value.

Moreover, there exists clear statistical evidence that the actual number of persons affected by at least some modern social problems has appreciably increased. Crime is more prevalent, divorce is more frequent, more children face juvenile court judges, more persons are permanently unemployable because they lack the physical or mental abilities required in order to meet modern societal demands of minimum adequacy.

The above paragraphs are not intended to convey the impression that modern life is necessarily inferior because it is different. It is only meant to document the fact that the accelerated rate of social change, the existence of great personal insecurities, and the rise of new values have made the modern world the kind of world in which the existence of many and serious social problems are normal and critical aspects of human life. To minimize either the normalcy or the criticalness of these social problems is to be naïve and unrealistic about the kind of a world in which we are living.

## SUMMARY

We began this chapter with the formulation of a working definition of the concept *social problem*. A social problem is a social condition over which there is a disagreement concerning desirability. Different groups are usually differentially affected by, and related to, a given social condition, and hence a clash of value judgment regarding the condition gives evidence of the existence of the social problem through popular discussion.

Badness, seriousness, and harmfulness of social conditions are matters of definition and judgment, and hence there is often a clash of values on the question whether a given condition is a problem condition at all, and, if so, which among several alternatives is the proper course of action with respect to it. Democratic values and the planning ideology seem to have strongly affected the thinking about social problems in America and other nations of similar culture.

In the process of making the members of a society aware of the existence and seriousness of a social burden, the social scientist may play an indirect part. Being a scientist, he does not usually enter vigorously into the realm of advocacy, but rather tends to play his rôle in terms of research and the diffusion of his findings through teaching, speaking, writing, and more recently, consultant work. Some persons, including some social scientists themselves, think this to be a mistake, and the immediate future may show a somewhat different rôle characteristically played by those in the field of social science.

Social problems have been the object of much sociological and other social scientific research. From these researches we have learned that:

1. Social problems consist of those social conditions which the current values so define, and are often not inherently problems at all;
2. Social problems usually have many causes, insofar as causes can be determined;
3. Solutions or adjustments to social problems also have many ramified effects, often being unpredictable at the time the solution is introduced;
4. Social problems are closely interrelated with social change, some of them resulting from social change, others bringing about social change, and social change resulting, sometimes, in the elimination or reduction of social problems;
5. Social problems affect the various groups and classes of a society differentially, some problems being in reality class problems which are made into general problems by the efforts to secure solutions to them;
6. Social problems are usually interrelated with one another, aggravating the severity of one another, and sometimes apparently "causing" one another;
7. Social problems may arise from social controls (laws) which are evaluated as good, on the whole, but have undesirable concomitants or by-products;

8. Individual persons by their own efforts cannot often protect themselves from the influence of social problems, all persons being more or less "in it together" in many cases.

It has been suggested that perhaps modern man is hypersensitive regarding his collective social conditions, that social problems may be made to appear more numerous and more severe than they "really are," and that modern social problems have had counterparts in past societies when less attention was given them. Probably modern man is somewhat more conscious of trouble areas in modern society now that he has the democratic ideal and the knowledge of the power to control social life. He probably is less willing to accept all existing sets of conditions as his unalterable destiny. In addition, considerable objective evidence exists to support the idea that many social problems are increasing in respect to the number of persons affected, and probably also in the severity of the effects. It seems not to follow from this, however, that modern life is per se less good than the past; it is instead only a different kind of world, a kind of world in which change is rapid, great personal insecurities are common, and new values about collective living make for a more dynamic approach to the conditions of life. It is quite as tenable that these characteristics may make the modern world a "better" one rather than a "worse" one. Many believe that a society which espouses democracy, as we do, should not long tolerate many of the conditions which we have here discussed, because the existence of these social problems constitutes a practical denial of equality of opportunity to many people.

## SUGGESTED READINGS

FULLER, Richard, "The Problem of Teaching Social Problems," *American Journal of Sociology*, XLIV, pp. 415-435. **A B**

Develops the thesis that social problems are defined by the culture through the clash of value judgments of the various persons and groups participating in the culture. Evaluation of the Fuller thesis by several other representative sociologists follows the main article.

FULLER, Richard, in Park, R. E., editor, *An Outline of the Principles of Sociology* (New York, Barnes and Noble, Inc., 1939), Part I, "Social Problems." **B**

A brief treatment of the whole field of social problems and a classification of social problems by the exponent of the "clash of value judgments" theory. Also treats social change and social planning in relation to the emergence and treatment of social problems.

MILLS, C. W., "The Professional Ideology of Social Pathologists," *American Journal of Sociology*, XLIX, pp. 165-181. **A**

A significant article in which the author examines the leading social problems textbooks with a view to discovering the values which the authors actually employ in their evaluation of social change and of the proposals to adjust to social change. Has deep implications for the student of social problems and social change.

Typical Textbooks in Social Problems:

The following textbooks, while they differ from one another in several respects, may be taken as representative of the scope and treatment of the subject by American sociologists. The student should be cautious in regarding any one of these books as "typical"; they are typical *as a group*, but singly show considerable variation.

BOSSARD, H. S., *Social Change and Social Problems* (New York, Harper and Bros., 1938).

GILLETTE, J. M., and RHINEHART, J. H., *Current Social Problems* (New York, American Book Co., 1937).

NORTH, C. C., *Social Problems and Social Planning* (New York, McGraw-Hill Book Co., 1932).

PHELPS, H. A., *Contemporary Social Problems* (New York, Prentice-Hall, Inc., 1938).

It should be noted that none of these books uses the definition of social problems which is used here and by Fuller, at least not expressly or consistently. This will be somewhat confusing, but knowledge is dynamic, and changes in basic theory are normal, even though at times confusing. Most of the existing books tend to regard social problems either as self-evident "harmful" conditions or as the conditions defined as harmful by the sociologists and other students of society. The theoretical and practical difficulties with this way of approaching the matter were treated in this textbook and need not be restated here.

## STUDY QUESTIONS

1. Why can we not define social problems simply as the undesirable conditions in a society? Illustrate.
2. To what extent are social problems really social class problems?
3. Illustrate the importance of rationalization in social problem discussions.
4. How are social problems defined in this chapter?
5. Explain what is meant by "the ideology of rational control of society."
6. Why is a "consensus" not the same as a "majority agreement?"
7. Why is it almost impossible to evaluate proposed solutions to social problems objectively?
8. What principles should one bear in mind when discussing the causes of social problems? Illustrate.
9. What is the rôle of the social problem expert in the "treatment" of social problems? What are his strengths and his weaknesses?
10. Explain: "Social problems are both cause and effect of social change."

11. Are we hyperconscious of social problems? Discuss *pro* and *con*.
12. Why is a genuinely democratic person, other things being equal, more likely to be conscious of social problems?
13. What do you consider to be the leading social problems in present American culture? Justify your choice.

# SUMMARY AND CONCLUSIONS

Summarizing an introductory textbook is an especially difficult task, because the book is itself a summary of many and highly varied materials. The difficulties notwithstanding, summarization will be attempted and a few overall conclusions will be drawn.

In the opening two chapters attention was devoted to such preliminary and basic matters as the point of view of modern sociology, objectivity, the scientific method, and the persistent problems of bias and values in sociological work. The rest of the book implemented these ideas as fully as seemed feasible in an elementary treatise. The student must understand, however, that these tools of the sociological trade are much more useful and precise than we have here demonstrated. In a measure the real test of the mastery of these sociological materials is revealed by the student's ability to utilize these concepts in his own thinking about social phenomena. Perhaps the effectiveness of his citizenship will be his ultimate "grade" in the course.

Part II, entitled "Background Understandings from Cultural Anthropology," introduced the basic concepts of *culture* and *society*. It showed how and why such social facts as are subsumed in these fundamental concepts are really basic to the understanding of human behavior and social organization. The non-rational or extra-rational nature of many values and the pervasive influences of ethnocentrism are of the essence if one is to comprehend the true nature of human nature. The antiquity of man and the inherent nature of change in social relationships are also fundamental derivative ideas from these materials.

Part III, entitled "Background Understandings from Social Psychology," presented in brief compass the underlying knowledges regarding the development of the individual human being. The multipotential or pluripotential nature of original nature was stressed, because it is the elemental psychological fact about man. Since popular folklore is so replete with fallacy, these data have been presented in a somewhat "debunking" manner. The various categories of behavior such as attitudes, values, rôles, self-ideas, and frustration have been treated in separate chapters for the purpose of special attention, but they are actually all part and parcel of one another. They are all group-related; they can be regarded as group products as well as evidence of group participation. The unconscious nature of much human learning and behavior was stressed throughout, especially in such phases of personality as the acquisition of attitudes, adjustment to frustration, and the assumption of social rôles. These become integrated into a life-pattern for the person which tends to be somewhat unified and persistent. Personal inadequacy, whether of the approved or disapproved forms, was presented in terms of two concepts—*deviancy* and *social definition of deviancy*. Persons differ from one another not categorically, but in degree, often by infinitesimal gradations. Deviancy is socially defined, and the deviant person reaps benefits or disprivilege largely because of the prevailing social valuation of his behavior attributes, not because of the attributes per se. It was stressed that deviancies cannot successfully be classified either on the basis of cause or their nature, and that control of deviancy is very difficult.

Part IV sought to describe and interpret the modern social "order." The somewhat theoretical chapter on the nature of groups was intended to supply the student with some of the specialized nomenclature which sociologists have found useful for describing and interpreting groups, and to outline some of the main characteristics and trends in groups in our and similar modern societies. Races and race relations were given a separate chapter not only because of their great present importance, but also because race relations illustrate many underlying facts about society and human behavior. Here we see the institutionalization of misinformation and the ease with which false inferences from social facts come into being and are perpetuated by cultural rationalization.

The chapters on population and urbanization constituted a brief unit treating some of the main understandings from the sub-field of sociology known as human ecology. The cardinal ecological fact is symbiosis, which in human society works itself out through the division of labor and is spatially revealed in such forms as the patterns of the city and the region. The treatment of urbanization illustrated the interrelationships of ecological and non-ecological factors in human affairs; both the value system and the symbiotic needs of the human being are inextricably interwoven.

Part V contained a brief description of some of the enduring institutions of society, government, the family, education, economic organization, and religion. In each of these chapters trends were emphasized, the interaction of the influences for perpetuation of the past and the impact of current pressures for change. The mental hygiene aspects of changing institutions and values were stressed because, for the individual, they often constitute the main impact of social change on his existence.

Part VI was concerned more directly than previous units with the problem aspect of society and human behavior. The chapter on "Social Organization" constitutes a sort of summary and theoretical formulation of many of the materials presented in Parts IV and V. Here the treatment has been of necessity somewhat general and abstract, because of the all-embracing scope of the understandings which were sought. Basically, it was shown that societies are "held together" by both symbiotic ties and value ties. The everchanging nature of culture results in the continuous modification of social organization and gives rise to problems. The process of change may be conceived in terms of "disorganization," of change per se, or as having attributes of both. Many of the conditions often regarded as "disorganization" in society are really only patterns of change which the observer does not approve or does not understand. Treatment of such social "processes" as competition, conflict, accommodation, assimilation, and coöperation was introduced so that the student might get some idea of the ways in which change operates in specific instances, as well as how society "works" in the channelizing of human behavior.

The final chapter on "Social Problems" is in a sense a summary of the book. It stresses the basic factor of social valuation as the source of problem-consciousness, and shows how the definition of social problems stems from the conflict of values among the persons and groups of a society. Man periodically, through culture, appraises the conditions of his existence and strives to control them. How successful he has been can only be judged by each person for himself in the light of the understandings he has.

Termination of the book with the chapter on social problems may or may not be sound. Yet it is easy to justify. For our day, with its turmoil of social change and panoramic adjustment to change, the emphasis on the processes by which man seeks to control his individual and collective destiny seems amply justified. In this process of evaluation and conscious modification of society, the student of sociology will play his part along with other citizens. Probably his somewhat more scientific understanding of the nature of human behavior and of social organization may make him a more realistic, if not more effective, participant in the process of social valuation. It can be hoped that the voice of the better informed may not always be lost in the clamor of the rabble for the freeing of social Barabbases.

# AUTHOR INDEX

# SUBJECT INDEX

( 3 )